inside out

NORTHERN CALIFORNIA

A BEST PLACES® GUIDE
TO THE OUTDOORS

D0972952

DENNIS J. OLIVER

SASQUATCH
BOOKS
SEATTLE

Acknowledgments

A special acknowledgment for Michael Carr, who not only helped research and write this book, but also loaned his invaluable California newcomer's perspective where it was needed. Thanks to editors Kate Rogers, Justine Matthies, Cynthia Rubin, and the rest of the Sasquatch staff for their hard work. Finally, thanks to the hundreds of people who were generous enough to share their favorite places with us.

Dedication

This book is dedicated to Michael W. Butler, who taught me how to explore; without his inspiration, it could not have been written.

First edition

02 01 00 99   5 4 3 2 1

ISSN: 1522-8576
ISBN: 1-57061-166-1

Cover photo: John Kelly/The Image Bank
Cover design: Karen Schober
Interior design: Lynne Faulk
Composition: Patrick David Barber
Maps: GreenEye Design

Important Note: Please use common sense. No guidebook can act as a substitute for experience, careful planning, and appropriate training. There is inherent danger in all the outdoor activities described in this book, and readers must assume responsibility for their own actions and safety. Changing or unfavorable conditions in weather, roads, trails, waterways, etc. cannot be anticipated by the author or publisher, but should be considered by any outdoor participants. The author and the publisher will not be responsible for the safety of users of this guide.

The information in this edition is based on facts available at press time and is subject to change. The author and publisher welcome information conveyed by users of this book, as long as they have no financial connection with the area, guide, outfitter, organization, or establishment concerned.

Sasquatch Books
615 Second Avenue
Seattle, WA 98104
(206) 467-4300
www.SasquatchBooks.com
books@SasquatchBooks.com

Contents

Introduction
and How to Use
this Book

This is an E-ticket ride.

It will take you 14,000 feet up to the snow-ravaged peak of Mount Shasta, from which the end of the Earth is visible. It will lead you down to the kelp forests of Monterey Bay to explore the edge of a vast and mysterious canyon carved into the ocean floor. You will glide, fly, bump, and drop through remote stretches of river for a look at canyons reachable only by those willing to brave the rapids. Along the gravel banks of the unrestrained Smith River, the best fly-fishing nooks in the state will reel you in. You will crane your neck, wide-eyed, to take in the awesome beauty of Yosemite Valley's granite walls, while the glacial valley's mighty falls chill you to the bone with spray and fill your ears with thunder. Exploring the old-growth redwood forests of the North Coast will take you back to their beginnings 1,000 years ago. And at Lake Tahoe's winter play paradise, you'll kick some powder around and then, when summer arrives, enjoy the lake's cobalt blue water. In a word, Northern California is boundless.

I am fortunate enough to have been born here, to be a real live California native. We had our Fourth of July family outings at Santa Cruz or Lake Tahoe, took weekend camping jaunts deep into the national forests of the Sierra, and enjoyed weekends boating and beachcombing at Brannan Island in the Delta or fishing on Clear Lake. In California, exploring is an intrinsic part of the culture. Having been introduced to the state's fabulous outdoor treasures as children, we natives feel compelled to continue exploring our home state. After 35 years, I am still discovering new places and having new experiences. Not only am I one of those weekend warriors, I am also fortunate to have a job writing about environmental issues in the state. As a result, my job often takes me to the same places I would spend a day off. I don't need a Club Med.

For me, writing a guidebook to the Northern California outdoors is like telling you about an old friend: these are my favorite places and this is my personal invitation to you to come explore them. When I complain about the crowds in the more touristy areas, remember that I do so not to try to lock out newcomers, but rather to let you know what to expect. The growing popularity of outdoor recreation coupled with both the state's expanding population and its increasing number of visitors means you must plan smart to avoid the crush—or at least be prepared for it. My survival tips for this are sprinkled throughout this book. You also will notice frequent references to environmental problems facing certain areas. This information is provided not to alarm you or make you feel guilty, but rather to make you better informed. I have tailored this book not for the Olympic athlete who is an expert at every sport, but rather for regular people like myself who either want to try certain outdoor activities for the first time or just need to know where to go to engage in their favorites. You will also find phone numbers, Web sites, addresses, and directions to the people and places who are best suited to make your visit to our state or your weekend outing a successful one. I also invite you—my guest—to contact me directly with your inquiries. My phone number in San Francisco is (415) 221-9412 and my email address is djo3@ix.netcom.com. A response is guaranteed.

Thank you, welcome to California, and have fun.

—*Dennis J. Oliver*

How to Use This Book

We have tried to make *Inside Out Northern California* an entertaining, informative, and easy-to-use guidebook. The state's geographical regions were divided into eight sections. Basic reference maps are featured at the beginning of each section. Each section is then subdivided into smaller, more manageable areas (or chapters) that are represented in the following manner.

Introduction

The introduction to each chapter offers a general description of the area and its primary towns and features. These sections should provide you with a sense of place and history, as well as give you an idea of what to expect when you visit. Directions to the area and transportation information are included in the **Getting There** sections, which are followed by **Adjoining Areas** to your destination that are found in this book.

Inside Out

The Inside Out sections make up the bulk of the book. We go to great pains to discover what the best year-round options are for outdoor activities in each area. We talk to locals, rangers, guides, and outdoor store owners to get the scoop on the most popular trails, lakes, stretches of river, beaches, ski slopes, and more. And we reveal some lesser-known gems as well.

These sections are divided into individual sports and activities, listed in order of prominence and appeal. Most chapters include **Hiking, Biking, Fishing, Camping, Skiing,** and **Rafting/Kayaking**—things that can be enjoyed in many parts of the state. Other chapters feature specialized activities, such as **Surfing, Gold Panning,** and **Hang Gliding.** Here, you can select your adventure and discover how to get out into the wilderness, outside, out-of-doors, just out!

The "Northern California Outdoor Primer," which follows on page viii, also provides safety tips and essential information on outdoor recreation and travel.

Outside In

After a long day enjoying the outdoors, you need to know where to go for some inside fun. The **Attractions** sections tell you about museums, hot springs, shops, and other sights in the area that will distract the kids, get you out of inclement weather, or are just plain interesting places.

The **Restaurants** and **Lodgings** sections provide star-rated reviews of the best places to eat and sleep. (See "About Best Places® Guidebooks" on page xx for a description of how we rate and choose the restaurants and lodgings.)

More Information

Finally, we wrap up each chapter with a list of useful phone numbers specific to that area. Ranger districts, chambers of commerce, visitors centers, and more are all included for your convenience.

Northern California Outdoor Primer

Whether you're setting out to explore Northern California's mountains, rivers, beaches, valleys, or forests, there is something to be said for spontaneity: Just point the rig in the direction you choose and hit the road. *Inside Out Northern California* is custom-built for adventurers who like to keep their plans flexible. Some level of preparation is always necessary, however, and following are some basic guidelines to help prevent your spur-of-the-moment road trip from ending up as a series of minor inconveniences or even as a medical emergency. Also included are pointers and general safety advice you may want to consider when engaging in specific activities.

The key to enjoying outdoor recreation is to use **common sense.** This means accepting our public lands for what they are—wild places where wildlife, terrain, and weather are untamed. A calm-looking river can sweep you away, and even an animal as seemingly gentle as a deer can be dangerous (as a matter of fact, the only documented case of a visitor being killed by an animal in Yosemite National Park involved a deer). Check forecasts and road condition reports before driving to areas where you may encounter weather extremes, and be sure you're properly outfitted for the activity in which you want to engage.

Getting There

Many areas discussed in this guide are prone to weather extremes: many are also fairly remote. In each chapter, the general character of roads and highways is discussed, and phone numbers are given for the local highway authority and public transportation agencies. It is important to check with these resources and plan your trip with current information in hand. Even driving on major highways to winter recreation areas such as Lake Tahoe can be trying. One good centralized source for current road information is the state Department of Transportation information center, (800) 427-ROAD (7623), or on the Internet at www.dot.ca.gov/hq/roadinfo/.

If the travel advisory says to carry chains, carry them. If the rangers say you need a four-wheel-drive vehicle or high ground clearance to travel a particular road, listen to them. Nobody wants to get stranded in the middle of nowhere, particularly in a blizzard.

Hiking/Backpacking

Obviously, there is a big difference between walking a few miles on a level trail in a county park close to the city, and hiking deep into the backcountry of a national forest. Each hike listed has a ranked **difficulty level,** with the distance indicated in round-trip terms unless otherwise noted. Expect **"easy"** hikes to be relatively level and easy to finish. On those hikes listed as **"moderate,"** expect to encounter some reasonably steep grades or a longer trek. Those hikes listed as **"difficult"** or **"extremely difficult"** usually involve strenuous climbing, numerous switchbacks, stream crossings, or potential weather extremes associated with high altitudes. With many hikes, we have given some indication of how long they take to complete, but that is going to vary depending on your physical condition and pacing. It is important in all cases to time your hike correctly so that you finish—or have your a backcountry camp set up—by the time sunset arrives.

Gear

Dress suitably, carry water, wear the correct footgear, and pack properly. The right footgear protects your ankles and feet in comfort, while packing equipment should keep the weight you are carrying concentrated at the hips and allow both hands to remain free. Even something as easy to carry as a water bottle should be attached to a utility belt or stowed away in a daypack to make walking more efficient.

On longer backpacking trips in particular, it is important to cover the basics. Most hiking clubs and backpacking outfitters recommend the same standard list of **"10 essentials"** as a guideline for what you should take with you. These are: **maps** (see below), **compass, flashlight** (with spare batteries and bulb), **extra food, extra clothing, sunglasses, first-aid kit, pocket knife, matches,** and **fire starter** (usually a candle).

Particularly in the summer when the trails can be dry, it is also a good idea to carry a **bandana** to cover your nose and mouth should dust get airborne. Also be sure to carry plenty of clean, fresh **water** with you and to bring a water filter if you plan to drink from streams and rivers (but make sure the streams and rivers are safe first!). A **hat, sunscreen,** and **insect repellant** also will come in handy, particularly during the dry season. Winter hikes and climbing will require additional essentials, such as **crampons,** an **ice axe,** proper winter camping gear, winter clothing, and more weather-resistant, heavy-duty boots. Ice or snow climbs, such as the Mount Shasta ascent, should not be attempted without a qualified guide.

Maps

The topographical maps most commonly used by outdoor enthusiasts are those published and sold by the **United States Geological Survey**

(USGS). Authorized dealers are located throughout the state, but it is also possible to **order maps** directly from the agency. There are 70,000 USGS maps in print and available, covering national parks, forests, and wilderness areas. To determine which maps would be most appropriate for the area you plan to visit, call (800) HELP-MAP to request a complete map index. Information is also available by mail; send requests to USGS Information Services, PO Box 25286, Denver, CO 80225. In addition, the USGS has map ordering instructions and a complete dealer list on the Web at www.mapping.usgs.gov/esic/to_order.html.

The **US Forest Service** publishes maps of all national forests and wilderness areas mentioned in this book. To **order by mail,** send $6 per map needed to US Forest Service, 630 Sansome St., San Francisco, CA 94111. (It's also a good idea to include a return address label with your order.) In portions of this guide where national forests and wilderness areas are discussed, we have listed the different maps available for each area covered. Note that these maps are also available from retail map dealers and at national forest ranger stations. At **ranger stations,** they are usually available without charge. We encourage travelers exploring national forests to begin any outing with a visit to the nearest ranger station. Not only can they provide good maps, directions, and advice, but they also are able to advise visitors of road conditions, trail conditions, and other timely information.

Regional and city parks generally provide trail maps at key trailheads. We have listed phone numbers for local and regional park agencies, clubs, and associations mentioned in this guide. Many of these resources will help locate maps, or send them to you if you call.

The USGS maps will include information on national parks, but **Yosemite National Park** has its own park maps and hiking guides, available through the Yosemite Association. It is easiest to order publications from the association's Web site at www.yosemite.org/ or call (209) 379-2648 to request a catalog.

Camping

With the rising popularity of outdoor activities and the growing number of visitors to California, a site in a developed campground can be difficult to come by. Don't let this discourage you from hitting the road, however. Many parks—including Yosemite National Park and Point Reyes National Seashore—have reservations policies that still make it possible to get a spot even at the last minute. The key to finding a site often is arriving as early as possible to snap up those reserved for drop-in visitors. (It is also often possible to score a site in the mid to late afternoon if the person who has reserved it never shows up.) Throughout this guide, we also point out which national forest camping areas are most suitable as overflow spots for main attractions.

National parks, national forests, and state parks in California all have centralized **reservations systems.** While these entities own and manage most of the campgrounds mentioned in this book, other independent campgrounds are also listed, with individual phone numbers to call for reservations. In areas where public campgrounds are scarce, we have listed the names and phone numbers of select private campgrounds. Visitors bureaus and chambers of commerce, listed with each chapter, also are able to make private campground recommendations should you need one.

State parks reservations

The state parks reservations system can be reached at **(800) 444-7275.** Reservations are available for most campgrounds up to **seven months in advance,** with a block of dates becoming available on the first of each month. This means campers who wish to reserve a site for April should call in the previous October, and so on. Reservations are canceled and changed daily. It may be worth your while to check with the reservations system periodically to see if sites have opened up because of last-minute cancellations.

National parks reservations

The campgrounds within **Redwood National Park** boundaries are managed by the state parks system because of a joint operating agreement between the state and federal agencies; see above for state parks reservations information.

As is explained in detail in the Yosemite National Park: Overview chapter, getting a reserved campsite in **Yosemite National Park,** especially in Yosemite Valley, can be a challenge. Sites can be reserved five months in advance with a block of dates opening up each month on the 15th. Call the Yosemite reservations center, **(800) 436-7275,** beginning at 7am Pacific Standard Time and try your luck at getting through. Mail reservations should be addressed to NPRS, PO Box 1600, Cumberland, MD 21502, but be sure to call the above number first to find out the exact price of the campsite of your choice. In addition to reserved sites, Yosemite retains **first-come, first-served sites** throughout the park. **Dispersed camping** is allowed only at least 4 miles away from developed areas of the park, and at least 1 mile away from roads. Groups are limited to 15 people on trails, and 8 people for cross-country bushwhacking. You'd be best advised to reserve a wilderness permit up to 24 weeks in advance. Call the permit office at (209) 372-0740, or write Wilderness Permits, PO Box 545, Yosemite, CA 95389. For more information on dispersed wilderness camping, call (209) 372-0200.

Sites at **Whiskeytown National Recreation Area** can also be reserved up to five months in advance, but with openings appearing on the 5th day of each month. Unlike Yosemite, it is necessary to call the general national park service reservations number at **(800) 365-2267.** Alternatively, it also is now possible to check reservations online for *all* national parks at www.reservations.nps.gov/.

National forest reservations

The US Forest Service national reservations phone number is **(800) 280-2267.** It is possible to reserve individual campsites 240 days in advance within all of Northern California's national forests, but the Forest Service also maintains select non-reservation sites for first-come, first-served campers. Throughout this guide, we list phone numbers for national forest ranger stations; call them for information about campsite availability in a specific area. At press time, the Forest Service is considering a number of possible changes to its reservations and fee policies. An Internet reservations site is in the works, and some forest units are considering collecting fees and taking reservations for such things as river rafting and wilderness permits.

Winter Sports

Winter sports in Northern California have come a long way since the Gold Rush days 150 years ago, when miners took to the snow-covered slopes of the northern Sierra using crude skis fashioned from scraps of wood. Major resorts are located throughout the mountain regions, from Mount Shasta to the Tahoe Basin to Mammoth Mountain. Because of the increasing popularity of winter recreation, most resorts are undergoing modernization and expansion, with new high-speed lifts and other amenities being added and new slopes being developed. The descriptions included in this guide cover not only the facilities and services provided at each resort, but also the general character of the terrain. Following is some general advice, basic survival tips, and suggested resources for those interested in experiencing the outdoors during the winter.

The most common mistake new winter recreators make is that they fail to adjust for the season. Winter means cold, wet extremes. Gear up for the conditions you will be playing in. This means not only equipment and proper attire. It also is essential that you seek instruction before hitting the slopes or wandering down a ski trail. Novices who think they're experts and who take unnecessary risks in foul weather are the most likely to be injured or to injure others.

It is crucial that those using ski resort areas not go out of bounds, as areas outside of open and groomed trails and runs have not been patrolled for **avalanche danger.** Avalanches typically occur on slopes between 30 and 45 degrees. Most avalanche-related accidents occur in the backcountry where unstable snow is not monitored, and the victim has unwittingly triggered the avalanche. Carrying avalanche safety equipment such as shovels and electronic homing devices is not enough. Those who plan to venture into the backcountry in winter should take an avalanche safety course. Call the National Forest Service Avalanche Center in Ketchum, Idaho, (208) 622-5371, or check with a local ranger station for a safety training schedule. Useful information also is posted at www.avalanche.org on the World Wide Web.

Season

The typical **ski season** in California is October to April, but because the weather can be unpredictable and because snowmaking equipment is becoming more advanced, the season often extends well into the summer. Call resorts to check on current conditions. You may find the upper slopes open in June some years.

Downhill skiing/Snowboarding

While the Tahoe Basin is by far the most talked-about ski area in the state, you will learn in the pages that follow that snow sports are enjoyed throughout Northern California, from the southern Cascade range to south of Yosemite. Each resort has a snow condition phone number; call before finalizing your ski plans, as the weather can vary significantly even between resorts that seem geographically near each other. The **National Ski Areas Association** offers this seven-part **responsibility code** for how to behave on the slopes. Take heed:

■   Always stay in control and retain your ability to stop to avoid collisions. This includes collisions with other people and with objects such as trees. If you don't have the skills to do this, you don't belong on aggressive terrain.

■   The people in front of you have the right of way. Respect that and you won't have a pileup.

■   Do not stop in the middle of a trail or where you are not visible to other skiers.

■   When starting downhill or merging onto a trail, make sure you do so when traffic from above is clear.

■   Prevent runaway equipment.

■   Stay out of closed areas; adhere to all postings.

■   Know how to load and unload properly before using ski lifts.

Cross-country skiing/Snowshoeing

Cross-country (or Nordic) skiing is one of the most physically demanding sports discussed in this guide, but it is also one of the most rewarding—a great way to enjoy winter scenery. Snowshoeing also has become quite popular, particularly since it is an activity that entire families can engage in together. Many resorts reviewed in this guide have designated Nordic ski trails. We also recommend a number of areas in national forestlands where designated sno-parks are found (see below). Groomed trails are the best for learning, and lessons are advised. The Cross-Country Ski Areas Association Web site, www.xcski.org, has much useful information.

Visitors are required to obtain a **sno-park permit** to legitimately use sno-park parking areas. The permit season runs from November 1 through May 30. A one-day permit costs $5, and a season pass costs $25. The California permit also is valid at sno-parks in the state of Oregon. Those who use parking areas without first obtaining a permit will be cited. Permits are available at most outdoor sporting goods stores or at any AAA office. For directions to the nearest outlet, call (916) 324-1222. You can also purchase an annual pass by sending a check for $26 (the extra buck is for postage and handling), payable to California State Parks Department, to Sno-Park Permits, PO Box 942896, Sacramento, CA 94296.

Biking

Road cyclists and mountain bikers alike are going to find a bounty of excellent rides in Northern California. The possibilities are quite literally boundless: Tar heads love their long country roads and secluded highways, while mountain bikers let it rip on Forest Service roads and single-track trails. In most biking sections, we name the land manager and biking resources in the area. Check in with them for information and advice about current road and trail conditions. It is also imperative that you make yourself aware of any special biking restrictions. For example, on East Bay Regional Park District trails, riders are required to both call out to other trail users and to have their bicycles equipped with bells. Being caught without a bell or breaking the call-out rule can result in a hefty fine. (On occasion the park police stage bell checkpoints and clock speeding cyclists with radar to see if they are exceeding the 15mph speed limit!) Bicycles must be adjusted and fitted properly: the crossbar on a bicycle should be about the same height as the crotch, and seats should be adjusted so that you get nearly a full extension of the leg with each downward pedal. Reputable rental outfits will match and adjust bikes for you; if they don't, insist. Test brakes before hitting the trails or heading downhill. Always carry a tire repair kit and air pump. In California, all bicyclists the latest conditions and regulations affecting the areas over which they have jurisdiction. Another decent resource for fly-fishing information is at www.greenfly.com/ on the Web, as the site includes numerous useful links dealing with the sport.

For lake fishing and deep-sea fishing, we have included key contacts for marinas, guides, rental boats, and other resources.

Wildlife

The wildlife with which we share our parks, forests, beaches, preserves, and rivers should be admired from a distance, and not approached or meddled with in any way if we are to be good custodians of our public lands. Throughout this guide, we identify some of the best bird-watching areas on the West Coast, and give a general idea of the other types of wildlife you can expect to see in a specific area.

To be suitably outfitted for **bird-watching,** you should consider investing in a National Audubon Society field guide, which includes photographs and background information on each species. The field guides are available at most major book stores, or by going to www.audubon.com on the Web. A good viewing scope with a tripod or binoculars can also make a bird-watching outing much more enjoyable. Local Audubon Society chapters and other resources are named throughout the guide. Also note that in national forest and wilderness areas, most ranger stations have compiled bird lists and make them available to visitors at no charge.

We have deliberately excluded from this guide information about hunting, but it should be noted that private hunting clubs own large tracts of marshlands in the Central Valley, much of it adjacent to the preserves also popular among bird-watchers. As distressing as it may be to think that other people get a thrill out of hunting down the same animals you enjoy observing in nature, duck clubs have been credited by environmental organizations and resource management agencies as instrumental in preserving crucial habitat needed by these creatures and for participating in restoration projects.

While odds are that your encounters with wildlife will be interesting and pleasurable, it is still wise to use basic precautions when visiting areas where potentially dangerous animals reside. The three most common such animals in Northern California are the mountain lion, the black bear, and the rattlesnake.

Mountain lions

Mountain lions—also commonly known as cougars—are found throughout most of the Sierra Nevada range and in coastal foothills. In recent years, much attention has been called to the growing potential for lion–human confrontations, as population numbers for both species rise and human developments encroach upon mountain lion terrain. While encounters are most likely to occur away from cities and developed parks, lion sightings have occurred surprisingly near urban areas. Mountain lion attacks, however, are extremely rare. Nonetheless, should you find yourself face-to-face with a lion, these are the precautions experts say you should take:

■ Make yourself look big. The easiest way to do this is to wave your arms and/or open your jacket in a fan to give the appearance of more bulk. A lion is less likely to pursue a larger animal.

■ Make noise. Yelling and clapping your hands will startle the lion and possibly send it to higher ground.

■ Group up. If you are with a group of people, gather everyone together while taking the other precautions listed above. This will look very intimidating to a cat. Small children are closer to the size of a lion's normal prey. For this reason, they should be picked up by adults so that they don't look vulnerable.

■ Throw objects. While the precautions listed so far are virtually guaranteed to chase a lion off, one more option is to throw things. Rocks, sticks, and other objects will send the lion scampering.

■ Campfire. If camping, be sure to keep a fire lit. A lion will know to stay away once it is noted that a camp is in the area.

Most experts also agree that you should not turn you back on a mountain lion or run away; a speedy retreat mimics the behavior of a lion's wild prey, and it will give chase.

Black bears

In many developed camping areas, the California black bear has become particularly savvy at finding and consuming improperly stored food. The problem is especially out of hand in Yosemite National Park, where there exists a higher number of inexperienced campers. There are a variety of procedures you can follow to keep a bear from visiting your campsite, all of which involve proper storage of food and personal items:

■ Use bear-proof canisters. These canisters, which are available at any outdoor supply store, are considered to be the best preventative measure you can take when it comes to bear-proofing a campsite. Personal items that emit odors, such as toothpaste, should also be stored with food.

■ Elevate food. This involves bagging food items in 8- to 10-pound sections, and then suspending them from tree branches too high for the bears to reach. When choosing a tree to use for this, make sure the branch extends away from the trunk and is not sturdy enough to support the weight of a cub. This technique will not stop bears from pursuing your food; it will, however, delay them.

■   Properly handle and dispose of garbage and food waste. Developed campgrounds in areas where bears have a known presence will be equipped with bear-proof garbage bins. Put all food waste and garbage in these. In more primitive camps, food scraps should be burned, not disposed of in a refuse pile or nearby woods. Dishes should be rinsed over the fire. Garbage that you cannot burn should be safely stored with food and packed out.

■   Do not store food or garbage in your car. A bear will attempt to rip your car open like a sardine can if it thinks it will get a snack out of it.

■   Visual triggers. This is especially important in campgrounds that receive regular bear visits. If a bear sees a container such as a grocery bag or an ice chest that it knows may contain food, it may go to great lengths to investigate. Keep these items, as well as water bottles and other objects associated with food preparation or storage, out of view. If storing items like these in your car, place them in the trunk.

Snakes

When it comes to venomous snakes, of which the rattlesnake is most common in California, the key to avoiding problems is staying out of the snake's way. Be careful when moving rocks or branches or when reaching into places where snakes may be found. Rattlesnakes generally prefer dry, arid settings and so are more common in the Sierra Nevada and other inland areas than on the coast. If you encounter a snake on a trail or elsewhere, make sure it knows you are there and give it enough time and distance to get out of your way. Usually, a snake will leave the area once it knows a potential predator is nearby. Don't do anything to make the snake feel trapped or threatened, and never tease or try to handle a snake in the wild. Also, keep in mind that a dead snake is not safe either, as reflex biting is not uncommon. If you are bitten, it is best to uncover the affected area, splint it if necessary, and immediately transport the victim for treatment. Snake bites are usually not fatal, but if symptoms such as pain and swelling are severe, the victim should be carried in order to minimize blood flow, which accelerates the spreading of the venom. Otherwise, it is generally safe to allow the patient to walk.

About Best Places® Guidebooks

The restaurant and lodging reviews in this book are condensed from Best Places guidebooks. The Best Places series is unique in the sense that each guide is written by and for locals, and is therefore coveted by travelers. The best places in the region are the ones that denizens favor: establishments of good value, often independently owned, touched with local history, run by lively individuals, and graced with natural beauty. Best Places reviews are completely independent: no advertisers, no sponsors, no favors.

All evaluations are based on numerous reports from local and traveling inspectors. Best Places writers do not identify themselves when they review an establishment, and they accept no free meals, accommodations, or any other services. Every place featured in this book is recommended, even those with no stars.

Stars

Restaurants and lodgings are rated on a scale of zero to four stars, based on uniqueness, loyalty of local clientele, performance measured against goals, excellence of cooking, value, and professionalism of service. Reviews are listed alphabetically.

☆☆☆☆	The very best in the region
☆☆☆	Distinguished; many outstanding features
☆☆	Excellent; some wonderful qualities
☆	A good place
no stars	Worth knowing about, if nearby

Price Range

All prices are subject to change; contact the establishment directly to verify.

$$$	Expensive (more than $80 for dinner for two; more than $120 for one night's lodgings for two)
$$	Moderate (between expensive and inexpensive)
$	Inexpensive (less than $35 for dinner for two; less than $70 for one night's lodgings for two)

Directions

Basic directions are provided with each review; contact each business to confirm hours and location.

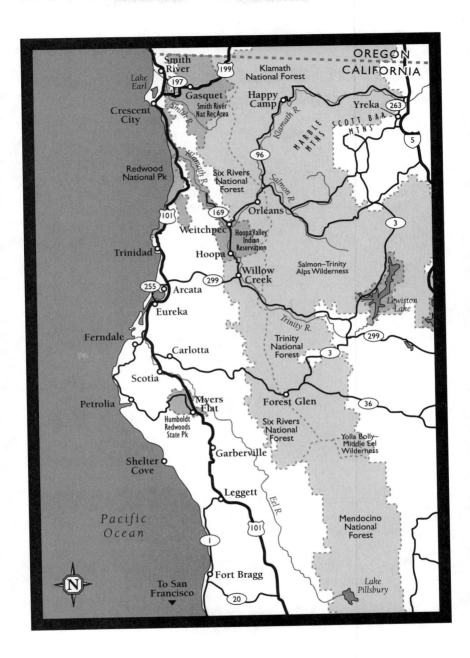

Redwood
Coast

Redwood Coast

Del Norte Coast

The stretch of redwood country extending from the Oregon border on the Redwood Highway (US Highway 101) south to the Humboldt County line through Crescent City, including Jedediah Smith Redwoods State Park, Del Norte Coast Redwoods State Park, Enderts Beach, and key portions of Redwood National Park.

The northwest tip of the state is a salty, cold, windblown five-acre stretch of wild sand dunes littered with driftwood. The water is too cold and the surf too rough for swimming. There are no volleyball nets or bikinis. If you're looking for a *Baywatch* scene, you took a wrong turn somewhere. Rather, Pelican State Beach on the west side of US Highway 101 5 miles south of the Oregon border, looks much the same as it has for centuries. It is a fitting gateway to a state where the "pave-to-improve" movement that began 150 years ago with the gold rush has run up against some of the most successful conservation victories in the country—most of these bad news for the region's economy but great news for wildlife and outdoor-lovers who want to explore. In Del Norte County, evidence of these victories abounds. The wild, untamed Smith River, the vast stands of old-growth redwoods in and around Jedediah Smith State Park, the more than 350,000 acres of naked wilderness preserved within the Smith River National Recreation Area, and even the lonely stretch of wild dunes at Pelican are definitive starting points for a Northern California tour.

One thing the coast traveler in this state quickly learns is that the farther north you go, the wetter, more lush, colder, and deeper green everything becomes. Del Norte being the northernmost stop, be prepared for extremes. More than 100 inches of rain fall annually here. As a result, the redwoods are fat and tall, and some stretches of river are temperamental. Crescent City, the closest thing to a population center in the region, has twice been wiped out, not by river floods, but by tsunamis flung ashore following Alaskan earthquakes at sea. What's more, government-imposed logging restrictions and the overseas exportation of milling jobs have decimated the area's job base over the past 10 years. Consequently, the city's center is a bizarre ramshackle of tilt-up buildings with no dominant style of architecture, some containing such curiosities as a combination bait and tackle/barber shop. The place has a funky yet friendly blue-collar feel.

Economic woes aside, steelhead and salmon fishing on the Smith, the longest dam-free river in the state—along with the chance to camp in a quieter redwood setting than busy Humboldt County to the south—have drawn enough visitors to keep the region in business. Head north and explore.

Getting There

US Highway 101 (US 101), also known as the Redwood Highway, is the main thoroughfare through this region, extending north from Humboldt County and south from the Oregon border through Crescent City. Near Crescent City this route intersects with US 199, which follows the Smith River east toward Jedediah Smith Redwoods State Park and the vast Smith River National Recreation Area. Redwood Coast Transit, (707) 464-9314, runs buses between Crescent City and Klamath with stops at several key points. Call for schedule information if you're hoofing it.

Adjoining Areas

SOUTH: **Humboldt Coast**

EAST: **Smith River National Recreation Area**

inside out

Parks/Beaches

Pigeon Point, at the northwest tip of the state, is one of those spots you visit just to say you did. Explore the dunes, enjoy the shorebirds and the ocean, feel the wind on your face, and brag to your friends that you've been to the upper lefthand corner of the best darn state in the USA. The beach is 5 miles south of the Oregon border, just west of US 101. Enjoy the sand between your toes and collect a piece of driftwood. Hey, why not?

The Smith River ends its 325-mile meandering journey through the Siskiyou Mountains at Tillas and Yontock Sloughs on the central shores of Pelican Bay. Add the 2,000-acre **Lake Earl Wildlife Area,** and what we have is a 10-mile stretch of coast containing two large lagoons, Lake Tawala, and Dead Lake. Tawala spills into the sea when heavy rains come. The Smith River/Lake Earl section of the coast is a great place to see nature up close. The area attracts a wide spectrum of wildlife, including interesting shorebirds and sea mammals. This is also where the salmon and steelhead return from the ocean en route to their upstream spawning grounds. You'll also find vast, wild sand dunes and the unique plant communities that support them. Boating, hiking, cycling, and limited camping are permitted around the lagoons. Public access to the river mouth, marsh, and lagoon areas is available all along Lake Earl Dr, and Lower Lake Rd from the Redwood Highway just north of Crescent City. **Kellogg Beach Park,** just northwest of Lake Earl, is accessible at the end of Kellogg Rd, left from Lower Lake Rd 8 miles north of the highway exit. For information about Lake Earl, call (707) 464-9533. Kellogg Beach is managed by Del Norte County, (707) 464-7237.

Redwood National Park extends 50 miles from just north of US 199 in Del Norte County to the vast Bridge Creek Ridge and surrounding peaks east of Patrick's Point State Park. Within its boundaries are Del Norte Redwoods State Park, Jedediah Smith Redwoods State Park, Enderts Beach, Prairie Creek Redwoods State Park (see Humboldt Coast chapter), large sections of the California Coastal Trail, and numerous other areas that are described separately throughout this section of the book. Still, vast areas of wilderness within the national park boundaries are maintained and managed separate from those owned by the state. These include the scenic Bald Hills Rd area, the Redwood Creek Trail, the Lady Bird Johnson redwood grove, and surrounding parklands. See Redwood National Park chapter in this section for an overview of the park and a description of activities in these areas.

Jedediah Smith Redwoods State Park is one of those "Wow! Look at that one" kind of places. What else would you expect to hear in a place where 9,500 acres of ancient virgin redwoods are flanked by the final run of the state's largest free-flowing river? The park contains the 5,000-acre National Tribute Grove, named for veterans of World War I. Its largest tree stands at a staggering 340 feet tall and 22 feet wide. What really blows you away about this place, however, is how quickly it can swallow you up. One second you're flying down US 199, the next you're in a big-tree wonderland that still looks much like it did centuries ago. Day visitors like to check out Jedediah Smith's entrancing nature walks or wade out into the river in the summer. Yet there's also every enticement to stay awhile. More than 100 campsites are available (see Camping, below) and there are over 20 miles of hiking trails to explore. Because Jedediah Smith borders the vast Smith River National Recreation Area, longer backpacking trips also may begin here. The park is east of Crescent City on US 199, 9 miles from the Redwood Highway intersection, on the south side of the road; you can't miss it. For information, call (707) 464-9533.

South of Crescent City, **Enderts Beach** is the premier place to explore tide pools along the North Coast. North of the rocky tide pool area is a nice sandy beach, beneath 500-foot grassy bluffs that make a great whale-watching spot during the southern migration. Nickel Creek Camp (see Camping, below) is a short hike away, offering secluded, primitive sites by the water. Adjacent **Crescent Beach** to the north has more sand and bluffs, along with a picnic area. Call (707) 464-6101 for information about both beaches. Both beaches are off Enderts Beach Rd, heading south from the Redwood Highway at Crescent City.

Del Norte Coast Redwoods State Park is perhaps the coldest, wettest redwood area of the Del Norte coast, featuring 6,500 acres of old-growth stands hugging the ocean on high bluffs above a rocky beach. It's a great place to get a cold mist shower if you venture in at the right (or, depending on your perspective, wrong) time of year. On clear days, how-ever, you'll be treated to dramatic vistas of the Pacific Ocean from forest and coastal hiking trails. In the section of the park on the east side of the Redwood Highway, family camping is available creekside (see Camping, below). The main park entrance is on the Redwood Highway 5 miles south of Crescent City, but you'll also find pullouts and staging areas north of there as well. Call (707) 464-9533 for information.

The **Klamath River,** the state's second largest watercourse and a notoriously great place for salmon and steelhead fishing, meets the Pacific Ocean just south of the Requa Overlook, a nice day-trip area with picnic facilities and access to the California Coastal Trail. The easiest way to get a look at the river is to exit the Redwood Highway at Requa Rd north of the Klamath River over-crossing, and head west to the overlook. There are numerous campgrounds along the river's edge, all private.

Camping

If you plan ahead, you're in for a major thrill here—especially if you're the kind of outdoor person who doesn't mind extremes of weather. In exchange for a chance to sleep among the ancient trees, you must often put up with chilly nights, fog that leaves a thick layer of dew on every-thing (even in the summer), and rain. Major hint: This is Del Norte

County, and the farther north you go in California, the wetter the climate. Because redwood country is such a popular camping destination, particularly in the summer, be sure to check other nearby options if the public parks in Del Norte are full. For backpackers, the Smith River National Recreation Area is a good alternative (see Smith River National Recreation Area chapter), since it not only has developed sites near the key redwood destinations but also allows wilderness camping just about anywhere, with a few restrictions. Also be sure to look at Humboldt Coast chapter for more options.

Jedediah Smith Redwoods State Park (see Parks/Beaches, above) has 108 sites (no hookups; RV limit 30 feet) amid incredibly huge and gorgeous old-growth redwoods, and is near a wide, calm stretch of the Smith River. Good winter fishing, summer swimming, and canoeing are nearby. Each site has a picnic table and fire pit. Piped water, flush toilets, and showers are available. *Call the state parks reservations system, (800) 444-7275. The park is 9 miles east of Crescent City on US 199, on the south side of the road.*

Del Norte Coast Redwoods State Park has 145 sites in its Mill Creek Campground (no hookups; RV limit 31 feet) in a pretty, mixed-redwood forest with a number of streams running through. Each site has a fire pit and a picnic table, and flush toilets and showers are available. *Call the state parks reservations system, (800) 444-7275. The campground is 5 miles south of Crescent City on the east side of the Redwood Hwy.*

You'll find 6 secluded hike-in sites and a horse camp large enough to sustain 16 riders at **Lake Earl** and adjacent **Lake Tawala** (see Parks/Beaches, above), 2 miles north of Crescent City on the Pelican Bay shoreline. Each site has a picnic table, food locker, and fire pit, but no running water. Nearby, the marshes surrounding the lakes are a supreme bird-watching area. Lake Earl is also a popular canoeing and kayaking destination. *Call (707) 464-9533 for reservations. The hike-in sites and horse camp are in two separate locations. To reach the hike-in camp, take the Redwood Hwy north from Crescent City 2 miles and exit west at Elk Valley Rd. At Lake Earl Rd, turn north for 1.5 miles to Lower Lake Rd. Go left on Lower Lake and continue 2.5 miles to Kellogg Rd. Turn left on Kellogg and continue 1 mile to the camp parking area on the right. The sites are a quarter mile in from the road. For the horse camp, continue north on Lower Lake Rd for 3 miles instead of turning on Kellogg. At Palo Rd, turn left and follow the road to the camp staging area.*

Flint Ridge Camp has 10 easy-to-reach hike-in sites on a bluff overlooking the ocean where the Klamath River meets the Pacific, in Redwood National Park, on the California Coastal Trail. Piped water and portable toilets are available. *Call Redwood National Park, (707) 464-6101, for* *reservations. The camp is a quarter-mile hike from the end of Coastal Dr. Take the Coast Hwy (Hwy 1) to the Coastal Dr exit near the Klamath River and head west up the drive 3 miles to the parking area on the east side of the road.*

Nickel Creek Camp has 5 hike-in sites on a bluff overlooking the ocean near Enderts Beach (see Parks/Beaches, above). Each has a picnic table and grill, but there is no piped water. Toilets are nearby. *Call Redwood National Park, (707) 464-6101, for reservations. The park is just south of Enderts Beach. Take the Redwood Hwy to Enderts Beach Rd, 2 miles south of Crescent City, and head west 1 mile to the trailhead. The hike to the campground is less than a mile.*

De Marin Camp, with 10 sites (for tents only) on a bluff overlooking the Pacific, is mostly used by those hiking along the California Coastal Trail. Running water is nearby, and there are storage lockers but few other amenities. No reservations are taken. *Call Redwood National Park, (707) 464-6101, for information. The camp is 2.5 miles from the trailhead, 20 miles south of Crescent City on the Redwood Hwy. Take the Wilson Creek Rd east to the end of the road, where the trail to the camp begins.*

Hiking/Backpacking

Quick. You've got exactly two hours to make the most of a trip through Del Norte County, and if you don't decide how to spend it your redwood memories will be of spotting really big, pretty trees through the car windshield as you whiz by. Even if you only have a half hour to spare, find some way to put some distance between you and your automobile. Even a short nature walk through a grove of centuries-old redwoods is well worth the detour. For a wider look at suggested hikes in the North Coast region, be sure to look at Smith River National Recreation Area, Redwood National Park, and Humboldt Coast chapters.

For such a short walk, the **Stout Grove Trail** (easy; 0.5-mile round trip) through Jedediah Smith Redwoods State Park (see Parks/Beaches, above) has amazingly large payoffs. It is quite simply the prettiest easy short walk you'll ever take. To be surrounded by these ancient giants is entrancing, especially in the off-season when there's nobody else around—just you and a lush, living community of trees too big for belief, blankets of moss, ferns dripping with condensation from the ocean fog, a carpet of rotting branches and needles half a foot thick, and all manner of creatures—particularly the ever-present banana slug, which despite its appearance is quite harmless (the slugs hate, however, to be picked up . . . and demonstrate that by curling into a ball). The trailhead is 2 miles in from the entrance to the park, 9 miles east of Crescent City on US 199, on the south side of the road. Call (707) 464-9533.

Yurok Loop Trail (easy; 1 mile round trip) in Redwood National Park is another easy, accessible trek among the big trees. It's also a more vibrant and active wildlife viewing spot than many other old-growth stands because of shorebirds attracted to the area by **Lagoon Creek,** which ponds at this location. To reach the creek and nature area, head south from Crescent City 15 miles on the Redwood Highway to the Lagoon Creek staging area on the east side of the road. The trail begins right at the parking lot. Being so near the highway, this is a popular tourist spot.

Nature Loop Trail (easy; 0.5 mile round trip) guides you through yet another stunning old-growth redwood grove, this one adjacent to the park headquarters at Del Norte Coast Redwoods State Park (see Parks/Beaches, above). Easy-to-follow interpretive panels mark the walk. The trail is clearly marked inside the park's main entrance, 5 miles south of Crescent City on the Redwood Highway, on the east side of the road. Call (707) 464-9533 for information.

Redwood forests and dramatic Pacific vistas aren't the only reason to take a walk in the Del Norte area. The **Lake Earl Interpretive Trail** (easy; 0.5 mile round trip), for example, is a nature tour of the freshwater marshes at the edge of Lake Earl (see Parks/Beaches, above), the largest of two lagoons found at the center of a vast coastal wildlife area north of Crescent City. A state Fish and Game wildlife center is adjacent. Take the Redwood Highway north from Crescent City to the Lake Earl Dr exit west, then go left at the Old Mill Rd turnoff to the wildlife center on the southern tip of the lake. Call (707) 464-2523 for information.

Damnation Creek Trail (difficult; 4.4 miles round trip) is just what the name suggests—one heck of a tough trek, 1,000 feet down (and back up!) a steep canyon of ancient redwoods, with a magnificent view of the ocean at the bottom. This walk, within Del Norte Coast Redwoods State Park (see Parks/Beaches, above), follows the same route Tolowa Indians used centuries ago. Despite the relatively short distance, allow at least half a day for this hike—and don't even try it unless you're properly outfitted and can handle strenuous exercise. The trailhead is 4 miles south of the main park entrance on the west side of the Redwood Highway at mile marker 16.0.

The **Hobbs Wall Trail** (moderate; 5.5-mile loop) passes through a mixed conifer forest between the Del Norte Coast Redwoods State Park visitors center and the Redwood Highway, peaking out at 1,000 feet for a nice vista of Mill Creek canyon. Begin the hike at the Mill Creek Campground, at the main park entrance, 5 miles south of Crescent City on the east side of the Redwood Highway. Call (707) 464-9533 for information.

The **Boy Scout Tree Trail/Fern Falls Trail** (moderately difficult; 7 miles round trip) takes you through the magnificent Boy Scout Tree area of Jedediah Smith Redwoods State Park, an ancient redwood forest with stunning giants tall and wide enough to blow your mind, then to the lovely Fern Falls, in nearby Jordan Creek. With this kind of scenery, you'll think you're on the film set for the next *Jurassic Park* sequel. But don't fret: The only reptiles in this forest are of manageable size. The trailhead is near the entrance to the park, 9 miles east of Crescent City on US 199, on the south side of the road. Call (707) 464-9533.

The **California Coastal Trail** sections that follow much of the Del Norte coast (moderately difficult; 22 miles, variable) offer a good mix of great vistas of the Pacific, long strolls deep within ancient redwood groves, and spring wildflower walks in open meadows. The northernmost trailhead is at Enderts Beach, the southernmost at the Klamath River overlook on Requa Rd (see Parks/Beaches, above). From Enderts, you'll find ocean-front walks, a wide meadow, and then a sudden change of scenery through a luscious redwood grove. If you go much more than 4 miles, however, be prepared for a steep climb into Del Norte Coast Redwoods State Park. From Requa, it's mostly high bluffs over a rugged and rocky coast, but the second leg of the journey features a nice swing through Del Norte Coast Redwoods State Park. Whether you're hiking north from Requa or south from Enderts, a great option is to make it a two-day affair and stay at the Redwood Hostel instead of camping out. Plan far enough in advance and you can reserve one of two private rooms; it's a great place to cook a hot meal, grab a shower, and start fresh in the morning. The trailhead at the Enderts end of the hike, known as the **Last Chance** section of the trail, is easily found at the end of Enderts Beach Rd; go west off the Redwood Highway, 2 miles south of Crescent City. The Requa leg of the hike, known as the Hidden Beach section of the trail, is 18 miles south of Crescent City at the west Requa Rd turnoff. Park a car at each end and take your time. Contact Redwood National Park, (707) 464-6101. The hostel takes reservations with a major credit card to hold the room; call (707) 482-8265.

Rafting/Canoeing/Kayaking

If you're looking for radical rapids, head east to the Smith River National Recreation Area or the Klamath area mountains (see Smith River National Recreation Area and Klamath Region chapters). Here, even the cantanker-ous **Smith and Klamath Rivers** become gentle and inviting as they make their way to the Pacific. That's not to say, however, that you shouldn't get out on the water anyway. Lunker Fish Trips, (800) 248-4704, rents Tahiti **rafts** during the summer from its riverside facility at 2095 US 199 in Hiouchi, near Jedediah Smith Redwoods State Park (see Parks/Beaches, above), a stretch of the Smith that at times seems more like a swimming pool than the huge, wild, and scenic body of water that it is. Bob around in the water and have fun—and maybe even reel in a cutthroat or two, the river's primary summertime catch. **Fort Dick,** just northeast of Lake Earl of the Redwood Highway, is another good access point for the river. River access points are clearly marked all along US 199.

On the westernmost stretch of the Klamath River, check with Klamath River Outfitters, (800) RIVER-35, about its **guided rafting, canoeing,** and **kayak tours.** Most of these will actually be closer to the Somes Bar stretch (see Klamath Region chapter), where the combination of rapids and calm water is a big draw for beginners. Still, the westernmost leg of the Klamath, although mostly a fishing area, is a suitable canoe run. River access is best along state Hwy 169, 25 miles south of Crescent City and east of the Redwood Highway, or along Alder Camp Rd, west of the Redwood Highway on the south side of the river.

Lake Earl Wildlife Area (see Parks/Beaches, above) is the spot for mist-shrouded canoe or kayak tours of some interesting freshwater lagoon marshes south of the Smith River mouth. Access to the lake is easy at Teal Point at the end of Kellogg Rd. Call the state Department of Fish and Game wildlife center at the lake, (707) 464-2523, for more information.

Fishing

Plainly said, the Smith River (also see Fishing in Smith River National Recreation Area chapter) is the best darn fishing river you're going to find in these parts. Wintertime **king salmon** and **steelhead trout** runs in the winter, and **cutthroat, perch,** and **flounder** fishing in the spring and summer make the Smith pretty much a sure thing all year. Although fish runs have declined dramatically over the past century all along the Pacific Coast, the Smith remains a favorite because of its unimpeded 325-mile course and recent efforts to protect its watershed from silting and other unfortunate environmental effects of logging. The best fishing access is either Jedediah Smith Redwoods State Park (see Parks/Beaches, above), 9 miles east of Crescent City on US 199, or just west of the Redwood Highway, 4 miles south of the Smith River town site at Fred D. Haight Dr. This location has boat rentals, fishing gear, and a boat ramp. Sandie's Marine and Sport, 110 Anchor Way, Crescent City, (707) 465-6499, should have the lowdown on where to go and a good supply of the things you'll need to take with you. Also check with Rick's Outdoor Store and Tackle, 929 Ninth St, Crescent City, (707) 464-2186.

You'll also find good fishing spots along the Pacific Coast from Pelican State Beach to Lake Earl and adjacent Lake Tawala (see Parks/Beaches, above). The lakes are unique in that they, too, contain **salmon** and **steelhead,** although why anyone would want to pass up the Smith for another spot escapes us. Still, there are other alternatives: At the west end of Pacific Ave in Crescent City proper, for example, **surf fishing** is good at Pebble Beach (not to be confused with the golfing mecca down the coast in Monterey). And Crescent City Harbor, just south of the city on the waterfront, has **pier fishing** spots, should the urge strike.

On the Klamath River, head to the Requa town site west of the Redwood Highway and due south of Crescent City, for fishing and boating access near the river mouth. Rivers West Outfitters, 70 Cedar St, Klamath, (707) 482-8635, should be able to guide the way.

To check on possible endangered and threatened species listings for both salmon and steelhead, always ask outfitters for a copy of the latest amended regulations. Alternatively, call the state Department of Fish and Game **river information** line at (707) 442-4502. Enderts Beach (see Parks/Beaches, above) is open for **clamming** in even-numbered years only, take limit is 20.

Wildlife

Enderts Beach (see Parks/Beaches, above) is a popular **gray whale**–spotting location during the 11,000-mile winter migration from the Bering Sea to Mexico, as is the Klamath River overlook at Requa. Sea mammals, including **harbor seals** and **otters,** are a common sight at Lake Earl and the Klamath and Smith River mouths.

The rocky intertidal zones off Enderts Beach (see Parks/Beaches, above) are the premier spot in all of the North Coast for **tidepooling**— which is kind of nice to know, since swimming and playing volleyball à la Venice Beach is pretty much out of the question. Cold, windy, wet, and rugged describe the beach scene here. Limpets, starfish, chitons, sea anemones, and bright orange opalescent nudibranchs (a funky, plantlike species) are found here, as are black turban snails and any number of brilliantly colored sea plants. Take to the rock zone only when it is safe to do so, as sudden tide shifts may leave you stranded and sudden sleeper waves may send you swimming for your life. Call Enderts Beach at (707) 464-6101 for information.

Shorebirds of every imaginable variety are the draw at Lake Earl Wildlife Area (see Parks/Beaches, above), which is managed by state wildlife officials. Look out for great blue herons, brown pelicans, terns, cormorants, arctic geese, and, of course, numerous varieties of duck. If your timing is right, you may even spy a rare snowy plover, one of five threatened species found in the redwood parks region. Lagoon Creek, which forms a busy pond at an easy-to-reach location off the Redwood Highway (see Yurok Loop Trail under Hiking/Backpacking, above), offers much the same type of birding experience with the added bonus of ancient redwood groves. Naturalists at the Lake Earl Wildlife Center, (707) 464-2523, can provide guidance for visiting birders.

The old-growth forests at Jedediah Smith Redwoods State Park and Del Norte Coast Redwoods State Park (see Parks/Beaches, above) are your best bet for spying a glimpse of the North Coast's most elusive and controversial birds, the **northern spotted owl** and the **marbled murrelet**, whose protection under the federal Endangered Species Act has caused hardship and headaches for Del Norte businesses reliant on the timber industry. More commonly seen in the ancient groves are the less-imperiled chickadees, juncos, kinglets, flycatchers, ospreys, and warblers.

Biking

A **mountain-biking** trek through the ancient redwoods is an unforgettable experience, but before setting out, be sure to check current maps for trail restrictions and—most important—to ask at the ranger station or visitors center about trail conditions. This is the wettest part of the state; some areas get more than 100 inches of rain annually, and that means mud, muck, and occasional trail washouts. Of course, there are those who prefer that sort of fun, and that's fine—just try to avoid an unpleasant surprise if you're not up for it.

A great ride follows along the Last Chance section of the **California Coastal Trail** (moderate; 12 miles round trip), from the trailhead on the Redwood Highway to Enderts Beach. This ride is toughest on the return because of a big, steep climb from Enderts, but the varied scenery makes it worth the work. You get deep forests, wide meadows, and stunning ocean vistas all in one trip—and the trailhead is easy to find, 5 miles south of the Del Norte Coast Redwoods State Park main entrance (see Parks/Beaches, above) on the west side of the road. Make this a one-way, mostly downhill ride by parking a car at each end of the course, one at the highway trailhead and the other at Enderts. Nickel Creek Camp (see Camping, above) is on the way if you want to make it a short ride/overnighter.

If you're more in the mood for a swampy marsh terrain with cool breezes, there also are numerous biking trails at **Lake Earl** (see Parks/Beaches, above).

A very nice **road-cycling route** is along **Alder Camp Road,** which starts at the Alder Camp Rd turnoff, west of the Redwood Highway just south of the Klamath River over-crossing, and traverses 8.5 miles of high bluffs overlooking the Pacific along Flint Rock. You have your choice between looping it back on the Redwood Highway where the road reconnects just inside Humboldt County or just turning back and riding the coastal route again—our favorite option, since there's less traffic.

US 199 east from Crescent City is also a suitable cycling route, taking you through ancient forest terrain following the Smith River. Rides can be taken in 5-, 10-, 20-, or even 30-mile sections of the highway, which extends to the Oregon border. Stop at any of a number of clearly marked river access points along the way, including at Jedediah Smith Redwoods State Park (see Parks/Beaches, above). For information, maps, or rentals, contact Back Country Bicycle, 1329 Northcrest Dr, Crescent City, (707) 465-3995, or Cycle Path, 1000 Northcrest Dr #6, Crescent City, (707) 464-5519.

Scenic Drives

One of the premier coastal drives on the Redwood Coast starts at the mouth of the Klamath River and runs 8 miles south towards Prairie Creek Redwoods State Park. If you're heading south on US 101, take the Alder Camp Road exit just south of the Klamath River bridge and follow the signs to the river mouth. North-bound travelers should take the **Redwood National and State Parks Coastal Drive** exit off the Newton B. Drury Scenic Parkway. Campers and cars with trailers are not advised. The narrow, partially paved drive winds through stands of redwoods, with spectacular views of the sea and numerous turnouts for picture-taking (sea lions and pelicans abound) and short hikes. Keep an eye out for the World War II radar station, disguised as a farmhouse and barn.

Just about everything is a scenic drive in these parts, but the **US 199** corridor east from Crescent City is also a favorite. Continue the 60 miles to Elk Valley, or just stay local and stop along the river. It's worth the gas.

As always, the drive-through trees are a winner with the kids. In Del Norte, do the **Klamath Tour Thru Tree,** just west of the Redwood Highway in Klamath at the Terwer Valley exit.

Horseback Riding

There are numerous horse trails in the Del Norte and Humboldt redwood parks. For information about day rides and extended camping trips, contact Tall Trees Outfitters in Orick, (707) 488-5785.

Adventure Calendar

US Nationals Inboard Jet Boat Races, early June: *Klamath,* (707) 482-2251.

Gasquet Raft Races, on the Smith River, mid-July: *Gasquet,* *(707) 457-9600.*

Salmon Festival, mid-August: *Klamath, (707) 444-0433.*

outside in

Attractions

Because it's the northern gateway to the popular Redwood National and State Parks, one might assume **Crescent City** would be a major tourist mecca, rife with fine restaurants and hotels. Unfortunately, it's not. Cheap motels, fast-food chains, and mini-malls are the main attractions along this stretch of US 101. The city is trying, however, to enhance its image. You won't want to make Crescent City your primary destination, but don't be reluctant to spend a day lolling around here, either; you'd be surprised what the town has to offer besides gas and groceries.

For starters, take a side trip to the **North Coast Marine Mammal Center.** This nonprofit organization was established in 1989 to rescue and rehabilitate stranded or injured marine mammals. Staffed by volunteers and funded by donations, the center is the only facility of its kind between San Francisco and Seattle, providing emergency response during environmental disasters and assisting marine researchers by collecting data on marine mammals. The center is open to the public daily year-round, and visitors are welcome to watch the volunteers in action, make a donation, and buy a nature book or two at the gift shop; located at the north end of Crescent City Harbor at 424 Howe Drive in Beach Front Park, (707) 465-MAML.

Other interesting local sites include the operational **Battery Point Lighthouse,** built in 1856 on a small island off the foot of A St. Guided tours of the lighthouse and the light-keeper's living quarters are offered Wednesday through Sunday from 10am to 4pm, tide permitting (you have to cross a tide pool to get there), April through September; (707) 464-3089. Take a shoreline tour along Pebble Beach Dr from the west end of Sixth St to Point St. George. You're bound to see a few seals and sea lions at the numerous pullouts. End the tour with a short walk though a sandy meadow to Point St. George, a relatively deserted bluff that's perfect for a picnic or beach stroll. On a clear day, look out on the ocean for the **St. George Reef Lighthouse,** reportedly the tallest (146 feet above sea level), deadliest (several lightkeepers died in rough seas while trying to dock), and most expensive ($704,000) lighthouse ever built.

From the looks of it, the town of **Klamath** hasn't recovered since it was washed away in 1964, when 40 inches of rain fell within 24 hours. All that remains are a few cheap motels, trailer parks, tackle shops, and boat rental outlets, kept in business by the numerous anglers who line the mighty Klamath River, one of the finest salmon and steelhead streams in the world.

Restaurants

Alias Jones ☆☆   Just when you were about to give up on Crescent City cuisine, along comes the answer to "Where's a good place to eat around here?" This small, lively cafe and bakery does just about everything right. *983 3rd St (between I and J Sts), Crescent City; (707) 465-6987; $.*

Beachcomber Restaurant ☆   If you can get past its tired nautical theme and blue Naugahyde booths, this place does a fair job of providing fresh seafood at reasonable prices. Set right on the beach. *1400 Hwy 101 S (2 miles S of downtown), Crescent City; (707) 464-2205; $$.*

Lodgings

Crescent Beach Motel ☆   Crescent City has the dubious distinction of being the only city along the coast without a swanky hotel. There is, however, an armada of cheap motels, the best of which is the Crescent Beach Motel. *1455 Hwy 101 S (2 miles S of downtown), Crescent City; (707) 464-5436; $.*

Requa Inn ☆   This venerable riverside inn was established in 1885 and is still going strong. The 10 spacious guest rooms are modestly decorated with antique furnishings and have private baths with showers or claw-footed tubs. The Requa Inn Restaurant is one of the only two decent restaurants in the region. *451 Requa Rd (from Hwy 101, take the Requa Rd exit and follow the signs), Klamath; (707) 482-8205; $$.*

More information

Crescent City–Del Norte County Chamber of Commerce: *(707) 464-3174.*
Del Norte Association for Cultural Awareness: *(707) 464-1336.*
State parks, Del Norte County section: *(707) 464-9533.*

Redwood National Park

Some 60,000 acres of federal land within Redwood National Park boundaries in northern Humboldt County east of Orick, including Tall Trees Grove, Redwood Creek, Lady Bird Johnson Grove, and the Bridge Creek Ridge Area.

Still wondering what a redwood tree looks like without an RV parked next to it? Well, this is one of the spots where you are guaranteed to find out. Trailers and motor homes can't handle the steep grades and sharp corners on nearby Bald Hills Road; as a result, the parking area at the Redwood National Park visitors center on US Highway 101 south of Orick looks like a used camper lot as the masses board shuttle buses that take them off to view some of the largest trees in the world. The attractions include a 367-foot-8-inch tall monster (in Tall Trees Grove on Redwood Creek), said to be the single tallest tree on the planet—a claim that has been neither tested nor disputed since the National Geographic Society measured the tree in 1964.

When it was established in 1968, Redwood National Park encompassed some 100,000 acres of forestland, including the old-growth stands found here. Today, with parkland additions, redwoods in state and national parks cover some 400 square miles of California, including 80,000 acres of old-growth groves that somehow survived the runaway logging through the North Coast range. Tall Trees and Lady Bird Johnson Groves, both found off Bald Hills Road, are considered the top of the line—which is why this place seems so much like a tree museum with gaggles of tourists lining up like crows on a fence.

From an anthropological point of view, this is a curious thing. We are people who will mow down nearly 2 million acres of magnificent ancient forest to build homes and furniture, only to later decide that perhaps we should have enshrined them instead.

If the spectacle seems a bit too much like a zoo containing trees instead of exotic animals, keep in mind that there are ways to avoid the crowds. During dry months, the long hike paralleling Redwood Creek or a horseback tour of the woods out of Orick are among the fine alternatives to herding onto a bus.

Getting There

From Crescent City, take US Highway 101 (US 101) south for 50 miles; from Eureka, take US 101 north 40 miles. Two miles past the Orick town site, head east at Bald Hills Road (motor homes and trailers not advised), where the main attractions are found for the next 10 miles. At the Redwood Information Center, (707) 464-6101, extension 5265, on the Redwood Highway near Orick, maps, information, and shuttles to some of the redwood groves off Bald Hills Road can be arranged. For information on other federal parklands, see Humboldt Coast and Del Norte Coast chapters.

Adjoining Areas

NORTH: **Del Norte Coast**

EAST: **Smith River National Recreation Area**

SOUTH AND WEST: **Humboldt Coast**

inside out

Hiking/Backpacking

There's no getting around it. If you want to see the biggest trees in the world, you're going to have to work for it. They haven't gotten around yet to building an escalator that will drop you off right at the entrance to the world-famous Tall Trees Grove. There are, however, a number of different ways to reach the grove, all of them a heck of a lot more enjoyable than waiting for a moving sidewalk to drop you off. Three of the hikes described here end up at the grove; choose based on how much work you want to put into it, and how much time you can stand being in a place so pretty you've got to pinch yourself every time you round another corner. Note: This chapter describes only hikes on the federal lands east of Orick. For hikes in Prairie Creek Redwoods State Park and on federal parklands near the coast, see Hiking/Backpacking in Humboldt Coast and Del Norte

Coast chapters. The Redwood Information Center, on the west side of the Redwood Highway south of Orick, can give you pointers; phone (707) 464-6101, extension 5265.

Tall Trees Grove Trail (moderate; 2.6 miles round trip) is the easiest way to reach the big stuff. You've got to plan it just right, however, to pull this one off, particularly in peak season when a lot of other people are running around redwood country with the same idea. Despite the trail's reasonably short length, allow at least half a day for the trip; it's a long, steep, winding drive to the trailhead. First order of business: Pick up a permit that will allow you to make that drive—only a limited number of cars are allowed on the trailhead's access road. Motor homes and trailers need not apply; it's just not possible to negotiate the narrow passages and steep grades. Permits for the access road are available on a first-come, first-served basis at the Redwood Information Center west of Orick on the Redwood Highway. Option two is to take a (gasp) shuttle bus from the center, but don't if you don't have to. It spoils the fun.

Once you have a permit, head north of town on the highway for 5 miles to the Bald Hills Rd turnoff east, and begin the defensive driving portion of the tour (the only real switchbacks are ones you'll have to negotiate behind the wheel). Five miles in, the Tall Trees access road on the right delivers you to the trailhead. From there, it is a pleasant walk descending 800 feet into the Redwood Creek canyon, where someone with a green thumb stuck some redwood tree seeds in the ground six or seven centuries ago. Behold. Enjoy. Take your time. This place is going to blow you away.

Lady Bird Johnson Grove Trail (easy; 1 mile round trip) is a pleasant and easy-to-reach self-guided nature tour through another impressive old-growth grove, the site where the First Lady dedicated the newly christened Redwood National Park in 1968. Take the Redwood Highway to the Bald Hills Rd turnoff, north of Orick on the east side of the road, and continue through about 2 miles of zigs and zags to the trailhead parking area on the left (north) side of the road.

Emerald Ridge Trail (moderate; 12 miles round trip) follows a switchbacky ridgeline path from Dolason Prairie to the Tall Trees Grove trailhead, where you then descend into a *Jurassic Park*–like set containing all things huge, ancient, and green. This is a good alternative to taking a shuttle bus to the grove on those occasions when no Tall Trees access road permits are available and you don't have time to hike all the way up via Redwood Creek (see above). The tough part is that the trailhead is 12 miles out on Bald Hills Rd, east from Orick off the Redwood Highway—the drive is half the work.

Lost Man Creek Trail (moderate to difficult, depending how far in you go; up to 10 miles round trip) follows a natural and unimpeded mountain creek through a well-forested and pristine setting on the western flanks of Hotler Ridge. It is best to take it in just a few miles, maybe find a nice pooled-up section of creek where you can sit down and gather your thoughts, then hike out. The trail ascends rather steeply after that, eventually connecting with Bald Hills Rd to the south near the Redwood Creek Overlook. The trailhead is 2.3 miles north of where Bald Hills Rd intersects with the Redwood Highway, north of Orick, on the east side of the road.

Redwood Creek Trail (moderate; 16 miles round trip) is pretty much a summer-only proposition because of hazardous winter creek crossings. You will notice spruce and alders mixed in with the redwood as you make your way through this lush thicket of ferns and poison oak—but never fear. Go the whole way (avoiding the poison oak), and the payoff is a stunning view of the Tall Trees Grove from a ridge directly across from the giant redwoods. The trail descends the ridge and heads into the grove itself. The trek is manageable as an all-day hike, but better as an overnighter. Camping permits are available at the Redwood Information Center. Camping is allowed only on creek-side gravel bars and must be at least a quarter mile from the grove itself; there are numerous other restrictions (apply for a permit and they will fill you in). We consider this hike the best option of all for reaching Tall Trees Grove; there is something mystical about being able to spy these magnificent trees from afar, then close in on them, and eventually stand beneath them as the hike unfolds. Also, working for it enhances the payoff. And the trails along the creek aren't anywhere near as crowded as the others in the Tall Trees area after the first few miles in. The trailhead is just northeast of Orick off Bald Hills Rd.

Camping

Primitive backpack camping is the only game in town (see Hiking/Backpacking, above). Developed sites are available at Prairie Creek Redwoods State Park just northwest of Orick, as well as in nearby Patrick's Point State Park, Del Norte Coast Redwoods State Park, and Jedediah Smith State Park. Check also with the less-traveled Smith River National Recreation Area sites east of Crescent City, and in Six Rivers National Forest south of there. Complete camping information about all of these areas can be found throughout this section in Humboldt Coast, Del Norte Coast, and Smith River National Recreation Area chapters.

Horseback Riding

Nice horseback routes are situated throughout the Redwood National Park trail system, from the Orick rodeo grounds into the thickets. A bonus for equestrians: Mountain bikes are not allowed on these trails, which approach Redwood Creek on its western flanks. The National Park Service has a concessionaire, Tall Trees Outfitters, (707) 488-5785, which offers guided day tours and longer camping expeditions.

Photography

Trying to do the Tall Trees Grove justice with a photograph can be intimidating. File a snapshot away in your memory first so you can see it again anytime you close your eyes. If you insist on returning home with a postcard-perfect snapshot, be advised that redwood forests are most photogenic on a cloudy day when there are no shafts of sunlight coming through the trees. Use a tripod for best results. Lost Man's Creek, because of its eerily deserted and pristine feel, is a great place to try and capture the moment on film.

Wildlife

Wildlife watchers would do best following the numerous creeks that traverse this area, namely Lost Man's Creek and Redwood Creek, since they seem to draw the most diverse range of birds and mammals. Hillsides along Bald Hills Rd are also a sure bet for birders who want to scope out raptors and other birds of prey.

Hike a few miles in from the trailheads along both Redwood and Lost Man's Creeks (see Hiking/Backpacking, above) to get the most out of a **birding** expedition through these forested canyons. In old-growth groves, look for the rare **marbled murrelet** or **northern spotted owl,** both of which have been spied in and around the Tall Trees Grove. Chickadees, dark-eyed juncos, ruby-crowned kinglets, flycatchers, ospreys, and warblers also may be spotted here. It is important, particularly on Redwood Creek, to hike in far enough that the voices of other visitors do not muffle the calls you will be listening for. Most park visitors don't go beyond the first few miles of trail.

The Redwood Creek approach to the Tall Trees Grove is preferred by birders for the same reason. The Redwood Region Audubon Society frequently schedules **guided birding tours** of North Coast hot spots. Write to PO Box 1054, Eureka, CA 95502, for schedule information. Also contact park visitors centers in whatever area you're interested in for outing announcements. The marshes around Humboldt and Arcata Bays (see Wildlife, Humboldt Coast chapter) and at Lake Earl (see Wildlife, Del

Norte Coast chapter) are also fantastic birding spots for those exploring the entire North Coast region.

While you're in the Orick area, it would be a shame not to head to Prairie Creek Redwoods State Park just northwest of here for a look at the magnificent **Roosevelt elk** herds found both there and on the adjacent Gold Bluffs Beach (see Humboldt Coast chapter). **Black bears, mountain lions, deer, raccoons,** and sometimes **beavers** are found in the forested areas around Redwood Creek. Observe all safety measures, especially when camping with food that may attract bears.

Biking

As of this writing, only **Lost Man's Creek Trail** (see Hiking/Backpacking, above) is open to **mountain bikes** in the forested areas east of Orick. Bikes are not allowed in the Redwood Creek area or in the horseback areas east of the Orick rodeo grounds. This significantly limits riders looking for a loop that is completely off-road. Because Lost Man's Creek Trail is so darn steep, riders not hoping for a major workout in advanced bike-riding territory won't want to go beyond the first few miles. There are, however, numerous other mountain-biking trails in and around the state and national parks adjacent to Orick (see Humboldt Coast and Del Norte Coast chapters). Also consider biking the forest roads in the Smith River National Recreation Area and Six Rivers National Forest (see Smith River National Recreation Area chapter). Note: The North Coast is a soggy place. If you're out mountain biking, there's a good chance you're going to pick up some mud along the way.

As for on-road riding, what's bad news for the motor home set is good news for **road cyclists** who want to bust out on a challenging, steep, 20-mile ride through some of the most beautiful forested lands in the world. Bald Hills Rd, you see, is closed to the big-homes-on-wheels you'll see whizzing by on the Redwood Highway. Ride the 10 miles to the 3,097-foot Schoolhouse Peak, then descend back toward Orick, or make a longer ride of it and follow the road all the way east to Weitchpec. Also see Del Norte Coast and Humboldt Coast chapters for road cycling routes. Outfitters in the area include Henderson Center Bicycles, 2811 F St, Eureka, (707) 443-9861, and Revolution Bicycle Repair, 1360 G St, Arcata, (707) 822-2562, but you're best off bringing your own equipment, since there are no rentals available on site.

Scenic Drives

If you're looking for something off the main thoroughfare and you aren't driving a motor home or pulling a trailer, consider exploring **Bald Hills**

Road (see Biking, above), which zigzags through Redwood Creek Canyon and some of the nicest ancient redwood forest groves in public ownership, then rises above the tree line and tops Schoolhouse and Coyote Peaks at over 3,000 feet. The road then descends 68 miles from its beginning at the US 101 interchange into the Klamath River Canyon near Hoopa Valley. In addition to the redwood groves described above, highlights include Gans Prairie, Elk Camp, Schoolhouse Pasture Rock (a good midpoint picnic spot), and French Camp Ridge, which provides great vistas of the Klamath. Connect at the end of the drive with Hwy 168, which will follow the Klamath north to Prairie Creek Redwoods State Park. This long, meandering drive takes a full day to complete, but provides a fantastic overview of the redwood region with beautiful vistas of the Pacific Ocean and the redwood-forested lands meeting the beaches, along with wide views of canyons meandering west from the mountains. To repeat the warning, do not attempt this in an RV or while pulling a trailer, as the road is extremely steep in places and windy. Also do not attempt it if you have not recently had the brakes on your vehicle inspected or if you have any doubts about its mechanical condition!

Fishing

Because of logging that occurred in the days before this area was preserved as a national park, the **steelhead** and **salmon** runs through Redwood Creek have been severely diminished in the past century. Consequently, anglers are going to have a better go of it on the Smith River in the Del Norte area (see Del Norte Coast chapter) or even the Eel or Klamath Rivers. That's not to say you shouldn't bring a rod and reel along on a Redwood Creek Trail overnighter, since the hike is short enough that there will be plenty of time for fishing. Just don't get your hopes up that the big one that got away is going to bite here. In summer, when backpacking Redwood Creek is more manageable, **cutthroat** is probably going to be the extent of it.

outside in

Attractions

The burl art capital of the world, **Orick** looks more like a huge outdoor gift shop than a town. What's burl art, you ask? Well, take a sizable chunk of redwood, do a little carving here and there with a small chain saw, and when it resembles some sort of mammal or rodent, you have yourself a piece of burl art. There are thousands of burl pieces to choose from here, ranging from the Abominable Burlman to Sasquatch and the Seven Dwarfs. Several roadside stands have viewing booths where mesmerized tourists watch the redwood chips fly. Orick is also the southern entryway to Redwood National and State Parks; 1 mile south of town off US 101 is the **Redwood Information Center,** where visitors can pick up a free park map and browse through geologic, wildlife, and Native American exhibits; open daily 9am–5pm, (707) 464-6101, extension 5265.

See the Humboldt Coast chapter for additional recommendations.

Restaurants

Rolf's Park Café ☆   Here among the redwoods is the place to find good bratwurst, Wiener schnitzel, and crêpes Suzette. There are also some unusual offerings such as wild boar, buffalo, and elk steak (the truly adventurous should get the combo platter featuring all three). *On US 101 about 2 miles N of Orick;* (707) 488-3841; $$.

More Information

Orick Chamber of Commerce: *(707) 488-2885.*
Redwood Information Center: *(707) 464-6101, extension 5265.*
Redwood National and State Parks: *www.nps.gov/redw.*
Redwood National Park Headquarters: *(707) 464-6101.*

Humboldt Coast

The Humboldt County coast from the Del Norte County border on the north to the Mendocino County line on the south, including Arcata and Humboldt Bays, Prairie Creek Redwoods State Park, Humboldt Redwoods State Park, and Avenue of the Giants.

Before he used $900 million worth of high-yield junk bonds to take over Pacific Lumber Company during that decade of excess, the 1980s, Texas financier Charles Hurwitz hired a team of surveyors to take an aerial tour of the 200,000 acres of redwood and mixed conifer forest he would own when the deal went through. He wanted to know, in board feet, just how much timber was out there so he could run the numbers to see if the investment would be a wise one. Sure enough, the amount of timber in the forested canyons on the eastern slopes of Humboldt County turned out to be a heck of a lot more than anybody realized, so when Hurwitz's Maxxam Corporation swallowed up Pacific Lumber, the chain saws started working overtime. That's about when the tree-huggers swung into big action. Radical environmental activists staged the tumultuous "Redwood Summer" protests, which gave way to the more recent battle to save Headwaters Forest, the largest remaining stand of old-growth redwoods still in private hands. The government ultimately purchased Headwaters Forest and adjacent lands. These, consisting of some 10,000 acres including two old-growth groves, are Northern California's newest preserve. There will be public access soon, through the US Bureau of Land Management. Despite this accomplishment, anti-logging protests continue. Logging jobs versus spotted-owl habitat. Corporate profits versus a nesting place for a goofy-looking seabird. Mix in a little savings-and-loan-failure debt, a gaggle of politicians, and a $380-million deal to rescue a bunch of trees, and it all starts to sound a little crazy.

While this is all important and should concern us, the visitor to Humboldt County is best off forgetting about it for a while and just having a good time. How can we say that? Yes, it is true that at one time there were more than 2 million acres of old-growth coastal redwoods covering a 30-mile-wide band along 500 miles of coast from southern Oregon to Big Sur. It's also true that only a fraction of those trees are left today. What many lose sight of in the heat of the current debate, however, is that more than a quarter million acres of redwood forestland are currently preserved forever in state, national, and county parks, and that includes some 80,000 acres of ancient trees in forests that the loggers never got—and never will get—a chance to mow down.

Rather than blow a gasket over what has been lost and get carried away in a debate that has no end in sight, it makes sense, for a visitor, to stand back and marvel at some of the most magnificent public forests in the world—while not forgetting to also take in the marshlands of Humboldt Bay and the countless special places where the redwoods stand at attention to face the Pacific along the coast. Whether you're gliding by in a canoe on a gentle stretch of the Eel River, taking a picturesque mountain-bike trek through the cool forests, camping at the base of a 300-foot giant, or just tracking the legendary Bigfoot, these are places we were meant to enjoy. So go for it and leave the hand-wringing for another day.

Getting There

It's simple; just get on the Redwood Highway (US Highway 101), point the car north, and drive. When the trees by the highway become so fat and tall that you can no longer resist the urge to pull over and just look at them, you've arrived. Another route, however, is to take the Coast Highway (Highway 1) all the way up from Mendocino, then join US Highway 101 (US 101) north of Ferndale. It's a matter of exchanging a big-tree drive for a longer and more lonely trek along some of the wildest, rockiest, most stunningly beautiful coast found anywhere. The two largest cities in this region are Arcata and Eureka. Smaller communities, however, are where the charm is. Along the US 101 corridor you'll find logging hamlets like Rio Dell, Orick, Carlotta (east on Highway 36), and Scotia (still owned by Pacific Lumber Company). Highway 36 follows the Van Duzen River east through the Six Rivers National Forest lands, and also passes nearest the infamous Headwaters Forest grove. To reach the Trinity region, consider a drive along the Trinity River east on Highway 299 from US 101 in Eureka. A key stop for information about your outdoor options is the Humboldt Redwoods State Park Visitors Center, on the Redwood Highway at Mattole Road, just north of Myers Flat, (707) 946-2263.

Adjoining Areas

NORTH: **Del Norte Coast**

SOUTH: **Northern Mendocino Coast**

EAST: **Smith River National Recreation Area**

Parks/Beaches

Redwood Highway

In the early-morning cold, the northwest corner of Humboldt County is almost spooky. On the forested ridges, trees 18 feet across and 300 feet tall vanish into the fog above, not unlike Jack's beanstalk. The condensation dripping from overhead branches makes the sound of a light rain. The forest floor is a spongy carpet of debris—layer after layer of fallen branches, twigs, and needles in a brew of rotting decay and damp soil—amid canyon walls where ferns grow taller than a man. At the edge of **Gold Bluffs,** the big, stormy Pacific is hardly visible; hidden behind a gray curtain, it crashes and moans. A herd of Roosevelt elk, huge and dark with oversized antlers and each weighing 1,000 pounds, stands picturesque and motionless, looking as unreal as a row of plastic reindeer on a suburban front lawn at Christmas. Such is the scene at **Prairie Creek Redwoods State Park,** 14,500 acres of old-growth redwoods, high ocean bluffs, a 6-mile ribbon of beaches, creeks that have carved deep redwood canyons thick with ferns, and open hilly meadows. We consider this a great spot to begin a tour of the Humboldt coast, not just because of its pristine condition and breathtaking beauty, but because the diverse landscape holds a little bit of everything redwood country has to offer: wild rivers, ancient forests, eroded cliffs meeting the sea—and the amenities to take it all in. There are 75 miles of trails for hiking and mountain biking, secluded river fishing spots, and 100 campsites quiet enough that all you hear are the ocean, the wind through the trees, and the rushing of streams—not highway traffic passing by. While a large section of the forest was wiped out by the 1998 El Niño floods, it's all patched together now for visitors' enjoyment. The park is 50 miles north of Eureka on the Redwood Highway; call (707) 464-6101 for information.

The 10-mile stretch of oceanfront extending south from Prairie Creek is a string of lovely lagoons and adjacent marshlands that are among the most productive shorebird habitats on the North Coast, as well as a busy stopover along the Pacific Flyway for migratory birds. Boating, fishing, bird-watching, and waterside picnics are primary activities here. The lagoons are divided among three main recreation areas: Humboldt Lagoons State Park, the adjacent Big Lagoon County Park, and the coastal Henry A. Merto State Recreation Area. For information about the state facilities, call (707) 488-2171. The county recreation area can be reached at (707) 445-7652. The lagoons all are adjacent to the Redwood Highway between Orick and Trinidad, north of Eureka.

A popular 2-mile hike (Rim Trail) along the high ocean bluffs at the 600-acre **Patrick's Point State Park,** 4 miles north of Trinidad, and half a mile west of the Redwood Highway, follows the same route that Yurok Indians used thousands of years ago. Stroll down Agate Beach (keep an eye out for the semiprecious stones), or climb the stone stairway up to the house-size Ceremonial Rock. The bluffs are a popular whale-watching spot, and the beaches are prime for tidepooling; there are also campsites, hiking and cycling trails, and a Native American cultural museum (see Attractions, below). Call the park at (707) 677-3570 for information.

South of Patrick's Point are 15 miles of coastal access that includes **Trinidad** and **Little River State Beaches, Mad River Beach,** and numerous access points for rock fishing, ocean-side picnics, and boating. You'll also find good clamming spots in ponds along the east side of the Redwood Highway. For information about the state facilities, call the park system office at (707) 488-2171. The county recreation area office can be reached at (707) 445-7652. South of Humboldt Bay, the Redwood Highway extends 20 miles inland. One nice spot off the beaten path is **Grizzly Creek Redwoods State Park,** a small but pretty set of old-growth groves south of Hwy 36. The reason these magnificent groves are in the public domain is that a Georgia-Pacific bigwig actually declared they were too pretty to cut down. Fishing and swimming in the Van Duzen River, well-developed hiking trails, and camping all are available here, about 15 miles east of Fortuna from the Redwood Highway. Call the park for information at (707) 777-3683.

Peace, quiet, and manageable crowds are *not* what you will find as you continue south to some of the most heavily used redwood parks on the North Coast. Still, the huge smattering of big trees on either side of US 101 some 10 miles north of Garberville is more than just a roadside curiosity. **Humboldt Redwoods State Park** covers more than 50,000 acres of some of the most stunningly beautiful ancient forest groves on earth. While the park's most popular attraction is the 32-mile **Avenue of the Giants** automobile tour (see Scenic Drives/Photography, below)—sort of a backpacking hike for couch potatoes—the biggest rewards await those who take the time to actually get out of their cars and look around or, better yet, make arrangements to stay awhile. There are numerous picnic sites among the giant trees. And while these groves are among the most visited anywhere, there is plenty of room to spread out and find some privacy among the cool, shaded canyons and creeks, the 3,379-foot summit of Grasshopper Peak, or along Mattole Rd, which follows Bull Creek deep into the woods, eventually leading to some wild and secluded sections of the Humboldt coast at Cape Mendocino. The park is on the Redwood Highway, 30 miles south of Eureka and 25 miles inland from Cape Mendocino. Call the park visitor center for information, (707) 946-2409.

Benbow State Recreation Area is centered around a 26-acre man-made lake south of Garberville. This is a popular swimming and picnicking spot—on those summer days when it gets warm enough for visitors to even think about taking a dunk. Call the recreation area at (707) 247-3318 for more information.

Humboldt's redwood tree row ends (or begins, depending on which way you're headed) at **Richardson Grove State Park,** 6 miles south of Humboldt Redwoods at the Mendocino County line. Richardson, which rests on the banks of the Eel River's south fork, encompasses over 1,500 acres of ancient redwoods mixed with Douglas fir, oaks, big leaf maples, and all of the add-ons that make these forests the treat that they are: tall ferns, creepy clumps of fungus growing on logs and rocks, and slithery banana slugs. There are two riverside campgrounds, but unfortunately they're within earshot of the Redwood Highway (quiet time in the campground ends at 6am, too). The best bet is to hike out as far away as possible from the motor home action. Call the park at (707) 247-3318 for more information.

South Humboldt oceanfront

The traveler heading south on the Redwood Highway faces a dilemma after passing Humboldt Bay: What will it be, more of the most beautiful ancient forests found anywhere in the world, or some of the most stunning wild beaches and eroding cliffs found anywhere in the world? The ideal solution would be to do both, but trying to do a turbo-tour of the Redwood Coast is extremely bad form. Day visitors are best off finding one or two spots to explore in depth rather than burning a tank of gas trying to see it all and coming away from the experience with little more than memories of pretty trees and rocky coast flying by at 50 miles per hour. Hang a left at the Hwy 1 junction with the Redwood Highway, 3 miles south of Loleta, to find the most primitive and stunning public access areas along the coast north of Big Sur. **Cape Mendocino,** where this stretch of Hwy 1 meets the ocean, is the westernmost point in all of California, extending even further west into the ocean than Point Reyes National Seashore in Marin. You'll find coastal access points just south of the cape, some with rugged paths leading down the high bluffs to the beaches below; it is best, however, to continue south on the highway to the official state beach access paths at **McNutt Gulch.** This is the southernmost part of the stretch of Hwy 1 that directly fronts the ocean—if the road veers east and you cross Mattole River, you've gone too far. You're better off using this part of the Humboldt coast for nature-viewing and beachcombing rather than any hard-core water sports, since the beaches are constantly changing size and shape under the weight of heavy surf and extreme ocean currents. Cape Mendocino has good whale-watching spots, however, and the surf fishing is excellent at any of the coastal access points from here to the Mendocino County line. There are pockets of private property mixed in with the public headlands and beaches, so pay close attention to signs. Major hint: Some spots along the highway may *look* like public access trails to the beach, but are actually private property. It is best not to try hiking any of these small, primitive trails—especially along the high bluffs, where the footing is often far from solid. The 1998 winter rains left many of these areas in particularly precarious condition. Legal public access points have the best-maintained trails, and all are wide enough for a confident hike to the beach. Look for proper signage; if it's not marked, move along to avoid having to be airlifted to the nearest trauma center by the Coast Guard.

Those who don't want to risk a hike from the road at all can still get to the beach by opting for the easiest coastal access point in the region: **Mattole Beach** at the mouth of the Mattole River, which has an actual parking lot! While this spot is away from the high, rocky bluffs that are the main attraction of the Humboldt coast, it has nice sandy dunes, with good surf fishing spots on the beach and river fishing spots upstream. The adjacent coastal marsh area is also good bird-watching territory. The beach is part of the vast 62,000-acre **King Range National Conservation Area,** a desolate area of high mountain peaks right on the ocean that's under the jurisdiction of the US Bureau of Land Management (BLM). This is also the northernmost section of northern Mendocino County's world-famous Lost Coast, whose name recalls the US government's relocation of the region's native people in order to open it up to logging and other money-making ventures during the California Gold Rush. Much of the Humboldt portion of the wilderness is difficult to reach by car; there are few paved roads, and those that exist are poorly maintained. It is, however, possible to hike south from Mattole or north from Shelter Cove (25 miles to the south) to reach more isolated beaches in between. Camps are located throughout the wilderness area for backpackers who wish to do so, but explorers should be sure to contact the BLM for information about current conditions before setting out, (707) 825-2300.

Shelter Cove, the southernmost coastal access point in Humboldt County, is within the King Range area but is privately owned. The beach area has a public boat launch and marina, however, with good surf fishing and tidepooling spots along the shore. Take Shelter Cove Rd west from Hwy 1 (Kings Peak Rd). Call the Shelter Cove marina, (707) 986-7432, for information.

Hiking/Backpacking

A good redwood experience doesn't necessarily have to involve a three-day backpacking pilgrimage deep into the wilderness. Most visitors to coastal Humboldt, in fact, opt for short treks of just an hour or two (and some never even get out of their cars!). A short walk is plenty, since excellent old-growth groves are situated along many easy, accessible trails. Longer and more difficult hikes, however, are your only option if you want to escape the crowds and really get a good snout full of the dank, decaying redwood wilderness just as it was before the chain saw and the Winnebago were invented. But don't attempt longer hikes without proper equipment and preparation. We call these places "parks," but they are wild in the true sense of the word. Northern Mountain Supply, 125 W Fifth St, Eureka, (800) 878-3583, is one of the more reputable outfitters in the region. Check in there for the essentials before you jump on a trail and vanish into the woods.

Rockefeller Loop Trail (easy; 0.5 mile round trip) in Humboldt Redwoods State Park (see Parks/Beaches, above) is a short but beautiful walking loop through part of the largest contiguous stand of old-growth forest still in existence (9,000 acres). The trail begins near the Redwood Highway, but once it crosses the Eel River it delves quickly into a cool, shady grove of ancient trees hugging the banks of both the river and Bull Creek. Don't be fooled by this trail's proximity to the highway. With the exception of some traffic noise and the presence of numerous other walkers, this section of forest is an excellent spot to get a feel for the redwoods. Those with the time and energy for a longer haul may continue deeper into the woods along Bull Creek via Bull Creek Flats Trail (see below).

Another excellent short walk in Humboldt Redwoods is along **Founder's Grove Nature Trail** (easy; 0.5 mile round trip), a self-guided nature tour just east of the Avenue of the Giants and near the Eel River fork. This section of trail includes the **Dyerville Giant,** which was more than 360 feet tall when it toppled in 1992 after being struck by a neighboring tree that gave way. This grove is named for the original founders of the Save-the-Redwoods League. Both trails are near the Redwood Highway intersection with Mattole Rd, 30 miles south of Eureka and 25 miles inland from Cape Mendocino, and are well marked. Call the park visitors center, (707) 946-2409, for more information.

Woodland Trail (easy; 1.6 miles round trip) in Richardson Grove State Park (see Parks/Beaches, above) is another sweat-free stroll through beautiful forestland right at the edge of the main highway. After crossing North Creek on a foot bridge near the park headquarters, the trail leads uphill some 200 feet (a mild grade), zigzagging around numerous impressively large trees. There is an optional half-mile side trail that crosses Laurel Creek just north of the Woodland grove. **Lookout Point Trail** (easy; 1.7 miles round trip) climbs up easy grades through forests just as lovely to a lookout over the Eel River; the key differences are the absence of creeks here, and the addition of a high view. Both trails begin at the park headquarters, west of the Redwood Highway at the Mendocino County line. Call the park, (707) 247-3318, for more information.

Proceeding north to just before the Del Norte County line, the **Fern Canyon Loop Trail** (easy; 0.75 mile round trip), meanders through a lush redwood canyon of incredibly tall and thick five-finger ferns. This is a soggy hike, as the canyon is dark, dank, and often misty. The trail is within Prairie Creek Redwoods State Park (see Parks/Beaches, above) and tops out at the Gold Bluffs overlooking the Pacific. Take the Davidson Rd (unpaved) turnoff west from the Redwood Highway 7 miles south of the Del Norte County border and follow to the end past the Gold Bluffs Campground to the trailhead. Call the park, (707) 488-2171, for more information.

For an interesting change of scenery, **Sanctuary Trail** (easy; 2 miles round trip) through the marshes on the north shores of Arcata Bay is a great stroll for birders who want a close-up view of the amazing biodiversity in the marshes and brackish waters near the rain-drenched North Coast. The marshes are a unique mixing zone where an unusual combination of migratory birds, nesting shorebirds, and species that nest primarily in redwood habitats can be found at close range. Take the New Navy Base Rd exit from the Redwood Highway west to I St, then continue south to the end of the road to reach the trailhead. Call the Audubon Society, (707) 826-7031, for information, including a schedule for interpretive walks. Another popular walk among birders and beachcombers alike is along the **Mattole River Trail** (easy; varied length with no loop), which extends along the banks of the Mattole River and dead-ends at the river mouth on Mattole Beach (see Parks/Beaches, above). You'll find numerous fishing spots and interesting bird-watching along a wide coastal wetland area. Stage from the end of Lighthouse Rd, 5 miles west of the Hwy 1 junction in Petrolia. Call (707) 825-3200 for more information.

While short walks through the redwoods are certainly satisfying and accessible, they are generally custom-made for the highway traveler, and at peak season these trails can be a lot like the aisles of a supermarket on the weekend before Thanksgiving. It takes only a second to *see* a redwood forest; to really explore one, however, requires quiet away from the crowds—and that means longer walks to where the sounds of mist spraying from high branches and old trees creaking as they sway is unbroken by voices, camera clicks, footsteps, or the squeals of excited children.

Bull Creek Flats Trail (easy; 9 miles round trip) in Humboldt Redwoods State Park (see Parks/Beaches, above) may seem precariously near some of the North Coast's most-traveled self-guided nature walks, but the crowds thin quickly if you make your way west from the highway. The trail follows Bull Creek through a lush canyon of redwoods and Douglas fir, with a passage through the park's famous Big Tree area. The trailhead begins near the Founder's and Rockefeller Grove trails just west of the park entrance, alongside Mattole Rd, on the Redwood Highway, 30 miles south of Eureka and 25 miles inland from Cape Mendocino. Another Humboldt Redwoods trail where the masses are unlikely to follow is **Allen's Trail** (difficult; 1 mile round trip), which catapults almost straight up from the banks of the Eel River, through the forest to the peak more than 1,200 feet overhead. The faint of heart should not attempt the hike; those who welcome the workout get solitude as their reward. The trailhead is 2 miles north of the Founder's/Rockefeller entrance to the park and east of the Redwood Highway, 30 miles south of Eureka and 25 miles inland from Cape Mendocino. Call the Humboldt Redwoods State Park visitors center, (707) 946-2409, for information.

James Irvine Trail (moderate; 9.5 miles round trip) is a great day hike for those who want to sample a little bit of everything the Humboldt Redwood Coast has to offer. It begins in a pretty, open meadow; passes through three different varieties of forest; skirts through the lush Fern Canyon; and tops out at Gold Bluffs Beach facing the Pacific—and there's a high likelihood of coming across a Roosevelt elk or two along the way! The trailhead is at the Prairie Creek Redwoods State Park visitors center (see Parks/Beaches, above), 50 miles north of Eureka and 6 miles north of Orick off the Redwood Highway; call (707) 464-6101.

At Disneyland, the rides that required an "E ticket" (before the park began charging only general admission) were the wildest and the scariest—the kind that could take your breath away or make your heart skip a beat. Well, if the three-day hike along the **Lost Coast Trail** from Mattole Beach south to Shelter Cove (difficult and dangerous; 25 miles one way) were a ride at Disneyland, it would be ranked right up there with Space Mountain and the Matterhorn. This hike is not, however, anything like a theme park. There are rattlesnakes to watch out for, sleeper waves that can tow a hiker right off the beach and out to sea, unsteady and rickety sections of cliff-side trail, streams to hop over, and slick rocks to navigate in places where the trail simply disappears. This is not the kind of hike you decide to do on the spur of the moment—especially if your gear is not up to par; they don't call it the Lost Coast for nothing. These high coastal mountain peaks covering more than 60,000 acres; deserted black-sand beaches; wild, meandering creeks dropping directly into the sea; and vast, uncharted forestlands—all strung across the longest section of wild coast in all of California—are a main Humboldt-area attraction for adventure-loving weekend warriors. Most of the route follows the coast, but every imaginable type of hiking terrain is encountered along the way—including sand. In the El Niño storms of 1998, the heaviest rains and most powerful ocean surges in a century, the entire California coast took a severe beating—resulting in unusually fast erosion on cliffs and stunning changes to beaches. Permits are not required, but in light of these recent events you should still check with the BLM, 1695 Heidon Rd, Arcata, CA 95521, attn: King Range Information, (707) 825-2300, for up-to-date information on trail conditions and suitable camping areas. Do not set out on this hike without proper gear and accurate maps. You can begin the journey either at Shelter Cove or Mattole, but Mattole is the traditional starting point, allowing hikers to keep the north wind to their backs. The trailhead is at the end of Lighthouse Rd, 5 miles west of the Hwy 1 junction in Petrolia.

Back in redwood country, a good overnighter is **Grasshopper Trail** (difficult; 12 miles round trip), which passes through some impressive redwood and mixed conifer forests to the highest point in Humboldt Redwoods State Park, Grasshopper Peak, at 3,379 feet. Be prepared for a 3,000-foot elevation gain over the course of 6 miles, almost half of it in the final mile. Some who make this journey from the Garden Clubs of America Grove, just west of the Redwood Highway, make a long day hike out of it. You are better off, however, arranging to stay overnight at Grasshopper Camp, one of five trail camps available to visitors on a first-come, first-served basis. Or there's the option of continuing through to other camps within the park boundaries over the course of several days. The Grasshopper hike offers all the quiet privacy and solace one can hope for in such a heavily traveled state park, and sweeping views of the surrounding groves from the peak are magnificent. Water is available at the peak's fire lookout and at the campground nearby. During the winter, the footbridge to the trail over the Eel River is removed. The trailhead is north of the Garden Club Grove, west of the Redwood Highway a mile from Myers Flat. Call the park visitors center, (707) 946-2409.

Camping

Planning is the key to having a decent camping adventure in Humboldt redwood country. The most obvious public campgrounds are precariously near the Redwood Highway, which can make for an unpleasantly noisy night of engines revving and headlights whizzing past, not to mention the buzz of motor home generators as late as 10pm and as early as 6am. So your first should be one of the campgrounds away from the highway (which doesn't require hiking 20 miles into the backcountry)—if you can get in. If you have to settle for a site in the highway corridor, at least be sure to ask for a spot as far back from the highway as possible, preferably next to the river.

Two of the three camping areas within **Prairie Creek Redwoods State Park** (see Parks/Beaches, above) are far enough away from US 101 to be quite peaceful. **Gold Bluffs Campground** has 25 sites (no hookups; RV limit 24 feet) near the beach, each with a picnic table, fire pit, and food locker, with showers nearby. Prairie Creek also has a **backpack camp** with 3 sites 8 miles from its main entrance in the quiet woods. While the site is intended for use by backpackers following the Coastal Trail, drop-ins are allowed. **Elk Prairie Campground** in Prairie Creek Redwoods State Park is closer to traffic noise. It has 75 car camping sites (no hookups; RV limit 24 feet; trailer limit 27 feet) in the forest groves adjacent to the Redwood Highway. Each site has a picnic table and fire pit with running water nearby. *Call state parks reservations, (800) 444-7275, to secure a drive-in site. For backpacker sites, call the park directly to check on availability, (707) 488-2171. Gold Bluffs camp is 6 miles northwest of the Redwood Hwy, at the end of the Davidson Rd (unpaved) turnoff north of Orick. The park is 50 miles north of Eureka on the Redwood Hwy, just within the Humboldt County line.*

Patrick's Point State Park has 124 car camping sites in a quiet forest west of the highway (no hookups; RV limit 31 feet). Each site has a fire pit and picnic table, with piped water nearby but ʌo showers. *Call state parks reservations, (800) 444-7275. The campground is 4 miles north of Trinidad, and a half mile west of the Redwood Hwy.*

Albee Creek Campground in **Humboldt Redwoods State Park** (see Parks/Beaches, above) has 38 car camping sites off Mattole Rd (no hookups; RV limit 33 feet), each with a picnic table and fire pit, with running water nearby. This is a best bet for pass-through campers since the sites are rented on a first-come, first-served basis only, with no reservations taken through the state parks reservations system. The park also has five trail camps south of Mattole Rd for use by backpackers—the most far-flung being the **Bull Creek Trail Camp** 4 miles out. Those wishing to use these camps must register at park headquarters and pick up a permit—mostly as a precaution, to prevent overcrowding and potential conflicts. The trail camps are the best option at Humboldt Redwoods. All have a secluded feel and the hikes out are easy to moderately difficult at most. The largest campground in the Humboldt redwoods region is **Hidden Springs,** just east of the Avenue of the Giants, on the banks of the south fork of the Eel River, also within Humboldt Redwoods State Park. It can be a bit noisier than the others because of its size and proximity to the Redwood Highway. The campground has 154 sites (no hookups; RV limit 24 feet), each equipped with a picnic table and fire pit with running water and showers nearby. Also at Humboldt Redwoods is the similarly equipped **Burlington Campground,** which has 56 sites (no hookups; RV limit 24 feet). *Albee Creek camp is 5 miles west of the Redwood Hwy on Mattole Rd. Go to park headquarters, on the Redwood Hwy 2 miles north of Myers Flat, to get a site, or call (707) 946-2409 (though just dropping in is probably a better bet). To reserve a site at Hidden Springs or Burlington, call the state parks reservations system at (800) 444-7275. The Hidden Springs campground is a half mile south of Myers Flat, on Avenue of the Giants just east of the Redwood Hwy. Burlington is near the park headquarters on the Redwood Hwy.*

Grizzly Creek Redwoods State Park (see Parks/Beaches, above) has 30 car camping sites (no hookups; RV limit 31 feet) in a pretty redwood grove on the banks of the Van Duzen River. *The campground is 17 miles east of the Redwood Hwy on Hwy 36. Call state parks reservations, (800) 444-7275.*

Benbow State Recreation Area has 75 sites (no hookups; RV limit 30 feet) in a popular summer water sports area on the Eel River's south fork. *The campground is 2.5 miles south of Garberville off the Redwood Hwy. Call state parks reservations, (800) 444-7275.*

Oak Flat Campground has 95 sites (full and partial hookups; RV limit 28 feet) for summer recreation on the Eel River in **Richardson Grove State Park** (see Redwood Highway under Parks/Beaches, above). Each site has a picnic table and fire pit. Running water, flush toilets, and hot showers are available. *Call state parks reservations, (800) 444-7275. The camp is west of the Redwood Hwy, 6 miles south of Humboldt Redwoods at the Mendocino County line.*

Wildlife

There are mysterious forces at work here.

As much as ecologists and naturalists have spent a lifetime studying and trying to explain how it all works, the delicately balanced web of life found in the ancient **redwood forests** is both a wonder and a curiosity. A good resource for general information is *Understanding Forests* by John J. Berger (Sierra Club Books, on the Web at www.sierraclubbookstore.com/html/). Additionally, *Redwoods, The World's Largest Trees* by Jeremy Joan Hewes is a 200-page primer with hundreds of color photos (available for $12.98; write to Redwood Technology, PO Box 1006, Huntsville, AL 35807).

There is more to looking at a big tree than just looking at a big tree. We mention trees under the wildlife heading because it is necessary to understand a few basics about how a redwood lives and behaves to fully appreciate encountering one in the forest.

One of the first things you notice when you enter an old-growth grove of redwoods is the cool—almost dank—climate. The redwood forest creates this climate by shading the forest floor from the sun. The water you see in the creeks and the cool, lush greenery all around are partly the result of moisture captured by the lower branches of the trees. The moisture drips earthward rather than evaporating; it lingers in the redwoods' shallow roots, moistens the thick carpet of rotting vegetation on the forest floor, runs through creeks kept cool by the forest shade, and nurtures the mosses, fungi, slithery banana slugs, and other creepy crawlers found under rocks and fallen trees. Even on a clear day, these trees are able to water themselves by creating their own rain. Call it nature's very own drip irrigation system.

The interplay between the coastal climate and the 30-mile band of redwoods here developed over thousands of years; John Steinbeck called these trees "ambassadors from another time." Old trees grow alongside young trees, but size is not a surefire way to tell them apart. A 100-year-old tree that has spent all its days in the shadow of its neighbors could grow to little more than two or three feet in circumference. The easiest way to spot an old tree is to look at its top branches: Those whose upper boughs have been battered the longest by strong Pacific winds show their age in the wide gaps in between branches. Younger trees are fuller on top. When a strong wind blast or a flood knocks down a tree or two, sunlight reaches the forest floor. New trees grow out of the fallen ones (called nurse logs); the most dominant among them receive more sun and become giants. The big trees have trunks up to two feet thick, giving them an incredible ability to withstand fire. Yet over the years natural fires sometimes swept through the forest floor, clearing the way for a new layer of fallen branches, needles, leaves, and twigs. Think of the forest floor as a big compost pile.

There is also a complex interplay between the trees and the wildlife. The anadromous fish that spawn in the creeks and rivers, for example, require the exact water flows and temperatures caused by the forest's special shade and drainage conditions in order to stay alive. Rare seabirds that fly too swiftly to safely land in a dense treetop are more at home on the wide branches at the tops of the older trees. Parasitic insects and invertebrates that thrive off the moist forest floor are food to unique bird species and fish. Because of fire suppression, many of the forest floors are overloaded with fuel; as a result fires burn too hot. Once in a while, an old tree falls across a river, changing the flow—and altering the entire cycle. Millions of dominos topple, and the web of life hangs in the balance.

This is why logging trees and damming rivers are considered so environmentally destructive. Land stripped of trees drains directly into the rivers and creeks, creating silt that destroys a migrating fish's ability to sniff out its spawning grounds. When rivers are diverted into reservoirs, water levels become artificially low and gravel needed for spawning does not accumulate where it is needed. Without the trees that normally shade the riverbanks, the water is the wrong temperature for native fish to survive. When old-growth trees are endangered, so are the birds that need their wide branches to nest. And so on.

Before they do anything else, **birders** making their way through the North Coast redwood areas have some decisions to make. Shall it be the old-growth forests, the freshwater lagoons, the rugged and rocky ocean shores, or the vast marshes of Humboldt and Arcata Bays? The forests are where you stand the best chance of spotting some of the region's more controversial feathered inhabitants: the **northern spotted owl** and the **marbled murrelet,** whose protection under the federal Endangered Species Act has been the hair trigger in the debate over logging restrictions of the past decade. There is only a random chance of spying one of these two at any given time; remote old-growth groves (see Redwood Highway under Parks/Beaches, above) are the best bet. Also look in the forests for chestnut-backed chickadees, dark-eyed juncos, ruby-crowned kinglets, flycatchers, ospreys, warblers, and the occasional **bald eagle,** which has been spotted in the vicinity of Dyerville at Humboldt Redwoods State Park (see Parks/Beaches, above).

At freshwater lagoons along the Humboldt coast, watch for **red-winged blackbirds, great blue herons,** and numerous varieties of **ducks.**

Along the Pacific shore, the wetlands at the mouth of the Mattole River and Mattole Beach (see Southern Humboldt oceanfront under Parks/Beaches, above) are spotting territory for **brown pelicans, terns, cormorants,** and rare **arctic geese,** which pass through in the winter and spring. We mention Mattole mostly because of its easy coastal access, but some of these same species might be glimpsed in any number of locations along the Humboldt oceanfront, including the Gold Bluffs area (see Redwood Highway under Parks/Beaches, above) and Cape

Mendocino, the westernmost point in all of California.

Finally, the marshes and river mouths of Humboldt and Arcata Bays are spotting grounds for the **Pacific black brant** and other **migratory waterfowl** and **shorebirds**. On the south side of the town of Arcata is the **Arcata Marsh and Wildlife Preserve**, a 154-acre sanctuary for hundreds of birds, including egrets and marsh wrens. Each Saturday at 8:30am the Audubon Society, (707) 826-7031, gives free 1-hour guided tours of the preserve—rain or shine—at the cul-de-sac at the foot of S I St and may help with other birding questions in the Humboldt forest and coastal regions. Also consult with the **Humboldt Bay National Wildlife Refuge,** 1020 Ranch Rd, Loleta, (707) 733-5406. Humboldt and Arcata Bays, being at the center of the county's most populated area, don't get the attention they probably deserve from tourists and outdoor enthusiasts, save for serious birders. Bird-watching is best at Arcata Marsh at the northeastern corner of Arcata Bay or at Humboldt Bay's south end, where expansive marshlands of the Humboldt Bay National Wildlife Refuge are found. Take the New Navy Base Rd exit from the Redwood Highway west to I St, then continue south to the end of the road to locate the Arcata Marsh. (You may also want to pick up the free self-guided walking tour map of the preserve, which doubles as Arcata's integrated wetland waste-water treatment plant; maps are available at the Arcata Chamber of Commerce, 1062 G St at 11th St, (707) 822-3619.) The Humboldt refuge is best accessed from the Table Bluff and Hookton Rd corridor west of the Redwood Highway.

Black bears are prevalent throughout the northern coast area. While they don't pose the same problem they do in Yosemite National Park, the bear-related policy is the same in redwood country: don't leave food out where the bears can get to it, but if you see a bear roaming around, enjoy the sight. **Mountain lions or cougars** are more reclusive than bears, but the big cats also can be spotted on occasion in the forests. They seldom attack people, but the advice is standard for those who come across them: do everything you can to make yourself look big and scary so the animal will run away instead of sizing you up as a meal. The biggest wildlife draw in this area is, luckily, easier to come across than other animals we have mentioned. **Roosevelt elk** can be found most easily at Prairie Creek Red-woods State Park (see Parks/Beaches, above) in the Newton B. Drury Scenic Parkway area. The elk also are commonly seen on adjacent Gold Bluffs Beach. Fall is the best time to look for them. Look, but don't approach. These guys weigh more than 1,000 pounds and they don't take kindly to humans snooping around their breeding areas.

Naturally, the best places along the coast to spot migrating **gray whales** headed south to their winter calving grounds in Baja California are high bluffs that extend west onto the ocean. Cape Mendocino (see Parks/Beaches, above), being the westernmost point in the whole state, has prime viewing. If you can't get there, head instead to Gold Bluffs (see Parks/Beaches, above). To get an even closer vantage point, head out from Humboldt Bay with a charter tour. Check with King Salmon Charters, 1121 King Salmon Ave, Eureka, (707) 442-3474, or Sailfish, 1821 Buhne Dr, Eureka, (707) 442-6682, for schedules.

Canoeing

If you're looking for radical whitewater action in Humboldt County, you took a wrong turn somewhere. The Upper Klamath, Smith, and Trinity Rivers are more the place for that (see Smith River National Recreation Area and Klamath Region chapters). There are nice canoe runs, however, on both the main and south forks of the **Eel River**—and a peaceful paddle tour is one of the most pleasant ways imaginable to view a redwood forest. The 20-mile stretch of the **south fork** from Richardson Grove State Park (see Parks/Beaches, above) to the small town of Weott north of Myers Flat at Humboldt Redwoods State Park (see Parks/Beaches, above) is a popular canoe run, as is the 15-mile stretch of the **main fork** between Dyerville Bar in Humboldt Redwoods and the logging town of Scotia; the bar near Founders Grove is a good put-in. During normal rain years, the canoe runs are best during the late spring to early summer runoff, but in the snow melt that followed the El Niño winter of 1998, all rules were off; rivers throughout the state were transformed into raging torrents, and water-sports accidents claimed many lives. The state Department of Boating and Waterways, (916) 445-2616, monitors **seasonal conditions** and issues safety advisories for paddlers when necessary. There are numerous outfitters in the area offering both rentals and guided tours, but the most reputable is Adventure's Edge, 650 10th St, Arcata, (707) 822-4673.

　　Kayak tours of Humboldt Bay and the adjacent portions of the Mad and Elk Rivers are also a treat, particularly if you're interested in wildlife viewing among the abundant marshlands found there, which includes beavers, otters, shorebirds, and a long list of other curiosities. Check with Hum-Boats, 25 W Third St, Eureka, (707) 443-5157, for marshland action.

Fishing

As splendid as it is to cast out in such a wonderful setting as an ancient redwood forest, you hear more complaints than praise about winter fly-fishing along the **Eel River.** Indeed, the **salmon** and **steelhead** runs along the river aren't what they used to be. Old-timers have a big fish story for every occasion, and whether you choose to believe every word or take it all with a grain of salt, there is no question that fisheries here and throughout the North Coast have been on the decline for decades. Erosion from logging, lousy fishery management, exotic fish species gobbling up eggs and babies, big floods of the past few years pushing the ecological reset button—you name it, there are undoubtedly many factors. Whatever the case, the inevitable scene along the Eel is this: lots of talk about salmon and steelhead in the winter, but quite possibly more anglers lining the riverbanks than fish in the river itself. Also, any quirk in the weather can spoil it for everyone; too much rain and the river silts up—and no fish. Same goes if temperatures turn unseasonably warm. In the summer, flows are small and so are the fish. Your best bet is to drive north to the Smith River (see Del Norte Coast and Smith River National Recreation Area chapters) where conditions are better.

Gerry Gray's "On the Fly" Guide Service in Trinity Center, (888) 286-7250, can arrange **guided fishing tours** on the northern rivers where big bites are more of a sure thing. In Humboldt, try heading east on Hwy 36 to spots along the **Van Duzen River,** or to where the Van Duzen and the Eel meet near Scotia. Be sure to check for the latest amendments to fishing regulations, as state officials have been wrangling over how to implement endangered species protections mandated by the federal government. As of this writing, stream fishing regulations in the northern portion of the state have been amended twice in less than a year because of the steelhead's threatened-species status listing. The Fish and Game department posts the most recent regulations on the Internet at www.dfg.ca.gov. Outfitters and tackle dealers have free copies of the latest regulations on hand; you can also get recorded information from the state at (707) 442-4502.

Rivers and creeks throughout the Humboldt redwoods are still a lot of fun for those who don't have a lot of ego wrapped up in the need to reel in a 50-pound salmon. Fishing **cutthroat trout, browns,** or **squawfish** can still be successful even along smaller creeks. Stop in at Eureka Fly Shop, 505 H St, Eureka, (707) 444-2000, for odds and ends.

Rock fishing and surf fishing along the coast for **surf smelt** or **redtail surfperch** is another option, particularly at numerous spots along the 15 miles of coastal access south of Patrick's Point (see Parks/Beaches, above), including Trinidad and Little River State Beaches and Mad River Beach. Lagoons along this stretch are stocked with **black trout** and **rainbows.** Also consider the southern end of the coast at Mattole Beach and Shelter Cove, near the Mendocino coast border. Shelter Cove has a marina and boat launch.

Another popular fishing area is along the **North Spit** jetty between Arcata Bay and the Pacific, with access from the southern end of New

Navy Base Rd (Hwy 255).

Deepwater **fishing charters** and tours are available from Humboldt Bay. Some reputable outfits are King Salmon Charters, 1121 King Salmon Ave, Eureka, (707) 442-3474, and Sailfish, 1821 Buhne Dr, Eureka, (707) 442-6682. From Trinidad, two sportfishing charter boats are the 36-foot *Jumpin' Jack,* (707) 839-4743 or (800) 839-4744, and the 45-foot *Shenandoah,* (707) 677-3625. Both charters offer morning and afternoon trips daily from Trinidad Pier, and walk-on customers are welcome. The 5-hour salmon or rockfish hunt costs about $60 per person, which includes all fishing gear. One-day fishing licenses can be purchased on board.

Boating

On Humboldt and Arcata Bays, the **Eureka Mooring Basin** has moorings and a boat ramp available for public use at the downtown waterfront (follow Broadway/US 101 to the elbow); call (707) 445-1910. There also is a public boat launch on the Bay at **Fields Landing,** west from the Redwood Highway at Railroad Ave. Hum-Boats, 25 W Third St, Eureka, (707) 443-5157, has rentals of all types. On the Pacific, **Trinidad Harbor,** 5 miles south of Patrick's Point off the Redwood Highway, has moorings and a boat launch for those who want to get out on the water at Trinidad Head; call (707) 677-3625. To the south, **Shelter Cove** has a public boat launch with rentals available, at the end of Shelter Cove Rd, west from the Hwy 1 corridor at the Humboldt/Mendocino County line; (707) 986-7432.

Biking

The cool climate and beautiful scenery make **mountain biking** in redwood country both comfortable and invigorating. And because most trail camps are open to cyclists, this is a great area for long hauls. The frequent rain also makes bike trips potentially messy, however. Always check with the visitors center and ranger station about trail conditions before setting out if you don't want to scuff up those designer cycling duds. If you don't care, just be careful and have fun. Backcountry fire roads and most trails wider than 60 inches are open to mountain bikes in the Humboldt redwoods area. Be sure to use up-to-date maps and obey all restrictions, however, to avoid trail conflicts with hikers and equestrians. The trek from the Albee Creek Campground area of Humboldt Redwoods State Park on Mattole Rd to the 3,379-foot summit of Grasshopper Peak via **Grasshopper Road** and **Squaw Creek Ridge Road Trail,** a challenging 8-mile loop up steep grades and through harrowing downhill switchbacks, has probably one of the best vistas in Humboldt redwood country. It is best to ascend on Grasshopper Rd. Once at the peak, rest and water up, then continue south beyond the peak a quarter mile to Preacher Gulch Rd, which meets Squaw Creek Ridge Road Trail after 1 mile. Then, it's all downhill, including one switchback that will have your bike pointing in two directions at once if you hit it too fast. Staging is from the Big Tree area at Humboldt Redwoods, 4 miles west of the Redwood Highway on Mattole Rd. In winter, make sure to call ahead or stop in at the visitors center on the main highway to check on trail conditions. The mud can make this ride next to impossible.

Road cyclists who want to tour the redwoods should consider doing so in the late fall or early winter when temperatures are still cool enough for a comfortable, long ride and forests are at their most lush. The 25-mile length of **Mattole Road** between Humboldt Redwoods State Park and Mattole Beach (see Parks/Beaches, above) begins in the cool shade of the redwoods at Bull Creek Canyon, catapults through an elevation gain of 1,000 feet in 1.5 miles, then descends toward the magnificent beaches of the southern Humboldt coast. Ride the reverse direction and end the journey camping among the redwoods. This ride also can be the inland leg of a tour along the Mendocino/southern Humboldt section of the Coast Highway. The 32-mile **Avenue of the Giants** (see Scenic Drives/Photography, below) is also an excellent choice for touring the redwoods by bicycle, but watch out for motor homes and minivans backing up and rounding corners. Important note: There are no bicycle rentals in the southern Humboldt County area. The nearest are in Eureka and Arcata, so make sure you're outfitted before heading out. Henderson Center Bicycles, 2811 F St, Arcata, (707) 443-9861, and Revolution Bicycle Repair, 1360 G St, Arcata, (707) 822-2562, can provide information and repairs.

Scenic Drives/Photography

The 32-mile **Avenue of the Giants** drive begins just north of Garberville and then travels east and west of the Redwood Highway through some of the most magnificent forests in the world. Get out the camcorder and the camera at Williams Grove north of Myers Flat, and Federation Grove north of Weott (location of the world-famous **Dyerville Giant**). Redwood forests photograph best on foggy days when there is no sunlight filtering through the trees to obscure detail. Use a tripod and slower film to avoid graininess. In Myers Flat, you can drive through the **Shrine Tree,** a great way to demonstrate to children just how big these trees are! Even better, stop and take a stroll along some of the numerous easy, short nature trails (see Hiking/Backpacking, above). All are well marked.

Motor homes and trailers are not permitted along **Davidson Road,** which leads 4 miles from the Redwood Highway to Gold Bluffs Beach and Fern Canyon from the turnoff 2 miles north of Orick. This drive offers not only fantastic forest views but also a good sampling of several types of North Coast scenery: redwoods, fern canyons, and rugged beaches and cliffs at the coast.

Perhaps the most memorable drive in the Humboldt region is the 25-mile stretch of **Mattole Road** leading from the Redwood Highway through old redwood stands to Mattole Beach, followed by a trip north on Hwy 1 to Cape Mendocino on roads hugging high oceanfront cliffs. We recommend several photo opportunities along the way: the Big Tree area of Humboldt Redwoods State Park on Mattole Rd, Mattole Beach, and Cape Mendocino. Finally, steer through the city of **Ferndale,** (see also Attractions, below) on the way back to the Redwood Highway at Fortuna, to check out the pretty Victorian buildings there. The Mattole/Cape Mendocino/Ferndale drive will appear on your road map as a loop beginning and ending on the Redwood Highway.

Adventure Calendar

Humboldt Redwoods Marathon and Half Marathon, early May and mid-October: *(707) 443-1220.*

Tour of the Unknown Coast bicycle race, mid-May: *(707) 443-5097.*

The Great Arcata to Ferndale Kinetic Sculpture Race, early June: *participants drive homemade contraptions, many of which fall apart on the course, (707) 443-5097.*

outside in

Attractions

(For recommendations in Orick, see Redwood National Park chapter.)

In the early 1850s **Trinidad** was a booming supply town with a population of 3,000; now it's one of the smallest incorporated cities in California, encompassing a little rocky bluff that a handful of anglers, artists, retirees, and shopkeepers call home. A sort of Mendocino-in-miniature, cute-as-a-button Trinidad is known mainly as a sportfishing town: trawlers and skiffs sit patiently in the bay, awaiting their owners or tourists eager to spend an afternoon salmon fishing. Scenery and silence, however, are the town's most desirable commodities; if all you're after is a little R&R on the coast, Trinidad is among the most peaceful and beautiful areas you'll find in California.

The **Humboldt State University Marine Laboratory** features various live marine life displays, including a touch tank and tide pools; it's open to the public daily and is located at Edwards and Ewing Sts downtown, (707) 826-3671. Then again, why not catch your own sea critters? If you're lucky enough to reel in a lunker salmon, haul it up to **Katy's Smokehouse,** just up the road from the pier at 740 Edwards St, (707) 677-0151. Katy herself will smoke it up and wrap it to go—or even send it via UPS to your home. Her salmon jerky ain't bad, either.

Five miles north of Trinidad off Patrick's Point Drive is Patrick's Point State Park (see Parks/Beaches, above), which was once a seasonal fishing village of the Yurok Indians. In 1990 descendants of the original Native American settlers reconstructed an **authentic Yurok village** within the park, and visitors are welcome. A map and guide to all of the park's attractions are included in the $5-per-vehicle day-use fee; call (707) 677-3570 for more details.

Home to the California State University at Humboldt, **Arcata** is like most college towns in that everyone tends to lean towards the left. Environmentalism, artistry, good beads, and good bagels are indispensable elements of the Arcatian philosophy, as is a cordial disposition towards tourists, making Arcata one of the most interesting and visitor-friendly towns along the North Coast.

The heart of this seaside community is **Arcata Plaza,** where a statue of President McKinley stands guard over numerous shops and cafes housed in historic buildings. A walk around the plaza—with its perfectly manicured lawns, hot dog vendor, and well-dressed retirees sitting on spotless benches—is enough to restore anyone's faith in small-town America. At the plaza's southwest end is its flagship structure, **Jacoby's Storehouse,** a handsomely restored 1857 brick pack-train station that now holds shops, offices, and restaurants; 791 Eighth St at H St. If you need a new book, the **Tin Can Mailman** is a terrific used-book store with 130,000 hard- and soft-cover titles, including a few collector's items; 1000 H St at 10th St, (707) 822-1307.

You can see (and touch!) three-billion-year-old fossils and view various California flora and fauna exhibits at Humboldt State University's **Natural History Museum** at 13th and G Sts downtown; (707) 826-4479. Savor a pitcher of Red Nectar Ale at the **Humboldt Brewing Company** (brewery tours are offered, too) at the corner of 10th and G Sts next to the Minor Theatre; (707) 826-BREW. A 2-minute drive east of downtown on 11th St will take you to Arcata's beloved Redwood Park, a beautiful grassy expanse complemented by a fantastic **playground** that's guaranteed to entertain the tots.

The best way to spend a summer Sunday afternoon in Arcata is at the **Arcata Ballpark,** where only a few bucks buys you nine innings of America's favorite pastime hosted by the Humboldt Crabs semipro baseball team. With the brass band blasting and the devoted fans cheering, you'd swear you were back in high school. Most games are played Wednesday, Friday, and Saturday evenings in June and July. The ballpark is located at the corner of Ninth and F Sts in downtown Arcata, but don't park your car anywhere near foul-ball territory; (707) 822-3619.

Named after the popular gold-mining expression "Eureka!" (Greek for "I have found it"), **Eureka** is the largest city on the North Coast (population 30,000). The heart of the city is **Old Town,** a 13-block stretch of shops, restaurants, and hotels, most of which are housed in painstakingly preserved Victorian structures; it's bordered by First and Third Sts, between C and M Sts. One of the finest Victorian architectural masterpieces is the multi-gabled-and-turreted **Carson Mansion,** built of redwood in 1886 for lumber baron William Carson, who initiated the construction to keep mill workers occupied during a lull in the lumber business. Although the three-story, money-green mansion is closed to the public (it's now a snooty men's club), you can stand on the sidewalk and click your Kodak at one of the state's most-photographed houses; it's located on the corner of Second and M Sts. For more Old Town history, stroll through the **Clarke Memorial Museum,** which has one of the top Native American displays in the state, showcasing more than 1,200 examples of Hupa, Yurok, and Karok basketry, dance regalia, and stonework; 240 E St at Third St, (707) 443-1947. A block away, there's more Native American artwork, including quality silver jewelry, at the **Indian Art & Gift Shop,** which sells many of its treasures at reasonable prices; 241 F St at Third St, (707) 445-8451.

If you need a good book at a great price, stop by the **Bootlegger,** a marvelous bookstore in Old Town with thousands of used paperbacks (especially mysteries, westerns, and science fiction), as well as children's books and cookbooks; 402 Second St, (707) 445-1344. Or if purple potatoes, cylindra beets, and other fancy foods are on your shopping list, then you're in luck, because you'll find them at the **farmers markets** held weekly from May through October in Eureka and Arcata. Most of the produce is grown along the local Eel and Trinity Rivers, and is sold at bargain prices at the Eureka Mall (on US 101 at the south end of Eureka) on Thursday from 10am to 1pm; in Eureka's Old Town on Tuesday from 10am to 1pm; and at Arcata Plaza on Saturday from 9am to 1pm.

Before you leave Eureka, be sure to take a bay cruise on skipper Leroy Zerlang's *Madaket,* the oldest passenger vessel on the Pacific Coast. The 75-minute narrated tour—a surprisingly interesting and amusing perspective on the history of Humboldt Bay—departs daily from the foot of C St in Eureka, and gets progressively better after your second or third cocktail. For more information, call Humboldt Bay Harbor Cruise at (707)

445-1910. Afterwards, stroll over to the **Lost Coast Brewery** for a fresh pint of Alleycat Amber Ale and an order of onion rings; 617 Fourth St, between G and H Sts, (707) 445-4480.

Even if **Ferndale** isn't on your itinerary, it's worth a detour off US 101 to stroll for an hour or two down its colorful Main St, browsing through the art galleries, gift shops, and cafes that are strangely reminiscent of Disneyland's "old town." Ferndale, however, is for real, and hasn't changed much since it was the agricultural center of Northern California in the late 1800s. In fact, the entire town is a National Historic Landmark because of its abundance of well-preserved Victorian storefronts, farmhouses, and homes. What really distinguishes Ferndale from the likes of Eureka and Crescent City, however, is the fact that US 101 doesn't pass through it—which means no cheesy motels, liquor stores, and fast-food chains.

For a trip back in time, view the village's interesting memorabilia—working crank phones, logging equipment, and a blacksmith shop—at the **Ferndale Museum,** 515 Shaw St at Third St, (707) 786-4466. Not officially a museum but close enough is the **Golden Gate Mercantile** at 421 Main St. Part of this general store hasn't been remodeled (or restocked) in 50 years, giving you the feeling that you're walking through some sort of time capsule or movie set.

In keeping with its National Historic Landmark status, Ferndale has no movie theaters. Rather, it has something better: the **Ferndale Repertory Theatre.** Converted in 1972 from a movie theater, the 267-seat house hosts live performances by actors from all over Humboldt County. The revolving performances run pretty much year-round and range from musicals to comedies, dramas, and mysteries. Tickets are reasonably priced and, due to the popularity of the shows, reservations are advised; 447 Main St, (707) 786-5483.

Restaurants

Abruzzi ☆☆   If you have trouble finding this place, just follow your nose: the smell of garlic and fresh bread will soon steer you to this friendly spot, where you'll be served an ample amount of artfully arranged food. *791 8th St (at H St in the Arcata Plaza), Arcata; (707) 826-2345; $$.*

Cove Restaurant ☆☆   At the north end of a small runway for private planes, this rather remote restaurant—selected by *Private Pilot* magazine as one of the nation's premier fly-in lunch spots—is situated in an A-frame beach house with a spectacular view. The menu's offerings are wide ranging and well prepared. *210 Wave Dr (off Lower Pacific Dr), Shelter Cove; (707) 986-1197; $$.*

Curley's Grill ☆☆   Curley's has been a hit ever since it opened in 1995. The reason? Curley doesn't fool around: the prices are fair, the servings are generous, the food is good, and the atmosphere is bright and cheerful. *460 Main St (between Washington and Brown Sts), Ferndale; (707) 786-9696; $.*

Eternal Treehouse Cafe ☆   Located in the tiny town of Redcrest on the scenic Avenue of the Giants, the Eternal Treehouse is an all-American cafe right down to the chocolate malts, house-made pies, and country western music flowing out of the kitchen. *26510 Ave of the Giants (from US 101, take the Redcrest exit), Redcrest; (707) 722-4247; $.*

Folie Douce ☆☆   To say Folie Douce just serves pizza is like saying Tiffany's just sells jewelry. Locals love this festive, brightly painted place, so reservations—even for early birds—are strongly recommended. *1551 G St (between 15th and 16th Sts), Arcata; (707) 822-1042; $$.*

Larrupin' Café ☆☆☆   Trinidad's finest restaurant—looking very chic with its colorful urns full of exotic flowers—draws crowds with its creative seafood dishes and fantastic pork ribs doused with a sweet and spicy barbecue sauce. *1658 Patrick's Point Dr (from US 101, take the Trinidad exit and head N on Patrick's Point Dr), Trinidad; (707) 677-0230; $$.*

The Mateel Cafe ☆☆   With its delicious, healthful food and lively atmosphere, the Mateel has become a social and cultural magnet for the southern Humboldt region. A worldly selection of food is served here. *3342 and 3344 Redwood Dr (from US 101, take the Redway exit to downtown), Redway; (707) 923-2030; $.*

Restaurant 301 ☆☆☆   Located on the first floor of Hotel Carter, Restaurant 301 prides itself on using ultra-fresh ingredients. Diners, seated at windowside tables overlooking the bay, may order from either the regular or the prix-fixe five-course dinner menu. *301 L St (at 3rd St in Old Town), Eureka; (707) 444-8062 or (800) 404-1390; $$$.*

Samoa Cookhouse   This venerable dining spot is the last surviving cook house in the West (it's been in operation for more than a century) and a Humboldt County institution, where guests are served lumber-camp-style in an enormous barnlike building. *On Cookhouse Rd (from US 101, take the Samoa exit—R St—in downtown Eureka, cross the Samoa Bridge, and turn left on Samoa Rd, then left on Cookhouse Rd), Eureka; (707) 442-1659; $.*

Stage Door Café ☆   This area's top soup 'n' sandwich shop is the tiny Stage Door Café. Daily specials are posted in the front window; if one of them happens to be Orange Wonder soup, Ferndale tradition requires that you order a bowl. *451 Main St (next to the Ferndale Theatre), Ferndale; (707) 786-4675; $.*

Lodgings

Benbow Inn ☆☆   From its sophisticated afternoon tea to its beautifully cultivated gardens, this elegant Tudor-style inn built in 1926 is a little slice of England nestled in the redwoods. A National Historic Landmark, the inn has 55 guest rooms. *445 Lake Benbow Dr (from US 101, take the Benbow Dr exit), Garberville; (707) 923-2124; $$$.*

Carter House / Hotel Carter / Carter House Cottage ☆☆☆☆   This trio of inn, hotel, and cottage offers a contrasting array of luxury accommodations, ranging from rooms with classic Victorian antique furnishings in the house and cottage to a softer, brighter, more contemporary decor in the hotel. *301 L St (at 3rd St in Old Town), Eureka; (707) 444-8062 or (800) 404-1390; $$$.*

An Elegant Victorian Mansion ☆☆☆   This inn is a jewel—a National Historic Landmark lovingly maintained by attentive owners. If you're a fan of Victoriana, be prepared for a mind-blowing experience. Each of the 4 guest rooms has a different theme, and the morning meal is a feast. *1406 C St (at 14th St), Eureka; (707) 444-3144; $$.*

The Gingerbread Mansion ☆☆☆   The awe-inspiring grande dame of Ferndale, this peach-and-yellow Queen Anne inn is a lavish example of Victoriana. Gables, turrets, English gardens, and architectural gingerbread galore have made it one of the most-photographed buildings in Northern California. *400 Berding St (at Brown St, 1 block S of Main St), Ferndale; (707) 786-4000 or (800) 952-4136; $$$.*

The Lady Anne ☆☆   Just a few blocks from Arcata Plaza in a quiet residential neighborhood, this exquisite example of Queen Anne architecture has been painstakingly restored. Five large and airy guest rooms are each decorated with antiques, stained glass, Oriental rugs, and lace curtains. *902 14th St (at I St), Arcata; (707) 822-2797; $$.*

The Lost Whale Bed and Breakfast Inn ☆☆☆   This Cape Cod–style building stands on a grassy cliff overlooking the sea, with a private stairway leading down to miles of deserted rocky beach. The 8 rooms all have private baths, and some have balconies or separate sleeping lofts. The owners also rent out two homes that can accommodate up to six people. *3452 Patrick's Point Dr (from US 101, take the Seawood Dr exit and head N for 1¾ miles on Patrick's Point Dr), Trinidad; (707) 677-3425 or (800) 677-7859; $$$.*

Scotia Inn ☆☆   This landmark three-story hotel constructed entirely of redwood is the pride of Scotia, one of the last company-owned towns in America. In fact, the whole town is built of redwood—no surprise once you discover the town's owner is the Pacific Lumber Company. *On Mill St (directly across from the mill; from US 101, take the Scotia exit), Scotia; (707) 764-5683; $$.*

The Shaw House Bed and Breakfast Inn ☆☆☆   This Carpenter Gothic beauty, the oldest house in Ferndale, is modeled after the titular manse of Hawthorne's *House of the Seven Gables*. It was built in 1854 and is listed on the National Register of Historic Places. Each of the 6 rooms has a private bath. *703 Main St (just E of the downtown area), Ferndale; (707) 786-9958 or (800) 557-SHAW; $$$.*

Shelter Cove Ocean Inn ☆☆   Snoozing seals, grazing deer, and migrating whales are just some of the sights you'll see in Shelter Cove, the Lost Coast's only oceanside community. At the end of the journey you'll reach this inn, a handsome Victorian-style facility built smack-dab on the shoreline. *148 Dolphin Dr (from Shelter Cove Rd, turn right on Upper Pacific Dr, left on Lower Pacific Dr, then right on Dolphin Dr), Shelter Cove; (707) 986-7161; $$.*

More Information

Arcata Chamber of Commerce: *(707) 822-3619.*
Eureka Chamber of Commerce: *(707) 442-3738.*
Eureka–Humboldt County Convention and Visitors Bureau: *(707) 443-5097.*
Ferndale Chamber of Commerce: *(707) 786-4477.*
Garberville-Redway Chamber of Commerce: *(707) 923-2613.*
Humboldt Redwoods State Park Visitors Center: *(707) 946-2263.*
Orick Chamber of Commerce: *(707) 488-2885.*
Rio Dell–Scotia Chamber of Commerce: *(707) 764-3436.*
State parks camping reservations: *(800) 444-7275.*
Windsor Chamber of Commerce: *(707) 838-7285.*

Northern Mendocino Coast

The northern portion of the Mendocino County coast from Highway 20 on the south to the Humboldt County line on the north, including Jackson State Demonstration Forest, Fort Bragg, and Sinkyone Wilderness State Park.

Even silly humans couldn't screw this place up. After more than a century of logging, these forested river canyons and hillsides of redwood and Douglas fir are still lush enough to take your breath away. The lumber towns have been transformed into quaint little artsy hamlets, while the wild, rugged cliffs where the land meets the Pacific remain agelessly unaffected by anything other than the slow massage of ocean waves. Instead of mutating into an ugly, industrialized urban center with a 16-lane interstate slicing through, which was the case with so much of California during the postwar economic boom, this stretch of the California coast has resisted the urge to pave itself over. As a result, it has become a favorite escape. Tourism is now a bigger business here than logging. Weary city dwellers are happy to hear that the largest city in northern Mendocino, Fort Bragg, has only 6,000 residents. That's hardly enough to fill one of those new subdivisions that keep springing up in the rest of America—much smaller, in fact, than the number of fans that can fill a baseball stadium.

Once recovered from the culture shock of a society without crowds and traffic jams, outdoor adventurers have a dilemma on their hands—what not to do. If you go for a romantic, thrilling horseback ride on the beach, there will be no time for a 20-mile-mountain bike ride through the redwoods. If you explore the pygmy forests and botanical gardens, there may not be time left for a lazy fishing trip up the Noyo River. Or, most tempting of all, for a foray into the vast Sinkyone Wilderness State Park at the very northern end of the Coast Highway, where you can hike for hours or days among black-sand beaches, wild mountain streams, and waterfalls dropping directly into the sea.

To look at it, an uninformed visitor would have no clue to the Mendocino coast's sordid past.

The coast was "discovered" by westerners quite accidentally during the Gold Rush, when a cargo ship loaded with porcelain and silk from the Orient slammed into rocks offshore. A San Francisco sawmill owner was among the businessmen who traveled 80 miles north to investigate the loss—and the coast redwoods he saw when he got there set off bells in his head. Before long, lumberjacks invaded the forests, pulling out 50,000 board feet a day from the virgin forests to help fuel the economic boom taking place in San Francisco. The Noyo Indians, who had occupied the area for nearly 10,000 years, were pushed aside to nearby Road Valley within 15 years.

The logging legacy didn't last, however. Fort Bragg's lumber industry base suffered during the Great Depression and never recovered. While logging still occurs there today, there is much less of it, and most of the scenic landscape along the coast has fallen into public ownership, so there's little or no danger that a shining megalopolis will ever emerge.

The result is a blue-collar resort area occupied by an interesting combination of fourth-generation logging families, retirees who bought their homes before land prices skyrocketed, and artists who enjoy the tranquility, natural beauty, and tourist money—which there is plenty of. Escape and enjoy.

Getting There

The Coast Highway (Highway 1) runs the entire 50-mile stretch of shore from the Highway 20 intersection south of Fort Bragg to near Sinkyone Wilderness State Park, at Usal Road, the unpaved entrance to pristine paradise. Quickest access is via Highway 20 from Willits on US Highway 101 (US 101).

Adjoining Areas

NORTH: **Humboldt Coast**

SOUTH: **Sonoma and Southern Mendocino Coasts**

EAST: **Mendocino National Forest**

inside out

Parks/Beaches

Major hint: Going north on the Mendocino coast, the Coast Highway bends east away from the ocean. Don't follow it. This is where you're supposed to leave the main road. Your reward will be more than 7,300 acres of coastal mountains, bluffs dropping 1,000 feet to the frothing surf below, and wild beaches where you stand no chance of seeing Pamela Anderson Lee keeping watch from atop a lifeguard tower. Usal Rd, a gravel cutaway left from the main highway, is the southern entrance to the vast **Sinkyone Wilderness State Park.** See where the rocks have been dramatically cut by creeks gushing toward the ocean, take long lonely walks through forests of alder and eucalyptus or high meadows teeming with wildflowers, visit deserted black-sand beaches where the sea caves are engorged with thundering surf. The geology, the wildlife, the heavy blankets of fog and strong winds off the ocean—all of this keeps this place wild and real, even though at several points in the not-so-distant past logging companies, railroads, highway builders, you name it, have done what they could to change it. Unpaved roads make getting in easy for everyone *except* RV campers, people pulling trailers, and tourists whose rental car insurance prohibits them from leaving the highway. We consider this place the official crown jewel of the Mendocino coast. There are 40 campsites along the beaches, and trail connections to the King Range National Conservation Area (see Humboldt Coast chapter). The Usal Rd turnoff northwest from the Coast Highway is 40 miles north of Fort Bragg at the northernmost point where the highway parallels the ocean. Call the park ahead of time for trail and road conditions, (707) 986-7711.

A string of overlooks, sandy beaches, private summer campgrounds, surf fishing areas, and surfing spots are found along the 40 miles of the Coast Highway between the Usal Rd turnoff and the city of Fort Bragg. Among the best places to stop on this stretch of magnificent coast is **Union Landing State Beach,** (707) 937-5804, a popular camping area on wind-sheltered bluffs overlooking the Pacific, with easy access to a sandy beach below that is a popular free diving area for abalone and rock cod or just plain summertime beachcombing. Adjacent is **Wages Creek Beach,** (707) 964-2964, with more camping and winter steelhead fishing on Wages Creek. These are 42 and 40 miles south of the Usal Rd turnoff to Sinkyone.

MacKerricher State Park is the longest stretch of sandy beach and dunes to be found in the northern Mendocino coast region and is adjacent to a forested lake area covering nearly six miles of coast just north of Fort Bragg. This is a popular coastal horseback riding and beachcombing area, with good fishing not only on the ocean shore but also on Lake Cleone. The park's highlight is the Laguna Point Seal Watching Station, a fancy name for a small wood deck overlooking numerous harbor seals sunning themselves on the rocks below. The park has 140 campsites in the coastal forest. Access points are all along the Coast Highway from near Fort Bragg to Mill Creek 6 miles north. The main entrances are 3 miles north of the city on both sides of the highway. The park can be reached at (707) 937-5804.

Sandy beaches, coastal scrub, and the marshes at the mouth of Jug Handle Creek make up 5.5 miles of coastline near Caspar Point, 6 miles south of Fort Bragg, known as **Jug Handle State Reserve.** This is a nice day-hiking area for outdoor explorers interested in seeing both the dramatic, eroded rocky coast Mendocino is famous for and the white-sand beaches that are perfect for barefoot surf walks on warm summer days. The river mouth marsh area is a good fishing and bird-watching spot, as well as a key location to observe sea mammals like harbor seals. The reserve access points are along the west side of the highway at the Caspar shore.

The largest of California's eight state forests, the 50,000-acre **Jackson State Demonstration Forest** is a fascinating cross between an outdoor public recreation area and a working forest for timber companies to test new forest management techniques. In fact, the forest's managers say there is an annual net gain of timber each year because, board foot for board foot, the trees grow faster than loggers can cut them down! Logging has been the primary activity on these lands since the Gold Rush days. The redwood, Douglas fir, hemlock, bishop pine, and alder groves offer numerous interpretive trails, two large camping areas, cross-country mountain biking routes, swimming holes on the Noyo River, and picnic areas. The forest's most unusual feature is a **pygmy forest grove,** where poor drainage and unusually acidic soil (both caused by natural conditions) are responsible for the vegetation's diminutive size. Because working logging areas are sectioned off, the untrained observer would never know this was a commercial forest. State Hwy 20 slices through the forest east from the Coast Highway just south of the Noyo River mouth, 2 miles south of Fort Bragg. Call the forest's administrative offices, (707) 964-5674, for more information. Camping reservations are not taken, and there is no charge.

Camping

Sinkyone Wilderness State Park has 40 primitive sites (no RV access) scattered among the wild beaches and dramatically eroded cliffs in the more than 7,300 acres of secluded wilderness west of the Coast Highway. Of those sites, 15 are at Usal Beach. Each of these has a picnic table and fire pit, with outhouse toilets nearby. There is no running water, so bring your own, or be prepared to treat creek water. The other 25 sites, most similarly appointed, are to the north along Usal Rd in various locations along the coast. No reservations are accepted. *Drive to the Usal Rd turnoff west from the Coast Hwy 40 miles north of Fort Bragg at the northernmost point of where the highway parallels the oceanfront. Call ahead for camp and weather conditions, (707) 986-7711. Usal is a gravel road with no access for trailers or RVs.*

Wages Creek Campground has 175 sites (no hookups; RV limit 31 feet) either on the creek banks or overlooking the ocean. Each site has a picnic table and fire pit, with running water, flush toilets, and showers nearby. *Call the park at (707) 964-2964 for information; reservations are through the state parks system, (800) 444-7275. The camp is located 30 miles north of Fort Bragg on the Coast Hwy.*

Union Landing State Beach has 100 sites (no hookups; RV limit 35 feet) on bluffs overlooking the ocean. Each has a picnic table and a fire grill, with running water and porta-potty toilets nearby. Reservations are not accepted. *Call (707) 937-5804 for information. The camp is 28 miles north of Fort Bragg on the Coast Hwy.*

MacKerricher State Park has 142 sites (no hookups; RV limit 35 feet) in a forest by the ocean with good fishing, hiking, and horseback riding nearby. Each site has a picnic table and fire pit, with running water, flush toilets, and showers nearby. *Call the park at (707) 865-2391 for information; reservations are through the state parks system, (800) 444-7275. The park is 3 miles north of Fort Bragg on the west side of the highway.*

Jackson State Demonstration Forest has 44 primitive sites (no hookups; RV access at 18 sites) in an interesting forest setting with river swimming holes, hiking trails along old logging roads, and wildlife viewing. Most sites are primitively appointed, with hike-in or horseback access. Each site has a picnic table and fire pit, with outhouse toilets nearby, but no running water. There are no fees, but reservations are accepted. *Call the forest office, (707) 964-5674, for information. The camp areas are situated throughout the forest along the Noyo River, 10 miles east from Fort Bragg and the Coast Hwy, along Hwy 20.*

Hiking/Backpacking

Botanical Gardens Trail (easy; 1.2 miles round trip) passes through gardens so unbelievably lush and colorful that you won't even care that a lot of the flowers and plants aren't indigenous to the Mendocino coast.

Flower mazes made of rhododendrons, azaleas, camellias, and others, along with ponded areas teeming with amphibians and birds, highlight the stroll. The walk starts at the botanical gardens entrance and follows a level, winding cut across Digger Creek, ending at high bluffs overlooking the ocean. It's a favorite among all those retired Wilmas and Harveys you see collecting state stickers for the back of the RV—but it's great for all ages, and if you go during the week or in the rain you'll enjoy it with some privacy. The gardens, covering 12 acres on the coast, are owned and managed by a nonprofit organization, and there is no charge for entry. Look for the trailhead west of the Coast Highway, 2 miles south of Fort Bragg. Call the Mendocino Coast Botanical Gardens, (707) 964-4352.

Chamberlain Creek Falls Trail (easy; 0.5 mile round trip) has big payoffs for relatively little work—you just have to leave the wonderful, wild Mendocino coast and enter Jackson State Demonstration Forest (where logging is still en vogue) to get there. The trail follows the creek up to a lovely 50-foot waterfall framed by redwood forest. It is most stunning in the winter months, though you'll have to contend with muddy, unpaved logging roads to see it at its best. The trailhead is 4 miles past the Chamberlain Creek Bridge on Forest Rd 200, south of Hwy 20, 10 miles east of the Coast Highway near Fort Bragg. Call the forest to check on road conditions since the mud can be a problem for passenger cars, (707) 964-5674.

La Laguna Trail (easy; 1 mile round trip) encircles Lake Cleone, a unique lagoon sealed off from the Pacific Ocean by a man-made barrier but still a popular stopping point for scads of interesting waterfowl and shorebirds, not to mention a lot of pond turtles and noisy frogs. The trailhead is east of the Coast Highway at the entrance to MacKerricher State Park (see Parks/Beaches, above), 3 miles north of Fort Bragg. Across the highway on the coastal portion of MacKerricher, **Laguna Point Trail** (moderate; 2 miles round trip) skirts Laguna Point, a popular whale-watching spot overlooking the longest stretch of sandy beach on this portion of the coast.

Most of the hikes you read about in this book will have specific trail names and routes mentioned. **Usal Beach** (moderate; 1 to 5 miles round trip, variable) is an exception. For one thing, it's an exceptional stretch of beach; for another, on sand, you can't leave a permanent trail. And here you won't need one—just follow the beach and rocky coast north from the mouth of Usal Creek, past stunning waterfalls dropping into the ocean from the cliffs, vibrant tide pools, and sandy beach strips where it can seem as if nobody has walked before. Note: It's essential to take this walk only at low tide, with enough time to return to the trailhead without beach access closing off, so check with the ranger station at Sinkyone

Wilderness State Park, located at the park entrance from Usal Rd, for information about ocean conditions. Do not rely on printed tide tables; they can be wrong, particularly if ocean temperatures are anomalously high. Sleeper waves are a concern, too—stay alert when on the rocks. And watch out for timber rattlers: These critters are known to hide under driftwood on the beaches, and getting bitten by one is not a good idea. The trailhead is at the mouth of Usal Creek, and the walk tops out at Big White Falls, 2.5 miles north. To find the beach, take the Coast Highway north from Fort Bragg 40 miles to the Usal Rd turnoff on the left, at the point where the highway begins to veer east away from the ocean. Follow Usal Rd 8 miles to the beach. Be sure to veer left after the first 2 miles. Call the park for information, (707) 986-7711.

Lost Coast Trail (difficult and dangerous; up to 25 miles round trip) can be accessed from the Usal Beach campground (see Camping, above) for some vigorous, butt-kicking steep climbs containing relentless switchbacks through forests of oak and Douglas fir, wild meadows, high oceanfront mountain peaks, and old-growth redwoods. It's a three-day hike between Shelter Cove and Mattole Beach in Humboldt County—but the long trip is normally taken from the Humboldt side to Mendocino because the hiker's back is to the wind when heading south. Nonetheless, day visitors to the Mendocino coast who want to experience some raw wilderness can opt to head even just a few miles in before doubling back, since this is a hike with big payoffs no matter how far you take it. To find the beach, take the Coast Highway north from Fort Bragg 40 miles to the Usal Rd turnoff on the left, at the point where the highway begins to veer east away from the ocean. Follow Usal Rd 8 miles to the beach. Be sure to veer left after the first 2 miles. Call the Sinkyone Wilderness State Park for information, (707) 986-7711. The long hike in enters the King Range National Conservation Area, managed by the US Bureau of Land Management (BLM). While the state rangers should have up-to-date information on the conservation area, it is prudent to obtain seasonal information regarding trail conditions and suitable camping areas there. Do not set out on this hike without proper gear and accurate maps. Call (707) 825-2300 or write BLM, 1695 Heidon Rd, Arcata, CA 95521, attn: King Range Information. Also see Hiking/Backpacking, Humboldt Coast chapter.

Diving/Fishing

Free diving for **abalone** and **rock cod** at Union Landing State Beach (see Parks/Beaches, above) is a big part of the Mendocino and Sonoma coast experience but, as you'll find out if you suit up for it, there is not much chance of doing it in the peak season without a lot of company. The

Mendocino coast is lined from end to end with abalone hunters. The ritual is to dive by day, and then eat by night—and the gaming law allows a big enough bounty for one meal. Because these are red abalone, however, be prepared to put a little work into cooking it; red abalone requires extensive tenderizing before it is edible, unlike white abalone found in more tropical waters. Dive spots are found south of Fort Bragg all the way to Bodega Bay. First-timers are best off taking a guided dive tour from one of any number of outfitters working the area. Bodega Bay Pro Dive, 1275 Hwy 1, in Bodega Bay, (707) 875-3054, is a complete outfitter conveniently located on the drive up from the Bay Area. This is also a good place to hook up with local guides. Adventure Sports Unlimited, operating out of Santa Cruz, (831) 458-3648, has area dives on the calendar several times each year. A state fishing license with an abalone stamp is required for all divers. The season starts April 1. Contact the North Coast Diving Club, PO Box 5091, Vallejo, CA 94591, for scheduled group outings.

Steelhead fishing is best at Wages Creek and Jug Handle Creek (see Parks/Beaches, above) or at the Noyo River mouth, where a sleepy fishing village and harbor sets a fine pace for relaxation and escape. *Tally Ho II,* an ocean-fishing charter, is berthed at Noyo for deep-sea fishing expeditions for **salmon, rock cod,** and **ling cod;** call (707) 964-2079. Wes Hee, a guide in Fort Bragg, leads river fishing trips through the area, (707) 964-1407.

MacKerricher State Park is the favorite **surf fishing** spot for those who would rather stay on shore. Those who opt for a solo trip can get outfitted at Noyo Fishing Center, 32450 N Harbor Dr, Fort Bragg, (707) 964-7609.

Boating/Canoeing

The harbor village at the Noyo River mouth is the place both to hire a fishing party and obtain a **boat rental.** Call the Noyo harbor marina, (707) 964-0167, for information. (Also consider boating out of Bodega Bay, described in Sonoma and Southern Mendocino Coasts chapter.)

In addition to being a great fishing and boating spot, the Noyo at one time attracted canoers looking for a lovely, lazy, effortless drift upstream. Those with their own canoes should put in at the end of North Harbor Rd, near Casa Del Noyo. Those without their own canoes are out of luck since the only canoe rental place in the village has gone out of business. As of this writing, the canoeless are better off trying the Little River 10 miles south of Noyo (see Sonoma and Southern Mendocino Coasts chapter); Catch A Canoe & Bicycles Too, 44850 Comptche-Ukiah Rd in Mendocino, (707) 937-0273, is the place to rent.

Wildlife

Don't forget the binoculars on any trip to this portion of the Mendocino coast during **whale-watching** season. There are numerous high points and bluffs from which to catch a glimpse of the whales during the southern migration January through March. Laguna Point (see Hiking/Backpacking, above) and Caspar Point south of Jug Handle State Reserve are two of the best viewing spots, particularly when the weather is clear. To reach Caspar Point, take Caspar Orchard Rd west from the Coast Highway, 3 miles south of the Hwy 20 intersection. **Harbor seals** also are commonly seen off the coast at these locations. You can also watch for whales from the westernmost peaks within Sinkyone Wilderness State Park, but don't make a special trip for that alone; getting up to the best spots takes a lot of work and preparation. For those who would rather get up close than watch from the shore, daily whale-watching trips leave from the Noyo Harbor village aboard the *Lady Irma II*, (707) 964-3854, or the *Patty-C* at the Sportsman's Dock, (707) 964-0669.

The freshwater marshes around Lake Cleone at MacKerricher State Park (see Parks/Beaches, above) attract a healthy stream of shorebirds and migrating waterfowl, including some of the beautiful **tundra geese** more commonly found farther south along the Sonoma/Mendocino region. Any of the river marsh areas along this section of coast, including the Noyo River harbor and Jug Handle Creek at Jug Handle State Reserve (see Parks/Beaches, above), are suitable birding spots. **Brown pelicans, murres, great blue herons, sandpipers,** and a wide variety of **ducks** and **gulls** are found in these areas.

The forested areas of Sinkyone Wilderness State Park or even Jackson State Demonstration Forest (see Parks/Beaches, above) are spotting ground for **flycatchers, ospreys, warblers,** and **robins,** and at Jackson you'll see the occasional **northern spotted owl** and **marbled murrelet** (according to forest managers). For more information, call the rare-bird hot line for the entire North Coast region at (707) 822-5666.

Horseback Riding

A few hours on horseback is a splendid way to explore the Mendocino oceanfront and redwood forests. **Ricochet Ridge Ranch** has daily rentals and guided rides along Ten Mile Beach through the MacKerricher State Park area, as well as redwood forest tours from its ranch at 24201 N Hwy 1, Fort Bragg, (707) 694-7669. All skill levels are welcome, and longer horseback vacations are also available.

Mountain Biking

The more than 40 miles of forest roads slicing through **Jackson Demonstration State Forest** (see Parks/Beaches, above) make for a delightful ride through second-growth coast redwoods, Douglas fir, bishop pine, and oak forestlands—but make it during the dry season unless you're really into getting messy. These roads get muddy.

The **Caspar/Little Lake Road** route between Caspar on the Coast Highway and Hwy 20 through the forest is a rugged 16-mile round trip covering a wide variety of forest types, including numerous canyons with wild streams cutting toward the sea. Dozens of smaller gravel and dirt roads are also accessible through the area. Be sure to get a forest map and check with the forest rangers on trail conditions and use restrictions before setting out. Areas of the forest being logged are closed to the public, as are active roads. Call (707) 964-5674 for information.

For beachfront rides, use either a road bike or, more preferably, a mountain bike, on the **Old Haul Road Trail** from Fort Bragg at MacKerricher State Park (see Parks/Beaches, above), which follows a long stretch of the northern Mendocino beachfront, including the Ten Mile Beach area. It is a level and easy ride, variable in length depending on where you start and how far you decide to go. Watch out for weekend traffic, though. Ocean Trail, Bikes & Rental, 1260 N Main B-4, Fort Bragg, (707) 964-1260, has a good selection of rentals and trail information for visitors.

Adventure Calendar

Fort Bragg Whale Festival, late March: *includes whale-watching excursions, lighthouse tours, food, and fun; (800) 726-2780.*

Fort Bragg Whale Run/Walk, late March: *a 10K and 5K run/walk benefitting local organizations; (707) 964-0994.*

Attractions

Like other coastal towns, **Fort Bragg,** Mendocino's bad-boy cousin to the north, hasn't been able to escape the relentless approach of gentrification. Originally built in 1855 as a military outpost to supervise the Pomo Indian Reservation, it's still primarily a logging and fishing town, proud of its century-old timber-and-trawler heritage. But not a year goes by in Fort Bragg without yet another commercial fishing vessel being converted into a whale-watching boat (the ultimate insult) or an unemployed logger trading his chain saw for a set of carving knives.

There are plenty of interesting things to do in and around Fort Bragg. If you've visited all of Mendocino's boutiques and still haven't shrugged the shopping bug, Fort Bragg's downtown area has enough shops and galleries—all within walking distance of each other—to keep you entertained for hours. Another dangerous place for a credit card is the **Fort Bragg Depot,** a 14,000-square-foot marketplace with more than 20 shops and restaurants, as well as a historical logging and railroad museum; 401 Main St at Laurel St, (707) 964-8324.

After you've dragged your feet up and down Fort Bragg's streets, give your tired dogs an extended rest aboard the city's popular **Skunk Train** (so named because the odoriferous mix of diesel fuel and gasoline once used to power the train allowed you to smell it before you could see it). Depending on which day you depart, a steam- or diesel-electric-engine train will take you on a scenic 8-hour round-trip journey through the magnificent redwoods to the city of Willits and back again (or you can take the 3.5-hour round-trip excursion to Northspur). Reservations are recommended, especially in the summer; 100 Laurel St Depot, (707) 964-6371.

Certainly among the most exciting things to come to Fort Bragg in years is the **Warehouse Repertory Theatre,** one of the hottest new theater groups in Northern California. Email them at theatre @warerep.org or call the 24-hour reservation and information line at (707) 961-2940 for a listing of performances ranging from modern comedies to Shakespearean classics.

Restaurants

Gardens Grill ☆☆ The perpetually packed parking lot is a dead giveaway to the popularity of this restaurant, located in the botanical gardens. The romantic alfresco seating on the elevated deck overlooking the flower gardens is the main attraction. *18220 Hwy 1 (in the Mendocino Coast Botanical Gardens, S of town), Fort Bragg; (707) 964-7474; $$.*

North Coast Brewing Company ☆☆ This homey brewpub is the most happening place in town, especially at happy hour, when the bar and dark wood tables are occupied by boisterous locals. *444 Main St (just S of the Grey Whale Inn), Fort Bragg; (707) 964-3400; $$.*

The Restaurant ☆ One of the oldest family-run restaurants on the coast, this small, unpretentious Fort Bragg landmark is known for its good dinners and Sunday brunches. The eclectic menu offers dishes from just about every corner of the planet. *418 N Main St (1 block N of Laurel St), Fort Bragg; (707) 964-9800; $$.*

Viraporn's Thai Café ☆   When this tiny cafe opened in 1991, Asian-food aficionados on the North Coast breathed a communal sigh of relief. Masterfully balancing the five traditional Thai flavors of hot, bitter, tart, sweet, and salty, Viraporn's works wonders with refreshing Thai classics. *500 S Main St (off Hwy 1, across from Rite Aid), Fort Bragg; (707) 964-7931; $.*

Lodgings

DeHaven Valley Farm and Restaurant ☆☆☆   This remote 1875 Victorian farmhouse, has a sublime rural setting and access to a secluded beach. The 5 guest rooms in the house and the 3 nearby cottages are decorated with colorful comforters and rustic antiques; some even have fireplaces. *39247 Hwy 1 (1.7 miles N of town), Westport; (707) 961-1660; $$.*

Emandal Farm ☆   Since 1908 this thousand-acre working farm situated along the Eel River has been a popular summer getaway for Bay Area families. The 13 rustic, redwood one-bedroom cabins and 4 two-bedroom cabins are nestled under a grove of oak and fir trees. They're not equipped with much just single- and queen-size beds, cold spring water, and electricity (and that's it). *16500 Hearst Post Office Rd (16 miles E of town; call or write for directions), Willits; (707) 459-5439 or (800) 262-9597; $$.*

Grey Whale Inn ☆☆   Wide doorways and sloped halls are the only vestiges of this popular inn's previous life as the town hospital. The stately four-story building is now one of the more comfortable and distinctive inns on the coast. Decorated with quilts, heirlooms, and antiques, the 14 large guest rooms have private baths and wonderful views of the town or sea. *615 N Main St (at 1st St and Hwy 1), Fort Bragg; (707) 964-0640 or (800) 382-7244; $$.*

More Information

Fort Bragg–Mendocino Coast Chamber of Commerce: *(707) 961-6300.*
Jackson Demonstration State Forest: *(707) 964-5674.*
Noyo Harbor fishing village: *(707) 964-4719.*
Sinkyone Wilderness State Park information: *(707) 986-7711.*
State parks camping reservations: *(800) 444-7275.*

Smith River National Recreation Area

The Smith River National Recreation Area wilderness and other key highlights from the entire 1.1-million-acre Six Rivers National Forest, which extends in a narrow ribbon 140 miles south to the Mendocino National Forest border and includes the Trinity, Smith, Mad, Klamath, Eel, and Van Duzen Rivers.

As poorly as some of the nation's national forests have historically been managed, the Smith River National Recreation Area, covering some 350,000 acres of lush woods, doesn't fit the stereotype of land raped by greedy logging companies who then charged American taxpayers for the pleasure. That's because in 1990, before anyone could get around to building another dam or bringing on the chain saws en masse, Congress passed legislation permanently protecting the Six Rivers forest area from everyone except those looking for a bit of outdoor adventure. Today, the area is the sole territory of rafters, hikers, birders, anglers, and campers looking to get in touch with something that seems increasingly unreachable these days: a wild, undisturbed paradise.

The crowning feature of this paradise is the Smith River, which runs 325 miles from its headwaters in Oregon's Kalmiopsis Wilderness through the ancient redwood groves of Del Norte County and out to the Pacific—unimpeded by irrigation, flood control, or water storage dams. This is saying a lot in California, where dams and water diversion are a way of life. Named for Jedediah Smith, the Gold Rush mountain man whose trading posts for miners marked the beginnings of settlement on the North Coast, the river is a wild ride for rafters who enjoy the excitement of unpredictable conditions found on uncontrolled waters. The pristine Smith also has arguably the best salmon and steelhead fishing in the state. Activities on the river and its tributaries, in fact, are a common draw for many of the people who come here. Visitors also camp on its banks and swim in its coves to get a feel for its unbridled flows.

This is also a place for nature lovers, who will find an odd mix of rare plant communities such as fire-adapted lodgepole and knobcone pines, along with growth-stunted groves of Port Orford cedars, whose diminutive size is a result of the serpentine soil conditions. Even in formerly logged areas, these unusual characteristics can be captivating. More than 300 documented species of wildlife live here, on seven different types of terrain.

The recreation area is managed by the Gasquet Ranger District in Del Norte County, with the remaining forested areas divided between the Orleans, Mad River, and Lower Trinity Ranger Stations. Off-road vehicles have the run of miles of roads in the Mad River area east of Fortuna in southern Humboldt County, access that is difficult to find in this age of increasingly restrictive wildlife habitat management,

Getting There

US Highway 199 (US 199), which follows the wild and scenic Smith River in a meandering cut northeast from Crescent City, is the main thoroughfare through the national recreation area. It connects to numerous forest service roads extending into the wilderness. To reach some areas, a sturdy truck or four-wheel-drive vehicle is often the best bet. Call (707) 442-1721 to check on road conditions before setting out. The remainder of Six Rivers National Forest is best accessed on Highway 299 between Arcata and Redding, and along Highway 96, which cuts north to south through much of the wilderness. Highway 36 east from southern Humboldt County also traverses the forest area in an east-west direction. Discovery Trail, 86 miles of forest roads open to off-road vehicles, is accessible from Highway 36 as well. The main ranger station for the Smith River National Recreation area is in Gasquet, on Highway 199, 18 miles east of Crescent City, (707) 457-3131.

Adjoining Areas

WEST: **Del Norte Coast, Humboldt Coast**

EAST: **Trinity Region, Klamath Region**

SOUTH: **Mendocino National Forest**

inside out

Camping

Backcountry hikers who don't mind roughing it look to the Smith River National Recreation Area as a godsend—particularly on those busy summer holiday weekends up north when the quiet riverside anglers are replaced by hordes of shrieking children in inner tubes. Not only do this recreation area and adjacent national forest offer 15 campgrounds away from the Redwood Highway and busy state campgrounds, they also allow backwoods camping just about anywhere you can find a spot level enough to pitch a tent—so long as the spot is at least a quarter mile away from developed camps. **Primitive camping** is limited to 30 cumulative days per person each year. A **permit** is required if you plan to use fire, including stoves or lanterns. Most of the developed sites are open only during the summer water-sports season, the exceptions being **year-round camps** at Patrick Creek, Panther Flat, and East Fork Trinity (see below). **Reservations** are taken only at Grassy Flat, Panther Flat, and Patrick Creek Camps (see below), through individual ranger districts or the Forest Service reservations system, (800) 280-2267. If you have backpacking in mind, it is best to hit the trails in the recreation-area portion of the forest, where the trails are better developed (see Hiking/Backpacking, below). The southern ranger districts of Six Rivers National Recreation Area are more of an overflow camping zone for those who want to be near the Humboldt redwoods (see Humboldt Coast chapter).

Six Rivers National Recreation Area

Panther Flat Camp has 39 sites (no hookups; RV limit 22 feet) and is a good location for winter fly-fishing on the state's premier salmon and steelhead river, the Smith. Each site has a picnic table and fire pit; running water, flush toilets, and hot showers are available nearby. Because of the location and amenities, this is one of the most popular campgrounds in the Six Rivers boundaries. It is open year-round. Reservations are a good idea. *Contact the Smith River National Recreation Area, Gasquet Ranger District, (707) 457-3131, or national forest reservations system, (800) 280-2267. The campground is 20 miles east of the Redwood Hwy on US 199 near Gasquet, entrance on the north side of the road at mile marker 16.75.*

Big Flat Camp has 28 sites (no hookups; RV limit 22 feet) on the banks of Hurdy-Gurdy Creek near the south fork of the Klamath, not far from good fishing spots and river sports. Each site has a picnic table and fire pit. No water. No reservations taken. Open May to September. *Contact* *the Smith River National Recreation Area, Gasquet Ranger Station for information, (707) 457-3131, or forest service reservations, (800) 280-2267. The camp is north of Crescent City on Big Flat Rd. Take US 199 north from the Redwood Hwy 10 miles, then head south on South Fork Rd, then go 15 miles to Big Flat Rd and east to the camp entrance on the north side of the road.*

Grassy Flat Camp has 19 sites (no hookups; RV limit 22 feet) in a popular winter fishing and summer water-sports area on the banks of the Smith River middle fork. Each site has a picnic table and fire pit, and running water is provided nearby. Reservations taken. The camp is open May to September only. No showers or flush toilets. *Call the Smith River National Recreation Area, Gasquet Ranger Station, (707) 457-3131, for information, or national forest reservations, (800) 280-2267. The camp is 25 miles north of the Redwood Hwy intersection on US 199; entrance is on the east side of the road at mile marker 18.87.*

Patrick Creek Camp is a small but well-appointed campground with 13 sites (no hookups; RVs okay) near where the creek meets the upper portion of the Smith River and not far from the Siskiyou Wilderness Area. Each site has a picnic table and fire pit, and there are running water and flush toilets nearby, but no showers. Be sure to make a reservation, particularly on holiday weekends and during the peak winter fishing months. The camp is open May to September only. *Call the Smith River National Recreation Area, Gasquet Ranger Station, (707) 457-3131. The campground is 25 miles north of the Redwood Hwy intersection on US 199, on the east side of the road and 9 miles past the town of Gasquet, at mile marker 22.*

Northeastern Humboldt County

Pearch Creek Camp has 11 sites (only 2 for RV, limit 22 feet; no hookups) on a tributary to the Klamath River with good fishing nearby. Each site has a picnic table and fire pit. No showers and no running water. No reservations taken. Open May to November. *Call Six Rivers National Forest, Orleans Ranger District, (530) 627-3291, to check on availability, or just drop in. The camp is 1 mile north of Orleans on Hwy 96, east side of road.*

There are 10 tent sites and 19 sites for RVs (no hookups; RV limit 35 feet) at **Aikens Creek Camp** off the Klamath River, along a good run for beginning rafters. Each site has a picnic table and fire pit, and there are flush toilets but no showers. *Reservations accepted through the Six Rivers National Forest, Orleans Ranger District, (530) 627-3291, or the national forest system, (800) 280-2267. The camp is 5 miles north of Weitchpec on Hwy 96, east side of the highway.*

Fish Lake Camp has 23 sites, 13 for RVs (no hookups; RV limit 35 feet) at a small fishing and swimming lake that is a popular destination for summer outings. Each site has a picnic table and fire pit. Running water is available nearby, but no showers. Open May to September only. *Reservations through the Six Rivers National Forest, Orleans Ranger District, (530) 627-3291, or the national forest system, (800) 280-2267. The camp is at the end of Fish Lake Rd, which is a turnoff west from Hwy 96, 7 miles north of Weitchpec.*

Southeastern Humboldt County

Boise Creek Camp has 20 sites, including 3 hike-in only (no hookups; RV limit 40 feet), near good fishing and rafting areas of the Trinity River. Each site has a picnic table and fire pit, with running water nearby but no showers or flush toilets. Sites given on drop-in basis only; no reservations taken. Open May to September. *Contact the Six Rivers National Forest, Lower Trinity Ranger District, (530) 629-2118. The campground is 39 miles east of the Redwood Hwy intersection on Hwy 299, north side of the road.*

East Fork Trinity Camp is small, with just 8 sites (no hookups; RVs okay) in a nice setting in the foothills right on the banks of the Trinity River. The camp is a favorite swimming spot in summer, and has good fishing during the winter migration. No reservations are taken. Open year-round. *Call the Six Rivers National Forest, Lower Trinity Ranger District, (530) 629-2118, for information. The camp is on the south side of Hwy 299, 6 miles east of the Redwood Hwy intersection in Arcata.*

Tish Tang Camp has 40 campsites (no hookups; RV limit 30 feet) near a popular swimming and water play area on the Trinity River. Each site has a picnic table and fire grill, and running water is available. Open May to September. No showers or flush toilets. No reservations taken. *Contact the Six Rivers National Forest, Lower Trinity Ranger District, (530) 629-2118, for information. The camp is 8 miles north of Willow Creek on Hwy 96, east side of the road.*

Grays Falls Camp has 32 sites (no hookups; RV limit 35 feet) at a popular summer water play area on the Trinity River. Each site has a picnic table and fire pit, with running water and flush toilets nearby, but no showers. No reservations taken. Open only May to September. *Call the Six Rivers National Forest, Lower Trinity Ranger District, (530) 629-2118, for more information. The campground is 12 miles past Willow Creek on Hwy 299, south side of the road.*

Hiking/Backpacking

This is the real thing here, so don't just go disappear down some trail in a pair of sneakers carrying no water. Get properly outfitted with gear and maps before exploring the more than 75 miles of hiking trails traversing the Six Rivers National Forest and Smith River National Recreation Area. First off, the best developed trails are in the northern reaches of the forest, within the 350,000-acre national recreation area. For a current **map** of the entire forest, send a written request and a check for $4.29 (for each map), payable to the Northwest Interpretive Association, to Six Rivers National Forest, Office of Information, 1330 Bayshore Way, Eureka, CA 95501. It is best to request both the Six Rivers National Forest and Smith River National Recreation Area maps, for a total of $8.58. While the Six Rivers area is largely a backwoods wilderness tract, numerous nice short walks and day hikes are possible there also, so don't be deterred just because you're not Grizzly Adams. Check in with the **Gasquet Ranger District,** (707) 457-3131, which manages the recreation area, for up-to-the-minute trail conditions and advice. For points south, contact the **Mad River Ranger District,** (707) 574-6233; **Orleans Ranger District,** (530) 627-3291; or **Lower Trinity Ranger District,** (530) 629-2118. For gear and good information, check with the area's most reputable outfitter, Northern Mountain Supply, 125 W Fifth St, Eureka, (800) 878-3583.

Smith River National Recreation Area

Stoney Creek Trail (easy; 1 mile round trip) is a great sweat-free way to take a gander at the wild and scenic Smith River north fork. There are also excellent fishing spots near where the creek meets the river. The trailhead is just south of US 199. Take Middle Fork Rd off the highway south, then go west on Gasquet Rd for 1 mile to the trail parking area on the right.

Myrtle Creek Trail (easy; 2 miles round trip) offers not only a lovely walk through a lush fern canyon, but also an interesting look at the aftermath of the California gold rush. Miners scavenged the creek for gold in the late 1800s after a legendary 47-ounce nugget was discovered there. The excitement generated a flurry of activity around the creek, with scars still visible today. The trailhead is directly north of US 199, just east of the Myrtle Creek Bridge, 12 miles east of the Redwood Highway at Crescent City.

McClendon Ford Trail (easy to moderate; 3 miles round trip) passes through a forest of old-growth Douglas fir and cedar to the rocky shores of the south fork of the Smith River at the confluence with Horse Creek. This is a nice pooled area for swimming during the summer and fly-fishing during the winter. The trail has an elevation gain of 250 feet over half a mile on the return. To get to the trailhead, take US 199 east for 13 miles from the Redwood Highway junction to South Fork Rd, then go north 14 miles on South Fork, and turn southeast on the gravel Forest Rd 15. Continue for 3 miles to Forest Rd 15N39, take a left, and continue another 2 miles to the trailhead. This is also the trailhead for South Kelsey Trail.

French Hill Trail (moderate; 5.5 miles round trip) is a brisk and steep hike catapulting 1,600 feet to the fire lookout areas east of the Gasquet Ranger Station. The walk is challenging, but the forest shade makes it more bearable. The payoff is a panoramic view of surrounding forests and canyons from 2,000 feet above. Look for the trailhead 4.5 miles east of US 199 on French Hill Rd outside Gasquet. The French Hill turnoff is left (east) from US 199 at mile marker 12.23.

Craig's Creek Trail (moderate; 7.5 miles round trip) is an old Gold Rush–era pack mule trail that climbs low ridges overlooking the Smith River south fork's confluence with Craig's Creek. The walk passes through varied terrain that includes rocky river shore, shady forests, and grassy knolls. To find the trailhead, take US 199 east for 13 miles from the Redwood Highway intersection to South Fork Rd. Head north on South Fork to the George Tyson Bridge; park on the north side of the bridge.

High Dome Trail (moderate; 8 miles round trip) is a daylong trek to an overlook 3,821 feet up Dome Mountain. The mountain is named after a wide grassy meadow that spreads out over its summit like a dome. From the top, old-growth forest canyons, rivers, surrounding peaks, and the Pacific Ocean unfold before you. This is a decent day hike, but camping is available for those who want to make an overnighter out of it. To reach the trailhead, take US 199 for 13 miles east of the Redwood Highway, then go north on Patrick Creek Rd 3 miles to Gasquet Toll Rd. Proceed left (west) for another half mile on Gasquet, then right on Holiday Rd. The trailhead is immediately to the right.

Elk Camp Ridge Trail (difficult and steep; 16.5 miles round trip) offers stunning views of the Smith River, surrounding old-growth forest canyons, neighboring peaks, and the Pacific Ocean following a 2,500-foot climb along what at one time was a gold rush pack trail leading to Illinois Valley, Oregon. The terrain is mostly serpentine rock; the lower portion passes through an interesting fire ecology zone, burned out in 1996. To reach the trailhead, go 6 miles east of the Redwood Highway on US 199, then south at Middle Fork Rd, right (west) at Gasquet Flat Rd, and 2.5 miles to Forest Rd 18N10. Turn left on 18N10, and continue 1.5 miles.

Island Lake Trail (difficult and steep; 10.4 miles round trip) catapults from Elk Creek to a strenuous 4-mile climb over a ridge of Jedediah Mountain, and then switches down to a pretty, hidden lake in the woods just within the Siskiyou National Wilderness. This is a good camping and fishing spot away from the masses, but you really have to work for it. To reach the trailhead, take US 199 for 27 miles east of the Redwood Highway intersection, then go south 10 miles on Little Jones Creek Rd. When that turns into Forest Rd 16N02, continue for 2.5 miles (no turns—stay on the main road), then turn left on Forest Rd 16N28 and continue another 1.5 miles to the staging area at the end of the road.

Little Bald Hills Trail (moderate to difficult; 19.2 miles round trip) begins near Stout Grove in Jedediah Smith Redwoods State Park (see Parks/Beaches, Del Norte Coast chapter) and then ascends gradually to

2,000 feet, where you'll find remarkable open prairies in the Siskiyou foothills surrounded by thick forests of fir and pine. This is a popular backpacking trip with birders, who enjoy watching raptors that use the area as their hunting fields. The trailhead is within Jedediah Smith; go 3 miles east of the Redwood Highway intersection on US 199, then south into the park at South Fork Rd. Cross two bridges, then turn right on Howland Hill Rd, and continue 2 miles to the trailhead.

South Kelsey Trail (difficult; up to 30 miles round trip, variable) is part of a 150-year-old mule trail that ran 200 miles between Siskiyou County and Crescent City, to bring gold out of the mountains for shipment to San Francisco. The first 7 miles of the hike are easy, following the Smith River's south fork past popular fishing holes around Horse and Buck Creeks. After that begins the 5-mile climb up steep terrain toward the 5,775-foot Baldy Peak, which offers panoramic views of the river canyons, surrounding peaks, and Pacific Ocean. The third leg of the trail continues another 3 miles to Harrington Lake on the eastern Smith River National Recreation Area boundary. The fourth optional leg of the hike continues for another 12 miles into the Klamath National Forest high country. Hiking camps are located throughout, and are prominently marked on recreation area maps (see Camping, above). To get to the trailhead, take US 199 13 miles east from the Redwood Highway junction to South Fork Rd, go north 14 miles on South Fork, and turn southeast on the gravel Forest Rd 15. Continue for 3 miles to Forest Rd 15N39, take a left, and continue another 2 miles.

Lower Trinity Ranger District

The overnight outing to Mill Creek Lake on the western slopes of the Trinity Alps on **Horse Ridge Trail** (moderate; 13 miles round trip) climbs gently through desolate woods toward Trinity Summit, where you'll have a great view of Hoopa Valley and the river canyons of Humboldt County. To reach the trailhead, take Hwy 299 east from Arcata and the Redwood Highway for 20 miles, then go north 9 miles on Hwy 96 to Big Hill Lookout Rd. Go east on Big Hill Lookout Rd for 10 miles; continue as the road changes to Forest Rd 18N01; it dead-ends at the trailhead.

South Fork Trail (moderate; 14 miles round trip) follows the route of an old gold rush mining trail along bluffs overlooking the Trinity River's south fork. The trail crosses the river twice, once at a nice shallow spot (during the summer, anyway), and the second time at a swinging footbridge that looks like something out of an Indiana Jones daredevil scene. There is a campsite at the bridge, 7 miles in from the trailhead. Be sure to check with the ranger district for maps and river conditions before setting out on this one. To find the trailhead, go south of Hwy 299 on South Fork Rd, just west of Salyer, for 13 miles. Continue for 3 miles after the road changes over to Forest Rd 5N03. At the end of the road, get out and walk a mile to the trailhead—unless you have a four-wheel-drive vehicle, in which case you may continue one more mile to a more convenient staging area.

Rafting/Kayaking/Canoeing

Since it is the longest free-running river in the state, whitewater action along the **Smith River**'s north and south forks can be both dicey and dangerous. On most other rivers through the North Coast and north mountain regions, scheduled releases from upstream reservoirs make it possible to scope out the temperament of any given run as much as two days in advance. Sudden water surges on the Smith, however, cannot be foretold, particularly if the weather forecast is faulty and an unexpected rain hits. This considered, amateur rafters and kayakers should take to the Smith, particularly the **north fork,** only with a skilled and reputable guide who knows when the time is right. Those who think they can handle the wild Class IV rapids of the north fork on their own, however, have a choice of put-ins along High Divide Rd in the extreme northern reaches of the Smith River National Recreation Area, with access via Rowdy and Low Divide Rds north from the Gasquet Ranger Station on US 199. Check with the ranger station, (707) 457-3131, for **river conditions, maps, directions,** and to register before heading up. Because the north fork's headwaters are in the Kalmiopsis Wilderness Area southwest of Grants Pass, Oregon, it is necessary to leave the state to get to rapids in the extreme northern reaches. This portion of Kalmiopsis is often out of reach because of weather, however, so don't make solid plans without checking first. Bigfoot Rafting Company in Willow Creek, (800) 722-2223, is one of the few **guided raft trip** companies that ventures up the north fork on a regular basis. If the river is right, these folks are likely to know about it and be planning an outing.

The Smith's **south fork,** at a Class III rating, is both easier to get to and easier for less experienced rafters and kayakers to contend with. The run between Jedediah Smith Redwoods State Park (see Del Norte Coast chapter) and the Redwood Highway, in fact, is tame enough for a **canoe run** when the river hovers at 700 cubic feet per second. More cantankerous runs are found between Coopers Flat and the confluence with Goose Creek. River access can be found along South Fork Rd at Second Bridge, Sand Camp, Redwood Flat, Rattlesnake Flat, and Goose Creek, all south of the US 199 crossing. Again, contact the Gasquet Ranger station, (707) 457-3131, for river information.

The Class IV runs on the upper **Klamath River** at Somes Bar and those on its tributary, the Salmon River, are considered to be among the most exciting in the north (see River Rafting, Klamath Region chapter). The middle fork of the Klamath River, however, with its Class II to Class III rapids, is also a major draw because the waters are generally calm enough under normal summer conditions. The run between Orleans and Weitchpec parallels Hwy 96, with numerous put-in spots along the public right-of-way. River Dancers, an outfitter out of Mount Shasta, (800) 926-5002, has regularly scheduled middle Klamath outings from June to September.

The **Trinity River**'s more moderate Class II whitewater runs, particularly the 5-hour trip from Tish Tang to Hoopa Valley, are more appropriate for less experienced rafters and kayakers, or those who want to get a child on the water for the first time. River access is easy along both Hwys 299 and 96 for the Tish Tang to Hoopa run, the Willow Creek to Tish Tang run, the Salyer to Willow Creek run, and the Hawkins Bar to Salyer run, all Class I and II rapids, with the exception of a low-key Class III rapid between Willow Creek and Tish Tang near Sugar Bowl Ranch. The Trinity is not only tamer than the Smith, it also offers prettier scenery, as the banks are more densely wooded than many of the Smith's upper runs. Check with the Six Rivers National Forest, Lower Trinity Ranger District, in Willow Creek, (530) 629-2118, for up-to-date **river conditions** and advice if you head out with no guide service. The outfitter Redwoods & Rivers, in Arcata, (800) 429-0090, takes frequent outings on the more popular Trinity runs.

Fishing

The **Smith River**, being the last major river in the state to run unrestricted, is the premier winter destination for anglers looking to reel in monster **salmon** and **steelhead.** But with more than 200 miles accessible to the public along with more than 40 tributaries, the number of super-special fishing spots—the ones where those legendary 80-pound monsters are most likely to bite—is limitless. Within the entire Six Rivers National Forest boundaries, there are 1,500 miles of riverfront. We can't promise that a king the size of a German shepherd is going to eat your rod and reel. What we can do is point out some key public access points along the Smith and strongly recommend that, if a big catch is absolutely necessary, you go out with a guided fishing tour. There are excellent fly-fishing spots both at the Smith's **middle fork** and **Stoney Creek** where the two waterways come together, as well as the area within half a mile of the Stoney Creek Trail trailhead (see Hiking/Backpacking, above). An even better spot in both winter and summer is on the Smith's south fork near Horse Creek, accessed via a 1.5-mile walk from the McClendon Ford Trail trailhead (see

Hiking/Backpacking, above). Also seek out the fishing spots around three Six Rivers National Forest camps on the Smith: Panther Flat, Grassy Flat, and Patrick Creek (see Camping, above).

Most visitors do best with a **guide service,** however. One of the best is Lunker Fish Trips, (800) 248-4704, which matches adventurers with experienced guides during the winter spawning season and rents Tahiti **rafts** during the summer from its riverside facility at 2095 US 199 in Hiouchi. Hiouchi Hamlet, 2100 US 199, Crescent City, (707) 458-3114, also has bait, tackle, supplies, and friendly advice on hand.

Fishing spots along the **Klamath River** within the Six Rivers forest area can be found by fanning out on either side of Big Flat near the south fork's confluence with Hurdy-Gurdy Creek, and also around the Pearch Creek Camp area (see Camping, above). On the **Trinity River,** access is easy at pullouts along Hwy 299 between Willow Creek and Junction City. Boise Creek and East Fork Trinity Camps (see Camping, above) are particularly well situated on the river.

While most North Coast river anglers tend to focus on the **winter** season, fly-fishing on rivers and bait fishing on small lakes throughout the Smith River National Recreation Area and the Six Rivers National Forest are popular summer activities as well. Just count on a lazier time, and a smaller catch. Fish Lake north of Weitchpec and Mill Creek Lake near Hoopa Valley (see Camping, above) are two good choices for stocked **rainbow trout** fishing, although Mill Creek involves a 2-mile hike and is best approached as a backpack camping/fishing excursion. Again, be sure to check for the latest amendments to fishing **regulations** before heading out. Outfitters and tackle dealers have free copies of the latest regulations on hand, or call the state Department of Fish and Game river information recording at (707) 442-4502.

Wildlife

The varied terrain within Smith River National Recreation Area and the Six Rivers National Forest—from rocky peaks and wide meadows to lush riverbanks, deep forests, and stillwater ponds—means a smorgasbord for **birders.** Among the oaks and hardwood forests, turkey vultures, sharp-shinned hawks, Cooper's hawks, ferruginous hawks (seen only rarely, in the fall), golden eagles, merlins, barn owls, western screech owls, great horned owls, the occasional rare northern spotted owl, woodpeckers, fly-catchers, and swallows are the main fare. Jedediah Smith Redwoods State Park (see Del Norte Coast chapter) and the surrounding woodlands to the east along US 199 are prime viewing spots for these species.

Closer to the rivers, particularly in the pooled areas and gentle currents that make good summer fishing holes, such as the Grassy Camp area of the Smith River (see Camping, above) or the Trinity River's east fork, look for swans, pintails, ducks, common mergansers, and scaups. These also might be found around the forest ponds and lakes, or at Hoopa Valley and Elk Creek.

The open, high prairies, such as those at Little Bald Hills (see Hiking/Backpacking, above), are good for spotted **predatory birds** like the red-tailed hawk, turkey vultures, and common nighthawk. Check with the North Coast Redwoods Interpretive Association, (707) 822-7611, extension 5300, or the Audubon Society, (707) 826-7031, for recent **bird count information** and word of any special **interpretive tours.**

In the untamed wilds of Six Rivers, the odds are likely that explorers are going to come across any variety of wild animals inhabiting the wooded canyons and mountainsides—maybe even the legendary **Bigfoot!** Expect to see **black-tailed deer, raccoons, gray foxes, gray squirrels, garter snakes, yellow-legged frogs,** and maybe **black bears** and **mountain lions** (heed the warnings about bears and lions spelled out in the primer at the beginning of this book).

Cross-Country Skiing

Shasta it's not, but when the snow is adequate, some decent cross-country skiing can be had in the open pine and cedar forests of **Horse Mountain,** which covers just over 1,000 acres of the Six Rivers National Forest's botanical preserves in the shadows of the Trinity Alps to the east. This is the wilds, so don't expect a four-star ski resort to be here waiting for you, and note that skiing conditions can be hit-or-miss between the 3,900 and 4,800 elevations. The scenery, however, is worth the gamble. The growth-stunted forests found around the serpentine rock terrain at Horse Mountain are a curiosity for botanists throughout the state. Take Hwy 299 east from Arcata 40 miles to Lord Ellis Summit, then go south 15 miles on Titlow Hill Rd (Forest Service Hwy 1) to the well-contrasted open woods. Check with the Lower Trinity Ranger District in Willow Creek, (530) 629-2118, on **snow conditions** before heading out. Ski **equipment** is available at the Outdoor Store, 876 G St, Arcata, (707) 822-0321, or the Sports World, 2824 F St, Eureka, (707) 443-4011.

Off-Road Vehicles

It is possible to explore the wilderness on 149 miles of Forest Service roads, about half unpaved, which follow the **Discovery Trail** route through much of the Mad River Ranger District portion of Six Rivers National Forest. The segment connects with another 86 miles of similar roads within the Mendocino National Forest to the south. Most roads within the forest are rugged, one-lane dirt roads that are subject to closure during wet weather, times of critical fire danger, periods when sensitive or rare wildlife must not be disturbed, or times when it is necessary to minimize impact on trees and vegetation. The Discovery Trail segment begins at the Mad River ranger station. Take Hwy 36 east 45 miles from the Redwood Highway to the station, 28 miles east of Bridgeville. From there, the trail follows the 100-year-old Butterfield Stagecoach route through mixed forest, oak woodlands, and pretty streams and meadows. There is a lot to look at—and endless places to get lost. Sign in and check on the latest **rules and regulations** at the ranger station, (707) 574-6233, before heading out. Only limited portions of the area are open to all-terrain vehicles, or **ATVs;** you will need a street-legal vehicle to make any distance. The Lost Coast 4X4 Club, 7177 David Ave, Eureka, (707) 442-9510, has information on driving skills and organizes off-highway adventures for those who would rather buddy up than vanish into the wilderness alone.

Mountain Biking

How could you resist? With seemingly endless and labyrinthine Forest Service roads traversing more than a million acres of wilderness, exploring on a mountain bike seems only natural. The opportunities here are pretty boundless; just be sure to check with the appropriate ranger station in whatever district you're in for the latest trail conditions because, as with the rest of the North Coast and mountains, roads and trails get mucky nearly to the point of impassability in the rainy season.

One route to consider is **Old Gasquet Loop Road,** a difficult 23-mile jaunt through Panther and Grassy Flats, Cedar Creek, and then up more than 2,000 feet and over 10 miles through the foothills of Cold Spring Mountain on a seldom-traveled gravel Forest Service road. The last 8 miles follow US 199. To get to the trailhead, go west of Gasquet about a half mile from the ranger station, then south on Middle Fork Rd a half mile (veering right at the fork) to Old Gasquet Toll Rd. Go west on Old Gasquet a quarter mile to the end, where the trail begins. After the first 15-mile leg of the ride, the trail meets US 199, and you have a choice between climbing the foothills again to return the way you came or riding with the highway traffic. Obviously, one is more work than the other—but some purists would rather turn a 23-mile ride into a 30-mile ride than share the road with the minivans and Winnebagos. Contact the Gasquet Ranger Station, (707) 457-3131, for more information and road conditions before setting out. Also be sure to carry maps (see Hiking/Backpacking, above) and a bike repair kit with you on this and all other long, bumpy rides in the wilderness.

Perhaps the most feared off-road biking route in all of the Six Rivers area is **the Bushwhacker,** a brutal 23.3-mile ordeal over two 3,000-foot peaks in the foothills southwest of Tish Tang Point outside Hoopa Valley. The ride begins in the Horse Linto area north of Hwy 299 on Forest Rd 8N03 (east from Arcata), then whips through creek crossings, sharp switchbacks, and steep grades. The best way to take the ride is to do the first leg on Forest Rd 7N30, hang a right turn from just past the beginning of Forest Rd 8N03, and follow the broken concrete, gravel, and dirt roads, making all right turns. Reconnect with Forest Rd 8N03 for the final downhill back to Horse Linto. Because of the numerous creek crossings, checking with the Lower Trinity Ranger District, (530) 629-2118, on **road conditions** is a necessity. Again, do not attempt this without maps and proper gear—and note that this ride really is for advanced mountain bikers only.

An easier ride is along the **Ruth Lake Bike Trail,** at the Ruth Reservoir on the Mad River, well marked at the south side of the road, 65 miles east of the Redwood Highway on Hwy 36 between Mad River and Forest Glen. Forest Rd 1S06 follows the west side of the lake for 8 miles, then connects with Trinity County Rd 502, where you can double back to the trailhead or keep exploring. The reservoir is a popular camping and summer water play area. Contact the Mad River Ranger District, (707) 574-6233, for more information.

More Information

Forest Service reservations system: *(800) 280-2267.*
Lower Trinity Ranger District: *(530) 629-2118.*
Mad River Ranger District: *(707) 574-6233.*
Orleans Ranger District: *(530) 627-3291.*
Six Rivers National Forest: *(707) 442-1721.*
Smith River National Recreation Area Visitors Center:
   (707) 457-3131.

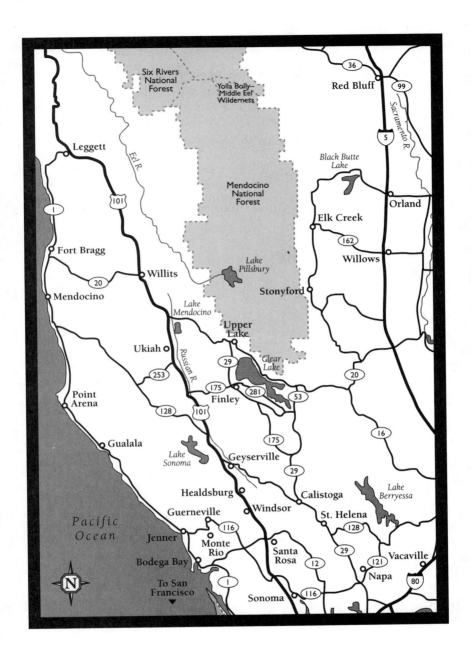

Six Rivers
National
Forest

Yolla Bolly–
Middle Eel
Wilderness

36

Red Bluff

99

Sacramento R.

Leggett

Eel R.

5

Black Butte
Lake

Mendocino
National
Forest

Orland

101

Elk Creek

Fort Bragg

162

Willows

20

Willits

Lake
Pillsbury

Mendocino

Lake
Mendocino

Stonyford

Upper
Lake

Ukiah

Russian R.

Clear
Lake

29

253

175

281

53

20

Point
Arena

128

Finley

101

175

16

Gualala

Lake
Sonoma

Geyserville

29

Lake
Berryessa

Pacific
Ocean

Healdsburg

Calistoga

St. Helena

Guerneville

116

Windsor

128

Jenner

Monte
Rio

Santa
Rosa

29

121

Vacaville

Bodega Bay

12

Napa

80

To San
Francisco

1

116

Sonoma

N

Wine
Country

Sonoma
and Southern
Mendocino
Coasts

From the Sonoma County border at Bodega Bay north to the Highway 20 divide near Fort Bragg in Mendocino County, including Russian Gulch and Mendocino Headlands State Parks, the Jenner coast, Manchester State Beach, and Fort Ross State Historic Park.

A grim-faced beachcomber was kind enough to shout this warning to us during a recent winter visit to the Sonoma and southern Mendocino coasts: "Never turn your back on the ocean here. You'll be sorry." The warning, while perhaps a bit alarmist, is justified. The most common mishaps afflicting visitors to these dramatically eroded rocky shores are run-ins with the Pacific, which gurgles and froths relentlessly when the weather is stormy and the tide is in. At least one or two people get washed out to sea each year, and many more have to be plucked from rocks where they have been stranded after adventuring a bit too far during low tide.

The curious thing about all this, however, is that one of the most popular outdoor activities for visitors is free diving for red abalone and rock cod. So on one hand you have people telling you to stay away from the water, and on the other you have them telling you to dive in—with no breathing apparatus—to fish for your dinner.

This is where common sense comes in.

You can survive a trip to the Sonoma and southern Mendocino coasts by playing it smart. That means calling ahead for information about current conditions before suiting up and diving in or climbing a rock and having to be airlifted to safety.

The first thing you notice when approaching this area from the urban Bay Area is that this is where the landscape really begins to change character. The open spaces get wider, the terrain gets greener due to heavier rainfall up north, and the people begin to lose that big-city edge. Repeat visitors are common, drawn by the rivers, the redwoods, the stormy coast, and the millions of places to get lost.

The community of Mendocino, with its postcard-perfect Victorian architecture and sleepy, time-passed-by atmosphere, is on the National Register of Historic Places—not just a few sites, mind you, but the whole town. It's worth breezing through—but do not get sucked into the cute gift shop and restaurant scene; instead, head west of the town proper and explore the best of what the coast has to offer. Plain and simple, this is a fantastic spot to walk and look at the ocean. The layered marine terraces here, and the fascinating pygmy forests that grow upon them, are much more interesting than any boutique and sometimes easier to get in and out of.

Upland hikes through the wilderness surrounding Fort Ross State Historic Park, site of a real Russian fort; surfing on Bodega Bay; canoeing on the wide and gentle rivers; camping on the edge of wind-protected bluffs overlooking the sea . . . the options away from town are wide and varied.

Getting There

Virtually all of the area covered in this chapter is accessed easily along the Coast Highway (Highway 1) between Bodega Bay and the Highway 20 intersection south of Fort Bragg—90 miles of rugged coast with narrow and curvy pockets where the going is slow. Most travelers to this region access the Coast Highway via Highway 20 from Willits or Highway 116, which meets the coast after passing through the Russian River area.

Adjoining Areas

NORTH: **Northern Mendocino Coast**

SOUTH: **Point Reyes National Seashore, Marin**

EAST: **Mendocino National Forest, Russian River**

inside out

Parks/Beaches

Along the Sonoma County portion of the coast, the southern third—from Bodega Bay to Russian Gulch, north of Jenner—is mostly public land. In contrast, much of the northern third of Sonoma's coast is privately owned, so public access is limited. Beaches along the Sonoma and southern Mendocino coasts are secluded and sometimes difficult to get to. During the less-crowded winter season, storms and driving rains make this a wet but beautiful place—but a summer visit is preferable, simply because the pale blue water rolling with white breaks makes the perfect backdrop for photographs that really say "California." During summer when the sun is shining, temperatures can climb into the 70s. But when the chilly fog rolls in around 5pm as it usually does, temperatures almost instantly plummet into the mid-50s, where they will remain until the fog burns off the next morning. Always carry a sweater, and keep heading north if where you are is too crowded for your mood.

Geologic oddities like the caves and wave tunnels covering the 2-mile stretch of coast at **Mendocino Headlands State Park** are just plain fascinating to look at. When the high-tide surf smacks against the wave-worn rocks, a froth of ocean shoots skyward as if ejected through a whale's blowhole. A rock arch forms a natural footbridge, an irresistible crossing for hikers exploring the shore (even though it leads to a dead end). The park is a mystical-looking place where the land meets the sea, with rugged cliffs, coves, and secluded beaches laden with driftwood. On the park's southern boundary, **Big River** flows from the coastal mountains and meets the Pacific. The headlands area, which is open for day use only, is a must-see for visitors who flock to the quaint seaside community of Mendocino. The best way to explore the coastline here is on foot; in fact, once you're off the trails and onto rocks you have to jump from flat surface to flat surface to get around. Bicycling is also popular, however, on trails leading to the shore. For a different vantage point, experienced kayakers pass through behind the breaks. From Albion, take Hwy 1 north to Mendocino. Turn left on Main St and proceed to the park at the street's end. Beach access is nearby, 1 mile south on the highway. For more information, call the park at (707) 937-4296.

The headlands are sandwiched on the coast between two nice state parks, both with camping areas. North of the headlands, **Russian Gulch State Park** has 15 miles of hiking trails covering a redwood-forested valley on the shore, with beach activities nearby. Pick up a trail map at the park entrance and find the path to Devil's Punch Bowl—a 200-foot-long, sea-carved tunnel that has partially collapsed in the center, creating an immense blowhole that's particularly spectacular during a storm. Horseback riding and diving are also popular here; there are camping facilities for equestrians and an underwater park for scuba. The park is west of the Coast Highway, 1.5 miles north of Mendocino. Call the park, (707) 937-4296, for information. (See Camping, below, for campground information.)

South of Mendocino, the odd pygmy forests of **Van Damme State Park** draw hordes of curious nature lovers to this 2,337-acre preserve blanketed with ferns and second-growth redwoods; so do the beach area on the mouth of Little River and an underwater diving park. There are also 15 miles of spectacularly lush trails—ideal for a stroll or a jog—that start at the beach and wind through the redwood-covered hills. Fern Canyon Trail is the park's most popular route (see Hiking/Backpacking, below). You can hike or drive (most of the way) to the peculiar Pygmy Forest, an eerie scrub forest of waist-high stunted trees. The park is on both sides of the highway with entrances 3 miles south of Mendocino. (To reach the Pygmy Forest by car, follow Hwy 1 south of the park and turn up Little River Airport Rd, then head uphill for 21 miles.) Call the park at (707) 937-5804.

Another sandy beach is found at the mouth of the **Navarro River,** 7 miles south of Mendocino. Primitive camping is permitted along the wide beach and adjacent estuary, which is a good wildlife viewing area. Albion Flat, a private water recreation area and boating center, is also adjacent.

Manchester State Beach covers nearly 1,000 acres northwest of the town of Point Arena. Birders enjoy watching waterfowl and migrating shorebirds on the beaches, vast coastal wetlands, and marshes. During the winter and spring rainy season, Alder Creek, Brush Creek, and the Garcia River flow heavily from the hillsides to the Pacific, creating a beautiful land- and seascape for visitors hiking the shore. Other activities at the beach include scuba diving, fishing, and camping. For more information, contact the beach at (707) 882-2437.

About 18 miles north of Jenner lies **Salt Point State Park.** The park's 6,000 acres range from rugged coastal terrain to grasslands and forests of pine, cypress, and redwood. But by far the park's most outstanding feature is Salt Point, a rocky promontory of tide pools, jutting out onto the Pacific. To the east of Salt Point lies the **Salt Point Underwater Reserve,** the first such reserve ever established in the state. Scuba divers flock to these sheltered waters, which are crawling with a wide array of sea creatures. Free diving for abalone (with no tank, per regulations) is also a big draw. You'll find camping and upland coastal hiking here too. At the north end of the park on Kruse Ranch Rd is the 317-acre **Kruse Rhododendron Preserve,** a forested grove of the wild pink and purple flowers that grow up to 18 feet tall in the shade of a vast canopy of redwoods. Peak blooming time varies yearly, but April or early May is usually the best time to see the world's tallest *Rhododendron californicum.* From Jenner, take the Coast Highway north about 18 miles to the park's southern boundary. Follow signs to the parking area and visitors center off the west side of the highway. For more information, contact the park at (707) 847-3221. For ocean conditions, call (707) 847-3222; the recording is updated daily between 7:30am and 9:00am.

Of the six public beach access points along Hwy 1 between Gualala and Sea Ranch, the one that offers the most bang for the $3 parking fee is 195-acre **Gualala Point Regional Park.** The park has 10 miles of trails through coastal grasslands, redwood forests, and river canyons, as well as picnic sites, camping areas, and excellent bird- and whale watching along the mostly deserted beaches; (707) 785-2377.

The beachfront at **Stillwater Cove Regional Park** is the premier abalone diving spot on the North Coast, not only because the harvest is bountiful but also because the surf and swells are smaller and calmer than in other spots along the Sonoma and Mendocino shores. The parking area is west of the Coast Highway, 14 miles north of Jenner. The beach is managed by the county parks department, (707) 847-3286.

Fort Ross State Historic Park lies roughly 11 miles north of Jenner, on a particularly rocky, windy section of the Sonoma coast where you've got to keep your eyes peeled for cows wandering around on the highway. The park's fascinating history dates from 1812, when a group of Russian merchants decided to build their homes and fort on the windswept coastal cliffs. Today, while some of those original buildings still stand as a monument to the region's past, the park is relatively devoid of new development. To explore, visitors must park in the dirt and hike cross-country—there are no hiking trails in the upland reaches of the 3,386 acres of bluffs and meadows. This is a place where one can literally get lost. The southern end of the park is characterized by steep bluffs dropping several hundred feet to the sea, while the **Fort Ross Cove** area contains a sheltered cove and protected beach. Upland of the coastal area, you'll find forests of bishop pine, Douglas fir, and redwood. Animals common to the upland area include bobcats, gray fox, black-tailed deer, and brush rabbit. Fort Ross also boasts a campground, as well as a 90-acre underwater preserve that makes for good diving. From Jenner, take Hwy 1 north, 11 miles to the park's southern boundary. Look for the visitors center on the west side of the highway, at Fort Ross Cove. For more information, contact Fort Ross State Historic Park, (707) 847-3286.

Sonoma Coast State Beach is actually a long series of smaller beaches and coves, extending 16 miles along Sonoma's damp coast, from Bodega Bay north to Russian Gulch. It is accessible from about two dozen areas along the Coast Highway, with miles of pristine sand and gravel beaches, tide pools, rocky bluffs, hiking trails, and one heck of a gorgeous drive. Although all the beaches are pretty much the same—divine—the safest for kids is **Doran Beach,** located just south of Bodega Bay. When the water's rough everywhere else, Doran is still calm enough for swimming, clamming, and crabbing (an added bonus: the adjacent Doran mud flats are a favorite haunt of egrets, pelicans, and other seabirds). Tide-pool trekkers will want to head to the north end of **Salmon Creek Beach** (off Bean Ave, 2 miles north of Bodega Bay) or **Shell Beach,** a small low-tide treasure trove 10 miles north of Bodega Bay near Jenner. If all you want to do is get horizontal in the sand, deciding which of the 14 beaches along Hwy 1 looks the best will drive you nuts; just pick one and park. But don't forget your windbreaker and an extra sweater. Rock fishing and surf fishing are favorite sports in these parts, as the rocky coves, bay, and river frontage, attract a wide variety of fish. Beachcombing and camping are also popular. Like most North Coast beaches, the Sonoma coast, with its steep waves, rocky shoals, and rip currents, is definitely not for swimming (except for Doran, mentioned above). To reach Sonoma Coast State Beach from Sonoma, take Hwy 116 east to Hwy 1. For more information, contact the park headquarters, (707) 875-3483.

Diving

For divers accustomed to modern conveniences—like oxygen tanks—the scene along the Sonoma and Mendocino coasts may take some getting used to. That's because state fishing regulations prohibit use of oxygen tanks while **abalone diving** . . . a way of preventing you from removing more than your share from the beds. Free diving is an experience worth the adventure—especially for those who like to lean back after scarfing their catch with the satisfaction of knowing they worked for their dinner. **Stillwater Cove** (see Parks/Beaches, above), because it is protected from the Pacific swells and breaks, attracts the most beginners. Van Damme State Beach and Salt Point and Russian Gulch State Parks (see Parks/Beaches, above) are other major abalone diving destinations protected from the heavy surf. If you require a beach entry, use Van Damme and Russian Gulch. Entries are steep and rocky elsewhere, and some have bumpy waters.

   Fully outfitted diving isn't completely banned, however, so if you're not diving for abalone go ahead and have at it in any of the coast's interesting dive parks. Salt Point Underwater Reserve is the best, but don't hesitate to check out Fort Ross Cove and **Manchester State Beach** (see Parks/Beaches, above). In addition to the abundant sea life and kelp forests, shipwrecks at Manchester make the underwater experience a bit more interesting. Manchester, however, has more open water than other dive areas—inexperienced divers should stay away. Also, don't hit the North Coast ocean expecting to find the water clarity and abundant sea life of Monterey Bay (see Monterey Bay chapter)—

this is murkier and even colder a lot of the time.

Salt Point has an **ocean conditions** hot line, (707) 847-3222, updated daily in the morning. Bodega Bay Pro Dive, 1275 Hwy 1, in Bodega Bay, (707) 875-3054, is a complete **outfitter** conveniently located on the drive up from the Bay Area. This is also a good place to hook up with local guides. Adventure Sports Unlimited, (408) 458-3648, also has guided Stillwater Cove dives on the calendar several times each year. A **state fishing license** with an abalone stamp is required for all divers; the season starts April 1. Contact the North Coast Diving Club, PO Box 5091, Vallejo, CA 94591, for scheduled group outings.

Kayaking/Canoeing

Most of the Northern California coast is exposed and rocky, making **sea kayaking** trips a test for those who aren't used to having to react to quickly changing conditions. Surf baths are not uncommon when you're getting out or coming in. The payoffs, however, are great if you can get past the breaks for a paddling tour of the rocky Mendocino coast, particularly at **Mendocino Headlands State Park** (see Parks/Beaches, above), where the wide view of the numerous sea caves and wave holes is a thrill to remember. Only intermediate-to-advanced kayakers should set out alone in areas that are not coved. Catch a Canoe & Bicycles Too, 44850 Comptche-Ukiah Rd, in Mendocino at the Little River, (707) 937-0273, can hook you up with a **rental** and help you find an experienced **guide** if you need one. Putting in is best from the beach access west of the Coast Highway just south of the headlands park.

The breaks on **Bodega Bay** tend to be smaller and more manageable than those on much of the coast, making it a better choice for paddlers with less experience. Check with the Bodega Bay Sport Fishing Center, 1500 Bayflat Rd, Bodega Bay, (707) 875-3344, for equipment rentals and guide information. **Doran Beach Regional Park,** west from the Coast Highway at Doran Park Rd, has access points, as do **Campbell Cove** and **Westside Regional Park.** Call Doran Beach, (707) 875-3540, for information.

The Russian, Gualala, and **Little Rivers** (see Russian River chapter) offer pleasant Class II **canoe** runs through the forested redwood canyons, which give way to open country where they meet the Pacific. On the Gualala River and Little River, head upstream from the Coast Highway crossings while the tide is in—that way you won't have to wrestle the tide on the return trip. These are calm, placid, enjoyable runs during normal weather years and ideal for beginners. Catch a Canoe & Bicycles Too (see above), (707) 937-0273, has kayak and canoe rentals available. In Gualala, try Adventure Rents, 45450 Pacific Woods Rd, (707) 884-4386 or (888) 881-4FUN, or Gualala Kayak at the river mouth, (707) 884-4705. Both will transport single- and two-person kayaks to and from the river and provide all the necessary gear and instruction. (Adventure Rents also carries canoes and bicycles, including tandems.)

Hiking/Backpacking

Most of the trekking options on the Sonoma and southern Mendocino coasts are day hikes along the rocky shores and sandy beaches; there are also a few nice forested hikes following the creeks and rivers. The serious backpacker who wants to get away from it all for a few days should consider a trek through Mendocino National Forest or through the Lake Sonoma area and Anderson Redwoods State Park. Consult the Mendocino National Forest and Russian River chapters for hike descriptions in those areas.

Along the coast, be aware that while there are numerous nice summer day hikes, it's hard to find any that aren't jammed with tourists on hot sunny days. Fortunately, some of these walks are particularly stunning during the winter.

Headlands Loop Trail (easy; 2 miles round trip) skirts the Gualala River, travels across high ocean bluffs where you can spot gray whales during the southern migration, and passes through pretty groves of cypress at Gualala Point. It is a pleasant walk for those who want to get a taste of the coast without spending all day working up a sweat. The trailhead is west of the Coast Highway just south of the river crossing near the town of Gualala.

Near Stillwater Cove Regional Park (see Parks/Beaches, above), follow **Stockoff Creek Trail** (easy; 1 mile round trip) through a redwood forest following the creek, crossing on two footbridges. There is beach access along the route, which also begins and ends at a parking area. Look for the Stillwater sign 15 miles north of Jenner on the west side of the Coast Highway.

Stump Trail (moderate; 4 miles round trip) follows high ocean-side bluffs with great views of the waves crashing against the rocky shore at Salt Point State Park, then drops down to the sandy beach popular with free divers. The trailhead is 15 miles north of Jenner; go through the Salt Point park entrance to the parking area. **North Trail** and **Pygmy Forest Trail** (easy; 4 miles round trip, combined) extend east from the same location. Combine all three for a longer day hike spanning pygmy forests in the uplands and taking in the ocean views on the coast. It takes twice the time but is doubly interesting. For other pygmy forest hikes, see the Northern Mendocino Coast chapter.

Bodega Head Trail (moderate; 2 miles round trip) at the southern-most edge of the head offers views of rocky coves and the chilly north Pacific beyond. This hike is the starting point for the rest of the coastal trail system, which covers 16 miles of the Sonoma Coast State Beach and spans from the mouth of the Russian River south to the Bodega Head area. The high bluffs make for good whale watching during the southern migration. To reach the trailhead, go 9 miles south of the Hwy 116 inter-section with the Coast Highway, then west on E Shore Rd for 1 mile.

Alder Creek Trail (easy; 4 miles round trip) is most often used by anglers trying to get down to the beach and lagoon area near Manchester State Beach for wintertime steelhead runs. This is one of those day hikes for those who enjoy weather—meaning if you've got your slicker in the trunk and you're looking for a good place to listen to the Pacific howl and moan, come on down. For those more sensitive to the extremes, it's a pleasant summertime walk too—just more crowded. To reach the trail-head, go 8 miles north of Point Arena on the Coast Highway, then left at the signs for Manchester State Beach.

Those in the mood for a little waterfall action should take the **North Trail** link to **Falls Trail** at Russian Gulch State Park (moderate; 7.5 miles round trip) through second-growth redwood forests, topping out at a pretty waterfall dropping down shade-shrouded rocky cliffs. This is one of the most popular and crowded hikes on the Sonoma and Mendocino coasts, especially during the summer when the Coast Highway is dotted with rental cars. The North Trail trailhead is easy to find, 7 miles south of Fort Bragg just past the park entrance. This is another hike you may want to do in the winter, when it's less crowded and the falls are more spectacular.

Another popular hike is along the Little River from Van Damme State Park on **Fern Canyon Trail** (moderate; 8 miles round trip). This trek also crosses through a nice redwood forest and creek drainage area overgrown with lush ferns. Expect to see lots of fanny packs and white tennies during the summer; this is another tourist romp, though most walk only the first mile or so before continuing down the coast via car. The trailhead is in the campground at Van Damme, 3 miles south of Mendocino on the west side of the Coast Highway.

Ecological Staircase Trail (easy; 5.5 miles round trip) takes you on an amazing nature tour of one of the Mendocino coast's most entrancing natural features—the pygmy forests of its layered marine terraces. Uplift-ing from the ocean for more than half a million years resulted in a series of staircaselike land formations on the coast. Combine that with the highly acidic soil types found here and less-than-ideal irrigation and drainage, and the result is a bizarre community of tiny trees dwarfed by the normal-sized forests nearby. The walk has an elevation gain of about 500 feet, but you'll be too enchanted to notice. There are five terrace levels, with pygmy trees on the top three. The trailhead is 5 miles south of Fort Bragg west of the Coast Highway at Jughead Creek. Call the state beaches office, (707) 937-5804, for information.

Goat Rock Trail (easy; 8 miles or less round trip), toward the northern edge of the **Sonoma Coast State Beach,** is an open, grassy peninsula between the ocean and the Russian River. Hiking along the beach to Goat Rock is very rewarding, as the Russian River estuary creates a unique environment for waterfowl and marine life, including harbor seals. You can start out from **Wright's Beach** or **Shell Beach.** Wright's Beach, which takes you through Shell Beach, is the longer route (easy; 8 miles round trip). For a shorter hike, starting out at Shell Beach will shave 3 miles off your day. To reach both Wright's Beach and Shell Beach, from Sonoma take Hwy 116 east to Hwy 1 south; look for signs for the Shell Beach trail after about a mile. Signs for Wright's Beach are about 2 miles farther, at the Ocean View parking area.

Hikers looking for solitude and undisturbed wilderness should head to **Fort Ross State Historic Park's** (see Parks/Beaches, above) 3,386 acres of coastal bluffs dropping 200 feet to the Pacific, along with meadows and upland forests of redwood, Douglas fir, and bishop pine. There are no hiking trails—just park the car and head out! Ocean access is at **Fort Ross Cove** in the midsection of the park and **Windermere Point** at the park's northern end. From Jenner, take Hwy 1 north and go 11 miles to the park's southern boundary. To reach Fort Ross Cove, follow signs to the visitors center on the west side of the highway. To reach Windermere Point, continue north on Hwy 1 about a mile and look for signs on the west side of the highway. For more information, contact Fort Ross State Historic Park, (707) 847-3286.

Surfing

With the bumpy water and rocky shores, there are portions of the Sonoma and Mendocino coasts where you'd have to be a lunatic to want to get out there on a surfboard. Bodega Bay, however, is the exception. Though the bay can kick up, it tends to be relatively calmer than the remainder of the Sonoma coast, and surfing is quite popular here, especially during the summer and fall months. Bob's Bodega Bay Surf Shack, in the town of Bodega Bay, (707) 875-3944, **rents** surfboards, wet suits, and body boards and provides **lessons.** Northern Light Surf Shop, 17190 Bodega Hwy, Bodega Bay, (707) 876-3032, is another reputable outfitter nearby.

Boating/Fishing

Manchester State Beach (see Parks/Beaches, above), a crossing point for anadromous fish moving upstream on Alder Creek and the Garcia River, is a good **surf fishing** spot on the Mendocino coast for salmon, steelhead, halibut, and rock cod. You'll also find shore access to the rivers and creeks, making the Manchester area a good two-for-one shot if you're feeling eclectic and come outfitted for inland fishing, too. **Steelhead** fishing is particularly good on Alder Creek and the Garcia River, just south of the park. For perch, smelt, steelhead, and salmon, try surf and rock fishing at Salmon Creek Beach and Shell Beach along the Sonoma Coast State Beach area, 1 and 6 miles, respectively, south of the Hwy 116 intersection with the Coast Highway. William Shandel, (707) 937-5400, is a licensed **fishing guide** in Comptche who specializes in surf casting. Steve Jackson (707) 869-2156, located in Guerneville, is also an experienced guide, who's particularly familiar with the lower Russian River area around Jenner. Be sure to check the most recent fishing regulations since those involving steelhead and salmon runs are in flux.

If a **sportfishing trip** on the open water is more to your liking, check in with the Boat House, 1445 Hwy 1, Bodega Bay, (707) 875-3495, which runs daily salmon and rock cod sportfishing trips out of Bodega Bay and whale-watching trips from January to April. Wil's Fishing Adventures in Bodega Bay, (707) 875-2323, charters a fishing boat into Bodega Harbor for sunset fishing daily.

Casini Ranch, a mile west of the town of Monte Rio on Hwy 116, has a boat launch and supplies on the Russian River, as does the Timber Cove Campground on the ocean in Jenner. The busiest boating area, however, is on Bodega Bay. Port Bodega Marina, 1500 Bay Flat Rd, (707) 875-2589, has a boat landing and bait-and-tackle shop. Doran Beach on Bodega Bay has a trailer sanitation station, fish cleaning station, boat launch, and boat washing area. Ocean access is available through the harbor's entrance, about a mile from the boat launch. Mason's Marina on Bodega Harbor, (707) 875-3811, has boat slips available by the day or the month, along with gas, diesel fuel, and propane.

Wildlife

The wetlands and marshes around Manchester State Beach (see Parks/Beaches, above) are a good spotting area for a wide range of water-fowl, including **tundra swans,** which arrive each winter near the Garcia River. The marshes around Bodega Bay are the other hot spot in this region, with large communities of both **migrating waterfowl** and resident **shorebirds.** The cast of characters here and at the river marshes to the north include but are not necessarily limited to geese, great blue herons, egrets, loons, oystercatchers, murres, guillemots, and brown pelicans. There is a **rare-bird hot line,** (707) 822-5666, for the entire North Coast region. Serious birders should consider continuing south to Point Reyes National Seashore (see Point Reyes National Seashore chapter) for some of the best birding on the West Coast.

Bodega Head, the southernmost tip of Sonoma Coast State Beach, provides a good vantage point for observing migrating **gray whales** between December and April. From Sonoma, take Hwy 116 east to Hwy 1 south and travel about 10 miles to Bodega Bay; follow signs to Bodega Head. For more information, call Sonoma Coast State Beach at (707) 875-3483. From Salt Point in Salt Point State Park, gray whales can be seen sporadically as they migrate from Alaska's Bering Sea to their breeding grounds off Baja California. Take US Hwy 101 (US 101) north from Jenner to Salt Point State Park; follow signs to the Salt Point parking area and visitors center on the west side of the highway. For more information, contact Salt Point State Park at (707) 847-3221. Be sure to consult the Point Reyes National Seashore chapter for more whale-watching sites reasonably nearby. (Because Point Reyes is situated farther west into the Pacific Ocean than other areas, spotting is less sporadic.) Still, your best chance to have a close encounter with one of these magnificent creatures is via a **chartered sea expedition** boat ride—but try to plan such a cruise well in advance, as they book up quickly. Bodega Bay Sport Fishing, (707) 875-3495, and Oceanic Society Expeditions, (415) 474-3385, take groups out from San Francisco and Bodega Bay throughout the season.

One of the major highlights of the Jenner area is beautiful Goat Rock Beach, a popular breeding ground for **harbor seals.** Pupping season begins in March and lasts until June, and orange-vested volunteers are usually on hand to protect the seals (they give birth on land) from potentially menacing dogs and passersby. They answer questions about the playful animals, and even lend out binoculars for a closer look. At the mouth of the Russian River on the Sonoma coast, harbor seals also crawl ashore on the protected beach to feed and pup from April through early September. From Guerneville, take Hwy 116 west to Hwy 1 north. Proceed to the Sonoma coast visitors center on the west side of the highway.

Horseback Riding

The upland prairies, dunes, and marshes around Bodega Bay are a great place for exploring on horseback. Chanslor Horse Stables, (707) 875-2721, has a 700-acre working ranch that covers all of that ground. The main ranch is at 2660 Hwy 1 in Bodega Bay.

Camping

Fort Ross State Historic Park has 20 campsites (no RV access) just south of Fort Ross Cove, in a wind-protected canyon. Tables, stoves, pit toilets, and footlockers are available. Sites are available on a first-come, first-served basis from March 15 through December 1. The campground is closed the rest of the year. *From Jenner, take Hwy 1 north, 11 miles to the park's southern boundary. Look for the visitors center on the west side of the highway, at Fort Ross Cove. For more information, contact Fort Ross State Historical Park at (707) 847-3286.*

Sonoma Coast State Beach has two camping areas, open year-round. There are 30 campsites at **Wright's Beach** (no hookups; RV limit 27 feet), which is right on the ocean. It is the most remote of the Sonoma coast's camping areas and gets very chilly, especially when the fog rolls in. Each site has a picnic area with fire pit, and running water is nearby. **Bodega Dunes** campground has 98 sites (full hookups; RV limit 31 feet), each with a picnic table, fire pit, and running water nearby. Showers are available. Reservations at both camping areas are encouraged during the summer and autumn. Summer camping stays are limited to 10 days; the limit during the rest of the year is 30 days. *For reservations, call (800) 444-7275. To call the campgrounds directly, phone the state beaches office, (707) 875-3483. To reach the campgrounds, from Sonoma, take Hwy 116 east to Hwy 1 south. You will see signs for Wright's Beach in about 3 miles, and for Bodega Dunes in about 8 miles.*

There are 30 sites in a wooded canyon near the ocean at **Russian Gulch State Park** (no hookups; RV limit 27 feet), each with a picnic table, fire pit, and running water nearby. Showers and rest rooms are available. *Call state parks reservations at (800) 444-7275. The state beaches number is (707) 875-3483. The campground is 2.5 miles north of Mendocino on the Coast Hwy, on the west side of the road.*

Salt Point State Park has two campgrounds, with 110 sites combined (no hookups; RV limit 31 feet). **Gerstle Cove Campground,** quieter and closest to the ocean, has 30 sites, each with a picnic table and fire pit, and showers and running water nearby. Farther inland and away from the cool evening ocean breezes is **Woodside Campground** with 80 sites, drinking water, and rest room facilities, but no showers. Sites at both campgrounds can be reserved between March 2 and November 30; call state reservations at (800) 444-PARK. *Take US 101 north from Jenner to Salt Point State Park. Follow signs to the Salt Point parking area and visitors center on the west side of the highway. Nearing the visitors center, you will see the Gerstle Cove Campground on your left. Woodside Campground is on the east side of Hwy 1, up the hill from Gerstle Cove. For more information,* *contact Salt Point State Park at (707) 847-3221.*

Manchester State Beach has 46 primitive campsites (no hookups; RV limit 32 feet) in a grassland/sand dunes area with Monterey cypress groves nearby. Reservations are encouraged during the summer and autumn. For reservations, call (800) 444-7275. *From Point Arena, take Hwy 1 north 8 miles. Follow signs to Manchester State Beach on the west side of the highway. For more information, contact the beach at (707) 882-2437.*

Doran Beach on Bodega Bay, with 114 campsites (no hookups; RV limit 31 feet) in a nice waterfront setting shielded from the ocean, is popular for fishing trips. No more than eight people may be registered at each campsite, and campers are limited to stays of 10 consecutive days. *From Salmon Creek, take Hwy 1 south. Follow signs to Doran Beach on the west side of the highway. For more information, contact the beach at (707) 527-2041.*

Gualala River Campground, in the county park on the river's mouth, has 25 sites, 18 open to vehicles (no hookups; RV limit 30 feet), each with picnic tables and fire pits; running water, showers, and rest rooms are nearby. Call Sonoma County Parks, (707) 785-2377, for information. *The camp is on the west side of the highway at the Sonoma/Mendocino County line.*

Stillwater Cove has 23 sites (no hookups; RV limit 35 feet) near the ocean in a popular free diving area (during abalone season). Despite its size, the camp comes well-appointed with showers, flush toilets, and running water. Each site has a picnic table and fire pit. *The camp is well-marked on the west side of the Coast Hwy, 15 miles north of Jenner. Call (707) 847-3245.*

Photography

You'll have trouble stopping yourself from snapping one shot after another, particularly if you're an Ansel Adams wannabe. Timber Cove Inn in Jenner was among Adams' favorite subjects, as was the rugged coast adjacent to the famous resort hideaway (which is quite expensive). Many photographers find the estuary areas around the **Russian River** and the **Garcia River** particularly appealing. However, our favorite area for photography is **Mendocino Headlands State Park.** The stark seascape, windswept fields, and backdrop of coastal mountains make for some great shots, particularly on summer days as the evening fog starts to roll in. To reach the park from Albion, take Hwy 1 north to Mendocino. Turn left on Main St and proceed to the park at the street's end. For more information, call (707) 937-4296.

Cycling

Bicycling the **Sonoma** and **Mendocino coastline** is a terrific **road cycling** ride. Unfortunately, the only route is Hwy 1, which can get a bit crowded on weekends, particularly around midday. Therefore, if you intend to ride along the coast, try to make it during the week, and start out in the morning before the tourist traffic hits. The terrain consists mostly of gentle rolling hills, with some steeper slopes and flat ground. One area particularly appealing to bicyclists is the stretch of highway from **Jenner** south to **Bodega Bay.** Another very appealing area is **Mendocino Headlands State Park.** This is a magical-looking place where the land meets the sea with rugged cliffs, coves, and secluded beaches laden with driftwood. The terrain is mostly flat, and riders can enjoy the contrast of the headlands solitude with the provincial bustle of the village nearby. From Albion, take Hwy 1 north to Mendocino. Turn left on Main St and proceed to the park at the street's end. For more information, call (707) 937-4296. Bicycles can be **rented** at Bob's Bodega Bay Surf Shack in Bodega Bay, (707) 875-3944.

Adventure Calendar

Bodega Bay Fisherman's Festival, mid-April: *(707) 875-3422.*
Sand Castle Contest, Sonoma Coast State Beaches, mid-September: *tied in with annual coast cleanup, a statewide event, (707) 875-3540.*

Attractions

Spend a few hours meandering through town and it becomes apparent that **Bodega Bay** is, for the most part, still a working-class fishing town—the sort of place where most people start their day before dawn mending nets, rigging fishing poles, and talking shop. As it stands, there is only one three-star lodge and restaurant, and the town's most venerable store sells taffy and kites. If all you want to do this weekend is breathe in some salty air and you couldn't care less about Gucci boutiques and dancing till sunup, come to Bodega Bay—there ain't much here, except beautiful scenery and golden beaches, which is precisely the point.

As you roll into Bodega Bay, keep an eye out for the Bodega Bay Area Chamber of Commerce, located in the center of town at 850 Hwy 1, (707) 875-3422. Load up on free maps, guides, and brochures, including the "Bodega Bay Area Map & Guide," which gives the exact locations of all the town's attractions. A great way to spend a lazy afternoon in Bodega Bay is at the docks, watching the rusty fishing boats unload their catches. **Tides Wharf Restaurant,** at 835 Hwy 1 in Bodega Bay, (707) 875-3652, has the most active dock scene, including a viewing room near the processing plant that allows you to witness a fish's ultimate fate—a swift and merciless gutting by deft hands, followed by a quick burial in ice. Just outside, sea lions linger by the dock hoping for a handout.

Worth half an hour of any Hitchcock fan's day is a quick trip to the town of **Bodega,** a few miles southeast of Bodega Bay off Hwy 1. The attraction is the hauntingly familiar Potter School House and St. Teresa's Church, both immortalized in Hitchcock's *The Birds,* filmed here in 1961.

The tiny town of **Freestone,** a county-designated historic district, boasts a population of 35 people and 10 cute-as-a-button restored Victorian farmhouses. And stirring things up a bit in this sleepy little farming community is the **Osmosis Enzyme Baths,** a spa offering massages and rare Japanese heat-therapy treatments in large wooden boxes filled with hot, fragrant cedar sawdust; 209 Bohemian Highway, (707) 823-8231.

About 16 miles north of Bodega Bay on Hwy 1 is what seems to be every Northern Californian's "secret" getaway spot: **Jenner.** Built on a bluff rising from the mouth of the Russian River, the tiny seaside town consists of little more than a gas station, three restaurants, two inns, and a deli, which means the only thing to do in town is eat, sleep, and lie on the beach—not a bad vacation plan. Perhaps Jenner's best attraction, however, is its location: it's two hours closer than Mendocino to the Bay Area, yet has the same spectacular coastal scenery and a far better selection of beaches.

The southernmost town in Mendocino County, **Gualala** also happens to have the most mispronounced name in Mendocino County. Keep the G soft and you end up with "wah-LAL-ah," the Spanish version of *walali,* which is Pomo Indian patois for "water coming down place." The water in question is the nearby Gualala River, a placid year-round playground for kayakers, canoeists, and swimmers.

Once an industrious, lively logging town, Gualala has been tamed considerably since the days when loggers would literally climb the saloon walls with their spiked boots. Though a few real-life suspender-wearing lumberjacks still end their day at the Gualala Hotel's saloon, the coastal town's main function these days is providing gas, groceries, and hardware for area residents. On its outskirts, however, are several excellent parks, beaches, and hiking trails; combine this with the region's glorious seascapes, and suddenly poor little mispronounced Gualala emerges as a serious contender among the better vacation spots on the North Coast.

Open to the public, the award-winning **Sea Ranch Golf Links** is a challenging Scottish-style course designed by Robert Muir Graves. Originally built as a 9-hole oceanside course, the Links expanded to a full 18 holes in August 1996. It's located along the Sea Ranch's northern boundary at the entrance to Gualala Point Regional Park, and is open daily; (707) 785-2468.

Fifteen miles north of Gualala is **Point Arena,** one of the smallest incorporated cities in California. Once a bustling shipping port, the three-block-long city is now home to only 400 or so people, mostly transplants from larger cities who have set up shop along Main St with neither the desire nor the intention of making much money. They're just here to enjoy the quiet small-town life. Since there is no direct inland road to Point Arena, few tourists pass through, ensuring that the city will never become as overloaded as Mendocino. Yet this ain't no cow town either. It has one of the hottest restaurants on the North Coast, historic lodgings, and even poetry readings at the local bookstore. So if you're tired of the crowded Mendocino scene yet want to spend a relaxing weekend on the coast, there's no better alternative than little Point Arena.

A cross between a bookstore, cafe, coffeehouse, and impromptu community center is **Bookends,** the dream-come-true enterprise of co-owner Alix Levine, an admitted bibliophile and town mother. Located within a beautifully restored Main St edifice, Bookends is the perfect place to start your day, whether you're staying in Point Arena or just passing through. Tofu scrambles and house-baked pastries are served for breakfast until 2pm on weekends, and an eclectic lunch menu featuring everything from croissant sandwiches to veggie stir-fries is offered until the doors close at 9pm (6:30pm in the winter). On sunny days, warm your bones on the outdoor patio; 265 Main St, (707) 882-2287.

While you're here, be sure to take a tour of the **Point Arena Lighthouse.** Built in 1870 after 10 ships ran aground here on a single stormy night, the fully operational lighthouse had to be rebuilt after the 1906 earthquake, but now it's solid enough for visitors to trudge up the six-story tower's 145 steps for a standout view of the coast (that is, if the fog has lifted). The dazzling, 6-foot-wide, lead-crystal lens is worth the hike alone. The lighthouse is open 11am to 3:30pm weekdays and 10am to 3:30pm weekends in the summer (11am to 2:30pm daily in the winter), and is located at the end of scenic Lighthouse Rd, about 5 miles northwest of downtown Point Arena off Hwy 1. The parking/tour/museum fee is only a few bucks; (707) 882-2777.

Once known as Greenwood, this tiny former logging town was renamed **Elk** by the postal service when someone realized there was another town in California called Greenwood. For a such a small community (population 250) it sure has a booming tourist trade: six inns, four restaurants, and one authentic Irish pub. Its close proximity to the big tourist town of Mendocino, a mere 30-minute drive up the coast, is one reason for its popularity. Elk's paramount appeal, however, is its dramatic shoreline; the series of immense **sea stacks** here create one of the most awesome seascapes on the California coast.

A renowned haven for pot growers until an increase in police surveillance and property taxes drove most of them away, **Albion** is more a free-spirited ideal community than an actual town. You'll know you're there when you cross a white wooden bridge; it was built in 1944 (steel and reinforced concrete were unavailable during World War II) and it's the last of its kind on Hwy 1.

Once a bustling logging and shipbuilding community, **Little River** is now more like a precious suburb of Mendocino. The town does a brisk business handling the tourist overflow from its neighbor 2 miles up the coast. Vacationers in the know reserve a room in serene Little River and make forays into Mendocino for dining and shopping.

The grande dame of Northern California's coastal tourist towns, **Mendocino** has surprisingly managed to retain much of its charm and allure as a refurbished replica of a New England–style fishing village—complete with a white-spired church. Motels, fast-food chains, and anything hinting of development are strictly forbidden here (even the town's only automated teller is subtly recessed into the historic Masonic Building), resulting in the almost-passable illusion that Mendocino is just another quaint little coastal community. Try to find a parking space, however, and the illusion quickly fades; even the 4-hour drive fails to deter hordes of Bay Area residents.

Founded in 1852, Mendocino is still home to a few anglers and loggers, although writers, artists, actors, and other urban transplants now far outnumber the natives. In fact, Mendocino County is rumored to have the highest percentage of Ph.D.s of any rural county in the country. Spring is the best time to visit, when parking spaces are plentiful and the climbing tea roses and wisteria are in full bloom. Start with a casual tour of the town, and end with a stroll around Mendocino's celebrated headlands. Suddenly the long drive and inflated room rates seem a trivial price to pay for visiting one of the most beautiful places on earth.

To tour Mendocino proper, lose the car and head out on foot to the **Tote Fête Bakery** at 10450 Lansing St at Albion St, (707) 937-3383. Fuel up with a double capp and cinnamon bun, then throw away your map of the town and start walking—the shopping district of Mendocino is so small it can be covered in less than an hour, so why bother planning your attack? One must-see shop is the **Gallery Bookshop & Bookwinkle's Children's Books,** one of the best independent bookstores in Northern

California with a wonderful selection of books for kids, cooks, and local-history buffs; it's located at Main and Kasten Sts, (707) 937-BOOK. Another is **Mendocino Jams & Preserves,** a town landmark at 440 Main St that offers free tastings—à la cute little bread chips—of its luscious marmalades, dessert toppings, mustards, chutneys, and other spreads; (707) 937-1037 or (800) 708-1196.

If you have a passion for plants and flowers, spend a few bucks on the admission fee to the **Mendocino Coast Botanical Gardens,** located 2 miles south of Fort Bragg, at 18220 Hwy 1, (707) 964-4352. The non-profit gardens feature 47 acres of plants—ranging from azaleas and rhodo-dendrons to dwarf conifers and ferns—as well as a picnic area, retail nursery, gift store, and the popular Gardens Grill restaurant.

After a full day of adventuring, why not top off the evening with a lit-tle nightcap and music? If you appreciate classical tunes and warm snifters of brandy, take a stroll down Mendocino's Main St to the elegant bar and lounge at the **Mendocino Hotel and Restaurant** (see Lodgings, below) at 45080 Main St, (707) 937-0511. If blue jeans and baseball caps are more your style, hang out with the guys at **Dick's Place,** which has the cheapest drinks in town and the sort of jukebox-'n'-jiggers atmosphere you'd expect from this former logging town's oldest bar; 45080 Main St, next to the Mendocino Hotel, (707) 937-5643. For a rowdy night of danc-ing and drinking, head a few miles up Hwy 1 to **Caspar Inn,** the last true roadhouse in California where everything from rock and jazz to reggae and blues is played live Thursday through Sunday nights starting at 9:30pm; take the Caspar Rd exit off Rd 1, 4 miles north of Mendocino and 4 miles south of Fort Bragg, (707) 964-5565.

Restaurants

The Bohemian Cafe ☆   When in Rome, do as the Romans do, and when traveling the Bohemian Highway, do as Occidental-area locals do and eat at the Bohemian Cafe. This converted old house is staffed by friendly free-spirits, who bring artistic expression even to their pizzas. *3688 Bohemian Hwy (at the S end of town), Occidental; (707) 874-3931; $$.*

Breakers Café ☆   For breakfast, park your fanny among the numerous plants in the sun-filled dining room and feast on yummy Belgian waffles. Lunch is mostly sandwiches, burgers, and soups, and dinner items range from fresh seafood to chicken, pasta, and vegetarian dishes. *1400 Hwy 1 (in the Pelican Plaza at the N end of town), Bodega Bay; (707) 875-2513; $.*

Cafe Beaujolais ☆☆☆   Cafe Beaujolais is one of the finer little breakfast and lunch spots in Mendocino. *961 Ukiah St (at Evergreen St, on the E end of town), Mendocino; (707) 937-5614; $$$.*

Chez Peyo ☆☆   Chez Peyo is renowned for its savory French country fare, and its Sunday champagne brunches have been a popular town attraction for years. Granted, Chez Peyo wouldn't survive long on the Champs-Elysées, but for Sebastopol, this is très bon. *2295 Gravenstein Hwy (on Hwy 116, 2 miles S of town), Sebastopol; (707) 823-1262; $$.*

The Duck Club ☆☆☆   Gastronomes up and down the coast are coming to the Bodega Bay Lodge to sample the menu here. "Sonoma County Cuisine" best describes Duck Club's penchant for local yields. *103 Hwy 1 (in Bodega Bay Lodge, at the S end of town), Bodega Bay; (707) 875-3525; $$$.*

The Food Company ☆   For fine dining in Gualala, go to the St. Orres or the Old Milano. For every other kind of dining, come here. Open all day, every day, the Food Company is a cross between a deli, bakery, and cafe. *38411 Hwy 1 (½ mile N of Gualala at the corner of Hwy 1 and Robinsons Reef Rd), Gualala; (707) 884-1800; $.*

Greenwood Pier Café ☆   Most of the herbs and vegetables served in this cafe come straight from the elaborate gardens behind the restaurant, and all of the breads and pastries are baked on-site. Prices are very reasonable, and the ambience is pleasantly informal and relaxed. *5926 Hwy 1 (in the center of town), Elk; (707) 877-9997; $$.*

The Ledford House Restaurant ☆☆   It's rare when an ocean-view restaurant's food is as good as the view, but this place manages to pull it off, serving Provençal-style cuisine in a wonderfully romantic cliff-top setting. *3000 Hwy 1 (take the Spring Grove Rd exit W off Hwy 1), Albion; (707) 937-0282; $$$.*

MacCallum House Restaurant ☆☆☆   Using the freshest ingredients— seafood straight from the coast, organic meats and produce from neighboring farms and ranches—this place offers some wonderful North Coast cuisine. *45020 Albion St (between Kasten and Lansing Sts), Mendocino; (707) 937-5763; $$$.*

Mendocino Café ☆   The Mendocino Café is one of the last vestiges of the Mendocino of the '60s. Everyone from nursing mothers to tie-dyed teenagers queues up for the cafe's eclectic mix of Asian and Mexican specialties, served fresh and fast. *10451 Lansing St (at the corner of Albion St), Mendocino; (707) 937-2422; $.*

955 Ukiah Street Restaurant ☆☆☆   This relatively unknown restaurant is described by local epicureans as "the sleeper restaurant on the coast." The dramatic interior sets the mood for the haute cuisine. *955 Ukiah St (next to Cafe Beaujolais), Mendocino; (707) 937-1955; $$$.*

Pangaea ☆☆☆☆   Although it's a relative newcomer to the area, Pangaea is already the talk of the North Coast, with exotic menu items à la Indonesia, Nigeria, and other far-reaching latitudes. *250 Main St (downtown, across from Bookends), Point Arena; (707) 882-3001; $$.*

River's End ☆☆   Don't bother looking for a better restaurant or bar in the area; for more than 20 years this oceanside establishment has been the local favorite. Who'd have guessed you could order roasted baby pheasant in tiny Jenner? *1104A Hwy 1 (just N of town), Jenner; (707) 865-2484; $$$.*

St. Orres Restaurant ☆☆☆   St. Orres Restaurant is one of the main reasons people keep coming back to this region. The constantly changing prix-fixe dinner menu focuses on wild game, and a distinctly Northern California rendition of French country cuisine. *36601 Hwy 1 (2 miles N of Gualala on the E side of Hwy 1), Gualala; (707) 884-3335; $$$.*

Lodgings

Agate Cove Inn ☆☆☆   Completely renovated in 1995 with light pine furnishings and "casual country" decor, the 10 cottages at Agate Cove offer seclusion, privacy, and views that in-town B&Bs just can't match. *11201 N Lansing St (½ mile N of downtown), Mendocino; (707) 937-0551 or (800) 527-3111; $$–$$$.*

Albion River Inn ☆☆☆   After a long period of ups and downs, this modern seaside inn, poised high above Albion Cove where the Albion River meets the sea, is now one of the finest on the California coast. All 20 of the individually decorated New England–style cottages are equipped with antique and contemporary furnishings. *3790 Hwy 1 (on the NW side of the Albion bridge), Albion; (707) 937-1919 or (800) 479-7944; $$$.*

Bodega Bay Lodge ☆☆☆   Granted, the competition isn't very fierce, but it's safe to say that the Bodega Bay Lodge provides the Sonoma coast's finest accommodations. It's the view that clinches it: all 78 rooms have private balconies with a wonderful panorama of Bodega Bay. *103 Hwy 1 (at the S end of town), Bodega Bay; (707) 875-3525 or (800) 368-2468; $$$.*

Bodega Harbor Inn ☆   A homey old-timer in a town of mostly modern accommodations, the Bodega Harbor Inn consists of four clapboard buildings (with a total of 14 guest rooms) set on a large lawn overlooking the harbor. *1345 Bodega Ave (off Hwy 1 at the N end of town), Bodega Bay; (707) 875-3594; $–$$$.*

Coast Guard House ☆☆   Poised high above Arena Cove, this historic Cape Cod–style cottage was originally built by the Life-Saving Service in 1901 to lodge crew members. The decor evokes memories of Point Arena's seafaring past, but the inn's 6 rooms remain simple and uncluttered. *695 Arena Cove (off Iversen Ave, 1 mile W of town), Point Arena; (707) 882-2442 or (800) 524-9320; $$$.*

Glendeven Inn ☆☆☆   A few years ago Glendeven was named one of the 12 best inns in America by *Country Inns* magazine, and rightly so. This stately 19th-century farmhouse resides among two and a half acres of gardens and headlands that extend all the way to the Pacific. The 10 spacious rooms and suites feature an uncluttered mix of country antiques and contemporary art. *8221 Hwy 1 (2 miles S of Mendocino), Little River; (707) 937-0083 or (800) 822-4536; $$$.*

The Gravenstein Inn ☆☆   This rustic three-story farmhouse has garnered National Historic Landmark status. The inn was built in 1872 and restored in 1989, when it opened as a 4-bedroom bed-and-breakfast hotel. *3160 Hicks Rd (off Hwy 116, at Graton Rd, 2¼ miles N of town), Sebastopol; (707) 829-0493; $$.*

Harbor House Inn ☆☆☆   In 1985, Helen and Dean Turner converted this palatial redwood house—perched on a bluff above Greenwood Landing—into the Harbor House Inn, adding 6 guest rooms, 4 cottages, and an exceptional restaurant. *5600 Hwy 1 (at the N end of town), Elk; (707) 877-3203; $$$.*

Heritage House ☆☆☆   Heritage House sits on a cliff overlooking a rocky cove, surrounded by acres of cypress trees, flower and vegetable gardens, and expansive green lawns. There are 3 guest rooms in the main building, 63 cottages, and a detached 1877 farmhouse. *5200 Hwy 1 (S of Van Damme State Park), Little River; (707) 937-5885 or (800) 235-5885; $$$.*

The Inn at Schoolhouse Creek ☆☆   Whereas most small inns located along the Mendocino coast have to make do with an acre or less, the Inn at Schoolhouse Creek has the luxury of spreading its 9 private, immaculate cottages amid 10 acres of beautiful flower gardens, lush meadows, and cypress groves. *7051 N Hwy 1 (just S of town), Little River; (707) 937-5525 or (800) 731-5525; $$.*

Inn at the Tides ☆☆   In Bodega Bay the architectural style of most structures is nouveau Californian—wood-shingled boxes with lots of glass—and the Inn at the Tides is no exception. Perched on a hillside overlooking Bodega Bay, it offers 86 units with bay views. *800 Hwy 1 (across from the Tides Wharf), Bodega Bay; (707) 875-2751 or (800) 541-7788; $$$.*

Jenner Inn & Cottages ☆   When people say they stayed at the cutest little place in Jenner, they're talking about Jenner Inn & Cottages. There are 16 guest rooms here, each dispersed within a cluster of cottages and houses perched above the Russian River or the ocean. *10400 Hwy 1 (1 mile N of the Hwy 116/Hwy 1 junction downtown), Jenner; (707) 865-2377 or (800) 732-2377; $$.*

Joshua Grindle Inn ☆☆☆   The most authentic of Mendocino's many New England–style B&Bs, this masterpiece was built in 1879. This two-story beauty has lovely bay windows and a wraparound front porch trimmed with gingerbread arches. *44800 Little Lake Rd (at the road's E end), Mendocino; (707) 937-4143 or (800) GRINDLE; $$$.*

Mendocino Farmhouse ☆☆   Once you emerge from deep within the redwood forest surrounding this secluded estate, you know you're going to be very happy here. The 5 rooms are filled with antique furnishings and fresh flowers from the house's English gardens, and, if you listen carefully, echoes of the nearby ocean. *43410 Comptche-Ukiah Rd (from Hwy 1 just S of Mendocino, turn E on Comptche-Ukiah Rd, drive 1½ miles to Olson Lane, and turn left), Mendocino; (707) 937-0241 or (800) 475-1536; $$.*

Mendocino Hotel and Restaurant ☆☆   The 51-room Mendocino Hotel, built in 1878, combines modern amenities with turn-of-the-century Victorian furnishings to create a romantic yesteryear setting with today's creature comforts. *45080 Main St (between Lansing and Kasten Sts), Mendocino; (707) 937-0511 or (800) 548-0513; $$$.*

The Old Milano Hotel ☆☆☆   Overlooking the sea above Castle Rock Cove, this picturesque Victorian bed and breakfast, built in 1905, is featured on the National Register of Historic Places. *38300 Hwy 1 (just N of the Food Company, 1 mile N of town), Gualala; (707) 884-3256; $$$.*

Rachel's Inn ☆☆   Strategically sandwiched between Van Damme State Park and the Mendocino headlands is this 1860s Victorian farmhouse, one of the best bed and breakfasts on the Mendocino coast. *8200 N Hwy 1 (2 miles S of Mendocino), Little River; (707) 937-0088 or (800) 347-9252; $$$.*

St. Orres ☆☆☆   Located just off Highway 1 and within walking distance of a sheltered, sandy cove, this dazzling copper-domed inn consists of 8 small, inexpensive rooms in the main lodge and 11 private cottages scattered throughout the 42 acres of wooded grounds. *36601 Hwy 1 (2 miles N of Gualala on the E side of Hwy 1), Gualala; (707) 884-3335; $ (lodge), $$$ (cottages).*

Sea Ranch ☆☆☆   A ritual among Northern California families and friends is to rent a vacation home along the 9-mile coastal stretch of the ritzy residential development called Sea Ranch. Approximately 300 homes are available as vacation rentals. *On Hwy 1 (between Stewarts Point and Gualala), Sea Ranch; (707) 785-2579; $$–$$$.*

The Stanford Inn by the Sea / Big River Lodge ☆☆☆   This parcel of prime coastal property and the former Big River Lodge is something more than a magnificent resort. It's a true ecosystem, a place where plants, animals, and people coexist in one of the most unforgettable lodging experiences in California. *At Hwy 1 and Comptche-Ukiah Rd (1 mile S of town), Mendocino; (707) 937-5615 or (800) 331-8884; $$$.*

The Valley Ford Hotel ☆   The pleasant, old-fashioned, 7-room Valley Ford Hotel, built in 1864 and completely renovated in 1990, is a good choice for travelers who prefer the privacy of a hotel to the more intimate quarters of a B&B. *14415 Hwy 1 (downtown), Valley Ford; (707) 876-3600 or (800) 696-6679; $$.*

More Information

Bodega Bay Area Chamber of Commerce: *(707) 875-3422.*
Fort Bragg–Mendocino Coast Chamber of Commerce: *(707) 961-6300.*
Russian River Region Inc. Visitor Information Centers: *(707) 875-2868.*
Sonoma Chamber of Commerce: *(707) 996-1033.*
Sonoma Coast Visitor Information: *(707) 875-2868.*
Sonoma County Convention and Visitors Bureau: *(707) 935-0758.*
State beaches: *(707) 875-3483.*
State parks camping reservations: *(800) 444-7245.*

Russian River

The Russian River recreation area, from Cloverdale through the river canyon at Guerneville, through Monte Rio to the Pacific Ocean at Jenner, including outlying areas such as Armstrong Redwoods State Reserve and Austin Creek.

If you were ever to custom-build a place for the sole purpose of basking in the sun and never wearing long pants, the Russian River resort area would be it. Part wine country, part swimmin' hole, and part lazy weekend paradise, this region seems to have a little bit of everything that is Northern California wrapped into one package. The river itself is placid enough for canoeing and tubing, or just taking a dip. The beach scene can be *Baywatch*esque during the height of summer. Go north of the resort town of Guerneville a short distance, however, and you'll swear you've reached Humboldt County, as the state park at Armstrong is a nicely preserved redwood forest, perfect for slow, meandering walks or bike rides in the cool shadows of giants. Another "California" component to the Russian River experience is sociological rather than geographic: numerous resorts along the river cater primarily to the Bay Area gay community, who use the Sonoma coast area as a weekend retreat. It is curious to see a relatively rural setting embrace a culture normally associated with big cities, but the blend works comfortably here, and therefore the river is also a popular family spot.

While most of the river frontage is privately owned, there are numerous public access points for anglers and canoers who don't want to spend time at a private resort. A 10-mile run will keep you busy all day, and if you put in far enough west you'll even get a taste of the ocean during your travels. From Cloverdale to Jenner on the Pacific coast, nearly 80 miles of river are suitable for canoeing, so the biggest dilemma is to bite off the right section. This is a place to drift, oars abandoned, soaking in the sun with one toe in the water.

Getting There

Several roads and highways follow the Russian River as it makes its way from its headwaters in the Mendocino mountains to its mouth at the Pacific Ocean in Jenner. The most popular areas and best access, however, are along River Road and Highway 116 in Sonoma County, both found west of US Highway 101 (US 101).

Adjoining Areas

NORTH: **Mendocino National Forest**

SOUTH: **Point Reyes National Seashore**

EAST: **Napa and Sonoma Wine Valleys**

WEST: **Sonoma and Southern Mendocino Coasts**

inside out

Parks

Nestled in the rolling hills and valleys adjacent to the Russian River canyon are two contiguous parks, comprising some 6,000 acres of forested hills. The magnificent redwood grove at **Armstrong Redwoods State Reserve** contains a self-guided nature trail that meanders among the trees, some of which are well over 1,000 years old. Exploring the cool, shaded, moist redwood grove at Armstrong is a true joy. From Santa Rosa, take US 101 north, and turn west on Hwy 12 (it becomes Hwy 116 at Forestville) to Guerneville. At Armstrong Woods Rd, turn right and drive 2.5 miles to the entrance of Armstrong Redwoods State Reserve. For more information, contact the park at (707) 869-2015.

Austin Creek State Recreation Area adjacent to Armstrong contains grasslands, riparian habitats, chaparral, conifer, and oak woodland. The park's only campground sits on a high ridge overlooking the forest. From the 20 miles of hiking trails through the Austin Creek area, you're likely to see an array of wildlife, such as the rare California spotted owl. To reach Austin Creek State Recreation Area, continue 3.5 miles through Armstrong Redwoods State Reserve (see above) to the entrance. For more information, call the park at (707) 865-2391.

Canoeing/Kayaking

You don't have to worry about people shooting down Class V rapids with a death wish when you visit the Russian River. Virtually its entire length is more suitable for canoes, sea kayaks, and even inflatable tubes. This makes the river a popular summer water play area for families with children. As it meanders through Guerneville, the river also attracts many gay tourists from the Bay Area; families tend to access the river farther west, near Monte Rio. For those looking for solitude, the western part of the river, downstream from Monte Rio is the place to go.

In addition to private resorts, there are a number of independent **outfitters** working the river. Gold Coast Kayak Rentals (707) 865-1441, located in Jenner, rents kayaks for exploring the lower Russian River, from Duncan Mills to the estuary where the river meets the Pacific. California Rivers Paddlesports, (707) 838-8919, located in Windsor, also rents kayaks for the lower Russian River. Burke's Canoe Trips, (707) 887-1222, in Forestville, rents canoes and kayaks that can be paddled downstream to Guerneville; from there, a complimentary shuttle will take you back to Burke's. The 10-mile trip takes about 3.5 hours if you do a straight run, or longer if you stop to picnic, swim, or explore the riverbank, as most canoers do. Kiwi Kayak Rentals, (707) 865-2104, is located in Monte Rio, which lies between the quaint bustle of Guerneville and the solitude of the lower Russian River. The Casini Ranch Family Campground, (707) 865-2255 or (800) 451-8400, in Duncan Mills, offers boat and canoe rentals. From May to October, you can rent canoes, kayaks, and paddleboats at Johnson's Beach in Guerneville, just under the main bridge; (707) 869-2022.

Do take note, however, of the Russian River's alter ego. Because no flood control measures are in place, the river spills over its banks on a regular basis. Disastrous winter flooding has occurred here in 50 of the past 100 years! Canoeing, therefore, is more of an April through September activity; in the winter floods, the river is more like a Class V rafting run.

Hiking

If you are looking for a short stroll through an old-growth redwood forest, with trees towering some 300 feet above your head, then check out **Pioneer Trail** (easy; 1.4 miles round trip) in Armstrong Redwoods State Reserve. The trail runs parallel to Fife Creek through the cool, dark, and damp redwood habitat. An alternate route back to the trailhead is via the **Pool Ridge Trail** and the **Discovery Trail,** which will add roughly 1 mile to your return trip. From Santa Rosa, take US 101 north, and turn west on Hwy 12 (it becomes Hwy 116 at Forestville) to Guerneville. At Armstrong

Woods Rd, turn right and drive 2.5 miles to the entrance of Armstrong Redwoods State Reserve. Proceed to the trailhead at the park station. For more information, contact the park at (707) 869-2015 or (707) 865-2391.

Contiguous to Armstrong Redwoods State Reserve, Austin Creek State Recreation Area has several trails that are seldom traveled, compared to the busy Armstrong Redwoods area. One noteworthy trail is the **Gilliam Creek Trail** (moderate; 8.2 miles round trip). This trail starts out at a 1,200-foot elevation and travels along the riparian habitat of Gilliam/Schoolhouse Creek down to a 200-foot elevation at the trail's end in Gilliam Creek Trail Campground. To reach Austin Creek State Recreation Area, continue 3.5 miles through Armstrong on Armstrong Wood Rd (see above) to the Austin entrance. The trailhead is near the parking area. For more information, contact the park at (707) 869-2015 or (707) 865-2391.

Horseback Riding

Miles of equestrian trails traversing Armstrong Redwoods State Reserve (see Parks, above) make it a must-see destination for those who want to explore by horseback. Armstrong Woods Pack Station offers 1.5-hour and half- and full-day horseback rides with gourmet lunches as well as overnight camping rides. Call (707) 869-2015 for information.

Camping

Most camping areas along the Russian River are in the hands of private resorts; unless you plan to stay at one of the few state parks in the area, it's smart to call either the Guerneville Chamber of Commerce, (707) 869-9000, or the Russian River Chamber of Commerce, (707) 869-3533, for a recommendation. That said, here are a few public and private campground recommendations of our own.

Austin Creek State Recreation Area has 24 sites for tents (showers and toilets available) or RVs (no hookups; RV limit 20 feet). Two and a half miles into the backcountry, there are 4 primitive campsites (no water; pit toilets) for use; just be sure to get a backcountry camping permit from the ranger station. *From Santa Rosa, take US 101 north, and turn west on Hwy 12 (it becomes Hwy 116 at Forestville) to Guerneville. At Armstrong Woods Rd, turn right and drive 2.5 miles to the entrance to Armstrong Redwoods State Reserve. Continue 3.5 miles through Armstrong Redwoods to Austin Creek State Recreation Area; the campground is just past the main parking area. For more information, contact the recreation area at (707) 865-2391.*

The **Faerie Ring Campground** is a private campground in Guerneville with 41 sites (showers and toilets available) for tents or RVs (hookups;

RV limit 31 feet). Water and a sanitary disposal station are available. Locationwise, this facility is in a central spot, just 1 mile from the Russian River and less than a mile from Armstrong Redwoods State Reserve. *From Santa Rosa, go north on US 101. Exit west on Hwy 12 (it becomes Hwy 116 at Forestville) to Guerneville. At Armstrong Woods Rd, turn right and drive 1.8 miles to the campground. For additional information, contact the campground at (707) 869-2746.*

The **Casini Ranch Family Campground** is a private campground in Duncan Mills with 225 sites (showers and toilets available) for tents or RVs (some hookups; RV limit 31 feet). Water, a sanitary disposal station, a laundromat, a grocery store, propane, and boat and canoe rentals are available. Some facilities are wheelchair accessible. *From Santa Rosa, take US 101, turn west on Hwy 12 (it becomes Hwy 116 at Forestville) to Duncan Mills. In Duncan Mills, turn left Moscow Rd and drive half a mile to the campground. For more information, contact the campground at (707) 865-2255 or (800) 451-8400.*

Fishing

Fishing is a year-round sport on the Russian River, with access points at major resorts and bridge crossings. In late September, **chinook** and **coho salmon** runs begin, and while recent endangered species listings continue to affect fishing regulations in the state, the sport has yet to be completely outlawed. Just be sure to check the latest regulations before setting out for the riverbanks. Bait and tackle dealers should have free copies of the latest amendments to the regulations. In November the **steelhead** runs begin on the Russian. In May, **shad** can be caught, and during the summer months, the popular catch are **striped bass, large-** and **smallmouth bass, bluegill,** and **catfish.** Kings Sport & Tackle in Guerneville, (707) 869-2156, arranges guided fishing tours on the river and also has information about current fishing conditions. There are numerous other areas along the Sonoma and Mendocino coasts for both surf fishing on the ocean and river fishing. (Check Sonoma and Southern Mendocino Coasts chapter for information about the whole region.)

Biking

Backcountry roads and riding trails in the redwood forest are the big draw along the Russian River for cyclists. Bianchi Bike Rentals, (707) 865-2104, is in Monte Rio, while Mike's Bike Rental, (707) 869-1106, is in Guerneville, conveniently close to Armstrong Redwoods State Reserve.

Ballooning

Ballooning is an ideal way for explorers to get that wide view of the **Russian River canyon.** Aerostat Adventures, (707) 579-0183 or (800) 579-0183, in Santa Rosa, offers flights over the vineyards of Santa Rosa's wine country at altitudes of 2,000 feet or more, depending on wind direction. Flights are scheduled seven days a week year-round, weather permitting.

outside in

Attractions

The tiny hamlet of **Forestville** is surrounded by redwoods and a nice base for trips on the river. On the town's itty-bitty main drag is **Brother Juniper's Bakery,** the home of the Russian River Valley's best breads; 6544 Front St, (707) 542-9012. Also worth a detour is **Koslowski Farms,** a family farm that has turned into a gourmet-food business. The Koslowski's apple butter, jams, and vinegars are sold in specialty shops throughout Sonoma County; 5566 Gravenstein Hwy, (707) 887-1587.

The longtime residents of **Guerneville**—one of the busiest logging centers in the West during the 1880s—have seen their town undergo a significant change of face in every recent decade. First it was a haven for bikers—the leather, not the Lycra, sort—then it became a hangout for hippies. Now it's a summer mecca for Bay Area gays and naturalists attracted by the beauty of the redwoods and the Russian River. The town is a good launching spot for nature expeditions and touring the area's **wineries.** Korbel Champagne Cellars, overlooking the vineyards and the Russian River, is one of the region's most popular wineries and offers free tastings of its bubbly; 13250 River Rd, (707) 887-2294. Johnson's Beach, just under the main bridge, is home to the wildly popular **Russian River Jazz Festival,** held every September; (707) 869-3940. Another crowd-pleaser is the annual **Stumptown Days Parade and Rodeo,** which takes place on Father's Day weekend; (707) 869-1959.

Restaurants

Topolos Russian River Vineyards Restaurant & Winery ☆☆   A Greek restaurant on the Russian River? Well, why not—especially when the chefs prepare the food the same way you'd get it on the Mediterranean. *5700 Gravenstein Hwy (on Hwy 116, ¼ mile S of town), Forestville; (707) 887-1562; $$.*

Lodgings

Applewood ☆☆☆ Set on a forested hillside, this 1922 California Mission Revival mansion is one of the Russian River Valley's finest accommodations, with an atmosphere far more relaxed than you would expect at such an elegant hotel. *13555 Hwy 116 (1 mile S of Guerneville), Pocket Canyon; (707) 869-9093; $$$.*

The Farmhouse Inn ☆ Don't let the Farmhouse Inn's 8 guest cottages fool you. At first glance these buildings look like nothing more than your everyday roadside motel cabins. Take a step inside and you'll see that they are actually quite luxurious. *7871 River Rd (at Wohler Rd), Forestville; (707) 887-3300 or (800) 464-6642; $$$.*

Santa Nella House ☆☆ This century-old Victorian farmhouse, hidden just off Hwy 116, is one of the better B&Bs in the valley—and it's only a short walk from the Russian River. Santa Nella's 4 turn-of-the-century guest rooms are decorated with antiques. *12130 Hwy 116 (1½ miles S of town), Guerneville; (707) 869-9488; $$.*

Timberhill Ranch Resort ☆☆☆☆ The honors continue to roll in for this secluded resort, perched high above the rugged Sonoma coast and surrounded by the 6,000 wilderness acres of Salt Point State Park. The Timberhill Ranch offers 15 elegant cedar cottages scattered throughout 80 private acres. *35755 Hauser Bridge Rd (from Hwy 1, take Myers Grade Rd for almost 14 miles to Hauser Bridge Rd and bear right), Cazadero; (707) 847-3258 or (800) 847-3470; $$$.*

The Willows ☆ The Willows prides itself on its convivial, hang-loose atmosphere. An immense lawn sweeps down from the back of the lodge to the shores of the Russian River, and the 13 guest rooms are simply decorated with wood furnishings and flowered quilts. The least expensive units are on a par with your average no-frills motel room. *15905 River Rd (½ mile E of the green bridge downtown), Guerneville; (707) 869-2824 or (800) 953-2828; $$.*

More Information

Guerneville Chamber of Commerce: *(707) 869-9000.*
Russian River Chamber of Commerce: *(707) 869-3533.*

Napa and Sonoma Wine Valleys

The wine-growing regions north of San Francisco, including the Napa Valley, Santa Rosa, the Sonoma Valley, and Lake Berryessa.

Topography, climate, and a bit of ingenuity on the part of European immigrants who missed the wines of their homelands have combined to make Napa one of the world's most famous and productive wine regions. Warm summer days are cooled when the coastal fog rolls in around twilight and fills the valley—a weather pattern said to resemble that of Bordeaux, and ideal for the grape harvest. The valley, however, at 30 miles long and from 1 to 15 miles wide, is big enough to hold more than a wine harvest, and it does.

For one thing, Napa is a terrific biking destination with long and challenging tours through the river canyons and ridge lands. Napa is also a place to pamper yourself while still getting a taste of the dirt: climb a mountain, then get a mud bath and massage in Calistoga. Stay in a bed and breakfast with doilies and big fluffy pillows or camp under the stars. You can have it both ways.

Napa County lies about an hour north of San Francisco, and thanks to ongoing efforts by the vast majority of local voters, the county has decided to remain primarily agricultural, confining most commercial and residential development to the existing cities. While this may sound promising to outdoor enthusiasts, unfortunately there is little public land in Napa. Hiking and camping spots are there if you look for them, but much of the open space you see is farmland.

An estimated 10,000 to 12,000 Wappos Indians lived in this region for 4,000 years. In 1831, the area's first European settler, George Yount, arrived and planted, for his own enjoyment, the first grapevines; today, there are more than 200 wineries in the Napa Valley. Many of them sponsor public tours of their vineyards and distilleries during the spring, summer, and fall. Unlike most of California, much of Napa County experiences four distinct seasons. Winters here are chilly and damp. (Visitors should dress for rain and bring extra clothing.) Summers, however, are dry and hot—temperatures routinely soar over 100 degrees in many areas during the day. The spring and fall are balmy and beautiful, making great conditions for golf, bicycling, hiking, and horseback riding.

Just as there is more to Napa Valley than the wine, there is also more to California wine country than Napa Valley: the oak woodlands and forested canyons of Sonoma County to the west, high peaks such as 4,300-foot Mount St. Helena, water sports and fishing on Lake Berryessa. Bring your loafers and your hiking shoes; drag the backpack and the tent out but don't forget the credit card. Leave twice as much time to have both kinds of fun.

Getting There

From San Francisco: Take US Highway 101 (US 101) north. Exit east at Highway 37 (the Napa turnoff). Proceed to Highway 121/12. Follow the signs to Napa. This is the most scenic route to Napa. In regular traffic conditions it will take an hour. During rush hour it will take considerably longer. If you are staying in downtown San Francisco, it is considerably less scenic, but quicker, to travel across the Bay Bridge and approach Napa from Oakland. From Sacramento and Oakland: Take Interstate 80 west from Sacramento, or east from Oakland. Exit Interstate 80 at Highway 37 and head west. Proceed to Highway 29 and head north to Napa.

Adjoining Areas

NORTH: **Mendocino National Forest, Sonoma and Southern Mendocino Coasts**

SOUTH: **East Bay**

EAST: **Marin**

WEST: **Russian River**

inside out

Cycling

It doesn't take long for outdoor enthusiasts visiting the Napa Valley and surrounding wine region to realize they're going to want to spend more time sipping out of water bottles on their bicycles than out of wine glasses in the tasting rooms. The cool canyons and gently sloping country roads make Napa an ideal cycling tour destination. Don't worry that the main highways are crowded with tourists buzzing from winery to winery in their rental cars—the best cycling routes are off the main highways anyway, and that's where you're advised to stay. The scenery is pleasant, rural, and quiet; long, low-slung canyons planted with vineyards dominate much of the landscape. Among the best areas to explore the looping country roads are in the valleys west of Hwy 121 and around the St. Helena area, west toward Sonoma. The best time of year to ride is either side of summer, particularly during the fall grape harvest season when the mornings stay cool longer and the afternoons are mild.

There are two ways to bike the valley: either contact a tour company for a complete cycle tour of the wineries and canyon roads, tasting included, or rent bicycles and explore freestyle. Some reputable **tour companies** and **outfitters** in the area include Getaway Bicycle Tours, 1117 Lincoln Ave, Calistoga, (800) 499-2453; Bicycle Trax, 796 Soscol Ave, Napa, (707) 258-8729; Napa Valley Bike Tours, 4080 Byway E, Napa, (800) 707-BIKE; St. Helena Cyclery, 1156 Main St, St. Helena, (707) 963-7736; and Detailed Destinations, 1734 Jefferson #C, Napa, (707) 256-3078. Another good resource is the Eagle Cycling Club, (707) 226-7066, www.napanet.net/~eccweb/, which organizes and sponsors numerous rides in the Napa Valley area each month.

One pleasant ride, of intermediate difficultly mostly because of its length, is the 40-mile trek through Wooden Valley along **Wooden Valley Road,** which begins at the Hwy 121 intersection and then follows Wooden Valley Creek and Suisun Creek to the west. There are numerous possible loop connections here that will bring you back to the highway, with most of the ride in lightly traveled countryside dotted with ranch buildings and croplands. Another favorite among road cyclists is **Dry Creek Road,** which takes riders from Oakville north of Yountville on Hwy 29 through scenic canyons and ridge lands separating the area from Glen Ellen in Somona County. There is a pleasant but long 50-mile loop beginning on Dry Creek at Oakville, through to Glen Ellen via **Trinity Road,** then back to the Hwy 29 corridor via **Napa Road.** All of this, of course, is through lovely ranchlands and open countryside best explored in the spring and early fall when temperatures tend to be moderate. **Petrified Forest Road** west of Calistoga near the Hwy 29/128 junction passes through the Chalk Mountain wilderness areas, with loop connections through **Alexander Valley** to Santa Rosa and then Napa.

In Sonoma County, there are some nice paved regional trails used by cyclists who aren't keen on sharing the open highways with motorists. The **Sebastopol–Santa Rosa Trail** covers 6 miles of abandoned railroad right-of-way transformed for recreational use by the county parks agency. It covers mostly farmland terrain between the two cities. Because the trail is a multiuse facility, count on encountering in-line skaters, baby strollers, and joggers along the way. The trailhead is near the Hwy 116/12 interchange in downtown Sebastopol. The county parks department in Sonoma can be reached at (707) 527-2041.

Mountain Biking

As much as road cycling appears to go hand-in-hand with doing the wine thing, there is always the option of saying to hell with the wineries and going off-road instead. Indeed, the ridge lands, peaks, and winding canyons surrounding the Napa Valley are ideal for mountain biking, some even featuring intense climbs for those who really want to sweat it. The chief conquest is, of course, the ride to the 4,343-foot summit of **Mount St. Helena** northeast of Calistoga, a moderately difficult 9-mile ride on the summit fire road (clearly marked) off Hwy 29 east of the town of St. Helena. This is the main fire road leading to both the south and north peaks of the mountain, which offers spectacular views of several high Northern California peaks—including Shasta, Lassen, Mount Diablo, and the Sierra Nevada—on clear, cool days.

The best route for expert bikers is the **Oat Hill Mine Road** in Calistoga, an old mining road turned bike trail that climbs from 400 feet to 2,200 feet in about 5 miles. Definitely bring plenty of water on this ride. The dirt-rock road is very rutted from the days of old mining wagons, and the property on either side of it is private, so do not stray from the trail. In the spring you will see plenty of wildflowers. From Calistoga, take Hwy 29 north about 1 mile and look for the trailhead to the east. Oat Hill Mine Rd is to the left of the Trailhead Store.

More advanced riders should consider the trails at **Skyline Park** in Napa. The park has no easy trails, and it sponsors bicycle races. In fact, it was the site of the Grundig–UCI World Cup Opener, in 1997 and 1998. The bike trails are maintained by volunteers, and after large bicycle races, such as Grundig–UCI, the trails are generally in very poor condition until the volunteers are able to rehabilitate them. Before taking a trip to Skyline, it is a good idea to call the park to check on conditions and the event schedule. A complete map of the park's trails is available at the visitors center. From the south, take Hwy 29 and exit north at Hwy 221/Soscol Ave. Turn right on Imola and proceed to the end. The park is on the right. For more information, contact the park at (707) 252-0481.

Angwin Park is the site of the Napa Valley Dirt Classic and the Napa Nobular races. It has several bicycle tracks, all of which are in great shape. One useful map of the area has been posted on the World Wide Web at www.apgar.net/biking/AngwinMap.html but any of the recommended outfitters (see Cycling, above) also have information on Angwin. To reach the park from Napa, take Hwy 29 north. Turn right on Deer Park Rd about 5 miles before Calistoga. Turn right on Cold Springs Rd. Make a slight left on Las Posadas Rd. In about a mile you will see an obvious parking area for cars and the entrance to the trails where the road curves to the right.

The **outfitters** listed above in Cycling are suitable for mountain bike equipment as well.

Ballooning

It's not exactly *Around the World in 80 Days,* but it's a great way to get a sprawling view of the Napa Valley and its environs: the meandering Napa River snaking toward San Francisco Bay, rolling hills of vineyards, the high peaks and mountain lakes. Three launching areas are located in Yountville. Above the West Ballooning, (800) 627-2759, offers smaller excursions of four to six passengers and complimentary shuttle service from selected Napa Valley lodgings. Adventures Aloft of Napa Valley, (800) 944-4408, offers excursions of larger parties of eight passengers per balloon, along with shuttles. Balloon Aviation of Napa Valley, (800) 367-6272, offers excursions for eight to nine passengers per balloon.

Parks

At the geographical center of Napa Valley between St. Helena and Calistoga, **Bothe–Napa Valley State Park** and **Bale Grist Mill State Historic Park** are good examples of what the region must have looked like before rangelands gave way to mile after mile of vineyard. The park is a woodland, with interesting oak habitat, big-leaf maples, and fir trees rather than the trademark vineyards that dominate so much of the landscape in this area. Bothe–Napa has a swimming pool, an unusual feature for a state park. Other activities in these parklands include camping, hiking, and bicycling through the shady canyons. The Bale Grist Mill State Historic Park is adjacent, a relic from early settlers who used primitive milling equipment here in the 19th century. From St. Helena, take Hwy 29 north about 3 miles. Turn left at the kiosk and proceed to the park entrance. For more information, contact Bothe–Napa Valley State Park at (707) 942-4575.

Annadel State Park is a large wilderness area of nearly 5,000 acres, encompassing 35 miles of horseback, hiking, and biking trails amid rolling hills, streams, meadows, and forests of Douglas fir. In springtime, wildflowers are in full bloom. During winter, the park is relatively quiet. However, even at its busiest moments, the park's massive size makes it a favorite among outdoor enthusiasts looking for solitude. **Lake Llsanjo** offers excellent fishing conditions for bluebill and black bass. From US 101 north, exit east on Hwy 12. Travel 4 miles then turn right on Montgomery Dr. Travel 3 miles then turn right on Channel Dr. Proceed to the park entrance. For more information, call Annadel State Park at (707) 938-1519.

Sugarloaf Ridge State Park, between Santa Rosa and Sonoma, covers much of the vast oak woodlands draining toward Sonoma Creek, but there are also some nice redwood groves here, along with 2,729-foot **Bald Mountain,** one of the valley's most prominent geologic features. You'll also find picnic facilities, biking, hiking, and equestrian trails; a campground (see Camping, below); and even a pretty 30-foot waterfall on the creek, but be advised that much of the park is open and exposed to the elements. So don't head out on a long bike trek without being properly prepared. The park is located 2.5 miles north of Hwy 12 on Adobe Canyon Rd, 8 miles east of Santa Rosa. Call the park, (707) 833-5712, for more information.

Jack London State Park, in the gently rolling hillsides outside the small town of Glen Ellen, southeast of Santa Rosa on Hwy 12, is named for the famed author, whose cabin home is still on-site. Hiking and equestrian trails, with horse rentals available, are the main recreational attraction here, although London's vineyards, piggery, other ranch buildings, and a house-turned-museum are also interesting to visit. The museum contains his art collection and mementos (including a series of rejection letters London received from several publishers, who must have fallen over backward in their cushy chairs the day they learned London had become the highest-paid author of his time). The park is about 1 mile west of Hwy 12 in Glen Ellen. Take Arroyoada Rd west from Hwy 12 for a quarter mile, turn right on Arnold St, then head to the intersection with Jack London Ranch Rd a quarter mile away. Turn left on Jack London Ranch Rd and continue to the end, where the park entrance is. Call the park at (707) 938-5216 for more information.

Visitors to Napa County who are interested in learning about the plants and animals will want to visit the **Carolyn Parr Nature Center** at the entrance to **Westwood Hills Park** in Napa. There are displays and exhibits about the region's natural habitats, as well as an extensive nature reference library. The center is open year-round on Saturday and Sunday, from 1pm to 4pm. During the summer it is also open Tuesday through Friday from 1pm to 4pm. Take Hwy 29 north through Napa and turn right on Browns Valley Rd. Proceed to Westwood Hills Park on your right. For more information, contact the nature center at (707) 255-6465.

Camping

Most camping opportunities within the Napa Valley are at private resorts and RV parks, but there are a few choice public campgrounds for those who know where to look. If the camps mentioned here are booked, it may be advisable to check with either the Napa Valley Tourist Bureau, (707) 944-1558, or the Napa Valley Chamber of Commerce, (707) 226-7455, for a private campground recommendation. Also see Mendocino National Forest and Clear Lake Region chapters for other nearby options.

Bothe–Napa Valley State Park (see Parks, above) has 50 sites (no hookups; RV limit 31 feet) near the oak and bay forests on the western slopes of the Napa Valley. Each site has a picnic table, grill, running water, flush toilets, and showers nearby. *Call state parks reservations, (800) 444-7275, or the park at (707) 924-4575, for information. The park is 5.5 miles north of St. Helena on Hwy 29, west side of the road.*

There are 50 RV sites at the **Napa County Fairgrounds** (full hookups; various RV lengths accomodated), which, while it looks like little more than your typical RV parking area, is still near enough to the main Napa Valley attractions to be an enjoyable stopover. The campground is closed during the annual fair in June and July. Call ahead during these months for exact dates. Hot showers, flush toilets, and full modern conveniences are provided. *Call the fairgrounds, (707) 942-5111, for information. No reservations are taken. The campground is in Calistoga, 31 miles north of Napa. Take Hwy 29 to Calistoga, then go south on Lincoln Ave in the downtown area to Fairway Dr, which continues east to the fairgrounds entrance.*

Spring Lake Regional Park in Santa Rosa (no hookups; various RV lengths accomodated) has 30 sites at Spring Lake, a popular boating and rainbow fishing spot. The lake, also known as Santa Rosa Creek Reservoir, has a regular fish stocking schedule during the outdoor season. Each site has a picnic table and fire pit, with piped water, showers, and flush toilets nearby. There are boat rentals and shopping for basics available on site. For reservations, call the park at (707) 539-8082. *The campground is east of US 101 in Santa Rosa at the Hwy 12 interchange. Take Hwy 12 for 0.75* mile east from US 101, continuing along Hoen Ave for another half mile to the intersection with Newanga Ave. Here, head north another half mile to the park entrance.

Sugarloaf Ridge State Park has 50 sites (see Parks, above) outside Santa Rosa (no hookups; RV limit 27 feet) in a nice area of oak woodlands with a redwood grove and Bald Mountain nearby. Each site has a picnic table and fire pit with running water and flush toilets nearby. You'll also find picnic facilities; biking, hiking, and equestrian trails; and a waterfall. *The park is 2.5 miles north of Hwy 12 on Adobe Canyon Rd, 8 miles east of Santa Rosa. Call the park, (707) 833-5712, for information.*

Lake Solano County Park has 85 sites (full hookups; RV limit 35 feet) near Monticello Dam at Lake Berryessa. Each site has a picnic table and fire grill, with running water, flush toilets, and showers nearby. Full boating facilities are also available, including rentals. *Call the park, (530) 795-2990, for reservations. To reach the park, take I-505 north from I-80 (between Vacaville and Davis) for 10 miles to Hwy 128, then continue west 5.5 miles to Pleasant Valley Rd. At Pleasant Valley Rd, turn south and continue a short distance to the park entrance.*

Hiking/Walking

In keeping with the wine-and-cheese picnic pace you'd expect in Napa Valley, the hiking here is more of an after-lunch stroll scene. Who ever heard of climbing a mountain with a belly full of wine and finger snacks? That considered, the strolls and walks in this area deserve equal billing with those daylong treks to the top of the mountain. The rule of thumb in Napa when it comes to hiking is that most outdoor physical activity is best done in the cool spring and fall mornings rather than in the summer, when the heat can be unbearable. Brewster's, 1008 Main St, Napa, (707) 253-9082, is a good **outdoors supplier.** Also check directly with the Napa Valley Tourist Bureau, (707) 944-1558, or the Napa Valley Chamber of Commerce, (707) 226-7455, for information about special events and **guided walking tours.** Napa County Landmarks, (707) 255-1836, a community preservation center, in downtown Napa, sponsors historical walking tours of the Napa region generally every other weekend in the spring, summer, and early fall.

Fern Springs Trail (moderate to easy; 3 miles round trip) at White Sulphur Springs Resort is tucked away in a deep canyon just west of St. Helena. The trail meanders through redwood groves, madrone, and oak forests. Other trails at the resort lead to year-round waterfalls and springs. A day-use fee gives visitors access to all the trails as well as to a sulfur pool, whirlpool, sauna, picnic areas, and showers. For additional information contact the resort at (707) 963-8588. To reach the resort, head west from Hwy 29, just south of downtown St. Helena, on Spring Rd. Follow the road 3 miles to where it changes to White Sulphur Spring Rd, where you'll find the entrance.

Bothe–Napa Valley State Park (see Parks, above) has several hiking trails. The **Ritchey Canyon Trail** (moderate; 9 miles round trip) follows a year-round stream through groves of redwoods, firs, and other plants that thrive in the cool, damp, shaded environment. The **Coyote Peak Trail** (moderate to difficult; 6 miles round trip) extends from the canyon floor up to 1,170-foot Coyote Peak, which offers sweeping views of the upper canyon and Napa Valley beyond. The **History Trail** (moderate to difficult; 2.4 miles round trip) extends from the park's picnic area up through a pioneer cemetery to the site where Napa Valley's first church was built in 1853. From this point, the trail leads up to the historic Bale Grist Mill. From St. Helena, take Hwy 29 north about 3 miles. Turn left at the kiosk and proceed to the park entrance. Follow signs to the "Trailhead Parking" area. For more information, contact Bothe–Napa Valley State Park at (707) 942-4575.

For hikers looking for solitude in the woods, there is no better place than **Annadel State Park**'s 35-mile trail network. The **Warren Richardson Trail** (moderate; 6 miles round trip) begins in a forest of Douglas firs, bays, and redwoods. The forest gives way to drier open meadows at about the 900-foot elevation level. The trail ends at **Lake Llsanjo,** an excellent fishing spot. You can return by backtracking along the Warren Richardson Trail, or you can loop back via **Steve's Trail** (moderate; 2 miles back to the Warren Richardson trailhead). From US 101 north, exit east on Hwy 12. Travel 4 miles, then turn right on Montgomery Dr. Travel 3 miles then turn right on Channel Dr. Proceed to the end of Montgomery. The trailhead is on the left side of the road. For more information, call Annadel State Park at (707) 938-1519.

At **Jack London State Park** (see Parks, above) near Sonoma, **Lake Trail** (easy; 1.5 miles round trip), is a pleasant stroll around a small pond on the grounds of London's Sonoma County retreat, a great way to try to capture the quiet and serenity of a great American author's workplace. Combine this walk with a tour of the grounds and museum. The park is about 1 mile west of Hwy 12 near Glen Ellen. Take Arroyoada Rd west from Hwy 12 for a quarter mile, turn right on Arnold St, then head to the intersection with Jack London Ranch Rd a quarter mile away. Turn left on Jack London Ranch Rd and continue to the end, where you will see the park entrance.

Bald Mountain Loop Trail (moderate; 8 miles round trip) provides what amounts to a grand tour of Bald Mountain—the dominant peak on the skyline to the south of Mount St. Helena—and Sugarloaf Ridge State Park north of Sonoma (see Parks, above). Redwood groves, oak woodlands, a waterfall on Sonoma Creek, and sweeping views of the Napa Valley and San Francisco Bay await you here. From the trailhead, where park maps are available, loop through the park using Bald Mountain, Meadow, Brushy, and Gray Meadow Trails. The trail system begins at the parking area for Sugarloaf. The park is 2.5 miles north of Hwy 12 on Adobe Canyon Rd, 8 miles east of Santa Rosa.

The premier challenge for hikers looking to make a day of it in the Napa Valley is the trek to the 4,343-foot summit of Mount St. Helena along **Mount St. Helena Trail** (difficult; 9 miles round trip), a sometimes steep and grueling climb to what has got to be the best view of the California wine region found anywhere. The trail is bike-free, and best tackled during the spring wildflower season—not only because it's so pretty but also because the summers at high noon are just plain unacceptable here. The mountain is slated for development as a state park someday, but for now it is more of a wilderness area with few recreational improvements beyond trail cuts. The trailhead can be found on the west side of Hwy 29, approximately 9 miles north of Calistoga. Call the local state parks office at (707) 942-4575 for information.

Another good, hearty trek that will take the breath out of you is the daylong or overnight climb along **Blue Ridge Trail** (difficult; 17 miles round trip), another journey best taken in the cooler spring wildflower season, not only because it's steep and rocky but also because that's when the terrain looks its best. The trail is relatively easy to track, but the grade is incredible in sections, including one 2,000-foot elevation gain that unfolds in less than 3 miles. The trailhead is in the foothills north of Lake Berryessa. From Hwy 20 at Wilbur Springs Station east of the town of Clearlake, head east 14 miles to the trailhead at Yolo County Park (clearly marked) on the south side of the road. For information, contact the US Bureau of Land Management (BLM) at (707) 462-3873.

Hikers can also stretch their legs at **Montgomery Woods State Reserve**, 1,142 acres of coastal redwoods with a self-guided nature trail along Montgomery Creek; it's located on Orr Springs Rd, off US 101, 15 miles northwest of Ukiah.

Boating/Fishing

Among the nicest geologic features of Napa and Sonoma Counties are the numerous small lakes and reservoirs found tucked away in the surrounding ridge lands and mountains.

Lake Llsanjo in Annadel State Park, for example, has excellent fishing for **bluegill** and **black bass,** with daily catches routinely weighing in at over 9 pounds. The solitude of this place is one of its finest assets; it can only be reached by foot. That, of course, means no boats, although it is possible to pack a raft in if you insist. The quickest way to get there is to hike in from the Warren Richardson Trail (see Walking/Hiking, above).

Roughly 20 miles northeast of Napa, **Lake Berryessa** on Putah Creek is more than 25 miles long and up to 3 miles wide in most areas. Its shoreline is dotted with marinas, providing adequate facilities, and its waters are stocked year-round with **largemouth** and **smallmouth bass.** While the largemouth bass can be found in a wide variety of areas around the lake, mainly in coves, the smallmouth bass primarily enjoy the placid waters of Pope Creek, Spanish Flat, and the rock slide near Skier's Cove on the eastern shore. In spring, look for **trout** and **salmon** action here. This is a particularly popular, and therefore crowded, spot during the summer so if you're looking for solitude and serenity, go find a small lake in the high country and hike to it! From St. Helena, take Hwy 128 east and exit north at the Spanish Flat/Lake Berryessa exit. The Lake Berryessa Marina Resort, 5880 Knoxville Rd, (707) 966-2161, or Markley Cove Resort in Winters, (707) 966-2134, are two good places to check on lake conditions and accommodations.

Lake Sonoma at Warm Springs Dam near Healdsburg is more of a kayaker/skier/boater lake than a fishing spot. The north end of the reservoir is the best area for anglers, who will find a diverse fare: in addition to **smallmouth bass** and **rainbow trout,** numerous varieties of **sunfish** are bred at the lake hatchery. Also look for a little **crappie** and **catfish** action here. You'll find a public boat ramp and full marina at Lake Sonoma Marina off Stewarts Point Rd, (707) 433-2200; bait, tackle and boat rentals are also available.

There are numerous good **outfitters** and suppliers located throughout the Napa region. A few reputable ones include Sweeney's Sports, 1601 Lincoln Ave, Napa, (707) 255-5544; Wind River Fly Fishing, 1043 Atlas Peak Rd, Napa, (707) 252-4900; and Thompson and Daughters Enterprises, 5100 Knoxville Rd, Lake Berryessa, (707) 966-0427.

Swimming

Unusual for a state park, **Bothe–Napa Valley State Park** has a swimming pool that is open from noon to 6pm from mid-June through Labor Day, with a lifeguard on duty. Pool visitors must first purchase a ticket at the visitors center. The pool tends to be on the cool side, as its water comes from the cool natural springs in the area. Showers and dressing rooms are available. From St. Helena, take Hwy 29 north about 3 miles. Turn left at the kiosk and proceed to the park entrance. Follow signs to the pool area on the left side of the road. For more information, contact Bothe–Napa Valley State Park at (707) 942-4575.

Golf

Kennedy Park in Napa contains a challenging 18-hole municipal golf course with many tight fairways. Water comes into play at 14 of the holes. The course measures 5,956 yards from the women's tees, 6,506 from the regular tees, and 6,730 from the championship tees. Lessons are available at the facility, and there are also a clubhouse, driving range, and practice greens. Take Hwy 29 north through Napa and turn left on Imola Ave. Turn right on Soscol Ave/Hwy 221. Turn right on Streblow Dr and proceed to the park entrance. For additional information, contact the park at (707) 257-9529.

The **Chardonnay Golf Club,** located south of Napa, has a 36-hole golf course, open to the public, called the Vineyards. The course is 6,800 yards long, par 71. Driving range and private lessons are available. From Napa, take Hwy 29 south and exit at Hwy 12 east. Travel 1.5 miles. The entrance is on the right. For more information, contact the club at (800) 788-0136.

Scenic Drives

It seems that every road in Napa is scenic, but we'll mention two of particular appeal. **Highway 29** runs north-south through Napa Valley, connecting its major towns of Napa, St. Helena, and Calistoga. Several crossroads intersect with Hwy 29, and just about any of them will get you off the beaten path and provide a picturesque drive.

Washington Street runs north-south parallel to Hwy 29, between Napa and Yountville. Travel on it is slower than on Hwy 29, but more scenic. To reach Washington St from Napa, turn right at the Washington St turnoff, just north of Napa on Hwy 29. Make an immediate left on Washington St and enjoy.

Adventure Calendar

Grundig–UCI World Cup mountain bike race, early April: *Skyline Park, (415) 367-7797.*

outside in

Attractions

The **Napa Valley** remains one of the most magical spots in Northern California and is blessed with an abundance of excellent restaurants, scores of welcoming bed and breakfasts, a couple of ultra-luxurious resorts, and enough interesting shops to keep gold cards flashing up and down the valley. You might grab a map to the region's numerous wineries and work on expanding the contents of your cellar. Or engage in that ultimate food-to-go experience, the **Napa Valley Wine Train,** where passengers sip fine wines and sup on an excellent meal while gazing out at the lush countryside on their cushy three-hour train ride; for dining information and reservations call (707) 253-2111 or (800) 427-4124.

Napa's **wineries** are mainly clustered along Hwy 29 and the Silverado Trail, two parallel roads running the length of the valley. The place is a zoo on weekends—especially in the summer and early fall, when the traffic on narrow Hwy 29 rivals rush hour in the Bay Area. With the increased number of visitors, most vintners now charge a small fee to taste their wines and some require reservations for tours (don't let the latter deter you—the smaller establishments just need to control the number of visitors at any one time and make sure someone will be available to show you around). A tip from veteran wine tasters: pick out the four or five wineries you're most interested in visiting over the weekend, and stick to your itinerary. Touring more than a couple of wineries a day will surely overwhelm and exhaust even the most intrepid wine connoisseur, although if you really want to see several wineries in a short period, skip the grand tours and just visit the tasting rooms. If you're new to the wine-touring scene, you'll be relieved to know you won't ever be pressured to buy any of the wines you've sampled—the vintners are just delighted to expose you to their line of products.

Winery maps, as well as details about parks, hot-air balloon rides, and other recreational pastimes, are readily available at many locations, including most hotels and the **Napa Valley Conference and Visitors Bureau** at 1310 Town Center Mall (off First St) in Napa, (707) 226-7459.

About half the residents of the Napa Valley live in the pretty, sprawling town of **Napa,** whose name has become synonymous with wine. Napa's downtown has plenty of imposing Victorian structures worth admiring, and you can pick up a walking-tour map at the Napa Valley Conference and Visitors Bureau (see above). For a break, amble over to the **ABC/Alexis Baking Company** for great espresso, pizza, fresh salads, and goodies like chocolate-caramel cake, pumpkin-spice muffins, and pistachio-apricot cake; 1517 Third St, (707) 258-1827. **Napa Valley Roasting Company** is another pleasant place to sip a cup of freshly brewed java; 948 Main St, (707) 224-2233. If you want a good read as you linger over a steamy mug, browse through **Copperfield's** for new and used books at reasonable prices; 1303 First St, (707) 252-8002.

The itsy-bitsy town of **Oakville** is a destination in itself, thanks to the famous **Oakville Grocery Co.**, which has turned the former Stars restaurant site next door into the Oakville Grocery Cafe to keep up with the demand for its tasty deli fare. Although the Oakville Grocery is disguised as an old-fashioned country market complete with a fading "Drink Coca-Cola" sign outside, step inside this extraordinary gourmet deli and you'll find a fine variety of local wines (including a good selection of splits), a small espresso bar tucked in the corner, and pricey but delicious picnic supplies ranging from pâté and caviar to sliced-turkey sandwiches and several freshly made sweets; 7856 St. Helena Hwy at the Oakville Cross Rd, (707) 944-8802.

Where else can you find a small farming town that sells $1,600 owl-skin Japanese lanterns? **St. Helena** has come a long way since its days as a rural Seventh Day Adventist village. On Main St, with its Victorian Old West feel, farming-supply stores now sit stiffly next to chichi women's clothing boutiques and upscale purveyors of home furnishings. Just off the main drag you can find more earthy pleasures at such shops as the **Napa Valley Olive Oil Manufacturing Company,** an authentic Italian deli and general store stuffed to the rafters with goodies ranging from dried fruit and biscotti to salami and fresh mozzarella. Be sure to pick up a bottle or two of the very reasonably priced extra-virgin California olive oil; the store is located at the corner of Charter Oak and Allison Aves, (707) 963-4173. Take your Italian treats to **Lyman Park** (on Main St between Adams and Pine Sts) and picnic on the grass or in the beautiful little white gazebo where bands sometimes set up for live summer concerts. About 3 miles north of town on Hwy 29 is St. Helena's popular tree-lined upscale outlet mall, where you'll find discounted designer wares by such familiar names as Donna Karan, Brooks Brothers, London Fog, and Joan & David; 3111 St. Helena Hwy, (707) 963-7282.

Mud baths, mineral pools, and massages are still the main attractions of the charming little spa town of **Calistoga,** founded in the mid-19th century by California's first millionaire, Sam Brannan. Savvy Brannan made a bundle of cash supplying miners in the Gold Rush and quickly recognized the value of Calistoga's mineral-rich hot springs. In 1859 he purchased 2,000 acres of the Wappo Indians' hot springs land, built a first-class hotel and spa, and named the region Calistoga (a combination of the words California and Saratoga). He then watched his fortunes grow as affluent San Franciscans paraded into town for a relaxing respite.

Generations later, city slickers are still making the pilgrimage to this city of spas. These days, however, more than a dozen enterprises touting the magical restorative powers of mineral baths line the town's Old West–style streets. You'll see an odd combo of stressed-out CEOs and earthier types shelling out dough for a chance to soak away their worries and get the kinks rubbed out of their necks. While Calistoga's **spas** and resorts are far from glamorous (you have to go to the Sonoma Mission Inn & Spa for rubdowns in luxe surroundings), many offer body treatments and mud baths you won't find anywhere else in this part of the state. Among the most popular spas are Dr. Wilkinson's Hot Springs, where you'll get a great massage and numerous other body treatments in a rather drab setting, 1507 Lincoln Ave, (707) 942-4102; Calistoga Spa Hot Springs (a favorite for families with young children), which boasts four mineral pools in addition to several body-pampering services, 1006 Washington St, (707) 942-6269; Indian Springs for pricey spa treatments in a historic setting and the best (and largest) mineral pool in the area, 1712 Lincoln Ave, (707) 942-4913; and Lavender Hill Spa, which provides aromatherapy facials, seaweed wraps, mud baths, and other sybaritic delights in one of the most attractive settings in town, 1015 Foothill Blvd (Hwy 29), (707) 942-4495.

Once you're rejuvenated, stroll down the main street and browse through the numerous quaint shops marketing everything from French soaps and antique armoires to silk-screened T-shirts and saltwater taffy. For a trip back in time to Calistoga's pioneer past, stop by the **Sharpsteen Museum and Brannan Cottage;** 1311 Washington St, (707) 942-5911. Just outside of town you can marvel at **Old Faithful Geyser,** which faithfully shoots a plume of 350°F mineral water 60 feet into the air at regular intervals; 1299 Tubbs Lane, 2 miles north of Calistoga, (707) 942-6463.

Other natural wonders abound at **The Petrified Forest,** where towering redwoods were turned to stone when Mount St. Helena erupted 3 million years ago (you can read about the fascinating event at the museum at the forest entrance); 4100 Petrified Forest Rd, off Hwy 128, 6 miles north of town, (707) 942-6667. For a bird's-eye view, hop aboard a **glider plane** for a stunning tour of the Wine Country at the Calistoga Gliderport; 1546 Lincoln Avenue, (707) 942-5000.

In the mood for a bit of Africa? The 240-acre **Safari West** animal preserve, west of Calistoga, is home to nearly 400 mammals and birds. Guests spend two and a half hours on an educational tram and walking tour of the preserve. Sunscreen and a hat are recommended during the spring and summer months. Walking shoes are also essential, and don't forget the binoculars if you plan to try this unique experience. Last we checked, the basic tour ran $48 for adults and $24 for children. From Santa Rosa, take US 101 north and exit east at the River Rd/Calistoga exit. In 7 miles, turn left on Franz Valley Rd. Proceed to the entrance gate. For additional information, contact Safari West at (707) 579-2551.

Many California enophiles would argue that when it comes to comparing the **Sonoma Valley** with Napa Valley, less is definitely more: Sonoma is less congested, less developed, less commercial, and less glitzy than its rival. Smitten with the bucolic charm of the region, Sonomaphiles delight in wandering the area's back roads, leisurely hopping from winery to winery and exploring the quaint towns along the way.

California's world-renowned wine industry was born in the Sonoma Valley. Franciscan fathers planted the state's first vineyards at the Mission San Francisco Solano de Sonoma in 1823 and harvested the grapes to make their sacramental wines. Thirty-four years later, California's first major vineyard was planted with European grape varietals by Hungarian Count Agoston Haraszthy at Sonoma's revered Buena Vista Winery. Little did the count know that one day he would become widely hailed as the father of California wine—wine that is consistently rated as some of the best in the world. Today more than 40 **wineries** dot the Sonoma Valley, most offering pretty picnic areas and free tours of their winemaking facilities. Before setting out for this verdant vineyard-laced region, stop at the **Sonoma Valley Visitors Bureau** for lots of free, helpful information about the area's wineries, farmers markets, historic sites, walking tours, recreational facilities, and seasonal events; 453 First St E, Sonoma, (707) 996-1090.

Sonoma's slide into gentrification has been slower than Napa's, though just as relentless. Designed by Mexican General Mariano Vallejo in 1835, **Sonoma** is set up like a Mexican town, with an 8-acre parklike plaza in the center. Several historic adobe buildings hug the perimeter of the plaza, most of which now house wine stores, specialty food shops, quaint boutiques, and restaurants. **Mission San Francisco Solano de Sonoma** (aka the Sonoma Mission), the northernmost and last of the 21 missions built by the Spanish fathers, is on the corner of the square at First St E and E Spain St; (707) 938-1519. After touring the mission and the plaza, stroll over to **The Coffee Garden** for a good cup of java and a quick bite on the pretty, vine-laced patio hidden in back; 415-421 First St W (across from the plaza's west side), (707) 996-6645. Not far from the plaza, **The General's Daughter** restaurant dishes out very good, moderately priced continental cuisine in the beautifully remodeled Victorian home built in 1878 by General Vallejo's daughter Natalia; 400 W Spain St, (707) 938-4004.

There are more places and things named after Jack London in Sonoma County than there are women named María in Mexico. This cult reaches its apex in **Glen Ellen,** where the writer built his aptly named Beauty Ranch, an 800-acre spread now known as **Jack London State Historic Park;** see Parks, above.

The tiny town of Glen Ellen was also the longtime home of the late celebrated food writer M.F.K. Fisher. It offers a couple of good restaurants, plus wine-tasting and antique-hunting excursions. The **Wine Country Film Festival,** a three-week summer splurge of screenings and parties throughout Napa and Sonoma, is headquartered here; call (707) 996-2536 for more information.

Santa Rosa is the closest thing Sonoma County has to a big city, but it's more like a countrified suburb. Oddly enough, it's got more than its share of offbeat museums. Botanists, gardeners, and other plant lovers will want to make a beeline to the popular gardens and greenhouse at the **Luther Burbank Home & Gardens.** Burbank, for those struggling to recall their elementary-school history, was a world-renowned horticulturist who created 800 new strains of plants, fruits, and vegetables at the turn of the century; the home is located at the corner of Santa Rosa and Sonoma Aves, (707) 524-5445. Pop culture fans will get a kick out of **Snoopy's Gallery & Gift Shop,** a "Peanuts" cartoon museum with the world's largest collection of Snoopy memorabilia, thanks to donations by the beagle's creator, Charles Schulz, who lives in Santa Rosa; 1665 W Steel Lane, (707) 546-3385. The tacky but fun **Robert L. Ripley Memorial Museum,** housed in the historic Church Built from One Tree, is filled with wacky displays and information about the late Santa Rosa resident who created the world-famous "Ripley's Believe It or Not" cartoon strip; 492 Sonoma Ave, (707) 524-5233.

For music, magicians, and a plethora of fresh-from-the-farm food, head over to the wildly successful **Thursday Night Farmers Market** on downtown Santa Rosa's Fourth St, which is closed to traffic every Thursday night for this festive event and draws folks from far and near from Memorial Day through Labor Day; (707) 542-2123. Another local crowd-pleaser is the annual **Sonoma County Harvest Fair,** a wine-tasting, food-guzzling orgy held at the fairgrounds from late July to early August; 1350 Bennett Valley Rd, (707) 545-4200.

Healdsburg is one tourist town whose charm seems completely unforced. Boutiques and bakeries surround a pretty, tree-lined plaza where you can sit and read the newspaper while munching on pastries from the marvelous **Downtown Bakery & Creamery;** 308-A Center St, (707) 431-2719.

Once noted only for sheep, apples, and timber, **Anderson Valley** has become the premier producer of cool-climate California wines such as chardonnay, gewürztraminer, and riesling. The enological future of this valley, whose climate is almost identical to that of the Champagne region of France, may also reside in the production of sparkling wine, now that some of France's best champagne-makers have successfully set up shop here. Most of Anderson Valley's **wineries** line the narrow stretch of Hwy 28 that winds through this gorgeous, verdant 25-mile-long valley before it reaches the Pacific Coast.

Boonville is a speck of a town in the heart of the Anderson Valley and is best known for a regional dialect called Boontling, developed by towns-folk at the beginning of the century. No one really speaks Boontling any-more, though a few old-timers remember the lingo. As in most private languages, a large percentage of the words refer to sex, a fact glossed over in most touristy brochures on the topic. Most people don't know what the Boontling word for beer is, but the folks at the **Anderson Valley Brewing Company & Buckhorn Saloon,** a fine little microbrewery across from the Boonville Hotel, probably do. It's at 14081 Hwy 128, (707) 895-BEER. While you're in town, grab a copy of the *Anderson Valley Advertiser,* a rol-licking, crusading (some say muckraking) small-town paper with avid readers from as far away as San Francisco and the Oregon border. **Boont Berry Farm,** an organic-produce market and deli in a small, weathered-wood building, turns out terrific treats; 13981 Hwy 128, (707) 895-3576.

There's not much to see in the hamlet of **Philo,** but about 2 miles west you'll find Gowan's Oak Tree, a great family-run roadside fruit-and-vegetable stand with a few picnic tables in back and a swing for road-weary tots; 6350 Hwy 128, (707) 895-3353.

Located in the upper reaches of the California Wine Country, **Ukiah** is still what Napa, Sonoma, and Healdsburg used to be—a sleepy little agricultural town surrounded by vineyards and apple and pear orchards. Peopled by an odd mix of farmers, loggers, and back-to-the-landers, Ukiah is a down-to-earth little burg with few traces of Wine Country gen-trification. That doesn't mean there aren't any **wineries,** however. Among them is Mendocino County's oldest winery; founded in 1932, Parducci Wine Estates produces a variety of reds and whites; 501 Parducci Rd, (707) 462-WINE.

Soak away the aches and pains of your long drive (Ukiah is a long drive from almost anywhere) at the clothing-optional **Orr Hot Springs,** 13201 Orr Springs Rd, (707) 462-6277, or in North America's only warm and naturally carbonated mineral baths at Vichy Springs Resort (see Lodg-ings, below). In town, the main attraction is the **Grace Hudson Museum and Sun House,** featuring Hudson's paintings of Pomo Indians and a col-lection of beautiful Pomo baskets; 431 S Main St, (707) 467-2836.

Restaurants

All Seasons Café ☆☆　Many restaurants in Napa Valley have elaborate wine lists, but none compare to this cafe's award-winning roster. The All Seasons' menu is even structured around wine. So much emphasis is placed on wine, in fact, that the food sometimes suffers. *1400 Lincoln Ave (at Washington St), Calistoga; (707) 942-9111; $$.*

Babette's Restaurant & Wine Bar ☆☆☆☆　In a region where aspiring restaurants put as much, if not more, thought into decor as cuisine, Babette's is proof of the old adage that looks aren't everything. But never mind. The cuisine is incredible, and the service is superb. *464 1st St E (down an alley between E Spain and E Napa Sts), Sonoma; (707) 939-8921; $$–$$$.*

Bistro Don Giovanni ☆　As the name suggests, there is a touch of French bistro in this friendly Italian trattoria. The service is remarkably attentive and the atmosphere is joyous. *4110 St. Helena Hwy (on Hwy 29, just N of Salvador Ave), Napa; (707) 224-3300; $$.*

Bistro Ralph ☆　In a town where restaurants have been afflicted with the revolving door syndrome, simple yet stylish Bistro Ralph continues to thrive. Housed in a slender storefront on the square, this intimate bistro serves consistently excellent food, with a focus on local ingredients. *109 Plaza St E (on the plaza), Healdsburg; (707) 433-1380; $$.*

Brava Terrace ☆☆　Brava Terrace offers lively French-Mediterranean cuisine in an idyllic setting: the beautiful dining room has vaulted ceilings with exposed wood beams, white walls with bright modern art, glowing hardwood floors and furniture, and a big stone fireplace. *3010 St. Helena Hwy (on Hwy 29, between St. Helena and Calistoga, next to Freemark Abbey), St. Helena; (707) 963-9300; $$$.*

Brix ☆☆　Hawaiian influences infuse the eclectic cuisine at this Napa Valley newcomer, a refreshing addition to a restaurant scene that typically veers towards Mediterranean-style fare. The airy dining room has a crisp, slightly Asian feel. *7377 St. Helena Hwy (on Hwy 29, just N of town), Yountville; (707) 944-2749; $$$.*

Caffe Portofino ☆　Caffe Portofino's handsome oak dining room is always bustling and crowded with patrons. The vast California-Italian menu features more than 30 entrees, including meat, poultry, seafood, and an array of pastas. *535 4th St (between Mendocino Ave and B St), Santa Rosa; (707) 523-1171; $$.*

Catahoula ☆　The discrepancy between the chef's formal training and Catahoula's down-home fare turns out to be serendipitous, resulting in a glorious, spirited brand of nouvelle Southern cuisine. Although plunked in the middle of the Mount View Hotel, with its Old-West-meets-art-deco flavor, the dining room has a sophisticated, urban feel. *1457 Lincoln Ave (near Washington St), Calistoga; (707) 942-2275; $$.*

Château Souverain Cafe at the Winery ☆   This brightly painted restaurant offers a small menu of roast chicken, grilled salmon, and a few pasta dishes. Although it's not worth going out of your way to dine here, it's still a great place for an inexpensive bite to eat. *400 Souverain Rd (S of town; from US 101, take the Independence Lane exit), Geyserville; (707) 433-3141; $$.*

Della Santina's ☆   In addition to the small, trattoria-style dining room, Della Santina's has a wonderful vine-laced brick patio tucked in back. The menu includes a good selection of light to heavy house-made pastas, and wonderful meats from the rosticceria. *133 E Napa St (off 2nd St), Sonoma; (707) 935-0576; $$.*

The Diner ☆   Terrific, belly-packing breakfasts (don't pass up the huevos rancheros) have secured this restaurant's reputation for years, but lunches and dinners are good, too, with hearty, well-prepared Mexican dishes and seafood specialties supplementing the typical diner fare. *6476 Washington St (near Oak St), Yountville; (707) 944-2626; $.*

Domaine Chandon ☆☆☆☆   Napa Valley's culinary reputation was born at this elegant restaurant. Rooted in traditional French techniques enlivened by California innovation, the creative and delicate cooking style is perfectly matched to Domaine Chandon's sparkling wines. *1 California Dr (just W of Hwy 29), Yountville; (707) 944-2892; $$$.*

Ellie's Mutt Hut & Vegetarian Cafe ☆   There are a few notable places in Ukiah for a good, quick, cheap bite to eat, and this is one of them. Try thinking of the Mutt Hut as the Wiener schnitzel of an alternate universe. *732 S State St (from US 101, take the Talmadge St exit, then head N on S State St), Ukiah; (707) 468-5376; $.*

Foothill Cafe ☆☆   This place earns kudos for its delicious, meticulously prepared food—a small menu of meat, seafood, and vegetarian dishes, with an emphasis on local produce. The decor borders on whimsical, with papier-mâché animals, oddball salt and pepper shakers, and plaid tablecloths. *2766 Old Sonoma Rd (W of Hwy 29, near Foster Rd), Napa; (707) 252-6178; $$.*

The French Laundry ☆☆☆☆   This is the place you dream of stumbling upon in the French countryside: an unassuming old stone house (with no sign announcing its purpose) draped in ivy and surrounded by herb gardens, offering magnificent meals, stellar wines, and faultless service.

6640 Washington St (at Creek St), Yountville; (707) 944-2380; $$$.

Glen Ellen Inn ☆☆   If you're staying in Glen Ellen, it's nice to know you don't have to go far to find a good meal. In fact, this tiny, romantic restaurant is worth a drive from farther afield. The menu changes frequently, but always features local cuisine at its freshest and in beautiful preparations. *13670 Arnold Dr (at O'Donnell Lane), Glen Ellen; (707) 996-6409; $$.*

Hopland Brewery Brewpub and Beer Garden ☆   California's first brewpub since Prohibition (and the second in the nation), the Hopland Brewery is a refreshing break from the crushed-grape circuit. This quintessential brewpub has tasty grub, foot-stomping live music on Saturday (everything from the blues to Cajun), and eight fine beers brewed on the premises. *13351 US 101 (downtown), Hopland; (707) 744-1015; $.*

John Ash & Co. ☆☆☆☆   This casually elegant restaurant has topped the list of Santa Rosa's best restaurants for many years. It's pricey, but the service is expert, the food is fabulous, and the dining room is serene. The menu is a classic California hybrid of French, Italian, Asian, and Southwestern cuisines. *4330 Barnes Rd (next door to Vintners Inn, off River Rd, at US 101), Santa Rosa; (707) 527-7687; $$$.*

Kenwood Restaurant and Bar ☆   This large, sun-filled dining room with polished wood floors, a natural-pine ceiling, white linens, and bamboo chairs is the showcase for a changing menu. *9900 Sonoma Hwy (on Hwy 12, 3 miles past Glen Ellen), Kenwood; (707) 833-6326; $$.*

La Boucane ☆☆   Housed in a restored Victorian, Napa Valley's bastion of classic French cuisine has a small teal-and-rose dining room that glows with candles. The wine list is perfectly matched to the French fare. Despite the restaurant's old-fashioned decor, the atmosphere is delightfully unstuffy. *1778 2nd St (1 block E of Jefferson St), Napa; (707) 253-1177; $$$.*

Las Conchitas Restaurant ☆   Granted, it's not worth making a detour to Middletown for a taco, but if you happen to be passing through, stop at this small cantina and sample its crispy tortilla chips and fiery salsa. *21308 Calistoga St (on Hwy 29), Middletown; (707) 987-9454; $.*

Lisa Hemenway's ☆☆   Don't let the rather drab shopping center setting fool you—centered within this boxy brown shrine to the '70s is a refreshingly light, airy restaurant with alfresco dining and an inviting menu. *714 Village Ct (in the Village Court Mall/Montgomery Village, at Farmers Lane and Sonoma Ave), Santa Rosa; (707) 526-5111; $$.*

Mes Trois Filles ☆☆   This wisp of a restaurant in a small, gray clapboard storefront holds its own with the big guys, thanks to the chef's skillful rendition of French country fare with a soupçon of Japanese style. *13648 Arnold Dr (at Warm Springs Rd), Glen Ellen; (707) 938-4844; $$.*

Mustards Grill ☆   Some critics call the wildly popular Mustards' feisty American regional cuisine "comfort food," but that's too complacent a description for the vigorous, spicy, vaguely Asian-influenced bistro fare served here. *7399 St. Helena Hwy (on Hwy 29, just N of town), Yountville; (707) 944-2424; $$.*

Pinot Blanc ☆☆   Inside, the dark wood wainscoting, black leather banquettes, and nouveau ironwork evoke a French bistro. The food usually shines. *641 Main St (off Hwy 29), St. Helena; (707) 963-6191; $$$.*

Ristorante Piatti ☆☆   Piatti is a deservedly popular chain of good, chic, nouvelle Italian restaurants with outlets in cute, touristy towns throughout Northern California. Piatti has a large, open kitchen and an L-shaped dining room decorated in soft Mediterranean colors, with terracotta tile floors, light woods, and plenty of natural light. *6480 Washington St (S of the Vintage 1870 shopping complex), Yountville; (707) 944-2070; $$. 405 1st St W (in El Dorado Hotel, at W Spain St, facing the plaza's W side), Sonoma; (707) 996-2351; $$.*

Schat's Courthouse Bakery and Cafe ☆   What separates this bakery from the rest are the huge, more-than-you-can-possibly-eat lunch items: made-to-order sandwiches, build-your-own baked potatoes, and house-made soups, all for around five bucks. *113 W Perkins St (from US 101 take the Perkins St exit W; ½ block W of State St, across from the courthouse), Ukiah; (707) 462-1670; $.*

Terra ☆   Housed in a historic stone building, Terra's subdued dining rooms have an ineffable sense of intimacy about them. Fervid tête-à-têtes, however, are more likely to revolve around Terra's fine Southern French/ Northern Italian food than around amore. *1345 Railroad Ave (between Adams and Hunt Sts, 1 block E of Main St), St. Helena; (707) 963-8931; $$$.*

Tra Vigne / Cantinetta Tra Vigne ☆☆☆☆   It's become fashionable to trash this now-too-famous Tuscan-inspired temple to food and wine, but if you've never eaten at Tra Vigne, you haven't really done the Wine Country. If you'd prefer a light lunch or want your food to go, amble over to the less-expensive Cantinetta Tra Vigne out front, which also has patio seating. *1050 Charter Oak Ave (off Hwy 29), St. Helena; (707) 963-4444 (restaurant) or (707) 963-8888 (cantinetta); $$.*

Trilogy ☆   Despite its humble storefront setting, Trilogy doesn't have to shout to be heard over the culinary din of Napa Valley's competitive restaurant scene. What it lacks in glitz it more than makes up for with inspired California-French cuisine. An ever-changing prix-fixe menu is offered daily. *1234 Main St (near Hunt Ave), St. Helena; (707) 963-5507; $$.*

Wappo Bar & Bistro ☆☆   This zesty bistro offers cuisine that is hard to pinpoint, merrily skipping as it does from the Middle East to Europe to Asia to South America to the good old USA. This is ambitious, imaginative cooking, and the talented chefs usually pull it off with aplomb. *1226-B Washington St (off Lincoln Ave), Calistoga; (707) 942-4712; $$.*

Willowside Cafe ☆   Hiding out in a funky roadhouse a few miles from downtown Santa Rosa, Willowside may be Sonoma's best-kept dining secret. Inside, the mood is simple yet sophisticated—the perfect match for the California-French cuisine. *3535 Guerneville Rd (at Willowside Rd), Santa Rosa; (707) 523-4814; $$.*

Wine Spectator Restaurant at Greystone ☆   The Wine Spectator rates high for authentic Wine Country atmosphere, with old stone walls and deep-set ceiling windows in the dining room. The menu cuts a wide swath through the Mediterranean, with a touch of Spain, the south of France, Italy, and Greece. *Culinary Institute of America at Greystone, 2555 Main St (at Deer Park Rd), St. Helena; (707) 967-1010; $$.*

World Famous Hamburger Ranch and Pasta Farm ☆   Rave reviews from satisfied customers all over the world paper the walls of this converted service station, which was voted the purveyor of Sonoma County's Best Burger by readers of the *Santa Rosa Press Democrat*. *31195 Redwood Hwy (at the N end of town at the top of the hill), Cloverdale; (707) 894-5616; $.*

Lodgings

Auberge du Soleil ☆☆☆☆   This exclusive 33-acre, 52-unit resort, inspired by the sunny architecture of southern France, is nestled in an olive grove on a wooded hillside above the Napa Valley. Its 11 original cottages have rough-textured adobe-style walls, white French doors and windows, and smashing views of the valley. *180 Rutherford Hill Rd (N of Yountville; from the Silverado Trail, turn right on Rutherford Hill Rd), Rutherford; (707) 963-1211 or (800) 348-5406; $$$.*

Belle de Jour Inn ☆   In a region where rampant Victoriana is all the rage, Belle de Jour's 4 romantic hillside cottages and large carriage house have a refreshingly spare, uncluttered feel. *16276 Healdsburg Ave (1 mile N of Dry Creek Rd, across from Simi Winery), Healdsburg; (707) 431-9777; $$$.*

The Boonville Hotel and Restaurant ☆ The decor of the Boonville Hotel is pleasantly austere. The beautiful wood bar downstairs and most of the exquisite furniture in the 10 guest rooms are the work of local craftspeople. The restaurant in the Boonville Hotel, a gathering spot for local winemakers, is still one of the best north of the Napa Valley. *On Hwy 128 (at Lambert Lane, in the center of town), Boonville; (707) 895-2210; $$$.*

Churchill Manor ☆☆ Churchill Manor is an elegant, meticulously maintained mansion, incongruously set in a modest neighborhood. This 1889 colonial revival house is listed on the National Register of Historic Places. *485 Brown St (at Oak St), Napa; (707) 253-7733; $$.*

Crossroads Inn ☆ The three most important factors in real estate—location, location, location—make the Crossroads Inn an ideal retreat. Perched on a hillside 500 feet off the valley floor, this modest and homey 4-room B&B wins for Best View in the Wine Country. *6380 Silverado Trail (1½ miles E of Yountville, at the Yountville Cross Rd), Napa; (707) 944-0646; $$$.*

El Dorado Hotel ☆☆ If you've had it with cutesy B&Bs, El Dorado Hotel is a welcome respite, offering 26 moderately priced rooms modestly decorated with terra-cotta tile floors, handcrafted furniture, and down comforters. *405 1st St W (at W Spain St, on the plaza's W side), Sonoma; (707) 996-2351 or (800) 289-3031; $$.*

Fountaingrove Inn ☆ The Fountaingrove's 84 rooms are elegant to the point of austerity, with gray carpets, gray bedspreads, mirrored walls, and pen-and-ink drawings of horses over the beds. It all seems very serious (and very '70s), perhaps because the motel caters more to business travelers than to tourists. *101 Fountaingrove Pkwy (at Mendocino Ave), Santa Rosa; (707) 578-6101 or (800) 222-6101; $$$.*

The Gables Bed and Breakfast ☆ This gothic Victorian is the house of not 7 but rather 15 gables. The 8 cheerful guest rooms in this historic landmark are decorated with antiques and old-fashioned furnishings. *4257 Petaluma Hill Rd (4 miles from the Rohnert Park Expwy), Santa Rosa; (707) 585-7777; $$$.*

Gaige House Inn ☆ From the outside, the Gaige House looks like yet another spiffed-up Victorian mansion. Inside, however, the Victorian theme comes to a screeching halt. All 11 rooms are spectacular, and each is individually decorated with an eclectic mix of modern art. *13540 Arnold Dr (from Hwy 12, take the Glen Ellen exit), Glen Ellen; (707) 935-0237 or (800) 935-0237; $$$.*

Glenelly Inn ☆☆   A graceful grove of oak trees forms the backdrop for this inn, originally built in 1916 as a lodging for railway travelers. The 8 guest rooms, each with private entrances, down comforters, and private bathrooms, open onto the elaborate garden or the veranda, which offers a fine view of the Sonoma Valley and the tree-covered mountains beyond. *5131 Warm Springs Rd (off Arnold Dr), Glen Ellen; (707) 996-6720; $$.*

Harvest Inn ☆   If you can't get enough of Merrie Olde England but demand all the conveniences of the 20th century, this is the place for you. With its Tudor-inspired architecture, the Harvest Inn works hard to evoke the spirit of an earlier time and another place. The 54 immaculate guest rooms are all outfitted with antiques. *1 Main St (off Hwy 29), St. Helena; (707) 963-9463 or (800) 950-8466; $$$.*

Healdsburg Inn on the Plaza ☆   Originally built as a Wells Fargo Express office in 1900, this surprisingly quiet inn on the plaza has high ceilings and a lovely old staircase leading from the ground-floor art gallery to the 10 attractive guest rooms upstairs. *110 Matheson St (on the plaza's south side), Healdsburg; (707) 433-6991 or (800) 431-8663; $$$.*

Hope–Bosworth House ☆☆   Across the street from its showier cousin, the Hope–Merrill House, the 4-room 1904 Queen Anne–style Hope–Bosworth House provides a cheery, informal, and less-expensive place to stay. *21238 Geyserville Ave (from US 101, take the Geyserville exit), Geyserville; (707) 857-3356 or (800) 825-4BED; $$.*

Hope–Merrill House ☆   Since nearly every mediocre shack built in the late 19th century gets dubbed "Victorian," it's easy to forget the dizzying architectural and design heights reached during this period. This beautifully restored 8-room 1870 Eastlake gothic will remind you. *21253 Geyserville Ave (from US 101, take the Geyserville exit), Geyserville; (707) 857-3356 or (800) 825-4BED; $$.*

Indian Springs Resort ☆   This historic inn offers 17 rustic and casually furnished wooden cottages with partial kitchens, which appeal to families eager to cavort in the resort's huge hot-springs-fed swimming pool. Indian Springs also offers a playground and the full gamut of spa services. *1712 Lincoln Ave (between Wappo Ave and Brannan St, next to the Calistoga Gliderport), Calistoga; (707) 942-4913; $$$.*

The Ink House Bed and Breakfast ☆   This gorgeous 7-room Italianate Victorian inn, built in the shape of an ink bottle by Napa settler Theron Ink in 1884, would merit three stars if it weren't for its no-star location alongside a busy, noisy stretch of Hwy 29. *1575 St. Helena Hwy (at Whitehall Lane), St. Helena; (707) 963-3890; $$$.*

Inn at Southbridge ☆ This new sister to the swanky Meadowood Resort fills the gap between Napa's ultra-luxe digs and its ubiquitous bed-and-breakfast inns. The 21 guest rooms are almost Shaker in their elegant simplicity. *1020 Main St (between Charter Oak Ave and Pope St), St. Helena; (707) 967-9400 or (800) 520-6800; $$$.*

Kenwood Inn ☆ This posh inn resembles a centuries-old Italian pensione. The 12 guest rooms are beautifully decorated, each with a fluffy feather bed, a fireplace, and a sitting area. *10400 Sonoma Hwy (on Hwy 12, 3 miles past Glen Ellen), Kenwood; (707) 833-1293; $$$.*

La Residence ☆☆ Set back in the trees along busy Hwy 29, this is one of the valley's most luxurious bed and breakfasts. Twenty guest rooms are scattered throughout two houses separated by a heated swimming pool and an elaborate gazebo. *4066 St. Helena Hwy (on Hwy 29, next to Bistro Don Giovanni), Napa; (707) 253-0337; $$$.*

Madrona Manor ☆ Surrounded by lush green lawns, exotic gardens, and a citrus orchard, Madrona Manor looks a lot like a cheerier version of the Addams Family's gothic abode. The inn's 21 rooms and 3 suites are divided between the main house and the carriage house. *1001 Westside Rd (at Dry Creek Rd), Healdsburg; (707) 433-4231 or (800) 258-4003; $$$.*

Maison Fleurie ☆☆ Built in 1873, this beautiful, ivy-covered brick-and-fieldstone hotel was reborn as Maison Fleurie in 1994 and endowed with a French country feel. Seven of the guest rooms are located in the main house; the remaining six are divided between the old bakery building and the carriage house. *6529 Yount St (at Washington St), Yountville; (707) 944-2056; $$$.*

Meadowood Resort ☆☆☆☆ Rising out of a surreal green sea of fairways and croquet lawns, Meadowood's pearl-gray, New England–style mansions are resolutely Eastern. The 85 exorbitantly priced accommodations range from one-room studios to four-room suites. *900 Meadowood Lane (off the Silverado Trail), St. Helena; (707) 963-3646 or (800) 458-8080; $$$.*

Oak Knoll Inn ☆ This French country–inspired hostelry is blessed with one of the most serene, isolated settings of any Napa Valley B&B: it sits amid 600 acres of spectacular vineyards. It may be just the ticket if you're seeking a respite from Victorian clutter or Wine Country cutesiness. *2200 E Oak Knoll Ave (off the Silverado Trail, 3 miles S of Yountville), Napa; (707) 255-2200; $$$.*

Philo Pottery Inn ☆☆ This 1888 redwood farmhouse is pure and authentic country—no frilly ruffles, no overdressed dolls, just a lavender-filled English garden in the front yard and bright handmade quilts and sturdy frontier furnishings in each of the 5 guest rooms. *8550 Hwy 128 (in town), Philo; (707) 895-3069; $$.*

Quail Mountain Bed and Breakfast ☆☆   Quail Mountain is a good choice for people who want to escape the bustle of the valley floor but still want to be near the action. The bad news is that this idyllic place is almost always booked; you'd be wise to make reservations several months in advance. *4455 St. Helena Hwy (from Hwy 29 turn left just after Dunaweal Lane and follow the signs), Calistoga; (707) 942-0316; $$$.*

Sanford House Bed and Breakfast ☆☆   There's something indisputably small-town about this tall, yellow Victorian inn on a tree-lined street just west of Ukiah's Mayberry-like downtown. Inside, antiques grace each of the 5 rooms. *306 Pine St S (from US 101, take the Perkins St exit, head W, and turn left on Pine), Ukiah; (707) 462-1653; $$.*

Scott Courtyard ☆☆   Just a short jaunt away from Calistoga's best shops, spas, and restaurants, the Scott Courtyard B&B offers 6 comfortable suites with private entrances and baths in a quiet, tree-lined residential neighborhood. *1443 2nd St (off Washington St), Calistoga; (707) 942-0948; $$$.*

Sonoma Chalet ☆☆   Every room in this secluded Swiss-style farmhouse overlooks the grassy hills of a 200-acre ranch. Fact is, you're three-quarters of a mile from Sonoma's town square. If you're looking for a low-key, rustic, and romantic retreat, it's a good choice, particularly if you reserve one of the cottages. *18935 5th St W (follow 5th St W to the end, then continue W on the gravel road), Sonoma; (707) 938-3129; $$.*

Sonoma Mission Inn & Spa ☆   With its ethereally serene grounds and elegant pink stucco buildings, the Sonoma Mission Inn feels a bit like a convent—except that novitiates wear white terrycloth bathrobes or colorful running suits instead of nuns' habits. *18140 Sonoma Hwy (on Hwy 12, at Boyes Blvd), Boyes Hot Springs; (707) 938-9000 or (800) 862-4945 (in California only), (800) 358-9022 (outside California); $$$.*

Thatcher Inn ☆   Built as a stage stop in 1890, this haughty cream-colored combination of gothic spires and gabled windows still looks like a luxurious frontier saloon-hotel. A wide, curving wood stairway leads from the lobby to 20 charmingly decorated guest rooms. *13401 Hwy 101 (downtown), Hopland; (707) 744-1890 or (800) 266-1891; $$$.*

Vichy Springs Resort ☆   These are North America's only naturally carbonated mineral baths. With such a distinction, one would expect the resort to be ringed by four-star accommodations and fancy bathhouses, but it is far from posh, though 5 new creekside rooms and a new two-bedroom cottage bring the accommodations up a notch. *2605 Vichy Springs Rd (from US 101, take the Vichy Springs Rd exit and head W), Ukiah; (707) 462-9515; $$$.*

Victorian Garden Inn ☆ This 1870s Greek revival farmhouse with a wraparound veranda has one of the most inviting small gardens you'll ever see. The inn's 4 guest rooms, decorated in white wicker and florals, are pretty, if a bit cloying. *316 E Napa St (between 3rd St E and 4th St E, 2 blocks from the plaza), Sonoma; (707) 996-5339; $$.*

Vintage Inn ☆☆ Spread throughout a 23-acre estate, the Vintage Inn provides the Napa Valley traveler with a host of creature comforts in a modern setting. The 80 large, cheery rooms, bathed in soothing earth tones and wood accents, are all equipped with fireplaces, Jacuzzi tubs, and plush private baths. *6541 Washington St (just E of Hwy 29), Yountville; (707) 944-1112 or (800) 351-1133; $$$.*

Vintage Towers Bed and Breakfast Inn ☆☆ Listed on the National Register of Historic Places, this beautiful mauve mansion located on a quiet residential street has 7 air-conditioned guest rooms. *302 N Main St (at 3rd St, off Cloverdale Blvd), Cloverdale; (707) 894-4535; $$.*

Vintners Inn ☆☆ The Vintners Inn combines the charm of a country inn with the conveniences of a modern hotel. Its four Provençal-style buildings are clustered around a central courtyard set amid vineyards. *4350 Barnes Rd (off River Rd, at US 101), Santa Rosa; (707) 575-7350 or (800) 421-2584; $$$.*

More Information

Calistoga Chamber of Commerce: *(707) 942-6333.*
Geyserville Chamber of Commerce: *(707) 857-3745.*
Napa Chamber of Commerce: *(707) 226-7455.*
Napa Valley Conference and Visitors Bureau: *(707) 226-7459.*
Napa Valley Tourist Bureau: *(707) 944-1558.*
Santa Rosa Chamber of Commerce: *(707) 545-1414.*
Sonoma Chamber of Commerce: *(707) 996-1033.*
St. Helena Chamber of Commerce: *(707) 963-4456.*

Clear Lake Region

The area surrounding Clear Lake, including Clear Lake State Park, Anderson Marsh State Historic Park, Sonoma and Mendocino Lakes, Cache Creek, and the Indian Valley Reservoir area.

Spend a lazy, warm afternoon in an aluminum fishing boat bobbing around in the pooled waters of a shady cove on Clear Lake, and the best way to keep track of time is to count the number of catfish you've snagged. We reeled in 16 in just a few hours. In fact, the biting was so regular and predictable it was almost annoying—we never got a chance to just sit there doing nothing, which is supposed to be the whole point of fishing in the first place, right? Clear Lake, the largest natural lake in the state, prides itself on its famed bass fishery anyway, so a bucket full of catfish is really nothing to brag about. At one time Clear Lake was primarily a resort area that cleared out during the off season. But with an increasing number of year-round residents, many of them retirees who have waited their whole lives for the day they could fish and do little else, the region is undergoing a metamorphosis of sorts. It now grapples with many of the same problems the big city must contend with: crime, unemployment, and environmental issues like the loss of natural wetlands. With a large number of private resorts and some well-appointed public recreation areas to choose from, however, this is among the best non-alpine lake settings anglers can hope to stumble upon.

Clear Lake State Park and the adjacent Anderson Marsh State Historic Park have superior lake access, while 100 miles of shoreline consist of numerous private marinas and resorts. There are also other options in the Clear Lake region at large—some of which have nothing to do with fishing! Lake Sonoma, Indian Valley Reservoir, and Lake Mendocino are viable alternatives to Clear Lake, each offering something a bit different: Indian Valley is more secluded and quiet, while Mendocino has more of a water sports emphasis. And, of course, there's no need to stick to lake action exclusively: Cache Creek, which drains from the lake region down the northern Sacramento Valley, is an ideal rafting spot, for example. There is no way to do it all, so just choose a place and activity and go with it.

Getting There

Clear Lake is bisected by Highway 20 and Highway 29. It can be approached easily from the northern Sacramento Valley (go west from Interstate 5 on Highway 20), from the US Highway 101 (US 101) corridor on Highway 20 (go east), or from the Napa Valley (go north on Highway 29). Highways 20 and 29 are little more than glorified country roads, so leave plenty of driving time and be careful. Stop in at the Clear Lake Chamber of Commerce, 4700 Golf Avenue, in the town of Clearlake, (707) 263-5092; or the Lakeport Chamber of Commerce, 290 South Main Street, Lakeport, (707) 263-5092, for information on day facilities and private resorts.

Adjoining Areas

NORTH: **Mendocino National Forest**

SOUTH: **Napa and Sonoma Wine Valleys**

EAST: **Sacramento Valley**

WEST: **Sonoma and Southern Mendocino Coast**

inside out

Fishing/Boating

Clear Lake, at nearly 70 square miles, is the largest natural lake in California, and because it tends to fill up faster than it drains during heavy rains, sometimes it literally overflows like a plugged kitchen sink, especially when El Niño is in town. With more than 100 miles of shoreline, it contains one of the finest **bass** fisheries in the state. **Nighttime fishing** under the full moon of summer is particularly rewarding here. While bass is the main fare, the **bluegill, catfish,** and **crappie** also bite a good percentage of the time. Clear Lake State Park and Horseshoe Bend, which lies to the east of the state park, are considered the best fishing spots for bass in early March through mid-June. These areas are also the main access points for recreation on the lake. **Public boat ramps** are located all around the lake: at Redbud Park in the town of Clearlake on Lakeshore Dr, (707) 994-8201; at Lakeside County Park in Kelseyville, on Park Dr; at five locations along the waterfront in Lakeport; at Lucerne Harbor County Park off Hwy 20 in Lucerne; and at H.V. Keeling County Park on Lakeshore Blvd in Nice. From Napa, take Hwy 175 north to Hwy 29 north. Proceed to Kelseyville and turn right on Main St. Turn right on Gaddy Lane, then right on Soda Bay Rd. Proceed to the park entrance. For more information, contact Clear Lake State Park at (707) 279-4293. There are numerous marinas and resorts around the lake with full fish and tackle shops, slips, and **boat rentals.** Among the most reputable are Ferndale Resort & Marina, 6190 Soda Bay Rd, Kelseyville, (707) 279-4866, and Talley's Family Resort, 3827 Hwy 20, Nice, (707) 274-1177.

Indian Valley Reservoir, about 15 miles east of Clear Lake, was formed in 1974 when Cache Creek was dammed. The lake is a bit smaller and less visited than Clear Lake because of its location off the main highway and its relative lack of amenities. As at Clear Lake, however, the **bass** and **bluegill** fishing, particularly top fishing at night, is quite good in the spring. There are a boat ramp and tackle facility near the dam; it's up to you to bring the rest. The lake's northern edge is a popular fishing spot in the spring; in the summer the west shore is more crowded. From the town of Clearlake, take Hwy 53 east, and exit north to Indian Valley. The US Bureau of Land Management (BLM) runs a campground on the lake (see Camping, below). Most facilities are near the dam. Call (707) 468-4000.

Lake Mendocino was created on the Russian River's east fork 40 years ago. The lake covers some 1,800 acres and supports a healthy fishery of striped, largemouth and smallmouth **bass, bluegill, catfish,** and **crappie.** There are two public boat launch areas on the lake, both with six lanes. One is at the Che-Ka-Ka section of the south shore on Lake Mendocino Dr. The other is at Lake Mendocino Marina, just east of Calpella on the north end of the lake, on Marina Dr. The marina also has **boat rentals** and slips and is the main gathering spot for those interested in sports such as waterskiing (equipment rentals are available). For information, contact the US Army Corps of Engineers office in Ukiah, (707) 462-7581, or the marina at (707) 485-8644. To reach the lake, head east on Hwy 20 from Calpella on the US 101 corridor or west on Hwy 20 from the Clearlake area. The lake is south of the highway at Lake Ridge Dr, clearly marked and easily accessible.

Naturally, there are a number of obvious options when it comes to **tackle and outfitters** in an area where bass fishing is so central. Our favorite way to scrounge up bait, however, is to scoop up crayfish living in the still, coved areas of the lake and just whittle them down into chunks.

This is particularly effective in summer catfish season. Among reputable bait and tackle dealers in the lake region, however, are Don's Bait Shop, 4531 Lakeshore Dr, Clearlake, (707) 994-6279; Lakeport Tackle, 1050 N Main St, Lakeport, (707) 263-8862; and Ron's Grocery & Tackle, 800 Lake Mendocino Dr, Ukiah, (707) 462-2622.

Rafting

The main river action in this part of the state is on the upper section of **Cache Creek,** which flows southeast through the canyons of the northern Sacramento Valley from just below Clear Lake. Good runs are possible all summer if timed correctly with flow controls out of Indian Valley Reservoir. The run is best taken on a two-day trip, mostly paralleling Hwy 16 between the towns of Rumsey and Madison. The creek is ideal for beginners who are not quite ready for the whitewater death-drops found on other Northern California rivers. One good **outfitter** running regularly scheduled trips on the Cache is Whitewater Adventures of Napa, (707) 944-2222. Trips are usually scheduled through September in normal water-level years. To run the creek freestyle, take Hwy 16 west from Woodland or east from Clear Lake, and look for **put-ins** at Rumsey, Guinda, and Brooks.

Parks

Clear Lake State Park sits on the south banks of Clear Lake, and as you might imagine, much of the park's activity revolves around boating and fishing. Camping and hiking are other outdoor activities that dominate this 500-acre park. **Mount Konocti,** an active volcano that has been quiet for the past 10,000 years or so, stands 4,200 feet above the water level. While the water's edge of the park can get quite crowded on warm summer days, the park's steep elevations of 1,320 to 1,600 feet keep most visitors away from the interior reaches, where the campgrounds and nature trails are found. From Napa, take Hwy 175 north to Hwy 29 north. Proceed to Kelseyville and turn right on Main St. Turn right on Gaddy Lane. Turn right on Soda Bay Rd. Proceed to park entrance. For more information, contact Clear Lake State Park at (707) 279-4293.

The 1,000 acres encompassing **Anderson Marsh State Historic Park** on Clear Lake (see Wildlife, below) contain freshwater marshes, grasslands, oak woodlands, and riparian woodlands. The diverse habitats within the park make it a nature-lover's paradise. By far, the park's most outstanding feature is the marshland. While 84 percent of Clear Lake's marshland has been destroyed, the Anderson Marsh provides breeding areas for many species of bird, mammal, reptile, and amphibian. The park is open 10am to 5pm Monday through Sunday. From Hwy 53 north, you'll find a parking facility at the park headquarters on the left side of the road. For information, contact the park at (707) 944-0688.

In 1949, the state purchased **Boggs Mountain Demonstration State Forest** from Claso Lumber Company. The forest at that time had been effectively clear-cut, with the exception of a few inaccessible valleys. Today the 3,493-acre forest is used for forestry experiments and for demonstrating the economic possibilities of good forest management. Outdoor enthusiasts with a penchant for forestry will want to see this area but also should venture to Jackson State Demonstration Forest near Fort Bragg. The forest sports several hiking and biking trails as well as a campground. From Kelseyville, take Hwy 175 south to Hobergs. Proceed south 0.75 mile to the forest entrance on the east side of the highway. For more information, contact the forest at (707) 928-4378.

Wildlife

Come to the Clear Lake area at the right time of summer and you'll swear the only wildlife here is the plain ol' mosquito. Bring repellent along, however, and there are plenty of other animals to watch, observe, and enjoy. The best bet for bird-watchers is to hit the trails at the Anderson Marsh State Historic Park on Clear Lake, where **mallard ducks** and **western grebes** make their foraging grounds. The riparian woodlands adjacent to the marsh house a wide variety of birds, including **great horned owls, bald eagles** in the winter, and **great blue herons.**

Also along the marsh and riparian woods at Anderson, watch for **pond turtles, muskrats, river otter,** and **gray fox.** Within the park's oak woodlands, find **deer** and **squirrel, black-tailed hare,** and **rattlesnakes.** The park is open from 10am to 5pm, Monday through Sunday. From Hwy 53 north, you'll find a parking facility at the park headquarters on the left side of the road. For information, contact the park at (707) 944-0688.

Hiking

For hikers looking to experience the sights and scenery of a freshwater marsh, there is no better place than **Anderson Marsh State Historic Park** (see Parks, above). **Cache Creek Nature Trail** (easy; 2.2 miles round trip) is a level hiking trail that meanders through the park's riparian ecological community, along the banks of a creek flowing into the marshland. The **Ridge** and **Marsh Trails** (easy; 2.5 miles round trip) travel along the marsh and up though a higher elevation of oak woodland, providing an up-close glimpse into the unique and rapidly diminishing freshwater marsh habitat. To reach the trailheads for all of these trails, take Hwy 53 north to the park's headquarters and parking facility on the west side of the road. For park information, call (707) 944-0688.

While **Clear Lake State Park** is relatively small at 500 acres, the park has a few trails that meander about its hilly terrain, as well as ranger-guided morning nature walks. **Dorn Trail** (easy; 2 miles round trip) winds through oak woodlands and provides hikers with beautiful views over Clear Lake. **Indian Nature Trail** (easy; 0.25 mile round trip) is a self-guiding nature trail near the park office, with explanations of how the local Indians used the native plants for their daily needs. From Napa, take Hwy 175 north to Hwy 29 north. Proceed to Kelseyville and turn right on Main St. Turn right on Gaddy Lane, then right on Soda Bay Rd, and proceed to the park entrance. Indian Nature Trail begins at the park office. The Dorn trailhead is at the visitors center. For more information, contact Clear Lake State Park at (707) 279-4293.

Camping

Clear Lake State Park has 150 sites divided into four sections (no hookups; varying RV lengths accomodated) around the lake's western shores, among oak woods and near a boat launch and good fishing spots. Each site is equipped with a picnic table and fire grill, with rest rooms, showers, and running water nearby. *Call state parks reservations, (800) 444-7275, to secure a spot; particularly during the summer. For general directions, the park may be reached at (707) 279-4293. To reach the campground, take Hwy 29 west from the town of Lower Lake for 8.5 miles to Soda Bay Rd. Continue north on Soda Bay another 9.5 miles to the park entrance, on the east side of the road.*

Blue Oak Camp has 6 sites (no hookups; varying RV lengths accomodated) in oak woods on the western banks of a nice fishing lake at **Indian Valley Reservoir** just east of Clear Lake, and it's popular with bass anglers who don't want to contend with crowds. Each site has a picnic table and fire pit, with running water and pit toilets nearby. There is a smaller camp on the east side of the lake, with just 1 site for tents only. *Contact the BLM, (707) 468-4000, for information. No reservations. To reach the camp, take Hwy 20 for 18 miles east of Clearlake Oaks, then go 4 miles north on Walker Ridge Rd; go west at the four-way intersection. It's another 3 miles to the campground on the north side of the road. This is a dirt road, so call ahead for conditions before taking the drive up.*

Cache Creek Regional Park has 45 sites (no hookups; varying RV lengths accomodated) on the banks of a popular rafting creek in the canyons north of Davis, in Yolo County. Each site has a picnic table and grill, with running water and flush toilets nearby. No reservations are taken. *Call the park at (530) 666-8115. To reach the camp, take I-505 north* *from I-80 (between Vacaville and Davis) for 20 miles to Hwy 16. Head west on Hwy 16 toward Lake Berryessa for 60 miles to the park.*

Boggs Mountain Demonstration Forest has 15 primitive campsites (no running water, but pit toilets are available) with fire rings at **Calso Camp.** Naturally, the campground generally attracts only experienced campers who are looking for a rugged, primitive camping experience. Surprisingly, however, the campground can fill up rather quickly, especially during the spring and summer season. Reservations are not taken. *From Kelseyville, take Hwy 175 south to Hobergs. Proceed south 0.75 mile to the forest entrance on the east side of the highway. For more information, contact the forest at (707) 928-4378.*

Biking

The Napa and Sonoma Valley wine regions are better suited for **road cycling** than the lake area to the north (see Napa and Sonoma Wine Valleys chapter), but there are some nice lakeside rides here nonetheless. **Soda Bay Road** takes off from the intersection of Hwys 175 and 29 south of Lakeport and traverses much of the south shore of Clear Lake, passing through Clear Lake State Park (see Parks, above). From the Hwy 175/29 junction, head east for 5 miles, then follow Hwy 281 to the Hwy 29 junction for the loop back. In all, it is a 15-mile ride, much of it on the waterfront or passing near Buckingham, Wright, Howard, and Sugarloaf Peaks.

Lake Mendocino, east of Ukiah, also has a nice road system surrounding it. Take **Marina** and **Lake Ridge Roads** south from the Hwy 20 junction with the lake for a pleasant 4-mile ride to **Coyote Dam** on the Russian River's east fork.

Mountain bikes are welcome in most parks in the Clear Lake area, but this is really not the place to rock and roll, as most lakeside trails are primarily used by campers, anglers, vacationing families, and the like. Still, because of the lake's size and the arrangement of recreation facilities, a mountain bike is a great way to get around. Those bent on tearing up the trails should head for Mendocino National Forest outside the wilderness areas (see Mendocino National Forest chapter). Bikes are not allowed in Anderson Marsh State Historic Park. Dave's Bike Shop, 846 S State St, Ukiah, (707) 462-3230, and Fetzer Cycles, 290 Seminary Ave, Ukiah, (707) 462-4419, are reputable **outfitters** on the US 101 side of the lake region. On the Clear Lake side, try the Bike Rack, 302 N Main St, Lakeport, (707) 263-1200. Another good resource is the Eagle Cycling Club, (707) 226-7066, www.napanet.net/~eccweb/, which organizes and sponsors numerous rides in the Napa Valley area each month.

Adventure Calendar

American Bass Team Tournament, mid-January: *at Redbud Park, Clearlake, (707) 837-0158.*

American Bass Pro/AAA, late March: *at Redbud Park, Clearlake, (707) 837-0158.*

WON Bass Tournament, late April: *at Redbud Park, Clearlake, (916) 442-9711.*

West Coast Bass Tournament, early May: *at Redbud Park, Clearlake, (916) 635-0111.*

Baja Racing Jet-Ski Race, late June: *Austins Beach, Clear Lake, (707) 994-3600.*

International Worm Races, July 4: *at Redbud Park, Clearlake; the first nightcrawler to inch its way out of a circle wins; $2 entry fee, (707) 994-3600.*

outside in

Attractions

California's largest freshwater lake, **Clear Lake** once had more than 30 **wineries** ringing its shore. Prohibition put an end to all that in 1919. The land was converted to walnut and Bartlett pear orchards, and only in the last few decades have the grapes (and the wineries) been making a comeback. This area may one day become as celebrated as Napa and Sonoma, but here's generally not a whole lot going on until the weekend boaters and anglers arrive. Clear Lake's big annual blowout is the **Fourth of July Festival,** when thousands of born-again patriots amass (and timorous locals split) for a three-day sunburnt orgy of flag-waving, fireworks, and waterskiing.

With its small, old-fashioned downtown, **Lakeport** is the prettiest town on Clear Lake. Formerly known as Forbestown (after early settler William Forbes), the town is usually very peaceful until people from out-lying cities pack up their Jeeps and station wagons and caravan out here in the summer for fishing, camping, swimming, and wine-tasting. Folks also flock to Lakeport every Labor Day weekend for the **Lake County Fair,** featuring 4-H exhibits, livestock auctions, horse shows, and a carnival; it's held at the fairgrounds, 401 Martin St, (707) 263-6181.

For more information on Clear Lake and its surrounding towns and wineries, call or drop by the **Lake County Visitor Information Center;** at 875 Lakeport Blvd, Vista Point, Lakeport, (707) 263-9544 or (800) LAKESIDE.

Restaurants

Park Place ☆☆   Ever since the Loon's Nest restaurant in nearby Kelseyville closed, there hasn't been much debate over Lake County's best restaurant. It's Park Place—a small lakeside cafe serving very good Italian food. *50 3rd St (off Main St, near the lake), Lakeport; (707) 263-0444; $$.*

Lodgings

Featherbed Railroad Company ☆   Nine cabooses that look as though they would be right at home in Disneyland are spread out underneath a grove of oak trees at this gimmicky but fun bed and breakfast. *2870 Lakeshore Blvd (off Hwy 20, at the SW end of town), Nice; (707) 274-8378 or (800) 966-6322; $$.*

The Forbestown Inn ☆   Located only a few blocks from the lake, this wisteria-draped, cream-and-brown Victorian house dates back to 1869, when Lakeport was still known as Forbestown. Each of the inn's 4 guest rooms is pleasantly decorated with fine American antiques, Laura Ashley fabrics, and piles of hand-stitched pillows atop queen- and king-size beds. *825 Forbes St (1 block W of Main St, downtown), Lakeport; (707) 263-7858; $$.*

Konocti Harbor Resort & Spa ☆   The Clear Lake area isn't known for its swanky accommodations and restaurants, but this 250-room mega-resort is the fanciest place around. The resort's accommodations range from standard no-frills rooms to suites, apartments, and beach cottages set on a large lawn that leads down to the lake. *8727 Soda Bay Rd (off Hwy 29), Kelseyville; (707) 279-4281 or (800) 660-LAKE; $$.*

More Information

Clearlake Chamber of Commerce: *(707) 994-3600.*
Clear Lake State Park: *(707) 279-4293.*
Lakeport Chamber of Commerce: *(707) 263-5092.*
State parks camping reservations: *(800) 444-7275.*

Mendocino National Forest

One million acres of wilderness, 35 miles wide and 65 miles long, extending north from Lake County, including the Yolla Bolly–Middle Eel Wilderness, Snow Mountain Wilderness, Lake Pillsbury, and the Corning, Covelo, Stonyford, and Upper Lake Ranger Districts.

A million of anything sounds like an awful lot. Imagine a million jelly beans. A million birds in the sky. A million strikes of lightning. In the case of Mendocino National Forest, a million acres of working wilderness—covering an area of mountains, lakes, meadows, and forests 65 miles long and 35 miles wide—means a million things to do. Hikers take to the deep wilderness trails, campers settle into secluded campgrounds or pack in to that secret spot, off-roaders take off on the rugged forest roads where you actually have to use the four-wheel drive. Mountain bikers contend with sometimes steep and rugged roads; a day ride becomes a two-day bike-camp expedition. Fishing, boating, hang gliding, you name it—you won't run out of outdoor options.

Most of the activity in Mendocino National Forest revolves around the two wilderness areas: Snow Mountain Wilderness, in the southern end of the forest near Clear Lake, and Yolla Bolly–Middle Eel Wilderness in the northern end. Take a hike 7,056 feet up to the summit of East Peak, passing through three distinct types of terrain in the more than 5,000-foot elevation gain. Dive off the top for some hang gliding. Go on a rock hunt. Or head to Lake Pillsbury, with 31 miles of shoreline and more than 2,200 acres of its surface, considered by many to be Mendocino's crown jewel—but don't rush to judgment so quickly. There are a million places to explore.

Getting There

Some forest roads traversing Mendocino National Forest are not suitable for travel in passenger vehicles, so check with ranger stations and obtain forest maps before venturing too far. Highway 20 between Upper Lake and Williams, west of Interstate 5, offers the most direct access to the south sections of the forest, including Lake Pillsbury. North of Williams on Interstate 5, the most direct access to the Snow Mountain Wilderness is on Forest Road M10 from Stonyford. Still north, Forest Road M4 from Paskenta and Forest Road FH7 from Covelo are the main access points to the Yolla Bolly–Middle Eel Wilderness. For a road map, stop in at any of the following locations, or send a written request with a $4 payment: Upper Lake Ranger District, Middlecreek Road (PO Box 96), Upper Lake, CA 95485, (707) 275-2361; Stonyford Ranger District, 5080 Lodoga Road, Stonyford, CA 95979, (530) 963-3128; Covelo Ranger District, 78150 Covelo Road, Covelo, CA 95428, (707) 983-6118; and Corning Ranger District, 22000 Corning Road (PO Box 1019), Corning, CA 96021, (530) 824-5196.

Adjoining Areas

NORTH: **Smith River National Recreation Area**

SOUTH: **Clear Lake Region**

EAST: **Sacramento Valley**

WEST: **Sonoma and Southern Mendocino Coasts**

inside out

Camping

As with most of the national forests in California, camping in Mendocino National Forest is allowed just about anywhere you can find a piece of ground flat enough to pitch a tent on—with just a few exceptions. While there are nearly 500 developed campgrounds to choose from, ranging from lake- and streamside settings to forested areas and rocky peaks, the best bet for those who don't mind packing in is to set up **wilderness camp** in one of the forest's two wilderness areas, the 37,000-acre Snow Mountain Wilderness at the southern end or the 154,000-acre Yolla Bolly–Middle Eel Wilderness up north. Be sure to tread lightly in protected areas; as always, stop in at ranger stations for **wilderness and fire permits.** Water must be treated, and trash must be burned or packed out (not buried); in other words, "leave no trace" of your presence behind. The best **maps** are available directly from the Forest Service; write US

Forest Service Information, Room 521, 630 Sansome St, San Francisco, CA 94111. There are three main maps for this forest: one full Mendocino National Forest map and one for each wilderness area. See the primer at the beginning of this book for more explicit ordering information. **Car campers** be advised: recent severe winters have affected many of the forest roads, and even during times of normal weather, tree blowdowns and washouts can make dirt roads difficult to pass. Periodic closures are unavoidable. Check with the relevant ranger station (see More Information, below) for updated **road conditions** before deciding on a site located deep within the forest property or away from the Lake Pillsbury area. It is best to enter remote areas only in vehicles with high ground clearance and, preferably, four-wheel drive. Road information is also available through a 24-hour recording at (530) 934-2350; this recording is also updated regularly with fire danger ratings, hunting season dates, and periodic campground closures. The Forest Service is currently reviewing its reservations and fees policies for this area, but generally no reservations are taken for any of the campgrounds listed below. Stays are limited to 14 days. Call the Forest Service **reservations** system at (800) 280-2267 or individual ranger stations for campsite availability information and reservations where applicable.

Covelo Ranger District, (707) 983-6118

Hammerhorn Lake Campground has 9 sites (no hookups; RV limit 16 feet) next to a pretty 5-acre fishing lake stocked with trout, in a mixed conifer forest at 3,500 feet elevation. Each site has a picnic table, fire ring, and stove. There is running water and outhouse-style toilets nearby. Trash must be packed out. Season is June 1 to October 1. No fee. *The camp is 18 miles north of the Eel River Bridge at Hwy 162, on Indian Dick Rd (Forest Rd M1).*

Little Doe Campground has 13 tent sites (no RV access) on the north end of Little Howard Lake, a popular trout-fishing spot between two ridges. Each site has a picnic table, fire ring, and stove. Outhouse-style toilets are nearby. There is no running water here, and you must pack out your garbage. Season is June 15 to October 1. No fee. *The camp is 12 miles north of the Eel River Bridge at Hwy 162, on Indian Dick Rd (Forest Rd M1).*

Eel River Campground has 16 tent sites (no RV access) near where the middle fork of the Eel meets Black Butte River, in the oaks at 1,500 feet elevation. Each site has a picnic table and stove. There is a gravity water system, and four outhouse-style toilets. The season is May 1 to October 1. No fee. *The campground is 13 miles east of Covelo on Hwy 162.*

Corning Ranger District, (530) 824-5196

Wells Cabin Campground has 25 sites (no hookups; RV limit 22 feet) in an area of red fir forest at 6,300 feet elevation and just a mile from the 6,900-foot Anthony Peak, which offers stunning views of both the Pacific Ocean and the inland valleys. Each site has a picnic table and fire ring, with running water and outhouse-style toilets nearby. Trash must be packed out. The season is July 1 to October 31. *The camp is 33 miles west of Paskenta at the east side of the forest near Corning. Take Forest Rd 23N02 from Paskenta to the intersection with Forest Rd 23N96, then head north 3 miles to the campground.*

Whitlock Campground has 3 sites (no hookups; RV limit 22 feet) in a mixed oak and pine forest at 4,300 feet elevation. Each site has a table, fire ring, stove, and grill, with running water and outhouse-style toilets nearby. Trash must be packed out. The season is June 1 to October 31. *The camp is 16 miles west of Paskenta, near Corning. Take Forest Rd 23N01 west from Paskenta to the intersection with Forest Rd 24N41, then head north to the camp.*

Stonyford Ranger District, (530) 963-3128

Plaskett Meadows Campground has 32 sites (no hookups; RV limit 16 feet) situated among two small fishing lakes in an area of pines and firs. Each site has a picnic table and fire pit, with outhouse-style toilets and a gravity water system nearby. The fee is $5. Trash must be packed out. The season is June 15 to October 15. *The camp is 36 miles northwest of Elk Creek, via Forest Rd 7.*

Some of the visitors to **Letts Lake Campground** are drawn by the folklore: The campground, with 42 sites (no hookups; RV limit 24 feet), is situated on the spot where the Letts brothers, prominent homesteaders in the 1800s, were murdered. Others are drawn by the beautiful location, adjacent to 34-acre spring-fed Letts Lake. Piped water and vault toilets are available, and each site has a fire grill and a picnic table. The lake is stocked with rainbow trout and black bass and there is a fishing pier. Motorboats are not permitted on the lake, but sailboats and canoes are. *The camp is 17 miles west of Stonyford on Fouts Springs Rd, on the east side of the lake.*

Visitors to Letts Lake who prefer solitude should check out **Mill Valley Campground.** Situated on Lilly Pond, about 1 mile from the main lake, Mill Valley has 15 sites (no hookups; RV limit 18 feet). Piped water is available except during the winter months. There are vault toilets, and each site has a fire grill and a picnic table. *To reach the camp, go 17 miles west of Stonyford on Fouts Springs Rd, then half a mile south on Forest Rd 17N02.*

Dixie Glade Group Horse Campground can accommodate groups of up to 50 people in either tents or RVs (no hookups; various RV lengths accommodated). Be sure to bring your own water, because the piped water in the camp area is for horses only! For horses there are troughs and a corral; for people, there are vault toilets, picnic tables, and fire pits with grills. Several riding trails leading throughout Snow Mountain Wilderness originate near the campground. *The camp is 12.5 miles west of Stonyford on Fouts Springs Rd, on the south side of the road.*

Campers looking for a more primitive experience may want to check out **Mill Creek Campground.** Adjacent to Mill Creek, it contains 6 tent sites (no RV access). There is no piped water in the area, so be sure to bring plenty of your own. Vault toilets, fire grills, and picnic tables are provided. *Contact the Mendocino National Forest Stonyford Ranger District, (530) 963-3128, for more information. The campground is 9 miles west of Stonyford on Fouts Springs Rd, on the north side of the road.*

Situated in a pine forest, **Fouts Campground** is just east of Snow Mountain Wilderness. It contains 11 sites for tents or RVs (no hookups; RV limit 16 feet), with piped water and vault toilets. Each site is equipped with a fire grill and table. Backpackers enjoy this campground because of its proximity to wilderness-area trailheads. *Go 8 miles west of Stonyford on Fouts Springs Rd, then 1 mile north on Forest Rd 18N03 to the campground entrance on the east side of the road.*

South Fork Campground lies adjacent to a network of off-road trails and, as you might imagine, is popular with off-road vehicle riders. So if you are looking for solitude, this campground will not do. South Fork contains 5 tent sites and no RV sites. There is no water in the area, so be sure to bring plenty of your own. Fire grills, picnic tables, and vault toilets are provided. If this campground is full, you may want to try Davis Flat Campground, described below, or Fouts, described above. *Go 8 miles west of Stonyford on Fouts Springs Rd, then 1 mile on Forest Rd 18N03 to the entrance on the north side of the road.*

Adjacent to a network of off-road trails, **Davis Flat Campground** is also popular with off-roaders. There are 75 sites for tents or RVs (no hookups; various RV lengths accommodated), and piped water and vault toilets. Each site has a fire pit and picnic table. Several hiking trails await in nearby Snow Mountain Wilderness. *Go 8 miles west of Stonyford on Fouts Springs Rd, then 1 mile north on Forest Rd 18N03 to the entrance on the east side of the road.*

Cedar Camp is located at the foot of Goat Mountain and contains 5 sites for tents or RVs (no hookups; RV limit 16 feet). Be sure to bring plenty of water, as you will not find any in this remote outreach of the forest. There are vault toilets, tables, and fire rings at each site, however. As one might imagine, this campground is popular with hikers and backpackers looking to conquer Goat Mountain. *Go 6 miles west of Stonyford on Fouts Springs Rd, then 13 miles south on Trough Springs Rd to the campground on the west side of the road.*

At Plaskett Lake, **Masterson Group Camp,** for up to 100 people, is open May to October. Contact the Stonyford Ranger District, (530) 963-3218, for more information and reservations. No single-site camping is available there.

Upper Lake Ranger District, (707) 275-2361

Fuller Grove Campground has 30 sites (no hookups; RV limit 22 feet) on the northwest shore of Lake Pillsbury, near boat launch facilities. Each site has a picnic table and fire ring, with outhouse-style toilets and running water nearby. *The camp is at the northwest end of the lake. From Hwy 20, take Potter Valley/Lake Pillsbury Rd 6 miles east to the campground entrance, 1 mile past the Forest Service information booth.*

Also on the banks of Lake Pillsbury, **Pogie Point Campground** provides a nice spot for swimming and fishing. There are 52 sites for tents or RVs (no hookups; various RV lengths accommodated). A few of the sites are wheelchair-accessible. Water is piped into the campground and readily available except during the winter season. The campground also contains vault toilets, and each site has a fire grill and a picnic table. There's a boat ramp a short distance south of the campground. *The camp is at the northwest end of the lake. From Hwy 20, take Potter Valley/Lake Pillsbury Rd 6 miles east to the campground entrance, 2 miles past the Forest Service information booth. The entrance is on the south side of the road.*

Sunset Campground has 51 sites for tents or RVs (no hookups; various RV lengths accommodated) at Lake Pillsbury. One of the reasons for its popularity is its location—a mere quarter of a mile from a boat ramp and adjacent to several of the forest's most attractive nature trails. Vault toilets and piped water (but no showers) are available, except during the winter season. Each site has a fire grill and a picnic table. *The camp is at the northwest end of the lake. From Hwy 20, take Potter Valley/Lake Pillsbury Rd 6 miles east to the campground entrance, 5 miles past the Forest Service information booth, on the south side of the road.*

For campers looking for solitude and a primitive camping experience, **Oak Flat Campground** half a mile from Lake Pillsbury is accessible only on foot or by bicycle. The campground contains 12 sites for tents. There is no water available, so be sure to bring plenty of your own. Picnic tables, fire grills, and vault toilets are provided. *The camp is at the northwest end of the lake. From Hwy 20, take Potter Valley/Lake Pillsbury Rd 26 miles east to the campground entrance, 4 miles past the Forest Service information booth.*

The entrance to Navy Campground (see below) is on the south side of the road. From there, hike half a mile (trail is clearly marked) to the campground.

Many consider **Navy Campground** one of the most scenic camping areas on Lake Pillsbury. Nestled in a shallow cove on the north shore, the campground has a beautiful southern exposure. Unfortunately, during the dry summer season, if the lake level drops significantly, the shallow waters bordering Navy Campground are the first to dry up, leaving the campground high and dry. The campground contains 20 sites for tents or RVs (no hookups; various RV lengths accommodated). Vault toilets and piped water are available. Each site has a fire grill and a picnic table. There's a boat ramp a short distance away. *The camp is at the northwest end of the lake. From Hwy 20, take Potter Valley/Lake Pillsbury Rd 26 miles east to the campground entrance, 4 miles past the Forest Service information booth, on the south side of the road.*

Campers looking for a quiet, primitive camping experience in the Snow Mountain area may also want to visit **Lower Nye Campground.** This tiny campground, with 6 sites for tents or RVs (no hookups; various RV lengths accommodated), is tucked away in the forest adjacent to Skeleton Creek. There is no running water, so bring plenty of your own. Vault toilets are available, and each site contains a picnic table and a fire grill. *The camp is at the northwest end of the lake. From Hwy 20, take Potter Valley/Lake Pillsbury Rd 17 miles east, then take Bear Creek Rd north for 7 miles. Turn left on Forest Rd 18N04 and go northwest 15 miles to the campground entrance on the right side of the road.*

Deer Valley Campground is located deep in the forest at an altitude of 3,800 feet and contains 13 sites for tents or RVs (no hookups; various RV lengths accommodated). There is no water available, so bring plenty of your own. Picnic tables, fire grills, and vault toilets are provided. *The camp is at the northwest end of the lake. From Hwy 20, take Elk Mountain Rd 12 miles east, then turn right on Forest Rd 16N01 and continue 4 miles south to the campground. Note: The drive contains a twisty section that may be difficult for large RVs or trailers.*

Tucked away in the forest near Middle Creek, **Middle Creek Campground** offers plenty of solitude. It has 13 sites for tents or RVs (no hookups; RV limit 20 feet). Piped water and vault toilets are available, and each site has a fire grill and a picnic table. *From Hwy 20 in Upper Lake, take Mendenhall Ave north 8 miles to the campground on the east side of the road.*

Bear Creek Campground, adjacent to Bear Creek, contains 18 sites for tents or RVs (no hookups; RV limit 18 feet). There is no water at the campground; bring plenty of your own. Vault toilets are provided, and each site is equipped with a fire grill and a picnic table. *From Hwy 20 in Upper Lake, take Mendenhall Ave north 17 miles, turn right onto Bear Creek*

Rd, and head east for 8.5 miles to the campground on the south side of the road.
For those traveling with a large group, the **Fuller Group Camp-ground,** on the banks of Lake Pillsbury, can accommodate groups of up to 60 in tents or RVs (no hookups; various RV lengths accommodated). The camp area contains piped water, vault toilets, picnic tables, and large fire pits with grills, for groups of people. A boat ramp is nearby, and the facility is wheelchair-accessible. *Contact the Mendocino National Forest Upper Lake Ranger District, (707) 275-2361, for reservations and information.*

Hiking/Backpacking

With more than a million acres to cover, and hundreds of miles of looping trails and forest roads to follow, the hiking and backpacking opportunities in Mendocino National Forest seem boundless. Naturally, it is impossible to list more than highlights here. We can, however, offer a few pointers that will make deciding where to go much easier. First, it is best to limit longer treks to the expansive wilderness areas, Yolla Bolly–Middle Eel and Snow Mountain, since they're protected from such activities as bear hunting, all-terrain vehicle use, and logging. The Lake Pillsbury, Middle Creek, Elk Mountain, Letts Lake, Fouts, Eel River, Plaskett Lake, and Lake Red Bluff recreation areas are also suitable spots to begin day hikes or longer back-country treks. No hike should begin until you are properly equipped, and that means packing in water, supplies, and—just as important—accurate maps. The best **maps** are available directly from the Forest Service; write US Forest Service Information, Room 521, 630 Sansome St, San Francisco, CA 94111. There are three main maps for this forest: one full Mendocino National Forest map and one for each wilderness area. See the primer at the beginning of this book for more detailed ordering information. It is best to check with the relevant ranger station for updated **road conditions** before heading out to a chosen trailhead; also, some roads may require vehicles with high ground clearance and four-wheel drive. Information on roads is also available from the 24-hour recording at (530) 934-2350, but do not rely on the recording for **trail condition information;** call ranger stations directly. Another good resource is the California Conservation Corps backcountry trail construction program Web page at www.ccc.ca.gov/bcpage.htm. If the Corps happens to have a trail construction crew in the area, weekly reports from the field will be posted to the site as work is finished. All that said, here are a few recommendations:

Overlook Loop Trail (moderately difficult; 8 miles round trip) departs from the Summit Springs Trailhead at Snow Mountain at an elevation of 5,200 feet in the shadows of the mountain's west peak, and ascends through sometimes steep, forested terrain of firs, oaks, and pines broken up by occasional meadows. This is a nice spring wildflower hike, and the meadow areas are quite lush well into the summer, since this portion of the Mendocino Range receives a lot of moisture from Pacific storms. Incredible vistas of surrounding mountain peaks and the northern Sacramento Valley are visible from the mountain crest at Cedar Camp (see Camping, above). On clear days, from the west or east summits (both at just above 7,000 feet), watch for the snow-draped peak of Mount Shasta to the northeast.

There is the option of continuing north along either **Milk Ranch Loop Trail** or **Waterfall Loop Trail** (moderate; 13.5 miles round trip) to the West Crockett trailhead area of the wilderness on its northern boundary, an additional distance of 6.8 to 7 miles, depending on the direction you choose. Waterfall Loop Trail, northeast of Summit Springs, is the best choice because of its superior views of Lake Pillsbury and a waterfall stop on the middle fork of Stony Creek. In addition to traversing the forested canyons, you also pass through Milk Ranch, which, while privately owned, is open to forest users on horseback and on foot. This hike is best taken between late spring and mid-autumn because of severe winters, but don't pass up the chance to explore this area on cold, clear winter days when the views are sharper and there is snow on the ground. To reach the trailhead at Summit Springs, take Fouts Springs Rd west from Stonyford or County Rd 301 north from Upper Lake to the Lake/Colusa County border on Forest Rd M10/18N01. Ranger stations located in both Stonyford and Upper Lake (see More Information, below) can provide maps, permits, and information.

East of the Snow Mountain peaks but in the same general area of the forest, the **Bear Wallow Trail** (moderate; 12 miles round trip) passes through chaparral and mixed pine, oak, and fir woodlands along ridges below the mountain at the 4,000- to 5,200-foot elevation range. It then drops to Bear Wallow Creek, near some good fishing spots. Additionally, the aforementioned 150,000-acre **Yolla Bolly–Middle Eel Wilderness,** with its 8,092-foot Mount Linn, has an elaborate looping trail system that passes through predominantly fir (red, white, and Douglas), pine, cedar, hemlock, and western juniper forestlands. Many hikes in this section of forest involve difficult, steep sections with rapid elevation gains and losses. Do not set out into this area without proper maps and basic map-reading skills. There are four entry points for Yolla Bolly–Middle Eel, but the easiest is from the southwest in the Covelo Ranger District area on Hwy 162; call (707) 983-9118. Check in first at the station, 22000 Corning Rd, for an update on road and trail conditions.

Traveler's Home Trail (moderate; 7.6 miles one way) passes through oak woodlands and open meadows, ending along the Eel River's middle fork in a secluded, pretty, undeveloped section of the wilderness. Access the trail on Forest Rd 24N21 from the Covelo station. To the southeast, **Hell Hole Trail** (moderate; 3 miles one way) leaves the Indian Dick Rd trailhead on Forest Rd 1N02, 15 miles east of Covelo, and traverses Hell-hole Canyon, which, as its name suggests, can get rather toasty during the summer. Pack in plenty of water. This can be a good overnighter, since the hike is short and there are camping spots in the canyon at the trail's end. Contact the Covelo ranger station for maps, directions, permits, and trail conditions.

In the eastern portion of the wilderness, **Poison Glade Trail** (difficult; 6 miles one way) is a rugged trek through oak-wooded Grindstone Canyon. Don't be fooled by the short distance on this one; the grades and primitively developed trails can make it a long trek. The trailhead is off Forest Rd 23N53 southwest of Log Springs. In the northeast section, **Lantz Ridge Trail** and **Peterson Trail** (adjoining; easy to moderate; 6 miles one way, combined) cover ponderosa pine, old-growth Douglas fir, and buck-eye forestlands; meadows; and Thomas Creek canyon. You'll also find numerous swimming holes, picnic spots, and camp areas, with elevations ranging from 2,000 to 3,850 feet. There are three trailheads for this route; one midway, one at the north end of Peterson, and one at the south end of Lantz. Contact the Corning Ranger District, (530) 824-5196, for maps, directions, trail conditions, and any required permits. Much of this section of the wilderness is best traveled with a four-wheel-drive vehicle.

Fishing/Boating

Fishing and hiking go hand-in-hand in these parts—because the best spots are **hike-in only**. The middle and south forks of Stony Creek are regarded as the most productive native **rainbow trout** fishery in the area, with numerous good fishing spots accessible within 4 miles of the West Crockett trailhead (see Hiking/Backpacking, above). In the northern portion of the Stonyford Ranger District are three nice fishing lakes, two at the Plaskett Meadows Recreation Area and one nearby at Keller Lake.

More good fishing lakes are within the **Eel River Recreation Area** in the Covelo Ranger District. While Lake Pillsbury may seem a more obvious destination because of its accessibility, these remote locations are less crowded in the peak outdoor season, and native **steelhead** runs are more healthy. For a prime experience, we suggest taking the extra effort to get to these spots—whether it means a drive on winding forest roads or a bit of a hike. To reach Lake Pillsbury, take Potter Valley/Lake Pillsbury Rd for 26 miles east from Hwy 20. To reach Keller, take Hwy 162 and go 3 miles south of Elk Creek.

Boaters will do best, however, to stick to the **Lake Pillsbury** area, where full boat-launching facilities and boating supplies are available. One easy-to-reach launch is at the Fuller camp area. From Hwy 20, take Potter Valley/Lake Pillsbury Rd 6 miles east to the campground entrance, 1 mile past the Forest Service information booth. Alternatively, **Letts Lake,** smaller and less crowded than Pillsbury, is also equipped with launch facilities, although no motorized boats are allowed here. Letts is stocked with **rainbow trout** and **black bass.** The lake is 17 miles west of Stonyford on Fouts Springs Rd; the launch and a fishing pier are on the east side of the lake.

Wildlife

Wildlife within the forest is varied and abundant. Look for **bald eagles** in the Lake Pillsbury and Eel River areas. The riverbanks and trails along the East Fork of the Trinity River are considered the best bird-watching turf in the forest, with wild turkeys, quail, doves, waterfowl such as geese and ducks, subtropical and tropical songbirds, eagles, hawks, ospreys, and owls. Best access to the river area is from Wildman Rd; take Hwy 36 for 32 miles east from Mad River, and make a right turn from the highway. But call the Covelo Ranger District, (707) 983-6118, for road condition information before you go.

Mountain Biking

Mountain bikers turn to Mendocino National Forest's abundant dirt forest roads for long, two- to three-day bike-camping treks and rigorous, butt-kicking day rides. Difficulty levels range from moderate to advanced. Advanced riders should consider taking the 16-mile ride from **Cold Springs Station** to the Thomes Pocket area along **Forest Road 23N01.** This ride has numerous dips and climbs, including a brutal 1,000-foot elevation gain covering 4 miles of the return trip. This is best taken as an overnighter, with camping at Thomes Pocket. Contact the Corning Ranger District (see More Information, below). A more moderate and much shorter ride is the 7-mile round trip through meadows and oaks along the **Traveler's Home National Recreation Trail,** which begins off Blands Cove Rd outside Corning and ends at the Eel River, with mild elevation gains on the forward ride, but one steep climb out on the return. To get there, take Plaskett Rd west from Corning for 14 miles, then follow the river northwest at Blands Cove. Loop rides are found at **Letts Lake** (easy; 7.5 miles), **Miner Ridge** (difficult; 7.5 miles), and **South End Loop** (difficult; 24 miles). Again, contact individual ranger stations for trail condition information and maps before setting out.

Rock Hunting

Rock hunters in the Mendocino National Forest can find **agate** and **jasper** along Big Stony Creek from Red Bridge to Mine Camp, **jadeite** and **nephrite** along the Eel River near Eel River Station and along Buttermilk Creek, **serpentine** along the eastern boundary of the forest at McCloud Ridge and Blue Banks, **quartz crystals** in the Big Butte–Shinbone area, and **chrome** just west of the town of Chrome in the Red Mountain area. Fossils can be found in the Rice Valley area. The US Geological Survey in Menlo Park, (650) 853-8300, has basic information on geology and rock types here and elsewhere.

More Information

Corning District Chamber of Commerce: *(530) 824-5550.*
Corning Ranger District: *(530) 824-5196.*
Covelo Ranger District: *(707) 983-6118.*
Forest Service reservations system: *(800) 280-2267.*
Lakeport Chamber of Commerce: *(707) 263-5092.*
Stonyford Ranger District: *(530) 963-3128.*
Upper Lake Ranger District: *(707) 275-2361.*

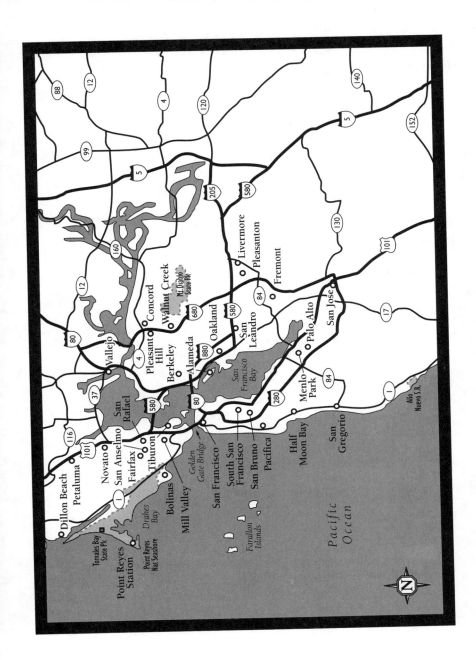

**Bay
Area**

San Francisco

All of the city and county of San Francisco, from the Bay Bridge landing west to the oceanfront border with San Mateo County, including the Golden Gate Bridge, Golden Gate Park, Presidio National Park, Ocean Beach, Alcatraz Island, and other points of interest.

You've seen San Francisco's skyline and the Golden Gate Bridge on a million postcards and calendars; that pointed Transamerica tower is unmistakable. "The city," however, has much more to offer than cityscapes. To many who know how to seek out the better side of life even in a metropolis, San Francisco is as much an outdoor playground as it is a cosmopolitan city.

Golden Gate Park and the Presidio consist of forests and greenery where no forests and greenery should be. Both are built on what used to be vast sand dunes covering the western end of the San Francisco peninsula—meaning it was originally a relatively treeless terrain, rolling however the wind chose to shape it, with low-slung scrub and bushes as the dominant plants. But truck in enough artificial irrigation, exotic foliage, soil, and willpower, and the seemingly impossible can happen. The Presidio began as one of the US Army's least desirable destinations, the desertlike, fog-shrouded desolation so unbearable that soldiers in the late 1800s didn't mind walking 10 miles each way to town. Today, you'd never guess it: since the Army turned the property over to the National Park Service in 1996, its prized forests and gardens, ample hiking and cycling trails, and coastal vistas have become an irresistible draw for outdoor adventurers.

Golden Gate Park was transformed from dunes to greenery as a way to keep the Pacific winds from scattering the city streets with sand. Today, remnants of that endless sandy terrain remain only in select pockets along the city's Pacific Coast. Most of the rest has been paved or greened over, and it is those greened-over portions that constitute San Francisco's so-called open space. Get over the fact that their origins aren't entirely "natural," and these are indeed fine parklands—fine enough that people who don't even live in San Francisco will travel great distances to enjoy them instead of settling for their suburban neighborhood parks. These lands are also an escape *within* the city—wild places to enjoy a lakeside stroll, a lazy afternoon on a blanket in the grass, a hike through forests and gardens, or a bike ride to the ocean.

The city's Pacific shoreline and the adjacent bay waterfront also are an outdoor recreation hub. From the Golden Gate south are 10 miles of virtually contiguous oceanfront public areas containing five beaches, walking and cycling trails, hang gliding facilities, and literally hundreds of great spots to simply sit and take in the sunset. East of the bridge are some of the best windsurfing and sailing areas on the West Coast, along with an amazingly jogger/cyclist/in-line skater–friendly waterfront. Fish, sail, cycle, swim, surf, hike—all without leaving the town!

Getting There

From the East Bay, follow Interstate 80 west or Interstate 880 or 580 north to the San Francisco–Oakland Bay Bridge. Pay the $2 toll and you're in. From Marin, the entry free is $3 but the bridge is a lot nicer—roll in on the world-famous Golden Gate. From the South Bay, enter free of charge on US Highway 101 (US 101) north. Other options include Bay Area Rapid Transit (BART) trains that travel in a tube beneath the bay to underground stations in downtown San Francisco, or CalTrain, which connects with the city's internal Municipal Railway (MUNI) south of the Bay Bridge. For BART information, call (650) 992-2278. CalTrain can be reached at (650) 660-4287; for MUNI, call (415) 673-6864. If you need transportation to or from the San Francisco International Airport (SFO), reserve a seat with one of the fast, reliable shuttle services, such as SuperShuttle, (415) 558-8500, and Quake City, (415) 255-4899.

Because Golden Gate Park is both the city's main outdoor attraction and contiguous with most of the others, here are simple pointers for how to get there. If you're driving, exit Interstate 80 or US 101 at Fell Street and head west 3 miles to the park entrance at John F. Kennedy Drive. From there, roads through the park will take you 3 miles to the Great Highway and the San Francisco oceanfront. Two public transportation options: Take BART into the city and transfer at any of the downtown stations to MUNI; take the N train west through the city's Sunset District (it stops at various points just south of Golden Gate Park) to the end of the line at Ocean Beach (near the park's westernmost section). Or take the 71 bus, which enters the park from the Haight-

Ashbury district and makes key stops inside. Note: San Francisco's public transportation system is notoriously unreliable. If you don't want to risk getting stranded in a subway tunnel because of a breakdown, take a cab instead.

Years of propaganda about sunny California have left millions of tourists freezing in the city by the bay. Although San Francisco's weather is usually mild and temperatures don't change drastically throughout the year (they rarely rise above 70°F or fall below 40°F), it's seldom warm enough to go without a coat or a sweater, especially at night. Spring and fall months are warmest. The summer is usually foggy, except at midday; locals beat the summer morning chills by dressing in layers.

For more details on San Francisco's outdoors and attractions, visit the tremendously helpful staff at the Visitor Information Center (open seven days a week, Monday through Friday 9am to 5pm, Saturday and Sunday 9am to 3pm) on the lower level of Hallidie Plaza, at Market and Powell Streets (near Union Square), or call them at (415) 391-2000.

Adjoining Areas

NORTH: **Marin**

SOUTH: **Peninsula and South Bay**

EAST: **East Bay**

inside out

Parks/Beaches

Golden Gate Park: Nothing like a strip of greenery to break up the concrete jungle. And boy, what a strip of greenery this is. As one of the largest urban parks in the world, Golden Gate covers 1,017 acres extending more than 50 blocks from the Pacific shore to the Haight-Ashbury area more than 3 miles inland. Forested with elms, live oaks, and redwoods, Golden Gate contains nine lakes; a series of grassy meadows; gardens of roses, fuchsia, tulips and dahlias; and facilities for numerous outdoor activities and sports including cycling, horseback riding, golf, handball, lawn bowling, tennis, soccer, horseshoe pitching, boating, fly casting, and picnicking—there's even a model boat club. On Sundays, a large section of Kennedy Dr, the main roadway leading through the park, is closed to automobile traffic and turned over to hundreds of in-line skaters, cyclists, joggers, and power walkers out to take advantage of a big, flat place with no cars. A thousand different escapes present themselves here; just step off any of the surrounding city streets and into the wild . . . you'll forget where you are. Golden Gate, which was built on an area of sand dunes over two decades beginning in the 1870s, doubles as a cultural center as well, with the Asian Art Museum, M. H. de Young Museum, Steinhart Aquarium, and Morrison Planetarium arranged around an open-air music concourse and fountain plaza (see Attractions, below). The park is not, however, without its problems. Homeless people, many of them mentally ill or struggling with substance abuse, have claimed sections of the park as home (camping is not allowed), and funding shortages in the city parks department have left some of its finest facilities, including the beautiful Victorian-vintage Conservancy of Flowers, crumbling from lack of maintenance. While police have attempted to crack down on the homeless problem, it naturally cannot be resolved with simple park sweeps (which tend to send the homeless from the park into the doorways of surrounding neighborhoods). Fact of the matter is that until a solution is found for some of the urban problems any major city has to deal with, those problems will also manifest themselves in the city parks. Use common sense when exploring here, and you're unlikely to have an unpleasant encounter. Where else can you take in an art exhibit and go for a paddleboat cruise while hiking from the city to the sea? To reach the park from the East Bay, take the Oakland–San Francisco Bay Bridge west to the Fell St exit, then follow Fell St west to the park entrance. From the South Bay, take US 101 north to Fell St, and continue to the park entrance. From the North Bay, cross the Golden Gate Bridge, then follow the state Hwy 1 route, or Park Presidio Blvd, into the park. For more information, call the park at (415) 221-1310 or (415) 750-5105. The park's main visitors center is along Middle Dr (at the center of the park) near Steinhart Aquarium and the California Academy of Sciences. A display on the history of the park is found at the Beach Chalet, on the Great Highway at the park's extreme western edge near the polo fields.

The Presidio: After more than 100 years as a military base, it's finally official: this block of prime coastal real estate—the forests, the golf course, the miles and miles of well-manicured grasslands and walking paths with their spectacular vistas of the Golden Gate Bridge—has been turned over to the National Park Service. Like Golden Gate Park, the Presidio grounds were historically sand dunes but were converted to grasslands and forests in the late 1800s for convenience and livability. The result was one of the country clubs of Army bases, with palatial homes overlooking the grounds and the waterfront in the distance, a golf course closed to the general public, an officer's club, walking paths, and gardens. As the park service takes over to transform the base into public land, most of the emphasis will be on environmental cleanup, rehabilitation and leasing of buildings, and establishing this area as a self-sufficient "city within a city." The main difference between the present day and the army-occupied Presidio is that now it is safe to stop for a picnic, take a bicycle tour, or hike the forests and gardens without being chased away by military police. This is a big piece of greenery, open 24 hours a day with no locked gates, for the public to enjoy. To reach the Presidio from the San Francisco–Oakland Bay Bridge, take the Fell St exit and continue west on Fell 3 miles to the Golden Gate Park entrance. Fell then curves left and changes to Lincoln Way; continue on it to 19th Ave (Park Presidio Blvd), turn right, go through Golden Gate Park, and continue north. From the South Bay, take the Fell St off-ramp from northbound US 101 and follow the same route. From the North Bay, take the Hwy 1 route from the Golden Gate Bridge, and enter the park on Park Presidio Blvd coming from the other direction. For more information, call the Presidio Information Center, (415) 561-4323. The main visitors center and the Presidio Museum are at the intersection of Funston St and Gerard Rd in the center of the property.

Crissy Field/Marina Green: This section of bay waterfront east of the Golden Gate Bridge and north of the Presidio is a historic airfield site featuring a thin, sandy strip of beach, picnic areas, walking, jogging and cycling trails connecting with the Golden Gate Bridge crossing, and access to some of the finest windsurfing waters anywhere. Just east of here, adjacent Marina Green, is prime picnic, kite-flying, volleyball, jogging, and cycling turf, all along the open waterfront and Fort Mason marina. The Crissy Field area, which is part of the Golden Gate National Recreation Area, is undergoing a transformation as park service officials restore tidal marshes, expand the beach, improve trails and picnic facilities, and remove pavement for a grassy meadow area. When all is complete, possibly as soon as next year, expect to pay for parking here. Now, parking is free. To reach Crissy Field and the Marina Green area from the East Bay, exit I-80 (from the Bay Bridge) at the Ninth St/Civic Center off-ramp, and follow the downtown corridor to Van Ness Ave. Turn right on Van Ness, and continue north to the waterfront area. Turn left on Bay St, and follow the waterfront traffic until it becomes Marina Blvd. Parking is easiest on the Crissy Field grounds straight ahead, west of the Marina. From the South Bay, take the downtown exit from US 101 and follow the same route. From the North Bay, take the downtown/US 101 exit off the Golden Gate Bridge to Lombard St. Turn right on Lombard and enter the Presidio through the Lombard Gate. Turn right on Presidio Blvd, then right on Halleck St to Crissy Field. For more information, call (415) 556-0865.

Ocean Beach: These 3 miles of sandy beach in the northernmost portion of San Francisco's Pacific shoreline and at the west end of Golden Gate Park are a great place for weekday-morning surfing before work or any other time that the water is right (watch for riptides), waterfront walks, jogging, kite flying, volleyball, watching the sunset—even sun-bathing on the few days of the year when the weather is warm enough. Because of the tides, however, swimming or even wading is *not* advisable here. (As of this writing, in fact, five people have drowned in the past year at this location, including three on the same day. There are posted warn-ings, but apparently they are not visible enough for some to heed.) Dune grass, which originally covered many of the now artificially vegetated areas of the city, thrives here. North of the beach, the historic Cliff House and the ruins of the famed Sutro Baths are open to the public. From the East Bay or South Bay, take the Fell St off-ramp, follow Fell to the Golden Gate Park entrance, and follow park roads all the way to the waterfront. Or veer left at the park entrance and follow Lincoln Way through the city's Sunset district to the ocean, then turn right on the Great Highway. Ample free parking is available the entire length of the beach. From Marin County and the North Bay, take the 19th Ave exit from the Golden Gate Bridge, follow Park Presidio Blvd south to Fulton St, then turn right and head to the shore (you'll be passing through the city's residential Rich-mond District). For more information, call (415) 239-2366.

Baker Beach: North of Ocean Beach and just below the western flanks of the Presidio, this mile-long sandy cove offers stunning views of the Marin Headlands and the Golden Gate. Picnic areas with tables and grills, gun-battery ruins, coastal walking trails, and surf fishing are favorite attractions here. On warm days, Baker is a favorite spot for sun-bathing—and parking around the beach trail areas can be very scarce. From the Lombard gate at the Presidio, go west on Lincoln Blvd. Follow Lincoln as it meanders through the Presidio. Turn right on Bowley and follow the signs to the Baker Beach parking area. For information, call (415) 556-0865.

Fort Funston: These rugged coastal headlands south of Ocean Beach are perhaps the best remaining example of what the white **sand dunes** that once covered much of the San Mateo and San Francisco coast must have looked like. Expansive areas of coastal scrub and wildflowers, high bluffs, and sand dunes as tall as 200 feet make this a great ecotouring spot. There are hiking trails, picnic facilities, and horse trails; March through October, also watch for hang gliders, since west winds flow through this area persistently enough for the spot to be rated a "hang III" site. A launch deck is available where you can watch the gliders do their thing. To reach Fort Funston from Hwy 1 (19th Ave/Park Presidio Blvd) in San Francisco, head west on Fulton St, Lincoln Way, or Noriega St to the Great Highway, then left (south) to where the highway intersects with Skyline Blvd. Park-ing areas for Funston and the adjacent Battery Davis will be on the right. For more information, call (415) 239-2366.

Alcatraz Island: In addition to grand tours of the legendary "escape-proof" federal prison on "the Rock" and a glimpse of the West Coast's very first lighthouse, visitors to this popular attraction can enjoy picnics among the island's historic gardens, wildlife viewing, tide pools, and some of the best bay views anywhere. Getting to the island is the tricky part: The public must use ferries departing on a regular schedule from San Francisco's Pier 41, and often reservations are necessary well in advance since tourists flock to the island en masse. Call (800) 229-2784 for ferry information, and (415) 705-1045 for park information.

Walking

San Francisco is a great place to see on foot, but before you set out there are a few things you need to know. The weather here is unpredictable. At times the morning fog can give way to afternoon sun that lasts only an hour or two before more fog comes rolling in. Expect to run hot and cold. Dress in layers. Also note that San Francisco can be a difficult driving town for visitors. Taxis or public transportation are often preferable, particularly if you're headed downtown or to the Fisherman's Wharf area. But however you get to your starting point, this is a great place to take a nice, long stroll. (See Attractions, below, for additional tours.)

There's no question: the most popular outdoor "activity" in San Francisco has got to be the walk across the city's most famous landmark—the **Golden Gate Bridge** (easy; 2.4 miles round trip). Tourists pull up by the busload to do it, and locals use it for jogging and cycling as well as a "thing to do" with relatives and friends from out of town. The vistas of the Pacific and the city and just the excitement of this historic place make it a frequent repeat outing. First opened to motorists on May 28, 1937, the 1.2-mile, 90-foot-wide suspension bridge is an engineering wonder that oddly enhances the natural landscape. The walk across is best combined with a visit to historic Fort Point, the Presidio, Crissy Field, or Baker Beach. It is easiest to stage from the San Francisco end of the bridge, in the unpaved parking lots just west of the bridge visitors center—but if the area is jammed (as it often is on weekends), try driving to the Marin side and staging from Fort Baker instead. To reach the bridge from the city, simply take the US 101 route (follow the signs) directly to the toll plaza exit, then drive slightly east of the pay parking areas for free unlimited parking in the dirt spaces provided. To stage from Marin, cross the bridge and exit at Fort Baker. For information on the bridge, call (415) 921-5858.

Another easy walk of variable length (easy; 4 miles round trip max), depending on how far you decide to venture before turning back, is the stroll along the **esplanade** following the seawall at Ocean Beach (see

Parks/Beaches, above). Beginning at the Cliff House just north of the beach, this is the perfect spot for **sunset strolls.** Kick off your shoes and make it a walk in the sand if you like, or just stay on the sidewalk in your dinner clothes. Also, don't hesitate to come out when the weather is bad; some people think that's the best time to experience the ocean. From the East Bay or South Bay, take the Fell St off-ramp, follow Fell to the Golden Gate Park entrance, and follow park roads all the way to the waterfront. Or veer left at the park entrance and follow Lincoln Way through the city's Sunset district to the ocean, then turn right on the Great Highway. Ample free parking is available the entire length of the beach. From the North Bay, take the 19th Ave exit from the Golden Gate Bridge, follow 19th Ave/Park Presidio Blvd south to Fulton St, then turn right and head to the shoreline through the residential Richmond District. For more information, call (415) 239-2366.

There's also the option of walking north from the Cliff House on the **Coastal Trail** to Fort Point and the Golden Gate Bridge (easy to moderate; 4 miles round trip). This walk includes spectacular vistas of the city's coastal bluffs and the bridge looking west, and passes through both the China Beach and Baker Beach areas (see Parks/Beaches, above). Because this walk is not completely level and is partly unpaved, check with the National Park Service to make sure it's open, and avoid it in the rain or fog. Fog, of course, can spoil the views—even wipe them out completely.

To enjoy the city's bay shore, walk along the **Golden Gate Promenade** leading from **Aquatic Park** to the Golden Gate Bridge (easy; 7 miles round trip). This walk, one of the most popular in the city, is like a San Francisco history tour; it passes through Civil War–era fortifications, the retired landing strip at Crissy Field, and the city's historic Marina district with its fabulous waterfront homes. The walk is paved most of the way, but watch out for construction activity in the Crissy Field area, as a restoration project is under way there. Also note that directly beneath the bridge an ongoing toxic cleanup has been taking place to remove lead contaminants left from overspraying of bridge paint through the decades. Aquatic Park is just north of one of the most frequented tourist shopping areas, Ghirardelli Square. The best way to get there is by public transportation. Take CalTrain or BART to downtown San Francisco, then switch to the Hyde St cable car line, which ends at Ghirardelli. For cable car information, call the San Francisco Municipal Railway (MUNI) at (415) 673-6864.

On the Presidio grounds (See Parks/Beaches, above), try the romantic stroll along historic **Lover's Lane** (easy; 2 miles round trip), which follows the same route lonely soldiers used in the mid- to late 19th century to reach the nightlife around the city's Mission Dolores District. While their original 12-mile path has long been lost to development, a 1-mile stretch of it, preserved over the years, passes through pleasant forested grounds and gardens between Barnard Ave on the Presidio's southeast edge and San Francisco's exclusive Presidio Heights neighborhood. The path is lit for evening strolls. The easiest way to reach the Lover's Lane area: Follow the US 101 signs through San Francisco to Geary St, head west on Geary 2 miles to Presidio Ave, then go north (right) into Presidio Heights. The walk begins at Presidio Blvd and W Pacific Ave.

If there is time, also walk along the Presidio's **Ecology Loop** (easy; 2 miles round trip) through more forested gardens beginning at the northwestern end of Lover's Lane. Contact the Presidio Visitors Center, (415) 561-4323, for more information and suggestions for other walking tours on the expansive grounds.

Finally, there are myriad good walking tours in **Golden Gate Park** (See Parks/Beaches, above), particularly the stroll around **Stow Lake** at the park's center. The best way to explore your options is to check in at the main concourse near the M. H. de Young Museum for a park map and guide, then have at it. Call (415) 221-1310 or (415) 750-5105 for information.

In-Line Skating

Each Sunday, **John F. Kennedy Drive,** the main entrance to Golden Gate Park (See Parks/Beaches, above) from the downtown area, is closed to automobile traffic—making it the perfect place to get out the in-line skates. Beginners have a wide, flat, smooth surface where they can practice with little worry of getting trampled. Skate dancers take over adjacent basketball courts; music is provided. Another area is sectioned off for roller hockey. It's crowded, but fun whether you skate or just watch. Skates on Haight, 1818 Haight St, (415) 752-8375, has **rentals** available just a few blocks from where all the action is. Also try Skate Pro Sports, 2549 Irving St, (415) 242-0706; Golden Gate Park Skate & Bikes, 3038 Fulton St, (415) 499-0320; and Mike's Bikes & Blades, 1 Maritime Plaza, (415) 668-6699. Another decent skating area is the city's waterfront along the **Embarcadero,** but Golden Gate Park has far less traffic congestion or danger of potential conflicts with pedestrians, cyclists, and joggers.

Cycling

Some of the best cycling in San Francisco are the routes that deliver you to the grand **Golden Gate Bridge** crossing—because once there, you can do just that—and continue the journey in some of Marin County's prime cycling areas (See Cycling, Marin chapter). From China Beach (See Parks/Beaches, above), the Cliff House, or the Palace of the Legion of Honor southwest of the Presidio, take the city's **El Camino Del Mar** up moderately difficult grades heading north toward the bridge. At the Baker Beach (See Parks/Beaches, above) entrance to the Presidio, the route changes to **Lincoln Boulevard,** which will take you through rolling, forested hills hugging the ocean to the San Francisco landing of the bridge. Depending on the day of the week, the side of the bridge open to bicycles alternates: try to do this ride on a weekend, when the side closest to the ocean belongs to bikes. The bridge ride is thrilling and exhilarating, but please keep in mind that this is not the place for a race, as mountain bikers, children, and tourists (some of whom have not been on a bicycle for a long time) share the lanes with in-shape road warriors looking to burn it up. There is limited space on the bridge and potentially dangerous automobile traffic just over the railing. (A few years ago, a young man involved in a bike wreck was thrown into the traffic lanes.) Be extra-careful, relax, shift down, and enjoy the salt breezes and the views; there is no need to blow a gasket. There are places to pull over if you really want to take in the moment.

Cycling is also popular on the routes leading through **Golden Gate Park** to the oceanfront Great Highway. All surface roads through the **Presidio** are excellent for cycling as well, with only moderately difficult grades. Park Cyclery, 1749 Waller St, (415) 221-3777, has rentals and tour planning information. For tours, contact Wheel Escapes, (415) 586-2377, or the Sierra Club at (510) 653-6127. Also consider Golden Gate Park Skate & Bikes, 3038 Fulton St, (415) 499-0320, and Mike's Bikes & Blades, 1 Maritime Plaza, (415) 668-6699.

Hang Gliding

The Pacific winds and well-developed dunes at **Fort Funston** (see Parks/Beaches, above), make this area among the best in the world for hang gliding, although it's less a spot for beginners than for those with intermediate or better hang-gliding skills. We have heard reports of gliders staying airborne here in excess of 90 minutes! For those who like to watch, there is a viewing deck. Winds are most vigorous here from late March through October. Several shops in the Fort Funston area offer sales, instruction, and other services. For information, contact the Bay Area Paragliding Association, (415) 756-7560; Airtime of San Francisco, 3620 Wawona St, (415) 759-1177; and Weather Fort Funston, Skyline Blvd, (415) 333-0100.

Windsurfing

One of the most popular windsurfing spots in the world is the beach at **Crissy Field** (see Parks/Beaches, above), just west of the Golden Gate, where ocean breezes pass through to the bay but currents are relatively calm. Late March to October is the best time to launch. Because the water can get crowded at times and because the winds here make it possible to really get some speed, this area is best reserved for those with intermediate or higher skill levels; beginners have plenty of alternatives in other parts of the Bay Area (see Surfing/Windsurfing, East Bay chapter, and Windsurfing, Marin chapter). The dance of sails, often in the shadow of passing oil tankers and cargo ships, is quite a scene here; just kicking back and watching can be a hoot. Cityfront Sailboards, 2936 Lyon St, (415) 929-7873, is a good place to check in for instruction, sales, rentals, and information. Also contact the San Francisco Board Sailing Association, (415) 522-9001, for advice on where and when to set sail and how to get outfitted. To reach Crissy Field from the East Bay, take the Bay Bridge west, exit I-80 at Ninth St, and follow the downtown corridor to Van Ness Ave. Turn right on Van Ness and continue north to the waterfront area. Turn left on Bay St and follow the waterfront traffic to Marina Blvd. Parking is easiest on the Crissy Field grounds straight ahead, west of the Marina. From the South Bay, take the downtown exit from US 101 and follow the same route. From the North Bay, take the downtown/US 101 exit off Golden Gate Bridge to Lombard St. Turn right on Lombard and enter the Presidio through the Lombard Gate. Turn right on Presidio, then right on Halleck St to Crissy Field.

Kite Flying

Getting a kite up is theoretically no problem anywhere along the city's windy waterfronts, but there are only a few spaces open enough to do it easily without getting tangled up with passersby or overhead wires. The best spots are the **Marina Green, Ocean Beach,** and **Fort Funston,** along with certain spots in **Golden Gate Park** (see Parks/Beaches, above). San Francisco has no shortage of kite retailers. Try Airtime Kites, 3620 Wawona St, (415) 759-9463; Buena Vista Kite Co, 301 Eighth Ave, (415) 626-3599; or Sundowners, 1590 Portola Dr, (415) 731-7604.

Surfing

The water is chilly and the surf breaks impressive, so don't even think about getting in the water with a surfboard off the San Francisco coast unless you know what you're doing. Beginners should head south to the San Mateo coast beaches (see Peninsula and South Bay chapter) where the breaks are less rowdy. At San Francisco's **Ocean Beach** (see Parks/Beaches, above), surfers will find the largest breaks in the area topping at over 10 feet in normal conditions. Smaller but still challenging conditions are at

China Beach and **Baker Beach** (see Parks/Beaches, above), but again, we caution against setting out there without some experience under your belt (and, most definitely, a wet suit on your bod). A general **surf report** is available 24 hours a day, at (415) 665-9473. Local outfitters include Big Yank Board Sports, 728 La Playa St, (415) 666-1616; City Front Sailboards, 2936 Lyon St, (415) 929-7873; O'Neill, 2090 Evans Ave, (415) 826-9091; Purple Skunk, 5820 Geary Blvd, (415) 668-7905; SF Surf Shop, 3809 Noriega St, (415) 661-7873; and the well-stocked Wise Surfboards, 3149 Vicente St, (415) 665-7745.

Sailing

San Francisco Bay offers some of the best sailing conditions in the world for the same reason it offers some of the best windsurfing: ocean breezes get through, but not the ocean currents. **Public moorings** with varying time limits are available at all key points, including Fort Mason Center, Pier 39, and the city port at the Embarcadero just north of the Bay Bridge. Day charters can be found along Fisherman's Wharf for quick **bay tours. Charters and lessons** can also be arranged through A Day on the Bay at the city marina, (415) 922-0227, or Sailing Education Adventures at Fort Mason, (415) 775-8779. For lessons and/or boat rentals, contact Spinnaker Sailing at Pier 40, (415) 543-7333, or Marine Chartering Co Inc, 781 Beach St, (415) 441-3100. The Pier 39 marina can be reached at (415) 705-5556.

Wildlife

With the exception of **seabirds** along the city's Pacific coast, most notably at the Cliff House and Ocean Beach (See Parks/Beaches, above), the wildlife scene here, oddly enough, centers around animals that have adapted to the altered state of affairs caused by human settlement. You're more likely, for example, to spot **sea lions** lounging around the piers east of Pier 39 than on Seal Rocks in the ocean near Cliff House. And some of the best bird-watching is on Alcatraz Island, where the rare **black-crowned night heron** nests among bushes that wouldn't be there had the federal government not blasted the rocky terrain to prepare for federal prison construction, then hauled soil in from neighboring Angel Island to get vegetation to take root. In Golden Gate Park (See Parks/Beaches, above), **great horned owls** nest in trees that wouldn't be there had the park not been planted atop the expansive sand dunes that once covered large sections of the western San Francisco peninsula. **Pond turtles** live in the park's man-made lakes, and **buffalo** graze its artificially planted meadows.

Fishing

San Francisco has it all: pier fishing on the bay, trout fishing on the city's stocked Lake Merced, surf fishing at the ocean beaches, and sportfishing adventure cruises on the Pacific. The best bet, particularly if children are involved, is to head to **Lake Merced,** where **trout** and **catfish** are most prolific in midsummer. Boat rentals, bait and tackle, and fishing permits are available on site. The lake sits on the San Francisco/Daly City border one block from the zoo. Take the Great Highway south from Ocean Beach till it ends at Skyline Blvd. Turn left on Skyline, then make an immediate right on Harding Rd. Lake Merced Boating and Fishing Co, 1 Harding Rd, (415) 753-1101, handles the full works.

Surf fishing for rockfish, perch, lingcod, wolf-eel, smelt, and silversides is popular at both Baker Beach and Ocean Beach (see Parks/Beaches, above). **Pier fishing** on the bay for striped bass, perch, jacksmelt, sturgeon, leopard shark, and flounder is best from the piers at Crissy Field (See Parks/Beaches, above), Fort Mason, Fort Point, or Aquatic Park. Fort Point is just west of Crissy Field beneath the Golden Gate Bridge, and Fort Mason is just east of Crissy Field and the city marina. Aquatic Park is adjacent to Fort Mason. Check with Gus's Discount Fishing Tackle, 3710 Balboa St, (415) 752-6197; Hi's Tackle Box, 3141 Clement St, (415) 221-3825; and Kaplan's Surplus and Sporting Goods, 1055 Market St, (415) 863-0127, for **supplies,** licensing, pointers, and updates on state fishing regulations. Or at the very least check in with the California Department of Fish and Game field office, (707) 944-5500.

Sportfishing **charters** leave the city's marina and piers daily for the open Pacific and the bay. Chucky's Pride Sport Fishing, (415) 564-5515; Captain Joey Sports Fishing, Pier 47, (415) 346-4422; Miss Farallones, (415) 346-2399; New Easy Rider Salmon Fishing, (415) 285-2000; New Edibob Sportfishing, (415) 564-2706; Quite-A-Lady, (415) 821-3838; and The Jacky Wacky, 473 Bella Vista Way, (415) 586-9800; are among the favorites.

Photography

Visitors to San Francisco quickly realize there's a photo op every second, so your choice will be to either load up on film and get busy or just pick the highlights. Obviously, the Golden Gate Bridge (see Parks/Beaches, above) is the most popular photo subject in the city (if not on the entire West Coast). Head up on a clear day—it will be expected of you. Also hit the infamous corner of Haight and Ashbury Sts for a shot beneath the most famous street sign in the Bay Area. For scenics, you can't go wrong with the city waterfront, from the ocean to the bay.

Adventure Calendar

San Francisco Examiner Bay-to-Breakers, May: *a wild and wacky 7.5-mile city to shore run (or walk) with many participants in costume such as two-legged Brillo boxes, centipedes, Snow White and the Seven Dwarfs, and a Whitney Houston clone in drag,* (415) 777-7950.

The San Francisco Marathon, July: (800) 722-3466

Golden Gate Bridge Swim, San Francisco to Marin, early August: (415) 868-1829.

outside in

Attractions

San Franciscans know they are uniquely blessed. In no other city in the country is the meeting of land and sea so spectacular. The late afternoon sun flashes off the dark blue bay and lights up the orange towers of the Golden Gate Bridge, and the magnificent sails of boats and windsurfers add color in brilliant flashes. Almost every evening the fog pours in from the Pacific, spilling over the towers of downtown like a white wave. Lovers of all persuasions kiss on street corners. Poets still scribble in coffee shops. No wonder this is one of the world's favorite cities.

Over the years, however, San Franciscans have begun to view this magnetism as something of a liability. Drawn by the city's fabled beauty, cuisine, art, and culture, newcomers from around the globe have poured into this hilly, 46-square-mile oasis. Housing prices have soared, forcing many middle-class families to move to distant suburbs. On bad days, it seems the city is entirely populated by frazzled workaholics, grumpy long-distance commuters, and legions of the homeless—but even on those days, most people are still smiling. What follows are a few highlights of San Francisco's attractions.

The Arts. TIX Bay Area sells half-price **tickets** to many of San Francisco's dance, music, and theater events on the day of the performance only (tickets for Sunday and Monday events are sold on Saturday). You must purchase the tickets in person and pay in cash or with travelers' checks. Advance full-price tickets are sold here, too, and may be purchased with Visa, MasterCard, or cash; call (415) 433-7827 for recorded information (which half-price tickets are available is not announced on the phone). TIX Bay Area is located at 251 Stockton St, between Post and Geary Sts on the east side of Union Square. Tickets to most dance and theater events are also sold by phone through the City Box Office, (415) 392-4400, and BASS

Ticketmaster, (510) 762-2277. For a 24-hour recording of the city's current events and activities, call (415) 391-2001.

Dance. The internationally renowned San Francisco Ballet kicks off its season in mid-December with the classic **Nutcracker,** and dances to more contemporary pieces beginning in February; performances are held at the War Memorial Opera House, 301 Van Ness Avenue at Grove St, (415) 703-9400. Ethnic dance troupes abound in the Bay Area, and they join together in June for the San Francisco Ethnic Dance Festival; for more information, call (415) 474-3914. For modern and contemporary performances, see the ODC/San Francisco dance troupe, (415) 863-6606, and for contemporary ballet, Lines is a local favorite and often performs at Yerba Buena Gardens' Center for the Arts, 701 Mission St at Third St, (415) 863-3040.

Music. The world-class San Francisco Opera alternates warhorses with rarities from September through January at the beautiful War Memorial Opera House, which was modeled on Garnier's Paris Opera and first opened on October 15, 1932, with a production of Puccini's *Tosca.* Subscribers grab up most of the seats, but fans with smaller bankrolls can stand in line early on performance mornings to buy one of the 200 standing-room tickets, which go on sale at 10am (50 of these inexpensive tickets are also sold two hours before the performance); 301 Van Ness Ave at Grove St, (415) 864-3330 (box office) or (415) 861-4008 (general information). The San Francisco Symphony performs from September through July at the modern Louise M. Davies Symphony Hall, a gorgeous concert hall with a wraparound glass facade; 201 Van Ness Ave at Grove St, (415) 431-5400.

On summer Sundays, families and couples tote blankets and picnic baskets to free outdoor performances (everything from jazz to opera and ballet) at the pretty Stern Grove; it's located at Sloat Blvd and 19th Ave, (415) 252-6252. The San Francisco Jazz Festival, one of the largest in the country, toots its horn every fall with concerts, dances, films, and lectures; call (415) 788-7353.

Theater. American Conservatory Theater (ACT), the city's best-known theater company, presents solid productions of new works and classics from late September to mid-June in the Geary Theater, 415 Geary St, (415) 749-2ACT. Broadway shows on tour are performed at the Golden Gate, Curran, and Orpheum Theaters; call (415) 551-2000 for the current lineup and ticket information. For off-Broadway acts, contact the Theatre on the Square, 450 Post St, between Powell and Mason Sts, (415) 433-9500, and Marines Memorial Theatre, 609 Sutter St at Mason St, (415) 771-6900. Theatre Rhinoceros specializes in gay and lesbian drama; 2926 16th St at S Van Ness Ave, (415) 861-5079. Summer and early autumn bring free outdoor performances by America's oldest political musical-comedy theater group, the Tony award–winning San Francisco Mime Troupe, at various venues, (415) 285-1717. The more serious Shakespeare in the Park theater group also performs for free in the summer in Golden Gate Park at Liberty Tree Meadow, off John F. Kennedy Dr just west of the Conservatory of Flowers, (415) 422-2221. Beach Blanket Babylon, the longest-running musical revue in the world, is a cabaret-style show full of silly jokes that's famous for its wild costumes and humongous hats. It remains a favorite of residents and visitors alike, so be sure to reserve seats several weeks in advance; Club Fugazi, 678 Green St near Powell St, (415) 421-4222.

Visual Arts. The San Francisco Museum of Modern Art (SFMOMA), housed in a dramatic modernist building designed by internationally acclaimed Swiss architect Mario Botta, offers more than 17,000 works of art, including gems by Picasso, Matisse, O'Keeffe, Rivera, Pollock, Warhol, Klee, De Forest, and Lichtenstein, to name just a few; 151 Third St, between Mission and Howard Sts, (415) 357-4000. The M. H. de Young Memorial Museum showcases American art from colonial times to the 20th century. It used to host many traveling international exhibits, but the popular museum, damaged by the 1989 earthquake, was declared unsafe for hosting those big shows by the federal government in 1997. De Young supporters are searching for a new home for the museum, and in the meantime all of its upcoming international exhibitions will be transferred to the California Palace of the Legion of Honor (see below); until further notice, the de Young is located in Golden Gate Park, off John F. Kennedy Dr, (415) 863-3330. On the west side of the de Young is the Asian Art Museum, the largest museum in the Western world devoted exclusively to Asian art, with many masterpieces from the Avery Brundage collection (note: the museum will move to the former San Francisco Main Library building in the Civic Center in the year 2001), (415) 668-8921.

The California Palace of the Legion of Honor, a three-quarter-scale replica of Paris' grand Palais de la Légion d'Honneur, reopened in 1997, after three years of extensive renovation and seismic work. The dazzling museum features European paintings (including works by Monet, Rubens, and Rembrandt), sculptures (more than 70 works by Rodin are on display), and decorative art. It also holds ancient art, the Achenbach Foundation collection of works on paper, plus traveling international shows; the museum is in Lincoln Park near 34th Ave and Clement St, (415) 863-3330 or (415) 750-3600. The city has several terrific folk-art museums, most notably the Mexican Museum, the first in the United States to feature Mexican and Chicano art; it's located at Fort Mason Center, in Building D, off

Marina Blvd at Buchanan St, (415) 441-0404. Photography buffs should not miss the Ansel Adams Center for Photography, where the work of the master himself, Imogen Cunningham, Dorothea Lange, and many other notables is showcased in five exhibition galleries; 250 Fourth Sts, between Howard and Folsom Sts, (415) 495-7000.

Major Attractions. The third-most-visited amusement attraction in the nation, **Pier 39** is packed with kitschy shops and overpriced, touristy restaurants, but it boasts beautiful views of Angel Island, Alcatraz, and the bay, and has great entertainment for kids with its Venetian Carousel, jugglers, mimes, the "motion theater" Turbo Ride, the fun (but slightly overrated and expensive) Underwater World aquarium, and an arcade stocked with every gizmo and quarter-sucking machine the young-at-heart could dream of. Once you've had your fill of the tourist-packed pier, hop aboard a **ferry** for the surprisingly fascinating audiocassette tour of Alcatraz (make advance reservations), a San Francisco Bay cruise, or a scenic trip to the pretty little towns across the bay, Sausalito and Tiburon; for tour information and ferry schedules, call the Blue & Gold Fleet at Piers 39 through 41, (415) 705-5444 or (415) 773-1188 (recordings), or (415) 705-5555 (reservations).

Just a short jaunt west of Pier 39 are the world-famous **Fisherman's Wharf, The Cannery,** and **Ghirardelli Square.** They're always mobbed with tourists, but they offer some interesting shops and are riddled with witty, wisecracking, watch-me-pull-a-rabbit-out-of-my-shoe street entertainers. And from mid-November through June, this is also where you'll see the city's highly touted (and delicious) Dungeness crabs boiling in large metal pots on the sidewalks lining the wharf. All three attractions are located side by side on the waterfront at the north end of the Embarcadero and next to Aquatic Park.

While tourists flock to Fisherman's Wharf and Pier 39, locals often head in the other direction to the extraordinary **California Academy of Sciences,** where under one roof you'll find the Natural History Museum, Morrison Planetarium, the Laserium, and the superb Steinhart Aquarium, offering one of the most diverse collections of aquatic life in the world— about 14,500 specimens, including seals, dolphins, and alligators; the science complex is located in Golden Gate Park, off Middle Dr E, between John F. Kennedy and Martin Luther King Jr. Drs, (415) 750-7145. Another San Francisco favorite is the **Exploratorium,** a unique interactive museum that brings scientific concepts to vivid life—it's a blast at any age. The Exploratorium's marvelous Tactile Dome, where visitors must feel their way through a maze of hurdles in total darkness, requires reservations and a certain amount of nerve. The Exploratorium is housed within the magnificent **Palace of Fine Arts,** designed by renowned architect

Bernard Maybeck for the 1915 Panama-Pacific International Exposition. Surrounded by a natural lagoon, the Palace is an ideal spot for a picnic and for tossing your leftovers to grateful swans, seagulls, and pigeons; 3601 Lyon St, between Jefferson and Bay Sts near the on-ramp to the Golden Gate Bridge, (415) 561-0360 (Exploratorium), (415) 561-0362 (Tactile Dome reservations).

In the southwest corner of the city, near the ocean and Lake Merced, is the popular **San Francisco Zoo.** Don't miss the famed Primate Discovery Center, where several species of apes and monkeys live in glass-walled condos. The zoo also has rare Sumatran and Siberian tigers, African lions (visit during their mealtimes), a children's petting zoo, and even an insect zoo; 45th Ave and Sloat Blvd, (415) 753-7061.

To get an up-close and personal look at some of the city's multi-ethnic neighborhoods and architectural masterpieces, strap on your heavy-duty walking shoes and hike around the **Russian Hill** neighborhood, starting at the top of the crookedest street in the world, **Lombard Street** (at Hyde St). Wind your way down Lombard's multiple, flower-lined curves and continue east until Lombard intersects with Columbus Ave, then turn right and stay on Columbus for a tour of charming **North Beach**—a predominantly Italian and Chinese neighborhood where residents practice tai chi in Washington Square on weekend mornings or sip espresso as they peruse Proust or the *Bay Guardian*'s really racy personal ads (guaranteed to make you blush—or send you running for the nearest pay phone). You can extend this tour by turning right off of Columbus onto Grant Ave, which will take you through the heart of the ever-bustling and fascinating **Chinatown**—the only part of the city where vendors sell live, 3-foot-long slippery eels next to X-rated fortune cookies and herbs meant to cure whatever ails you.

For a different tour: instead of turning off Lombard onto Columbus, keep following Lombard St east all the way up to **Coit Tower** on the top of Telegraph Hill, then reward yourself for making the steep ascent with a trip (gasp, gasp) in an elevator to the top of the tower for a panoramic view of the Bay Area; (415) 362-0808. Too worried about getting lost on your self-guided walking tour? Then call City Guides, which offers numerous guided tours through San Francisco year-round—and they're free to boot; phone (415) 557-4266 for details. See also Walking, above, for additional suggestions.

If you'd rather ride than walk the hills of San Francisco, an outside perch on one of the city's famed **cable cars** is always a kick. The three cable car routes are named after the streets on which they run (you can take them in either direction) and operate daily from 6:30am to 12:30am, rain or shine. The Powell–Mason line starts at Powell and Market Sts and terminates at Bay St near Fisherman's Wharf; the Powell–Hyde line also begins at Powell and Market Sts, but ends at Victorian Park near Aquatic Park and the bay, making it the most scenic route; and the California line runs from California and Market Sts through Chinatown to Van Ness Ave, the widest street in the city. Expect very long lines during peak travel times, especially when the weather is warm. For more information on the cable cars call the Visitor Information Center at (415) 391-2000 or MUNI at (415) 673-6864.

In the heart of the city, across from the Museum of Modern Art, is **Yerba Buena Gardens,** a 5-acre urban park featuring a walk-through waterfall leading to a beautiful memorial for Martin Luther King Jr., a sculpture garden, and terrace cafes. Look for the new Yerba Buena Children's Center with a carousel, ice-skating rink, bowling alley, technology and arts center, and a children's garden, as well as Sony's Metreon Entertainment Complex, featuring a 15-screen cinema, an IMAX theater, and a children's play center designed by author/illustrator Maurice Sendak. Tours of Yerba Buena Gardens, located at Mission and Third Sts across from the Moscone Convention Center, are available by appointment for a nominal fee; for more details call (415) 541-0312.

Shopping. The famous and oh-so-trendy Union Square area and the nearby San Francisco Shopping Centre at Market and Fifth Sts, (415) 495-5656, together boast many major department stores (including Macy's, Nordstrom, and Neiman Marcus) and more specialty shops than Imelda Marcos has shoes. A short walk away is the chichi Crocker Galleria, a 70-foot-high glass-domed trilevel shopping mall (with Ralph Lauren, Versace, and similar boutiques), which was modeled after Milan's 1867 Galleria Vittoria Emmanuelle; it's bounded by Post, Kearny, Sutter, and Montgomery Sts. The vast Embarcadero Center is a sophisticated triple-level, open-air neo-mall well worth a spree; it's located between Clay, Sacramento, Battery, and Drumm Sts.

Outdoor enthusiasts should check out The North Face outlet for skiwear, sweaters, sleeping bags, and other high-quality outdoor gear; 1325 Howard St, between Ninth and Tenth Sts, (415) 626-6444.

Good bookstores include City Lights, still Beat after all these years, 261 Columbus Ave at Broadway, (415) 362-8193; A Clean Well-Lighted Place for Books, 601 Van Ness Ave, in Opera Plaza between Golden Gate Ave and Turk St, (415) 441-6670; Stacey's Bookstore, 581 Market St at Second St, (415) 421-4687; the massive Borders Books & Music, 400 Post St at Powell St in Union Square, (415) 399-1633; and Rand McNally Map & Travel Store, 595 Market St at Second St, (415) 777-3131.

Nightlife. Great clubs abound in San Francisco, the city that never seems to sleep. Most of San Francisco's clubs offer an ever-changing lineup of bands or recorded music, so call ahead for up-to-date recorded listings at each venue. The Be-At Line recorded hot-line will also tell you where you can find the night's hot musical acts, (415) 626-4087. Locals tend to pick up a copy of the free *San Francisco Bay Guardian* weekly newspaper (available at cafes and most major street corners) for the straight scoop on the city's wild and ever-changing club scene.

When San Franciscans need something to cut the chill of those long foggy nights, many head to North Beach, which has more than its fair share of popular watering holes, including Little City, a great spot for flirting over drinks and plates of antipasti; 673 Union St at Powell St, near Washington Square, (415) 434-2900. There's also the Tosca Cafe, where locals hang out (and celebs hide in the back room) to sip the house specialty: coffeeless cappuccinos made with brandy, milk, and chocolate, 242 Columbus Ave, between Pacific Ave and Broadway, (415) 391-1244. When the fog burns off and the weather heats up, grab a chair on the patio of Cafe Flore in the Castro District and order a glass of white wine or a latte; 2298 Market St at Noe St, (415) 621-8579. Or get the full array of spirits on the outdoor decks of such funky local favorites as The Ramp, 855 China Basin St off Third St, (415) 621-2378, and Pier 23, on the Embarcadero between Broadway and Bay St, (415) 362-5125.

Union Square's best bustling bars are at Kuleto's restaurant, 221 Powell St, between Geary and O'Farrell Sts, (415) 397-7720, and the Compass Rose on the first floor of the Westin St. Francis Hotel, 335 Powell St, between Post and Geary Sts, (415) 774-0233 or (415) 397-7000.

Spectator Sports. Bay Area sports buffs are justly proud of their champion San Francisco 49ers football team, which plays home games at 3Com Park; for 49ers ticket info (don't get your hopes up—they're hard to come by), call (415) 468-2249. The San Francisco Giants take over during baseball season until the year 2000, when the construction of their new state-of-the-art Pac Bell Park stadium in China Basin is expected to be completed; call (415) 467-8000 for more details on the Giants.

Restaurants

Acquerello ☆☆☆   Acquerello offers contemporary regional Italian cooking in a tranquil, refined setting. The small, innovative menu changes often, and stellar entrees are beautifully presented. *1722 Sacramento St (near Polk St), San Francisco; (415) 567-5432; $$–$$$.*

Antica Trattoria ☆☆☆   This simply decorated restaurant with dark wood floors and cream-colored walls has developed a deserved reputation as one of the city's best Italian trattorias. It's well-prepared and reasonably priced. *2400 Polk St (at the corner of Union St), San Francisco; (415) 928-5797; $$.*

Aqua ☆☆☆   Aqua was the first restaurant in the city to elevate the humble fish house to a temple of haute cuisine. The attractive dining room is sleek as a shark, and culinary creations are marked by a refreshingly light touch with herbs and sauces. *252 California St (at Battery St), San Francisco; (415) 956-9662; $$$.*

Betelnut ☆☆   This sumptuously decorated Asian "beerhouse" has the ever-so-slightly tarty feel of an exotic 1930s Shanghai brothel. The mixed menu is Pan-Asian, with an array of authentic dishes from Vietnam, Singapore, China, Thailand, Indonesia, and Japan. *2030 Union St (near Buchanan St), San Francisco; (415) 929-8855; $$.*

Bizou ☆☆☆   Bizou means "a little kiss" in French, but San Francisco foodies seem to have planted a big fat wet one on this lively bistro with the rustic Mediterranean menu. The service can range from boffo to beastly. *598 4th St (at Brannan St), San Francisco; (415) 543-2222; $$.*

Boulevard ☆☆☆   Big, bustling Boulevard serves hearty American-style cuisine with French and Italian influences. The Parisian-inspired interior design is capped with a sweeping view of the Embarcadero and the Bay Bridge. *1 Mission St (in the Audiffred Bldg, at the Embarcadero, on the corner of Steuart St), San Francisco; (415) 543-6084; $$$.*

Bruno's ☆☆☆   This swanky 1950s supper-club–style dining room has giant cherry-red booths that seem to be made for snuggling. But ambience isn't the only thing that makes Bruno's such a hot spot—it offers a marvelous French and Italian menu. *2389 Mission St (between 19th and 20th Sts), San Francisco; (415) 550-7455; $$$.*

Cafe Kati ☆☆☆   This tiny cafe has garnered a monsoon of kudos for weird and wonderful arrangements of numerous cuisines. Fortunately, it tastes as good as it looks. Don't make any plans after dinner because the kitchen takes its sweet time preparing your objet d'art. *1963 Sutter St (near Fillmore St), San Francisco; (415) 775-7313; $$.*

Chez Michel ☆☆☆   Sophisticated without being pretentious, Chez Michel has a sleekly tailored look. The superb French cuisine and the knowledgeable staff make this spot so inviting that it has even lured locals into the Fisherman's Wharf area for dinner. *804 North Point (at Hyde St), San Francisco; (415) 775-7036; $$$.*

Eos Restaurant & Wine Bar ☆☆☆   The Euro-Asian fusion theme is hardly original, but the portions (generous) and presentations (brilliant) have brought throngs of visitors to Eos. The stark deco-industrial decor amplifies the nightly cacophony. *901 Cole St (at Carl St), San Francisco; (415) 566-3063; $$–$$$.*

Farallon ☆☆☆   This dazzling restaurant offers seafood dishes that are as innovative as the elegant aquatic-themed decor, a dramatic but enchanting stage for excellent coastal cuisine. *450 Post St (between Powell and Mason Sts, 1 block W of Union Square), San Francisco; (415) 956-6969; $$$.*

Firefly ☆☆   Inside, an eclectic array of modern art surrounds small tables laden with an equally eclectic display of food, which the owners call "home cooking with few ethnic boundaries." *4288 24th St (near Douglass St), San Francisco; (415) 821-7652; $$–$$$.*

Fleur de Lys ☆☆☆☆   This is definitely a Grand Occasion restaurant, with fantastic food, formal service, breathtaking decor, and a superb wine list. Many of the contemporary French dishes are near-miracles. *777 Sutter St (between Taylor and Jones Sts), San Francisco; (415) 673-7779; $$$.*

Flying Saucer ☆☆☆   This hip bistro specializes in attitude as well as excellent food. The menu can be quite eccentric and changes often, but most of it works well. That attitude sometimes extends to the service, which can be maddeningly rude. *1000 Guerrero St (at 22nd St), San Francisco; (415) 641-9955; $$–$$$.*

Fringale ☆☆☆☆   This tiny French restaurant has plenty of charm emanating from its blond-wood-trimmed interior and its friendly waitstaff. Fringale (French for "a sudden pang of hunger") is packed at dinnertime. *570 4th St (between Bryant and Brannan Sts), San Francisco; (415) 543-0573; $$.*

Greens ☆☆   As the Savoy Grill in London is to the roast beef connoisseur, so is Greens at Fort Mason to the vegetarian aesthete. *Fort Mason Center, Bldg A (off Marina Blvd at Buchanan St), San Francisco; (415) 771-6222; $$–$$$.*

Harris' ☆☆   Not just another steak house, Harris' is a living monument to the not-quite-bygone joys of guiltless beef-eating. The formal club setting boasts dark wood paneling, plush carpets, and large brown tufted booths. *2100 Van Ness Ave (at Pacific Ave), San Francisco; (415) 673-1888; $$$.*

Hawthorne Lane ☆☆☆   Ever since it opened, this has been one of the city's hottest restaurants, its popularity fueled by its lovely design and the contemporary American menu with Asian and Mediterranean influences. *22 Hawthorne St (off Howard St, between 2nd and 3rd Sts), San Francisco; (415) 777-9779; $$$.*

House of Nanking ☆☆   Nanking's food is outstanding and the prices are some of the most reasonable in the city, but the service is downright terrible at this tiny, wildly popular hole-in-the-wall. *919 Kearny St (between Jackson St and Pacific Ave), San Francisco; (415) 421-1429; $.*

Infusion Bar & Restaurant ☆☆☆ This trendy, noisy SoMa bar and restaurant was named after the house specialty, vodka-based infusions. European, Asian, Mexican, and Caribbean influences add interesting grace notes to the New American fare. *555 2nd St (between Bryant and Brannan Sts), San Francisco; (415) 543-2282; $$.*

Jardinière ☆☆☆ Jardinière was a smashing success as soon as the highly stylized glass doors swung open. The two-story brick building, elegantly framed with violet velvet drapes, is an impressive setting for the French-California cuisine. *300 Grove St (at Franklin St, behind Davies Symphony Hall), San Francisco; (415) 861-5555; $$$.*

Kyo-ya ☆☆☆ This elegantly austere restaurant in the Palace Hotel serves some of the best sushi and sashimi in town. Catering to well-heeled business execs visiting from the other side of the Rim, Kyo-ya's food is fresh, authentic, and delicious. *2 New Montgomery St (in the Palace Hotel, off Market St, between 2nd and 3rd Sts), San Francisco; (415) 392-8600; $$$.*

La Folie ☆☆☆☆ The intimate, whimsical dining room is an appropriate stage for the creative and exuberant, but disciplined, menu. The wine list is extensive but the prices are steep, and while the service is attentive, it's not seamless. *2316 Polk St (between Union and Green Sts), San Francisco; (415) 776-5577; $$$.*

La Taqueria ☆☆ Among colorful fruit stands, thrift shops, and greasy panhandlers lining bustling Mission Street sits La Taqueria, the Bay Area's best burrito factory. It's all fresh, delicious, and guaranteed to fill you up. *2889 Mission St (at 25th St), San Francisco; (415) 285-7117; $.*

Masa's ☆☆☆☆ This is probably San Francisco's most expensive restaurant. That said, the prices accurately reflect the precious ingredients, generous portions, stunning presentations, and labor-intensive nature of the elegant French-California cuisine. *648 Bush St (in the Hotel Vintage Court, between Stockton and Powell Sts), San Francisco; (415) 989-7154; $$$.*

Mecca ☆☆ Mecca is a magnet for those who want an abundance of atmosphere with hearty American bistro fare—and this sexy, silver Mission Street supper club lined with chocolate brown velvet drapes delivers. *2029 Market St (between 14th and Dolores Sts, across from Safeway), San Francisco; (415) 621-7000; $$$.*

One Market ☆☆ Dozens of waiters and waitresses dart from one end of this vast dining room to the other trying to keep as many as 230 customers satisfied with very good (and sometimes excellent) contemporary American fare. *1 Market St (at Steuart St, across from the Ferry Bldg), San Francisco; (415) 777-5577; $$$.*

Pane e Vino ☆☆☆   This dark-wood-trimmed trattoria framed by a cream-colored awning is a local favorite. The two tiny dining rooms fill up fast, providing first-rate service and rustic Italian fare. *3011 Steiner St (at Union St), San Francisco; (415) 346-2111; $$.*

PlumpJack Cafe ☆☆☆   This exotic California-Mediterranean bistro is one of San Francisco's leading restaurants, with consistently excellent food and a surprisingly extensive wine list with fine bottles offered at near-retail prices. *3127 Fillmore St (between Greenwich and Filbert Sts), San Francisco; (415) 563-4755; $$$.*

Postrio ☆☆☆   Postrio is a splashy slice of Hollywood set in the heart of San Francisco, with superglitzy decor, delightful California/Asian/ Mediterranean culinary combinations, and the perpetual hope of catching sight of some celeb at the next table. *545 Post St (in the Prescott Hotel, between Mason and Taylor Sts), San Francisco; (415) 776-7825; $$$.*

Rose Pistola ☆☆☆   This sleek and sexy addition to the Columbus Avenue promenade is as pleasing to behold as it is to dine in. The food is rustic Italian with a California flair (less fats, more flavors) inspired by the cuisine of Liguria. *532 Columbus Ave (between Green and Union Sts), San Francisco; (415) 399-0499; $$–$$$.*

Rubicon ☆☆☆   This Financial District restaurant received so much advance publicity that San Franciscans were setting dates to eat here long before it opened. The French-inspired menu features a pair of prix-fixe menus and a tasting menu. *558 Sacramento St (between Montgomery and Sansome Sts), San Francisco; (415) 434-4100; $$$.*

The Slanted Door ☆☆   This small, bilevel restaurant specializes in country Vietnamese food. The stylish, narrow dining room has green-stained wood tables, and the unique fare attracts droves of people for lunch and dinner. *584 Valencia St (near 17th St), San Francisco; (415) 861-8032; $–$$.*

Swan Oyster Depot ☆   This is where diehard San Francisco shellfish fans gleefully slurp down fresh oysters, clams, and delicious clam chowder. It's a one-of-a-kind San Francisco experience, the type of place tourists tend to unknowingly walk past. *1517 Polk St (at California St, next to See's Candies and the Royal Theatre), San Francisco; (415) 673-1101; $$.*

Thep Phanom ☆☆☆   A creative touch of California enters the cultural mix here, resulting in sophisticated preparations that have a special sparkle. The tasteful decor, informal atmosphere, and eclectic crowd are all very San Francisco. *400 Waller St (at Fillmore St, near Haight St), San Francisco; (415) 431-2526; $$.*

Ton Kiang ☆☆   Ton Kiang has established a solid reputation in San

Francisco as one of the best Chinese restaurants in the city, particularly when it comes to dim sum. Ton Kiang's dim sum is phenomenal—fresh, flavorful, and not the least bit greasy. *5821 Geary Blvd (between 22nd and 23rd Aves), San Francisco; (415) 387-8273; $$.*

Woodward's Garden ☆☆☆   In what is arguably one of the least desired commercial spaces in the city stands what is certainly one of the Bay Area's best restaurants. The American/Mediterranean-influenced menu changes weekly. *1700 Mission St (at Duboce Ave, under the highway overpass), San Francisco; (415) 621-7122; $$$.*

Yank Sing ☆☆   Yank Sing's fare is as good as any dim sum you'll get in Hong Kong, and the prices (and service) are much better than in nearby Harbor Village. Make reservations or prepare to wait and wait and wait. *427 Battery St (between Clay and Washington Sts), San Francisco; (415) 781-1111 or (415) 362-1640; $$.*

Zuni Cafe ☆☆   Before it got famous, Zuni was a tiny Southwestern-style lunch spot in a low-class neighborhood. Today, it's nearly as quintessential a San Francisco institution as Dungeness crab and sourdough bread. *1658 Market St (between Franklin and Gough Sts), San Francisco; (415) 552-2522; $$.*

Lodgings

The Bed and Breakfast Inn ☆☆   San Francisco's first bed and breakfast maintains the convincing illusion that it's a charming old English inn somewhere in Cornwall. The main difference, of course, is that this 11-room B&B is tucked into a cul-de-sac just steps away from Union Street, one of the city's most popular shopping areas. *4 Charlton Court (in a cul-de-sac off Union St, between Buchanan and Laguna Sts), San Francisco; (415) 921-9784; $$.*

Campton Place Kempinski Hotel ☆☆☆☆   The lobby, reminiscent of a gallery with its domed ceiling, miles of marble, crystal chandeliers, and striking Asian art, is worth the price of admission alone. The 117 guest rooms are very comfortable, and the custom furnishings help create a pervasive air of luxury. *340 Stockton St (between Sutter and Post Sts, at Union Square), San Francisco; (415) 781-5555 or (800) 235-4300.*

Clift Hotel ☆☆☆☆   As you step up to the entrance of this resplendent 17-story mansion, a doorman will politely usher you into the lobby, a vast gilded chamber replete with sparkling chandeliers and fine Oriental carpets. Each of the 326 guest rooms is individually designed and boasts luxurious furnishings. *495 Geary St (at Taylor St, 1½ blocks from Union Square), San Francisco; (415) 775-4700 or (800) 332-3442; $$$.*

Commodore International Hotel ☆☆   The relatively new 113-room Commodore is a fun and surprisingly affordable hostelry. If you're on a tight budget, stick with the plain but pleasant rooms on the first four floors; otherwise, break out an extra Jackson and live it up near the top, where the interiors echo the neo-deco theme. *825 Sutter St (between Jones and Leavenworth Sts), San Francisco; (415) 923-6800 or (800) 338-6848; $$.*

El Drisco ☆☆☆   This six-story structure, perched on one of the most coveted blocks in San Francisco, was originally built in 1903 and is now one of the finest small hotels in the city. The 24 rooms and 19 suites are bathed in soothing shades of alabaster, celadon, and buttercup yellow and feature rich fabrics and quality antiques. *2901 Pacific Ave (at Broderick St), San Francisco; (415) 346-2880 or (800) 634-7277; $$$.*

Hotel Bohème ☆☆   Hopelessly chic is perhaps the best way to describe the Hotel Bohème, one of the sexiest small hotels in the city and a favorite retreat of visiting writers and poets. Hovering two stories above Columbus Avenue, the 15-room Bohème artfully reflects North Beach's bohemian flair dating from the late 1950s and early '60s. *444 Columbus Ave (between Vallejo and Green Sts), San Francisco; (415) 433-9111; $$.*

Hotel Diva ☆☆☆   When it first opened in 1985, Hotel Diva was the prima donna of San Francisco's modern hotels, winning Best Hotel Design from *Interiors* magazine for its suave, ultramodern design. Even the 111 guest rooms are works of art, decorated with handsome Italian modern furnishings. *440 Geary St (between Mason and Taylor Sts), San Francisco; (415) 885-0200 or (800) 553-1900; $$$.*

Hotel Monaco ☆☆☆☆   "Wow!" is a common exclamation among first-time guests of Hotel Monaco. The 201-room Monaco has received nothing but kudos for its sumptuous, stunning decor. Expect a melding of modern European fashion with flourishes of the American Beaux Arts era. The entire hotel is truly a feast for the eyes. *501 Geary St (at Taylor St), San Francisco; (415) 292-0100 or (800) 214-4220; $$$.*

Hotel Triton ☆☆☆   The Hotel Triton has been described as modern, whimsical, sophisticated, chic, vogue, neo-Baroque, ultra-hip, and retro-futuristic—but the words just don't do justice to this unique hostelry-cum-art-gallery that you'll simply have to see to appreciate. The 133 rooms and 7 designer suites continue the theme. *342 Grant Ave (at Bush St, near the gateway to Chinatown), San Francisco; (415) 394-0500 or (800) 433-6611; $$$.*

Huntington Hotel ☆☆☆   The small, modest lobby of this imposing Nob Hill landmark belies its lavish interiors. The 12-story hotel's 140 individually decorated rooms are spacious, with imported silks, 17th-century paintings, and stunning views of the city and the bay. *1075 California St (at the top of Nob Hill, across from Grace Cathedral), San Francisco; (415) 474-5400 or (800) 652-1539 (in California only), and (800) 227-4683 (outside California only); $$$.*

Inn on Castro ☆   This convivial bed-and-breakfast inn, catering to the gay and lesbian community for nearly two decades, has developed an ardent following. The restored Edwardian exterior is painted in a pleasing medley of blue, rose, and green. The 8 rooms are equally festive, with contemporary furnishings, original modern art, and exotic plants. *321 Castro St (H block N of Market St), San Francisco; (415) 861-0321; $$.*

Jackson Court ☆☆   Tucked away behind a brick archway and a white-trellised garden courtyard, this three-story brownstone is set in the heart of the exclusive Pacific Heights residential neighborhood. All 10 blissfully quiet guest rooms have handsome architectural details and pleasantly spare high-quality antiques. *2198 Jackson St (at Buchanan St, in Pacific Heights), San Francisco; (415) 929-7670; $$$.*

Mandarin Oriental ☆☆☆   The 158 rooms at the award-winning Mandarin Oriental (perched on the top 11 floors of San Francisco's third tallest skyscraper), are comfortable and deceptively austere: well hidden among the simple blond-wood furniture and fine Asian artwork are all the latest luxury amenities. *222 Sansome St (between Pine and California Sts, in the Financial District), San Francisco; (415) 885-0999 or (800) 622-0404; $$$.*

The Prescott Hotel ☆☆☆   The Prescott puts pressure on Union Square's neighboring luxury hotels by offering first-rate accommodations at a fairly reasonable price. The 154 rooms, decorated with cherry-wood furnishings, black-granite-topped nightstands and dressers, and silk wallpaper, have rich color schemes of hunter green, deep purple, cerise, taupe, and gold. *545 Post St (between Taylor and Mason Sts), San Francisco; (415) 563-0303 or (800) 283-7322; $$$.*

The Ritz-Carlton, San Francisco ☆☆☆☆   This 1909 17-columned neoclassical beauty earned a seventh-place ranking in *Condé Nast Traveler's* 1997 list of the top 25 hotels in North America (and a first-place ranking in San Francisco). The 336 guest rooms are not high fashion, but they're sinfully plush and loaded with high-society amenities. *600 Stockton St (at California St, on Nob Hill), San Francisco; (415) 296-7465 or (800) 241-3333 (reservations only); $$$.*

San Remo Hotel ☆   Hidden in a quiet North Beach neighborhood, the San Remo is within easy walking distance of San Francisco's main attractions. Combine the locale with an inexpensive price tag, and you have one of the best room bargains in the city. This well-preserved, charming three-story Italianate Victorian has 62 rooms reminiscent of a European pensione. *2237 Mason St (at Chestnut St), San Francisco; (415) 776-8688 or (800) 352-REMO; $.*

Savoy Hotel ☆☆   Originally built in 1913, the Savoy is now a posh French country–style inn with a gorgeous facade of richly veined black marble, beveled glass, mahogany, and polished brass. The 83 guest rooms and suites are small but beautifully appointed, with heavy French cotton bedspreads, imported Provençal furnishings, and plump feather beds. *580 Geary St (between Taylor and Jones Sts), San Francisco; (415) 441-2700 or (800) 227-4223; $$.*

Tuscan Inn ☆☆   You won't find the glitz of San Francisco's downtown hostelries or even a terrific view here, but the Tuscan's 221 attractive guest rooms (including 12 deluxe suites) offer every creature comfort one could need. Armchairs, writing desks, honor bars, remote-control TVs, direct-dial phones, and private bathrooms are standard features of every room. *425 North Point St (at Mason St), San Francisco; (415) 561-1100 or (800) 648-4626; $$$.*

Union Street Inn ☆   This delightful bed and breakfast wins a prize for overall ambience. Although the two-story Edwardian mansion is situated amid the bustle of trendy Union Street, it's set high above the traffic. There are 5 large guest rooms and a deluxe carriage house across the garden, each with its own theme and color scheme. *2229 Union St (between Fillmore and Steiner Sts), San Francisco; (415) 346-0424; $$$.*

The Washington Square Inn ☆☆   The Washington Square Inn's prime location in the middle of the historic North Beach district is its best asset. And behind the inn's plain, inconspicuous facade is a delightful European-style bed and breakfast. The 15 comfortable, modest rooms are furnished with European antiques and bright flower-print bedspreads. *1660 Stockton St (at Filbert St, in North Beach), San Francisco; (415) 981-4220 or (800) 388-0220; $$$.*

More Information:

Golden Gate National Recreation Area: *(415) 556-0560.*
San Francisco Convention and Visitors Bureau: *(415) 391-2000.*
San Francisco Department of Parks and Recreation: *(415) 666-7200.*
San Francisco neighborhood profiles: *www.sanfrancisco.sidewalk.com.*
San Francisco Tourist Guide: *(415) 821-4414.*

Marin

From the Golden Gate Bridge's north landing and Angel Island to the south, heading north to Tomales Bay on the west and the mouth of the Petaluma River on the east, including Mount Tamalpais and China Camp State Parks, Muir Woods National Monument, and the Marin Headlands.

Take a good look at the San Francisco skyline. The trademark Transamerica Pyramid building, historic Coit Tower, and the Golden Gate and Bay Bridges are among the distinctive features setting the city apart aesthetically from other internationally significant cities around the world. Now, try to imagine what this all looked like 150 years ago, before pavement and skyscrapers replaced the grasslands and coastal scrub on the hills, and ports and warehouses replaced the marshes along the bay. If you're having trouble picturing this, just turn your attention north and take a gander at the vast, undeveloped areas of Marin County. Areas of San Francisco's less populated and more carefully developed neighbor, found conveniently at the other end of the Golden Gate Bridge, look much the way San Francisco did when the first western explorers arrived. From the bluffs and beaches of the Marin Headlands, where the remnants of military fortifications still stand, to the 2,610-foot peak of Mount Tamalpais, and from the ancient trees of Muir Woods to the stunning vistas from atop Angel Island State Park's Mount Livermore, Marin is the quintessential outdoor playland. One visit and you'll wonder why they charge a toll on the Golden Gate Bridge to enter San Francisco from Marin instead of the other way around.

Marin is where the mountain bike was invented in the late 1970s, and Tamalpais is still considered one of the world's chief off-road biking regions. From Kirby Cove just west of the Golden Gate to Dillon Beach north of the mouth of Tomales Bay, Marin's ocean beaches are largely wild and undeveloped, and virtually all have public access. In select places very good surfing conditions exist, especially compared to points south where heavy surf and sometimes-unpredictable riptides can give beginners and intermediates the jitters. On the bay shore, the Marin coast offers some of the best windsurfing and boating conditions in the San Francisco region.

While the climate tends to be significantly wetter here than in the rest of the Bay Area, the rain turns out to be another thing Marin County and the rest of the North Bay region have going for it. Wet days, you see, frighten the masses away, leaving the spoils for those of us who don't mind a little muck or mud if it means a chance to get out on the trails or hit the beaches without fighting the weekend crowds. Keep in mind, however, that summers are hotter and winters colder here as well.

Indeed, Marin is San Francisco's favorite escape hatch. And Bay Area residents who appreciate the outdoors know how to take advantage of that.

Getting There

From San Francisco, take the Golden Gate Bridge north to Marin on US Highway 101 (US 101), which has turnoffs for all major outdoor recreation areas. From the East Bay, take Interstate 580 to the Richmond–San Rafael Bridge, which lands just south of the US 101 corridor in northeastern Marin. From Sonoma County, take Highway 1 or US 101 south, and from Napa take Highway 37 west to the US 101 interchange. Much of the open space falls under the jurisdiction of the Golden Gate National Recreation Area, (415) 556-0560, with visitors centers in San Francisco at the Cliff House on the Great Highway just north of Ocean Beach and at Fort Point, beneath the Golden Gate Bridge. For Mount Tamalpais, stop in at the Pantoll Ranger Station, at the crest of the Panoramic Highway near the summit, (415) 893-1580.

Adjoining Areas

NORTH: **Sonoma and Southern Mendocino Coasts**

SOUTH: **San Francisco**

EAST: **Napa and Sonoma Wine Valleys**

WEST: **Point Reyes National Seashore**

inside out

Mountain Biking

The mountain bike was invented here, okay? So, as much as other points around the state and even the world try to pass themselves off as prime off-road biking destinations, keep this in mind: this is where it all started in the late 1970s. For nostalgia's sake, any trip to Marin should involve a mountain bike. Don't, however, get caught up in the "scene." Somehow during the past two decades, mountain biking became more than a sport in Marin, it mutated into a fashion statement. Watch for those who wear the costume and spend heartily on the equipment, but never break a sweat on the trails. These are the people you will pass on the difficult climb to the top of **Mount Tamalpais.** Bikes have long been banished from the mountain's single-track trails, where the sport actually was born, but rides are spectacular and challenging even on the wider fire roads.

A 15mph speed limit is strictly enforced on the fire roads covering Tamalpais, which traverse the mountain from every possible direction, with difficult to moderately difficult routes over and around the 2,560-foot west peak. You have numerous options of where to stage, so get suggestions from the park ranger station, (415) 288-2070. Also check in with the Marin Municipal Water District, which owns adjoining properties with trail connections to the mountain, (415) 459-5267.

On the mountain, the **Old Railroad Grade Trail** to the summit (difficult; 13 miles round trip) is a popular route, starting from West Blithedale Ave in Mill Valley. Count on a strenuous climb, steep with numerous switchbacks in the last 2 miles.

Mountain-biking routes for all skill levels also run throughout the adjacent **Marin Headlands,** and on the bay, **Angel Island State Park** (see Parks, below) is another favorite biking area, just a short ferry ride from the Marin town of Tiburon. To get outfitted with gear or **rentals** along with **trail information,** drop in at Start to Finish, Miller Ave at US 101, Mill Valley, (415) 388-3500; A Bicycle Odyssey, 1417 Bridgeway, Sausalito, (415) 332-3050; or Sausalito Cyclery, 1 Gate Six Rd (at US 101), (415) 322-3200. Bicycle rentals on Angel Island are available at Ayala Cove, right where the ferry drops off visitors. The **Bicycle Trails Council of Marin,** (415) 456-7512, is also a good resource for planning outings, particularly in the headlands and on "Tam," pet name for the mountain among locals.

Trails and fire roads covering the vast headlands area are managed by the Golden Gate National Recreation Area. Keep in mind that these trails are heavily patrolled, and the 15mph speed limit is taken very seriously by park rangers. As much as the temptation will be difficult to resist, this is not the place for the rabid downhill racing veteran mountain bikers like to rhapsodize about. **Bobcat, Coyote Ridge, Marcinello, and Tennessee Valley Trails** all are popular legal mountain bike routes within the headlands, of moderate aerobic and technical difficulty on most alignments. Call the headlands visitors center, (415) 331-1540, for maps and **trail condition information.** North and just east of Point Reyes National Seashore, **Bolinas Ridge Trail** (moderate; 22 miles round trip) offers nice vistas overlooking Kent Lake and Olema Valley. With no switchbacks or difficult climbs, and sparse use on weekdays, this is a good ride for beginners who have the strength for the climb but lack the technical skills necessary to keep from wiping out on steep downhill grades and tricky corners. Stage at the end of Bolinas-Fairfax Rd; from Sir Francis Drake Blvd, turn right into Fairfax, then left on Broadway. Turn left at the stop sign onto Bolinas-Fairfax Rd, and follow it to the end. Before setting out on this adventure, however, check with the Olema Valley ranger station, (415) 663-1092, for updated trail condition information, as this trail is particularly vulnerable to inclement weather and is often partially closed.

On Angel Island the off-road biking scene is completely different. You will want to use a bicycle just to get around this mile-wide island parkland in enough time to catch the ferry back to the mainland (miss the last ferry and you're stranded). **Perimeter Trail** encircles the island, covering 10 miles, with cutoffs toward the peak of Mount Livermore, 781 feet above the geographic center of the bay. You cannot ride all the way to the peak, however. For trail information, call the park office, (415) 435-5390, or the Angel Island Association, (415) 435-3522. For information on the Tiburon ferry service, contact the Angel Island–Tiburon Ferry, in Tiburon at (415) 435-2131. For information on the San Francisco and Vallejo ferries, contact the Blue and Gold Fleet at (415) 773-1188.

Cycling

Let's make one thing perfectly clear: while some do see Marin as the mountain biking center of the universe, possession of a mountain bike is not required for admission. In fact, some of the best road cycling in the Bay Area is also here among the headlands beginning at the Golden Gate Bridge landing, and along the scenic roads and highways following the full length of the Marin coast. There are many routes to choose from. Perhaps the most important advice we can offer (aside from a few suggested tours): try to avoid biking the coastal areas on weekends if at all possible. Competing with automobile traffic on congested, winding, and at times narrow roads can be trying, particularly when many of those drivers are from out of town and unfamiliar with the area. Tourists looking for the perfect overlook to snap their next Kodak moment or who have been circling a little too long trying to park are famous for sudden moves behind the wheel on the headlands roads.

The strenuous 15-mile ride from the foot of the bridge over the headlands on **Conzelman Rd** begins with a catapult up a rigorous 12 percent grade past Battery Rathbone–McIndoe and the Bicentennial Camp (see Camping, below), then takes a fast descent to Bunker Rd, which flattens out toward East Fort Baker (you will pass through a one-lane tunnel with the bicycle lane marked). At the fort, relax waterside before reconnecting easily with the bridge via the **Bay Trail.**

Road cycling is also popular along the 30-mile **Stinson Beach Loop,** along Hwy 1, through Olema Valley, and along Bolinas-Fairfax Rd. Write Marin Cyclists, PO Box 2611, San Rafael, CA 94912, for **tour suggestions.** See Mountain Biking, above, for local cycle shop suggestions and other resources.

Beaches

The stretch of the Coast Highway (Hwy 1) winding around Mount Tamalpais State Park and slicing through the cliffs overlooking the Pacific between Muir Woods and Point Reyes is a beachcomber's paradise. Coldwater swimming, surfing, sandy jogs on the smooth white sand, wildlife viewing, secluded picnics, you name it! Add in the coastal portions of the Marin Headlands and you'll be exploring for days. Keep in mind, however, that these are wild places. Heavy and unpredictable surf makes swimming precarious—and even coved or reefed areas are susceptible to strong undertows. Don't turn your back on the water, because a sleeper can nail you at any time. For a complete rundown of beachfront opportunities in this region, contact the Golden Gate National Recreation Area, (415) 556-0560, or the Gulf of the Farallones National Marin Sanctuary at (415) 556-3509. Here are some beach highlights:

Stinson Beach: The smell of scented suntan oil often overpowers the salt breezes of the Pacific at this wide, sandy beach at the end of Panoramic Highway. Stinson is one of the most popular in the Bay Area for summer sunbathing, swimming, walking, or jogging along its 3 miles of smooth, white sand. This portion of the Marin coast is also prime for surfers and boogie-boarders, as the beach is protected by Duxbury Reef. Volleyball equipment is available at the lifeguard towers, free of charge. With easy **trail connections** to Mount Tamalpais State Park and Muir Woods National Monument, Stinson also is the perfect stopover point for daylong hiking and mountain-biking trips in the coastal region. In peak season, however, this place is probably best reserved for weekday trips, as weekend crowds can spoil the experience with traffic and people jams. Parking places are usually full by midmorning on peak days. Other features include picnic tables, rest rooms, a snack bar, and wheelchair access. No pets allowed. Lifeguards are on duty May to September. Call the Stinson Ranger Station at (415) 868-1922 for information; for surfing and parking conditions, call (415) 868-1922. The beach is easily found at the junction of the Coast Highway and Panoramic Highway, north of Mount Tamalpais State Park.

Muir Beach: This sandy beach in a cove just south of Mount Tamalpais State Park is a popular spot for tidal fishing, picnics, sunbathing, and wildlife viewing. Whale watching is popular nearby from the **Muir Beach Overlook,** long ago the location of military watch stations guarding the Pacific Coast from enemy vessel traffic. There are lovely pine groves facing the ocean, rest rooms, and handicapped access. This area can get windy, so be prepared to batten down the hatches just in case. Call the beach office at (415) 556-3509 for information. The beach entrance is on the Coast Highway near Muir Woods Rd.

Rodeo Beach: Wildlife viewing and coastal hikes are most popular at this sand-and-pebble beach adjacent to **Rodeo Lagoon.** Trails through the bluffs connect easily to the Marin Headlands trail systems. An environmental education center here, open 10am to 4pm daily, offers guided interpretive walks and environmental education programs. Call (415) 331-1540.

Kirby Cove: Considering its location within sight of the Golden Gate Bridge, you'd expect beachcombers to be climbing over each other to get to this sand-and-pebble, coved beach below the eastern portion of the Marin Headlands. But the crowds don't flock here, mostly because the beach is difficult to get to: those without camping reservations (see Camping, below) must walk or hike more than half a mile down a gravel access road—and climb all the way back up to leave. Picnic facilities and rest rooms are available. Access is a half mile west of US 101, on Conzelman Rd; proceed to the locked gate. Parking is limited. Call Golden Gate National Recreation Area, (415) 556-0560, or the Marin Headlands park office, (415) 331-1540, for more information. Most of the time, there is no park personnel on site.

Surfing/Windsurfing

Fort Cronkhite, Stinson Beach (see Beaches, above), and **Bolinas** are the prime **surfing** spots along the Marin coast, the latter two ideal for beginners because much of the time they are shielded from the torrents of the Pacific by Duxbury Reef. Don't be fooled, however. Even the protected spots can get bumpy, although these areas are calmer and less crowded than Bay Area points south. And remember, this is not Florida or Hawaii: the water is cold, and you'll need wet suits and the whole works. Contact Marin Surf Sports, 254 Shoreline Hwy, Mill Valley, (415) 381-9283; Fat Kat Surf Shop, 42 Bolinas Rd, Fairfax, (415) 453-9167; or Double Overhead Association of San Francisco, (415) 665-7745, for **equipment,** pointers, and information on where to get lessons if you need them. The **Stinson surf report** line is (415) 868-1922. For a general surf report, call (415) 665-9473.

It is possible to **windsurf** in Marin on the San Francisco Bay shore. The prime launching spots are from **Larkspur Landing** in San Rafael, **China Camp State Park** just outside San Rafael (see Parks, below), and the bay shore near the San Rafael Rod and Gun Club. Park on Sir Francis Drake Blvd, along the waterfront for the gun club area. Morning conditions are best for beginners here. Watch out for submerged rocks, harbor seals, and ferryboats. Also keep in mind that San Quentin State Prison is adjacent to the sailing grounds. Going ashore there is not a good idea. Along the China Camp shoreline, putting in at low tide is not advisable— the area turns to salt marsh—so be sure to check tide tables before setting out from there. Two local **sailboarding shops** can help out with details and rental equipment: Boardsports Marin, 2233 Larkspur Landing Circle, (415) 925-8585, and Windsports, 1595 Francisco Blvd, San Rafael, (415) 459-1171.

Clamming/Fishing

Feel like digging for your dinner? Lawson's Landing near Dillon Beach on Tomales Bay is a prime place to get out the pump gun and garden shovel and pull up meaty 6- to 8-inch **horseneck clams,** famous for their size and texture. Head out at minus-low tide, anytime from January to July. A barge leaving Lawson's periodically throughout the day drops clammers at key spots along the mudflats for just $2. Don't just show up expecting to go at it, though, because conditions have to be right; if the flats aren't properly exposed, you'll be wasting your time. Call Lawson's, (707) 878-2443, to check on conditions and equipment rentals. The resort also keeps a tide calendar. Tomales Bay State Park's (see Parks, below) ranger station also will be able to point you to other spots around the bay suitable for clamming, (415) 669-1140. A state fishing license is required.

Varied fishing spots also are found throughout the Marin bay shore and along the Pacific Coast. At **East Fort Baker** east of the Golden Gate

Bridge, fishing for **perch, flounder,** and **salmon** is good both along the shoreline and from the public pier. Tidal fishing at Muir Beach for **rockfish, surf perch, lingcod, wolf eel, smelt,** and **silversides** is also a favorite. But before setting out, be sure to call the state Department of Fish and Game for the latest sportfishing regulations, as this portion of the Pacific is subject to strict restrictions, and those restrictions are likely to change as new endangered and protected species listings are taken into account. Check with the Fish and Game office in Menlo Park, (650) 688-6340, and be sure to pick up a free copy of the latest regulations and any amendments at your bait-and-tackle shop. For charter adventures offshore, contact New Merrimac Charter Boat, 40 Starbuck Dr, Muir Beach, (415) 388-5351, or Seeker Sport Fishing, 205 Laurel Dr, Fairfax, (415) 453-7335. Both are reputable and have been in business for more than 20 years.

On the bay, fishing from the **piers** and beachfront at China Camp State Park (see Parks, below) is a big draw. While this portion of the shore has historically been known for its impressive yield of grass shrimp, which were harvested en masse in the mid- to late 1800s when a fishing village existed on the site, **striped bass, perch, jacksmelt, sturgeon, leopard shark, flounder,** and other common bay dwellers are the fare today (shrimp gathered here is mostly used as fish bait). Contact the park, (415) 456-0766, for tide and facilities information. Loch Lomond Live Bait House, 110 Loch Lomond Rd, San Rafael, (415) 456-0321, can set you up with bait, tackle, and useful advice.

Parks

In Marin, "park" often also means pristine, wild, open, and huge. From the Pacific Coast to the bay, there is a little something for everybody.

Angel Island State Park: In what may be considered the geographic center of San Francisco Bay, this hilly, forested island was used as a fishing, hunting, and camping site by the Miwok Indians for thousands of years. Later, the island was used for military purposes, from the Civil War era through World War II. It also served a stint as the Ellis Island of the West—a stopping place for immigrants from Asia who often were detained for months or years before being allowed to enter the country. Among the sloping fields of wildflowers and thickets of oak, fir, cypress, and coyote brush, a large variety of government buildings remain in varying states of disrepair—reminders of the island's life before it became a state park in 1950. Today, Angel Island is known for its trails (see Mountain Biking, above), beaches, picnic facilities, and mountaintop vistas instead of its batteries and barracks. And the chief spot, of course, is at the 750-foot summit of the island's Mount Livermore, with its views of peaks around the Bay Area, the Golden Gate, and the Marin skyline. Work a little for it: lug your picnic onto a ferry to Ayala Cove, take in the scenery on the trek to the top, and turn a simple outing into a trip seemingly to the top of the world! Bring binoculars and a camera (but leave the in-line skates at home, as they're prohibited here). Three ferry services go to the island: one departs Pier 41 in San Francisco, one from Tiburon in Marin, and a third from Vallejo in the East Bay. For information on the Tiburon ferry service, contact the Angel Island/Tiburon Ferry at (415) 435-2131. For the San Francisco and Vallejo ferries, contact the Blue and Gold Fleet at (415) 773-1188. Call the park office, (415) 435-5390, or the Angel Island Association, (415) 435-3522 for additional information.

Samuel P. Taylor State Park: Shaded groves of coast redwoods along the cool banks of Lagunitas Creek, along with adjacent open grasslands with oak and madrone, make this attractive 2,600-acre park on the site of a Gold Rush–era paper mill a worthwhile stopover en route to Point Reyes National Seashore (7 miles west), as well as a suitable camping area for those unable to secure one of the small number of backpacking camps in the more popular seashore area. Don't, however, write Taylor off as a main destination. It has a paved path ideal for family bike rides, an elaborate system of trails and fire roads offering scenic vistas of both surrounding valleys from 1,400 feet above the creek bed, and a pleasant creekside picnic area. From US 101, take the Sir Francis Drake Hwy exit west for 15 miles to the park office and visitors center on the right. Call (415) 488-9897 for information.

Muir Woods National Monument: This 560-acre preserve of ancient coastal redwoods is the Cadillac of day-trip destinations, but don't expect a quiet time away from the crowds. The monument, named for naturalist John Muir, is tour bus central, the parking areas overflowing with visitors to California whose agenda includes seeing what a redwood tree looks like. And that's really all there is to do here: look at trees. Picnics are prohibited, as is leaving the walking trails to roam unescorted through the forest. Also leave pets, bicycles, camping gear, and radios at home; they're banned too. Despite the rules and the heavy weekend crowds, however, this is the definitive place for a crash course in redwood forest ecology and the history of the California coastal range, which at one time extended 500 miles south from the Oregon border in a continuous 30-mile-wide band. Watch migratory rainbow trout spawn in Redwood and Fern Creeks; see black-tailed deer, Steller's jays, and chipmunks living among the lush fern and green mossy shade of giant trees. There are 6 miles of walking trails, with enough loops and connections to make this a safe bet for small children and their grandparents; routes are level throughout with only one (optional) exception. There is a $2 entry fee. To reach the woods, take the Stinson Beach exit west from US 101 and continue 4 miles to the Muir Woods turnoff on the right. It is a windy but pretty drive. Call (415) 388-2595 for information.

Tomales Bay State Park: Four surf-free beaches lining the western shores of Tomales Bay are the big draw at this 1,000-acre outdoor recreation area adjacent to Point Reyes National Seashore. Picnicking among groves of bishop pine, swimming, coastal hikes, and kayaking (see Kayaking, below) are all popular here, as is the small hike-in campground (see Camping, Point Reyes National Seashore chapter). Dogs are not permitted on beaches or in nature areas. To reach the park from US 101, exit west on Sir Francis Drake Blvd, then go 25 miles, through the town of Inverness and into the Point Reyes complex. Turn right at Pierce Point Rd, and continue 5,000 feet to the park entrance on the right. Call (415) 669-1140 for information.

China Camp State Park: Some of the least-altered bay-shore watersheds can be found here, on a 1,500-acre preserve hugging the southwest shore of San Pablo Bay. Once the site of a Gold Rush–era Chinese fishing village (a few dilapidated buildings from the settlement remain), the oak/laurel forestlands, open meadows, small redwood groves, and salt marsh area are a favorite among bicyclists, hikers, and picnickers. Fishing, swimming, boating, and windsurfing are popular along the open waterfront. A walk-in campground (see Camping, below) is also available, as are day-use picnic areas. Call the China Camp ranger station, (415) 456-0766, for more information.

Wildlife

Some of the best **bird-watching** in Marin County is on the Point Reyes National Seashore peninsula (see Wildlife, Point Reyes National Seashore chapter). Don't hesitate, however, to venture to surrounding areas for some prime viewing. Within the Marin Headlands, for example, is **Hawk Hill,** one of the most remarkable avian sites in the western United States and the biggest hawk lookout in western North America. Record count in 1992 was more than 20,000 birds, including **21 species of hawks.** The best time to visit is during September and October, when thousands of birds of prey soar over the hill each day. The hill is located above Battery 129, where Conzelman Rd becomes a one-way street. For a current schedule of the free ranger-led walks through the Marin Headlands—with topics ranging from bird-watching to wildflowers and war relics—call (415) 331-1540.

A short drive north of Stinson Beach on Hwy 1 leads to **Bolinas Lagoon,** a placid saltwater expanse that serves as refuge for numerous shorebirds and **harbor seals** sprawled out on the sandbars. Across from the lagoon is the Audubon Canyon Ranch's Bolinas Lagoon Preserve, a 1,014-acre wildlife sanctuary that supports a major rookery of **great blue herons;** see also Point Reyes National Seashore chapter. This is the premier spot along the Pacific Coast to watch immense, graceful seabirds as they court, mate, and rear their young, all accomplished on the tops of towering redwoods. Admission is free, though donations are requested; open mid-March to mid-July on Saturday, Sunday, and holidays, 10am to 4pm, and by appointment for groups. Located at 4900 Hwy 1, just north of Stinson Beach; (415) 868-9244.

A side trip near Bolinas offers some terrific **tide pools.** Just before entering downtown Bolinas, turn right (west) on Mesa Rd, left on Overlook Rd, and right on Elm Rd and you'll dead-end at the Duxbury Reef Nature Reserve, a rocky outcropping with numerous tide pools harboring a healthy population of starfish, sea anemones, snails, sea urchins, and other creatures that kids go gaga over.

At Tomales Bay State Park (see Parks, above) north of the national seashore, the rare **spotted owl** has been seen among the pine forests. Other species spotted here include band-tailed pigeons, horned larks, goldfinches, summer warblers, bitterns, woodpeckers, meadowlarks, pelicans, and scoters.

Wild Birds Unlimited in Cupertino, (408) 252-5712, is a good **resource** for birders anywhere in the Bay Area. Also check in with individual park ranger stations for information about naturalist programs. For Angel Island, information about interpretive services may be obtained at (415) 435-1915; at Tomales Bay, call (415) 669-1140. Also, be sure to check in with the National Audubon Society, (415) 383-1770, or the Sierra Club, (510) 653-6127.

Sailing/Boating

San Francisco Bay is, of course, one of the best sailing areas on the West Coast, with relatively small swells compared to the open sea breezes. And because of its position just around the corner from the Golden Gate and the open Pacific, Sausalito is a popular place to get on the water. **Moorages, launches,** and **boat services** abound along the Sausalito waterfront, so take your choice. Call the Sausalito Sailing Club, (415) 331-6266, for ideas to plan an outing on the water. Modern Sailing Academy, 2310 Marinship Way, Sausalito, (800) 995-1668, is a good place for instruction. Well-equipped marinas include the Clipper Yacht Harbor, Sausalito, (415) 332-3500; Kappas Marina, Sausalito, (415) 332-5510; Loch Lomond Marina, San Rafael, (415) 454-7595; and Marina Plaza Harbor, Sausalito, (415) 332-4723. One unique boating adventure in Marin is the short trip to Ayala Cove at Angel Island State Park, where boaters may stay overnight on buoys for $9 or just dock for the day for a park visit. Call the park at (415) 435-3522 for mooring availability and details. (For additional San Francisco Bay boating information, see Sailing, San Francisco chapter).

Kayaking

The bumpy waters off much of the Pacific Coast in Marin are hardly prime for sea kayaking, especially for the inexperienced, but don't allow that to stop you from putting in at some of the region's prime spots around San Francisco Bay, Tomales Bay, or Drakes Bay. From **Shoonmaker Point Marina Beach** in Sausalito, experienced riders can paddle beneath the Golden Gate to **Kirby Cove** (see Beaches, above), a thrilling ride that you should not attempt unsupervised unless you know what you're doing. Surf and currents at the Golden Gate can be hazardous enough to send a cargo ship off course, so you need only imagine what can happen if a kayaker tries to paddle through at the wrong moment! A more serene, or significantly less bumpy, paddle can be had within the waveless, virtually current-free confines of **Tomales Bay** north of Point Reyes National Seashore, where overnight kayaking/camping trips, wildlife viewing around Hog Island, and access to quiet beaches reached only from the waterfront make the experience for beginner and intermediate paddlers quite exceptional. The best put-ins on Tomales are at Nick's Cove on the bay's northern shores 40 miles north of Olema on Hwy 1 and Heart's Desire Beach off Sir Francis Drake Blvd in Point Reyes National Park. For tours, rentals, and lessons on Tomales Bay, including for beginners, check out Blue Water Kayaking, 12398 Sir Francis Drake Blvd, Inverness, (415) 669-2600, or Tomales Bay Kayaking, in Marshall, (415) 663-1743, www.tamalasaka.com on the Web. For Tomales Bay conditions, call (415) 669-1140. For information about other areas, check with Bay Area Sea Kayakers, San Francisco, (415) 457-6094, or Sea Trek, San Francisco, (415) 488-1000.

Scott Tye, a kayak instructor for Off the Beach Boats in downtown **Stinson Beach,** offers 2-hour lessons on the basics of sea and surf kayaking. Rentals are surprisingly cheap (about $25 for 4 hours for surf kayaks), and they even rent a kayak that can hold an entire nuclear family. Call (415) 868-9445 or drop by the shop at 15 Calle del Mar next to the Stinson Beach Post Office.

Scenic Drives

They don't call it **Panoramic Highway** for nothing. From US 101, take the Stinson Beach exit, then follow Panoramic Highway for 6 panoramic miles through the shaded woodlands south of Mount Tamalpais's West Peak, with places along the way to stroll, take pictures, or make a pit stop. Stellar views of the Pacific await once you round that final bend toward the beach. The zigs and zags drop you at the Coast Highway. Make a right here and head back to the urban center with overviews at **Rocky Point, Muir Beach** (see Beaches, above), and **Slide Ranch** along the way. Allow three hours to cover the 22 miles; you'll want to stop numerous times. Hwy 1 meanders back to US 101 from the Muir Beach Overlook. This compact loop drive shows off two of Northern California's best features: its striking mountain woodlands and its rugged, pristine coast.

One of the most scenic drives on the Marin coast is along **Dillon Beach Road** from Tomales. The 4-mile drive passes through windswept meadows with wonderful vistas of Tomales Bay, Point Reyes, and the Pacific before ending at the privately owned Dillon Beach campground. For a proper grand finale to the drive, turn right on **Oceana Drive** in Dillon Beach and continue to a vacant cul-de-sac. On a clear day you can see all the way to Bodega Bay.

Hiking

Since mountain bikers still flock to Marin for the nostalgia of it all, one key to hiking and backpacking is to try to avoid trails where you run the risk of coming head to head with the downhill daredevils. This is actually easier than it sounds, since on **Mount Tamalpais,** through the **Marin Headlands,** and on just about all other public land, bicycles are allowed only on fire roads. Walks, rambles, and long hauls, abound from the bluffs overlooking the Pacific to the high peaks and redwood canyons to the bay shore. Frankly, there are boundless opportunities here so we can't list them all, just our favorites. The Mount Tamalpais Interpretive Association leads **guided hikes** through the area every weekend, (415) 258-2410. The Greenbelt Alliance, the Bay Area's leading land conservation group, also sponsors numerous free outings in the open spaces of Marin, announced on an outings hot line, (415) 398-3730. Another resource is a Web site maintained by the outdoor retailer, REI, listing hikes throughout the Bay Area region, www.rei.com/MORE_STORE/hikes/sanfranhktemp.html.

Here are a few suggestions and highlights:

Tennessee Valley Trail through Tennessee Valley in the **Marin Headlands** (easy; 4 miles round trip) is custom built for families—easy and flat enough for children to make the trip! The walk follows the valley of scrub and brush all the way to the Pacific Ocean, a mile or so along a pleasant lagoon. Note, however, that mountain bikes *are* allowed on this trail. Watch out for them. Otherwise, enjoy sweeping views of the Pacific without having to work too hard for them. The trailhead is at the end of Tennessee Valley Rd, a left (west) turn off the Coast Highway north of Marin City.

Another stroll offering fantastic views of the Marin coast is found along the paved **Fort Cronkhite Trail** (easy to moderate; 5.2 miles round trip), which leads through coastal grasslands to a 960-foot summit overlooking Rodeo Beach. This is a shared trail, so, again, watch out for downhill racing bicycles. Stage from the Fort Cronkhite parking lot. From US 101, go west on Alexander Ave, then up Conzelman Rd for 1 mile. Go left on McCullough Rd, then make an immediate left on Bunker Rd. Continue 2.5 miles to the end.

A series of cascading waterfalls, shady canyons, and an overlook of Alpine Lake are the highlights of a half-day hike on the **Cataract Falls Trail** loop (difficult; 6.5 miles round trip) on the northern coastal slopes of **Mount Tamalpais**. This is perhaps the most stunning hike of any among the mountain's 50 miles of trails that are open to hiking. The first mile is a 750-foot climb from the lakeshore to the falls on Cataract Trail, which crosses Cataract Creek in two places, shooting straight up to the falls at 1,400 feet. Get rested, and let the spray of the falls cool you off, then loop back to where you started through wooded canyons on **Willow Meadow Trail,** which meets **Kent Trail.** Along the lake shore, **Helen Markdt Trail** takes you back to the trailhead, a level and soothing walk to top off all the hard work you've done. Extreme weather can easily wash out this trail, so be sure to check with the park, (415) 388-2070, if you have reason to believe heavy rains may have done damage. From Sir Francis Drake Blvd, turn right into Fairfax, then left on Broadway. Turn left at the stop sign onto Bolinas-Fairfax Rd, toward the lake. The trail beginning is west of the dam, right side of the road, in the middle of the hairpin turn.

One butt-kicker of a hike (but well worth it) is the **Dipsea Trail** (difficult; 6.6 miles one way) from Mount Tamalpais at Mill Valley to **Stinson Beach** (see Beaches, above), through Muir Woods. Along the way, contend with a 672-step stairway, and a nearly 500-foot climb in less than half a mile (over a point affectionately referred to as "Cardiac Hill"). Pass through coastal bluffs, redwood canyons, and finally Steep Ravine along the way to Stinson; then enjoy the beach and catch a ride home (you won't feel like hiking both ways). Stage from Old Mill Park in Mill Valley. From US 101, exit east on E Blithedale Ave, which becomes Throckmorton Rd, and continue to the park. Be certain to check with one of the hiking information resources listed above before venturing out on this one, and don't do it without a map and good instructions. Also check on weather conditions at the beach, (415) 868-1922, before hitting the road.

Also on Mount Tamalpais, the loop hike along **Bootjack** and **Ben**

Johnson Trails (moderate to difficult; 6 miles round trip) takes you through meadows, grasslands, oaks, and redwoods. Begin at the Bootjack/ Panoramic Highway crossing north of the Pantoll Ranger Station on the mountain. Head downhill on Bootjack Trail 0.75 mile along Redwood Creek to meet Ben Johnson Trail within Muir Woods National Monument. This trail doubles back for a sometimes steep trip back to where you started, but much of the 500-foot climb is in the shade of towering redwoods. When the trail becomes **Stapelveldt Trail,** the climb back to the ranger station is nearly complete. Take a left on **Alpine Trail** to return to where the hike started without having to walk along the highway, which can get busy with automobile traffic, particularly on weekends. Take the Stinson Beach exit from US 101, then go west to the Panoramic Highway. The trailhead is slightly east of the Pantoll Rd intersection.

Camping

Despite Marin's proximity to the busy urban centers, many camping areas here are surprisingly secluded, quiet, and pristine. Car camping, however, is oddly scarce. Most campsites are walk-in only for backpackers.

Kirby Cove is just a stone's throw from the Golden Gate Bridge. This beachside camping area at the foot of the Marin Headlands just west of the bridge has 4 family campsites equipped with tent pads, fire pits, picnic tables, pit toilets, and barbecue grills. No water or RV hookups here, and car access is limited without a camping permit. Due to high demand, reservations must be made 30 days in advance; call (415) 331-1540. *Kirby Cove is below Conzelman Rd, 0.5 mile west of East Fort Baker. Day use access limited to foot or bicycle.*

Haypress Backpack Camp has 5 two-tent sites located in the coastal scrubs above Tennessee Valley in the Marin Headlands, accessible only via an easy quarter-mile hike from the trailhead or a longer hike from Muir Beach (See Beaches, above) or Coyote Ridge Trail. Toilets and picnic tables are available, but there are no barbecues or water, and no fires are allowed. Reservations and permits are required. Call the Golden Gate National Recreation Area, (415) 331-1540, for reservations and information. *The trailhead to the Haypress Camp is located at the end of Tennessee Valley Rd. Take US 101 north from the Golden Gate Bridge to the Hwy 1 turnoff. Head west toward Stinson Beach. About 1.5 miles west of US 101, turn left on Tennessee Valley Rd and follow it to the end. From the staging area at the end of the road, hike approximately half a mile on Tennessee Valley Trail.*

Bicentennial, also a walk-in camp (just a short distance from the parking area), is in a forested area overlooking Bonita Cove. It has 3 sites, each big enough for just two people. Toilets and picnic tables are available, with water nearby. No fires allowed. Register 90 days in advance, (415) 331-1540. *To reach Bicentennial Camp from Fort Baker at the foot of the Golden Gate Bridge, take Conzelman Rd west for about 3 miles to the point at which it becomes a one-way passage at Bonita Cove. Park at the side of the road where there is room, and walk to the campground just left of the road.*

China Camp State Park (see Parks, above), on the shores of San Francisco Bay and on the east side of the Marin coast, has 30 walk-in sites for tent camping; gear must be carried in from the parking area, a distance of about 100 yards. RV parking is allowed in the lot, but there are no hookups. Picnic tables, food lockers, fire pits, and water are available. *Make reservations through the state parks reservations system, (800) 444-7275; for information, call (415) 456-0575. Take San Pedro Rd 3.5 miles east of US 101 in San Rafael.*

Mount Tamalpais State Park, like the rest of Marin, has very little car camping. **Pantoll Camp** on the Panoramic Highway, however, has 16 walk-in sites with picnic tables, stoves, food lockers, and tent pads. The sites are a few hundred feet from the parking area. Water and flush toilets are available, but no showers. RV parking is allowed in the lot (no hookups; RV limit 25 feet). *No reservations are taken. Call the ranger station, (415) 388-2070, for information. Pantoll Camp is located on the Panoramic Hwy, 4 miles west of Hwy 1.*

A more popular attraction at Tamalpais is the **Rocky Point–Steep Ravine Environmental Campground,** a walk-in camp overlooking the Pacific Ocean, just south of Stinson Beach (see Beaches, above). There are 6 campsites with tent pads, food lockers, picnic tables, and fire pits. Water and toilets are nearby. Ten cabins are also available, each with wood stove, picnic table, bunks, and barbecue. This camp is very popular, at one of the most stunning spots on the California coast, and fills up fast. *There is a short walk from the parking area. For reservations, call (800) 444-7275. The campground is west of Hwy 1 at Rocky Point Trail.*

RV camping is scarce in Marin parklands. Check with Marin Park Inc, San Rafael, which has 89 full RV hookups, a pool, showers, a laundromat, and supplies, at (415) 461-5199.

outside in

Attractions

When you consider that the San Francisco Bay Area has more people than the entire state of Oregon, and that Marin County has the highest per capita income in the nation, you would expect its coastline to be lined with gated communities and fancy resorts. Truth is, you won't find even a Motel 6 along the entire Marin coast, due partly to public pressure but mostly to the inaccessibly rugged, heavily forested terrain. The only downside to the Marin coast's underdevelopment is the scarcity of affordable lodgings; expensive B&Bs reign supreme, which is fine if you don't mind blowing $150 a night or more for a bed and a bagel.

On a sunny San Francisco day, there's no better place to spend time outdoors than in the **Marin Headlands.** For more than a century following the Civil War, this vast expanse of grass-covered hills and rocky shore was off-limits to the public, appropriated by the US Army as a strategic base for defending the bay against invaders. Remnants of obsolete and untested defenses—dozens of thick concrete bunkers and batteries recessed into the bluffs—now serve as playground and picnic sites for the millions of tourists who visit each year. Refer to the Inside Out sections above, and buy the handy $1.50 "Marin Headlands Map and Guide to Sites, Trails, and Wildlife," at the Information Center at Fort Barry (follow the signs in the headlands), and plan your day from there. The center is open daily from 9:30am to 4:30pm, (415) 331-1540.

A popular Marin Headlands attraction is **The Marine Mammal Center,** a volunteer-run hospital for injured and abandoned mammals-of-the-sea. It's virtually impossible not to melt at the sight of the cute sea lions and elephant and harbor seals as they lie in their pens (the center's staff, being no dummies, take donations right on the spot). Signs list each animal's adopted name, species, stranding site, and injury—the latter of which is usually human-caused. Located at the east end of Fort Cronkhite near Rodeo Lagoon, the Marine Mammal Center is open daily from 10am to 4pm and admission is free; (415) 289-SEAL.

Closed to the public for several years due to storm damage, the precariously perched 1877 **Point Bonita Lighthouse** is once again thrilling those tourists who are brave enough to traverse the long, dark tunnel and seven small footbridges leading to the beacon. (Because the cliffs along the passageway are so steep, one 19th-century lighthouse keeper rigged ropes around his children to prevent them from slipping into the raging sea below.) The reward for such bravery is, among other things, a rare and sensational view of the entrance to the bay. Call for tour times, and be sure to inquire about the full-moon tours, which take place twice a month by reservation only; (415) 331-1540.

A sort of retirement community for aging rock stars, spent novelists, and former hippies, **Bolinas** is one of the most reclusive towns in Northern California. Residents regularly take down highway signs pointing the way to their rural enclave, an act that ironically has created more publicity for Bolinas than any road sign ever did. As a tourist, you don't have to worry about being chased out of town by a band of machete-wielding Bolinistas, but don't expect anyone to roll out the welcome mat either. The trick is to not look like a tourist, but more like a Bay Area resident who's only here to buy some peaches at the People's Store.

What's the **People's Store,** you ask? It's a town landmark that's famous for its locally grown organic produce and exceptional service—the antithesis of the corporate supermarket. It's a little hard to find, hidden at the end of a gravel driveway next to the Bolinas Bakery (don't confuse it with the much larger general store down the street), but it's worth searching out just to see (and taste) the difference between Safeway and the Bolinas way; open 8:30am to 6:30pm daily, (415) 868-1433.

Tomales is also a hugely popular stop for fresh raw and barbecued oysters. Since 1909 the **Tomales Bay Oyster Company** has been selling its wares right off the shore at 15479 Hwy 1, just south of Marshall and 5 miles north of Point Reyes Station. The oysters range from bite-size cocktails to big ol' hunkin' cowboys and are sold by the dozen or in sacks of 100, should you be feeling randy enough. Those in the know bring their own knife, lemons, cocktail sauce, and even bags of charcoal for the nearby barbecue pits; open daily from 9am to 5pm, (415) 663-1242.

Restaurants

Bubba's Diner ☆☆   There's nothing on the menu at Bubba's that you probably couldn't make at home, but chances are you just couldn't make it as well. This is classic diner food with decor to match: red Naugahyde booths and a black-and-white tile floor. *566 San Anselmo Ave (downtown), San Anselmo; (415) 459-6862; $.*

Buckeye Roadhouse ☆☆☆   The decor here combines a reserved elegance with over-the-top Marin kitsch—lofty ceilings, mahogany beams, and a huge stuffed yellowfin tuna. The cuisine, likewise, is both classic and eclectic. *15 Shoreline Hwy (from Hwy 101 take the Stinson Beach–Mill Valley exit), Mill Valley; (415) 331-2600; $$.*

Creekside Bistro ☆☆   This pretty bistro perched over rippling San Anselmo Creek has garnered raves since it opened in 1996. The chef has a flair for nearly flawless meat and fish entrees. *636 San Anselmo Ave (downtown), San Anselmo; (415) 456-2952; $$.*

Guaymas ☆☆   Guaymas serves Mexican classics as well as California-inspired variations. Dine on the deck and take in the incredible view of the bay, as you sip one of the mighty margaritas. *5 Main St (on Tiburon Harbor at the ferry landing), Tiburon; (415) 435-6300; $$.*

Half Day Cafe ☆☆   Breakfast in this beautifully renovated, plant-filled mechanic's garage features a number of first-rate dishes. The only complaint is that you may have to wait a stomach-growling hour for a table on a busy weekend morning. *848 College Ave (across from the College of Marin), Kentfield; (415) 459-0291; $.*

Il Fornaio ☆☆   This handsome branch of the popular restaurant chain offers well-prepared Italian standards, especially those items that come from the rotisserie. *223 Corte Madera Town Center (from Hwy 101, take the Paradise Dr exit), Corte Madera; (415) 927-4400; $$.*

Insalata's ☆☆   In a large, handsome building, dazzling Mediterranean fare is showcased behind floor-to-ceiling windows. The sunny, airy dining room is highlighted by paintings of lemons, plums, and pears. *120 Sir Francis Drake Blvd (at Barber St), San Anselmo; (415) 457-7700; $$$.*

Las Camelias ☆☆   The delicious, authentic Mexican cuisine dished up at this pleasant, casual cafe comes straight from the recipe file of the owner/chef's mother in Jalisco, Mexico. *912 Lincoln Ave (between 3rd and 4th Sts), San Rafael; (415) 453-5850; $.*

Left Bank ☆☆☆   This is a fun, vibrant restaurant with a French bistro-style menu that changes seasonally, prompting patrons to return again and again for the latest rendition of the wonderful, traditionally prepared fare. *507 Magnolia Ave (at Ward St), Larkspur; (415) 927-3331; $$.*

Mikayla ☆☆   In a bright, pleasant interior designed by artist Laurel Burch, patrons are treated to a view of Angel Island. It's all very romantic and engaging, and the experience is enhanced with American, French-influenced fare. *801 Bridgeway (downtown), Sausalito; (415) 331-5888; $$$.*

The Parkside Café ☆   During the day this popular neighborhood cafe bustles with locals and Bay Area beach-goers who stop for an breakfast or lunch before shoving off to the beach around the corner. *43 Arenal Ave (off Calle del Mar downtown), Stinson Beach; (415) 868-1272; $.*

The Pelican Inn ☆☆   One of the better ways to spend a Sunday afternoon in the Bay Area is at this homey little English pub. Grab a table at the glassed-in patio or by the fireplace, and gorge yourself proper on a steaming shepherd's pie. *10 Pacific Way (off Hwy 1 at the entrance to the beach), Muir Beach; (415) 383-6000; $$.*

Piazza D'Angelo   This is one of Mill Valley's most popular restaurants, with large (often noisy) crowds of Marinites packing the pleasant, airy bar. They don't necessarily come for the Italian food, mind you, but for the charged atmosphere. *22 Miller Ave (on the square), Mill Valley; (415) 388-2000; $$.*

The Rice Table ☆☆☆   Decorated with rattan screens and bright batik tablecloths, this small, popular, dimly lit restaurant offers dozens of wonderfully aromatic Indonesian dishes that are a treat for the soul as well as the palate. *1617 4th St (at G St), San Rafael; (415) 456-1808; $$.*

Sushi Ran ☆☆☆   To the loyal patrons of this south Marin culinary landmark sushi is not just food—it's a way of life. The sushi served here is impeccable, prepared with aplomb and served with a flourish. *107 Caledonia St (next to the Marin Theater), Sausalito; (415) 332-3620; $$.*

Tony's Seafood Restaurant   Don't bother ordering anything but the barbecued oysters at Tony's—they're so tasty they're worth the drive to this ramshackle building on the east shore of Tomales Bay. *18863 Hwy 1 (1 mile S of town), Marshall; (415) 663-1107; $.*

Lodgings

Casa del Mar ☆☆☆   This beautiful Mediterranean-style haven overlooks Stinson Beach. Each of the 6 sun-drenched rooms has large windows (with views of Mount Tamalpais, the ocean, or the terraced garden), French doors that open onto a private balcony, and a private bath. *37 Belvedere Ave (heading N into Stinson Beach, turn right at the fire station), Stinson Beach; (415) 868-2124 or (800) 552-2124; $$$.*

Casa Madrona ☆☆☆☆   Each of the 34 lavish rooms here is unique; the rooms in the Victorian cottages, which dot the hillside, and in the 110-year-old mansion on top of the hill are more rustic than those in the 15-year-old blue stucco building below. The hotel offers everything you could possibly desire: sweeping bay vistas, an outdoor Jacuzzi, and all the amenities of a citified hotel. *801 Bridgeway (downtown), Sausalito; (415) 332-0502 or (800) 567-9524; $$$.*

Mountain Home Inn ☆☆   Perched on the side of Mount Tamalpais, this inn has 10 guest rooms decorated in what might best be described as Marin Modern, with plush carpeting and wood-paneled walls. A full breakfast is included with your stay. *810 Panoramic Hwy (call for directions), Mill Valley; (415) 381-9000; $$$.*

Panama Hotel ☆☆   With slowly churning ceiling fans, balconies lined with old wicker chairs, and mismatched antiques, the Panama Hotel looks as if it should be the backdrop for a noir film. There are 15 individually decorated guest rooms located in two 1910 vintage homes connected by a tropical garden patio. *4 Bayview St (at the end of B St, 3 blocks W of 2nd St), San Rafael; (415) 457-3993 or (800) 899-3993; $$.*

The Pelican Inn ☆☆   This 16th-century English Tudor country inn, named after Sir Francis Drake's ship, has 7 small yet cozy rooms with canopy beds, leaded-glass windows, heavy brocade curtains, and English antiques. *10 Pacific Way (off Hwy 1 at the entrance to the beach), Muir Beach; (415) 383-6000; $$.*

Stinson Beach Motel ☆   If you can't afford the Casa del Mar, try this place. The motel has 5 small rooms and 1 apartment nestled in a cute little garden setting, each individually decorated with aging yet homey furnishings and private baths. *3416 Hwy 1 (at the S end of town near the fire station), Stinson Beach; (415) 868-1712; $$.*

U.S. Hotel ☆   With nothing more to go by than a photograph of the original Western inn—which burned down in 1920—the owners built the U.S. Hotel from the ground up in 1989, resulting in a place wonderfully evocative of a bygone era. Each of the 8 rooms has high ceilings, a private bath, and simple yet attractive furnishings. Continental breakfast included. *26985 Hwy 1 (in the center of town), Tomales; (707)878-2742; $$.*

More Information

Bicycle Trails Council of Marin: *(415) 456-7512.*
Corte Madera Chamber of Commerce: *(415) 924-0441.*
Fairfax Chamber of Commerce: *(415) 453-5928.*
Golden Gate National Park Association: *(415) 776-0693.*
Golden Gate National Recreation Area: *(415) 556-0560.*
Gulf of the Farallones National Marine Sanctuary: *(415) 556-3509.*
Marin County Convention and Visitors Bureau: *(415) 472-7470.*
Marin Headlands Visitors Center: *(415) 331-1540.*
Marin Municipal Water District: *(415) 459-5267.*
Mill Valley Chamber of Commerce: *(415) 388-9700.*
Mount Tamalpais Headquarters: *(415) 893-1580.*
San Rafael Chamber of Commerce: *(415) 454.4163.*
Sausalito Chamber of Commerce: *(415) 331-7262.*
State parks camping reservations: *(800) 444-7275.*
West Marin Chamber of Commerce: *(415) 663-9232.*

Point Reyes National Seashore

Along the Marin County coast from Bolinas north to Dillon Beach on Tomales Bluff, and inland along Tomales Bay, including Bolinas Ridge and Audubon Canyon Ranch east of the Coast Highway.

Go ahead and pack the mountain bike, the tent, the beach towel, and the kayak—but it is probably more important to pack the spotting scope and the binoculars if you're considering a trip to Point Reyes National Seashore. These 30 miles of unique coastline on the Marin seashore are seemingly limitless in what they have to offer those looking for a rugged, breathtaking adventure in the wild. But the most compelling reason to come here is to observe a stunningly beautiful and incredibly diverse wildlife area, whether you're a weekend warrior bent on losing your breath on a challenging climb or a more passive nature lover who would prefer to take it all in without breaking a sweat. Point Reyes is sea lion country and mountain lion country all rolled into one. It is a place to watch migrating whales off the coast and spot rare migrating birds overhead. It is rugged bluffs overlooking the ocean, dense alder and pine forests dipping into expansive canyons, and open meadows of grass and rare wildflowers. So go ahead and camp. Feel free to ride and hike the trails. Take a cross-country trip on horseback. But don't forget to take a pause and really look around, because the highlight of any trip to this unique place is to study the wildlife and ecology and gain at least a layperson's understanding of how it all works. There are two environmental education centers within the preserve, so no excuses.

These 70,000 acres of nearly pristine coastal wilderness are preserved forever because of legislation signed by President John F. Kennedy in 1962. The natural forces that together create the Point Reyes experience, however, have been at work for many thousands of years. Elemental to them is the tension between the Pacific and North American tectonic plates, which cause the Point Reyes peninsula to slip two inches northwest—out toward the Pacific Ocean—each year. The infamous San Andreas Fault running between the two plates bisects the Point Reyes peninsula from the rest of the Marin coast; thus the movement outward. Look at a map of California, and note that Point Reyes appears to protrude west of the rest of the coast. This protrusion into the sea is the reason such a wide variety of bird species—more than 400 by one estimate—inhabit the seashore and the waters around it. Many are lost, having accidentally collided with Point Reyes while migrating along the Pacific Flyway. This randomly balanced interplay between seismic forces and wildlife ecology is also the reason you can stand on the beaches and watch gray whales pass by offshore.

Point Reyes is indeed a living textbook for those interested in wildlife, nature, and ecology. After a fire caused by an illegal burn at a campsite ravaged some 13,000 acres of the preserve in 1995, naturalists seized upon the opportunity to closely observe as wildlife and plants recovered. Then they created an interpretive program to explain their observations to visitors. From the resilient bishop pines, which need fire to reproduce, to the rare burrowing mountain beavers and nesting songbirds, regeneration of life throughout the fire zone has been swift and promising.

In all, there are more than 140 miles of diverse hiking trails winding through the Point Reyes complex, connecting its rugged beaches with its peaks and canyons, and its forests with its grasslands. The terrain is not unlike what you would find in the Tehachapi Mountains, but overlooks the ocean instead of the Mohave Desert.

There is, however, a downside to all of this: Point Reyes is perhaps too popular. With an estimated 2.6 million visitors each year, the seashore is one of the most often visited of all national parks. This means competition and crowds in some areas, especially on weekends and during summer holidays. It also means that if you plan to visit here, you should plan your visit carefully and in advance, especially if you expect to find a campsite or to commune with nature without standing shoulder-to-shoulder with school kids, who are bussed here by the gaggle for science class field trips. Don't be discouraged, however. There are ways to avoid the crowds. Just use good planning and common sense. The only thing you will find a shortage of here is limits (although there is no shortage of rules). Just about anything goes.

Getting There

Point Reyes National Seashore is west of the Coast Highway (Highway 1) between the towns of Bolinas and Tomales, 20 miles north of San Francisco. From San Francisco, take US Highway 101 (US 101) north to Sir Francis Drake Boulevard in San Rafael, then head west to Olema. From Sonoma County or the north state, take US 101 south to Point Reyes–Petaluma Road, then head west to the seashore. The main information headquarters for Point Reyes is the Bear Valley Visitors Center, on Bear Valley Road just north of Olema, at the park's main crossroads entrance. The center can be reached at (415) 663-1092.

Adjoining Areas

NORTH: **Sonoma and Southern Mendocino Coasts**

SOUTH: **San Francisco**

EAST: **Marin**

inside out

Point Reyes National Seashore Rules and Regulations

You will find no gates or toll booths on the roads leading in and out of Point Reyes; access is free and relatively unlimited, but you will not be allowed to park your car overnight here since **car camping** is prohibited (although the rangers won't stop you from taking an innocent midnight stroll on a clear night). Most of the rules here are aimed at one of two goals: protecting park visitors who lack common sense from injuring themselves and protecting rare and endangered wildlife from being trampled or otherwise disturbed by their admirers. Here are the basics: **Dogs** are allowed only on Kehoe, Palomarin, North, South, and southern Limantour Beaches, but must be kept on leashes at all times. Do not take your dog on any hiking trails within the seashore boundaries. **Camping** is limited and very closely regulated. If you don't have a reservation and a permit for one of the four small backpacking camps in the park, you will not be allowed to spend the night. Permits are required for all **fires,** including beach fires. **Bicycles** are allowed on just 35 miles of the park's more than 140 miles of trails, and cyclists are require to yield right-of-way to every other class of trail user (especially equestrian). The 15mph bicycle speed limit is strictly enforced. Finally, disturbing or harassing any **wildlife** in the park is strictly prohibited. Observe seasonal **beach closures** and **trail restrictions** that may become necessary to protect nesting, breeding, or molting animals . . .

if it looks like something you wouldn't want to do in front of an audience, stay away. To plan your visits, contact one of three visitors centers: **Bear Valley Visitors Center,** Bear Valley Rd, (415) 663-1092; the **Ken Patrick Visitors Center,** mile 14, Sir Francis Drake Blvd, (415) 669-1250; or the **Lighthouse Visitors Center,** end of Sir Francis Drake Blvd, (415) 669-1534.

Camping

There are two words to describe camping within the Point Reyes preserve: fantastic, and scarce. That is to say, if you plan to do it you're best off planning as far in advance as possible. Because park policy is to do whatever is necessary to preserve the natural beauty and pristine condition of the peninsula, there are just 39 campsites on the entire 70,000 acres, all within four sparsely equipped backpacking camps—no car camping allowed. Sleeping on the beach also is not allowed, so if you don't have a permit to use one of the park's approved sites, you're out of luck. Any camping trip within Point Reyes must begin with a call to the **Bear Valley Visitors Center,** where reservations are taken and drop-in campers are assigned sites (should they be lucky enough to drop by when there happens to be an opening). The center can be reached at (415) 663-1092, or found just off Bear Valley Rd west of Olema. **Reservations** are taken up to two months in advance; limit is four nights. The camping fee is $10 per site each night, and group sites are available for 9 to 25 people.

The camp nearest the beach is **Wildcat Camp,** with 3 group sites and 5 individual sites, a 6.5-mile hike from the Bear Valley area. The camp is on an open meadow very near Wildcat Beach, which means ocean sounds at night instead of the mutter and bustle of other campers. The other campsite near the beach is **Coast Camp,** with 2 group sites and 12 individual sites, a 1.8-mile walk from the Point Reyes Hostel area (see Attractions, below). East of the beach are **Sky Camp,** with 1 group site and 11 individual sites, on the west side of Mount Wittenberg, and **Glen Camp,** with 12 individual sites in a forested valley that is a 6.5-mile hike from the visitors center.

In the likely event that campsites are not available, or if you're more comfortable car camping, there are alternatives nearby. The best is **Samuel P. Taylor State Park,** 6 miles east of Point Reyes on Sir Francis Drake Blvd; it has 61 sites (25 with full RV hookups) and is open April 1 to October 31. Showers are available, and dogs are allowed. Call the park at (415) 488-9897 or call Park Net at (800) 444-7275 for information and reservations. *The park is located on both sides of Sir Francis Drake Blvd, 15 miles west of US 101.*

Mountain Biking

Within Point Reyes, count on sharing the main trails with hikers and equestrians. This means yielding the right-of-way and obeying a 15mph speed limit at all times. Difficult trails are generally less crowded for bikers, but keep in mind that for every advanced mountain biker willing to take on a challenging trail there is bound to be an experienced hiker or horseperson willing to do the same. Riding is prohibited on single-track trails, and allowed only on those trails clearly marked as bicycle approved.

For a ride that includes spectacular ocean views with not much of a sweat, take the 5.6-mile **Coast Trail** from the Point Reyes Hostel area off Limantour Rd to the bluffs overlooking **Santa Maria Beach.** This is a casual ride across relatively level terrain starting off in a forest of red alders and ending in the open bluffs. It is also a great ride for those who would like to combine a little off-road biking with some relaxation on the beach. Coast Camp is at the end of the trail, so there is the option of staying even longer if you so desire; just plan for it if that is what you have in mind (see Camping, above). The trailhead is 6 miles west of the park headquarters. Take Bear Valley Rd north to Limantour Rd, then follow signs to the hostel. Stage from the hostel or the nearby Clem Miller Environmental Education Center.

Of course, there is no need to take it easy. This area is known for some challenging and adventuresome rides. Take, for example, the strenuous uphill ride from the **Five Brooks** area through Douglas fir forests and onto open bluffs overlooking Wildcat Beach along **Stewart Trail,** a difficult 11.4-mile round trip. This is one of those physically challenging rides where you definitely won't feel guilty resting along the way; stopping to rest, as a matter of fact, may be the highlight, because you're going to want to slow down and take in your surroundings anyway. There is a 1,200-foot elevation gain, along with equally impressive downhill drops in both directions—so you have to climb twice to get back to where you started. Note, however, that this trail is also heavily used by horseback riders. Take the Coast Highway south from Olema 3 miles to the Five Brooks trailhead, which also provides direct access to the **Olema Valley** and **Bolinas Ridge Trails,** both also moderately difficult off-road rides.

A less challenging ride within the park is along **Estero Trail** (moderate; 8.8 miles round trip) from Sir Francis Drake Blvd to **Drakes Head,** which overlooks Limantour Spit and Drakes Bay, facing directly south. Single-track riding is allowed on portions of this course, and there are only a few steep climbs to contend with. The rest is rolling hills in an open grassland and scrub terrain. The trailhead is 10 miles northwest of Olema. Take the Coast Highway north to Sir Francis Drake Blvd, then head west on Sir Francis another 8 miles to the Estero turnoff on the left.

Cycling is also popular along **Inverness Ridge** north of the park boundaries and in locally managed open space areas along the Coast Highway. Check at any park visitors center for a free trail map. For **bike rentals,** try 88 Bear Valley Rd, in the park, (415) 663-1958; Building Supply Center, 11280 Hwy 1, Point Reyes Station, (415) 663-1737; or Cycle Analysis, on Main St, Point Reyes Station, (415) 663-9164.

Hiking

Considering that there are more than 140 miles of trails at Point Reyes suitable for hiking, we will not attempt to list them all here. Even if you're planning just a day hike, first thing on the agenda should be to stop by the **Bear Valley Visitors Center,** (415) 663-1092, on Bear Valley Rd just west of Olema for an official trail map. Let's just make it clear from the get-go that the hiking opportunities at the seashore are a series of trade-offs. While the most popular hikes here offer breathtaking views of the Pacific, Drakes Bay, Tomales Bay, or any number of canyon vistas, trails can be crowded during the peak season, especially on weekends. Since some hikes can take several hours, it's also important to be prepared for sudden changes in the weather. Even during summer months, Point Reyes can be warm and sunny one moment and cool and drizzly the next. Dress in layers.

Tomales Point Trail at the extreme north end of the park on Tomales Point (easy with mild grades; 6 miles round trip) can be a wildlife fancier's dream. This is one of the hikes that lets you feel the uniqueness of Point Reyes, as the point extends so far out into the ocean you'll swear you're on a small island in the middle of nowhere by the time you're at the midway mark. Tule elk are abundant in this area, and you stand a good chance of spotting a few during the three hours it takes to complete the journey. Your reward at the end of the hike is a stunning view from the point—of the Pacific overlooking Bird Rock to your left and an equally breathtaking overlook of the mouth of Tomales Bay. The hike begins at the end of Pierce Ranch Rd. Take Sir Francis Drake Blvd west from the Bear Valley Visitors Center, through Inverness, turn right on Pierce Point Rd and drive 7 miles to the trailhead, which is also very near a beach access.

Another easy hike with great rewards is the **Rift Zone Trail** (easy; 10 miles round trip). Here walkers follow the path of the San Andreas Fault zone where the ground is said to have shifted 20 feet as a result of the San Francisco quake of 1906. Notice the difference in vegetation on opposite sides of the fault, along with twin ridge formations that seem set together like bookends. The trailhead can be found just east of park headquarters, at the Bear Valley Visitors Center. Follow Sir Francis Drake Blvd west through Olema and turn left on Bear Valley Rd, then left at the visitors center entrance, which is clearly marked.

Olema Valley Trail (easy; 11 miles round trip) also leads through the fault zone, along Pine Gulch Creek, through more pretty forested landscape, ending at Hwy 1. There are no vistas here, but the canyon is loaded with curious geologic formations and interesting plant communities and wildlife. The trail begins at Five Brooks trailhead, 3 miles south of Olema on the Coast Highway.

For the more experienced hiker who wants to get away from the crowds, we recommend **Sky Loop Trail** (moderate; 8.5 miles round trip), a rocket trip 1,400 feet up Mount Whittenberg that begins with shaded forest cover, then gives way to open bluffs with ocean views. This hike is full of options and possibilities; allow a minimum of five hours to explore. Drop down to **Kelham Beach** below Point Resistance before making your way back toward park headquarters, or cut the hike short on any number of turnoffs that will loop you back to where you started without having to make the climb to the top of the mountain. The trailhead is located 3 miles west of park headquarters. Take Sir Francis Drake Blvd to the Bear Valley Rd turnoff west of Olema, then continue 1 mile to Limantour Rd. Follow Limantour Rd west another mile to the trailhead turnoff on the left side of the road. Time these hikes carefully. If it's afternoon already, it's probably too late to even try a lot of the better ones without risking getting stranded by nightfall.

Inverness Ridge Trail (moderate; 6 miles round trip, but variable depending on options chosen) follows the ridgeline combing the northeastern flanks of Point Reyes National Seashore, with vistas of both the Pacific Ocean and Tomales Bay from 1,200 feet up. Mount Vision, at 1,282 feet, is visible immediately south of this hike. Elevation gains are mild. Be sure to dress in layers for this hike, as weather conditions can shift abruptly. From up here, you can actually see the weather coming! At the trail's end, 3 miles in toward Limantour Rd, you have the option of continuing an additional 9 miles on adjoining Bayview Trail. The trailhead is 4 miles up Mount Vision Rd from Sir Francis Drake Blvd, 6.5 miles north of Olema.

Scenic Drives

It would be a shame to come to a place like Point Reyes and not get a chance to ditch the car for at least a few hours . . . but if a scenic drive is all you have time for, there are two excellent options. One is to take the 15-mile drive from the town of Inverness to the **Point Reyes Lighthouse** on Sir Francis Drake Blvd. Numerous overlook points are marked along the way; the best is at the end of the line where you will come face to face with the Pacific Ocean as it meets the rocky cliffs of the peninsula's southern extremes. Canyon overlooks and a breathtaking roadside view of **Drakes Estero** greet you along the way. However, this is probably not a drive you will want to attempt during the height of the whale-watching season in mid-January and mid-March, since the lighthouse area is a prime viewing spot and can become so crowded that park visitors are required to ride shuttles.

Another scenic option is the 8-mile drive from just south of **Inverness Park** through wooded canyons and coastal scrub to the shores of **Drakes Bay** on Limantour Rd, ending at **Limantour Beach.** While the route to the waterfront is not as direct as Sir Francis Drake Rd, and the road is a little more windy, this drive gives a better overview of the diverse landscape at Point Reyes, taking you through forests, scrubs, open canyon vistas, and finally the bay, open to the sea.

Wildlife

Naturally, there is more to the wildlife scene at Point Reyes than birding and whale watching. **Elephant seals** can commonly be found molting during summer months and breeding during the winter at South Beach, Chimney Rock, and Lifeboat Station. Watch but don't get too close: 5,000-pound bulls have been known to charge if angered or startled. Park officials suggest you stay at least 100 yards away. During pupping season, beach areas colonized by the seals are closed.

Back inland, be on the lookout for **tule elk,** particularly in the reserve area adjacent to Tomales Point, and be advised that **mountain lions** roam the entire Point Reyes area. One of the more unusual wildlife features here is a unique species of **albino deer,** introduced to the area in the late 1800s by area ranchers. This bizarre creature looks identical to a common deer except for the color—and running into one unexpectedly can be a surreal experience. Also be on the lookout for snakes, frogs, and lizards, as 28 different species of reptiles and amphibians have been documented within the park, including the rare **rubber boa** and the **western terrestrial garter snake.**

Its unique position along the Pacific Flyway makes Point Reyes one of the best bird-watching regions in the United States. During the fall and winter, Tomales Point is a prime area for spotting birds of prey, such as the rare **peregrine falcon** and numerous varieties of **owls** and **hawks.** Wintering **waterfowl** such as geese, shore birds, egrets, and herons can be found much of the year along Tomales Bay and Bolinas Lagoon. Catch a glimpse of the endangered **snowy plover,** which nests during the spring and early summer on Abbott's Lagoon. Migrating species such as **murres, pigeon guillemots, loons,** and **scoters** are abundant along the rocks and cliffs at the south end of the seashore, where **brown pelicans** can be found in the fall and **black oystercatchers** all year. Remember, however, that there are more than 400 different species of bird documented here—which means the entire region is like an E-ticket ride at Disneyland to the avid birder. The forests and canyons are songbird country, the marshes and lagoons waterfowl territory, the bluffs and cliffs a hunting bird's haven.

Be certain to check out **Point Reyes Bird Observatory,** a research facility at the park's southern boundary, at the end of Mesa Rd west of Bolinas. Bird banding can be observed here through the spring and summer. Call (415) 868-1221. Nearby, east of Bolinas on Hwy 1, and bounded on the north by Bolinas-Fairfax Rd, is Audubon Canyon Ranch, a 1,500-acre bird sanctuary and wildlife preserve with rare vistas of an oddly diverse avian nesting community among wooded canyons. Self-guided tours, well-marked nature trails, or scheduled guided walks are open to the public from March through mid-July. Call (415) 868-9244.

This is where those binoculars will come in handy. Again, because Point Reyes protrudes 10 miles west of the surrounding coastline, **California gray whales** can easily be spotted offshore while migrating to their calving grounds in Baja California in winter and then north to their feeding grounds in the Bering and Chukchi Seas during spring. Point Reyes Lighthouse, Tomales Point, and South Beach are prime viewing spots during the southern migration, particularly in mid-January. For the migration back north, also try watching from the Chimney Rock area, the peak viewing time being mid-March. Because a lengthy hike is required to reach Tomales Point, it tends to be less crowded than the other whale watching vantage points—but don't come here during the prime season and expect to find yourself gazing out at the ocean alone. Whale watching has become incredibly popular in recent years, with people lined up like crows on a fence trying to get a glimpse of these awesome sea mammals. Also, be forewarned that whale watching requires patience and careful attention. Watch for spouts and flukes as they pass—don't expect a whale to glide right up in the shallows to say hello. Aside from being in the right place at the right time when the occasional confused whale enters San Francisco Bay (which happens at least once a year), your best chance to have a close encounter with one of these magnificent creatures is to pay for a whale-watching **charter**—but try to plan such a cruise well in advance, as they book up quickly. Bodega Bay Sport Fishing, (707) 875-3495, and Oceanic Society Expeditions, (415) 474-3385, take groups out from San Francisco and Bodega Bay throughout the season.

Horseback Riding

Numerous trails within the seashore boundaries are approved for equestrian use, most of them moderate rides of between 5 and 14 miles. Horse rentals are available at the Five Brooks Stables, 3.5 miles south of Olema on Hwy 1, (415) 663-1570, and guided rides leave the Five Brooks area several times a day. Also visit the Morgan Horse Ranch, (415) 663-1763, near the Bear Valley Visitors Center for tours of a working ranch where park service employees train and care for horses.

Beaches/Swimming

If you have swimming on your mind, the beaches along the Pacific seashore between Tomales Point and the Point Reyes Headlands are not where you want to be unless you have a death wish. Strong rip currents, unpredictable surf, and a lack of lifeguards make these areas potentially hazardous even for experienced water sportsters. However, **Drakes Beach,** below the white cliffs on the east side of the park's southern peninsula facing Drakes Bay, is suitable for swimming and wading. Beach fires are allowed. Picnic tables, rest rooms, even ranger-led walks are available here, with easy access from the parking area at the Kenneth C. Patrick Visitors Center off Sir Francis Drake Blvd. To get away from the minivans loaded with families, opt for a more remote beach locale (preferably with hike-in access only) starting from any number of vantage points. Two good choices include **Santa Maria Beach** and **Sculptured Beach,** both located near where Coast Trail, Fire Lane Trail, and Woodworth Valley Trail converge at the Coast Camp (see Camping, above) on the northeastern shore of Drakes Bay. On the Pacific shore, **Kehoe Beach** and **McClures Beach** are accessible by short hikes from marked parking areas along Pierce Point Rd. Swimming is particularly unsafe at McClures, which is at the bottom of a steep trail, but this is a fantastic place to observe tide pools and the varied sea life and avian communities that make this region such a remarkable nature lover's destination.

Canoeing/Kayaking

Again because of the rough ocean currents, sea kayaking off the Point Reyes shore is out of the question—but if you set your sights on the smaller bodies of water surrounding the peninsula, the canoeing and kayaking can be quite impressive, particularly when it comes to viewing wildlife from offshore.

Bring your canoe to **Abbotts Lagoon,** but be prepared to carry it 2 miles to the beach. Once on the water, your course is a placid waterfowl habitat shielded from the ocean by a small band of beach. The lagoon is 2 miles out on Pierce Point Rd, west of Tomales Bay State Park. Kayaking along the more than 10 miles of coves and sandy beaches at **Tomales Bay** is easily accessible from staging areas all along the northeastern perimeter of the seashore, including at **Hearts Desire Beach** in **Tomales Bay State Park** off Sir Francis Drake Blvd 3 miles west of Inverness, or **Chicken Ranch Beach** and **Martinelli Park** closer to town. Larger boats can be launched from a half mile east of Hamlet Oyster Pen on Hwy 1, 13 miles north of Point Reyes Station on the east side of the bay.

On **Drakes Estero**, a lagoon adjacent to Drakes Bay, paddle among tide pools, seals, rays, leopard sharks, and an array of other marine life and waterfowl. Drakes Estero is best accessed from the Limantour Beach area at the end of Limantour Rd. All of these waterways are relatively calm and easily navigable, with abundant protected coves for beginners to get the hang of paddling while enjoying secluded beaches with no easy access from land. For **guided tours, lessons,** and **equipment rentals,** call Pacific Currents in Bodega Bay at (800) GO-KAYAK.

outside in

Attractions

On the westernmost tip of Point Reyes at the end of Sir Francis Drake Blvd is the **Point Reyes Lighthouse,** the park's most popular attraction. Visitors have free access to the lighthouse via a thigh-burning 308-step staircase; open 10am to 4:30pm, Thursday through Monday, weather permitting, (415) 669-1534.

That mighty pungent aroma you smell on the way to the Point Reyes Lighthouse is probably emanating from **Johnson's Oyster Farm.** It may not look like much—a cluster of trailer homes, shacks, and oyster tanks surrounded by huge piles of oyster shells—but that certainly doesn't detract from the taste of fresh-out-of-the-water oysters dipped in Johnson's special sauce. Eat 'em on the spot, or buy a bag for the road—either way, you're not likely to find California oysters as fresh or as cheap anywhere else. The oyster farm resides within Drakes Estero, a large saltwater lagoon on the Point Reyes peninsula that produces nearly 20 percent of California's commercial oyster yield. It's located off Sir Francis Drake Blvd, about 6 miles west of Inverness, and is open 8am to 4pm Tuesday through Sunday; (415) 669-1149.

There are four towns in and around the Point Reyes National Seashore boundary—Olema, Point Reyes Station, Inverness Park, and Inverness—but they are all so close together that it really doesn't matter where you stay, because you'll always be within a stone's throw of the park. While the selection of lodging in Point Reyes is excellent, it's also expensive (most rooms cost well over $100 per night). Be sure to make your reservation far in advance for the summer and holidays, and dress warm: Point Reyes gets darn chilly at night regardless of the season. If you're having trouble finding a vacancy here, call the **West Marin Network** at (415) 663-9543 for information on available lodgings. For additional recommendations in the area, see the Outside In sections in the Marin chapter.

Another option is the **Point Reyes Hostel,** located within the seashore boundaries and conveniently near trailheads and key park attractions on Limantour Rd, 5 miles due west of park headquarters. As with most hostels, a full kitchen and hot showers are included with your dorm-style bunk. Call (415) 663-8811, or drop in daily after 4:30pm to check on availability and make reservations.

Restaurants

Manka's Inverness Lodge ☆☆☆   Dining at Manka's is like being in a Jack London novel. To complement the hunting lodge illusion, they serve "unusual game"—from wild boar sausages grilled in the wood-burning fireplace to pan-seared elk tenderloin, black buck antelope chops, and Canadian pheasant—as well as local seafood. *On Argyle St (off Sir Francis Drake Blvd, 3 blocks N of downtown), Inverness; (415) 669-1034 or (800) 58-LODGE; $$$.*

The Station House Café ☆☆   For more than two decades this place has been a favorite stop for West Marin residents and San Francisco day trippers. The menu changes weekly, but you can count on daily wonders with local produce, seafood, and organic beef. *11180 Shoreline Hwy (on Main St, in the center of town), Point Reyes Station; (415) 663-1515; $$.*

Taqueria La Quinta ☆   Mexican folk music fills the air and bright colors abound at this exuberant restaurant, where most of the fare costs less than *seis dólares.* The service is fast, the food is fresh, and the salsa is *muy caliente. 11285 Hwy 1 (at 3rd and Main Sts), Point Reyes Station; (415) 663-8868; $.*

Lodgings

Blackthorne Inn ☆☆☆   With its four levels, 5 rooms, multiple decks, spiral staircase, skybridge, and fire pole, the Blackthorne Inn is more like a tree house for grown-ups than a B&B. *266 Vallejo Ave (off Sir Francis Drake Blvd, ¼ mile up Vallejo Ave), Inverness Park; (415) 663-8621; $$$.*

Dancing Coyote Beach ☆☆☆   This bayside bed and breakfast is hidden in a pine-covered cove and within easy walking distance of downtown Inverness. The 4 adjoining natural-wood cottages are painted in pastels and equipped with simple furniture, private decks, fireplaces, and full kitchens. *12794 Sir Francis Drake Blvd (just N of downtown), Inverness; (415) 669-7200; $$.*

Holly Tree Inn ☆☆☆   Hidden in a 19-acre valley with a meandering creek and wooded hillsides is the blissfully quiet Holly Tree Inn. This family-owned B&B has 4 cozy guest rooms, each with a private bath (one with a fireplace) and decorated with country antiques. *3 Silverhills Rd (off Bear Valley Rd, 1 mile from Point Reyes Station), Inverness Park; (415) 663-1554; $$$.*

Manka's Inverness Lodge ☆☆☆☆   This former hunting and fishing lodge is one of the most romantic places to stay in California. A dozen accommodations (rooms, cabins, or a boathouse) offer a variety of amenities. Friendly, refreshingly unpretentious, and surprisingly affordable, this is the idyllic weekend getaway. *On Argyle St (off Sir Francis Drake Blvd, 3 blocks N of downtown), Inverness; (415) 669-1034 or (800) 58-LODGE; $$$.*

Point Reyes Seashore Lodge ☆☆   For folks who want the beauty of the countryside combined with the creature comforts of the city, this is the place. Built in 1988, the three-story cedar inn has 21 guest rooms. *10021 Hwy 1 (at Sir Francis Drake Blvd), Olema; (415) 663-9000 or (800) 404-LODG; $$$.*

More Information

Bear Valley Visitors Center: *(415) 663-1092.*
Ken Patrick Visitors Center: *(415) 669-1250.*
Lighthouse Visitors Center: *(415) 669-1534.*
Point Reyes Field Seminars: *(415) 663-1200.*
West Marin Visitor Bureau: *(415) 669-2684.*

East
Bay

All of Alameda and Contra Costa Counties, including the waterfront from the Santa Clara County line on the bay shore east to the beginning of the Sacramento–San Joaquin River Delta, and including the East Bay hills and Mount Diablo State Park.

When the Bay Area is socked in with low-lying morning fog, as it so often is during the summer months, you don't need to wait for the fog to lift to can enjoy the California sunshine. Instead, rise early and head to Wildcat Canyon Road, which slices between the hills separating Berkeley in Alameda County from Orinda in Contra Costa County. It is a winding drive leading up above the crowded freeways and into quiet canyons of eucalyptus and pine. Halfway between Inspiration Point and the Lake View picnic area is a turnout for Seaview Trail. From there, a 20-minute hike or a 10-minute mountain bike cruise will lead you to a sunny spot 1,300 feet above it all; we're talking blue skies with a floor of mashed potatoes, obstructed only by the occasional jumbo jet taking off or landing at one of the Bay Area's three international airports. Cancel your morning appointments. Relax. Take it in. Enjoy. You have discovered a secret hiding place. This is just one of the thousands of special spots tucked in around the vast open spaces of the East Bay that locals know about and visitors need only stray a few minutes off the beaten path to discover.

There is no getting around the fact that this is an urban area with more than 2 million people. The aforementioned freeways are jammed with commuters in the morning, oil refineries line much of the Contra Costa County waterfront, and new subdivisions are replacing farmland in the inland valleys south and east of Mount

Diablo, the region's highest peak. Even as urban expansion takes its toll, however, there remains another side to the East Bay—one that holds an amazing array of outdoor recreation opportunities, with the rolling grassy hills and shady canyons preserved as state and regional parks. Because of the way the open spaces are situated, there quite literally is no danger of becoming stranded—and yet, in what has shaped up to be one of the nation's busiest urban areas, you're never more than a few miles from somewhere that makes you feel smack-dab in the middle of God's country.

From the 3,849-foot summit of Diablo, watch the Bay Area's urban landscape unfold—and on a clear day, also take in stunning vistas of the Central Valley, the snowcapped peaks of the Sierra Nevada, and the Pacific Ocean beyond. The East Bay, like so much of urban California, truly has the best of both worlds; there are places to fish, windsurf, hike, camp, cycle, swim, and fly a kite all within minutes of the Pacific Stock Exchange (across the bridge in San Francisco).

Between the East Bay Regional Park District, which manages and owns more than 70,000 acres of open space throughout the two counties, and the state and city park systems, you will find no shortage of greenery here—and we're talking quality as well as quantity. In Sunol Regional Wilderness, for example, tucked away in Alameda County's southeast corner, is a scenic gorge called "Little Yosemite" where, when you can't make it to the Sierra, the mini-peaks and complementary waterfalls serve as a suitable substitute for the real thing. Stocked fishing lakes and creeks abound, and hundreds of miles of backpacking, hiking, and mountain biking trails lead far into the wilds. And thankfully, property owners for the most part have managed to put aside bureaucratic politics and turf wars to develop a regional trail system that cuts across park and water districts as well as private ranch lands. The trail user on a long hike has no idea when a park district boundary ends—it's all simply open and available.

As great as all of this must sound, the even better news is that there's more to come. It seems everywhere you look in the East Bay region open space areas are being expanded or improved, wildlife areas are being restored or enhanced, and trail systems are being developed with improved links. Among the most exciting recent changes is the addition of the vast watershed area for the new Los Vaqueros Reservoir in eastern Contra Costa County, which opened to the public in 1998. Then there's the planned Eastshore State Park on the Berkeley and Emeryville shoreline, which eventually will transform a ramshackle waterfront plagued by contaminated sediment and beaches of broken rock to a first-class waterfront recreation area along the shores east of the San Francisco–Oakland Bay Bridge.

Getting There

From San Francisco, take the San Francisco–Oakland Bay Bridge east to Oakland, where Interstates 80, 580, and 880, along with Highway 24, lead to their respective portions of the East Bay region. From the Peninsula south of San Francisco, take the Hayward–San Mateo Bridge east to the junction of Interstate 880 and Highway 92, where connections to other parts of the East Bay are made. From San Jose, take Interstate 680 or Interstate 880 north. From Sacramento, take Interstate 80 west. Virtually all area parks are accessible both by car and public transportation, but keep in mind that public transportation in some areas of the East Bay can be both dangerous and unreliable, particularly in the Oakland and Richmond areas. For information on AC Transit bus service, call (510) 839-2882. For information on Bay Area Rapid Transit (BART), call (510) 465-2278. For information on the East Bay Regional Park District's bus program, call (510) 635-0138.

Adjoining Areas

NORTH: **Napa and Sonoma Wine Valleys**

SOUTH: **Peninsula and South Bay**

EAST: **Sacramento Valley, San Joaquin Valley, The Delta**

WEST: **San Francisco**

inside out

Parks/Beaches

With the exception of Mount Diablo State Park, the open spaces mentioned here are managed by the East Bay Regional Park District. Founded in 1934, the district today has 50 parks and 20 regional trails covering more than 70,000 acres in Alameda and Contra Costa Counties. What is particularly exciting about these parklands is the variety of terrain they cover. Included are marshlands on the bay shore, riverfront fishing piers, attractive lakeside campgrounds, deep wilderness canyons with waterfalls, meadows with spring wildflowers, and high peaks accessible only to those willing to sweat. While most of these areas cover undeveloped open space, parks geared toward recreation are also plentiful. **Dogs** are allowed in most of the district's parklands, but they must be leashed in picnic areas, developed park areas, and anywhere a leash sign is posted. **Camping** is by permit only. Be prepared for extremes of weather, particularly in the inland valleys, where summer temperatures can reach over 100 degrees (don't forget the water). Likewise, in the wintertime, temperatures can be surprisingly cold; snow is not unusual atop many of the higher peaks.

Mount Diablo State Park is *the* place. The biggest draw here is the mountain's 3,849-foot peak, said to overlook the most sprawling panorama in the world next to Africa's Kilimanjaro—and you can drive all the way to the top for a look if biking or hiking for hour doesn't appeal. Diablo is indeed the crown jewel of the East Bay, if not the entire Bay Area region. You can almost see the curvature of the globe from up top, as the Central Valley rivers meander in a snakelike pattern toward the horizon and the ocean looms high and wide in a blue strip beyond. It is stunning, cold, windblown, and fantastic. And as incredible as the view is, there is much more to these nearly 20,000 acres of meadows, canyons, peaks, waterfalls, streams, caves, and sandstone formations. Hundreds of miles of hiking, horseback riding, and cycling trails, rock climbing areas, campgrounds, picnic sites, and wildlife areas exist here (see Camping, below). A world-class observatory is under construction on one of the mountain's west-facing slopes. Adjoining regional park and open space areas cover much of the surrounding foothills, and trail connections are well developed and continue to be improved. The park is open from 8am to sunset daily, but closed some summer days because of high fire danger. The summit is closed in winter when dusted by the occasional snowstorm. Campsites may be reserved up to 12 weeks in advance through the state's reservations system, (800) 444-7275. To check on conditions, call the park's main ranger station at (925) 387-2525. To reach the park from Oakland, take Hwy 24 east to the Diablo Valley. As you approach the I-680 interchange in Walnut Creek, the mountain will be visible to the southeast (you can't miss it!). From here, take I-680 south to Diablo Rd in Danville, and head east on Diablo Rd for 3 miles to the entrance. Alternatively, exit Hwy 24 at Ygnacio Valley Rd, continuing 3 miles to Walnut Ave. Turn right, and follow Walnut Ave to North Gate Rd, approximately 4 miles, which leads to the park gates. The entry fee is $5 per car, plus $1 for dogs.

Finding a place to get lost is indeed no problem in **Del Valle Regional Park,** which is contiguous with **Sunol** and **Mission Peak Regional Wilderness Areas.** These wildlands make it possible to hike from the bay shore to the region's easternmost point just over the hill from the Central Valley. Nestled in a canyon of oak trees, **Lake Del Valle** looks more like an alpine lake in the Sierra Nevada than one you would come across in the vast, arid hills of the East Bay. The 5-mile-long, quarter-mile-wide lake is surrounded by nearly 4,000 acres of parkland encompassing 28 miles of trails for hiking, horseback riding, and bicycling. Year-round swimming is allowed along most of the lakefront, along with fishing, boating, and windsurfing. Three campgrounds with 150 sites also lie on the banks of the reservoir (see Camping, below). To the southwest are Sunol and Mission Peak Regional Wilderness Areas, together comprising a large preserve of native wildlife and plants covering more than 10,000 acres of forested canyons and grassy hills with outstanding vistas, horseback and hiking trails, and a host of naturalist programs. To reach Del Valle from Oakland, take I-580 east to S Livermore Ave, then head 3 miles south to Mines Rd. Turn right on Mines Rd and right on Del Valle Rd. Proceed to the gate of the park. To reach Sunol Wilderness Area, take I-680 south from the I-580 interchange to the Calaveras Rd exit. Proceed south on Calaveras Rd to the park entrance. For additional information, contact the East Bay Regional Park District at (510) 562-PARK.

Briones Regional Park's best asset is its size. At 5,756 acres, it is one of the region's largest open space areas, surrounded on all sides by suburban development. Black-tailed deer, coyote, squirrels, red-tailed hawks, vultures, and a host of more reclusive creatures inhabit its grassy knolls, woodlands and canyons. Springtime brings acres and acres of wildflowers and is the perfect time to take advantage of ranger-led nature and history tours. Briones is ideal for horseback riding, hiking, and bird-watching. The low peaks in the park's eastern reaches offer stunning morning sunrise views of Mount Diablo, which looms black and silhouetted over the Walnut Creek skyline. The park is most conveniently reached from Oakland or San Francisco via Hwy 24. Take Hwy 24 east to the Happy Valley Rd exit. Take Happy Valley Rd north for about 3 miles to where it intersects with Bear Creek Rd. Turn left at Bear Creek Rd and travel half a mile to the Bear Creek staging area. Here you can find water, park information, picnic areas, and a horse staging area. To visit a more remote part of the park, take Hwy 24 east, past the Happy Valley Rd exit, to Pleasant Hill Rd. Exit at Pleasant Hill Rd and proceed north. Signs will guide you to the Lafayette Ridge Staging Area, where you can pick up park information, about a quarter of a mile from the highway on the left side of Pleasant Hill Rd. For an even more remote parking area, continue past this first parking area and make a left on Reliez Valley Rd, continuing for about 3 miles. Signs will guide you to an unnamed parking area on the left side of the road. For more information and maps of Briones, contact the East Bay Regional Park District at (510) 562-PARK.

Anthony Chabot and **Redwood Regional Parks** offer a wealth of outdoor recreation just 20 minutes from downtown Oakland. This combined 6,000-acre wilderness area can get a bit crowded at times, and with good reason. Anthony Chabot has a 315-acre lake at its center that is open for fishing and boating year-round, along with a trail system encircling the water and a 6-mile creek that meets with San Francisco Bay. The park also boasts a marksmanship range (offering a hunting safety course), horse rentals, and campgrounds. The Oakland Zoo and Lake Chabot Municipal Golf Course are adjacent. Park visitors can explore miles of hiking, horseback, and bicycle trails through grassy fields and shady eucalyptus groves.

Redwood Regional Park is quieter than the lake area of Chabot. This cool, shady grove of 150 second-growth coast redwoods, assorted evergreens, chaparral, and grasslands is bisected by meandering Redwood Creek, which attracts an array of wildlife including deer, raccoons, golden eagles, and rabbits. To get from Oakland to Chabot, take I-580 south to Lake Chabot Rd, exit east, and travel 2.5 miles to the Lake Chabot Marina on the left side of the road. To get from Oakland to Redwood, take I-580 south, exit east at Joaquin Miller Rd, and proceed to the park entrance. For additional information on either of these parks contact the East Bay Regional Park District at (510) 562-PARK.

The extreme eastern reaches of the East Bay offer access to the San Joaquin River Delta. **Antioch Regional Shoreline** is a quaint 7-acre waterfront park on the Delta with a 500-foot pier. Striped bass fishing is best from November though January, and flounder move in during the warm summer months. Or just enjoy a waterside picnic here. From Oakland take Hwy 4 east to Antioch; exit north at Bridgehead Rd. For additional information contact the East Bay Regional Park District at (510) 562-PARK.

Browns Island Regional Shoreline, covering 595 acres, is located at the confluence of the state's two largest rivers, the Sacramento and the San Joaquin, which meet to form the Delta leading to San Francisco Bay. Wildlife viewing is a favorite activity here, as is picnicking—but be certain to bring something to sit on, as this is a primitive site with no facilities of any kind. We're talking remote, quiet and rustic. Six rare and endangered plant species are found on the island, which is located off the Pittsburg shoreline. From Oakland, take Hwy 24 east to I-680, continue to Hwy 242, then go east on Hwy 4 toward Stockton. Exit east on Railroad Ave, and follow to the waterfront and marina area. For additional information contact the East Bay Regional Park District at (510) 562-PARK.

Contra Loma and **Black Diamond Mines Regional Parks** lie in the foothills east of Mount Diablo and are increasingly being encroached on by urban sprawl. But there's no danger of losing all the green. Large sections of wildlands have been preserved forever in these contiguous parts. Contra Loma's 776 acres include an 80-acre reservoir, open all year for windsurfing, boating, fishing, and swimming. The sandy beach has a refreshment stand, picnic area, and changing rooms. The lake is stocked with catfish, bluegill, trout, sunfish, and striped bass. Horseback riding and hiking trails from Contra Loma extend northwest to Black Diamond Mines Regional Preserve, 3,905 acres of foothill canyons containing three small ghost towns—remnants of a coal mining community from the last century that fueled California's industrial revolution. The park boasts numerous hiking and riding trails, beautiful vistas, a historic cemetery, mine programs, and geologic features such as exposed beds of sandstone and coal. The northernmost strand of Coulter pines and the desert olive are found here, as are eagle and mountain lion habitats. From Oakland take Hwy 24 west to Hwy 242, then go north to Hwy 4 east; continue on Hwy 4 roughly 12 miles. From there, to reach Black Diamond, exit at Somersville Rd, and continue south directly into the park's main entrance. To reach Contra Loma, exit Hwy 4 at Lone Tree Way. Head 2 miles south and turn right on Frederickson Lane. Proceed to the gate of the park. For additional information contact the East Bay Regional Park District at (510) 562-PARK.

Coyote Hills Regional Park, 976 acres of open space on the banks of a bay salt marsh, provides a window to the past, when tidal marshes encircled all of San Francisco Bay. The vast majority of these marshes have been filled in for salt production, farming, and building. Within Coyote Hills also lie preserved Indian sites and numerous exhibits describing how the Native Americans lived along the banks of the marsh, including a reconstructed tule reed house, shade shelter, dance circle, and sweat lodge. There are two picnic areas and a stunning 3.5-mile hiking trail along a marsh abundant with aquatic wildlife and waterfowl. From Oakland take I-880 south to Hwy 84, then head east on Hwy 84 for roughly 2.5 miles. Exit Hwy 84 at Paseo Padre Pkwy, then head north to Patterson Ranch Rd and turn right. Proceed to the gate of the park. For additional information contact the East Bay Regional Park District at (510) 562-PARK.

Tilden and **Wildcat Canyon Regional Parks** are the showcase centerpieces of the East Bay Regional Park District lands. They sit on the high ridges of the Berkeley and Oakland hills, covering nearly 4,500 acres with unparalleled views of the bay and eastern foothills. Hiking, bicycling, horseback riding, golf, pony rides, and swimming at Lake Anza are favorites among the visitors to these contiguous parks. From the hilltops of Tilden, one can stand above the fog. Tilden is topographically beautiful with its high ridges and hillsides and deep river-cut canyons. Sweeping vistas seem to abound at every turn. Tilden also boasts a world-class botanical garden and group campsites. From Oakland take I-80 north, exit east on University Ave and travel 2 miles to Shattuck Ave. Turn left on Shattuck Ave and right on Marin Ave. Continue to Grizzly Peak Blvd. Turn right and continue to Shasta Rd. Turn left and continue to the Tilden visitor information area. For additional information, contact the East Bay Regional Park District at (510) 562-PARK.

One of the most contentious growth battles in all of the Bay Area has centered around the wildlands adjacent to **Pleasanton Ridge Regional Park,** just north of Sunol. This 3,163-acre preserve of pastoral grasslands lures equestrians, bicyclists, and hikers, who come to enjoy its ridge-top vistas and deep canyon streams. In the past it has been eyed by developers for potential residential building. The park's grasslands support an abundance of wildflowers that blossom in early spring. Scattered throughout the park are small ponds and springs that support various animals requiring a wetland habitat. During summer, be prepared for extreme heat. From Oakland, take I-580 east to I-680, then head south on I-680 to Castlewood Dr. Go west on Castlewood Dr to Foothill Rd; turn left on Foothill Rd, and continue another 4 miles to Kilkare Rd. Turn right and proceed to the park entrance. For additional information, contact the park at (510) 862-2963.

On the bay shore, **Crown Memorial State Beach** is the East Bay's premier spot for sun worshipers. The centerpiece of this park is a 2.5-mile-long beach along Alameda's warm southwest-facing waterfront. Unique for its flat, long, sandy shore, an oddity for San Francisco Bay, this park is not for people in search of an area where wooded hills and trees meet the sea; it's more the type of coast you find in Southern California. Windsurfing is popular, along with fishing and swimming. Paved walking and bike trails hug the well-maintained shoreline. The beach is easily accessible and naturally quite busy on warm summer days. From Oakland, take I-880 south to the Webster St exit. Proceed through the Webster tunnel to Alameda Island, then continue to Central Ave. Turn left on Central Ave and right on Eighth St. Proceed to the park entrance. For additional information, contact the East Bay Regional Park District at (510) 562-PARK.

More on the wild side, **Las Trampas Regional Wilderness,** covering 3,638 acres, is a remote wilderness area with outstanding vistas and hiking and riding trails. It's also home to a wide variety of animals, including mountain lions and golden eagles. Bollinger Creek meanders through the center of the park, with scattered picnic areas along its edges. The picnic area at the end of Bollinger Canyon Rd is the most developed portion. The northeast corner of the park consists of densely forested canyons known as the Corduroy Hills. Group camping only. From Oakland, take Hwy 24 east to I-680, south. Exit I-680 at Bollinger Canyon Rd, and continue to the park entrance 6 miles ahead. For additional information, contact the East Bay Regional Park District at (510) 562-PARK.

Point Pinole Regional Shoreline juts out into the waters of San Pablo Bay. This 2,147-acre peninsula is equipped with a fishing pier and miles of hiking and riding trails. Enjoy bird-watching and vistas across the Bay, adjacent to three densely populated urban communities. Expect crowds, especially around the pier and picnic facilities on warm summer days. From Oakland, take I-80 north to San Pablo Ave west. From San Pablo Ave, turn left on Atlas Rd. Continue to the Giant Highway, where a right turn leads to the park entrance. For additional information, contact the East Bay Regional Park District at (510) 562-PARK.

Carquinez Strait and **Martinez Regional Shorelines** make the perfect combination road-bike outing and history tour. The 1,304 acres of the Carquinez Strait Regional Shoreline encircle the quaint and historic village of Port Costa, where the remnants of a once-bustling rail stop and port center in the late 1800s today are now offered up as trendy restaurants and offbeat junk stores. The shore is suitable for nice waterfront walks, and the lightly traveled country roads leading into the area are nice for cycling. But the historic charm is the reason to make the trip. Just east is the Martinez Regional Shoreline, a 343-acre waterfront that, while considerably smaller, comes equipped with a horse arena, pond, exercise course, and trails through a salt marsh. From Oakland, take I-80 north to eastbound Hwy 4. Continue on Hwy 4 to the Cummings Skyway exit. Take Cummings Skyway about a mile and a half. Turn right on Crockett Blvd and proceed to Pamona St. Turn left on Pamona St. The road turns into Carquinez Scenic Drive. Follow signs to Bull Valley Staging Area on the left side of the road to reach the Carquinez Strait Regional Shoreline. To reach the Martinez Regional Shoreline, stay on Carquinez Scenic Drive about 3 miles and turn left on Escobar St. Travel about 400 yards and turn left on Ferry St. Proceed to the park entrance. For additional information, contact the East Bay Regional Park District at (510) 562-PARK.

Miller/Knox Regional Shoreline, despite its name, is more of a hillside than a waterfront romp, simply because its uplands are much nicer. The shoreline, called Keller Beach, is paved with railroad tracks and is actually inaccessible except for a small patch of bay front; it's in the northwest corner of the 295-acre property. The park has a saltwater lagoon for fishing and swimming, plus several hiking and riding trails. From Oakland, take I-580 north, exit at W Cutting Blvd, and turn left. Proceed to Gerrard Blvd and turn left. This turns into Dornan Dr and leads to the park entrance. For additional information, contact the East Bay Regional Park District at (510) 562-PARK.

Martin Luther King Jr. Regional Shoreline has a small piece of the marshland that once surrounded San Francisco Bay preserved within its 1,220-acres on the shore of San Leandro Bay. The 50-acre Arrowhead Marsh, which is undergoing a large restoration, is a stopover for a host of migratory birds. The park has picnic areas with barbecue pits, a boat launch ramp, a fishing area, a sunbathing beach, and biking and hiking trails. Along the banks of Doolittle Pond, birders love to watch the daylight antics of the native birds. From Oakland, take I-880 south and exit west at Hegenberger Rd. Continue for 1 mile, then turn left at Doolittle Dr. Proceed to the park entrance. For additional information, contact the East Bay Regional Park District at (510) 562-PARK.

Finally, there's **Hayward Regional Shoreline,** an 843-acre park comprising the largest salt marsh restoration on the West Coast. This is a nature lover's delight; the marshy park teems with wildlife that can be viewed from its hiking and bicycling trails. If you are looking to see wildlife in the raw, this is the spot to do it. From Oakland, take I-880 south to W Winton Ave west. Continue on W Winton Ave about 4 miles to the park entrance. For additional information, contact the East Bay Regional Park District at (510) 562-PARK.

Hiking/Backpacking

Just have a look around. The East Bay is literally an embarrassment of riches with high peaks sporting panoramic views, deep lush canyons, waterfall vistas, and wildflower meadows. The Greenbelt Alliance, the Bay Area's leading land conservation group, sponsors numerous free outings in the open spaces. These **guided excursions** are worthwhile even for experienced hikers since each is led by a knowledgeable naturalist. The alliance maintains an outings hot line with information about planned events, (415) 398-3730. The Sierra Club Bay Chapter also makes hiking information easily available to the public and organizes regular outings. For a hiking guide, send a self-addressed stamped envelope to 1525 Berkeley Way, Berkeley, CA 94703, or call the area hiking coordinator at (925) 631-0751. Another resource is the Berkeley REI store at 338 San Pablo Ave, (510) 527-4140. REI maintains a thorough staff-written Web site, www.rei.com/MORE_STORE/hikes/sanfranhktemp.html, with information on local hikes. All of that said, here are the hiking highlights we recommend in the East Bay:

The **East Ridge Loop** (moderate; 4 miles round trip) rambles 900 feet up to the top of East Ridge, in **Redwood Regional Park,** in the Oakland hills, then down into a forested canyon of second-generation redwoods (most of the redwoods in the East Bay were hacked down in the mid-1800s to build up San Francisco during the Gold Rush). From the trailhead, take Canyon Trail about half a mile to East Ridge Trail, then go up the ridge and down into the canyon, where Redwood Creek runs through the park. Return to the trailhead on Stream Trail. The trailhead is at the Canyon Meadow staging area to the park, 3 miles east of Hwy 13 on Redwood Rd. To get there from downtown Oakland, take Hwy 24 east to the interchange with Hwy 13, then go south to the Redwood Rd exit, heading left.

The **Stewartville Townsite Trail** loops through the southeastern portion of the **Black Diamond Regional Preserve** (moderate; 9 miles round trip) in eastern Contra Costa County and covers expansive ridge lines, narrow and secluded canyons, and open meadows, with views of the delta from the peaks and interesting remnants of the Gold Rush–era coal-mining communities that once existed here along the way. Most of the hike is on wide fire roads, but there are two sections of single-track hiking to contend with along the way. Stage at the end of Fredrickson Lane in Antioch, just outside the entrance to adjacent Contra Loma Regional Park. From there, hike west on Stewartville Trail about 2 miles over the ridge and another third of a mile to Canyon Trail. At Lower Oil Can Trail, turn left for about a half mile, walking toward the canyon, and then climbing on a single-track trail to Upper Oil Canyon Trail above. Turn right, and descend back to rejoin Stewartville Trail, then go left on Stewartville for an easy quarter-mile canyon-floor walk to the Miner's Trail turnoff on the right. Climb 600 feet on a sometimes steep single-track trail from the canyon floor to Ridge Trail, which at 1,100 to 900 feet above sea level provides nice views of both the Stewartville area and the Delta. Follow Ridge Trail just under 3 miles to rejoin Stewartville Trail, about a third of a mile from where the journey began; turn right, and walk back to the staging area. Watch out for cows on this hike, as the park district continues to allow area ranchers to disperse cattle throughout its parklands. We've seen trampled streams, meadows strewn with manure and flies, and in this area in particular, aggressive cows that will actually try to *chase you away* if they're in a bad mood. Traditionally most of the open ranges in the East Bay have been used as ranchlands, and as the government has purchased areas for open space, ranching families have retained the right to work the land. Also, it's believed that cows keep fire danger down. Whatever the case, be prepared. To reach the trailhead from the Oakland area, take Hwy 24 east through the Caldecott Tunnel to the I-680 interchange, follow I-680 to Hwy 242, then go east on Hwy 4 to the Lone Tree Way exit. From there, head 2 miles west to Fredrickson Lane, turn right, and follow to the dead end and trailhead. Call the Black Diamond office and ranger station at (925) 757-2620.

The **Fire Interpretive Trail** loop (easy; 0.5 miles round trip) encircles the Mount Diablo summit, with stopping points along the way to help hikers enjoy some of the most stunning vistas in all of North America and Europe. On a clear day, the Golden Gate Bridge and the Farallon Islands off the San Francisco coast are visible to the west, the Santa Cruz Mountains to the south, Mount St. Helena in Napa Valley to the north, and even the Sierra Nevada to the east—including Yosemite National Park's Half Dome. No need to sweat it; the summit is accessible by car;

there is no need to walk all the way up. The trail is found at the Mount Diablo State Park summit parking area, top of the mountain. See Parks/ Beaches, above, for driving directions.

The hike along **Mission Peak Trail** in **Mission Peak Regional Preserve** (difficult, 7 miles round trip) is one of the most physically challenging hikes in the Bay Area, but the hard work is well rewarded with wide views of San Francisco and the bay, the Sierra Nevada, and the Santa Cruz mountains. Park at Ohlone College (lots D and H are closest), where the trailhead for **Spring Valley Trail** is found, and then head up—and we really mean up: a more than 2,000-foot ascent in the first 4 miles of hiking leads to the summit along Mission Peak Trail. Two warnings: there is no drinking water available along the way, so carry plenty; and watch out for feral goats that roam the hillsides, wildflowers, meadows, cliffs, and the crisp high altitudes. To reach the trailhead from Oakland, take I-580 to the I-680 interchange in Dublin, then go south on I-680 to Mission Blvd east. Continue 3 miles to Ohlone College on the right.

In the foothills south of Mount Diablo, and adjacent to the Los Vaqueros Reservoir watershed, **Volvon Loop** and **Manzanita Trails** (moderately difficult; 6 miles round trip) lead through sandstone hills adorned with more than 90 varieties of wildflower in the spring, offering vistas of the Livermore Valley, the Altamont Pass—and on clear days, from select vantage points, the Sierra Nevada 200 miles to the east. Begin the hike at the Morgan Territory Rd parking area, and follow Volvon Trail to Blue Oak Trail through bald ridge lands. Turn right, taking Manzanita Trail—the most challenging portion of the hike, with a steep grade—to the 2,317-foot peak and overlook. From the overlook, switch back to Valley View Trail, which reconnects with Volvon and the staging spot. From I-580 in Livermore, take the N Livermore Ave exit north, following the road as it veers west. Turn right (north) on Morgan Territory Rd, and follow it 10.7 miles to the parking area.

In addition to the numerous hikes through the East Bay's foothill and mountain regions, access to the bay shore is plentiful in this area. The best is the interpretive walk (easy; 3 miles) through **Cogswell Marsh** at the **Hayward Regional Shoreline** between the mouth of San Lorenzo Creek and the San Mateo Bridge. View rare shorebirds and enjoy excellent views of the bay along the trail route, which follows the bay shore and then loops through the restored marsh before connecting back to the shore trail. The trails are level and well managed. Guided interpretive walks are also available through the shoreline's interpretive center, (510) 783-1066. Stage from the Grant Ave parking area. From I-880, exit south on Washington Ave in San Leandro, turn right on Grant Ave, and follow to the end. Parking is on the right.

The three-day journey along the **National Skyline Trail** (moderate; 31 miles one way) passes through several regional parks, including some of the most stunning open spaces in the East Bay, from **Wildcat Canyon** in the foothills south of Richmond to **Chabot Regional Park** in Castro Valley. Before attempting this hike, call the East Bay Regional Park District at (510) 562-PARK for pointers on where to stage, park conditions along the way, and special instructions, although no permits are required for this particular jaunt. Sleeping spots and water are scarce along the way, and multiple-use trail crossings do not extend along the entire route, so the only way to do the whole thing is by foot. With the logistics properly sorted out, however, this is a unique haul through amazingly pristine and seldom-used parklands tucked in the canyons and ridges of the East Bay. The route begins at the Alvarado entrance to Wildcat. From Oakland, take I-80 to McBryde Ave east, then follow 3 miles to Park Ave on the left at the fork in the road. The park entrance is before you, with the Skyline route leaving directly from the parking area. From here, the journey south passes through Tilden Regional Park, Redwood Regional Park, Chabot Regional Park, and adjoining open spaces, ending at Chabot's Proctor gate. Expect to encounter horses, mountain bikes, campers, and even automobile traffic along the way (the trail crosses some roads)—and, again, don't even set out on this one without first getting maps and special instructions from the park district.

Another three-day journey through the wilderness follows the **Ohlone Wilderness Trail** (difficult; 28 miles one way) east from the Fremont hills at **Mission Peak** through the Sunol and Ohlone Wilderness Areas, ending at **Lake Del Valle** south of the Livermore Valley. A permit is required for this haul through grasslands, mountains, and canyons of southern Alameda County, which are populated by tule elk, mountain goats, mountain lions, bald eagles, and deer. The trail tops out at Rose Peak, which at 3,817 feet is only slightly lower than Mount Diablo. Call (925) 636-1684 for reservations and campsite and permit information before setting out. Trail maps are available with reservations. Note: Fresh water is available at only two points between Mission Peak and Del Valle, and sections of this hike are very strenuous, with numerous switchbacks between Mission and Rose Peaks. For directions to Mission Peak or Del Valle, see the Mission Peak Trail, above, and Parks/Beaches, above.

Mountain Biking

Sure, the mountain bike was invented on the other side of the bay in Marin, but don't let that diminish your interest in the East Bay for fine off-road adventuring. Be warned, however, that some of the area's best off-road riding opportunities are far inland, meaning bikers must contend with summer heat that is usually not a concern in coastal areas like Marin and the Peninsula. Here are some of our favorite off-road treks:

Mount Diablo State Park, with over 100 miles of trails and fire roads open to two-wheelers, is perhaps the prime East Bay destination for mountain bikers—and it actually has something that the more popular Mount Tamalpais in Marin doesn't: Three single-track trails were opened to limited mountain biking last summer. They are **Ranch Trail, Buckeye Trail,** and **Oyster Point Trail,** all easy to moderate rides in the park's northeast end. Before you let loose on those trails, though, check in with the park ranger station at the junction of North Gate Rd and South Gate Rd, (925) 837-2525, because bike traffic is restricted at times depending on weather conditions. A good overview ride begins on **Pine Ridge Trail,** the fire road leading from the park's Macedo Ranch Staging Area off Green Valley Rd in Danville. To find the staging area, take the Diablo Rd exit from I-680 in Danville and follow the signs east. From the staging area, it's a moderate 4-mile ride through the Pine Ridge and Cook Canyon areas, through Wildcat Camp, and then on to **Summit Trail,** but keep in mind that you cannot get to the summit itself without at some point switching over to South Gate Rd and taking the last third of the journey on (gasp!) tar roads. The climb all the way to the top is difficult, so don't try it unless you're prepared and have time. The view is worth it, but there is also a whole network of connected and looping fire roads to enjoy below the summit peaks. Another good option is to enter the park from the end of Mitchell Canyon Rd in Clayton, then ride west toward the summit trails through Donner Creek or Mitchell Canyon, both about a 5-mile, moderate to difficult ride toward the summit area. To reach the staging area from this end, take Ygnacio Valley Rd from the Hwy 24/I-680 interchange in Walnut Creek and head east 6 miles to Clayton Rd, turn right, and head south on Clayton Rd 1 mile to Mitchell Canyon Rd. Turn right and follow the road to the end for the park staging area (you have the option of parking on the street or entering the parking area for a $2 fee). Once you're here, your best bet is to brave the difficult 3,000-foot ascent up **Mitchell Canyon Trail.** Follow it 3 miles, then contend with numerous switchbacks through steep terrain as you enter the Deer Flat area and come to Juniper Campground. Turn around at the campground and descend the mountain through Bald Ridge and Meridian Ridge.

In the Diablo area, contact California Pedaler, 495 Hartz Ave, Danville, (925) 820-0345, for cycling **information, gear,** and **rentals.** Other shops to check are A Sports Rack USA, 2040 Mount Diablo Blvd, Walnut Creek, (925) 939-9900, and California Bike and Snowboard, 490 Ygnacio Valley Rd, Walnut Creek, (925) 934-2453.

Black Diamond Regional Preserve and **Tilden Regional Park,** with adjacent **Wildcat Canyon Regional Park,** also offer terrific mountain biking opportunities (see Parks/Beaches, above, for directions to all three). In Tilden, begin your ride at **Inspiration Point** midway along Wildcat Canyon Rd. Trail maps, water, and rest rooms are available at the trailhead, as is plenty of parking, both in the lot and at roadside. Riding here is restricted to fire roads, and then only those outside of designated nature and camping areas. The 15mph speed limit is strictly enforced, as is a "call-out" law requiring you to warn others of your approach on the trail. The paved **Nimitz Trail** leading from Inspiration Point can be crowded with walkers, runners, and in-line skaters for the first few miles, but you can make important connections here to less crowded and more enjoyable riding trails, most notably **Havey Canyon Trail** in the Wildcat portion of the park. Riding in Black Diamond is typically less crowded but certainly more arid—downright hot in the summer, the preserve being in the eastern foothills of Mount Diablo. Diablo Cyclists, at (925) 274-DIAB, arranges weekly group rides on and around the mountain. Another valuable resource is the East Bay Bicycle Coalition, (925) 939-5181 or (510) 530-3444.

Cycling is also popular in the East Bay, mostly on country roads leading through the inland valleys and into the undeveloped canyons in southeast Alameda County. Be alert, however, as many of these country roads double as commuter shortcuts for drivers trying to avoid the region's overstressed freeway system. That said, "tar heads" have some choices to make if they wish to tour the East Bay. One particularly nice road ride is the 35-mile trek, easy to moderate in difficulty, through **Palomares, Niles,** and **Eden Canyons** in southern Alameda County. Stage along Eden Canyon Rd, just south of the stretch of I-580 leading from Castro Valley to Dublin. Ride east to Foothill Rd, then south through the canyons at the foot of **Pleasanton Ridge** to Niles Canyon Rd 10 miles away. Take Niles Canyon Rd, which runs alongside Alameda Creek, 8 miles to Palomares Canyon Rd, a hairpin turn to your right. Palomares Canyon Rd takes you back north to where you started. This final 10-mile leg of the ride is the highlight, following a narrow and woodsy canyon of ranchettes and vineyards.

The aforementioned Diablo Cyclists and East Bay Bicycle Coalition are good resources for this sport as well (see above). Castro Valley Cyclery, 20515 Stanton Ave, Castro Valley, (510) 538-1878, is a good local resource for road cycling **equipment, maps,** and **rentals.** Another good bet is Hank & Frank Bicycles, 3377 Mount Diablo Blvd, Lafayette, (510) 283-2453.

Road cycling is also popular through and around **Mount Diablo State Park,** in the East Bay hills on park and county roads, and in eastern Contra

Costa County, through the Vasco Rd area, **Dougherty Valley,** and **Morgan Territory.** Also consider the country roads along the Contra Costa County waterfront, namely those adjacent to the **Martinez Regional Shoreline** (see Parks/Beaches, above). Again, however, watch out for commuters who don't watch out for you.

Camping

From the bayfront ridges to the inland valley parklands to the slopes of Mount Diablo, camping sites around the East Bay are nicely equipped and situated in the most spectacular surroundings you can imagine. Be aware, however, that because of their proximity to the suburbs, you run the risk of finding parks overrun with families, Scouts, pets, and noise. We suggest checking to make sure there is no jamboree in town before picking a day to sleep under the stars. The Berkeley REI store at 338 San Pablo Ave, (510) 527-4140, is a good resource for local camping options. Also call the East Bay Regional Park District, (510) 562-PARK, for overall park information.

Del Valle Regional Park has 150 sites for tents or motor homes (21 with full hookups), in a lake setting with boating, windsurfing, fishing, hiking, and horseback riding at arm's reach. Hot showers and flush toilets are available. Sites are arranged among five camps, two of them literally on the lake's edge. Call (925) 636-1684 to make reservations up to 14 days in advance. Bring your own drinking water and precut firewood. *Take I-580 east from Oakland to N Livermore Ave, then go south on N Livermore Ave to Mines Rd. Turn right and follow Mines Rd 3 miles to the park entrance.*

Sunol and **Ohlone Regional Wilderness Areas,** west of Del Valle and east of Fremont, are more quiet and secluded. Sunol has just 4 hike-in tent sites available among rolling oak woodlands and grasslands, among them "Little Yosemite," an area of rock cliffs and waterfalls on Alameda Creek. These are primitive sites, but running water is available. Call (925) 562-2267 for reservations. *From Oakland, take I-580 to I-680, then go south to Sunol. Take the Calaveras Rd exit, then go 4 miles south to Geary Rd. Turn left and continue another 2 miles to the park entrance.* Ohlone has both group and backpacking sites similar to those found at Sunol. To reach Ohlone, see directions under Parks/Beaches above.

Mount Diablo State Park has a total of 58 campsites suitable for tents or RVs (full hookups; RV limit 24 feet) in three campgrounds situated on the mountain's western flanks. Running water and flush toilets are available. Leave the beer at home, however: alcohol is prohibited in the park. Camping is first-come, first-served only during the summer because of intermittent park closures for fire danger. **Live Oak Campground** has

18 sites in an oak grove near the park's south entrance. Each is equipped with a picnic table and cooking grill, with running water and vault toilets nearby. This camp is closed in the winter. **Juniper Campground** has 34 sites in a grove of laurels and oaks just north of the access road to the summit; it's higher up on the mountain than the others. Each site has a picnic table and fire grill with running water and vault toilets nearby. There are pull-through slots here for RV camping. **Junction Campground** is the smallest, with 6 sites in a wooded area near the park ranger station at the junction of North Gate Rd and South Gate Rd. Each has a picnic table and fire pit, with running water and flush toilets nearby. This is a peaceful and quiet spot at night, but because the park office is the center of activity during the day it is not as out-of-the-way as a nature outing should be. *The state reservations system, (800) 444-7275, takes reservations up to eight weeks in advance October through May. Call the park directly, (925) 837-2525, for information. From Oakland, take Hwy 24 east to I-680 south. Exit I-680 at Diablo Rd, then go 5.5 miles to the park entrance (follow the signs).*

    Anthony Chabot Regional Park has 43 sites for tents or RVs (12 with partial hookups) and 10 walk-in sites among eucalyptus forests surrounding the lake. Grills, picnic tables, flush toilets, and showers are available. Hiking, boating, and equestrian facilities are all nearby. *Call (510) 562-2267 for reservations and information. From Oakland, take I-580 south to 35th Ave, then go east on 35th Ave to Redwood Rd (straight ahead). Continue 6 miles to the park entrance, a turnoff to the right.*

    The camping scene at **Redwood Regional Park, Tilden Regional Park,** and **Las Trampas Regional Wilderness,** being centered almost entirely around scouting and group activities, is not for the single weekend warrior seeking solace away from the concrete jungle. The Las Trampas camp is most popular with equestrian groups. To organize a big camp-out at Redwood, call (510) 636-1634. For Tilden, the reservations line is (510) 540-0220. For Las Trampas, call (925) 636-1684. Go elsewhere if scads of shouting kids isn't your idea of a good time! For driving directions, see Parks/Beaches, above.

Fishing

It's true. There is fishing all around San Francisco Bay, whether it be from the omnipresent public piers, by private boat, or by sportfishing tour. But the fishing scene in the East Bay is most active away from the bay. The region's numerous upland lakes, most of them well-stocked and managed by the regional park district, are where the action is. **Lake Chabot** in the hills between Castro Valley and Oakland, covering 300 acres, has an aggressive **trout** stocking program, with the best trout fishing from fall to spring. Summer fishing includes **catfish, crappie,** and **bluegill.** Check in at the Lake Chabot Marina, a short walk from the park entrance off Lake Chabot Rd (accessible east of I-580 from Oakland, see Parks/Beaches, above), for daily permits, boat rentals, bait, and other supplies. There is no hard and fast rule here: You can fish anywhere there is waterside access along the trail systems encircling the lake, or boat out to a suitable spot, preferably at the northern end of the lake, for more quiet and privacy— and perhaps better luck! Chabot is a great place to unfurl one of those low-slung portable fishing chairs on a lazy summer day and half-snooze while waiting for a tug on the line. Popular with geezers and kids alike.

Lake Del Valle in the hills east of Livermore is another popular spot for **trout** anglers, particularly in early spring before the valley's hot summers warm the lake. Here, head for the south end of the lake at the reservoir intake or along **Shallow Rock Cove.** Summer bait fishing is excellent here for **catfish** and **bluegills,** along with **largemouth bass** and numerous varieties of **panfish.** Prime fishing time here, however, is winter, as regular trout stocking occurs from October through May.

One less-traveled fishing spot is **Lake Don Castro** in the Castro Valley hills west of Lake Chabot. Anglers can find **trout, bass, bluegill,** and **catfish** here, particularly during stocking months. A swimming lagoon is located adjacent to the fishing lake.

Numerous other fishing spots are found throughout the East Bay hills, from the Oakland region east to the inland ridges south of Pleasanton, include **Briones Reservoir, Lafayette Reservoir, Contra Loma Reservoir,** and **Shadow Cliffs Lake.** Call (925) 248-FISH for complete park district concessionaire information on fishing activities at the lakes.

While the lake fishing is certainly desirable because of the stocking operations, bay fishing from the East Bay's numerous public piers is also a worthy enterprise. The **Point Isabel Regional Shoreline** is one such spot; **striped bass, perch, jacksmelt, sturgeon, leopard shark,** and **flounder** frequent the waters of the coved **Richmond Inner Harbor.** To reach Point Isabel from Oakland, take I-80 east to Central Ave, then head west to the waterfront. West of there, try the city parklands off the **Berkeley marina.** The marina is off I-80, west of University Ave. For even bigger adventures, hop a **sportfishing charter** for saltwater fishing outside the Golden Gate. From the East Bay, Emeryville Sport Fishing at the Berkeley marina is a good choice. Call (510) 654-6040. Other local fishing areas include Point Pinole, Antioch, Browns Island, and Miller/Knox Regional Shorelines, and Crown Memorial State Beach (see Parks/Beaches, above, for directions and contact information).

Horseback Riding

Riding trails can be found in most regional parks of the East Bay and all through **Mount Diablo State Park,** which has two horse camps. Your first choice, however, should probably be one of the parks less frequented by mountain bikers; call the stables at **Anthony Chabot Regional Park,** (510) 638-0610, or **Las Trampas Regional Wilderness,** (925) 838-7546, for information on riding and boarding throughout the East Bay region. The Livermore Area Recreation and Park District also runs **Robertson Park,** with full equestrian facilities and rodeo grounds, (925) 373-5700. Also see the Peninsula and South Bay chapter for information about horse rentals on the oceanfront within reasonable driving distance from the East Bay.

Windsurfing

Between the bay shore and the numerous lakes throughout the East Bay region, the windsurfing spots are numerous and diverse, covering every skill level—there is a little something for everyone. Because all areas of the bay, even the coved ones, can be choppy and extraordinarily windy at times, beginners are best off taking **lessons** at one of the lakeside parks managed by the East Bay Regional Park District. **Contra Loma** in eastern Contra Costa County, and **Lake Del Valle** in the Livermore hills are all good choices for beginners; each has rentals and regularly scheduled and supervised **lessons** during the summer sports season. To find Contra Loma, see Parks/Beaches, above. Also, call (925) 757-0404 for water conditions and sailboard availability. The windsurfing shack at Del Valle can be located by following the park directions in Parks/Beaches, above; call Windsurf Del Valle, (925) 455-4008, for rates, equipment, availability, and current lake conditions.

If you already have your board and sail strapped to the top of the car and are ready to rip, windsurfing spots on the bay are your best bet. One good spot for all skill levels is the **Berkeley/Emeryville waterfront,** a relatively calm strip of open bayfront just east of the San Francisco–Oakland Bay Bridge and accessible from the Berkeley marina at the foot of University Ave, north of I-80. Launch easily from nice but crowded public docks onto relatively calm (but always unpredictable) coved waters. Watch out for submerged rocks and pilings in this area. If you're unfamiliar with it, ask around about tides and current surf conditions; there may be areas you should avoid. Contact Berkeley Windsurfing, 1411 San Pablo Ave, (510) 527-9283, or Berkeley Boardsports, 843 Gilman St, (510) 527-7873, for **equipment rentals and lessons** in this area. **Crown Beach** in Alameda is also a prime spot for beginners and intermediate-level sailboarders—but if you set sail here, be aware that there's high potential for mixing it up with other classes of park user. Sunbathers, hikers, walkers, and bikers cover the beach and trails on nice summer days. Low tide also can be a problem here because of the muddy marsh areas off the beach, so timing is everything. Call (510) 636-1684 for details about the park, facilities, conditions, and rentals. See the park description in this section for directions to the beach.

Canoeing/Kayaking

Watching the huge cargo ships moving through the **Oakland Estuary,** you'd never think this waterway was the place to launch a tiny little kayak or canoe. But crazy as it sounds, the estuary, because of its prime location at the booming waterfront and its cover from bay currents, is becoming all the rage. There are even **moonlight paddles** guided by California Canoe and Kayak, 409 Water St, Oakland, (510) 893-7833, which is owned and operated by Olympic gold medalist Greg Burton. The estuary is a good place for beginners to learn and a popular workout spot for crew clubs and teams. Some good put-in spots are at the end of Franklin St, from the public docks at Jack London Square and the end of Alice St just south of that location. Canoeing and kayaking are also popular on **Lake Chabot,** with rentals at the Lake Chabot Marina, (510) 582-2198.

Lake Merritt in Oakland is one of the largest saltwater tidal lakes in the world; the lake is bounded by Grand Ave, Lake Shore Ave, and Lakeside Dr. Here you can rent a sailboat, rowboat, paddleboat, or canoe at the lake's Sailboat House, (510) 444-3807. The lake is also home to flocks of migrating ducks, geese, and herons and provides a great place for a leisurely stroll or jog.

Scenic Drives

The drive to the summit of **Mount Diablo** stands out as the most spectacular drive in the region—but for those with the time and gasoline, we recommend the windy and remote 40-mile drive from the mountains south of Livermore through the historic **San Antone Valley,** land of the one-room schoolhouse, the 10,000-acre family homestead, and the most vast undeveloped region in the Bay Area. Wild oak woodlands, sweeping pastures, deep, lush canyons, and finally the 4,209-foot peak of **Mount Hamilton** in Santa Clara County await; just leave a whole day for the adventure. From Oakland, take I-580 east to Livermore, exit at S Livermore Ave, and continue south through the downtown to Mines Rd, which rises high out of the Livermore Valley and into the wilds, where four county lines and three mountain peaks come together. Five hours later (more if you stop to take in the views), you emerge via San Antonio Valley

Rd into the Alum Rock section of San Jose. Stay alert: these are twisting, sometimes steep backcountry roads.

In-Line Skating

In the Bay Area, the in-line hot spot is San Francisco's Golden Gate Park, but there are nice blading areas in the East Bay as well. The **Iron Horse Trail,** which when complete will stretch 30 miles from the Martinez shoreline in Contra Costa County to **Shadow Cliffs Regional Recreation Area** in Pleasanton, is ideal for a skate outing, particularly on weekday mornings when there are fewer walkers out. We really mean it—walkers on these trails and within the regional parks as a whole have become extremely vocal in recent years about bikers, bladers, and other fast-moving trail users who whiz past them a little too quickly for their liking. This has prompted the park district board to pass one of the silliest ordinances we've seen—a law requiring you to call out a warning or ring a bell when passing slow-moving walkers. The reason it's silly? Well, inevitably, when we've used our mandatory bike bells or called out on the trails before passing walkers, the walkers have become startled and then stepped aside—*into* the path we were planning to take. The bells and "call-outs," therefore, may be more dangerous than just slowing down, and gliding past with a polite "good morning." In any case, slow down, be nice, and use common sense—particularly when you see seniors on the trails! For **skate rentals** and **tips** on the best trail sections, contact California Bike & Snowboard, 1469 Danville Blvd, Alamo, (925) 743-1249; Dublin Surf and Skate, 7752 Dublin Blvd, Dublin, (925) 828-8353; or Inline, 3506 Old Santa Rita Rd, Pleasanton, (925) 227-0750. The most contiguous completed sections of the trail can be found west of I-680 through the San Ramon Valley. From Oakland, take Hwy 24 east to the I-680 junction, then take I-680 south toward the San Ramon Valley. Exit at Livorna Rd west, Stone Valley Rd west, Diablo Rd west, or Bollinger Canyon Rd east to find trail crossings and staging areas.

Bird-Watching

In some parts of the East Bay, you're the odd one out if you don't have feathers and a set of wings. Since the region extends from the bay shore to the high peaks in the eastern valleys, bird-viewing opportunities are quite diverse. To view **waterfowl** of every imaginable variety, head to the salt marshes, tidal sloughs, and salt ponds of the **Don Edwards San Francisco Bay National Wildlife Refuge.** Stop in at the refuge visitors center near the Dumbarton Bridge toll plaza in Fremont, (510) 792-0222. The refuge and associated environmental education center offer numerous interpretive walking tours throughout the southern end of the region. Because of the area's position along the Pacific Flyway, bird varieties here change with the seasonal climate. **Grebes, snowy egrets, lesser scaups, black-bellied plovers,** and **western sandpipers** are common here during the spring. In winter, look for **willets, least terns, sandpipers, Bonaparte's gulls, starlings,** and **song sparrows.** This is one area where the faces are always changing. Perhaps a more exciting outing, although it's not as much of a sure thing, is to head for **Lake Del Valle** (see Parks/Beaches, above) in the hills south of Livermore where a pair of nesting **bald eagles** has been established for the past several years. Naturalist-led programs are scheduled year-round at the park, (925) 373-0332. For more information on birding in the area, call Wild Birds Unlimited in Cupertino, (408) 252-5712, or check out its Web site at www.wbu.com.

Adventure Calendar

International Arabian Horse Association Competitive Trail Ride, early April: *Sunol Regional Wilderness Area,* (925) 930-6889.

Devil Mountain Run, early May: *to the top of Mount Diablo, one of Danville's biggest events,* (925) 837-4400.

Skip to Skip Mountain Challenge Mountain Bike and Foot Race, early May: *Antioch to Clayton,* (925) 825-5401.

Diablo Vista Endurance Trail Ride, late May: *Mount Diablo, equestrian,* (925) 930-6889.

Great American Bike Ride, early June: *benefit for the American Lung Association, Livermore,* (925) 935-0472.

Crown Beach Sand Castle Contest, late June: *on the beach in Alameda, a competition among the more creative beach-mongers,* (510) 748-4565.

outside in

Attractions

You can still buy tie-dyed "Berserkley" T-shirts from vendors on Telegraph Ave in **Berkeley,** but the wild days of this now middle-aged, upper-middle-class burg are gone. In some respects, the action has moved from the campus to City Hall, where the town's residents—many of them former hippies, student intellectuals, and peace activists—rage on against everything from Columbus Day (Berkeley celebrates Indigenous People's Day instead) to the opening of a large video store downtown (too lowbrow and tacky).

If you're a newcomer to Berkeley, start your tour of the town at the world-renowned **University of California at Berkeley** campus (also known as Cal), the oldest and second-largest of the nine campuses comprising the UC system. Driving through the university is virtually impossible, so park on a side street and set out on foot. The campus isn't so huge that you'd get hopelessly lost if you wandered around on your own, but without a guide you might miss some of the highlights, such as Sproul Plaza, Sather Gate, and the Hearst Mining Building. So pick up a self-guided walking packet at the UC Berkeley Visitor Information Center (open Monday through Friday), or attend one of the free 1.5-hour tours offered Monday through Friday at 10am (meet at the visitors center) and on Saturday at 10am and Sunday at 1pm (meet in front of the Campanile in the heart of the campus); the visitors center is at 2200 University Ave at Oxford St, University Hall, Room 101, (510) 642-5215 or (510) 642-INFO.

Museums. The University Art Museum has a small permanent collection of modern art and frequently hosts peculiar but riveting exhibitions by artists such as Robert Mapplethorpe; 2626 Bancroft Way, (510) 642-0808. The Judah L. Magnes Museum, the third-largest Jewish museum in the West, offers numerous exhibitions of Jewish art and culture, including a Holocaust show and a display of modern Jewish paintings; 2911 Russell St, (510) 849-2710. Hands-on exhibits exploring everything from bats to holograms are featured at the Lawrence Hall of Science; while you're there, duck outside to hear (and see) the giant, eerie wind chimes and take a peek at the Stonehenge-like solar observatory; located in the hills above UC Berkeley on Centennial Dr, (510) 642-5133.

Music and Theater. The Berkeley Symphony blends new and experimental music with the classics at Zellerbach Hall on the UC Berkeley campus; for tickets call (510) 841-2800. Live rock, jazz, folk, reggae, and other concerts are frequently held at UC Berkeley's intimate, open-air Greek Theatre, a particularly pleasant place for sitting beneath the stars and listening to music on warm summer nights; located on Gayley Rd off Hearst Ave, (510) 642-9988. Cal Performances presents up-and-coming and established artists of all kinds—from the Bulgarian Women's Chorus to superstar mezzo-soprano Cecilia Bartoli; the concerts are held at various sites on the UC Berkeley campus, (510) 642-9988.

The Berkeley Repertory Theatre has a national reputation for experimental productions of the classics and innovative new works, 2025 Addison St, (510) 845-4700, and the Black Repertory Group offers a range of plays, dance performances, and art by African Americans; 3201 Adeline St, (510) 652-2120. Every summer the California Shakespeare Festival performs in an outdoor theater in the Berkeley hills near Orinda (bundle up 'cause it's usually freezing); 100 Gateway Blvd, (510) 548-3422. For up-to-date listings of cultural events, pick up a free copy of *The Express,* the East Bay's alternative weekly, available at cafes and newsstands throughout the city.

Shopping. With its recent profusion of chichi stores and upscale outlets (Smith & Hawken, Crate & Barrel, Dansk, Sur la Table, Pottery Barn, The Garden, Sweet Potatoes, et cetera), the Fourth St area has become a shopping mecca—a somewhat ironic development considering the city's traditional disdain for conspicuous consumption. Another favorite shopping area is in south Berkeley, near the Berkeley/Oakland border, in the small Elmwood neighborhood, which stretches along College Ave and crosses over Ashby Ave. Poke your head into the tiny Tail of the Yak boutique for a look at the fabulous displays of Central American and other art treasures, 2632 Ashby Ave, west of College, (510) 841-9891, then stroll along College, where you can pet the lop-eared baby bunnies and squawk back at the beautiful parrots at Your Basic Bird, 2940 College Ave, north of Ashby, (510) 841-7617; dip into the huge candy jars at Sweet Dreams, 2901 College Ave at Russell, (510) 549-1211; munch on fantastic fresh-fruit cheese danish at Nabolom Bakery, 2708 Russell St at College, (510) 845-BAKE; shop for clothes at numerous boutiques; and indulge in Bott's freshly made ice creams, 2975 College Ave, south of Ashby, (510) 845-4545. On the other side of Berkeley, where the northwest border meets the little town of Albany, is Solano Ave, a popular mile-long street lined with shops and cafes frequented by locals.

For some of the best bread in the Bay Area, go to Steve Sullivan's famous Acme Bread Company, 1601 San Pablo Ave, (510) 524-1327; or if you're a bagel lover, this is where Noah's Bagels, 3170 College Ave, (510) 654-0944, and 1883 Solano Ave, (510) 525-4447, got its start.

Literature. Most folks around here agree that if you can't find what you want to read at Cody's Books, Berkeley's best bookstore, it probably isn't worth reading; 2454 Telegraph Ave, (510) 845-7852. Almost every night, nationally known literary and political writers appear at Cody's and at Black Oak Books, a popular purveyor of new and used books; 1491 Shattuck Ave, (510) 486-0698.

Coffee and Beer. Like many university towns, this one seems to run on coffee. Peet's Coffee & Tea, with its sizable selection of beans and teas, is the local favorite; 2124 Vine St, (510) 841-0564; 2916 Domingo Ave, (510) 843-1434; and 1825 Solano Ave, (510) 526-9607. Caffé Mediterraneum churns out excellent cappuccinos and captures the bohemian flavor of Telegraph Ave, still a haunt of students, street people, runaways, hipsters, professors, tarot readers, and street vendors; 2475 Telegraph Ave, (510) 549-1128. Some of the best beer in the Bay Area is brewed at the frat-packed Triple Rock Brewery, 1920 Shattuck Ave, (510) 843-2739, and the hipper, more experimental Bison Brewing Company, which has such unusual offerings as honey-basil ale on tap and chocolate stout in magnums, not to mention hearty bistro food; 2598 Telegraph Ave, (510) 841-7734.

Emeryville, a tiny town slivered between Oakland, Berkeley, and the bay was once a dowdy industrial area, but a dozen years of manic redevelopment has turned it into one of the most intriguing urban centers in the Bay Area; computer jockeys, artists, and biotechies now abound here in their live-work spaces. Emeryville's town center is a nouveau ultramall called the **Emerybay Public Market.** The center offers great ethnic food stands, stores, a 10-screen cinema, and the hot **Kimball's East,** (510) 658-2555, a jazz and blues club with national headliners; take the Powell St exit from I-80.

Several years ago, in an effort to improve the city's image, the mayor of **Oakland** ordered the city to change all of the vaguely threatening "Entering Oakland" signs to read "Welcome to Oakland." Some folks scoffed at the effort and said improving the city's wretched schools or cutting its alarming murder rate would be a better way to improve the city's reputation, but others appreciated the gesture. Most residents agree that Oakland has gotten a bad rap. While the media keep close tabs on the body count, few seem to notice Oakland's peaceful, integrated neighborhoods and richly diverse cultural life.

Oakland's premier tourist destination is **Jack London Square,** a sophisticated seaside spread of boutiques, bookstores, restaurants, hotels, cinemas, and saloons that is refreshingly void of the touristy schlock that pervades San Francisco's Pier 39. Must-see stops along the promenade include Heinold's First and Last Chance Saloon, 56 Jack London Square, (510) 839-6761, a decidedly funky little bar crammed with faded seafaring souvenirs, and the recently overhauled USS *Potomac*, the 165-foot presidential yacht that served as FDR's "Floating White House." For information on tours of the ship or the bay, call (510) 839-8256.

Downtown's **Paramount Theatre,** a restored architectural masterpiece built in 1931 and restored in 1973, offers everything from organ concerts and rock concerts to plays and films from Hollywood's Golden Age. Guided tours of the 3,000-seat theater are given the first and third Saturday of each month, excluding holidays. No reservations are necessary—just show up at 10am at the box office entrance at 2025 Broadway at 21st St, (510) 893-2300.

The highly regarded **Oakland Symphony** offers classical and choral concerts at the Paramount Theatre and the Calvin Simmons Theater, 10 10th St; call (510) 446-1992 for symphony schedules.

The sunken building that holds the **Oakland Museum,** a spectacular specimen of modern architecture designed by Kevin Roche in 1969, features innovative displays of the art, history, and ecology of California, and also boasts beautiful terraced gardens; 1000 Oak St between 10th and 12th Sts, (510) 238-3401.

Pretty Lake Merritt (see Canoeing/Kayaking, above) is the site of the popular **Festival at the Lake,** an annual celebration of dance, arts, and music held at the beginning of June, (510) 286-1061. Tots will get a kick out of Lake Merritt's Children's Fairyland, a kid-sized amusement park that supposedly inspired Walt Disney to construct Disneyland; it's located off Grand Ave, (510) 452-2259. Youngsters will also thrill to the beasts at the **Oakland Zoo**; 9777 Golf Links Rd, (510) 632-9525.

Those hotshot boys of summer, the **Oakland A's,** are usually knocking 'em dead at the Oakland Coliseum (from I-80 take the Coliseum exit or, better yet, avoid the freeway crawl by taking a BART train); for tickets call (510) 638-0500. And the sparkling Oakland Coliseum Arena is the home of the tall guys: the **Golden State Warriors,** (510) 986-2200.

In genteel North Oakland, the Rockridge neighborhood running along College Ave boasts numerous bookstores, cafes, antique stores, expensive clothing boutiques, and a gourmet's paradise that rivals North Berkeley. Stroll through the **Rockridge Market Hall,** a chic multivendor market offering fresh pastas, gourmet cheeses, chocolates, fresh cut flowers, delicious deli sandwiches and salads, breads from the great Grace Baking Company, exquisite produce, and a wide selection of wine; 5655 College Ave at Shafter Ave, across from the Rockridge BART station, (510) 655-7748. Grittier but just as interesting is downtown Oakland's **Chinatown** (tour the area between 7th and 10th Sts and Broadway and Harrison), which is not as congested (with cars or tourists) as San Francisco's Chinatown.

Restaurants

Ajanta ☆   This brightly lit and attractive restaurant was once voted the Bay Area's best Indian restaurant in a *San Francisco Focus* magazine readers' poll. Part of its appeal lies in its changing specialties from different regions of India each month. *1888 Solano Ave (near The Alameda), Berkeley; (510) 526-4373; $$.*

Amforafino Caffe and Bar ☆☆   The staff is as exuberant as the decor in this bustling Italian-Mediterranean cafe (formerly known as Alexander Ristorante), where a shocking bolt of blue neon runs across the width of the dining room. *65 Moraga Way (in town, next to the Union 76 gas station), Orinda; (925) 253-1322; $$.*

Asmara Restaurant and Bar ☆   Asmara has a split personality: Eritrean expatriates seem to prefer the bar, while locals enjoy the restaurant's African decor. Both groups get caught up in the communal spirit of the place, sharing their meals with fellow diners. *5020 Telegraph Ave (at 51st St), Oakland; (510) 547-5100; $.*

Bay Wolf Restaurant ☆☆☆   Located in an attractive Victorian house with dark wood wainscoting and pale yellow walls, the Bay Wolf is a local favorite with a tradition of subdued Mediterranean-California cuisine. *3853 Piedmont Ave (between 40th St and MacArthur Blvd), Oakland; (510) 655-6004; $$$.*

Bette's Oceanview Diner ☆☆   There's not even a view here, but what this small, nouveau-'40s diner does have is red booths, chrome stools, a checkerboard tile floor, hip waitresses, the best jukebox around, and darn good breakfasts. *1807-A 4th St (between Virginia St and Hearst Ave), Berkeley; (510) 644-3230; $.*

Bighorn Grill ☆☆   As the name suggests, this pleasant Western-themed restaurant attracts big beef eaters. Freshly tossed salads and pasta and fish dishes are also on the menu, though the Bighorn primarily beckons to carnivores. *2410 San Ramon Valley Blvd (near Crow Canyon Rd), San Ramon; (925) 838-5678; $$.*

Blackhawk Grille ☆☆   This glamorous, offbeat restaurant is a testament to California's adoration of the automobile. There's an eclectic but down-to-earth menu of wood-fired pizzas, satisfying pastas, and competently prepared entrees. *3540 Blackhawk Plaza Circle (from I-680, take the Crow Canyon exit, head E on Crow Canyon, drive 7 miles to Camino Tassajara, and bear right to Blackhawk Plaza Circle), Danville; (925) 736-4295; $$$.*

Britt-Marie's ☆☆   As inviting as a pair of favorite slippers, Britt-Marie's offers comfort food from many corners of the globe. The decor recalls the sort of European wine bar where intellectuals gather to talk politics ad infinitum. *1369 Solano Ave (between Ramona and Carmel Sts), Albany; (510) 527-1314; $$.*

Bucci's ☆☆   Located in a beautifully restored former warehouse, Bucci's has soaring ceilings, an open kitchen, and a small patio garden. At lunch nosh on focaccia sandwiches and crisp thin-crust pizzas; dinner offers more elaborate fare from a daily changing menu. *6121 Hollis St (between 59th and 61st Sts), Emeryville; (510) 547-4725; $$.*

Café Fanny ☆☆   Alice Waters' diminutive corner cafe can handle fewer than a dozen stand-up customers at once, but that doesn't deter anyone. This popular spot recalls the neighborhood cafes so dear to the French, but Fanny's food is much better. *1603 San Pablo Ave (between Cedar and Virginia Sts), Berkeley; (510) 524-5447; $.*

Café Rouge ☆☆   This bistro offers everything from duck braised in white wine and smoked trout with frisée and leeks to hot dogs and cheeseburgers. All ingredients are high quality, so it's hard to go wrong with anything on the small but beguiling menu. *1782 4th St (between Hearst Ave and Delaware St), Berkeley; (510) 525-1440; $$$.*

Cambodiana's ☆☆   There aren't many Cambodian restaurants even in Cambodia, where wayfarers rely on teahouses and noodle shops, and traditional dishes may be sampled only in private homes, so this restaurant is hot property. *2156 University Ave (between Shattuck Ave and Oxford St), Berkeley; (510) 843-4630; $$.*

Chez Panisse ☆☆☆☆   The most famous restaurant in Northern California, Chez Panisse has been at the forefront of the California cuisine revolution since 1971, with simple, exquisitely orchestrated meals using the finest natural ingredients available. *1517 Shattuck Ave (between Cedar and Vine Sts), Berkeley; (510) 548-5525 (restaurant), (510) 548-5049 (cafe); $$$ (restaurant), $$ (cafe).*

Christopher's Nothing Fancy Cafe ☆   The exterior of this Mexican restaurant is as humble as the name, but inside lies an amiable dining room with a pleasant south-of-the-border feel. *1019 San Pablo Ave (near Marin St), Albany; (510) 526-1185; $.*

Citron ☆☆☆   An immediate hit when it opened in 1992, Citron has settled in for the long run. The intimate dining room, bathed in soothing shades of lemon yellow, sets the stage for the equally small menu of contemporary French-Mediterranean fare. *5484 College Ave (between Taft and Lawton Sts), Oakland; (510) 653-5484; $$.*

Fatapple's ☆   When local carnivores hear the call of the wild and nothing but a big, rare burger will do, they head for this comfortable, informal spot. Fatapple's is also famous for its all-American breakfasts. *1346 Martin Luther King Jr. Way (at Rose St), Berkeley; (510) 526-2260; $. 7525 Fairmount Ave (at Colusa St), El Cerrito; (510) 528-3433; $.*

Flint's ☆   If you've got a hankering for a sinful serving of juicy barbecued ribs doused in a sinus-blasting sauce, this is the place for you. This nitty-gritty rib joint has red-eye hours (open till 2am on the weekends) and the best barbecue in town. *6609 Shattuck Ave (at 66th St), Oakland; (510) 653-0593; $.*

Jade Villa ☆☆   Ever since Lantern restaurant closed, the title of Oakland's top dim sum house has been transferred to Jade Villa. You'll be charged by the plate, and you can afford to experiment here—two people

can eat with abandon for about 20 bucks. *800 Broadway (at 8th St),
Oakland; (510) 839-1688; $$.*

Kirala ☆☆   A no-reservations policy often means a long wait at this
small restaurant with the down-at-the-heels facade and plain-Jane decor.
Once you snag a seat, however, get ready to taste some of the best
Japanese food in town. *2100 Ward St (near Shattuck Ave), Berkeley; (510)
549-3486; $$.*

Lalime's ☆☆   It's hard to pass Lalime's at night without stopping to stare
at the radiant, pale-pink dining room and a crush of sleek patrons leaning
intimately over candle-lit, white-linen-cloaked tables. The menu changes
nightly. *1329 Gilman St (between Neilson and Peralta Sts), Berkeley; (510)
527-9838; $$$.*

Mama's Royal Cafe ☆   Diehard regulars don't even question the 40- to
60-minute wait required on weekends to get a seat at this landmark
known simply as Mama's. Good food served in large portions attracts a
crowd. *4012 Broadway (at 40th St), Oakland; (510) 547-7600; $.*

Mudd's Restaurant ☆☆   Fresh herbs from the garden complement
every aspect of this American-style fare, from the unique flavorings to the
delicate, edible herb-and-flower garnishes adorning every plate. *10
Boardwalk (just off Crow Canyon Rd and Park Pl, 1 mile W of I-680), San
Ramon; (925) 837-9387; $$.*

O Chamé ☆☆☆   Even jaded Berkeley food fanatics are bewitched by
the fare in this exotic restaurant. The chef spent years studying Buddhist-
Taoist cooking in Taiwan. This soothing cafe is crafted in the style of a
rustic wayside inn from Japan's Meiji period. *1830 4th St (near Hearst
Ave), Berkeley; (510) 841-8783; $$.*

Oliveto Cafe and Restaurant ☆☆☆   Oliveto has always been a top East
Bay destination, thanks in part to its obvious passion for the Italian table
and careful interpretations of Italy's rustic cuisine. The restaurant has the
air of a Florentine trattoria. *5655 College Ave (at Shafter Ave, across from
the Rockridge BART station), Oakland; (510) 547-5356; $$.*

Picante Cocina Mexicana ☆☆   Energetic and invested with an
engaging neighborhood feel, Picante Cocina Mexicana (literally "spicy
Mexican kitchen") packs 'em in because of both the *muy bueno* food and
the *muy pequeño* prices. *1328 6th St (just S of Gilman St), Berkeley; (510)
525-3121; $.*

Pizza Rustica ☆   Housed in a white postmodern building with red
Corinthian columns, this jazzy nouveau pizza joint has a cramped, noisy

dining room with tiny, knee-bruising tables, bright pop art on the walls, and California pizzas. *5422 College Ave (between Kales and Manila Sts), Oakland; (510) 654-1601; $.*

Pleasanton Hotel ☆ An oasis in the surrounding fast-food desert, the graceful, turn-of-the-century Pleasanton Hotel is the sort of place that makes you want to linger over lunch or dinner. *855 Main St (from I-580, take the Santa Rita exit and head S for 2 miles), Pleasanton; (925) 846-8106; $$$.*

Prima ☆☆ In addition to the high-quality, freshly made northern Italian specialties, Prima features an encyclopedic wine list—more than 1,200 California, Italian, and French bottles with several available by the taste or the glass. *1522 N Main St (downtown, near Lincoln St), Walnut Creek; (925) 935-7780; $$.*

Rivoli ☆☆☆ Rivoli offers relaxed yet refined ideas about California-Mediterranean cuisine. a tantalizing menu that changes every two weeks, and features numerous entrees for less than $14. *1539 Solano Ave (between Peralta Ave and Neilson St), Berkeley; (510) 526-2542; $$.*

Soizic Bistro-Cafe ☆☆☆ This handsome converted warehouse is a Paris salon straight out of The Moderns, with warm, golden colors and rich details. Named after a French friend of the owners, Soizic (SWA-zik) offers a wonderful mix of Mediterranean-style cuisine. *300 Broadway (near Jack London Square), Oakland; (510) 251-8100; $$.*

Tied House Cafe and Brewery ☆ This better-than-average brewery restaurant draws crowds with its high-quality beers and something-for-everyone menu. *On Triumph St (on the water, next to the Oakland Yacht Club), Alameda; (510) 521-4321; $$.*

Tsing Tao ☆ A favorite Sunday-night destination for local Chinese-American families, Tsing Tao delivers high-quality Cantonese cooking. It's a far cry from fancy, but it's a definite step up in quality and service from many Oakland Chinatown restaurants. *200 Broadway (at 2nd St), Oakland; (510) 465-8811; $$.*

The Union Hotel, Bar, and Restaurant ☆☆ It's nice to sit in the lovely dining room of this 1882 establishment and savor the nostalgia for a few hours. The chef is as much a throwback as the hotel is; he uses fresh, local ingredients in his dishes but adds a bit of frontier resourcefulness. *401 1st St (at D St), Benicia; (707) 746-0100; $$.*

Venezia ☆ Children love Venezia—the trompe l'oeil murals depicting an Italian piazza complemented by a real fountain and clothesline, the amiable bustle of the dining room, and the free crayons all add up to a pleasurable family dining experience. *1799 University Ave (at Grant St), Berkeley; (510) 849-4681; $$.*

Vi's Restaurant ☆   Located on a bustling street in the heart of Chinatown, this is where the professionals from places like Chez Panisse come to get their fix of Vietnamese steamed rolls, five-spice barbecued chicken, and Vi's famous braised duck noodle soup. *724 Webster St (in Chinatown, between 7th and 8th Sts), Oakland; (510) 835-8375; $.*

Wente Vineyards Restaurant ☆☆☆   This exquisite neo-Spanish colonial restaurant is set among the vineyards and rolling hills of the 1,200-acre Wente estate. The daily changing menu is a pleasant blend of traditional and experimental. *5050 Arroyo Rd (follow L St until it turns into Arroyo Rd, about 4½ miles S of town), Livermore; (925) 456-2450 (restaurant), (925) 456-2400 (estate); $$$.*

Zatis ☆☆☆   Zatis is a real find, discreetly tucked into a narrow spot on Piedmont Avenue. It's hardly noticeable during the day; only at night does the elegant ice-blue neon light entice you in, where the aroma of roasted garlic and olive oil will convince you to stay. *4027 Piedmont Ave (between 40th and 41st Sts), Oakland; (510) 658-8210; $$$.*

Lodgings

The Berkeley City Club ☆   This 1927 building, with hallways graced by soaring buttresses, tall lead-paned windows, and garden courtyards, was designed as a women's club to rival the poshest male enclave. Today both genders are welcome through its stately portals, not only as members but as bed-and-breakfast guests. *2315 Durant Ave (between Dana and Ellsworth Sts), Berkeley; (510) 848-7800; $$.*

Captain Walsh House ☆☆☆   This gorgeous pre-Victorian gothic revival bed and breakfast made its debut on the cover of *Better Homes & Gardens* in the summer of '94, and the inn is definitely worth a journey here. Each of the 5 guest rooms is startlingly original. The living room and dining room feature subtly painted hardwood floors and hand-sponged walls with elaborate hand-painted stripes. *235 East L St (at 2nd St), Benicia; (707)747-5653; $$$.*

The Claremont Resort and Spa ☆☆☆   This proud prima donna of a hotel holds fast to its Edwardian roots. The posh lobby is made for loitering and gaping, while the 22 acres of gorgeous grounds invite leisurely strolling. Amenities include everything you'd expect in a grand hotel. *41 Tunnel Rd (at the intersection of Ashby and Domingo Aves), Berkeley; (510) 843-3000 or (800) 551-7266; $$$.*

The French Hotel The French Hotel offers 18 guest rooms with modern, comfortable furnishings, large bathrooms, and either a small balcony or patio with a table and chairs. Avoid the noisy first-floor rooms facing Shattuck Ave. *1538 Shattuck Ave (between Cedar and Vine Sts), Berkeley; (510) 548-9930; $$.*

Gramma's Rose Garden Inn ☆☆   This attractive bed and breakfast surrounded by beautifully landscaped lawns started out as a restored Tudor-style mansion furnished with wonderful old furniture and period antiques; then it swallowed the house next door and added a couple of cottages and a carriage house, giving Gramma's 40 guest rooms. *2740 Telegraph Ave (between Ward and Stuart Sts), Berkeley; (510) 549-2145; $$.*

Hotel Mac ☆☆☆   Built in 1911, this imposing three-story, red-brick edifice on the National Register of Historic Places was remodeled in 1995 and now offers 7 lovely guest rooms (including 2 deluxe suites) that cost half as much as what you'd pay for a similar room in San Francisco. Each unit is individually decorated with rich, colorful fabrics. *10 Cottage Ave (at Washington Ave), Point Richmond; (510) 235-0010; $$.*

Lord Bradley's Inn ☆☆   Rebuilt after the devastating earthquake of 1868, this atmospheric Victorian-style hotel offers a good sense of what it must have been like to live in the Bay Area during the 19th century (though it's considerably more comfortable). The 8 individually decorated guest rooms have antique bedsteads and private baths. *43344 Mission Blvd (at Washington Blvd, just past Mission San Jose), Fremont; (510) 490-0520; $.*

Plum Tree Inn ☆   Located smack in the middle of old town, this restored 1890s Victorian has 6 unique suites—each with its own private bath, a tasteful collection of antiques, a TV, and a phone. Ask for one of the rooms overlooking the patio in back, especially the Cherry Room. Plead for their Belgian waffles. *262 W Angela St (just W of Main St), Pleasanton; (925) 426-9588; $$.*

The Secret Garden Mansion ☆☆☆   This lovely bed and breakfast is nestled behind elegant white wrought-iron gates at the end of a quiet street and is a peaceful Victorian retreat with 7 guest rooms. *1056 Hacienda Dr (from I-680, take the Ygnacio Valley Rd N exit and turn right on Homestead Ave, then left on Hacienda Dr), Walnut Creek; (925) 945-3600; $$$.*

Waterfront Plaza Hotel ☆☆   Our top recommendation for an Oakland-based lodging is this small luxury hotel perched on the water's edge at Jack London Square. Granted, it's not the fanciest hotel you'll ever stay in, but it comes with all the essential amenities at a reasonable price. *10 Washington St (at Jack London Square), Oakland; (510) 836-3800 or (800) 729-3638; $$$.*

More Information

Alameda Chamber of Commerce: *(510) 525-1771.*
Albany Chamber of Commerce: *(510) 525-1771.*
Antioch Chamber of Commerce: *(925) 757-1800.*
Berkeley Chamber of Commerce: *(510) 549-7000.*
Castro Valley Chamber of Commerce: *(510) 537-5300.*
Concord Chamber of Commerce: *(925) 685-1181.*
Danville Area Chamber of Commerce: *(925) 837-4400.*
Dublin Chamber of Commerce: *(925) 828-6200.*
East Bay Regional Park District: *(510) 562-PARK.*
Fremont Chamber of Commerce: *(510) 795-2244.*
Hayward Chamber of Commerce: *(510) 537-2424.*
Livermore Chamber of Commerce: *(925) 447-1606.*
Mount Diablo Interpretive Association: *(925) 933-5289.*
Oakland Chamber of Commerce: *(510) 874-4800.*
Pleasanton Chamber of Commerce: *(925) 846-5858.*
State parks camping reservations: *(800) 444-7275.*
Tri-Valley Convention and Visitors Bureau: *(510) 846-8910.*
Walnut Creek Chamber of Commerce: *(925) 934-2007.*

Peninsula
and South Bay

All of San Mateo and Santa Clara Counties, from the San Francisco city/county boundary on the north to the Santa Cruz County line on the south, including the Pacific Coast, the bay, San Bruno Mountain, Sweeney Ridge, Año Nuevo State Preserve, and Henry W. Coe State Park.

Sometimes, it seems as if Mother Nature is out for revenge. Take the 60 miles of California coast from the San Francisco border south to the Santa Cruz County line. Most of it is undeveloped, wild, publicly owned, and here for the pleasure of anyone who wants to enjoy it—surfers, beachcombers, campers, and equestrians, just to name a few.

But when powerful El Niño storms were unleashed on Northern California in winter 1998, it was one of the coast's few *developed* stretches—not the pristine areas—that began dropping into the Pacific, along with a few really nice beachfront homes. So another small stretch of the lovely California coast was reclaimed; now, that stretch looks a little more like the rest of the open beaches and stunning rocky cliffs found through this section of the Coast Highway. Easy to get to and simple to use, this part of the coast serves as both a day-trip escape for Bay Areans on a sunny weekend afternoon and a destination for vacationers who want to top off a trip to California with a close-up look at the Pacific. They come to see the most productive sea lion breeding grounds in Northern California, to hook up the RV for some oceanfront camping, or just to get their feet wet and smell the cool salt breezes.

But there's more to this coast than beaches. Look away from the shore to the mountainous ridges that tower over it, and you'll notice a bonus: tens of thousands of acres of shady redwoods, high mountain peaks, and deep river canyons that even decades of nearby logging, irrigation, and urbanization have not affected. Indeed, state, regional, and county parklands throughout San Mateo and Santa Clara Counties contain a little bit of everything: lonely roads for long bike rides, remote ponds for high-country fishing, secluded campgrounds that seem a world away from the city, and hundreds of miles of deep wilderness backpacking trails. Much of the open space is former ranchland that has come into public ownership over the past 100 years, the result of hard work by preservationists determined to see that the Bay Area metropolis never paves its way over the hills. And even with the strong tug of the rampant Silicon Valley economy, which has housing and job markets spinning out of control, that hasn't happened yet.

So steer west, roll the top back, and head on into the big blue. That's what it's there for, and it's boundless.

Getting There

This is a wide area hugging San Francisco Bay in an elbow-shaped band, then extending west to the Pacific Coast and east to the redwoods of the Santa Cruz Mountains. From San Francisco, US Highway 101 (US 101) south follows the bay through the Peninsula and to the South Bay region. Highway 1, the Coast Highway, extends from San Francisco south along the entire Pacific coast of the Peninsula and on into Santa Cruz. The main roadway connecting the bay shore with the Pacific Coast on the Peninsula is Highway 92, which runs from San Mateo to Half Moon Bay. From US 101 in the South Bay, Highway 17 passes south over the Santa Cruz Mountains to Santa Cruz.

There is no tried and true way to use public transportation to get around this area, particularly along the ocean, but CalTrain service is available from San Francisco through the Peninsula and on to San Jose. The trains connect easily to San Francisco's municipal railway system (MUNI), which in turn links with Bay Area Rapid Transit (BART). San Mateo County Transit (SamTrans) has bus lines through the entire region, including the coast, but as with so many of the subregional transportation services around the Bay Area, trying to make connections between them all can be dicey and time-consuming—and frankly not worth the frustration. For BART information, call (650) 992-2278. CalTrain can be reached at (650) 660-4287. SamTrans can be reached at (800) 660-4287. For MUNI information, call (415) 673-6864.

Adjoining Areas

NORTH: **San Francisco**

SOUTH: **Santa Cruz**

EAST: **East Bay**

inside out

Beaches

The nearly 60 miles of largely undeveloped coast between San Francisco and Santa Cruz county offer stunning bluffs and overlooks, wide beaches, great surfing spots for all skill levels, and fantastic wildlife viewing opportunities . . . all unbelievably near the Bay Area's most densely populated areas. Most of the coast is publicly owned, with easy beach access. On warm summer days, expect overflowing parking lots, traffic jams on the Coast Highway and feeder roads, and tight crowds on some of the more popular beaches. Don't be discouraged, however: there's so much of it that there's plenty of room to spread out—and no section of this coast is "undesirable" or second-rate. Some areas are just more popular than others because of their proximity to Hwy 92, a well-used route to the Bay Area's population centers. Head a little south of there, and fear not—the masses all tend to congregate on the beaches closest to Half Moon Bay. Important information: don't head down this coast thinking you're going to take a dip in the ocean; the water is too cold and the rip currents are too strong. As a matter of fact, it's an awfully good idea to stay plenty alert anytime you're on the water's edge, as some sections of this coast are known for the occasional sleeper wave.

There are several ways to reach the San Mateo coast from other parts of the Bay Area. From San Francisco, simply follow the Coast Highway south to I-280. Continue south, following the Hwy 1 route to Pacifica. Once back on the Coast Highway, it's a straight shot all the way to Santa Cruz. From the East Bay, take I-880 to Hayward, then head west on Hwy 92 (across the San Mateo Bridge). Hwy 92 enters the San Mateo Mountains, crosses them, and T-bones into the Coast Highway at Half Moon Bay. A left turn from here takes you toward Pescadero, Año Nuevo State Reserve, and Santa Cruz. A right turn (north) points you toward San Francisco. From the South Bay, take I-280 or US 101 north to Hwy 92, then continue west to the coast. For public transportation information, see Getting There, above. Here are some favorite spots on the San Mateo coast, going north to south.

Two miles south of the San Francisco city border, **Thornton State Beach's** high bluffs and wide sandy shores, with adjacent wind-shielded valley, are a popular picnic, sunbathing, hiking, kite-flying, and model-airplane-launching area (no passenger-size gliders allowed!). Note, however, that the main entrance to the beach is down a steep walkway. The easiest way to reach Thornton is to park on Skyline Blvd just south of Fort

Funston (see Parks/Beaches, San Francisco chapter) in the vicinity of John Daly Blvd, and walk from there to the coastal access points across the way. For more information, call the beach directly at (650) 755-5525 or the state parks office in Half Moon Bay, (650) 726-6238.

Rockaway Beach: You'll lose your breath, coming around the bend on the Coast Highway outside Pacifica and finding yourself face-to-face with the big blue. If you're driving, be prepared to pull to the side of the road—some have dropped right off the cliffs in this area, and there's a running suspicion that the reason isn't the hazardous driving conditions, cell phones, or even impaired driving, but the distraction of the view. Rockaway is a narrow strip of beach popular among surf anglers and surfers (breaks are often small enough for beginners). Take Rockaway Beach Ave west from Hwy 1 in Pacifica for parking and easy access down the stairs. From the highway, it looks like a shopping mall/roadhouse motel site, but don't be fooled. Once you're past the concrete and ultramodern strip mall construction on the highway, there really is a beach there. For information, call Pacifica Parks and Beaches, (650) 738-7381.

San Pedro Beach: Just south of and contiguous with Rockaway is an equally stunning and popular surfing and surf fishing spot. Access is from the Coast Highway between Crespi Dr and Linda Del Mar Blvd, in Pacifica. For information, call Pacifica Parks and Beaches, (650) 738-7381.

Gray Whale Cove State Beach: Between mid-April and mid-May, gray whales can often be seen offshore of this 800-foot, privately managed sunbathing (clothing optional) strip of sand. Parking is on the east side of Hwy 1 only, and there's a $5 per person entrance fee. For more information, call (650) 728-5336. The beach is half a mile south of Devil's Slide in Montara.

Montara State Beach: Sunbathing, picnics, surf walking, and nature viewing are the main draw at these 2 miles of sandy beach just north of the popular Montara Lighthouse Hostel. There are two access points from Hwy 1 about half a mile apart—one near the Chart House Restaurant and the other to the north. For more information, call (650) 726-8819. The hostel phone number is (650) 728-7177.

Half Moon Bay State Beaches: These 4 miles of broad, sandy beaches at Half Moon Bay are by far the most often used along the San Mateo coast. Sunbathing, fishing, and picnics are the main fare but there's also a coastal campground (see Camping, below) with 55 sites at Francis Beach, which can be found at the end of Kelly Ave, off the Coast Highway just south of the Hwy 92 interchange. Horseback riding is popular along trails between Dunes Beach and Francisco Beach, with rentals nearby (see Horseback Riding, below). You'll also find jogging trails, bicycling trails, interpretive programs, and more. Just watch out for crowds; this is not the spot for the rugged outdoorsperson, so if that is you, head north or south. Call the beach ranger station, (650) 726-8800, for more information.

San Gregorio/Pompano State Beaches: Some 5 miles of gently sloping sandy beaches just south of the Hwy 84 junction with the Coast Highway are downstream of two freshwater creeks, making them an important marsh wildlife habitat area and interesting nature study spot. High sandstone bluffs containing deep ridges make this a great place to watch the sea meet the land—but be sure to stay out of the water, as this stretch of the coast is known for strong rip currents and the occasional unexpected sleeper wave. Picnic, barbecue, sunbathe, and hike here. San Gregorio is a state historical landmark, commemorating the passage of Spanish explorer Gaspar de Portola in 1769. Parking and beach access areas are along Hwy 1 between San Gregorio Rd and Pescadero Creek. For more information, call the state parks office in Half Moon Bay, (650) 726-6238.

Pescadero State Beach and Marsh Preserve: Two miles of sandy beach, with rocky outcroppings and wide dunes, are adjacent to a 500-acre wildlife preserve consisting of a freshwater/brackish marsh at Pescadero Creek. Interpretive trails through the preserve are marked to keep visitors from trampling important rare plants and habitat for migrating birds that stop over while passing along the Pacific Flyway. Picnic tables and rest rooms are provided; dogs are not allowed. There are parking areas west of the Coast Highway and south of Pompano. For more information, call (650) 879-0832.

Bean Hollow State Beach: This is the perfect spot for a combination geology and wildlife lesson, with rare honeycomb-patterned rock formations and expansive easily accessed tide-pool areas. Wildflowers abound here in the spring—but don't stop expecting to find a wide, sandy beach to stroll. This is a particularly rocky and pebbly area because of the way tectonic upthrusting and ocean currents work together, creating unusual rock formations. Call it a trade-off, but it's interesting. The beach is 18 miles south of Half Moon Bay. Call (650) 879-2170.

Gazos Creek coastal access area: Gazos Creek, which winds through the redwood canyons of the coast near Santa Cruz, meets the sea here to form a unique freshwater lagoon sunken into the sand. A trickling, meandering stream then meets the surf. This is a popular sunbathing and picnic area. Rest rooms are provided, but no other facilities. To the south is a good surf fishing spot. East of the highway is the 4,000-acre Cascade Ranch preserve. The parking area is west of the Coast Highway at Gazos Creek Rd. Call (650) 879-0227.

Año Nuevo State Reserve: In the summer this 4,000-acre spread of dune fields, high and rugged bluffs, and sandy coved beach hugging a wide bay on the Pacific seems like a beachcomber's paradise. But return between December and March to discover the real attraction: elephant seals—damn big ones—rule this place. A huge colony of the 1,200- to 2,000-pound sea mammals use this spot as annual breeding and calving grounds, a spectacle that draws in excess of 100,000 visitors each year. Guided interpretive tours (also see Wildlife, below) are available, and hiking trails through the dune fields are marked with interpretive plaques. When the seals aren't around, the main attractions are the unusual rock formations, varied bird life, and historical points of interest; this is not a picnic or beach recreation area. December through March, the reserve is open *only* to those who have reserved a spot on a guided elephant-seal tour. Drop-in visitors are accepted in the summer and fall. Important note: The elephant seals are a very popular attraction, and tours fill up fast, so don't even bother trying to get on one without a reservation. Guided-tour reservations are taken by the state parks reservations system, (800) 444-7275. To contact the reserve directly, call (650) 879-0227. The reserve is located 25 miles south of Half Moon Bay and 20 miles north of Santa Cruz on the Coast Highway. Driving from San Francisco, you know you've gone too far if you see Big Creek Lumber Company on the east side of the highway or you cross the Santa Cruz county line.

Surfing

Much of the San Mateo coast surf is too bumpy with breaks far too large for beginner- or even intermediate-level surfers, but there are a few exceptions. **Rockaway Beach** (see Beaches, above) has breaks small enough that it's often okay for less experienced surfers to venture in; so does **San Pedro Beach** (see Beaches, above) to the south. Check in with Nor-Cal Surf Shop, 5460 Coast Highway, Pacifica, (650) 738-9283, and Sonlight Surfshop, 575 Crespi Dr, Pacifica, (650) 359-0353.

El Granada Beach just south of Half Moon Bay has breaks small enough *some* of the time for intermediate-level surfers to venture out. Nearby, however, is another surfing spot that is outrageous, with monster breaks at times in excess of 25 feet. Those who don't know where it is probably have no business being out there on a surfboard, so we won't even name it here. Just be warned: there are places, including this one, along the California coast where even world-class surfers can at times put themselves in serious jeopardy—anyplace where boards break can also be a place where skulls crack. This spot has proven fatal in the past, so, honestly, use your head to think before you end up using it to land on. If you don't know what you're doing, stay out of the water. Aqua Culture Surf and Beach Shop, 3032 Cabrillo Hwy N, Half Moon Bay, (650) 726-1155; Cowboy Surf Shop, 2830 Cabrillo Hwy N, Half Moon Bay, (650) 726-6968; and Mavericks

Surfboards, 530 Main St, Half Moon Bay, (650) 726-0469; all can help with outfitting, rentals, and pointers . . . including where *not* to go.

Fishing

With nearly 60 miles of oceanfront and 40 miles of bay shore to explore—not to mention lakes and reservoirs—the biggest dilemma anglers face on the Peninsula and in the South Bay is the same one they face everywhere else in the Bay Area: so many choices, and so few days of the week. **Surf anglers** need only roll out onto the Coast Highway and have at it . . . it's as simple as that, since access to the coast is liberal and most of it is publicly owned. The best spots along the Pacific to cast off are Rockaway Beach, San Pedro Beach, the Half Moon Bay State Beaches, and the coastal areas around Gazos Creek, Montara, Bean Hollow, and Pescadero (see Beaches, above). **Rockfish, croaker, perch, lingcod, wolf-eel, smelt,** and **silversides** are the normal fare. Important note: Avoid Half Moon Bay, Rockaway, and Pescadero during peak beachcombing or surfing season, as the potential for conflict with other beachgoers is higher at these spots. Much of the coast is without commercial outlets, so it is best to get outfitted before heading too far south of Half Moon Bay. Do that at Coastside No 2 Bait and Tackle, 1604 Francisco Blvd, Pacifica, (650) 359-9790; Pacifica Community Pier Bait and Tackle Concession, 2100 Beach Blvd, Pacifica, (650) 355-0690; or Hilltop Grocery and Fishing Supplies, 251 San Mateo Rd, Half Moon Bay, (650) 726-4950.

Pier fishing on the comparatively sleepy and placid bay shore is also plentiful, but be advised: the Environmental Protection Agency has warned the public to limit consumption of fish taken from the bay because of mercury poisoning. Easy access to public areas abound. The two best are Candlestick Point State Recreation Area, which has two piers and cleaning facilities, and Coyote Point north of there, a well-managed county recreation area that has public put-ins, a marina, and a fishing pier as well. Depending on the season, catches at both locations include **halibut, shark, striped bass, sturgeon, perch,** and **flounder.** To reach Candlestick Point from the South Bay or San Francisco, take US 101 to the 3Com Park exit in South San Francisco and head west. Call (650) 671-0145 for information. To reach Coyote Point, take US 101 to the Coyote Point Dr exit and head west to the park's main entrance. The fishing area is along the breakwater north of the marina. Call the park at (650) 573-2593 or (650) 573-2593 for more information. Sun Valley Bait and Tackle, 620 S Norfolk St, San Mateo, (415)343-4690; Armanino's, 329 Grand Ave, South San Francisco, (415)588-0245; and Colombo's Liquors, 507 Linden Ave, South San Francisco, (415)583-0236, are good places to stop in for supplies and gear.

Naturally, there are numerous **sportfishing tours** leaving the Half Moon Bay area daily. Check with Captain John's Deep Sea Fishing, Half Moon Bay, (650) 726-2913.

Lake fishing for largemouth bass, sunfish, and bluegill is best at the more than 20 high-country ponds scattered throughout the 80,000-acre wilderness of Henry W. Coe State Park (see Parks, below). Be prepared for a hike, however; the nearest spot is Frog Lake, a 1.5-mile trek from the park's main entrance. Call the park visitors center, (408) 779-2728, for the most up-to-date information.

Sailing

San Francisco Bay offers some of the best sailing conditions in the world because ocean breezes come through without the bumpiness of ocean currents. (Also see Sailing, San Francisco chapter.)

On the Peninsula, Coyote Point Marina in San Mateo, (650) 573-2594; Oyster Marina Park in South San Francisco, (650) 952-5540; Pete's Harbor in Redwood City, (650) 366-0922; and Peninsula Marina in Redwood City, (650) 369-8646; are the best places to check for **public moorings** and slips on the bay. Pillar Point Harbor in Half Moon Bay, (650) 726-5727, is the main boating center on this stretch of the Pacific Coast.

For rentals and charters south of the city, check in with Galleon Charters in South San Francisco, (650) 871-4819, or Spinnaker Sailing, 1 Seal Ct, San Mateo, (650) 570-7331.

Parks

Unlike San Francisco, where most of the big open spaces are artificially built scads of greenery on top of erstwhile expansive sand dunes, the vast majority of outdoor areas along the coast, on the Peninsula, and in the South Bay are pristine and preserved—just the way they might have looked 150 years ago when westerners first began settling the area (with a few modern improvements like roads and trails). The Mid-Peninsula Regional Open Space District—with over 41,000 acres of shoreline and foothill parklands in San Mateo and Santa Clara Counties and a small portion of Santa Cruz County—has the most diverse and best-appointed outdoor play spaces in the region. Add numerous county parks, state lands, beaches (see Beaches, above), and protected watersheds, and what emerges is a vast hiking, cycling, and equestrian playground, and more. There are places to get lost among the redwoods, view wildlife, grab a picnic, or just plain get away from it all, with easy access from urban and suburban parts of the Bay Area. For **trail maps** and details about the district's lands, call (650) 691-1200, or go to the agency's Web site at www.openspace.org. Other important outdoor activities **resources** are the REI stores in San Jose and San Carlos. Each has an extensive public information and guidebook section. In San Carlos, go to 1119 Industrial Rd, or call (650) 508-2330. The San Jose store is at 400 El Paseo de Saratoga, (408) 871-8765. The San Mateo County Parks and Recreation Division, (650) 363-4020, also oversees vast areas of open space, including the San Francisco Water Department's Crystal Springs Reservoir watershed area adjacent to I-280, a favorite hiking and cycling route among the Peninsula's forested foothills. What follows are descriptions of what we consider the prime open spaces west and south of the bay.

If there were a hard and fast requirement that a "crown jewel" had to be named for every sub-region of the state, this area would have to have two: Henry W. Coe State Park and the **Crystal Springs Reservoir** watershed area. The 6-mile-long reservoir, which provides water to San Francisco and its suburbs, is nestled like a necklace of jewels in the San Mateo County mountains separating the bay and ocean coasts. While we're sure this was a lovely river canyon before the dam-builders got to work, it is better just to enjoy the lake and accept that it's here than to get carried away wishing things were different. A well-developed waterside trail system traverses dozens of miles of watershed lands, forested with groves of Monterey cypress and pines, eucalyptus, and redwoods. Stunning open meadows yield a wide variety of spring wildflowers, some unique to this area because of the high magnesium content of the soils. Some 160 species of bird have been documented here, making it a popular area for nature walks as well as horseback and bicycle rides. Also look for exposed areas of the infamous San Andreas Fault, which bisects the watershed lands. Virtually all of the trail sections are easy to get to, with numerous access points from I-280, and easy to use—the maximum grade on most of them is about 10 percent. For Crystal Springs trail information, call (650) 589-4292. The easiest access point is from Hwy 92, which crosses the reservoir at midpoint. From the South Bay or San Francisco, take I-280 to the Hwy 92 junction. Two parking areas are located south of the highway on the banks of the upper reservoir.

The biggest mistake you can make an outing at **Henry W. Coe State Park** is to show up expecting to be able to drive around to see its forested ridges, wide meadows, and lush canyons, then pull off some nice paved road at a developed picnic area for sweat-free relaxation. Nope. Not going to happen. That's because this is not only the largest state park in Northern California—more than 80,000 acres—it's also one of the least developed. Cars are not allowed beyond the visitors center, so the only choices left for those who want to explore far and wide are long hikes, bike trips, or treks on horseback. And don't even think about drinking the water on a hike up one of the four 2,500-plus-foot peaks—there is no treated drinking water along the way. This place is quite plain and simply open and wild. So don't venture here without being properly outfitted with plenty of water (springs dry up in the summer, so sometimes a filter will be of no use), gear, food, maps, and backcountry experience. The park visitors center, (408) 779-2728, will have up-to-date information on trail conditions, fire danger, wildlife, and other pertinent matters, and calling or stopping by before your hike is pretty much a requirement, as washouts, slides, and other vagaries of Mother Nature can often make trails inaccessible. Once prepared and properly informed, however, you're in for a treat: grand vistas of the Bay Area backcountry, fishing in more than 20 ponds and lakes, and remote camp-out spots. To reach the park, take US 101 south from San Francisco (I-880, I-280, and I-680 from the East Bay and the Peninsula intersect with US 101) to the E Dunne Ave exit in Morgan Hill, then head 13 miles out to the park entrance and headquarters just beyond Anderson Reservoir. Limited car camping is allowed near the park headquarters. Beyond that, plan on a rugged outing among the blue oaks, pines, and rare California nutmegs.

Follow the Hwy 35 route (Skyline Blvd) south along the mountain ridges beginning at Hwy 92 southwest of Crystal Springs Reservoir and what unfolds before you are 40 contiguous miles of open space, most of it publicly owned with easy access for hikers, cyclists, and horseback riders. This is truly county park and regional preserve row, the highlight being south of Portola Valley where 12 contiguous open-space parks and preserves covering more than 10,000 acres unfold as far as the eye can see. **Skyline Ridge Open Space Preserve,** with 1,612 acres of dense forests of Douglas fir, two reservoirs, vast grasslands, and spectacular sandstone rock outcroppings, is at the center of these expansive open wilds. Along with the adjacent **Russian Ridge Open Space Preserve** (1,580 acres), **Los Trancos Open Space Preserve** (274 acres), **Monte Bello Open Space Preserve** (2,700 acres), **Wunderlich County Park** (940 acres), **Long Ridge Open Space Preserve** (1,600 acres), and **Upper Stevens Creek County Park** (850 acres), the Skyline area is a treasure trove of unique outdoor adventures, including self-guiding earthquake fault tours, ridgetop views of the Santa Clara Valley, wildflower walks, bird-watching, and backpacking. This area makes the perfect day trip, and it is easy to find. From US 101 or I-280, take Hwy 92 or Hwy 84 west approximately 5 miles to the Skyline Blvd intersection, then head south through the embarrassingly rich assortment of public play areas. At Alpine Rd, just west of Los Altos Hills, is the center of it all—parking areas and a limitless range of stuff to do in all directions! The best central source for information about this area is the Mid-Peninsula Regional Open Space District, (650) 691-1200.

Large pieces of the bay shore in San Mateo and Santa Clara Counties are preserved and restored as open space, much of it former salt-harvesting grounds taken out of production over the past 40 years. The **Don Edwards San Francisco Bay Wildlife Refuge** features tracts of marshland north of the Dumbarton Bridge in Menlo Park, south of the San Mateo Bridge in Redwood City (a recent acquisition, no public access yet), and through the Alviso area north of San Jose and south of Fremont. These are prime bird-watching spots, particularly along the Alviso marshes, which during wet months are an impressively productive waterfowl roosting area. Call the main refuge office, (510) 792-0222, for information about interpretive tours, environmental education programs, and the best shoreline access. Perhaps the most accessible and popular waterfront nature areas on this portion of the bay are the **Mountain View Shoreline** and adjacent **Palo Alto Baylands Nature Preserve,** each with well-developed shoreline trail systems for bike rides, hiking, and bird-watching. Take US 101 to the Shoreline Blvd exit in Mountain View, then head east to the shoreline and preserve parking areas. Don't forget the scope. This spot is noisy and busy. The best contact point for these areas is the national refuge office mentioned above. Also call the City of Palo Alto parks department, (650) 329-2376.

Just northwest of the San Francisco Water Department lands on the Peninsula is a 12,000-foot-high expanse of coastal scrub and wild grasses called **Sweeney Ridge**—famous not only for its well-appointed hiking areas of ravines and high peaks, but also for being the very spot where Spanish explorer Gaspar de Portola first caught a glimpse of San Francisco Bay in the late 1700s (a plaque at the ridge summit marks the spot where this historic event took place). The view today is much the same as Portola would have seen it, with the exception, of course, of the vast human development that has since taken place. Mount Tamalpais, Mount Diablo, San Pedro Point, and the Montara Mountains all are visible from this spot, which also offers simultaneous vistas of the Pacific and the bay. The ridge is a popular spring wildflower and bird-watching area. Beside hiking, other popular activities here include picnicking, mountain biking, and horseback riding. The ridge is just east of Pacifica and northeast of Linda Mar off the Coast Highway. Trail access is possible from two points. The easiest is from the park gates directly off the Coast Highway; they're easily marked before the city of Pacifica, on the righthand side coming north and the lefthand side traveling south. Rockaway Beach (see Beaches, above) is a mile north of this entrance, at Shelldance Nursery. Alternatively, visitors may enter the ridge area from the parking lot at Skyline College. From the Coast Highway, head east 1.5 miles on Sharp Park Rd a half mile north of Pacifica. Turn right on Skyline Blvd, then right again on

College Dr. The parking area for Sweeney Ridge is midway along the southern portion of the college loop road. For information, call the Golden Gate National Recreation Area, (415)239-2366.

San Bruno Mountain, northeast of Sweeney Ridge in Brisbane, is a 2,300-acre open-space island of coastal scrub and numerous rare plants, such as the San Bruno Mountain manzanita, that are important habitat for several rare breeds of butterfly, including three endangered species. At one time the mountain was slated for massive development, as it was in private hands and the subject of numerous speculative investments. Environmentalists won out, however—the mountain is now a San Mateo County open space area, and one that is rather hard to miss. Developed flatlands encircle the mountain on all sides, and at twilight it looms as a huge and almost out-of-place lump in the midst of it all. The 1,314-foot summit offers wide vistas of San Francisco Bay and the city skyline, along with other Bay Area peaks in clear weather. Picnic facilities, barbecue pits, and a day camp make the mountain a favorite stopover for families and youth groups. There also are 12 miles of hiking and riding trails, including a disabled-access trail near the park entrance. Easiest access to the mountain is from the Cow Palace (west) exit from US 101 near Brisbane, just south of San Francisco, off Guadalupe Pkwy. Call the park at (560) 363-4020 for more information.

You don't have to go far from the coast scrub of Sweeney Ridge and San Bruno Mountain to find lush redwoods—forests so secluded and away from it all that it seems impossible they are less than an hour's drive from most of the Bay Area's densely-populated regions. **Portola State Park**—named for the same Spanish explorer who stumbled on San Francisco Bay by climbing to the top of Sweeney Ridge and looking east—is a 2,800-acre oasis of old-growth and second-growth redwoods, some nearing 2,000 years old. Among the shady, cool canyons and wild creeks found here are stunning waterfalls, dense huckleberry, tall ferns, and unique marine fossil deposits from untold eons ago when all of this was beneath the sea. Camping, picnicking, hiking, limited horseback riding, wildlife viewing, and ecology lessons are the fare here—but don't even think about bringing your fishing pole. State authorities have declared the wild streams within the preserve to be off-limits to anglers until an exhaustive study of the watershed and ecosystem is completed. The park is in San Mateo County's southern end. Take I-280 to the Page Mill Rd exit near Mountain View, then go west on Page Mill 4 miles to the park entrance. The final stretch of the drive is steep and downhill on narrow roads, so heads up. Access is also available on Hwy 9 from San Jose or Skyline Rd from Sky Londa, Redwood City, or the Hwy 92 interchange at Crystal Springs Reservoir. Call the park, (650) 948-9098, for more information on this and adjacent redwood parklands.

Camping

With such a wide variety of open space in this area—from the Pacific Coast to the redwood forests to the inland backcountry—camping options also run the gamut.

The best bet for those who want to be rocked to sleep by the sound of the ocean is **Half Moon Bay State Beaches** (55 sites; some partial RV hookups; RV limit 36 feet), with prime access to fishing, surfing, and hiking near. A warning, however: This place fills up quickly with families, so while it's likely that the sound of the ocean will rock you to sleep here, it is equally likely that the sounds of children will wake you up—and earlier than appreciated! This is pretty much a family place, so if you're a grump or just a single, move to higher ground and camp among the redwoods instead. Each Half Moon Bay site has a picnic table and grill. Toilets are available, but no showers. *Call (650) 726-8820 or (415)330-6300. Take Hwy 1 one mile south of the Hwy 92 intersection, then go west on Kelly Ave to the park entrance.*

Redwood campers have more to choose from. Given its popularity, **Memorial County Park** (136 sites; no hookups; RVs okay) offers a remarkably peaceful setting among the redwood canyons 10 miles east of the Pescadero-area oceanfront. Each site has a picnic table and grill, and showers are provided. *Call (650) 879-0212 or (415)363-4021. Follow Hwy 1 for 15 miles south of Half Moon Bay, then go east on Pescadero Rd to the park entrance 10 miles inland.*

Portola State Park (52 sites; no hookups; RV limit 24 feet) is much more remote and less traveled than other redwood camp areas along this stretch of coast—but getting to it is also harder: The only way in and out by car is along a steep, windy, narrow road. Observe the RV limit! Sites have picnic tables and grills; showers are available. *Call the state parks reservation system, (800) 444-7275. The campground can be contacted directly at (650) 948-9098. Take I-280 to the Page Mill Rd exit near Mountain View, then go west on Page Mill Rd 4 miles to the park entrance. The final stretch of the drive is steep and downhill on narrow roads. Access is also available on Hwy 9 from San Jose, or via Skyline Rd from Sky Londa, Redwood City, or the Hwy 92 interchange at Crystal Springs Reservoir.*

Butano State Park has 39 sites, 18 hike-in only (no hookups; RV limit 31 feet). Because the park is so much easier to get to than other redwood camp areas in this portion of the coast, Butano is popular among families with small children and pets. It is indeed a lovely place to acquaint children with the redwoods without having to drive far from the urban centers. Grills and picnic tables are at each site; there are no showers. *Call state reservations, (800) 444-7275. The campground may be contacted directly* *at (650) 879-2040. Take Hwy 1 for 15 miles south of Half Moon Bay, then go east on Pescadero Rd. Just after the town of Pescadero, turn south on Cloverdale Rd, then continue to the park entrance on the east side of the road.*

The most rugged backcountry camping scene in perhaps the entire Bay Area is in the largest, least developed park in Northern California, **Henry W. Coe State Park,** which has 20 car camping sites (no hookups; 13 sites for RVs, limit 27 feet), 50-plus hike-in sites for use by permit, and a horse camp (see Parks, above). Car and RV camping are limited to the developed area near the park headquarters. This park is run with the avid outdoorsperson in mind: the backpacking camps are remote and in some cases difficult to get to. Come prepared with proper gear and supplies, and be sure to get a permit before venturing into the more than 80,000 acres of oak woodlands, deep ravines, ponds, high peaks, and wild country. *Call state parks reservations, (800) 444-7275. The park can be contacted directly at (408) 779-2728. Take US 101 south from San Francisco (US 101 intersects with I-880, I-280, and I-680 from the Peninsula and the East Bay) to the E Dunne Ave exit in Morgan Hill, then head 13 miles out to the park entrance headquarters just beyond Anderson Reservoir.*

Memorial County Park has 156 sites (no hookups; RV limit 35 feet) in the redwood forests near La Honda at the Santa Cruz/San Mateo County line. This area was hit particularly hard during the El Niño winter storms of 1998, but as of this writing things were well on their way to being patched together. No reservations are taken. *Call (650) 879-0212 for information. To reach the park, take the Coast Highway 15 miles south from the Hwy 92 junction to the intersection with Pescadero Rd, then head east 10 miles to the park entrance in the foothills.*

Hiking/Backpacking

If there was ever a perfect place to wear out a pair of hiking boots, this is it. Follow trails along the bluffs over the Pacific. Take to the peaks overlooking the ocean and the bay. Trek deep into backcountry where cool mountain streams and hidden swimming holes are the only relief from the heat. The Golden Gate Park Association, (415) 776-0693, can provide pointers on where to head outdoors for a walk or outing that suits specific needs and skill levels. Another good **resource** for hikers is the Greenbelt Alliance, a leading Bay Area land conservation group that sponsors numerous group outings in the Peninsula and the South Bay. These outings are worthwhile even for experienced hikers since each is led by a knowledgeable guide/naturalist. The alliance maintains an outings hot line with information about planned events, (415) 398-3730. The Sierra Club Bay Chapter also makes hiking information easily available to the public and organizes regular outings. For a **hiking guide,** send a self-addressed stamped envelope to 1525 Berkeley Way, Berkeley, CA 94703, or call the area hiking coordinator at (925) 631-0751. Finally, also consider checking in with the two REI stores in the Peninsula/South Bay region. In San Carlos, go to 1119 Industrial Rd, or call (650) 508-2330. The San Jose store is at 400 El Paseo de Saratoga, (408) 871-8765. REI maintains a thorough staff-written Web site at www.rei.com/ MORE_STORE/hikes/sanfranhktemp.html, with information on local hikes. On a smaller scale the folks at Friendly Hiking Services, 90 Spruce Ave, South San Francisco, (650) 742-6294, also can recommend places to go and how best to prepare for outings.

As the official San Francisco Bay discovery site, **Sweeney Ridge Trail** (moderate; 4.8 miles round trip) on Sweeney Ridge (see Parks, above) is a good combination hike and history tour for outdoor enthusiasts visiting the Bay Area. A plaque on the 1,200-foot summit marks the spot where Spanish explorer Gaspar de Portola first looked down and saw the bay in 1769. It is best to begin this hike through coastal scrub and wildflowers from the Skyline College parking area on the park's northern boundary, and double back from the summit instead of continuing to the southern end of the ridge—but if you have the time and energy, go ahead and explore the entire length of this trail. Or take a side trip on one of four others traversing the park. From the Coast Highway, head east 1.5 miles on Sharp Park Rd a half mile north of Pacifica. Turn right on Skyline Blvd, then right again on College Dr. The parking area for Sweeney Ridge is midway along the southern portion of the college loop road. For information and trail maps, call the Golden Gate National Recreation Area, (415) 239-2366.

To get a similar view from about 114 feet higher, try out the **Summit Trail** (easy to moderate; 3.1 miles round trip) and trek to the top of nearby **San Bruno Mountain,** a wildlife and rare plant habitat northeast of Sweeney Ridge. From the parking area south of Guadalupe Canyon Pkwy, there are actually a few options for reaching the summit. On warm days, make the 700-foot climb via **Eucalyptus Loop Trail** and **Dairy Ravine Trail,** which after numerous switchbacks connects with Summit Trail for the final half mile to the top. To follow the summit trail the entire length is to see much more of the park, but it also takes longer. Take the Cow Palace (west) exit from US 101 near Brisbane, just south of San Francisco, to Guadalupe Pkwy. Call the park at (560) 363-4020 for trail maps or more information.

They say the drinking water in San Francisco is good enough to bottle and sell—so it must also be good enough to walk next to while it's still sitting in San Andreas Lake or Crystal Springs Reservoir. Lakeside strolls along **Sawyer Camp Trail** (easy; up to 12 miles round trip) are peaceful, relaxing, and cooling—the waterside and the shade of the forest make this a popular retreat on warm summer days, with plenty of places to sit along the way. Numerous paved sections also make this a decent baby stroller outing—but watch out for speeding cyclists. Failure to stay to the right of the trail can result in a nasty collision. Sawyer Camp links with numerous adjoining trails and parklands. The easiest access point is from Hwy 92, which crosses the reservoir at midpoint. From the South Bay or San Francisco, take I-280 north or south to the Hwy 92 junction. Two parking areas are south of the highway on the banks of the upper reservoir. To the north is **San Andreas Trail** (easy; 7 miles round trip, variable), which, while more difficult, is less cluttered with trail users going the opposite way; it follows San Andreas Reservoir. Contact the San Mateo County Department of Parks and Recreation, (650) 363-4020, for information and trail guides.

These strolls are only one type of waterside walk to choose from in these parts. As an alternative, who can resist a nature walk among the marshes of San Francisco Bay? There are numerous access points for the **Don Edwards San Francisco Bay Wildlife Refuge,** which occupies vast portions of the south, east, and north bay lands. The **South Bay Nature Trail** (easy; 2.5 miles) loops on raised levees through the wild tidal marshlands at Alviso north of San Jose and south of Fremont. The refuge environmental education center is at this location, and guided walks are scheduled often. Take US 101 to the Hwy 237 exit outside San Jose, then go toward the waterfront. The center is on Zanker St, left from the highway. Call the main refuge office, (510)792-0222, for information. The **Mountain View Shoreline Trail** system (varying distances; all easy) is also a popular spot to access the bay shore. Take US 101 to the Shoreline Blvd exit in Mountain View, then head east to the shore and preserve parking areas.

Along the Pacific coast, there's a boundless choice of places to walk in the surf, among the tide pools, and along the bluffs (see Beaches, above). Among the best is the **Plover Overlook Trail** (easy; 2.3 miles round trip), which extends from just south of Francis Beach at Half Moon Bay north along the bluffs over Venice, Dunes, Roosevelt, and Miramar Beaches. Visible as you go are the Santa Cruz Mountains to the southeast, Pillar Point Harbor, and the point at where Pilarcitos Creek meets the ocean at Venice Beach. Historical points of interest are highlighted along the way.

The half-day trek up **Montara Mountain** (difficult; 7.5 miles round trip), adjacent to Montara State Beach (see Beaches, above), rockets 2,000 feet above the Pacific shore along the coastal ridge—but once at the summit, you're rewarded with spectacular views of surrounding Bay Area peaks and a wide vista of the big blue. The mountain is a favorite spring wildflower walk. Begin the hike on a fire road across the highway and slightly north of Montara Beach (parking at the beach lot is the best bet). From there, it's a straight shot to the top—but the climb is best taken in easy-to-swallow bites. In fact, a sprint straight to the top is out of the question because of the steepness. Find the beach and mountain trail along the Coast Highway south of Pacifica, near the Chart House Restaurant. For more information, call (650) 726-8819.

For another hearty half-day trek through redwood forests, grasslands, and oaks, try out **Meadow Trail** (moderate; 5.5 miles) through **Wunderlich County Park** north of Portola Valley and west of Hwy 84 near Woodside. No bikes allowed! Trail maps are available at the park office on the west side of Woodside Rd, 2.5 miles west of I-280 on the Hwy 84 route through the mountains. The park is adjacent to numerous open space preserves lining Skyline Ridge. Call the San Mateo County Parks department, (650) 363-4020, for more information.

The **Coastal Trail** section between San Gregorio Beach and Pigeon Point (moderate; 21 miles round trip) follows some of the most stunningly beautiful and secluded beaches of this region. Most of the walk is on the sand itself or (during high tide when the beach is inaccessible) along detours on the shoulder of the Coast Highway. At low tide, it can be completed its entire length on the beachfront. This hike is best done one-way, with a car parked at either end. Along the 10.5 miles you will come across quiet coved beach sections with dramatically high cliffs overhead, interesting tide-pool areas, and four large creek and river mouths where they meet the ocean. Along the way are Pompano, Sand, Pescadero, Pebble, Bean Hollow, and Pigeon Point Beaches; this is a grand tour! We recommend beginning at the northern point (San Gregorio), since winds tend to come out of the west or northwest. The beach is between San Gregorio Rd and Pescadero Creek.

Iverson Trail (moderate; 5.5 miles round trip) follows Pescadero Creek from the redwood groves at Memorial Park in the San Mateo coast mountains east of Pescadero Beach. We rank this hike as moderate in difficulty not because its particularly strenuous, but because there are occasional gaps and fallen trees to navigate around or climb over along the way. Those not in the mood for a half-day hike can cover just the first mile and relax at creekside instead. The trailhead is at the park entrance. Take Pescadero Rd 25 miles east from the Coast Highway in Pescadero and turn right (south) at the park entrance. Call the Mid-Peninsula Regional Park and Open Space District, (650) 691-1200, for additional information.

As tempting as it is, there's no need to depart the urban jungle completely to see the wilds. Long, lonely backpacking treks through the vast Bay Area wilderness (also see Hiking/Backpacking, East Bay chapter) can be just as rewarding as in the Sierra Nevada range or the North Coast red-woods—and perhaps a better choice depending on the snow level or rains. One example in the southern Bay Area is the **Gill Route,** beginning in the southeastern corner of **Henry W. Coe State Park** (extremely diffi-cult; 59 miles round trip). With elevation gains of 2,400 feet and 1,950-foot elevation drops, this is the longest and most challenging backpacking route in all of the Bay Area, covering deep canyons carved by wild streams, high forested peaks, and wide meadows with primitive backpack-ing camps along the way. Other popular backpacking routes at Henry Coe include **Rooster Comb Loop** (extremely difficult; 20.2 miles round trip), **Interior Route** to Mississippi Lake (difficult/advanced; 14 miles round trip), **Pacheco Route** (extremely difficult; 33.4 miles round trip), and **Northern Heights Route** (extremely difficult; 25.6 miles round trip). Backpacking **permits** are mandatory since camp space is limited. A spe-cial word of caution—this area gets warm during spring and summer months, climbs are vigorous, and developed facilities are either limited or nonexistent. Do not, repeat, *do not,* venture into the deep wilds of Henry Coe if you are not properly outfitted, in good physical condition, and accustomed to backpacking. If you do, you may end up injured or dead. These outings must be planned, not undertaken on a whim. Call the park ranger office at (408) 779-2728. To reach the park, take US 101 south from San Francisco (US 101 intersects with I-880, I-280, and I-680 from the Peninsula and the East Bay) to the E Dunne Ave exit in Morgan Hill, then head 13 miles out to the park entrance headquarters just beyond Anderson Reservoir.

Wildlife

Back when the marshes were undisturbed and before the Peninsula was urbanized, grizzly bears would fish for salmon at the bay's edge, migrating fish would clog the streams reaching into the highlands, and a thick band of centuries-old coast redwoods hugged the mountain ridges meeting the sea. Whether it is an old wive's tale or something closer to the truth, his-torical accounts claim that so many birds migrating along the Pacific Fly-way would make the stopover at the bay's edge that day would turn to night when they took to flight. While all of this has obviously changed significantly over the past two decades of human settlement here, the South Bay and Peninsula still offer numerous nature and wildlife viewing opportunities. From the Pacific coast to the backcountry wilderness above the inland valleys, variety abounds. Below are some of the standouts.

Talk about nature in the raw! One of the largest colonies anywhere of northern **elephant seals** is found at **Año Nuevo State Reserve** (also see

Beaches, above), 60 miles south of San Francisco on the Pacific Coast. The huge and elusive sea mammals—males can reach up to 5,000 pounds!—take care of most of their day-to-day business out at sea. Their most important business, however, is done here: these monsters come ashore by the thousands to mate, molt, and give birth to their young. The spectacle is quite a draw. At the height of the mating and **calving season** from December to March, the beaches are wall-to-wall blubber. First, the bulls arrive to engage in violent battles to sort out which of them will get top billing when the females arrive. After the males have duked it out, impregnated females return to the sea; it takes nearly a year for them to carry a pup to term. The beach is then transformed to a sea mammal maternity ward as pregnant females come ashore to give birth. In less than a month, their pups balloon from under 100 pounds to nearly 400 . . . just in time for the mating call. By March, the bulls, females, and new pups have deserted the beach, although they come ashore periodically during the summer to molt. Access to the preserve during the December-to-March mating and pupping season is by guided tour only. Tour reservations are taken by the state parks reservation system, (800) 444-7275. To contact the reserve directly, call (650) 879-0227. The reserve is 25 miles south of Half Moon Bay and 20 miles north of Santa Cruz on the Coast Highway. From San Francisco, you know you've driven too far if you see Big Creek Lumber Company on the east side of the highway or cross the Santa Cruz County line.

As environmental awareness has caught on, ecology outings have become increasingly popular. Marshes, creek beds, and in particular **tide pools** are a growing attraction not only along the ocean but also along the bay. The ecology tour program centered around the tide pools at **Bean Hollow State Beach** (see Beaches, above) is a great outing for schoolchildren to "practice" the watershed awareness they've learned in a science class. Not that tidepooling isn't for big kids, too; grown-ups also enjoy viewing the assorted invertebrates, sponges, sea anemones, mollusks, starfish, and other creatures commonly discovered in the tide-pool environment. As this activity has become more popular, however, park officials have had to do some quick thinking to keep growing crowds from adversely affecting the tide pools and their occupants: the "look but don't touch" approach is catching on, and expeditions are sometimes restricted to designated areas. Bean Hollow has monthly **interpretive tours.** Call (650) 879-2170.

Pescadero State Beach, and **Montara State Beach** (see Beaches, above) are other popular tidepooling spots on the Pacific Coast. The **Fitzgerald Marine Reserve** at Moss Beach also has tide pools worth exploring (and, if you can tear yourself away from the starfish, follow the south-side cliff trail to the eerily beautiful cypress forest and go down the rough-hewn stairs to another lovely little stretch of beach). Look for the signs on Hwy 1 announcing the reserve; for more information call (650) 728-3584.

On the bay, check out **Windharp Hill** at **Candlestick Point State Recreation Area** for tide-pool and mudflat walks and special bay ecology interpretive programs. To reach the park, take US 101 south from San Francisco to 3Com Park and follow the signs to the recreation area. For information, call (650) 671-0145.

For seasonal **whale watching** (approximately December through March), call Huck Finn's Sport Fishing Tours, (650) 726-7133, or Captain John's, (650) 726-2913; both are located on Pillar Point Harbor, about 4 miles north of Half Moon Bay.

A pristine redwood forest ecosystem has it all—the wild, meandering creeks and rivers loaded with migrating salmon and trout; rare birds dependent on the widely spaced branches of old-growth trees; and the thick, moist carpet of fallen branches and vegetation. Interesting mosses and fungi, tall ferns, thick banana slugs, you name it! **Pescadero Creek**, which meanders through numerous expanses of redwoods, including **Portola State Park** (see Parks, above), is a great place to observe all of this at work. When fall rains begin, spawning trout and salmon can be seen making their way through the creek, which until 30 years ago was blocked by a dam in the highlands. The rare **marbled murrelet** nests here, as do **dippers, woodpeckers,** and **kingfishers.** The stream canyons also are home to numerous mammals such as **bobcats, raccoons,** and **squirrels,** and a wide variety of **reptiles.** To reach this area, take I-280 to the Page Mill Rd exit near Mountain View, then go west on Page Mill Rd 4 miles to the park entrance. The final stretch of the drive is steep and downhill on narrow roads. Access is also available on Hwy 9 from San Jose or via Skyline Rd from Sky Londa, Redwood City, or the Hwy 92 interchange at Crystal Springs Reservoir.

Point Reyes National Seashore (see Point Reyes National Seashore chapter) in northern Marin is by far the bird-watching capital of the Bay Area, if not the entire Pacific Coast. San Francisco Bay, however, has numerous sanctuary lands where **waterfowl** of every imaginable variety can be viewed.

The best South Bay and Peninsula salt marshes, tidal wetlands, and brackish ponds for bird-watching are in the **Mountain View Regional Shoreline** and the Alviso portion of the **Don Edwards San Francisco Bay National Wildlife Refuge** (see Hiking/Backpacking, above). The refuge and associated environmental education center at Alviso offer numerous interpretive walking tours at the southern end of the bay. Because of its position along the **Pacific Flyway,** bird varieties here change with the seasonal climate changes. Grebes, snowy egrets, lesser scaups, black-bellied plovers, and western sandpipers are common here during the spring. In winter, look for willets, least sandpipers, Bonaparte's gulls, starlings, and song sparrows. For more information on birding in the area, call Wild Birds Unlimited in Cupertino, (408) 252-5712, or check out its Web site at www.wbu.com. Call the main refuge office, (510) 792-0222, for information about **interpretive tours,** environmental education programs, and up-to-date shoreline access. To reach the refuge area in Alviso, take US 101 to the Hwy 237 exit outside San Jose, then go toward the waterfront. The center is on Zanker St, left from the highway. Keep in mind that Alviso floods often when heavy rains move through, but the birds love it, so if the area is inaccessible, it's probably one of the most interesting times to head out. To reach the Mountain View shore, take US 101 to the Shoreline Blvd exit in Mountain View, then head east to the shore and preserve parking areas.

The wilderness area of **Henry W. Coe State Park** (see Parks, above) is the best place to view **birds of prey.** Red-tailed hawks, vultures, golden eagles, prairie falcons, wild turkeys, great horned owls, and even bald eagles have been spotted among the expansive forests and high ridges of this 80,000-acre wilderness. However, this is not exactly a low-key nature stroll kind of place; be prepared for some serious backcountry backpacking hauls to really see the creatures in the thick of it all.

Windsurfing

Candlestick Point in South San Francisco and **Coyote Point** in San Mateo are the best sailboarding spots in this section of the bay. But visitors to both should be aware of two potential hazards. First, because both are also popular fishing spots, sailboarders run the risk of becoming ensnared in fishing lines. Second, winds here are not as constant as in the more popular (but more advanced) windsurfing area near Crissy Field (see Windsurfing, San Francisco chapter), and that means possibly getting stranded. It's easy to go from "catching it" to barely anything; as a result, the Coast Guard is regularly having to pluck stranded sailboarders out of the bay in these parts after a sudden change in wind conditions takes them by surprise. Contact the San Francisco Board Sailing Association, (415)522-9001, for advice on where and when to set sail and how to get outfitted. To reach Candlestick Point from the South Bay or San Francisco, take US 101 to the 3Com Park exit in South San Francisco and go west. Call (650) 671-0145 for information. To reach Coyote Point, take US 101 to the Coyote Point Dr exit and head west to the park's main entrance. Call the park at (650) 573-2593 or (650) 573-2593 for more information.

Mountain Biking

Despite this region's multitude of wide-open spaces, it's hard to find off-road cycling areas where you don't face some potential for conflicts with other trail users. So the most important advice we can dole out is this: don't be a jerk on the trails. Horseback riders, hikers, walkers, and joggers frequent all of the places that mountain bikers frequent; keep the speed down and don't buzz people. Many of the good cycling trails in the San Mateo/Santa Clara County area are managed by the Mid-Peninsula Regional Open Space District, (650) 691-1200, with Web access at www.openspace.org; the San Mateo County Parks and Recreation Division, (650) 363-4020; or the state parks department at Henry Coe, (408) 779-2728.

Probably the most frequently used trails in the central Peninsula are those traversing the San Francisco watershed lands west of San Mateo in the shadow of Skyline Ridge. **Sawyer Camp Trail** and the contiguous **San Andreas Trail** follow an 8-mile stretch of the water's edge along San Andreas and Lower Crystal Springs reservoirs. The easy to moderately difficult ride is a good choice for beginners, and there's nice lakeside scenery and a peaceful setting despite its proximity to I-280. The Sawyer Camp section of the ride is paved, so don't expect a rugged, off-road free-for-all—especially since pavement also attracts families with kids and baby strollers and elderly amblers as well. The easiest staging area is from just west of the I-280 junction with Hwy 92. Parking areas are also available along Skyline Blvd, west of the interstate. Call the county parks department in San Mateo, (650) 363-4202, for more information.

A nice bay shore ride, also easy and ideal for beginners, is along the loop trail at **Coyote Point Park** in San Mateo, a 2.5-mile cruise over flat terrain with nice bay views and pleasant eucalyptus groves. Call Coyote Point Park, (650) 573-2593, for more information. Exit US 101 at Coyote Point Rd, go east to the bay shore, and follow the signs to the park.

A good ride that is easy to get to is the **Saddle Trail/Old Guadalupe Trail** loop on San Bruno Mountain, a moderate 2-mile huff-and-puff climb with big rewards. Add another 3 miles and another 725 feet of elevation to the ride by continuing on the **Summit Loop Trail** section before coasting easily back to earth. It's a tough climb and it more than doubles the length of the ride—but why even bother climbing a mountain if you don't plan to go all the way to the top? Just be sure you're ready for the challenge. Call San Bruno Mountain park, (650) 363-4020, for more information. Take the Cow Palace (west) exit from US 101 near Brisbane, just south of San Francisco, to Guadalupe Pkwy.

The 26-mile (round trip) ride along **Old Haul Road** within **Portola**

State Park, a mild and gentle climb through redwood country, is cool and easy to handle, and downhill all the way back—but don't let go the whole way (too many people around, and it's against the trail regulations anyway). The park is in San Mateo County's southern end. Take I-280 to the Page Mill Rd exit near Mountain View, then go west on Page Mill Rd 4 miles to the park entrance. The final stretch of the drive is steep and downhill on narrow roads. Access is also available on Hwy 9 from San Jose or Skyline Rd from Sky Londa, Redwood City, or the Hwy 92 interchange at Crystal Springs Reservoir. Call the park, (650) 948-9098.

Henry W. Coe State Park offers more than 200 miles of looping trails through rugged, wild backcountry—most of it difficult enough that we must declare it off-limits to beginners and those not in good physical condition. Heat exhaustion and heatstroke are not unheard of among these 80,000 acres of wilderness. The trail routes are steep, rocky, and full of switchbacks—in short, very demanding. After checking in with the park visitors center, (408) 779-2728, for information on trail conditions, fire danger, and other essentials, consider the 15-mile ride from the park headquarters to the 3,000-foot **Monument Peak,** and then on to the 3,500-foot peak of **Mount Sizer**—a killer with a more than 1,500-foot gain in less than a mile! From there, dip into **Poverty Flat** and then climb another 1,000 feet back to the park entrance. Rest along the way and don't even think about taking to the trails without a map because getting lost here is even more common than heat exhaustion.

Cycling

Despite the scary drivers and traffic along the 60 miles of **Coast Highway** between San Francisco and Año Nuevo State Preserve, road cyclists can enjoy a lengthy trek along the water. The 36-mile round trip between Half Moon Bay and Pescadero is particularly pleasant, mostly level with a few dips and turns, with plenty of salt breezes to keep cool along the way. Stage from any of the beaches in the vicinity of the Hwys 1 and 92 intersection, and stay alert. Another popular cycling route is the 23-mile trek from San Gregorio Beach to the I-280 intersection with the **Hwy 84 route** through the Woodside/Portola Valley mountains—a beautiful, forested, shady ride from the seashore to the bayfront, with nice bay vistas once you've survived the steep grades over the hill. Be warned, however, that bike/car conflicts are a problem here; residents of the exclusive countryside communities in the hills have become particularly annoyed with tar heads hogging the roads. A couple of bike shops in the area where **maps, gear,** and **information** are readily available: Bike Route Inc, 568 San Mateo Ave, San Bruno, (650) 873-9555; Ocb Bikeworks, 2260 Valleywood

Dr, San Bruno (650) 583-1863; and Performance Bicycle Shop, 2535 El Camino Real, Redwood City, (650) 365-9094.

In-Line Skating

On numerous Sundays between March and December, the San Mateo County Department of Parks and Recreation closes a 4-mile stretch of **Cañada Road** west of Crystal Springs Reservoir to all motor vehicles. The result: a nice, flat, long, paved piece of ground in as scenic a setting as you can find anywhere—all the ingredients of great blading turf. The road closures are effective 9am to 4pm on select dates only. Call (650) 361-1785 to check the schedule. A good Sunday alternative is San Francisco's Golden Gate Park, where large areas of pavement are off-limits to cars that day (see San Francisco chapter). Check with Western Skate Supply, 189 Constitution Dr, Menlo Park, (650) 324-0881, to get outfitted. To reach Canada Rd, take I-280 to the Hwy 92 junction, then proceed west to the reservoir shore. Parking areas are available here and 4 miles south at I-280 and Edgewood Rd.

Horseback Riding

The Peninsula/South Bay region is a great place to explore public lands on horseback, and there is no shortage of horse trails or horse camps (see Parks, above). The most popular and easily accessible equestrian adventure in these parts, however, is at Sea Horse Ranch or Friendly Acres Ranch in Half Moon Bay, where **coastal trail rides** are the main fare. The ranches have 200 horses and ponies on hand to accommodate all riding skills; kids welcome. Both ranches are located on Hwy 1 a mile north of Half Moon Bay and the Hwy 92 intersection. Call (650) 726-2362, or (650) 726-8550.

For rugged backcountry riding, the obvious choice is **Henry W. Coe State Park** (see Parks, above), which boasts more than 200 miles of trails open to equestrians (as well as hikers and bicycles), along with a well-appointed horse camp. **Portola State Park** and the regional open spaces along Skyline Ridge also offer horse trails and special accommodations. Contact the Henry Coe visitors center, (408) 779-2728, or the Mid-Peninsula Regional Open Space District, (650) 691-1200, for trail maps and camp information.

Adventure Calendar

Crystal Springs Trail Day, last weekend in May: *a time to show appreciation for the reservoir setting by using it en masse, (650) 363-4027.*

Tour de Peninsula, early August: *a 33-mile charity bike ride, (415) 759-2690.*

outside **in**

Attractions

Old Victorian houses and small boutiques line downtown **Half Moon Bay,** the oldest city in San Mateo County, while produce stands, U-pick farms, and well-stocked nurseries ring its perimeter (artichokes, broccoli, and pumpkins are the town's prime crops). Every October, thousands of Bay Area families make their yearly pilgrimage to this picturesque seacoast town in search of the ultimate Halloween pumpkin. The Half Moon Bay **Pumpkin Festival** features all manner of squash cuisine and crafts, as well as the World Heavyweight Pumpkin Championship, a weigh-in contest won recently by a 375-pound monster. During the spring and summer months, the **weekend flower market** is a big draw, while year-round the city's fine restaurants lure folks from "over the hill" (the Coastsiders' term for inland San Mateo County).

The home of notable restaurants, fine-art galleries, foreign-movie houses, great bookstores, a thriving theater troupe, and some of the best shopping this side of heaven, **Palo Alto** is a beacon of cosmopolitan energy shining on the suburban sea. Much of the fuel for this cultural lighthouse comes, of course, from **Stanford University,** which offers tours of its attractive campus on a fairly regular basis. Highlights of the university include the Main Quad, Hoover Tower (there are great views from its observation platform), the huge bookstore, and gorgeous Memorial Church; call the campus at (650) 723-2560 for more tour information.

If you didn't find the tome you were looking for at the Stanford bookstore, Palo Alto and its neighbors contain many other outlets for bibliophiles, one of which is **Kepler's Books and Magazines,** 1010 El Camino Real, Menlo Park, (650) 324-4321, a wonderland for serious bookworms. For authentic coffeehouse atmosphere and great espresso try Cafe Borrone, located right next to Kepler's, 1010 El Camino Real, Menlo Park, (650) 327-0830. If you'd like to surf the Web while you sip your cappuccino, head to Cybersmith, where you can connect to the Internet, try out the latest software, or don a helmet and gloves for a voyage into virtual reality; 353 University Ave, Palo Alto, (650) 325-2005.

If you prefer your **performances** live, check out the local Theatreworks troupe, (650) 463-1950, the Lively Arts series at Stanford University, (650) 725-2787, or the top-name talents currently appearing at the Shoreline Amphitheater, 1 Amphitheater Pkwy, Mountain View, (650) 967-3000. If you have nothing to wear for the show (or, indeed, if you have any other shopping need), Palo Alto won't let you down. **University**

Avenue and its side streets contain a plethora of interesting stores. The Stanford Shopping Center, just north of downtown on El Camino Real, (650) 617-8585, is a sprawling, beautifully landscaped temple of consumerism (stores include Bloomingdales, Macy's, Nordstrom, Ralph Lauren, The Gap, Imaginarium, Crate & Barrel, the Disney Store, and many more).

All the boomers who grew up with Dionne Warwick's "Do You Know the Way to San Jose," a paean to the relaxed small-town **San Jose** of yesteryear, may be shocked to see the city's newly gentrified chrome, glass, and pastel downtown and its sprawling, freeway-locked suburbs. Some may mourn the loss of the orchards and the sleepy, mañana attitude, but most San Joseans seemed puffed up with understandable pride at the city's energetic new look and feel. First-class restaurants, a state-of-the-art light rail system, a flourishing arts scene, and a dazzling sports arena (go Sharks!) have all contributed to the city's revitalization, helping it emerge at last from the long cultural shadow cast by San Francisco, its cosmopolitan neighbor to the north.

Museums. The newly renovated **San Jose Museum of Art** provides a handsome setting for contemporary European and American art; 110 S Market St, (408) 294-2787. The lively and ever-so-loud Children's Discovery Museum, painted in Easter-egg purple, offers kids the opportunity to explore exhibits of urban life: traffic lights, fire engines, a post office, a bank, and even a sewer (spanking clean and minus any errant rats or Ninja turtles). A Wells Fargo stagecoach, a farmhouse, and rural diversions like corn-husk doll-making help youngsters experience what the valley was like when it produced major crops instead of microchips; 180 Woz Way, (408) 298-5437. The Tech Museum of Innovation is a terrific hands-on science museum where adults and kids alike can play with robots, gain insight into genetic engineering, or design a high-tech bicycle; it's located across from the Convention Center, 145 W San Carlos St, (408) 279-7150. Fans of the supernatural might enjoy a tour of the Winchester Mystery House: after inheriting $20 million from her husband's repeating-rifle company, Sarah Winchester became convinced that the ghosts of people killed by Winchester rifles were coming back to haunt her. Her paranoia led her to have additions built to her home 24 hours a day for 38 years to house their restless spirits. The lovely if somewhat unorthodox Victorian mansion is a 160-room labyrinth of crooked corridors, doors opening into space, and dead-end stairways; 525 South Winchester Blvd, (408) 247-2101.

Theater, Dance, and Music. San Jose has a thriving community of theater, ballet, and opera groups, most of which may be found at the San Jose Center for the Performing Arts; 255 Almaden Blvd at Park Ave, (408)

277-3900. The San Jose Civic Light Opera, (408) 453-7108, puts on musicals and other frothy diversions, while Opera San Jose, (408) 437-4450; the San Jose Cleveland Ballet, (408) 288-2800; and the San Jose Symphony Orchestra, (408) 288-2828; offer more classical cultural enrichments. Los Lupeños de San Jose dance company reflects the Spanish heritage of the city; 34 N First St, (408) 292-0443. For drama, the San Jose Repertory Theatre offers innovative productions of new works and classics; 1 N First St, (408) 291-2255. The San Jose Stage Company, 490 S First St, (408) 283-7142, primarily showcases American contemporary drama and comedy, while the City Lights Theatre follows the more experimental route; 529 S Second St, (408) 295-4200.

Nightlife. Once the red-light district, the area around Market and First Sts has gradually developed into a clean, hip home for many nightclubs and a slightly more alternative scene. If you want a little bit of everything, visit the Pavilion, where under one roof you'll find a deluxe, eight-screen movie theater, a virtual-reality theme park, and a smattering of shops, bars, and restaurants, as well as San Jose Live, a popular nightspot with two dance floors, a sports bar with 11 big-screen TVs, a cafe serving California fare, a cigar and martini bar, dueling piano players on baby grands, an arcade, pool tables, and even a basketball court; 150 S First St, (408) 294-5483.

Restaurants

Agenda ☆☆☆   At this chic and beautifully designed restaurant in the city's SoMa district (yes, San Jose's got one, too), stylish types sip cosmopolitans at the sculptured wood bar. But sampling the eclectic food is what's really on everyone's agenda. *399 S 1st St (at San Salvador St), San Jose; (408) 287-3991; $$.*

Amber India Restaurant ☆☆   Located in a small, unprepossessing shopping center, Amber India offers an escape into a serene, exotic realm. The food is a cut above the fare typically found in Bay Area Indian restaurants, in terms of both quality and variety. *2290 El Camino Real (between Rengstorff and Ortega Aves), Mountain View; (650) 968-7511; $$$.*

Barbara's Fish Trap ☆   Situated on stilts above the beach, the Fish Trap has panoramic views of Half Moon Bay. The decor is classic fish 'n' chips style, but the food is a cut above. *281 Capistrano Rd (4 miles N of Half Moon Bay on Hwy 1, and W on Capistrano Rd), Princeton; (650) 728-7049; $$.*

Bella Mia ☆   A large and lovely brick patio and a lively bar scene are two of the principal draws at this cheery Italian restaurant. The menu encompasses everything from wood-grilled meats to flatbread pizzas. *58 S 1st St (at San Fernando St), San Jose; (408) 280-1993; $$.*

Bella Saratoga ☆☆ A pretty two-story Victorian house in the center of town is the homey setting for this popular Italian restaurant. Pasta is its forte, but you'll also find a selection of salads, pizzas, and meat and poultry items. *14503 Big Basin Way (between 3rd and 4th Sts), Saratoga; (408) 741-5115; $$.*

Beppo ☆☆ This place has a maze of eating areas drenched in Christmas lights, statues glazed in neon colors, and an exuberant, young waitstaff plunking down huge platters of traditional Italian food on the red-and-white-checked tables. *643 Emerson St (between Forest and Hamilton Aves), Palo Alto; (650) 329-0665; $$.*

Bistro Elan ☆☆☆ The dining room is decked out in a spare Parisian neighborhood-bistro style, and the kitchen's forte is a small, ever-changing repertoire of carefully crafted, subtly flavored dishes—classic French bistro, with an occasional dash of California cuisine. *448 California Ave (just off El Camino Real), Palo Alto; (650) 327-0284; $$.*

Bistro La Luna ☆☆ Flickering candlelight illuminates the spare, golden-hued dining room, but the kitchen's what really shines at this small restaurant. The globe-trotting fare melds Italian, French, and California flavors with a heavy dose of *sabor Latino*. *1137 Chestnut St (between Santa Cruz and Oak Grove Aves), Menlo Park; (650) 324-3810; $$.*

Blue Chalk Cafe ☆ Although a taste of California and even the Far East sneak into the menu now and then, this engaging cafe's culinary strength lies in its satisfying Southern comfort food. *630 Ramona St (between Hamilton and Forest Aves), Palo Alto; (650) 326-1020; $$.*

Buffalo Grill ☆☆ There's no denying the appeal the sophisticated and playful Southwestern decor lends to this mallside restaurant. Good American regional cuisine—and plenty of it—is dished up in a friendly, high-voltage atmosphere. *66 31st Ave (in the Hillsdale Mall, off El Camino Real), San Mateo; (650) 358-8777; $$.*

Cafe Trio ☆☆☆ This engaging California bistro has black-and-white floor tiles, green marbleized wallpaper, and crisp table linens. The essentially California menu is infused with French and Italian touches. *15466 Los Gatos Blvd (in the Village Square shopping center, between Lark Ave and Los Gatos–Almaden Rd), Los Gatos; (408) 356-8129; $$$.*

California Sushi and Grill ☆☆ This chic sushi spot is popular with the downtown crowd, who want something fast and delicious and don't mind parting with a chunk of change to get it. *1 E San Fernando St (between 1st and 2nd Sts), San Jose; (408) 297-1847; $$.*

Carpaccio ☆☆　Carpaccio holds tightly to its Northern Italian roots. The wood-burning oven (with bricks imported from Italy) turns out divine pizzas with premium toppings laced together with fresh mozzarella, *1120 Crane St (between Oak Grove and Santa Cruz Aves), Menlo Park; (650) 322-1211; $$.*

Chef Chu's ☆☆　Take a culinary tour of mainland China without ever leaving your table. Feast on dim sum from Guangzhou, banquet dishes from Shanghai, stretched noodles from Xian, and spicy favorites from Sichuan and Hunan. *1067 N San Antonio Rd (at El Camino Real), Los Altos; (650) 948-2696; $$.*

Creo La. ☆☆☆　It took awhile for this restaurant serving terrific New Orleans–style food to catch on in San Carlos, but now that folks know to ignore its inauspicious location and humble facade, Creo La. is coming into its own. *344 El Camino Real (just N of Holly St), San Carlos; (650) 654-0882; $$.*

Duarte's Tavern ☆☆　This rustic gem, built in 1894, is still set in an Old West–style wood-and-stucco building—and the bar is still dark and loud—but the restaurant serves terrific coastal fare. *202 Stage Rd (at Pescadero Creek Rd), Pescadero; (650) 879-0464; $$.*

Evvia ☆☆☆　This warm and welcoming restaurant has a sun-drenched, Mediterranean feel. Greece has succumbed to California's culinary charms here, resulting in an emphasis on fresh produce and interesting twists on traditional dishes. *420 Emerson St (between Lytton and University Aves), Palo Alto; (650) 326-0983; $$.*

Flea Street Café ☆　Flea Street has come a long way since it was accused years ago of serving tasteless organic food. Now it wins respect for its unique brand of feisty California cuisine. Organic ingredients are still the rule. *3607 Alameda de las Pulgas (near Santa Cruz Ave), Menlo Park; (650) 854-1226; $$.*

Gibson ☆☆☆　Lively and sophisticated, this corner restaurant specializes in a gutsy brand of California cuisine enhanced by Mediterranean and Asian influences. Service is polished and professional from the moment you walk in the door. *201 E 3rd Ave (at Ellsworth St), San Mateo; (650) 344-6566; $$$.*

Gombei Restaurant ☆☆　Among the many worthy restaurants in San Jose's Japantown, tiny, lively Gombei stands out with its unparalleled noodle dishes and the near-volcanic energy of its devoted patrons and staff. *193 E Jackson St (between 4th and 5th Sts), San Jose; (408) 279-4311; $. 1438 El Camino Real (3 blocks off Santa Cruz Ave), Menlo Park; (650) 329-1799; $.*

Hangen ☆☆   Mountain View's Castro Street is undeniably saturated with Asian restaurants of all descriptions, but this delicate and tasty Sichuan fare still has managed to carve out a distinctive niche. *134 Castro St (just W of the Central Expwy), Mountain View; (650) 964-8881; $$.*

Higashi West ☆☆   It's East meets West at this small, slick restaurant, where lamb chops are marinated in shallots and plum wine, mashed potatoes are infused with wasabe, and ravioli comes bathed in an herb-miso cream sauce. *636 Emerson St (between Hamilton and Forest Aves), Palo Alto; (650) 323-WEST; $$.*

I Gatti ☆☆☆   With its sponge-painted mustard and red-brown walls, weathered wooden shutters, and terra-cotta floor tiles, I Gatti evokes a Tuscan patio on a sunny afternoon. The kitchen serves a variety of refined and intensely flavorful Italian dishes. *25 E Main St (near University Ave), Los Gatos; (408) 399-5180; $$$.*

Il Postale ☆☆   Although the owner insists that his welcoming little trattoria serves Italian-American bistro food, that designation doesn't begin to describe the ambitious, interesting menu. *127 W Washington St (near Murphy Ave), Sunnyvale; (408) 733-9600; $$.*

Invitation House ☆☆   Set on Rockaway Beach, this large, two-level restaurant serves very good Korean and Japanese food in a modern setting softened by Asian artifacts. *270 Rockaway Beach Ave (just W of Hwy 1), Pacifica; (650) 738-8588; $$.*

John Bentley's Restaurant ☆☆☆   Housed in Woodside's first firehouse, John Bentley's resembles a snug cabin inside and out. In keeping with the atmosphere of backwoods elegance, the fare is bold yet refined. *2991 Woodside Rd (between Hwy 280 and Cañada Rd), Woodside; (650) 851-4988; $$$.*

L'Amie Donia ☆☆☆   At this amiable, bustling French bistro and wine bar, expect traditional favorites such as onion soup and steak bordelaise with pommes frites dished up in a pleasant space that's dominated by a zinc bar. *530 Bryant St (between University and Hamilton Aves), Palo Alto; (650) 323-7614; $$$.*

La Taqueria ☆☆   Don't expect a wide variety here, for the staff just churns out what it does best: fresh and delicious burritos, taco, and quesadillas. *15 S 1st St (at Santa Clara St), San Jose; (408) 287-1542; $.*

Lark Creek Cafe ☆☆   This inviting, casual-chic cafe serves what the owner likes to call "seasonal farm-fresh American fare," a concept that translates into updated versions of classic stick-to-your-ribs dishes. *50 E 3rd Ave (near El Camino Real, in the Benjamin Franklin Hotel), San Mateo; (650) 344-9444; $$.*

Los Gatos Brewing Company ☆   This cheery, upscale techno-barn of a restaurant has something for everyone: good, house-made beers and ales for the thirsty, a lively singles scene for the action-oriented, and good pub fare for the hungry. *130-G N Santa Cruz Ave (at Grays Lane), Los Gatos; (408) 395-9929; $$.*

Maddalena's Continental Restaurant ☆☆☆   If your mood is romantic, your culinary craving continental, and your wallet well padded, it's time to slip on your glad rags and head over to Maddalena's. *544 Emerson St (between University and Hamilton Aves), Palo Alto; (650) 326-6082; $$$.*

Michaels at Shoreline ☆   On a warm, sunny day, an alfresco lunch at this upscale cafeteria is like a mini-vacation. The food, while nothing fancy, is quite good, and the setting wonderfully relaxing. *2960 N Shoreline Blvd (near Rengstorff House), Mountain View; (650) 962-1014; $.*

Moss Beach Distillery ☆☆   With its blue-painted walls, cozy dining alcoves, and windows affording magnificent ocean views, this cliff-side landmark has a beguiling 1920s beach-house atmosphere and tasty, creative California-Mediterranean dishes. *On Beach Way at Ocean Blvd (from Hwy 1, take the Cypress Ave turnoff and turn right on Marine Blvd, which turns into Beach Way), Moss Beach; (650) 728-5595; $$.*

Orlo's ☆☆☆   If dining on new American cuisine in a splendid Old World setting appeals to you, Orlo's is well worth the trip. The seasonal menu, which stresses fresh, first-rate ingredients, stops just short of fussy. *200 Edenvale Ave (from Hwy 101, turn W on Blossom Hill Rd, then right on Lean Ave, which turns into Edenvale Ave), San Jose; (408) 226-3200; $$$.*

The Palace ☆☆☆   The Palace is an apt enough name for this amazing endeavor. The interior has the feel of a grand movie set, and the inventive tapas menu is as delicious as it is beautifully presented. *146 S Murphy Ave (between Washington and Evelyn Aves), Sunnyvale; (408) 739-5179; $$.*

Paolo's ☆☆☆   A longtime San Jose institution, Paolo's handsome facility may have a bit of a Corporate America feel, but the flavorful food is authentically Italian. *333 W San Carlos St (between Woz Way and Almaden Blvd), San Jose; (408) 294-2558; $$$.*

Peninsula Fountain & Grill ☆   After its recent remodeling, this longtime downtown favorite looks suspiciously like those faux-'50s diners cropping up all over the place, but make no mistake about it: this is the genuine article. *566 Emerson St (at Hamilton Ave), Palo Alto; (650) 323-3131; $.*

Pigalle ☆☆   Playing off its name, some Los Gatos residents have affectionately dubbed this French bistro "Pig Alley" because of the generous, reasonably priced portions served here. *27 N Santa Cruz Ave (near Main St), Los Gatos; (408) 395-7924; $$.*

The Redwood Cafe & Spice Company ☆☆   This pretty blue Victorian house with lovely gardens is celebrated for its wonderful breakfast dishes. The cafe also attracts a sizable lunch crowd. *1020 Main St (at Middlefield Rd), Redwood City; (650) 366-1498; $.*

Ristorante Piacere ☆☆   This mid-sized restaurant serves good Northern and Southern Italian cuisine in an attractive, modern setting that somehow manages to be stylish enough for a special night out yet friendly enough for family dining. *727 Laurel St (near Cherry St), San Carlos; (650) 592-3536; $$.*

San Benito House ☆☆   This pastel blue Victorian on Main Street has a candle-lit dining room that's one of the prettiest on the central coast. At lunch, the deli cafe turns out topnotch sandwiches; at dinnertime, interesting California-Mediterranean fare. *356 Main St (at Mill St), Half Moon Bay; (650) 726-3425; $$.*

San Jose Tied House Cafe and Brewery ☆   This better-than-average brewery restaurant draws crowds with its high-quality beers and something-for-everyone menu. The noisy, boisterous atmosphere may prove a little wearing if you enjoy hearing yourself think. *65 N San Pedro St (between Santa Clara and Saint John Sts), San Jose; (408) 295-2739; $$.*

Sent Soví ☆☆☆☆   The dining room is a study in understated elegance, with copper wainscoting, and dramatic dried flower-and-fruit garlands, but Sent Soví's principal draw is the contemporary French cuisine. *14583 Big Basin Way (at 5th St), Saratoga; (408) 867-3110; $$$.*

71 Saint Peter ☆☆   Spanish floor tiles, flowers, exposed brick walls, and crisp linens help create a feeling of rustic elegance at this tiny and romantic Mediterranean bistro, a theme echoed by the robust yet refined cuisine. *71 N San Pedro St (between Saint John and Santa Clara Sts), San Jose; (408) 971-8523; $$.*

Spiedo Ristorante ☆☆   Good Italian regional fare is served in an attractive, modern setting at this family-friendly restaurant. The owners are justly proud of their mesquite-fired rotisserie, and the kitchen also has a pleasant way with pasta. *223 4th Ave (between Ellsworth and B Sts), San Mateo; (650) 375-0818; $$.*

Sushi Main Street ☆☆   The food is Japanese, the decor is Balinese, and the background music might be anything from up-tempo Latin to bebop American. Hard to envision, but these elements come together beautifully at this funky yet tranquil oasis in the heart of town. *696 Mill St (just off Main St), Half Moon Bay; (650) 726-6336; $$.*

Tavern Grill ☆☆   This upscale bar and grill opened in 1995 and immediately won raves for its stylish ambience and delicious Cal-Med-American fare. The menu's focus is now on American bistro dishes. *1448 Burlingame Ave (4 doors E of El Camino), Burlingame; (650) 344-5692; $$.*

Tony & Alba's Pizza and Italian Food ☆   When newly arrived East Coast transplants start complaining about California's dearth of good pizza joints, one way to shut them up is to spirit them to Tony & Alba's. *619 Escuela Ave (between El Camino Real and Latham St), Mountain View; (650) 968-5089; $. 3137 Stevens Creek Blvd (at Winchester Blvd), San Jose; (408) 246-4605; $. 864 Blossom Hill Rd (in the shopping plaza, at Santa Theresa Blvd), San Jose; (408) 227-8669; $.*

2030 ☆☆   One of the best spots to grab a bite on this stretch of Broadway is 2030, a stylish restaurant serving generous portions of California and American regional food. Dinners feature an exciting lineup of ever-changing entrees. *2030 Broadway (between Jefferson and Main Sts), Redwood City; (650) 363-2030; $$.*

2 Fools Cafe and Market ☆☆   This small, pleasantly modern restaurant is a favorite with locals and visitors alike. Breakfast includes waffles and breakfast burritos, while the lunch menu concentrates on fresh salads and sandwiches. Dinner entrees run the gamut of satisfying, home-cooked meals. *408 Main St (near Mill St), Half Moon Bay; (650) 712-1222; $$.*

Vietnam Restaurant ☆   Yes, the walls could use a coat of paint, some new linoleum wouldn't hurt, and those paper lanterns have seen better days, but this family-run restaurant is still one of the best spots on the Peninsula for Vietnamese food. *1010 Doyle St (at Menlo Ave), Menlo Park; (650) 326-2501; $.*

Viognier ☆☆☆   This light and airy 160-seat dining room echoes the intriguing menu's Mediterranean theme, with garlands of dried flowers and herbs, polished ash floors, a dramatic central fireplace, and an open kitchen. *222 4th Ave (at B St), San Mateo; (650) 685-3727; $$$.*

Lodgings

Cypress Inn on Miramar Beach ☆☆☆   This cheerful wooden building, literally 10 steps away from Miramar Beach, has skylights, terra-cotta tiles, colorful folk art, and 12 rooms with warm, rustic furniture made of pine, heavy wicker, and leather—sort of a Santa-Fe-meets-California effect. *407 Mirada Rd (drive 3 miles N of the junction of Hwys 92 and 1, turn W on*

Medio Rd, and follow it to the end), Half Moon Bay; (650) 726-6002 or (800) 83-BEACH; $$$.

The Garden Court Hotel ☆☆☆ If you like elegance, pampering, and a happening location (well, some people may not), this is a darn good place to stay. A flower-laden courtyard, providing the balcony view for most of the 62 Mediterranean modern rooms, is studded with colorful tile work and hand-wrought-iron fixtures. *520 Cowper St (between University and Hamilton Aves), Palo Alto; (650) 322-9000 or (800) 824-9028; $$$.*

Hotel De Anza ☆☆☆ Renovations that took 10 months and $10 million brought this 1931 grande dame back to life after years of decay. The richly colored Moorish ceilings in the De Anza Room and the Hedley Club are art deco jewels, and the same design influence can be felt in the 99 guest rooms. *233 W Santa Clara St (at Almaden Blvd), San Jose; (408) 286-1000 or (800) 843-3700; $$$.*

Hyatt Sainte Claire ☆☆☆ This gracious Spanish revival–style hostelry was built in 1926. The 170 recently refurbished guest rooms (including 14 one-bedroom suites and a grand suite boasting two fireplaces and a library) feature feather beds, dual phone lines with high-speed modems, safes, and minibars among the other usual first-class amenities. *302 S Market St (at San Carlos St), San Jose; (408) 885-1234 or (800) 233-1234; $$$.*

Madison Street Inn ☆☆ Two gigantic pepper trees and a white picket fence studded with roses guard this restored Victorian house just minutes from downtown. The 6 guest rooms are small and quaint. If the smallness of the rooms begins to get to you, you can lounge by the pool and hot tub. *1390 Madison St (at Lewis St), Santa Clara; (408) 249-5541 or (800) 491-5541; $$.*

Old Thyme Inn ☆ A comfortable and informal B&B, this 1899 Victorian house sits on the quiet southern end of Main Street. Floral wallpapers and bedspreads, rustic antiques, and lots of teddy bears grace the 7 cozy guest rooms, each of which is named after one of the fragrant herbs in the inn's garden. *779 Main St (near Filbert St), Half Moon Bay; (650) 726-1616; $$–$$$.*

Oyster Point Marina Inn ☆☆ This small, pleasant Cape Cod–style inn works hard to accentuate the positive (30 rooms decked out in a snappy nautical color scheme, a spectacular bay setting) and diminish the negative (the fact that you have to wade through an industrial park to get here). *425 Marina Blvd (take the Oyster Pt Blvd exit off US 101, head toward the bay, and turn right at Marina Blvd), South San Francisco; (650) 737-7633; $$$.*

Pillar Point Inn ☆☆   Located on a bustling harbor, this modern inn is surprisingly quiet. Cheery and reminiscent of Cape Cod, the inn's 11 sunny, smallish rooms have harbor views, private baths, gas fireplaces, feather beds, and televisions with VCRs. *380 Capistrano Rd (4 miles N of Half Moon Bay on Hwy 1, then W on Capistrano Rd), Princeton; (650) 728-7377 or (800) 400-8281; $$$.*

Rancho San Gregorio ☆☆   This Spanish Mission–style bed and breakfast, with its terra-cotta tile floors, heavy oak antiques, and redwood-beamed ceilings, is a well-tended, unpretentious home-away-from-home. The 4 guest rooms are decorated in Native American, Southwestern, and Early California motifs. *5086 San Gregorio Rd (about 5 miles inland on Hwy 84), San Gregorio; (650) 747-0810; $$–$$$.*

Seal Cove Inn ☆☆☆   This gracious, sophisticated B&B somehow manages to harmoniously blend California, New England, and European influences in a spectacular seacoast setting. The large, vaguely English-style country manor has 10 bedrooms that overlook a wildflower garden. *221 Cypress Ave (6 miles N of Half Moon Bay on Hwy 1, then W on Cypress Ave), Moss Beach; (650) 728-7325; $$$.*

Stanford Park Hotel ☆☆☆   Cedar shingles, dormer windows, serene courtyards, and a copper-clad gabled roof distinguish this gracious low-rise hotel near Stanford University. Some of the 163 rooms have fireplaces, balconies, or courtyard views and all are appointed with handsome English-style furniture and splashed with accents of green and mauve. *100 El Camino Real (just N of University Ave), Menlo Park; (650) 322-1234 or (800) 368-2468; $$$.*

The Zaballa House ☆☆   The oldest building in Half Moon Bay, this 1859 pastel blue Victorian offers a few amenities that go beyond the usual B&B offerings—including the ghost that reportedly walks through the wall in room 9 now and then. Homey, pretty, and unpretentious, the nine guest rooms in the main house are decorated with understated wallpaper and country furniture. *324 Main St (at the N end of town), Half Moon Bay; (650) 726-9123; $$–$$$.*

More Information

Brisbane Chamber of Commerce: *(650) 467-7283.*
Burlingame Chamber of Commerce: *(650) 344-1735.*
Half Moon Bay Chamber of Commerce: *(650) 726-8380.*
Henry W. Coe State Park: *(408) 779-2728.*
Mid-Peninsula Regional Open Space District: *(650) 691-1200,*
    www.openspace.org.

Morgan Hill Chamber of Commerce: *(408) 779-9444.*
Mountain View Chamber of Commerce: *(650) 968-8378.*
Pacifica Chamber of Commerce: *(650) 355-4122.*
Palo Alto Chamber of Commerce: *(650) 324-3121.*
San Bruno Chamber of Commerce: *(650) 588-0180.*
San Jose Convention and Visitors Bureau: *(408) 295-9600.*
San Jose Metropolitan Chamber of Commerce: *(408) 291-5250.*
San Mateo Chamber of Commerce: *(650) 341-5679.*
San Mateo County Parks and Recreation Department: *(650) 363-4020.*
State beaches: *(650) 726-8800.*
State parks camping reservations: *(800) 444-7275.*
Sunnyvale Chamber of Commerce: *(408) 736-4971.*

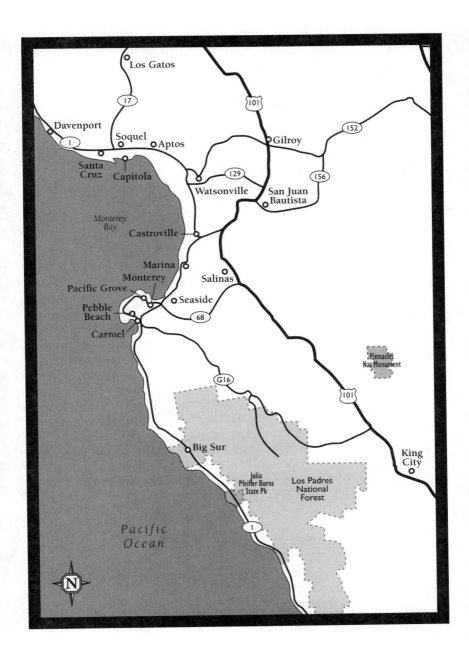

Big Sur

Santa Cruz

The Santa Cruz County coast and mountains from the San Mateo County and Santa Clara County borders to the north, and from the Monterey County border to the south, including Henry Cowell and Big Basin Redwoods State Parks, and the Santa Cruz beach and boardwalk areas.

Roller coasters, vampires, and hippies—this could easily be the image you have of Santa Cruz. There is much more to this place, however, than the Santa Cruz Beach Boardwalk amusement park with its thrill rides, B horror films like *The Lost Boys,* and Summer of Love holdouts who have migrated south from San Francisco in the past 30 years.

First of all, it was here—in the Santa Cruz Mountains, not in Humboldt County—that the campaign to save the redwoods began a century ago, when logging companies (yes, that's right) donated large tracts of lands to form Big Basin Redwoods State Park (California's first). And while logging has taken its toll here as elsewhere throughout the state, stunning old-growth groves are preserved permanently in the mountains north of town—no need to head way north to see one. Logging, in fact, has an anomalous reputation in these parts: Santa Cruz is the home of Big Creek Lumber Company, an operation that seldom draws the ire of environmentalists because it has a reputation for practicing sustainable forestry (the *Wall Street Journal* calls them "the friendly loggers.") A layperson venturing into some of the company's previously logged groves wouldn't immediately be able to see anything amiss, because the company practices selective logging in which the forest is "thinned" but not clear-cut.

Second, it is a known fact that the best thrill ride in town is not on a roller coaster, but on the breaks all along the 40-mile coast, which boasts some of the most consistently good surfing in Northern California. State and local beaches on the Pacific and the Monterey Bay contain enough varied surfing spots that all skill levels are covered; some are also staffed with lifeguards during the summer peak season and are protected enough for swimming.

Third, Santa Cruz is happening enough to have its own University of California campus, just like Berkeley and Los Angeles do (though for the most part it's not as prestigious). Because of this, expect to see college students—not just traveling families and hippies—sharing the beaches, campgrounds, and trails.

On a perfect day in Santa Cruz, the fishing rod, the mountain bike, the surfboard, the ice chest, the suntan lotion, the backpack, and the tent are all going to come in handy. Camp on the beach; take a two-day hike from the redwood-forested mountains to the ocean. When you peel away this town's undeserved reputation as a washed-out hippie enclave crawling with rambunctious children scurrying from ride to ride at the amusement park, you will find that there's a wealth of outdoor beauty to enjoy.

And you don't even need a ticket to ride.

Getting There

From the San Francisco Bay Area, take Highway 17 through the Santa Cruz Mountains south from San Jose. Highway 1, the Coast Highway, is the main thoroughfare from San Mateo to the north and Monterey to the south. These are the main thoroughfares moving traffic in and out of the region. There is no rail system in Santa Cruz, but the Santa Cruz Metropolitan Transit District, (831) 425-8600, runs buses throughout, including along the beachfront.

Adjoining Areas

NORTH: **Peninsula and South Bay**
SOUTH: **Monterey Bay**
EAST: **San Joaquin Valley**

inside out

Beaches/Swimming

Wide, sandy beaches with waters calm enough for swimming. Narrow, rocky shores where the surf and rips are wild, the bluffs tall, and great whites lurk offshore. Roller coasters and Ferris wheels; wildlife sanctuaries and marine preserves; surfboards and inflatable rafts—in 40 miles along the Santa Cruz coast, you'll find all of the above. It is a grab bag of contradictions, but that's a plus, because it means a family stuffed in a minivan can have just as much fun here as the hardcore outdoor sportster whose SUV doesn't even have power steering. Most of the larger beaches are owned and managed by the state parks department; the Santa Cruz district office can be reached at (831) 429-2850. Some popular spots are also owned and managed by the cities of Santa Cruz and Capitola. Santa Cruz city lifeguards have daily **weather and surf information,** (831) 429-3460.

Just a few miles within the northern end of Santa Cruz County along the Coast Highway, the fun begins. **Waddell Creek Beach,** adjacent to Big Basin Redwoods State Park (see Parks, below), is the first coastal access point in the Santa Cruz region, just a mile past the San Mateo County line. The beach is a prime spot for surfing, sailboarding, rock fishing, and—because of a nice wetland area and easily accessible tide pools—viewing a variety of aquatic wildlife. It's a little too cool and breezy most of the time for sunbathing, however. The beach parking area is near the Big Creek Lumber Company lumber yard and north of the quaint little seaside town of Davenport, where the corporate headquarters and main processing plant for Odwalla juices is located. Along the next 10 miles of coast are a series of small, undeveloped beaches, the nicest being **Scott Creek Beach,** because of its expansive wetland area and seclusion from the highway. Access is by roadside trail only, however, and the sand is just a sliver. The beach is at the spot where Scott Creek meets the Pacific, west of the Coast Highway and some 3 miles north of Davenport Landing. Park on the side of the highway, but only where safe. **Wilder Ranch State Park,** just west of the University of Santa Cruz and Henry Cowell Redwoods State Park (see Parks, below), has 20 miles of easily accessible hiking trails and a well-developed beachfront accessible enough that its no problem getting Grandma and the baby down to the bottom of the bluffs (although there are some stairs). Wilder Ranch is not, however, a wild beach experience: it has historical buildings, a dairy museum, rest rooms, and a pay parking lot, so don't go there expecting to be alone with the ocean. The beach is 4 miles north of the city of Santa Cruz; look for the parking area signs. For information, call (831) 429-2850.

Another good nature-viewing area is **Natural Bridges State Beach,** where—as the name would suggest—"natural bridge" rock formations are an interesting spectacle. This is also a study area for **monarch butterflies,** which migrate through in the winter and early spring; guided tours of the butterfly preserve are given on weekends. You'll find expansive tide-pool nature study areas here as well. The beach is west of the Coast Highway; take the Mission St turnoff west just south of the Long Marine Laboratory, then turn west on Natural Bridges Dr. Call (831) 423-4609 for information.

The **city of Santa Cruz beaches** are located just south of Natural Bridges, with access along the west side of W Cliff Dr (all streets heading west of the Coast Highway meet the city's waterfront). Just around the bend from Point Santa Cruz, where the surfing museum (see Attractions, below) and **Lighthouse Field State Beach** are located, you will find **Cowell Beach.** This 1.5-mile band of sandy beach, rocky shores, picnic and rock fishing spots, and coastal hiking trails between the point and the city's municipal pier are more like a suburban community recreation area than pristine oceanfront wilderness, especially on warm summer days. Keep heading south, and the municipal wharf, beach, boardwalk, and amusement park come into clearer view. While the beaches here are coved and calm enough for swimming in the summer (lifeguards are on duty during peak season), the water is just as chilly as along the rest of the Northern California coast. And the Disneyland atmosphere of the **boardwalk amusement park** (see Attractions, below) draws scads of people who aren't necessarily here for the sand and surf. If the family fun and screaming teens on summer break aren't your scene, head north or south. The beach and boardwalk are owned and managed by a private entertainment company. Call (831) 426-7433 for information.

At **Twin Lakes State Beach** and the adjacent **Schwan Lagoon,** both south of the boardwalk area, the coast starts to feel a bit more wild. The beach at Twin Lakes includes the popular **San Lorenzo Point** walkway, which extends out from the east side of the San Lorenzo River mouth onto Monterey Bay, offering stunning vistas of the marine sanctuary. The lagoon area is a waterfowl preserve, and the point where it meets Monterey Bay on the Twin Lakes beach is an interesting spot to study marine plants and invertebrates. Volleyball nets and beach fire rings are available. Call (831) 429-2850 for information. Take Soquel Dr from the Coast Highway west to Seventh Ave, then follow Seventh to E Cliff Dr, and the beach parking areas.

On toward the south, a string of city and county beaches with access points along 3 miles of E Cliff Dr includes two popular surfing spots: **Pleasure Point Beach** and **Opal Cliffs Key Beach.** Take 41st Ave west from the Coast Highway in Soquel to reach this area directly. Other popular activities along this stretch of scenic overlooks, rocky cliffs, and wide, sandy beaches include biking, tidepooling, hiking, and surf walks. The overlook at the end of 41st Ave is a great place to watch surfers.

Another mile to the south are the **Capitola City Beach** and adjacent municipal fishing wharf, popular areas for volleyball, swimming (lifeguards on duty during peak season), kayaking, boating, sailing, and fishing. Note, however, that the Capitola beach is lined with trendy shops, restaurants, and art galleries. This area is best accessed west from the Coast Highway on Bay Ave in Capitola. Call (831) 462-2208.

This is where the character of the Santa Cruz coast really begins to lose its ambience of a Disneyland-on-the-sea and take on more of a rural feel. Along the Coast Highway, artichoke fields replace the beachfront as the roadway departs the shore and heads into an agricultural zone. Don't fret, however. The beaches are still there, you just have to work to find them. **New Brighton State Beach** is a popular seaside camping spot (see Camping, below) just south of Capitola—and off the beaten path a bit; the retail establishments that dominate the boardwalk and downtown Capitola areas are absent here. In their place is a large wildlife area with regularly scheduled interpretive tours. Call (831) 429-2850 for information. New Brighton is west of the Coast Highway on Park Ave in Capitola.

Between Capitola and the mouth of the Pajaro River, both **Manresa Beach State Park** and **Sunset State Beach** are nice camping spots on the shore (see Camping, below). While this end of the Santa Cruz shore is not recommended for swimmers because of the powerful rip currents, it is a popular rock-fishing area. Cyclists can enjoy the 10 miles of trails following the Pajaro River. Call (831) 429-2850 for information. The best driving access to this stretch of coast is either west on San Andreas Rd from the Coast Highway in La Selva Beach or on Beach Rd in Watsonville.

Surfing/Windsurfing

The Santa Cruz coast has numerous consistently good **surfing** spots, some small and at times shielded adequately enough from ocean breezes to be suitable for beginners. In general, the larger, wilder breaks occur at the northern reaches of the coast, such as at **Waddell Creek Beach** (see Beaches/Swimming, above) just south of the San Mateo County line and the popular and infamous **Steamer's Lane** north of the Santa Cruz beach and boardwalk area. Both of these spots are considered expert surf turf, with breaks in excess of 20 feet not unheard of—so don't jump in unless you're experienced enough to know how to blend in and adhere to the local surfers' pecking order. Fatal freak accidents involving experienced surfers have been tallied at both locations, and Waddell has seen its share of sharks. Both are flanked by rocky shores. A more suitable beginner's spot is **Cowell Beach** (see Beaches/Swimming, above), a family surfing area where the breaks are small and tame enough for parents to bring their children out to test the waters. **Pleasure Point Beach** and **Opal Cliffs Key Beach** are also popular surf spots south of the boardwalk, but often too rough for beginners.

Santa Cruz is a sort of tough bet for beginning **board sailors** because of the high winds and large breaks at many of the popular beaches. **Waddell Creek Beach** (see Beaches/Swimming, above) is an expert windsurfing site, also popular with surfers. Rips, large breaks, direct ocean winds, and rocky shores make this a place where you must be alert at all times if you jump in. The inexperienced are better off watching and practicing elsewhere first (see Windsurfing, East Bay chapter). The one local spot a beginner may find suitable, however, is **Cowell Beach** (see Beaches/Swimming, above), which is not as wide open. Once you're up, however, a lot of the time you'll be ready to move on.

The Santa Cruz shores get both north and south swells, so be sure to check on conditions before venturing out. Santa Cruz city lifeguards have daily **weather and surf information**, (831) 429-3460. Another good resource is the Surfrider Foundation Santa Cruz chapter Web site, www. gate.cruzio.com/~surfride/, which posts up-to-date **surf condition reports.** Also note that as with virtually all of the Northern California coast, the water off these beaches is downright chilly—don't venture in without a full wet suit. And finally, watch out for fishing lines, board sailors, boats, and other potential hazards in the water.

Club Ed Surf School, on Cowell Beach, is one of numerous good places to check for **instruction, rentals,** and good advice, (831) 459-9283. Also try Cowell Beach N Bikini Surf Shop, 109 Beach St, (831) 427-2355, or, farther south, O'Neill, 2222 E Cliff Dr, (831) 476-5200.

Boating/Sailing

Boating in and around Santa Cruz is mostly centered around sportfishing—but there is life here for sailors, too, as the bay has suitable ocean breezes and smooth spots for learning. The **Santa Cruz Small Craft Harbor** offers 1,000 berths and a boat ramp that is open 24 hours. Boat rentals are also available at the harbor, west of the Coast Highway via either Morrissey Blvd or La Fonda Ave. Call (831) 475-6161. Santa Cruz Boat Rentals at the harbor has skiffs, bait, and tackle available, (831) 423-1739. More public **moorings** and **rentals** can be found at the Capitola Bay Marina, 1400 Wharf Dr, (831) 462-2208.

Charters are also available around the bay. Chardonnay Sailing Charters, Santa Cruz Harbor, offers luxury yacht whale-watching excursions and ecology tours. Pacific Yachting and Sailing, 790 Mariner Park Way, (831) 423-7245, offers both charters and a **sailing school** for beginners and advanced sailors. Another way to get out on the water is on the harbor **water taxi,** a free shuttle service that stops at numerous locations around the bay and along the Santa Cruz coast, homeported out of the city harbor, (831) 475-6161.

Fishing

The best game in town is river fishing for **steelhead** (and sometimes **salmon**) on the San Lorenzo River in Henry Cowell Redwoods State Park (see Parks and Camping, below). From October to March, the river is stocked and open to anglers. A year-round campground is located near the best fishing spots, or just drop in for a day outing. This area is perfect for children just learning, and there's plenty of room to spread out and find your own spot despite the popularity of the San Lorenzo. Another nice spot, also stocked with steelhead, and particularly suitable for **young anglers** who are just learning, is Camp Evers Fishing Park in Scotts Valley on Glenn Canyon Rd, not far from Cowell, (831) 438-3251.

This is, however, the Monterey Bay sanctuary area—meaning **rock fishing, pier fishing** from the shore, and **ocean fishing** are the main fare for anglers. **Rock cod** and **lingcod** bounties are terrific in this area, and decent **salmon** fishing in the bay and its environs is not unheard of, just a little less predictable. As we were reminded in the winter of 1997–98, unusual sea surface temperatures can send the fisheries out of whack; as El Niño brought more tropical varieties of fish to these shores. Popular rock fishing sites include Waddell Creek Beach and the adjacent Greyhound Rock fishing area established by the state Department of Fish and Game. Take the Coast Highway 2 miles south from Waddell Creek Beach, and descend from the highway on a stairway to the beach at Greyhound. Pier fishing is allowed along the Santa Cruz Municipal Wharf, which has boat rentals and fishing licenses available on site, (831) 423-1739, and the Capitola fishing wharf south of the Capitola City Beach, which has a tackle shop on site. If you'd rather try your luck out at sea, visit Capitola Boat & Bait at the end of the pier. Even if you don't know an outboard from a Ouija board, the friendly staff has faith that you'll bring their fishing boats back in one piece. Rates are reasonable and include fuel, safety equipment, and a map of the hot fishing spots. You can also rent fishing gear and purchase one-day licenses, so there's no excuse not to brave the open ocean just for the halibut; closed January to mid-February, 1400 Wharf Rd, (831) 462-2208. Manresa Beach State Park and Sunset State Beach (see Beaches/Swimming, above) are also good rock fishing points—especially since there are rarely swimmers or surfers to watch out for.

To hit the open waters with a **sportfishing excursion,** check with Santa Cruz Sportfishing at Santa Cruz Harbor, (831) 426-4690; Shamrock Charters, 2210 E Cliff Dr, (831) 476-2648; or Stagnaro's Fishing Trips, on the Santa Cruz Municipal Wharf, (831) 427-2334.

Parks

As corny as it sounds, it's really true. There's something about the **red-woods**—those ancient giants facing the Pacific—that helps you appreciate just how wide, and deep, and mysterious our wild places are. Once a 30-mile-wide band stretching from just past the Oregon border through the Monterey coast 500 miles south, the redwoods have unquestionably suffered from more than 150 years of timber-harvesting that exploded with the gold rush population boom. Thanks to the work of preservationists beginning nearly a century ago, however, the trees were not completely lost: millions of acres of virgin forest have been locked up in public parks and preserves.

In fact, **Big Basin Redwoods State Park,** northeast of Santa Cruz, is where the "Save the Redwoods" campaign began in California in 1900. Two years later, Big Basin became the very first state park, as area logging companies agreed either to sell or donate toeholds of virgin forest as open space. Today, Big Basin has expanded to nearly 20,000 acres, and is still growing. There are more than 80 miles of hiking trails (easy, short walks and butt-kickers both) and camping areas diverse enough to suit everyone from the serious backpacker to the family on an outing (see Camping, below). Deep river canyons, waterfalls, high exposed ridges, and a rare coastal freshwater marsh at the mouth of nearby Waddell Creek (see Beaches/Swimming, above) make this an ideal place for the redwood experience. There are horseback riding trails and camps, a nature education program, picnic areas, and fishing holes. To reach the park, take Hwy 9 from the Coast Highway just north of Santa Cruz to Hwy 236 (left), which continues to the park entrance. For more information, call the park at (831) 338-8860.

On Hwy 9 before Big Basin is another prime Santa Cruz redwood forest recreation area, **Henry Cowell Redwoods State Park.** While Cowell is smaller, with just 15 miles of hiking and riding trails to Basin's 80, it has the added interest of a spring wildflower meadow near the entrance and a more diverse range of plant life, including a rare stand of ponderosa pine. The park is named for Henry Cowell, a Gold Rush–era entrepreneur who at the turn of the century was the wealthiest resident of Santa Cruz County, and its principal landholder. In the 1950s his heirs donated some 1,600 acres of the park to the state. Today, riverside picnic areas, campgrounds (see Camping, below), a nature center, and a self-guided redwood forest ecology tour make Cowell an excellent choice for parents who want to teach their children about the forest and its inhabitants. Salmon fishing in the San Lorenzo River, which passes through the park, has been lousy the past several years, but the in-season steelhead trout fishing (see

Fishing, above) can still be strong. Call the park at (831) 335-4598.

Forest of Nisene Marks State Park near Aptos covers some 10,000 acres of formerly logged redwood forests extending from the coast to peaks 2,500 feet above Monterey Bay. There are 30 miles of trails, some through areas where remnants of the erstwhile logging operation are still apparent. A formerly logged redwood area is a great place to study redwood forest ecology. Second-growth trees sprout in a crown from the stumps of larger felled trees, and numerous examples, along with other logging aftereffects, can be found here. Take the Coast Highway to Aptos Creek Rd, then go north 4 miles to the park entrance. Call the park at (831) 763-7062 for more information.

Camping

What an ordeal: having to choose between sleeping by the beach or sleeping in the redwoods. In Santa Cruz, how about a night or two of each?

Henry Cowell Redwoods State Park (see Parks, above) has 112 sites situated around a peak above the San Lorenzo River floodplain (no hookups; RV limit 35 feet). Each site has a fire pit and picnic table; running water, showers, and toilets are nearby. *Call the state parks reservations system, (800) 444-7275. The park may be contacted directly at (831) 335-4598. From Santa Cruz, take the Central Santa Cruz turnoff from the Coast Hwy to Hwy 9 east, and continue about 3 miles to the park entrance.*

Big Basin Redwoods State Park has 107 car camping sites (no hookups; RV limit 27 feet), 48 backpacking sites (only 10 of those a long haul), and a nice horseback camp. There also are tent cabins for rent. Each of the 107 main sites has a fire pit and picnic table with showers, rest rooms, and toilets nearby. *Call the state parks reservation system at (800) 444-7275 for campsites. For tent cabin information, call the park directly at (800) 874-8368. The park is 23 miles east of Santa Cruz city on Hwy 236. Take Hwy 9 from the Coast Hwy, then head north (left) on Hwy 236 another 10 miles to the park headquarters.*

New Brighton State Beach (see Beaches/Swimming, above), has 112 car camping sites (partial hookups; RV limit 31 feet) on bluffs overlooking the beaches and Monterey Bay in Santa Cruz County's agricultural southern end. Each site has a picnic table and a fire pit, with showers, toilets, and running water nearby. *Call state parks reservations at (800) 444-7275. The beach may be contacted directly by calling (831) 429-2850. Take the Capitola–New Brighton Beach exit west from the Coast Hwy to the campground entrance.*

Seacliff State Beach's campground is smaller and therefore more desirable, on bluffs overlooking the bay, with just 6 sites (full hookups;

RV limit 40 feet). Each site has a table and a fire pit, with showers, toilets, and running water nearby. *Call the state parks reservations at (800) 444-7275. The beach may be contacted directly at (831) 688-3222. Take the Seacliff Beach exit from the Coast Hwy west to the park entrance.*

Manresa Beach State Park south of Capitola has 64 sites (no hookups; RV limit 31 feet), each with a picnic table and a fire pit, with running water, showers, and toilets nearby. The campground is on a wooded bluff area overlooking Monterey Bay. *Make reservations and arrive early to get a beachfront site. Call state parks reservations, (800) 444-7275. The beach may be contacted directly at (831) 724-3750. From the Coast Hwy south of Capitola, take the San Andreas Rd exit to Sand Dollar Dr and go west to the park entrance.*

Sunset State Beach has 90 car camping sites (partial hookups; RV limit 31 feet) on bluffs overlooking Monterey Bay. Each has a picnic table and a fire pit, with running water, toilets, and showers nearby. *Call state parks reservations, (800) 444-7275. The beach may be contacted directly by calling (831) 763-7063. From the Coast Hwy, take the Riverside Dr exit to Beach Rd, then take San Andreas Rd right to the beach area.*

Hiking/Backpacking

With more than 100 miles of hiking trails, the redwood state parks northeast of Santa Cruz provide some of the best outdoor romps anywhere in Northern California. Leave plenty of time, however, to explore the coast, which also has its share of nice trails for exploring the waterfront of Monterey Bay.

The best hikes in the Santa Cruz region are without question within **Big Basin Redwoods State Park,** not only because the forested canyons are cool and shady and gorgeous, but also because of the waterfalls, which push this place so far over the top you'll be pinching yourself to make sure you aren't in a dream. A waterfall is a great reward for day hikers who like to rest in the cool spray of the river before sweating it back to the trailhead. Got half a day to kill? A great way to spend it is by trekking off to take a gander at **Berry Creek Falls** in Big Basin along the **Skyline-to-Sea Trail** (moderate; 12 miles round trip, variable depending on return route). The first few hours of this hike are spent making your way over a 1,200-foot ridge following Kelly and West Waddell Creeks, then descending into Berry Canyon, an area of thick redwoods, tall ferns, and dark mosses 600 feet below. The 70-foot waterfall at the bottom is the first of four along **Berry Creek Trail,** which climbs to the 2,300-foot peak at Sunset Trail Camp. From the camp, it's a straight shot (figuratively speaking) back to park headquarters where the hike started along **Sunset Trail,** which parallels Skyline.

A shorter waterfall that you can get to much more easily is along **Sequoia Trail** (easy; 1.5 miles round trip), a pleasant nature walk through redwood groves around Sempenvirons Creek; the walk also begins at the park headquarters. The walk to **Sempenvirons Falls** is an ideal choice for kids old enough to handle the distance.

Another popular hike within Big Basin that can be completed in under three hours is the **Meteor Trail** hike (easy to moderate; 5 miles round trip). It also begins at park headquarters, via the **Skyline-to-Sea Trail** (in the opposite direction of Berry Creek), which ascends 600 feet to Meteor, which spills off the Middle Ridge View overlook—a great place to take a look at the Pacific (if it's not fogged in, which can often be the case on mornings in the early summer).

A popular long haul at Big Basin is the **Howard King Trail/MCrary Ridge Trail/Skyline-to-Sea Trail** route (moderate to difficult; 12 miles round trip) from the Big Basin park headquarters to Waddell Creek Beach (see Beaches/Swimming, above), following the Waddell Creek watershed to the ocean. It's best to make arrangements and camping reservation for this long trek with a park ranger at one of three trail camps found along the way, (831) 338-6132. The journey, which can be accomplished as a day hike but is best as an overnight backpacking trip, follows Howard King Trail around the north flanks of the park's stunning **Mount McAbee Overlook,** then descends to the Waddell Creek canyon on McCrary Ridge Trail, which meets the western end of Skyline-to-Sea Trail at Camp Herbert Trail Camp, the first of the three camps, on the banks of Waddell Creek. The hike and camps are a fantastic way to enjoy both the redwoods and the wild beaches of the Santa Cruz coast. They're also good for wildlife viewing; the redwood-lined creeks upstream and the wide freshwater marshes at the mouth of Waddell Creek can tell you more than any ecology textbook.

It's not as easy to get lost in **Henry Cowell Redwoods State Park,** but it can certainly satisfy a hiker's thirst for some excellent redwood scenery— just note that the trails are short and interlocking, covering a small geographic area. Pick up a **trail map** at the park headquarters campground reservation kiosk, then plot a few hours of walking according to how much time you have. Be sure to get to two essential highlights: the banks of the San Lorenzo River and the park overlook. **Eagle Creek Trail** (easy; 1 mile round trip) makes a long 400-foot drop from the park campground to the banks of the river, the park's nicest feature. From the river, connect easily to **River Trail** (easy; 1.6 miles from the campground), which ends at the **Rincon Fire Road** for another easy walk 4 miles to **Ridge Fire Road.** Another 2 miles and 400 feet up along Ridge Fire Rd takes you to the park's overlook and observation deck, which provides sweeping vistas of the

Santa Cruz region and Monterey Bay. From the overlook, return to the campground below on **Pine Trail** (easy; 1 mile one way). Special hiker's note: Cowell has no bridges at **river crossings,** so when the runoff is heavy, crossing can be dicey at times. The park does, however, have two entrances—one at the main gate and another at the campground, so visitors who know which side of the river they want to visit can avoid an unwanted swim by doing a little extra planning. The park office can be reached at (831) 335-4598. Cowell is 4 miles north of Santa Cruz near Felton on Hwy 9. Take the Coast Highway south to the Hwy 9 turnoff, then head northeast to the park's main gate. The campground also can be reached via Mount Herman Rd from Hwy 17 at Scotts Valley.

The hike to **Maple Falls** along **Bridge Creek Trail** (difficult; 8 miles round trip) in **Nisene Marks State Park** (see Parks, above) follows the creek through a formerly logged but picturesque redwood canyon. At 1.5 miles, switch off to **Loma Prieta Trail** after entering a clearing with old buildings once associated with the logging operation (on left), climb up the ridge through Loma Prieta's switchbacks, then on to the falls. Another popular hike within the park is the long haul to the Sand Point Overlook along **Aptos Creek Trail** (difficult; 13 miles round trip), an overnighter through the 70-year-old second-growth redwood groves, with a backpacking camp along the way. Register with the park for a permit and map before taking this one. To reach the park office, take the Coast Highway to Aptos Creek Rd, then go north 4 miles to the park entrance. Call the park at (831) 763-7062 for more information.

A nice walk along the coast is **Old Cove Landing Trail** (easy; 1.5 miles round trip) at **Wilder Ranch State Park,** an area of historic buildings on the site of a former coastal dairy farm. Cross to the east side of the Coast Highway, and **Eucalyptus Loop Trail** (moderate; 4.5 miles round trip) extends into the park's upper reaches, toward the border with Empire Grade Rd and Henry Cowell Redwoods State Park in the Santa Cruz foothills. Call the park, (831) 423-9703, for more information. Wilder Ranch is 4 miles north of the city of Santa Cruz. Just look for the signs marking the parking areas.

Wildlife

Santa Cruz is a terrific place to observe a wide variety of wildlife. Many area parks and beaches have nature programs and ecology tours, and the National Oceanic and Atmospheric Administration's sanctuary office is a resource for extensive public **information** materials and **special events,** (831) 647-4201. The state Department of Fish and Game also has an office in Monterey, (831) 649-2870.

Bring your **birding** scope with you on any visit to the Santa Cruz–area redwood parks. Big Basin Redwoods and Henry Cowell Redwoods State Parks (see Parks, above) both present fantastic opportunities to observe the important interplay between the giant, ancient trees and select bird life. The rare **marbled murrelet,** for example, protected under the Endangered Species Act, is a fast-flying seabird whose best hope for nesting is to land in the high, widely spaced branches of old-growth redwood trees. (Younger redwoods are fuller at the tops because they have had less exposure to the ocean breezes.) Bird lovers also will come across jays, woodpeckers, quail, red-tailed hawks, owls, swallows, hummingbirds, doves, great blue herons, and numerous other species commonly found among either the cool, sheltered forests or the open peaks above them. In all, there are nearly **100 different types of seabird** documented within the Monterey sanctuary region, many attracted to the coastal redwoods habitat. The state parks nature center located within Henry Cowell's boundaries has educational materials and naturalists available to guide park visitors, (831) 335-7077.

Beaches and coastal marshes are also prime wildlife viewing areas. It is not unusual to find entire sections of the beaches north of the city overrun with **brown pelicans.** Large seasonal populations of **migratory birds** stop in along the marshes, most notably those at Waddell Creek Beach (see Beaches/Swimming, above) and **Schwan Lagoon,** a waterfowl preserve adjacent to Twin Lakes State Beach (see Beaches/Swimming, above). Endangered **clapper rails** and rare **caspian terns** are also found in this region.

With the Santa Cruz coast's many rocky shores and varied tidal zones, **tide-pool viewing** is a favorite. Most interesting are the intertidal zones, where scouters will come across any variety of odd-colored algae; bizarre invertebrates like limpets, giant green anemones, and mossy chitons; and rock-dwelling fishes like rockweed gunnels, snubnose sculpin, and the monkey-faced eel. If all of this sounds like Greek to you, call the marine sanctuary office in Monterey at (831) 647-4201, or consult an excellent joint publication of the sanctuary and the Monterey Bay Aquarium (see Attractions, Monterey Bay chapter), *A Natural History of Monterey Bay,* available from the Monterey Bay Aquarium Press, 886 Cannery Row, Monterey, CA 93940, www.mbayaq.org. The aquarium bookstore can be reached at (831) 648-4952. The best tide-pool viewing is at Waddell Creek Beach and Natural Bridges State Beach, as well as Pleasure Point Beach and Opal Cliffs Key Beach along the south shore of Santa Cruz (see Beaches/Swimming, above).

While Point Reyes National Seashore (see Point Reyes National Seashore chapter) is a far better place to catch a glimpse of migrating gray whales, **whale-watching** boat tours are easy to come by in Santa Cruz.

Many are offered by charters that also specialize in sportfishing trips or **ecology tours** of the marine sanctuary. Santa Cruz Sportfishing, at Santa Cruz Harbor, (831) 426-4690; Shamrock Charters, 2210 E Cliff Dr, (831) 476-2648; and Stagnaro's Fishing Trips, on the Santa Cruz Municipal Wharf, (831) 427-2334, can get you out to the whale viewing spots, as can Chardonnay Sailing Charters, Santa Cruz Harbor, which takes whale watchers out on a luxury yacht.

Biking

There are numerous good **road cycling** choices in the Santa Cruz region, most notably the stretch of the **Coast Highway** between Waddell Creek Beach and the Santa Cruz Beach and Boardwalk—a curved-out 25-mile seaside trek of gentle uphill grades and moderate downhills ending in the city's central recreation and entertainment area. Another good ride is at the southern end of the Santa Cruz coast along the **Pajaro River Trail,** which follows the river for 7 miles and continues into the valley for another 3 miles, with easy grades and unobstructed paved pathways. The trail begins at the mouth of the Pajaro near Palm Beach. Take the Coast Highway to San Andreas Rd south of Aptos, then continue 8 miles to the intersection with Beach Rd. Go right to the end of Beach Rd to find a place to stage. The city's **boardwalk area** surface streets are a bit too congested to get up much speed, but a bicycle is a good way to get around this area, particularly crowded on summer days when parking lots are overflowing.

Mountain bikers may want to consider the difficult 18-mile trek to China Ridge and **Sand Point Overlook** from the Seacliff State Beach area near Aptos. Take the Coast Highway to the Seacliff Beach and Pier exit, and head west a quarter mile to the trail beginning. Also consider the crisscrossing system of wide fire roads in **Henry Cowell Redwoods State Park** (see Parks, above), with excellent vistas of the bay and coast. Bontrager Cycles, 104 Bronson St, (831) 427-2121, or Santa Cruz Mountain Bikes, at the same location, (831) 459-7560, can help with **rentals, equipment, maps,** and pointers.

Adventure Calendar

Wharf to Wharf Race, fourth Sunday in July: *annual run between Santa Cruz and Capitola, limited to first 14,000 registrants,* (831) 423-1111 or (831) 475-6522.

Roughwater Swim, early August: (831) 429-3747.

Aloha Races and Polynesian Festival, late August: *canoeing competition,* (831) 423-1111.

outside in

Attractions

Santa Cruz is a chimerical place, skittering from diamond-bright beach to swampy slough to moody redwood grove to cafe society to rustic farm in just about the time it takes to say "Surf's up, dude!" The city rings the north end of Monterey Bay and is bisected by the San Lorenzo River, which spills into the sea. Santa Cruz (Spanish for "holy cross") was founded by Father Junípero Serra when he built the **Mission of the Holy Cross** here in 1791. The mission was destroyed by earthquakes in 1857 and 1858, but a half-size replica of the building (built in 1931) is open to the public every day except Monday, offering morning masses and an opportunity to view some of the mission's original books and vestments; on the corner of Emmet and High Sts, (831) 426-5686. Despite its holy beginnings, Santa Cruz is now a devil-may-care, saltwater-taffy seaside resort.

Santa Cruz attracts more than 3 million visitors each year, and most of them flock to the half-mile-long, 100-year-old **Santa Cruz Beach Boardwalk,** the last remaining beachfront amusement park on the West Coast. Take a spin on the Giant Dipper, one of the best and oldest wooden roller coasters in the country (with a great view at the top), then grab a seat on one of the intricately hand-carved horses on the 1911 Looff Carousel (both rides are listed on the National Register of Historic Places). Of course, the Boardwalk (now a cement walk) also caters to hard-core thrill-seekers who yearn for those state-of-the-art, whirl-and-twirl rides that do their best to make you lose your lunch. Buy the reasonably priced day pass and stand in line for rides like Riptide and the Bermuda Triangle, and you won't be disappointed. The white-sand beach fronting the Boardwalk has tame breakers and free volleyball courts and barbecue pits. In the center of the action is the 85-year-old Municipal Wharf, where you can drive your car out to the shops, fish markets, and seafood restaurants. If you're among the crowds here on a Friday night in the summer, don't miss the Boardwalk's free concerts, featuring the likes of the Shirelles, Chubby Checker, and Sha Na Na. The Boardwalk is at 400 Beach St; call (831) 423-5590 for current prices and events.

On the south end of W Cliff Dr is Lighthouse Field State Beach, the reputed birthplace of American surfing. This beach has several benches for sitting and gazing, a jogging and bicycling path, and a park with picnic tables, showers, and even plastic-bag dispensers for cleaning up after your dog (it's one of the few public places in town where canines are allowed). The nearby brick lighthouse is now home to the tiny **Santa Cruz Surfing**

Museum (the first of its kind in the world), which is chock-full of hang-ten memorabilia (admission is free); located on W Cliff Dr at Lighthouse Point, (831) 429-3429.

The **Pacific Garden Mall** (aka Pacific Ave) is Santa Cruz's main shopping district, and until the Loma Prieta earthquake hit in 1989, it was a charming amalgam of Victorian houses, street musicians, bag ladies and gentlemen, inexpensive restaurants, bookstores, antique shops, and New Age head shops. It's recuperating slowly from the apocalypse (the earthquake's epicenter was only 10 miles away), but there's still plenty to gawk at. As you make your way down the mall, look for the Octagon Building, an ornate, eight-sided Victorian brick edifice built in 1882 that has survived numerous quakes. The building once served as the city's Hall of Records and is now part of the **McPherson Center for Art and History,** where museums showcase 10,000 years of the area's past as well as contemporary art of the Pacific Rim; 705 Front St at Cooper St, (831) 429-1964. Next door is the excellent Visitors Information Center; 701 Front St, (800) 833-3494.

The nearby **Bookshop Santa Cruz** has an inventory worthy of any university town, with a particularly good children's section, an adjacent coffeehouse, and plenty of places to sit, sip, and read a bit of your prospective purchase; 1520 Pacific Ave, (831) 423-0900. Another town highlight is the small aquarium and marine exhibits at the **Joseph M. Long Marine Laboratory,** where you can handle mollusks and other small sea creatures. You can also see scientists studying dolphins and sea lions in the lab's marine mammals pools; 100 Shaffer Rd, (831) 459-4308.

Locomotive lovers, kids, and fans of Mother Nature should hop aboard the historic narrow-gauge Roaring Camp Train for a 6-mile round-trip excursion up some of the steepest grades in North America. The **steam-powered train** winds through stately redwood groves to the summit of Bear Mountain. Another train, called the Big Trees Railroad, offers an 18-mile round-trip ride through mountain tunnels and along ridges with spectacular views of the San Lorenzo River before stopping at the Santa Cruz Beach Boardwalk. To reach the Roaring Camp and Big Trees Narrow-Gauge Railroad center, take Hwy 17 to the Mount Herman Rd exit, then turn on Graham Hill Rd (near the town of Felton). Train schedules vary seasonally; call (831) 335-4400 for more details.

For a different sort of recreation, visit a few Santa Cruz-area **wineries.** It's easy to get lost on your way to Roudon-Smith Winery, but its estate-grown chardonnay is worth the risk; 2364 Bean Creek Rd (near Scotts Valley), Santa Cruz, (408) 438-1244. For a list of other wineries, check with the Visitors Information Center, above.

Just east of Santa Cruz sits **Capitola-by-the-Sea,** a tiny, very popular resort town nestled around a small bay. The intimate downtown is only a few blocks long; it's a quaint, jumbled mix of restaurants, gift shops, and beachwear boutiques reminiscent of resort towns of yesteryear. Capitola's broad, sandy beach attracts lots of sun worshipers, primarily because it's sheltered from the wind; it's also bordered by a charming promenade. At the west end of town is the bustling 867-foot-long Capitola Pier—a great place to hang out, admire the view of the town, and, on weekends, listen to live music.

Will Rogers called **Gilroy** the only town in America where you can marinate a steak just by hanging it out on the line—and, yes, when the wind's blowing in the right direction, the aroma from the area's garlic fields is just about that strong. So it only made sense that the people of Gilroy decided in 1979 to celebrate their odoriferous claim to fame with the now-famous **Garlic Festival,** held the last weekend in July. The three-day-long festivities attract throngs of people eager to try such oddities as garlic ice cream and garlic chocolate and to enter their own stinking-rose recipes in the Great Garlic Cook-Off. You may also buy any number of garlic-based foodstuffs and doodads; call (831) 842-1625 for more festival facts. To find out about Gilroy before the age of garlic, visit the Gilroy Historical Museum; located on the corner of Fifth and Church Sts, (831) 848-0470. If bargain hunting, not garlic, happens to set your heart aflutter, be sure to stop at the newly expanded Pacific West Outlet Center, with scores of attractive outlets for big-name retailers on Leavesley Road, just east of US Hwy 101 (US 101); (831) 847-4155.

San Juan Bautista is a sunny little town and home to one of the most beautifully restored missions in California. Built just 2 feet away from the main trace of the San Andreas Fault, **Mission San Juan Bautista** was nearly destroyed by the 1906 quake, but locals raised the money to rebuild it. With its pretty chapel and gardens, the mission sits on a broad plaza surrounded by other well-preserved Spanish colonial buildings. Fans of Alfred Hitchcock's *Vertigo* will want to explore the bell tower from which Kim Novak's character fell to her death. On the first Saturday of the month, docents dress in period costume and give tours; call (831) 623-2127 for more information. San Juan Bautista is also home to the world-famous theater troupe **El Teatro Campesino**; 705 Fourth St, (831) 623-2444. El Teatro Campesino director Luis Valdez left the San Francisco Mime Troupe in the '60s to form this political theater group composed of migrant farmworkers. The group puts on plays throughout the year and is most famous for its Christmas plays, *La Virgen del Tepeyac* and *La Pastorela,* presented at the mission.

Restaurants

Bittersweet Bistro ☆☆   This new, large space features a patio for dining alfresco and a stylish mahogany, lacquer, and black granite bar area. The menu ranges but is always seasonal, and desserts are scrumptious. *787 Rio Del Mar Blvd (take Hwy 1 south of Santa Cruz to the Rio Del Mar exit), Rio Del Mar; (831) 662-9799; $$$.*

Cafe Sparrow ☆☆   This quaint French Country restaurant is a gem of a dining spot. Two charming rooms, decorated in a casual yet elegant style, provide a romantic backdrop for spirited culinary creations. *8042 Soquel Dr (near Trout Gulch Rd), Aptos; (831) 688-6238; $$.*

Casablanca Restaurant ☆☆   There's nothing very Moroccan about this boardwalk bastion of California-continental cuisine, except, perhaps, the palpable air of romance. Soft music fills the candlelit dining room, and stars wink on the water outside the window. *101 Main St (at Beach St, on the waterfront), Santa Cruz; (831) 426-9063; $$$.*

Ciao! Bella!! ☆☆   This exuberant restaurant, nestled in a mountain redwood grove, serves what the owner describes as "new California-Italian" cuisine. The staff is friendly and eager to please. *9217 Hwy 9 (just S of town), Ben Lomond; (831) 336-9221; $$.*

Crow's Nest ☆   This large, multilevel seaside restaurant offers a heated, glassed-in deck that's an uncommonly pleasant place to watch boats cruise in and out of Santa Cruz Harbor. The food isn't exactly gourmet, but it's competently prepared and tasty. *2218 E Cliff Dr (at the Santa Cruz Harbor), Santa Cruz; (831) 476-4560; $$.*

El Palomar ☆☆   Even on a rainy day, this lovely, vibrant restaurant hidden at the back of a former '30s hotel manages to create a sunny atmosphere. El Palomar is known for its seafood dishes, but traditional Mexican favorites are also outstanding. *1336 Pacific Ave (in the Pacific Garden Mall, near Soquel Ave), Santa Cruz; (831) 425-7575; $$.*

Felipe's California & Mexican Cuisine ☆   One of several Mexican places on San Juan Bautista's main street, this crowded storefront restaurant serves all the standard Mexican fare, but its Salvadoran dishes are what set it apart from its neighbors. *313 3rd St (between Mariposa and Polk Sts), San Juan Bautista; (831) 623-2161; $.*

Gayle's Bakery & Rosticceria ☆☆   Take a number and stand in line. It's worth the wait at this wildly popular self-service bakery and deli, which is packed with local folk on weekend mornings. *504 Bay Ave (by Capitola Ave), Capitola-by-the-Sea; (831) 462-1200; $.*

Harvest Time Restaurant ☆ The entrance to this former hotel ballroom is dominated by a large horseshoe-shaped bar and a hand-carved stagecoach. Inside you'll find a comfortably elegant Old West decor. The menu is a good jumble of American and Continental dishes. *7397 Monterey Rd (at 6th St), Gilroy; (831) 842-7575; $$.*

Inn at Tres Pinos ☆☆ Tres Pinos is one of those blink-and-you'll-miss-it towns, but it's worth keeping your peepers wide open to catch this intriguing restaurant, which features a continental menu with an Italian accent. Rustic but surprisingly elegant, the inn wins high praise for both its desserts and its romantic atmosphere. *6991 Airline Hwy (5 miles S of Hollister), Tres Pinos; (831) 628-3320; $$$.*

O'mei Restaurant ☆☆☆ Named after a mountain in the Sichuan province of China, this acclaimed Chinese restaurant is a wondrous little paradox tucked into one of Santa Cruz's many strip malls. *2316 Mission St (near Fair Ave), Santa Cruz; (831) 425-8458; $$.*

Oswald ☆☆☆ Thanks to adept cooking, reverence for fresh produce, and restrained spicing and saucing, this small, arty California-French bistro will remind you of Berkeley's celebrated Chez Panisse. *1547 Pacific Ave (use the parking lot on Cedar St and enter the restaurant through the courtyard), Santa Cruz; (831) 423-7427; $$.*

Ristorante Avanti ☆☆☆ Newcomers who take one look at this unpretentious restaurant set in a humble strip mall may be forgiven for thinking, "Three-star restaurant? I don't think so." Ah, but wait until they've tasted the food and sampled the considerate service—they'll be sorry for doubting our stellar designation. *1711 Mission St (near Bay St), Santa Cruz; (831) 427-0135; $$.*

Shadowbrook Restaurant ☆☆ While locals are forever undecided about the quality of the food, they nevertheless insist that all Santa Cruz visitors dine here at least once. Lately, Shadowbrook has been paying more attention to the food, resulting in a well-crafted, seasonal California-Mediterranean menu. *1750 Wharf Rd (near the end of Capitola Rd), Capitola-by-the-Sea; (831) 475-1511; $$$.*

Sinaloa ☆☆ Don't let the truck-stop exterior trick you, and once you're inside, pay no attention to the well-worn linoleum or blaring TV. Folks don't pack the place for the ambience—they come for the top-notch Mexican food. *19210 Monterey Rd (about 1 mile N of town), Morgan Hill; (831) 779-9740; $.*

Tony & Alba's Pizza and Italian Food ☆ This friendly, family-run restaurant chain features huge brick ovens and heavenly pizzas. *817*

Soquel Ave, Santa Cruz; (831) 425-8669; $. 1501 41st Ave (at Capitola Rd), Capitola-by-the-Sea; (831) 475-4450; $. 226 E Mount Herman Rd, Scotts Valley; (831) 439-9999; $.

The White Cockade Public House ☆ The White Cockade earns high marks for authenticity in the pub department. It's a homey watering hole where there's always a cozy fire and a friendly game of darts in progress. *18025 Hwy 9 (about 15 miles S of Saratoga, and 4½ miles N of town), Boulder Creek; (831) 338-4148; $.*

Lodgings

The Babbling Brook Inn ☆☆ Secreted in a fantastical garden with waterfalls, wishing wells, gazebos, and, of course, a babbling brook, Santa Cruz's oldest B&B offers 13 rooms, mostly named after famous artists. *1025 Laurel St (near California St), Santa Cruz; (831) 427-2437 or (800) 866-1131; $$–$$$.*

Bayview Hotel Bed and Breakfast Inn ☆ Built in 1878 on former Spanish land-grant property, the oldest hotel on Monterey Bay combines Old West ambience with up-to-date comfort. *8041 Soquel Dr (at Trout Gulch Rd), Aptos; (831) 688-8654 or (800) 4-BAYVIEW; $$–$$$.*

Cliff Crest Bed and Breakfast Inn ☆ History, the allure of an antique-laden Victorian house, and views of the Santa Cruz Boardwalk and the bay beyond are all a part of this welcoming 5-room B&B. *407 Cliff St (near 3rd St), Santa Cruz; (831) 427-2609; $$–$$$.*

The Darling House: A Bed and Breakfast Inn by the Sea ☆☆ There are probably no better views (and no softer carpeting) in all of Santa Cruz than those you'll find at the Darling House, a Spanish Revival mansion. *314 W Cliff Dr (between the pier and the lighthouse), Santa Cruz; (831) 458-1958 or (800) 458-1958; $$$.*

The Davenport Bed & Breakfast Inn ☆☆ This pretty, rustic spot has a simple charm befitting this laid-back region of the coast. The dozen rooms are decorated in a pleasing mélange of Native American, Victorian, and country motifs. *31 Davenport Ave (right off Hwy 1), Davenport; (831) 425-1818 or (800) 870-1817; $$.*

The Inn at Depot Hill ☆☆☆ Located in a turn-of-the-century train station, this is a dream of a place. The 12 guest rooms, lavishly designed to evoke international ports of call, seem to have sprung directly from the pages of *Architectural Digest*. *250 Monterey Ave (near Park Ave, next to the railroad tracks), Capitola-by-the-Sea; (831) 462-3376 or (800) 572-2632; $$$.*

Mangels House ☆☆   Set on an imposing green lawn in the middle of a redwood forest, this Italianate mansion has 6 guest rooms decorated in an artful, whimsical way that enlivens the house's stately Victorian demeanor. *570 Aptos Creek Rd (on the road into the Forest of Nisene Marks State Park, ½ mile above town), Aptos; (831) 688-7982 or (800) 320-7401; $$–$$$.*

Seascape Resort ☆☆   This condo-resort complex on 64 cliff-side acres offers spacious accommodations and plenty of creature comforts. The more than 200 guest suites are available in studio or one- or two-bedroom configurations. *1 Seascape Resort Dr (at Sumner Blvd), Aptos; (831) 688-6800 or (800) 929-7727; $$.*

More Information

Aptos Chamber of Commerce: *(831) 688-1467.*
Capitola Chamber of Commerce: *(831) 475-6522.*
Santa Cruz–area state parks: *(831) 429-2850.*
Santa Cruz Beach and Boardwalk: *(831) 426-7433.*
Santa Cruz Chamber of Commerce: *(831) 423-1111.*
Santa Cruz City Conference and Visitors Council: *(800) 833-3494.*
Santa Cruz County Conference and Visitors Council: *(831) 425-1234.*
State parks camping reservations: *(800) 444-7275.*
Surf conditions: *(831) 429-3460, www.gate.cruzio.com/~surfride/.*
Tourist info, Santa Cruz County: *(831) 458-0800.*

Monterey
Bay

From the Monterey County line at the Pajaro River south to Carmel on the Monterey Bay, including Seaside, Marina, and Pebble Beach.

Most of us look at astronauts who have orbited Earth or set foot on the moon as the ultimate explorers and adventurers. But when Dr. Sylvia Earle, the noted oceanographer and National Geographic sea explorer-in-residence, thinks about uncharted territory, she looks to deep ocean waters. "We really don't know enough about what's out there," said Earle, who is participating in a five-year National Oceanic and Atmospheric Administration project to delve into the nation's marine sanctuaries, including the one at Monterey, in search of answers to some of nature's deepest mysteries. "The one thing I can say for sure is that we're going to be discovering things we've never seen before," she adds.

Indeed, there is plenty right here at the Monterey coast for Earle to explore. An underwater canyon, vast and deep enough to swallow 10 Grand Canyons, extends 100 miles into the ocean from the bay shore, its black 10,000-foot depths holding the secrets of a 30-million-year-old ocean floor. Exploration is really what the Monterey Bay area is all about.

Don't jump in just yet, though. Before you swim side-by-side with curious sea lions, take in the dazzling colors and bountiful sea life of the kelp forests, or kayak through the teeming marshlands at Elkhorn Slough, consider a visit to the world-famous Monterey Bay Aquarium, which does a fantastic job of bringing it all together and explaining just what it is you are looking at. A little bit of education goes a long way to enhance the experience of actually diving in.

Once famous for its sardine fishery with blue-collar cannery workers like those in John Steinbeck's *Cannery Row*, Monterey has over the past 50 years become part science center, part outdoor recreation center, and part high-society resort town (if you factor in nearby Pebble Beach and Carmel). Today, marine science is Monterey's chief commodity, as is tourism. Froufrou boutiques and fancy restaurants abound. Despite the pretentiousness of a few far-flung corners, however, this is also a place for hard-core outdoor fun. And lucky for us, what begins in out-of-reach ocean depths can be seen in the kelp forests, rich marshlands, and wild sand dunes here. So suit up and take a dive.

Getting There

Take the Coast Highway (HIghway 1) north from Big Sur or south from Santa Cruz, or Highway 156 west from the Salinas Valley and US Highway 101 (US 101) corridor. The main public transportation service in this area is Monterey/ Salinas Transit, (831) 899-2555. Cannery Row and the Monterey Bay Aquarium have the most complete tourist information. Take the Pacific Avenue exit from the Coast Highway, then head west 3 miles to the bay shoreline center at David Avenue. Call (800) 840-4880 for information.

Adjoining Areas

NORTH: **Santa Cruz**

SOUTH: **Big Sur Coast**

EAST: **San Joaquin Valley**

inside out

Scuba Diving

Sure, it's pretty to look at—but visitors who come to Monterey Bay without jumping for a close-up of one of the world's most productive marine ecosystems are having their salad with no dressing or croutons. The best view of the sandy seafloor and kelp forests of the **Monterey Bay National Marine Sanctuary** is from beneath the water's surface. This is some of the best scuba country in North America, and you don't necessarily need a boat to enjoy it, as there are numerous shore dive locations at public beaches throughout the Monterey and Carmel areas, including some suitable for beginners. The area is also loaded with good expert resources, including guided dives, gear shops with rentals, schools with Professional Association of Diving Instructors (PADI)–certified teachers, and some of the best marine life research institutes in the world. Before setting out to get instruction, however, newbies should first pursue information about diving to see if it is the sport for them. Scuba is sort of like skydiving, rock climbing, parasailing, and bungee jumping that way; it is better to discover that it's not your cup of tea *before* you have slipped into a wet suit and spent a lot of money on equipment rentals and lessons. There are two excellent resources on the Internet with **basic dive information** and answers to diving-related questions. One is the National Oceanic and Atmospheric Administration's "Online Diving Manual" at www.uw-sports.ycg.com/reference_library/noaa/. Another is the FAQ (frequently asked questions) section of the PADI site at www.padi.com/ on the Web.

The fascinating kelp forests, abundant and varied sea life, and amazing water clarity in and around Monterey Bay combine to make scuba the primary outdoor activity here. One popular dive you can take directly from shore is at the **breakwater** adjacent to the city's historic Cannery Row. **Sea lions** frequent this spot, often boldly approaching divers. The current here is calm, and the sea life interesting because of numerous small openings in the granite bottom for **eels, urchins, crabs, octopuses,** and hundreds of other bay inhabitants to slither around in. **Stillwater Cove** and **Lover's Point** are also popular dive spots from the shore—Stillwater in particular since the conditions there hold up to the name of the place. Both are north of the Cannery Row complex in central Monterey, along Central Ave. **Bat rays** are a common treat at both locations—a thrilling sight for new divers, particularly when a large school passes through, moving not unlike a flock of birds.

Getting to some of the best **kelp forest** spots requires a **boat dive.** Places to ask about when scouting around for a tour are **Mono Lobo** and **the Pinnacles** (off Carmel). Pinnacles is a particularly colorful spot, with visibility approaching 100 feet during winter when plankton growth is minimal because of shorter periods of sun. Keep in mind, however, that numerous other factors can affect visibility, so wintertime does not necessarily guarantee ideal conditions. At the boat dive spots, look for **sunfish, blue sharks,** numerous varieties of **kelp fish,** and a wide selection of unusual **anemones, amphipods, sea stars,** and **sponges.**

The choice of **outfitters** and excursion companies is wide. Aquarius, which has locations both at 32 Cannery Row and 2040 Del Monte Ave, (831) 375-1933 and (831) 375-6605, has tour options, rentals, instruction, and a good variety of equipment for sale. The shop also maintains a dive conditions hot line, including tide, wind, surge, and visibility information around the bay region, (831) 657-1020. Numerous dive boats are for hire out of Monterey. Check with *Silver Prince,* (831) 394-4235; *Cypress Sea,* (408) 244-9433; or *Beach Hopper II,* (888) 422-2999. Bamboo Reef, 614 Lighthouse Ave, (831) 372-1685, and The Monterey Express, (888) 422-2999, also are worth a call.

Tidepooling

You'll find evidence of the rich marine life here not only in the kelp forests offshore but also in the vast **intertidal zones** along the rocky portions of the coast. That's a good thing, since tidepooling is one way of gaining an appreciation for the biodiversity of Monterey's aquatic sea life without having to take a dunk. There are four prime tidepooling areas along the Monterey coast, where you can find all manner of odd-colored algae; bizarre **invertebrates** like limpets, giant green anemones, and mossy chitons; and **rock-dwelling fishes** like rockweed gunnels, snubnose sculpin, and the monkey-faced eel. The spots are **Lover's Point, Asilomar State Beach, Carmel Beach,** and, best of all, **Point Lobos State Reserve** south of Carmel. To reach Lover's Point, take the Coast Highway through Monterey to the Pacific Ave exit southwest of the Cannery Row area, then exit right (west) on Pacific and follow it 3.5 miles to 17th St. Turn right (west) on 17th St and follow it to the waterfront. Call (831) 372-4212. To reach Asilomar State Beach from Lover's Point, take Ocean View Blvd west 1.5 miles to where it veers south along Point Piños on the oceanfront and continue another 1 mile south on Sunset Dr to the beach and conference center on your right. Call (831) 372-8016. To reach Carmel Beach, take the Coast Highway south from Monterey 2.5 miles to the Ocean Ave exit in Carmel, and then head west to the beachfront. Call (831) 624-3542. To reach Point Lobos State Reserve, take the Coast Highway south from Carmel to 2 miles south of the intersection with Carmel Valley Rd, and look for the park entrance on the highway at the right (west) side of the road on the oceanfront. Call (831) 624-4909. Point Lobos has an interpretive center. Call the Monterey Coast Guard office (831) 647-7300, for information about tides. Numerous resources offer basic information on marine life. Consult the marine sanctuary office in Monterey at (831) 647-4201, or check out a joint publication of the sanctuary and the Monterey Bay Aquarium, *A Natural History of Monterey Bay,* available from the Monterey Bay Aquarium Press, 886 Cannery Row, Monterey, CA 93940, www.mbayaq.org. The aquarium bookstore can be reached at (831) 648-4952. (See Attractions, below.)

Wildlife

The entire Monterey Bay region is a rich wildlife smorgasbord above and below water (see Scuba Diving and Tidepooling, above).

The Monterey Peninsula Audubon Society has a birding hot line that is updated weekly with current information about rare bird sightings and even gives directions to the hot spots, (831) 375-9122. The wide tidal slough east of Moss Landing, Elkhorn Slough, is a busy spot for **migrating birds** along the Pacific Flyway. Avocets, terns, great blue herons, sandpipers, willets, and even the rare **California brown pelican,** clapper rail, and peregrine falcon can be seen among the 1,400 acres of productive salt marsh bordering the **Moss Landing Wildlife Area** and Kirby Park. These coastal wetlands are not strictly a bird-watching zone, however. Also look for interesting land animals such as **coyotes, muskrats, jackrabbits, weasels,** and **mule deer,** and sea mammals like the **sea otter** and **sea lion.** Interpretive tours led by naturalists are available along some 5 miles of walking paths within the slough boundaries. Call (831) 728-2822 for Elkhorn, (831) 649-2870 for Moss Landing, or (831) 728-5939 for Kirby Park. To reach Moss Landing, take the Coast Highway north from Monterey 8 miles to the Jetty Rd exit, then head east along Bennett Slough to the wildlife center office. To reach Kirby, continue north on the Coast Highway another 1.5 miles and exit east at Salinas Rd. Follow Salinas Rd east for a half mile to Elkhorn Rd and turn right (south) on Elkhorn to the park entrance.

At **Point Lobos State Reserve** (see Tidepooling, above) south of Carmel, a vast area of Monterey cypress forest, rocky cliffs, and sandy coves, **seabirds,** and mammals also abound. An offshore island is reserved as a bird sanctuary, and nearly 1,300 acres of unique and pristine headlands habitat, much different from the tidal marshes at Elkhorn, are preserved. Point Lobos also has an interpretive program, (831) 624-4909.

About 11 miles north of Monterey on the Coast Highway, at the mouth of the Salinas River, the **Salinas River National Wildlife Refuge** encompasses more than 500 acres of salt marsh, lagoon, and meadows that also are an excellent birding site, with **pelican** roosting grounds, **plover** nesting, and a stopover point along the flyway. Spring wildflower walks, hiking, and surf fishing are among the favorite activities here. The refuge is west of the Coast Highway on Del Monte Ave, (831) 384-7695. As much of a draw as the coast is, the Monterey area also has some interesting wildlife viewing areas upstream. We recommend the forested slopes and open grasslands of **Fremont Peak State Park,** 10 miles south of Hwy 156 near San Juan Bautista, in the foothills directly east of Monterey proper. The 3,169-foot peak is best known as an observation spot for astronomers, but in addition to a sprawling view of the Monterey area, you'll get a sense of the wide biodiversity in the upland areas adjacent to the marine sanctuary. **More than 100 bird species** are found among Fremont's oak, manzanita, Coulter pine, and madrone woodlands. A short list includes great horned owls, sparrows, roadrunners, hawks, hummingbirds, golden eagles, finches, jays, and woodpeckers. **Deer, bobcats, foxes, coyotes,** and **raccoons** are among mammals found at Fremont, which also has one of the least-discovered campgrounds in the Monterey region (see Camping, below). Call the park office, (831) 623-4255.

Boating/Sailing

Boating in and around Monterey Bay (also see Boating/Sailing, Santa Cruz chapter) is mostly centered around sportfishing—but there is life here for sailors, too, as the bay has suitable ocean breezes and smooth spots for beginners. **Moss Landing Harbor** has guest moorings and a boat ramp. Take Sandholdt Rd west from the Coast Highway, (831) 633-2461. A hoist is available at the **Monterey Municipal Wharf,** (831) 375-6201, and the **Monterey Marina** has public ramps, moorings, and numerous amenities for fishing needs. Call (831) 646-3950. **Charters, rentals,** and **excursions** are numerous in the Fisherman's Wharf area. Some good options to consider are Carrera Sailing, which has a **sailing school** and runs group charters from the Monterey wharf area, (831) 375-0648, and Sea Life Tours, 90 Fisherman's Wharf, (831) 372-7150, which offers unique glass-bottomed-boat tours. Stillwater Cove at Carmel Bay is also popular among boaters. Check with the Monterey Peninsula Yacht Club, (831) 372-9686, for charter boat and sailing lessons.

Fishing

The Monterey Bay and its infamous Cannery Row were built on the abundant sardine fishery. Today the area is getting more of a reputation as a sanctuary and preserve, particularly with the growing popularity of eco-tourism and politicized environmentalism. Anglers should not fret, however: fishing has not yet been outlawed, although increasingly stringent wildlife recovery efforts prompted by recent endangered species listings are likely to make regulations more difficult to keep track of, particularly with both state and federal bureaucrats trying to come up with new and improved ways of applying them. Surf fishing, rock fishing, and **deep sea excursions** are all popular in and around the Monterey Bay area. Catch a sportfishing tour out of Monterey's Fisherman's Wharf for **albacore, salmon,** and **rock cod.** Chris's Fishing Trips, 48 Fisherman's Wharf, (831) 375-5951; Monterey Sport Fishing and Cruises, 96 Fisherman's Wharf, (831) 372-2203; and Sam's Fishing Fleet Inc, Fisherman's Wharf No. 1, (831) 372-0577, are places to check in with for the deepwater action.

Surf fishing and **rock fishing** for perch, kingfish, sole, flounder, halibut, jacksmelt, lingcod, cabezon, salmon, and steelhead are best at Kirby Park on the north end of Elkhorn Slough; within the Salinas River National Wildlife Refuge (see Wildlife, above); and at Zmudowski State Beach, Marina Dunes State Beach, Lover's Point, and Stillwater Cove (see Beaches, below). Seiner's Hold Bait and Tackle, 32 Cannery Row (831) 375-6958, and the Compass, at Fisherman's Wharf, (831) 647-9222, both have tackle, bait, and supplies.

Cycling

The best road-cycling spots are right along the ocean edge, where cool salt breezes and stunning vistas are your companions. The world-famous **17-Mile Drive,** which hugs most of the coast between Pacific Grove and Pebble Beach, is a great choice not only because of what it has—great oceanside views and shady pine and cypress forest groves—but also because of what it lacks: motorists moving at highway speed. Even better, cyclists get to take the ride for free—unlike drivers who have to fork over $7.25 for the privilege—and there are no challenging grades along the way. Note, however, that cyclists are required to use the Pacific Grove gate on weekends and holidays. See Scenic Drives, below, for more about the road. The 5-mile stretch of the **Coast Highway,** from Pacific Ave to Ocean View Blvd between Seaside and Lover's Point, is also a popular road-cycling route. A longer and more challenging ride is along the gravel **Old Coastal Road,** which takes an inland route through forested hills and meadows beginning south of Carmel and ending where the Coast Highway crosses Big Sur River. The return trip is north on the Coast Highway; the round trip is 19 miles. Adventures by the Sea, 299 Cannery Row, (831) 372-1807, is a good **cycling tour** outfit in town. Also consider Bay Sports, 640 Wave St, (831) 646-9090, or Baycycle Tours, (831) 649-1700.

Beaches

The wild dunes, vast marshes, and rocky cliffs spanning the Monterey Bay–area coast are arguably the most beautiful in all of California, if not for their pristine condition and rich wildlife then for the variety and range of experience available among them. While the surfing scene is not comparable to what's up north in Santa Cruz, shorefront diving, surf fishing, wildlife viewing, hang gliding, boating, and horseback riding are all excellent here. Note: As along so much California's Pacific Coast, **swimming** is not advised here. Currents are strong and unpredictable, and sleeper waves can easily wash unsuspecting beachcombers out to sea. Be extra careful and keep children accounted for.

South of the Pajaro River, which runs along the Santa Cruz County line, **Zmudowski State Beach, Moss Landing State Beach,** and **Salinas River State Beach** encompass 500 nearly contiguous acres of steep dunes and sandy beaches bisected by Elkhorn Slough (see Wildlife, above) and the harbor at Moss Landing. Zmudowski is one of the few spots on the Monterey side of the bay that's popular among surfers, and naturalist-led interpretive tours are available. There is also a good surf fishing spot. Take the Stuve Rd turnoff from the Coast Highway just north of the slough, then go west on Gilbertson Rd to the end. Just south is Moss Landing, which, while about a third the size of Zmudowski, is also a popular surfing beach and marshland bird-watching spot. Take the Jetty Rd exit from the Coast Highway. Salinas River Beach is less than a mile south of the Moss Landing Harbor area; it too is a popular birding and surf fishing spot. For information on all three beaches, call (831) 649-2836.

Marina Dunes State Beach is perhaps the best place to experience the wild dunes. Mother Nature's handiwork is on open display here; erosion from the mountains surrounding Monterey, onshore Pacific breezes, and strong bay currents have conspired over time to form some of the most awesome sand dunes along the California coast—some towering 150 feet above the beach and the Coast Highway. Nature walks, tidepooling, picnics, surf fishing, and hang gliding are popular among the 170 acres here, as are bird-watching and sunbathing on warm days. Great lengths have been taken, however, to discourage beach visitors from trampling the delicate native plants that are so crucial to the dunes habitat. State parks officials have begun an aggressive habitat restoration program—removing ice plant, which is not native to the area, and reestablishing the native grasses, vines, and shrubbery, such as sea rocket and sand verbena. To find the beach, head north from Monterey or south from Santa Cruz on the Coast Highway and exit at Reservation Rd, which dead-ends at the beach parking area. Call (831) 384-7695 for more information.

Closer to the city and much less hilly than the spots to the north, **Monterey State Beach**—actually three sandy waterfront areas spanning a mile of the bay—is more of a picnic/volleyball/kite-flying spot than a place for hard-core water sports or fishing, although it offers access to good diving. Call (831) 649-2836. The beach area is west of the Coast Highway at Canyon Del Rey Rd. Two other picnic/beachcombing spots are right in the middle of the shoreline's most developed area, on either side of historic Cannery Row: **San Carlos Beach Park** and **Macabee Beach.** San Carlos has nice waterfront picnic areas for families; Macabee is a jump-in point for divers who don't want to venture out too far from civilization. Call (831) 373-1902.

North of the Cannery Row and Monterey Bay Aquarium zone, the coast begins to change over from an area of wide dunes and marshes to rocky shores, higher bluffs, and thinner bands of sand. **Lover's Point** has family picnic areas on a high bluff and a fishing pier at the water's edge near three small beaches. Take Pacific Ave west from the Coast Highway to the waterfront area north of Lover's Point, or follow the Hwy 68 corridor west from the Coast Highway to the Sunset Dr/Ocean Dr corridor. Lover's Point is between Perkins Park and Berwick Park; all are run by the city. At **Asilomar State Beach,** south of the Lover's Point area, the coast becomes more rugged and rough, with rocky shores and small beach areas exposed to the open ocean. Tidepooling is popular here, as are nature viewing and diving—but it is not the place for a swim because of rips. Take Hwy 68 west from the Coast Highway to the beach where Sunset Dr bends north.

Due south of Pebble beach, the coved areas of Carmel Bay are also a popular diving, fishing, wildlife viewing, and beachcombing area. **Stillwater Cove** is a particularly popular diving and fishing spot with a boat launch and a nice sandy beach. Call (831) 625-8507. The **Carmel City Beach,** also a popular beachcombing and volleyball area, is adjacent to Stillwater. Avoid this spot on sunny weekends if you have an aversion to upscale crowds—fashionable swimwear, designer/scented suntan oils, and expensive name-brand sunglasses are a prerequisite for entry. Call (831) 624-3543, however, if that's your scene. **Carmel State Beach** south of there is more interesting for wildlife viewers because of the San Jose Creek mouth at its southern end, (831) 624-4909. All three beaches are easily found off the Carmel city waterfront. Take Ocean Ave west from the Coast Highway and explore from the T in the road.

The shore becomes a bit more rustic and wild once the Carmel scene is well behind you. In fact, the spectacular headlands at **Point Lobos State Reserve** are a pleasant change of scenery from the exclusiveness of the Carmel Bay waterfront. The reserve contains nearly 1,300 acres of cypress groves, tide pools, and small sandy coves with trails, picnic areas, and an adjacent interpretive center offering guided nature tours—all once the site of a whaling station and an abalone cannery. This gateway to the Big Sur coast also comes equipped with a stunning underwater reserve area for divers to enjoy. Take Riley Ranch Rd west from the Coast Highway. For more information, call (831) 624-4909.

Surfing

Santa Cruz is where the action is, but **Moss Landing and Zmudowski State Beaches** are two of the few spots along the Monterey coast where the breaks are enough to make a surf outing south of the Pajaro River worth the trouble. (See Surfing, Santa Cruz chapter, for the real thing.) Sunshine Surf and Sport, 443 Lighthouse Ave, (831) 442-3033, has equipment for sale and rent.

Camping

Pickings are slim in the Monterey area for public campgrounds, so most weekend warriors who insist on a tent instead of a motel room or B&B end up in adjoining areas (see Camping, Big Sur Coast and Santa Cruz chapters). There are, however, a few alternatives to hitting the highway north or south.

Fremont Peak State Park (see Wildlife, above), has 25 car camping sites (no hookups; RV limit 26 feet). Each site has a picnic table and a fire pit. Portable toilets are provided, but no showers. Piped water is nearby. *Contact state parks reservations, (800) 444-7275. To reach the park directly, call (831) 623-4255. Take Hwy 156 east to San Juan Bautista, then go south 10 miles on San Juan Canyon Rd.*

Those who insist on staying near Monterey have a few **private camp-grounds** to choose from. Marina Dunes RV Park, near the beach, has 65 sites (full hookups), with rest rooms, showers, and numerous conveniences not found on the backpacking trail (including cable TV). Call (831) 384-6914. The Laguna Seca Recreation Area has 170 sites (partial hookups), also with rest rooms, showers, and numerous recreational facilities nearby. Call (831) 422-6138.

Hiking/Walking

If you're looking for a challenging day hike or a long backpacking trip, your best bet is to head north to Santa Cruz or south to the Big Sur area (see Santa Cruz and Big Sur Coast chapters). Around Monterey Bay proper, however, there are plenty of nice oceanside walks.

Grove Trail in **Point Lobos State Reserve** (easy; 1 mile round trip) is more of a nature stroll than a serious hike, but it's one you just *have* to take if you're in the area and have an hour to kill. You'll find stunning groves of Monterey cypress along this trail, as well as countless curiosities along its other walking paths—particularly those with views of the rocks offshore, where, without fail, numerous sea mammals such as **otters** and **sea lions** can be seen sunning themselves and engaging in any number of sea mammal antics; quite a show. It is best just to grab a trail map and explore on your own. Take Riley Ranch Rd west from the Coast Highway to the preserve entrance. The trailhead is at the west end of the parking lot, to the right. For more information, call (831) 624-4909.

Another very nice, level walk along the coast on the **Elkhorn Slough Interpretive Trail** (easy; 1 mile round trip) at Elkhorn Slough (see Wildlife, above). Elkhorn is a prime birding area, with 15 miles of interpretive trails among some of the most productive salt marsh habitat on the Northern California coast. Start with this main trail, which has interpretive signs throughout. The slough is just east of Moss Landing, off the Coast Highway. Call (831) 728-2822 for information.

The highest peak on the Monterey shore area is at **Jack's Peak County Park**, with 10 miles of hiking trails over 525 acres of oak and pine forests. **Skyline Nature Trail** (easy; 2.2 miles round trip) leads to the summit, which offers spectacular views of the Monterey Bay area. The trail is well manicured and not at all switchbacky, meaning big rewards for not too much work at all. Take Olmstead County Rd north from Hwy 168 southeast of Monterey to the park entrance. Call (831) 647-7799.

Golfing

Because the sport's most prestigious tournaments are held at Pebble Beach, this is golf country—and greens fees at big-name courses can give sticker shock to the road warrior on a budget. Still, there are affordable golf links in the area. The **Laguna Seca** course in Monterey, for example—known as the "sunshine course" because of its reputation for perfect golfing weather—has greens fees ranging from $30 to $55, compared to the $175 to $320 you'd pay at the prestigious Spyglass Hill or Pebble Beach. Call the Laguna Seca course, (831) 373-3701, to check on greens conditions and the size of the crowd before just dropping in. Another fine choice are the two courses at **Rancho Cañada** in Carmel Valley, both flanked by the Carmel River. Pine trees on the west course and four lakes on the east make both quite challenging, and par-3 holes on both courses are considered among the best in the region; call (831) 624-0111.

Hang Gliding

It's kind of the antithesis of diving, which the Monterey area is known for, but why not? The strong onshore winds and the high bluffs and dunes along the south beaches of Monterey Bay make this area the perfect place to take in the sights while soaring above it all. **Marina State Beach** is the best spot to take flight, with launch areas, rentals, and lessons available. Intermediate to experienced gliders who have discovered this spot can regularly be seen hovering over the dunes from the Coast Highway. Lessons and information on hang gliding are available at Western Hang Gliding, Reservation Rd at Hwy 1, (831) 384-2622. Mission Soaring Center, 1116 Wrigley Way, Milpitas, also has a presence at Marina, (408) 262-1055.

Sea Kayaking

The best way to view the amazingly productive marshes of **Elkhorn Slough** is by sea kayak; paddling birders glide through virtually unnoticed, getting a fresh view of nesting and roosting areas. The slough is placid enough even for beginners to take to the water. Kayakers who want to tour the kelp forests of Monterey Bay, however, should be at an intermediate skill level, if not because of the swells and rocky shores in some areas, then because the kelp itself can be confusing to tangle with. A close encounter with an otter or a harbor seal is a good possibility! Kayak Connection, at the Elkhorn Yacht Club, 2370 Hwy 1, Moss Landing, (831)

724-5692, offers guided tours of both the slough and the bay and has **rentals** for paddlers who want to venture out on their own. The Elkhorn Slough Foundation, (831) 728-5939, offers interpretive kayak tours of the slough as well. Other choices are Monterey Bay Kayaks, 693 Del Monte Ave, (831) 373-5357, and Adventures by the Sea, 299 Cannery Row, (831) 372-1807.

Scenic Drives

The famous **17-Mile Drive** drive through Del Monte Forest and along the Pebble Beach coast provides dramatic ocean vistas and a good opportunity to gawk at fancy houses, too. To reach the starting point, take the Coast Highway south through Monterey and past Carmel. Just past the Hwy 68 intersection between Carmel and Pacific Grove, the entrance to the drive is clearly marked at the right (west) side of the road. Admission is about $7 for automobiles, but pedestrians and cyclists (see Cycling, above) get in free.

If you decide to pay the toll, you'll see everything from a spectacular Byzantine castle with a private beach (the Crocker Mansion near the Carmel gate) to several tastefully bland California Nouvelle country-club establishments in perfectly maintained forest settings. Impressive natural highlights include the often-photographed gnarled Lone Cypress clinging to its rocky precipice above the sea; miles of hiking and equestrian trails winding through groves of native pines and wildflowers, with glorious views of Monterey Bay; and Bird Rock, a small offshore isle covered with hundreds of seals and sea lions (bring binoculars). Self-guided nature tours are outlined in a variety of brochures, available for free at the gate entrances and at the Inn at Spanish Bay and the Lodge at Pebble Beach. And then there are the golf courses. This area is a bit of heaven to golfers, who flock to such famous courses as Spyglass Hill (see Golfing, above).

Pebble Beach has five guarded entrance gates, and the entire drive takes about three hours (though you can whiz by the highlights in 30 minutes). The most famous stretch is along the coast between Pacific Grove and Carmel, and your best bet is to avoid the busy summer week-ends and come midweek. For more information, contact Pebble Beach Security at (831) 624-6669, or call (831) 624-3811 for information.

Also be ready for a treat on the stretch of the **Coast Highway** between Carmel and Big Sur—you'll have trouble keeping your eyes on the road!

Rock Climbing

Experienced and beginning climbers can find places to test their stuff all along the Monterey peninsula. A good beginner's spot is the south end of

Garrapata State Beach (6 miles south of Carmel), with its short 15- to 20-foot cliffs above the sand. Experienced climbers may prefer to head to Pinnacles National Monument (see Ventana Wilderness chapter), on Hwy 146 east of the Monterey Bay area. Call Peak Experience, (831) 462-2023, in Monterey for climb information at both locations.

Adventure Calendar

Monterey Whalefest, January to February: *learn all you ever wanted to know about whales, and see them too,* (831) 644-7588.

AT&T Pebble Beach National Pro-Am, late January: (831) 649-1533.

Pebble Beach Spring Horse Show, late March: (831) 624-2756.

Monterey Sea Otter Classic, late March: *road cycling, mountain biking, and in-line skating race and exposition,* (831) 622-0700.

Poppy Century Bicycle Ride, early May: (831) 373-1839.

Monterey Human Race 8K Walk, mid-May: (831) 655-9234.

The Great Monterey Squid Festival, late May: (831) 649-6544.

CA Golf Association Senior Amateur Championship, late June: (831) 625-4653.

Pebble Beach Equestrian Classic, late July: (831) 624-2756.

The Triathlon at Pacific Grove, mid-September: (831) 373-0678.

Fall Fun Fest & Bed Races, early October: (831) 394-6501.

Pebble Beach Invitational Pro-Am Golf Tournament, late November: (831) 484-2151.

outside in

Attractions

Established in 1889 as a retreat for pious Methodists, **Pacific Grove** is a beautiful Victorian seacoast village that retains its decorous old-town character, though it's loosened its collar a bit since the early days, when dancing, alcohol, and even the Sunday newspaper were banned. Less tourist-oriented than Carmel, less commercial than Monterey, P.G. (as locals call it) exudes peace and tranquillity—here's no graffiti, no raucous revelers, and not even an unleashed dog in sight.

The town is famous for its Victorian houses, inns, and churches, and hundreds of them have been declared historically significant by the Pacific Grove Heritage Society. Every October, some of the most beautiful and artfully restored are opened to the public on the **Victorian Home Tour;** call (831) 373-3304 for details. If you can't make the tour, you can at least admire the faces of these lavish lovelies clustered along Lighthouse Ave, Central Ave, and Ocean View Blvd.

At the tip of Point Piños (Spanish for "Point of the Pines") stands the Cape Cod–style **Point Piños Lighthouse,** the oldest continuously operating lighthouse on the West Coast, built in 1855. This National Historic Landmark is open to the public Thursday through Sunday, from 1pm to 4pm, and admission is free; on Asilomar Blvd at Lighthouse Ave, (831) 648-3116.

Pacific Grove bills itself as Butterfly Town, USA, in honor of the thousands of **monarchs** that migrate here from late October to mid-March. Two popular places to view these lovely orange-and-black insects are the Monarch Grove Sanctuary (at Lighthouse Ave and Ridge Rd) and George Washington Park (at Sinex Ave and Alder St). To learn more about the monarchs, visit the charmingly informal and kid-friendly Pacific Grove Museum of Natural History, which has a video and display on the butterfly's life cycle, as well as exhibits of other insects, local birds, mammals, and reptiles (admission is free); located at the intersection of Forest and Central Aves, (831) 648-3116.

For good books and coffee, amble over to the nearby **Bookworks,** which also has an extensive array of magazines and newspapers; 667 Lighthouse Ave, (831) 372-2242.

If you arrive in **Monterey** looking for the romantically gritty, working-class fishing village of John Steinbeck's Cannery Row, you won't find it. Even though the town was the sardine capital of the Western Hemisphere during World War II, overfishing forced most of its canneries to close in the early '50s, and the city began trawling for tourist dollars instead. The low-slung factories of Cannery Row and Fisherman's Wharf have been turned into tacky clothing boutiques, knickknack stores, and yogurt shops. But the town itself, set on the south end of Monterey Bay, still has more than its fair share of breathtaking seacoast vistas, pretty Victorian buildings, historic adobes, and secret gardens full of succulents, herbs, and native plants. To catch the town at its best, come in the spring or during the sunny Indian summer months; at other times, expect it to be foggy and slightly cool.

The glory of the town is the amazing, high-tech, 221,000-square-foot **Monterey Bay Aquarium,** the largest aquarium in the United States, with more than 350,000 fascinating fish and other denizens of the (local) deep. It also boasts one of the world's largest indoor, glass-walled aquarium tanks. The bat-ray petting pool (not to worry, their stingers have been removed) and the two-story sea otter tank will thrill the kids (and adults), particularly when the sea otters get to scarf down a mixture of clams, rock cod, and shrimp at 10:30am, 1:30pm, and 3:30pm every day. Try to visit midweek to escape the crowds that consistently flock to this beloved institution. Reservations are recommended in the summer and on holidays; 886 Cannery Row (follow the signs). Call (800) 756-3737 for advance tickets and (831) 648-4888 for more information.

To get the flavor of Monterey's heritage, follow the 2-mile **Path of History,** a walking tour of the former state capital's most important historic sites and splendidly preserved old buildings—remember, this city was thriving under Spanish and Mexican flags when San Francisco was still a crude village. Free tour maps are available at various locations, including the Custom House, California's oldest public building (at the foot of Alvarado St, near Fisherman's Wharf), and Colton Hall, where the California State Constitution was written and signed in 1849 (on Pacific St, between Madison and Jefferson Sts); call Monterey State Historic Park at (831) 649-7118 for more information. Nautical history buffs should visit the **Maritime Museum of Monterey,** which houses ship models, whaling relics, and the two-story-high, 10,000-pound Fresnel lens used for nearly 80 years at the Point Sur lighthouse to warn mariners away from the treacherous Big Sur coast; 5 Custom House Plaza, in Stanton Center, near Fisherman's Wharf, (831) 373-2469.

The landmark **Fisherman's Wharf,** the center of Monterey's cargo and whaling industry until the early 1900s, is awash today in mediocre (or worse) restaurants and equally tasteless souvenir shops. Serious shoppers will be better off strolling Alvarado St, a pleasantly low-key, attractive downtown area with a much less touristy mix of art galleries, bookstores, and restaurants. Alvarado St is also the site of the popular **Old Monterey Farmers Market and Marketplace,** a good spot for free family entertainment and picnic-basket treats; it's held Tuesday year-round from 4pm to 8pm in the summer and 4pm to 7pm in the winter.

Children will love the **Dennis the Menace Playground,** designed by cartoonist Hank Ketcham himself. He created enough climbing apparatuses to please a monkey; it's at Camino El Estero and Del Monte Ave, near Lake El Estero. For fun on the water, take your Curious Georges on a paddleboat and pedal around Lake El Estero; (831) 375-1484. You can rent bicycles and in-line skates at the Monterey Bay Recreation Trail, which runs along the Monterey shore for 18 miles to Lover's Point (see Inside Out activities, above) in Pacific Grove.

For a terrific, toe-tappin' time, visit Monterey on the third weekend in September, when top talents such as Wynton Marsalis, Etta James, and Ornette Coleman strut their stuff at the **Monterey Jazz Festival,** one of the country's best jazz jubilees and the oldest continuous jazz celebration in the world. Tickets and hotel rooms sell out fast, so plan early (die-hard jazz fans make reservations at least six months before show time); call

(800) 307-3378 for tickets and (831) 373-3366 for more information. Monterey also hosts a Blues Festival in late June, which attracts a respectable but smaller crowd; (831) 649-6544.

You'll find plenty of references to Nobel prize–winning author John Steinbeck (*The Grapes of Wrath, Cannery Row, East of Eden*) all over town, but you'll have to go to the nearby town of Salinas to check out the writer's birthplace, **Steinbeck House,** which is now a luncheon restaurant run by the Salinas Valley Women's Guild; 132 Central Ave, Salinas, (831) 424-2735. Also in Salinas, the John Steinbeck Library has a large collection of his letters and first editions; 350 Lincoln Ave at W San Luis St, Salinas, (831) 758-7311.

How much are a room and a round of golf at **Pebble Beach** these days? Let's put it this way: if you have to ask, you can't afford it. This exclusive gated community of 6,000 or so residents even requires a $7.25 levy to trod on its gilded avenues. If you have no strong desire to tour corporate-owned hideaways and redundant—albeit gorgeous—seascapes along the famous 17-Mile Drive, save your lunch money; you're not really missing anything that can't be seen elsewhere along the Monterey coast. Then again, some folks swear that 17-Mile Drive is one of those things you must do at least once in your life, and that the enclave of mansions and manicured golf courses is worth the admission just to contemplate the lifestyles of the very rich. See Scenic Drives, above, for more details.

Years ago, **Carmel-by-the-Sea** was a quaint little seaside town with a relaxed Mediterranean atmosphere conducive to the pursuit of such arts as photography, painting, and writing. Luminaries such as Robert Louis Stevenson, Robinson Jeffers, Mary Austin, Sinclair Lewis, Edward Weston, Upton Sinclair, and Ansel Adams at one time called Carmel home. Today, though, the very name of this city has become synonymous with a spectacular fall from grace, and antidevelopment folks up and down the coast use the term "Carmelization" with their lips curled in disgust. The charmingly ragtag bohemian village (which once banned skateboards, high heels, and ice-cream cones) has long since given way to a cute but conservative and very wealthy coastal tourist village filled with frozen yogurt stands, T-shirt stores, and chichi house-and-garden marts offering ceramic geese and other essentials. Traffic—both vehicular and pedestrian—can be maddeningly congested during the summer and on weekends, and prices in the shops, hotels, and restaurants tend to be gougingly high.

But if you hit Carmel on the right day—preferably midweek in the off-season, when the sun is shining and a good, stiff breeze is blowing in from the sea—you'll discover all the charm that made the burg so famous. Stroll the streets in the early morning or early evening to avoid the crowds and admire the varied, eccentric architecture that gives the town its unique look. Flowers abound in every season. And then there's the setting: even the city's firmest detractors have to admit that Carmel boasts one of the most beautiful curves of beach on the central coast.

Part of Carmel's charm lies in its unusual city ordinances, which ban sidewalks, streetlights, franchises, billboards, and even residential addresses. That's right—no one living within city limits has a numerical street address. Instead, people have homes with names like Periwinkle and Mouse House, and residents go to the post office to pick up their letters and magazines, gossiping all the while about celebrity citizens like former mayor Clint Eastwood, Kim Novak, and Doris Day. If you don't feel like rambling through town on your own, knowledgeable local Gale Wrausmann conducts leisurely, two-hour **guided walking tours** Tuesday through Saturday; call (831) 642-2700 for details.

Carmel is also a little bit o' heaven for **shoppers.** Not only is its downtown packed with interesting little stores, but just outside of town lie two luxe suburban malls: The Barnyard (on Hwy 1 at Carmel Valley Rd) and The Crossroads (on Hwy 1 at Rio Rd). Ocean Ave has its share of tourist-schlock shops, it's true, but hit the side streets for some fine adventures in consumerland.

Mission Trails Park supports 5 miles of winding paths, with wildflowers, willows, deer, and redwoods. It's adjacent to the restored Mission San Carlos Borromeo del Río Carmelo, better known as the **Carmel Mission.** Established in 1770, this was the headquarters of pioneer priest Father Junípero Serra's famous chain of California missions, and his favorite (Serra is buried in front of the altar in the sanctuary, which is marked with a plaque). The vine-covered baroque church with its 11-bell Moorish tower, completed in 1797, is one of California's architectural treasures. Be sure to see the main altar, with its gothic arch and elaborate decorations, and Serra's restored cell, where he died in 1784. The mission houses three extensive museums, and its surrounding 14 acres are planted with native flowers and trees. The cemetery has more than 3,000 graves of Native Americans who worked and lived in the mission; in place of a gravestone, many plots are marked by a solitary abalone shell; 3080 Rio Rd at Lasuén Dr, several blocks west of Hwy 1, (831) 624-3600.

Other interesting structural landmarks include the **storybook cottages** Hugh Comstock constructed in 1924 and 1925 to indulge his wife's love of fairy tales and dollhouses; the Carmel Business Association can provide a list of the houses if you drop by its office in the Eastwood Building on San Carlos St, above Hog's Breath Inn, between Fifth and Sixth Aves, or call (831) 624-2522. Tor House, the former home of poet Robinson Jeffers, is a rustic granite building that looks as though it were transplanted from the British Isles. Constructed over several years beginning in

1914, today it's the residence of one of Jeffers' descendants. Even more intriguing is the nearby four-story Hawk Tower, which Jeffers built for his wife, Una, with huge rocks he hauled up from the beach below. Guided tours of the house and tower are available for a fee on Friday and Saturday by reservation only (no children under 12 admitted); 26304 Ocean View Ave at Stewart Way, (831) 624-1813.

Carmel has an active **theater** scene, perhaps best represented by the Pacific Repertory Theatre company, which puts on an outdoor musical and Shakespeare festival each summer and performs other classics such as *Amadeus* and *Death of a Salesman* in its indoor theater year-round. Call (831) 622-0700 or (831) 622-0100 for details. A thick cluster of quality **art galleries** is located between Lincoln and San Carlos Sts and Fifth and Sixth Aves. Particularly noteworthy is the Weston Gallery, which showcases 19th- and 20th-century photographers' works, including a permanent display featuring such famous Carmelites as Edward Weston, Ansel Adams, and Imogen Cunningham; located on Sixth Ave at Dolores St, (831) 624-4453.

The annual monthlong **Carmel Bach Festival** offers numerous concerts, recitals, lectures, and discussion groups—some are even free. In addition to Bach masterpieces, you'll hear scores by Vivaldi and Scarlatti, and some by those young whippersnappers Beethoven and Chopin. The classical music celebration begins in mid-July; series tickets are sold starting in January, and single-event tickets (ranging from $10 to $50) go on sale in April. Call (831) 624-2046 for tickets, and (831) 624-1521 for additional festival facts.

Restaurants

Cafe Fina ☆☆   Many locals swear this is the only restaurant worth dining at on Fisherman's Wharf. The food is delicious and carefully prepared, the atmosphere is casual and fun, and the view is a maritime dream. *47 Fisherman's Wharf (on the wharf), Monterey; (831) 372-5200; $$.*

Casanova Restaurant ☆☆   This sunny cottage with a Mediterranean feel attracts happy throngs of locals and tourists alike. Casanova specializes in Italian and French country–style dishes. *On 5th Ave (between San Carlos and Mission Sts), Carmel-by-the-Sea; (831) 625-0501; $$.*

Crocodile Grill ☆☆   Drawing on the exotic flavors of the Caribbean and Latin America, this exciting cuisine caters to the tender sensibilities of *norteamericanos* without sacrificing authenticity. Tropical plants, photographs, and dozens of crocodile tchotchkes set the mood for fiery, flavorful, fish-focused meals. *701 Lighthouse Ave (at Congress Ave), Pacific Grove; (831) 655-3311; $$.*

Fandango ☆☆   Fandango, the name of a lively Spanish dance, is the perfect moniker for this kick-up-your-heels restaurant specializing in Mediterranean country cuisine. It's a big, colorful place with textured adobe walls and a spirited crowd. *223 17th St (near Lighthouse Ave), Pacific Grove; (831) 372-3456; $$$.*

Fishwife ☆   Locals swear by this bustling and casual seaside restaurant, with its long roster of (mostly) seafood dishes. Try the justly famous Boston clam chowder. *1996½ Sunset Dr (in the Beachcomber Inn at Asilomar Beach), Pacific Grove; (831) 375-7107; $$.*

Flying Fish Grill ☆☆   Hidden on the ground level of the Carmel Plaza shopping center, this ebullient spot is worth seeking out for its fun, stylish atmosphere and its delicious Pacific Rim seafood. *On Mission St (between Ocean and 7th Aves, in Carmel Plaza), Carmel-by-the-Sea; (831) 625-1962; $$.*

Fresh Cream ☆☆☆   One of the most highly rated restaurants on the California coast, Fresh Cream features French cuisine with hints of California, exquisitely prepared and presented. *99 Pacific St (Suite 100C in the Heritage Harbor complex, across from Fisherman's Wharf), Monterey; (831) 375-9798; $$$.*

Gernot's Victoria House ☆☆   Located in the beautiful Hart Mansion, Gernot's has the kind of quiet charm and gracious service that the town's trendier restaurants just can't match. All of the continental entrees come with soup, salad, and hot country rolls. *649 Lighthouse Ave (at 19th St), Pacific Grove; (831) 646-1477; $$.*

Hog's Breath Inn ☆   You'll always find a horde of tourists and locals cruising, carousing, and plowing their way through the better-than-average pub grub here at movie star and ex-Carmel mayor Clint Eastwood's place. *On San Carlos St (between 5th and 6th Aves), Carmel-by-the-Sea; (831) 625-1044; $$.*

La Dolce Vita ☆☆   Those in the mood for authentic Italian food in a casual atmosphere will enjoy this restaurant, a local favorite. The main dining room resembles a cozy trattoria with slate floors, light wood furniture, and walls bedecked with garlic braids. *On San Carlos St (between 7th and 8th Aves), Carmel-by-the-Sea; (831) 624-3667; $$.*

Melac's ☆☆☆   This transplanted slice of France, with its brick fireplace, white-lace cafe curtains, and soldierly rows of wine bottles lining the walls, is a masterly combination of exquisite cuisine and elegant presentation. *663 Lighthouse Ave (at 19th St), Pacific Grove; (831) 375-1743; $$$.*

Montrio ☆☆☆   All's welcoming here, from the curved lines and soft-sculpture clouds that define the decor of this converted 1910 firehouse to the insightful, cordial waitstaff. The only thing even slightly edgy is the food, which has lusty, rough-yet-refined flavors. *414 Calle Principal (near Franklin St), Monterey; (831) 648-8880; $$$.*

Pasta Mia ☆☆   A century-old Victorian house provides a homey backdrop for Pasta Mia's hearty Italian fare. The house-made pastas include some intriguing choices. *481 Lighthouse Ave (near 13th St), Pacific Grove; (831) 375-7709; $$.*

Peppers ☆   This Pacific Grove hot spot with strings of red chile peppers dangling from the ceiling is known for its house-made tamales and chiles rellenos. The service is always friendly even though the place is usually packed. *170 Forest Ave (by Lighthouse Ave), Pacific Grove; (831) 373-6892; $.*

Red House Café ☆☆   This 103-year-old, brick house in downtown PG is the setting for some of the most adroit cooking in the area. The Red House offers a handful of humble-sounding dishes at breakfast and lunch, but you'll soon realize how even the simplest fare can be transporting. *662 Lighthouse Ave (at 19th St), Pacific Grove; (831) 643-1060; $.*

Rio Grill ☆☆   This noisy Southwestern-style grill is packed with a lively, young crowd from opening to closing. While the atmosphere may be chaotic, the service isn't, and the grill boasts a large wine list. *101 Crossroads Blvd (in the Crossroads Shopping Center, at Hwy 1 and Rio Rd), Carmel-by-the-Sea; (831) 625-5436; $$.*

Robert Kincaid's Bistro ☆☆☆   The master chef who created Monterey's ever-popular Fresh Cream restaurant returned to the peninsula in 1995 to open this charming temple to earthy haute cuisine. *217 Crossroads Blvd (in the Crossroads Shopping Center, at Hwy 1 and Rio Rd), Carmel-by-the-Sea; (831) 624-9626; $$$.*

Sans Souci ☆☆☆   True to its name (French for "without worry"), you'll never have to fret about the food or the service at this charming restaurant, which specializes in both classic and contemporary French cuisine. *On Lincoln St (between 5th and 6th Aves), Carmel-by-the-Sea; (831) 624-6220; $$$.*

6th Avenue Grill ☆☆☆   This breezily sophisticated restaurant turns out casual contemporary California-Mediterranean cuisine. The dining room is a cheerful stage for the chef's inspired cooking, with its Milano-modern furnishings and textured ocher walls. *On 6th Ave (at Mission St), Carmel-by-the-Sea; (831) 624-6562; $$.*

Stokes Adobe ☆☆☆   A historic adobe built in 1833 is the setting for one of Monterey's most engaging restaurants. Inside, it's a soothing and lovely showcase for the terrific contemporary rustic Mediterranean fare. *500 Hartnell St (at Madison St), Monterey; (831) 373-1110; $$.*

Tarpy's Roadhouse ☆☆☆   This exuberant restaurant features a broad, sunny patio shaded by market umbrellas out front and a handsome Southwestern decor inside. The menu indulges in a creative approach to traditional American food. *2999 Monterey-Salinas Hwy (at Hwy 68 and Canyon Del Rey), Monterey; (831) 647-1444; $$$.*

Taste Cafe & Bistro ☆☆☆   The Taste Cafe has developed a loyal and enthusiastic word-of-mouth following that is the envy of other restaurants in town. You won't find higher quality food—a combination of rustic French, Italian, and California cuisines—for the same price anywhere else on the coast. *1199 Forest Ave (at Prescott Ave), Pacific Grove; (831) 655-0324; $$.*

The Whole Enchilada ☆   Fresh seafood is the focus of this upbeat restaurant on Hwy 1 with gaily painted walls, folk-art decorations, and leather basket chairs that lend an engaging south-of-the-border ambience. *7902 Hwy 1 (at Moss Landing Rd), Moss Landing; (831) 633-3038; $$.*

Lodgings

Carmel River Inn   Families favor these 24 cottages and 19 motel units that offer utilitarian but homey accommodations at reasonable prices. Though the inn's close to the highway, noise isn't a problem because it is set back along the Carmel River and surrounded by trees. *On Hwy 1 (at the bridge, S of Rio Rd), Carmel-by-the-Sea; (831) 624-1575 or (800) 882-8142; $$.*

The Centrella ☆☆   The aptly named Centrella (located smack in the center of town) combines the down-home glow of an Old West boardinghouse with the comfort and attentive service of a modern hotel. *612 Central Ave (at 17th St), Pacific Grove; (831) 372-3372 or (800) 233-3372; $$$.*

Cypress Inn ☆☆   This charming Mediterranean-style inn in the center of town recently has been treated to a much-needed renovation that brought its 33 guest rooms up to date while preserving its Old Carmel charm. *On Lincoln St (at 7th Ave), Carmel-by-the-Sea; (831) 624-3871 or (800) 443-7443; $$$.*

Grand View Inn ☆☆☆   Even in a town as rich in resplendent Victorians as Pacific Grove, this pristine and romantic inn stands out. Built in 1910, it has a cheerful blue exterior and 10 guest rooms, all with bay views. *557 Ocean View Blvd (at Grand Ave), Pacific Grove; (831) 372-4341; $$$.*

The Green Lantern Inn ☆   Built in 1925, these rustic buildings are nestled among lush gardens just a few blocks above Ocean Beach. A member of the Best Western hotel chain, the 18-room inn maintains an Old Carmel charm. *On Casanova St (at 7th Ave), Carmel-by-the-Sea; (831) 624-4392; $$.*

Highlands Inn ☆☆☆   This exquisite luxury hotel began as a clutch of cabins in 1916, but its rustic days are long gone. Set high above the rocky coastline south of Carmel with fine views of Yankee Point, the Highlands Inn is now a sprawling modern complex of glowing redwood and soaring glass. *On Hwy 1 (4 miles S of town), Carmel-by-the-Sea; (831) 624-3801 or (800) 682-4811; $$$.*

Hotel Pacific ☆☆☆   Like a Modigliani looming angular and bold in a gallery full of Fra Angelicos, this somewhat modern, neo-hacienda hotel stands out in the midst of Monterey's authentic old adobes. *300 Pacific St (between Scott St and Del Monte Blvd), Monterey; (831) 373-5700 or (800) 554-5542; $$$.*

The Inn at Spanish Bay ☆☆☆   This sprawling modern inn has 270 luxuriously appointed rooms and suites perched on a cypress-dotted bluff, with gas fireplaces, quilted down comforters, and elegant sitting areas. *2700 17-Mile Dr (near the Pacific Grove entrance), Pebble Beach; (831) 647-7500 or (800) 654-9300; $$$.*

The Jabberwock ☆☆   Set well back from the hubbub of nearby Cannery Row, this whimsical 1911 former convent has 7 guest rooms, 5 with private baths. *598 Laine St (at Hoffman Ave), Monterey; (831) 372-4777 or (888)428-7253; $$.*

La Playa Hotel ☆☆☆   Almost regal in its splendor, this imposing 1904 luxury hotel spills down a terraced, bougainvillea-and-jasmine-strewn hillside toward the sea. The 75 guest rooms feature Spanish-style furnishings. To do La Playa right, invest in one of the 5 more private cottages. *On Camino Real (at 8th Ave), Carmel-by-the-Sea; (831) 624-6476 or (800) 582-8900; $$$.*

Lighthouse Lodge and Suites ☆☆   Less than a block from the ocean, the lodge, a Best Western property with a heated pool, consists of 68 motel-like rooms. Those seeking more luxurious accommodations should spring for one of the 31 newer suites down the road. *1150 and 1249 Lighthouse Ave (at Asilomar Blvd), Pacific Grove; (831) 655-2111 or (800) 858-1249; $$ (lodge), $$$ (suites).*

Los Laureles Lodge and Restaurant ☆☆   Believe it or not, the more than two dozen white clapboard guest rooms here were once actually stables. The hay and the flies have been replaced by knotty pine paneling and country antiques, but the property retains a refreshing ranch house ambience. *313 W Carmel Valley Rd (10½ miles E of Hwy 1), Carmel Valley; (831) 659-2233 or (800) 533-4404; $$–$$$.*

The Martine Inn ☆☆☆   Perched like a vast pink wedding cake on a cliff above Monterey Bay, this villa with a Mediterranean exterior and a Victorian interior is one of Pacific Grove's most elegant bed and breakfasts. *255 Ocean View Blvd (4 blocks from Cannery Row), Pacific Grove; (831) 373-3388 or (800) 852-5588; $$$.*

Mission Ranch ☆☆☆   This peaceful, Western-style spread offers everything a guest needs to feel comfortable and not a single silly frill. The 31 rooms, distributed among a clutch of pretty, immaculately maintained buildings, are sparsely but tastefully appointed. *26270 Dolores St (at 15th Ave), Carmel-by-the-Sea; (831) 624-6436 or (800) 538-8221; $$–$$$.*

Old Monterey Inn ☆☆☆   Even those who feel they've seen it all on the bed-and-breakfast circuit are likely to be awed by the elegantly appointed Old Monterey Inn. Nestled among giant oak trees and gardens, this 1929 Tudor-style country inn positively gleams. *500 Martin St (near Pacific St), Monterey; (831) 375-8284 or (800) 350-2344; $$$.*

Robles del Rio Lodge ☆☆   Set on an oak-covered ridge 1,000 feet above Carmel Valley, this classic 1920s Western lodge, constructed of river rock and timber, makes guests feel as if they've stepped back to a time of simple pleasures. *200 Punta Del Monte St (from Hwy 1, take the Carmel Valley Rd for about 13 miles to Esquiline Rd, then follow the signs to the lodge), Carmel Valley; (831) 659-3705 or (800) 833-0843; $$–$$$.*

Rosedale Inn ☆   While its name may conjure up images of pink petals and white lace, the Rosedale is more like an upscale motel, with woodsy flourishes such as a huge carved-redwood bear that welcomes guests. *775 Asilomar Blvd (at Sinex Ave), Pacific Grove; (831) 655-1000 or (800) 822-5606; $$.*

Spindrift Inn ☆☆☆   With its soaring four-story atrium and rooftop garden, this former bordello is an unexpected and elegant refuge amid the tourist bustle of Cannery Row. All 42 rooms have feather beds. *652 Cannery Row (at Hawthorne St), Monterey; (831) 646-8900 or (800) 841-1879; $$$.*

The Stonehouse Inn ☆☆   This ivy-covered stone structure is one of those inns people return to again and again—and many have been coming back since it opened as a hostelry in 1948. The 1906 building has 6 guest rooms, named after local writers and artists. *On 8th Ave (between Monte Verde and Casanova Sts), Carmel-by-the-Sea; (831) 624-4569 or (800) 748-6618; $$.*

Stonepine ☆☆☆☆   This exquisite Mediterranean villa has 16 guest rooms and rises in terraced splendor against the oak-covered hills of the Carmel Valley. During the day, float in the jewel-like swimming pool, play tennis, explore the ranch's 330 acres, or visit their equestrian center. *150 E Carmel Valley Rd (13 miles E of Hwy 1), Carmel Valley; (831) 659-2245; $$$.*

More Information

Carmel Area Tourist Information Center: *(831) 624-1711.*
Carmel Chamber of Commerce: *(831) 624-2522.*
Carmel Valley Chamber of Commerce: *(831) 659-4000.*
Monterey Bay National Marine Sanctuary, *(831) 647-4201.*
Monterey Peninsula Chamber of Commerce: *(831) 649-1770.*
Old Monterey Business Association: *(831) 655-8070.*
Visitors Underground Information: *(408)372-3621.*

Big Sur Coast

Northern Big Sur from south of Point Lobos State Reserve to Julia Pfeif-
fer Burns State Park, including Point Sur, Andrew Molera State Park,
Pfeiffer Beach, and the campgrounds of the Coast Highway corridor.

The Spanish settlers who descended on the Monterey Bay area in the late 1700s took one look at the Big Sur region and said, "Forget it." Lucky for us. The qualities that kept Spanish missionaries away are those that attract hordes of outdoor adventurers today. The Spanish settlers looked at the rocky, inaccessible Big Sur coast below and the steep forested hillsides above and could see no value in a place where there was no wide plateau to farm and no sheltered bay to use as a harbor. Today, needless to say, things are different. Public campgrounds, commercial resorts, easily accessed hiking trails, and a booming tourist industry draw vacationers and weekend road warriors to what once was a sleepy hamlet. Listen carefully enough, and you can hear the shopkeepers grumble over what seems an insolvable dilemma: they need the money tourists bring in, but the tourists ruin the blissful quiet and solitude that used to be Big Sur.

An especially telling moment came during the El Niño winter of 1998, when severe storms washed out large sections of the Coast Highway, cutting Big Sur off from the rest of the world. For nearly three months, state crews waited for the storms to back off before moving in to make repairs. When the media found a back way in to talk to the locals about the inevitable distress they must be feeling, the consensus was anything but. We like it this way, the locals claimed. It's like a vacation! When the roads opened up again, however, it was back to business.

But forget all the tourists and remember the gift the Spanish left for us: the forests, canyons, and rocky cliffs make Big Sur one of the best escapes for solitude and adventure around.

Getting There

There really aren't many options from getting in and out of the Big Sur coast area: the Coast Highway (Highway 1) south from Carmel or north from San Luis Obispo is the only direct access. Public transportation ranges from limited to nonexistent.

Adjoining Areas

NORTH: **Monterey Bay**

EAST: **Ventana Wilderness**

inside out

Parks/Beaches

If Alice in Wonderland had driven south on a secluded highway winding around the edges of ocean cliffs instead of falling down a rabbit hole, this is a lot like the ride she would have taken. Just follow the Coast Highway south from Monterey and see for yourself. The waterfalls cascading off cliffs into the ocean, wild rivers slicing through the woods, shots of light turning the trees golden, and an absolute silence broken only by the sounds of nature seem like something out of a fairy tale. This is the result of many years of western settlers basically leaving the Big Sur coast alone, although they do seem to be visiting in annoyingly large numbers these days. Even with the big weekend crowds, however, there is enough space out here to get off the highway and find some quiet privacy without an unreasonable amount of effort. Just remember, despite the pavement, the occasional roadside business, and the fact that these public areas are called parks, this is the wild. Leave things as you find them and, most important, don't do anything silly. There are no hospitals in Big Sur, and very few places to dial 911. Cell phones don't seem to work here either.

The 1,276-acre **Point Lobos State Reserve** juts into the Pacific with its magnificent cliff sides, sandy coves, tide pools, and Monterey cypress groves. Pets are not allowed in the park, and for good reason. This fragile wildlife area is home to more than 250 bird and animal species and 300 species of plants. As one might suspect, Point Lobos is paradise found for bird-watchers and wildlife enthusiasts. From Sea Lion Point, one can watch the sea lions on the rocks offshore. Bird Island is a sanctuary for waterfowl, and sea otters can frequently be seen from most of the bluffs. Guided tours of the park are available during the summer. From Carmel, take the Coast Highway south for 3 miles and proceed to the park's entrance on the west side of the highway. For additional information, contact the park at (831) 624-4909.

Garrapata State Park 4 miles south of Point Lobos is a great spot for whale watching from the cliffs above the beach and tidepooling down below. The park covers 4 miles of coastline and extends inland over nearly 3,000 acres of hilly terrain. Its best feature is the views of the coast from the cliffs above the beach. Sea otters also can be found here, quite often in large numbers. Watch carefully for the pullout for this one, 2 miles south of the Malapaso Creek crossing on the Coast Highway. Call (831) 667-2315 for more information.

Andrew Molera State Park is a 4,749-acre parkland of meadows, mountains, flatlands, and sandy beach along 2.5 miles of coast. An abundance of plant and animal life is found here, much of it visible from the main hiking trails. Bird-watching is particularly popular at the mouth of the Big Sur River, which flows out of the coastal hills and into the ocean at a lagoon that has been designated a bird sanctuary. Surf casting is another popular activity at this park, particularly during the January steelhead season. The damp month of January is also when visitors can stand on the beach and see migrating gray whales offshore. Though Andrew Molera is a day-use park and closes at sunset, it does have a few rustic, primitive campsites where visitors can stay overnight with permits (see Camping, below). From Carmel, take the Coast Highway south for 24 miles and proceed to the park's entrance on the west side of the highway. For additional information, contact the park at (831) 667-2315.

For those who like hiking and history, **Point Sur State Historic Park** should be on the agenda for any visit to the Big Sur coast. This spot's central feature is the historic lighthouse, built in 1889, which watches over the rocky shore once nicknamed the "Graveyard of the Pacific" because so many shipwrecks have occurred there. The Point Sur Lighthouse was managed by four families until it became an automated lighthouse in 1974. Each Sunday, tours are given of the lighthouse, the homes where the former light keepers lived, and the old workshops. But the natural surroundings shouldn't be overlooked. Point Sur's 34 acres provide hikers with seemingly endless vistas up and down the Big Sur Coast and out to the ocean beyond. From Carmel, take the Coast Highway south for 20 miles and proceed to the park's entrance on the west side of the highway. For additional information, contact the park at (831) 667-2315.

Pfeiffer–Big Sur State Park is one of the state's smaller parks at 821 acres. But size isn't everything, and the park is surrounded by an enormous undeveloped wilderness area made up of numerous privately held tracts of land. Raccoons, deer, bobcats, and gray foxes inhabit the area, which includes a spectacular redwood grove along the Big Sur River which cuts a deep canyon through the center of the park. Like any park containing a redwood grove, Pfeiffer–Big Sur is a popular hiking spot, particularly since the trails are easy to get to, such as the one to the 60-foot-high Pfeiffer Falls. There's also a large campground (see Camping, below), and guided walks through the park are available during the summer season. From Carmel, take the Coast Highway south for 27 miles and proceed to the park's entrance on the west side of the highway. For additional information, contact the park at (831) 667-2171.

Pfeiffer Beach is one of the easiest direct access points to the coast, with interesting rocky cliffs and caves surrounding a nice sandy cove. The adventurous will try to surf or kayak from here, but the surf and riptides are generally too rough and the water too cold to warrant the significant risk of being flipped over. We recommend enjoying the scenery instead. The beach is managed by Los Padres National Forest. For more information, call (831) 385-5434. Take Sycamore Canyon Rd west from the Coast Highway; the beach is at the end.

Without question, **Julia Pfeiffer Burns State Park** encompasses the most spectacular stretch of coast in the Big Sur area. Situated on 3,580 acres, the park includes a 1,680-acre underwater reserve, an 80-foot-high waterfall that dramatically plunges into the ocean from granite cliffs, and hiking trails that run along the coast and up through the coastal mountains covered with redwoods, sycamores, big-leaf maples, cottonwoods, and willows. It's open daily from sunrise to sunset (no camping), and while summer is the most crowded time of year, visitors should aim for spring, when the hillsides are lusciously green and the streams flow vigorously. From Carmel, take the Coast Highway south for 35 miles and proceed to the park's entrance on the east side of the highway. For additional information, contact the park at (831) 667-2315.

Hiking

As stunningly beautiful as the Big Sur coast is by car, you really can't see it unless you actually park and go for a walk in the wilds. Hundreds of miles of walking and hiking trails traverse the coastal parks, providing a good mix of easy walks and mild sweat–breakers—all with big rewards in exchange for little work. Longer backpacking hauls in the deep wilderness are more plentiful in the Ventana Wilderness to the east (see Ventana Wilderness chapter).

At Andrew Molera State Park (see Parks/Beaches, above), the **Beach**

and Headlands Trail (easy; 3 miles round trip) is a great choice for the day adventurer who wants to get a little taste of everything the Big Sur coast has to offer. The first half mile follows the north banks of the wild and pristine Big Sur River, where spawning salmon and steelhead can be seen during the winter run. The next leg passes through a forest of willows, then on to Molera Point, which overlooks the beach, the rocks, and the crashing waves. Next, enjoy the beaches, being careful not to get foolishly washed out to sea. The final segment of the loop returns on the opposite side of the river through open grasslands leading back to the park's main entrance. Take as long as you like and meander, because the more you look, the more you see. From Carmel, take the Coast Highway south for 24 miles and proceed to the park's entrance on the west side of the highway. The trail loop starts at the parking lot, where free maps are available. For additional information, contact the park at (831) 667-2315.

Another nice, quick walk is along **Soberanes Loop Trail** (easy; 1.8 miles round trip) at Garrapata State Park (see Parks/Beaches, above). The trail cuts directly through to some nice overlooks where visitors can take in the splendor of waves crashing against the rocks below, along with a wide view of Point Sur and the coast to the south. This is also a favorite whale-watching spot during the winter migration. The park is 2 miles south of the Malapaso Creek crossing on the Coast Highway. Call (831) 667-2315 for more information.

A favorite among the pass-through adventurers who have only an hour or two to explore Big Sur is one of two walks to the waterfalls in Julia Pfeiffer Burns State Park (see Parks/Beaches, above). The easiest way to get to McWay Falls is via **McWay Falls Trail** (easy; 1 mile round trip), which can be tricky to find, since it begins on the east side of the highway and you have to park in the lot to the west. Just go through the walking path tunnel under the road and it's a straight shot to the falls, which drop to the beach below from the creek at trailside. The other route to McWay Falls is a longer walk, but the falls are more impressive from that perspective. Take the **Pfeiffer Falls Trail/Valley View Trail loop** (easy; 1.8 miles round trip) from the park office through a path of strictly mild grades and shady creek crossings slicing through the redwood forest to a nice upward vista of the 60-foot falls and the cliff face behind them. Continue the loop toward an open ridge for more views of the canyons and coast, then follow the loop back to the starting point. For those with less time to kill, take the short half-mile nature walk through the forest along **Nature Trail** (easy; 0.5 mile round trip), which starts at the park main entrance. All trails are well marked. From Carmel, take the Coast Highway south for 35 miles and proceed to the park's entrance on the west side of the highway.

Maps for all hikes are available at the park entrance. For additional information, contact the park at (831) 667-2315.

To the north, **Grove Trail** in **Point Lobos State Reserve** (easy; 1 mile) is another nice nature stroll. You'll find stunning groves of Monterey cypress along this trail, plus countless curiosities along its other walking paths, particularly those with views of the rocks offshore, where without fail numerous sea mammals can be seen sunning themselves. It is best to just grab a trail map and explore on your own. Take Riley Ranch Rd west from the Coast Highway. More information, (831) 624-4909.

Rocky Ridge Trail (moderate; 4 miles round trip) catapults more than 1,500 feet above Garrapata State Park (see Parks/Beaches, above) on the east side of the Coast Highway, and while the trail climbs in the opposite direction of the coast, it tops out at a great overlook that reveals a wide vista of the Monterey coast north to Soberanes and Yankee points, as well as Point Lobos. The trailhead is not marked, so look for pullout 14 east of the highway, using the Malapaso Creek crossing on the Coast Highway north of the park as a landmark. Call (831) 667-2315 for more information.

At Julia Pfeiffer Burns State Park, climb to the Pfeiffer Ridge coastal overlook on **Buzzards Roost Trail** (moderate; 3 miles round trip), which ascends from the redwoods and open-meadowed western flanks of the park to an open vista looking down upon it all. The walk is not at all switchbacky or unreasonably difficult, but the trail is not well manicured and leaves you exposed to cold ocean winds. A more strenuous hike in this park is along **McWay Canyon Trail** (moderately difficult; 4 miles round trip), which jets up (with occasionally steep grades) to 1,800 feet above the forested canyons and rocky ocean shores—a nice day trip or even a good first leg for a longer haul through the adjacent Ventana Wilderness (see Ventana Wilderness chapter). Both hikes begin at the park entrance, 35 miles south of Carmel, on the west side of the Coast Highway. **Tan Bark Trail** (moderately difficult; 6.5 miles round trip), is only suitable for a day hike if you head out before noon. Be sure to take plenty of water and a snack. The payoff for navigating the steep ascent of over 2,000 feet in a little more than 3 miles, through numerous switchbacks, is more stunning vistas of the forests and oceanfront below, and the satisfaction of being able to say you got out of your car for more than a few hours. This hike starts a mile north of the main entrance to Julia Pfeiffer Burns State Park, east from the Partington Cove pullout on the Coast Highway. Pick up a trail map at the main park entrance before heading up. For additional information, contact the park at (831) 667-2315.

Camping

Reservations are a must at **Pfeiffer–Big Sur State Park.** The 218 sites for tents or RVs (no hookups; RV limit 32 feet) fill up with incredible speed, as this is one of the most popular state parks in California. The campground has a laundromat and grocery store. Each site has a picnic table and a fire pit, with running water and showers nearby. Propane gas is also available. For those looking for a more rustic experience, there are several primitive sites (no showers, pit toilets) that can be reached on foot or by bike. *Reservations are taken through the state system, (800) 444-7275. From Carmel, take the Coast Hwy south for about 25 miles. Proceed to the park entrance on the west side of the highway. For additional information, contact the park at (831) 667-2315 or (831) 649-2836.*

Ventana Campground has 70 sites (some hookups; RV limit 22 feet) in the woods not far from the ocean. Each site has a fire pit and picnic table, and there are showers and flush toilets nearby. *From Carmel, take the Coast Hwy south, roughly 28 miles to the campground entrance. For additional information, contact the campground at (831) 667-2688.*

Andrew Molera State Park has several primitive campsites (no showers, pit toilets) for those looking for a rustic camping experience. The sites are accessible on foot only, via a 0.3-mile walk from the parking area. There is running water in the camp area, and each site has a fire pit. Reservations are not taken. *From Carmel, take the Coast Hwy south about 21 miles to the park entrance. Permits (required) are issued on a first-come, first-served basis from the park office at the main entrance. For additional information, contact the park at (831) 667-2315 or (831) 649-2836.*

Options for RV campers in the Big Sur coast area are somewhat limited and fill up quickly, but a few **private campgrounds** are available:

Fernwood Park is a privately owned facility with 16 tent sites (showers, toilets) and 49 RV sites (some hookups; various RV lengths accommodated). Each site has a fire grill and a picnic table. A grocery store is nearby. *From Carmel, drive 28 miles south on the Coast Hwy to the campground. For more information, contact the park at (831) 667-2422.*

The **Big Sur Campground** has 40 sites (full hookups; various RV lengths accommodated), rest rooms, showers, a dump station, and a laundromat. Each site has a fire grill and a picnic table. *From Carmel, take the Coast Hwy south about 27 miles to the campground entrance. For additional information, contact the park at (831) 667-2322.*

Riverside Campground has 46 sites for tents (showers, toilets) or RVs (some hookups; various RV lengths accommodated). Each site has a fire grill and a table. *From Carmel, take the Coast Hwy south about 25 miles to the campground entrance. For additional information, contact the park at (831) 667-2414.*

Wildlife

When it comes to wildlife in Big Sur, it seems timing is everything. Between **gray whales** off the coast, **Monarch butterflies** in the forests, **waterfowl** in the marshes, and **steelhead** and **salmon** in the rivers, you've got to catch most of the interesting creatures as they pass through in their annual migrations. Monterey Bay National Marine Sanctuary, (831) 647-4201, is the main clearinghouse for wildlife information and data in the entire sanctuary region. Other than that, individual ranger stations and interpretive centers at key public spaces, chief among them the nature center at Point Lobos State Reserve, (831) 624-4909, are also helpful and informative resources. Most have handouts on local wildlife, where to find animals, and what to do and not to do if you come face-to-face with them.

The best bet for catching a glimpse of marine mammals is to head to one of the more easily accessed coastal areas. Pfeiffer Beach and the beach and headlands areas at Andrew Molera State Park, Garrapata State Park, and Point Lobos State Reserve (see Parks/Beaches, above) are good choices. From any of these spots, gray whales can be spied on the winter migration to Baja California, while **dolphins** and **porpoises** can commonly be seen frolicking just offshore. **Seals, sea lions,** and **elephant seals** come ashore by the herd, and are commonly seen sunning themselves on the rocky islands off the coast. **Sea otters** are more bashful and difficult to spot at times, but look for them. They have been known to swim right alongside divers on those rare occasion that the rips and surf are calm enough for a scuba dive from the shore.

The marsh areas at Andrew Molera State Park and Point Lobos State Reserve are the key spots along the Big Sur coast for viewing migratory **shorebirds,** while adjacent forested areas are prime spotting grounds for others. The Monterey Peninsula Audubon Society has a **birding hot line** updated weekly with current information about rare bird sightings, and even gives directions to the hot spots, (831) 375-9122. Among birds to look for in these parts are chestnut-backed chickadees, juncos, hummingbirds, California quail, white-crowned sparrows, scrub jays, white-throated swifts, kestrels, red-tailed hawks, turkey vultures, brown pelicans, oystercatchers, great blue herons, and great and snowy egrets.

The amazing and complex micro-world of the coasts intertidal zones is a favorite attraction for children. The best and most easily accessed **tide pools** along the Big Sur coast are at Point Lobos State Reserve and Garrapata State Park. Look for interesting algae, invertebrates, rock-dwelling fishes, and sometimes eels among these rocks. (Also, beware of sleeper waves and potentially hazardous surf.) Point Lobos has an interpretive center, (831) 624-4909. The marine sanctuary office in Monterey,

(831) 647-4201, can help with pointers and information about tide pools and wildlife in general that will help make your exploring more informed. Also consult a joint publication of the sanctuary and the Monterey Bay Aquarium (see Attractions, Monterey Bay chapter), *A Natural History of Monterey Bay,* available from the Monterey Bay Aquarium Press, 886 Cannery Row, Monterey, CA 93940, ww.mbayaq.org. The aquarium bookstore can be reached at (831) 648-4952.

It is difficult to suggest a place to go where you won't see some kind of wildlife in Big Sur's wooded areas, but among the best bets for viewing lots of creatures are the trails through eastern Pfeiffer–Big Sur State Park and at Point Lobos. The cast of characters is long and diverse, but don't be surprised if you come across any of the following in your travels: **coyotes, raccoons, badgers, weasels, mountain lions, bobcats, black-tailed deer,** and numerous small rodents, including shrews.

Water Sports

This is going to sound a lot like a lecture from an overprotective parent, but going into the water off this coast is a risky proposition—especially for those who are inexperienced, out of shape, or both. We don't recommend **surfing** or **kayaking** off the Big Sur coast for those who aren't highly experienced, since breaks are big and bad, and rocks are sharp virtually everywhere here (see Monterey Bay and Santa Cruz chapters for better pickings). The bets are pretty solid that on any given day trying to paddle offshore in Big Sur, getting past the breaks is going to be a major drama . . . and even if you manage to, bringing a kayak back in for a beach landing without getting rolled would be sheer luck. If you insist, however, try surfing or kayaking at **Pfeiffer Beach** or offshore of **Andrew Molera State Park** (see Parks/Beaches, above). Whichever the choice, there are no **outfitters** in Big Sur itself. In Monterey, Monterey Bay Kayaks, 693 Del Monte Ave, (831) 373-5357, and Adventures by the Sea, 299 Cannery Row, (831) 372-1807, are the closest and best bet for water sportsters. Also try Sunshine Surf and Sport, 443 Lighthouse Ave, (831) 442-3033.

As a general rule, **swimming** off the Big Sur coast is also a bad idea. The water is cold, and the currents rough. No joke: people really *do* get swept out to sea along the California coast, so be awake, alert, and smart—especially here. **China Cove** in Point Lobos State Reserve (see Parks/Beaches, above) is a protected area where the water is relatively shallower and warmer than on the rest of this coast, however, so if it's one of those rare hot summer days on the wild coast you might try taking a dunk there. Other potential swimming areas are along the **Big Sur River** in Pfeiffer–Big Sur State Park (see Parks/Beaches, above)—but again, be careful.

Because of the powerful currents and wild surf off the Big Sur coast, only divers with advanced skills and a good rundown on current conditions should consider jumping in here. Besides, some of the best **scuba diving** in the world is a short drive north in Monterey Bay (see Scuba Diving, Monterey Bay chapter). Still, Virg's Landing, with its dive boat *Princess,* gets up to Big Sur from Morro Bay from time to time, 1215 Embarcadero, Morro Bay, (805) 772-1222. Aquarius, with locations both at 32 Cannery Row and 2040 Del Monte Ave in Monterey, (831) 375-1933 and (831) 375-6605, has tour options, rentals, instruction, and a good variety of equipment for sale—but don't expect any outfitters from Monterey to be enthusiastic about putting a beginner in the waters off Big Sur.

Scenic Drives

There's nothing like a winding, hilly highway hugging the coast at the top of wild, rocky cliffs overlooking the ocean. The 25-mile stretch of the **Coast Highway** both north and south of central Big Sur may well be the prettiest drive in all the state. There are numerous turnouts along the way to take it in—those with time to spare really can't help themselves. Take it all the way to San Luis Obispo if heading south, or just keep track of your time and distance so you know where to turn around and head back. Before heading out for a drive here, however, keep in mind that the roads into and out of Big Sur are particularly susceptible to rock slides and washouts, as the cliffs above and below them are constantly eroding. In the El Niño storms of 1998, central Big Sur was literally cut off from the rest of the world for more than two months because of road failures north and south of the peninsula. It may be prudent to check on highway conditions before beginning any Big Sur coastal journey. The Big Sur Chamber of Commerce, (831) 667-2100, or any California Highway Patrol office should have up-to-date information on highway conditions.

Fishing

Winter fly-fishing in the Big Sur area can be dicey—not because there aren't fish in the rivers, but rather because of increasingly stringent and confusing regulations. Before setting out to snag a few **steelheads** from the **Big Sur River,** check in with the local state Department of Fish and Game office, (831) 649-2870. As of this writing, open season on the river ran from the last Saturday in April to November 15—with a five-fish limit on steelhead and a two-fish limit on salmon. But regulations throughout the state are in a constant state of flux, so visitors have to check on the latest. Cameron and Smith Outfitters, 215 Grand Ave, Pacific Grove, (831) 657-0931, leads guided fishing outings in the Big Sur area.

Surf fishing spots along the Big Sur coast are limited, naturally, to those areas where you can actually get to the water. But heed this warning: bring all the equipment you will need with you, as pickings are slim once you've arrived in Big Sur. There are **bait and tackle** dealers in the Monterey Bay Area, including Seiner's Hold Bait & Tackle, 32 Cannery Row, (831) 375-6958, and the Compass, at Fisherman's Wharf, (831) 647-9222. A stop at one of these places or, even better, some advance planning will save you a headache and a wad of money. Now, for the fishing spots: we suggest the beaches at **Pfeiffer–Big Sur** and **Garrapata State Parks** (see Parks/Beaches, above) as surf- and rock-fishing spots for **perch, kingfish, jacksmelt, lingcod, salmon,** and **steelhead.** For a deepwater fishing gig, hook up with one of the charters out of Monterey or Santa Cruz (see Fishing, Monterey Bay and Santa Cruz chapters).

Horseback Riding

The wilderness adjacent to the Big Sur coast is so expansive and wild that heading out on horseback may actually be preferable to hoofing it—especially on long hauls into the backcountry (see Ventana Wilderness chapter). Molera Big Sur Trail Rides has rentals and guided tours through the expansive riding trails at **Andrew Molera State Park,** (831) 625-8664. There are also numerous outfitters with rentals and tour packages available just north of Big Sur proper. Ventana Wilderness Ranch and Expeditions, 1780 Prescott, Monterey, (831) 372-4974, and Ventana Wilderness Outfitters and Guides, 38655 Tassajara Rd, Carmel Valley, (831) 659-2153, give riding tours both on a private ranch in the valley and, for the more adventurous, out in the Ventana backcountry.

Adventure Calendar

Big Sur International Marathon, late April: *along the Coast Highway,* (831) 625-6226.
Big Sur River Run, late October: (831) 667-2345.

Attractions

There isn't exactly a Big Sur in Big Sur . . . not a town by that name, anyway. Originally El Sur Grande (Spanish for "the Big South"), Big Sur encompasses 90 miles of rugged, spectacular coastline stretching south from Carmel to San Simeon. A narrow, twisting segment of Hwy 1 (built with convict labor in the 1930s) snakes through this coastal area, and the mist-shrouded forests, plunging cliffs, and cobalt sea bordering the road make the drive one of the most beautiful in the country—if not the world. The region is so scenic that some folks favor giving it national park status; others, however, recoil in horror at the thought of involving the federal government in the preservation of this untamed land and have coined the expression "Don't Yosemitecate Big Sur."

Despite Big Sur's popularity, the area miraculously has remained sparsely populated, and most people journey here for only a few days to camp or backpack—or to luxuriate in the elegant (and, in some cases, exorbitantly priced) resorts hidden in the hills. The bumper-to-bumper traffic on summer weekends is reminiscent of LA's rush hour; to avoid the crowds, come midweek or in the spring, when the gold, yellow, and purple wildflowers brighten the windswept landscape. Check in with the folks at the **Big Sur Land Trust,** (831) 625-5523, to find out where you can pick up an audiotape offering a guided tour of the region.

Whether you're cruising through for the day or plan to hide out in a resort, be sure to check out where Hwy 1 crosses Bixby Creek via the 268-foot-high, 739-foot-long **Bixby Bridge** (also known as the Rainbow Bridge), a solitary, majestic arch built in 1932 that attracts lots of snap-happy photographers. Nearby is the automated **Point Sur Lighthouse,** built in 1889 and situated 360 feet above the surf on Point Sur (see Parks/Beaches, above), a giant volcanic-rock island. Inexpensive (though physically taxing) 2.5-hour guided lighthouse tours, some under spectacular moonlight, are offered on weekends year-round and on Wednesdays in the summer (be sure to take a jacket, even in the summer months); located off Hwy 1, 19 miles south of Carmel, (831) 625-4419.

If you'd rather be shopping, visit the **Coast Gallery,** a showplace for local artists and craftspeople featuring pottery, jewelry, and paintings, including watercolors by author Henry Miller, who lived nearby for more than 15 years. The author's fans will also want to seek out the Henry Miller Library. In addition to a great collection of Miller's books and art, the library serves as one of Big Sur's cultural centers and features the art, poetry, prose, and music of locals; it's open Tuesday through Sunday, and is located just beyond Nepenthe restaurant on the east side of Hwy 1, (831) 667-2574. Seekers of other sorts flock to **Esalen Institute,** the world-famous New Age retreat and home of heavenly massages and hot springs that overlook the ocean; call (831) 667-3000 for general information, and (831) 667-3047 for hot springs reservations. The springs are accessible to non-guests daily in the wee hours only, from 1am to 3:30am.

Lodgings

Deetjen's Big Sur Inn ☆   Located in a damp canyon, most of these redwood cabins are divided into two units, with dark wood interiors, hand-hewn doors without locks or keys, and nonexistent insulation. Some have shared baths, and many are quite charming in a rustic sort of way. *On Hwy 1 (3 miles S of Pfeiffer–Big Sur State Park), Big Sur; (831) 667-2377; $$.*

Post Ranch Inn ☆☆☆☆   *Travel & Leisure* magazine has hailed the 98-acre Post Ranch Inn as "the most spectacular hotel on the Pacific Coast," and that might not be hyperbole. It is one of the new breed of eco-hotels, where the affluent can indulge in sumptuous luxury and still feel politically correct. *On Hwy 1 (30 miles S of Carmel), Big Sur; (831) 667-2200 or (800) 527-2200; $$$.*

Ripplewood Resort ☆   With its 16 spartan cabins clustered along a rugged section of Highway 1, Ripplewood Resort is a wonderful place to go with a large group of friends. During the summer the popular units are typically booked four months in advance. *On Hwy 1 (about 1 mile N of Pfeiffer–Big Sur State Park), Big Sur; (831) 667-2242; $$.*

Ventana Country Inn Resort ☆☆☆☆   Set on a chaparral-covered hill in the Santa Lucia Mountains, this modern inn is almost too serene and contemplative to be called decadent, yet too luxurious to be called anything else. *On Hwy 1 (28 miles S of Carmel, 2½ miles S of Pfeiffer–Big Sur State Park), Big Sur; (831) 667-2331 or (800) 628-6500; $$$.*

More Information

Big Sur Chamber of Commerce: *(831) 667-2100.*
Big Sur coast state parks and beaches: *(831) 667-2315.*
State parks camping reservations: *(800) 444-7275.*

Ventana Wilderness

Some 164,503 acres of mountain wilderness located within the Los Padres National Forest and just east of the Big Sur coast in the Santa Lucia Mountains, including the Ventana Cones, Tassajara Hot Springs, and the Cone Peak areas.

Ventana Wilderness, part of the 2-million-acre Los Padres National Forest complex that extends from the Big Sur region to the Los Angeles County line, holds the southernmost stand of coast redwoods. It is that mixing zone where the lush, forested northern and central coast give way to the arid desert climate of sunny Southern Cal. Ventana consists of 164,503 acres of rugged terrain in the Santa Lucia Mountains, a coastal range running the length of Monterey County. Without actually visiting Ventana, it is difficult for most people to visualize its awesome diversity. Geologic uplifting and faulting have fragmented the landscape, creating unique rock formations. Blocks of sandstone emerge from the earth to form a moonscape that in the wilderness silence at dusk seems eerie and impossible.

Some portions of the wilderness are at sea level. Others top out at 6,000 feet. The result of this stratification is an interesting mix of plant communities inhabiting the same area. Groves of redwoods, for example, are found on the banks of the Carmel, Little Sur, Big Sur, and Arroyo Seco Rivers, all of which flow furiously in springtime along their narrow paths through the wilderness toward the ocean. Just a few miles away at the area's highest elevations, visitors can find a host of subalpine plants scattered throughout the barren, rocky landscape. Ventana is home to the rare and spirelike Santa Lucia fir; this is its only natural habitat in the world. Much of the wilderness area is covered by dense brush and meadows, a result of the Marble Cone fire, which scorched over 90 percent of the wilderness for 21 days back in 1977. Even two decades of rebirth has not reestablished the forested terrain that was here before, but the afterburn makes Ventana a wonderful ecology laboratory. (Naturally, the poison oak has had little trouble rebounding!)

Since Ventana is a designated national wilderness area, legislation mandates strictly minimal user impact on the environment. Permanent structures are generally not allowed—meaning no campground improvements beyond the essential. Also, motor vehicles are not permitted. Therefore, nature-loving visitors will be pleased to find a nearly complete absence of human interference.

As with so many of our wild places, the rules intended to protect and preserve the natural pristine beauty of this area are exactly what make it that quiet place where we can disappear to discover ourselves. So strap on the backpack, take a few days off, and come on in for a spiritual tune-up.

Getting There

Given the size of Ventana Wilderness, there are a number of ways to get in. From the Coast Highway (Highway 1) in Carmel, take Carmel Valley Road east along the Carmel River canyon for access to Ventana's northeastern extremes. From here, choose any number of canyon roads cutting west into the wilderness area. A more direct access route is 10 miles south of Carmel on Palo Colorado Road, which bisects the forest and wilderness area. The Monterey Ranger Station is in King City, on US Highway 101 (US 101) 70 miles south of Salinas, 406 South Mildred Avenue, (831) 385-5434. For visitors approaching from the Big Sur area, however, it may be best instead to stop at the Forest Service outpost on the Coast Highway in Big Sur just north of Pfeiffer–Big Sur State Park. The Forest Service roads here are easiest to travel in passenger vehicles. RVs often have a slow go of it due to twists and turns and occasional steep grades.

Adjoining Areas

NORTH: **Monterey Bay**

EAST: **San Joaquin Valley**

inside out

Camping

Some people only fantasize about "disappearing" into the woods long enough to mutate into a Charles Manson look-alike by the time they see civilization again. Of those who actually get the time to drop out for a while, however, this is perhaps the premier place to do it. Within the wilderness area boundaries, camping must be done in a "leave no trace" spirit. There are no developed campgrounds here, though some are located in adjacent woods in Los Padres National Forest. As with all national forests, stays are limited to 14 days, and camping in unimproved areas is encouraged so long as it is at least a quarter mile from a developed site. All campers must have proper permits for use of fire. They are available from the ranger station outpost in Big Sur, just north of Pfeiffer–Big Sur State Park on the west side of the Coast Highway. To check in by phone, call the Monterey Ranger District, 406 S Mildred Ave, King City, (831) 385-5434. **Campground and trail conditions** in Ventana and the Santa Lucia range in general are subject to severe weather and fire, so it is best to check ahead just in case.

Bottchers Gap campground is on Mill Creek in the northwestern region of the forest, just outside Ventana. There are 11 sites (no hookups; various RV lengths accommodated), with vault toilets and no showers. Water is piped in, and each site has a picnic table and a fire grill. Reservations are not taken. *From Carmel, take Hwy 1 south for roughly 10 miles. Turn right (east) on Palo Colorado Rd and drive 9 miles to the campground.*

White Oaks campground is on Anastasia Creek in the northeastern region of the forest, just outside Ventana. There are 8 tent sites (no RV access), with vault toilets and no showers. Water is piped in, and each site has a picnic table and a fire grill. Reservations are not taken. *From Carmel, travel south on Hwy 1. Turn east on Carmel Valley Rd and travel about 25 miles. Turn right (south) on Tassajara Rd and proceed to the campground about 9 miles ahead (veer left at the fork in the road).*

China Camp is located due south of White Oaks campground just outside Ventana. There are 8 sites (no hookups; various RV lengths accommodated), with vault toilets and no showers. Water is piped in, and each site has a picnic table and a fire grill. Reservations are not taken. *From Carmel, travel south on Hwy 1. Turn east on Carmel Valley Rd and travel about 25 miles. Turn right (south) on Tassajara Rd and proceed to the campground about 11 miles ahead (veer left at the fork in the road).*

Arroyo Seco campground is located along Arroyo Creek just outside the eastern side of Ventana. There are 51 sites (no hookups; various RV lengths accommodated), with vault toilets and no showers. Each site has a picnic table and a fire grill, and supplies are available less than a mile away in the town of Arroyo Seco. Reservations are not taken. *From Salinas, travel south on US 101 to the town of Greenfield. Exit west on to Greenfield–Arroyo Seco Rd. Proceed to the campground 1 mile west of the town of Arroyo Seco.*

Escondido Campground is centrally located, nestled between two sections of the Ventana Wilderness. There are 9 tent sites, vault toilets, no showers, and no RV access. Each site has a picnic table and a fire grill. No reservations are taken. *From Salinas, travel south on US 101 to the town of Greenfield. Exit west on to Greenfield–Arroyo Seco Rd. Travel roughly 20 miles to Indians Rd. Turn left (south) and proceed to the campground roughly 10 miles ahead.*

Hiking/Backpacking

The northern region of Los Padres National Forest has so many remarkable trails, it would be impractical to list them all. What follows are the highlights—but that doesn't mean a trail not listed is not worth visiting. On the contrary, we often found ourselves splitting hairs or flipping a coin to decide which trails to mention. For a more comprehensive listing of trails in Los Padres, contact the Los Padres National Forest, Monterey Ranger District, 406 S Mildred Ave, King City, (831) 385-5434. Before embarking on a hike through Los Padres, contact the ranger district to get proper **permits** (day permits are required, as well as overnight permits for camping) and **current trail information.** There is a ranger station outpost on the Coast Highway, just north of Pfeiffer–Big Sur State Park for those who cannot get to the main ranger station, which is south of Salinas on US 101. As with any wilderness area, bring plenty of water, particularly during summer when even the most durable of streams can dry up overnight. Hikers and backpackers in Los Padres and Ventana stage mainly from three areas: Bottchers Gap area, Los Padres Dam area, and the China Camp area. Good trail **maps** are available directly from the Forest Service. Write US Forest Service Information, Room 521, 630 Sansome St, San Francisco, CA 94111. Note that there are different Los Padres maps, including one specifically detailed for the Ventana/Monterey Ranger District area. Be sure to specify which one you're ordering, particularly since one of them excludes the Santa Lucia Mountains.

On the eastern side of the forest, the **China Camp–Sulphur Springs Trail** (difficult; varying lengths) takes hikers through several river crossings that can be difficult to maneuver during heavy runoff. Most of the terrain is made up of wide meadows, steep V-shaped canyons, and forests of pine. Some of the more popular destinations hikers choose include **Pine Valley Camp** (moderate; 11 miles round trip), **Round Rock Camp** (moderate; 19 miles round trip), or **Sulphur Springs Camp** (moderate; 28 miles round trip). There are several swimming areas along the trail, as well as a waterfall. Very occasionally, winter snow may dust this area; on the other hand, summer can bring very hot temperatures, particularly along the unshaded sandstone cliffs in Pine Valley. This hike is especially popular for its diversity; it takes hikers through cool river areas with dense foliage as well as desert areas with boulders and brush. To reach the trailhead from Carmel, travel south on Hwy 1. Turn east on Carmel Valley Rd and travel about 25 miles. Turn right (south) on Tassajara Rd and proceed to the trailhead about 11 miles ahead (veer left at the fork in the road) at China Camp.

The **China Camp–Los Padres Dam Trail** (moderate; varying lengths) also has several popular destinations with hikers, such as **Miller Camp** (moderate; 15 miles round trip), **Bluff Camp** (moderate; 22 miles round trip), and the **Los Padres Dam** (moderate; 33 miles round trip). Much of this route follows the meandering Carmel River, with numerous crossings and switchbacks. Warning: With winter rains, the river often becomes completely impassable, getting up to 5 feet deep in areas, and swiftly sweeping away those who venture in. In the past, hikers have become stranded along the trail, unable to cross the raging waters. So always check the weather, and check in with the forest rangers, before taking to the wilderness here. This hike is most rewarding for those who love rivers and the wildlife that they attract. During the summer, when temperatures can get into the high 80s, the river is relatively shallow and tame, and hikers can get a drink and cool off on its shady, rocky banks. Though the route is an easy downhill slope to the Los Padres Dam, the moderate climb back to China Camp will take longer. From Carmel, go south on Hwy 1. Turn east on Carmel Valley Rd and travel about 25 miles. Turn right (south) on Tassajara Rd and proceed to the trailhead about 11 miles ahead (veer left at the fork in the road) at China Camp.

On the western side of Los Padres, the **Bottchers Gap–Big Pines Camp Trail** (difficult; varying lengths) begins at the Bottchers Gap campground. Depending on your taste, hiking into the Ventana Wilderness along this route can be a one- or two-day affair, depending on when you decide to turn around. Or meander and camp out for two weeks. Most hikers pick **Devil's Peak** (difficult; 9 miles round trip), **Comings Camp** (difficult; 12 miles round trip), or **Big Pines Camp** (difficult; 16 miles round trip) as their ultimate destination. A few primitive campgrounds (pit toilets, no water) exist in the area, with cool streams nearby to swim in. No matter which destination you pick, the trail is decidedly uphill, through oaks that give way to chaparral and beautiful vistas over the mountains and ocean. Mill Creek Canyon lies along the Palo Colorado fault, where a wall of granite rock on one side of the canyon has been separated from metamorphic rock on the other side. From Carmel, take Hwy 1 south for roughly 10 miles. Turn right (east) on to Palo Colorado Rd and drive 9 miles to the trailhead at Bottchers Gap campground. For additional information, contact Los Padres National Forest, Monterey Ranger District at (831) 385-5434.

The **Bottchers Gap/Ventana Trail** (difficult; varying lengths) also begins at the Bottchers Gap campground. As mentioned earlier, hiking into Ventana from Bottchers Gap is an expedition that can take one or more days, depending on when you decide to turn back. Most hikers pick **Little Pines Camp** (moderate; 19 miles round trip), **Lone Pine Camp** (very difficult; 27 miles round trip), or **Ventana Double Cone** (very difficult; 35 miles round trip) as their ultimate destination. The climb to Little Pines, through ponderosa pine and oak, is relatively easy compared to the sharp incline that hikers encounter en route to Lone Pine and Ventana. Only the most determined attempt these hikes, and therefore the route is seldom traveled, making for a very solitary and peaceful experience. The views are awe-inspiring: from the summit at Ventana Double Cone (elevation 5,575 feet), hikers can watch the evening fog as it rolls in to the shore and fills the valleys below. From Carmel, take Hwy 1 south for roughly 10 miles. Turn right (east) onto Palo Colorado Rd and drive 9 miles to the trailhead at Bottchers Gap campground.

On the northern boundary of Los Padres, the **Los Padres Dam Trail** (difficult; varying lengths) enters Ventana from the opposite direction of Bottchers. This, too, can be a one-day affair or take several days, depending on how soon you turn around. Popular destinations with hikers include **Bluff Camp** (difficult; 9 miles round trip), **Sulphur Springs Camp** (difficult; 12 miles round trip), and **Round Rock Camp** (difficult; 21 miles round trip). What makes this route so rewarding (and also quite dangerous at times) is the meandering Carmel River: water is pretty much always in sight or just a stone's throw away, and river wildlife abounds. The trail also crosses the river in numerous places. Once again, during the rainy season, the river can become impassable. Check in with the forest rangers before taking to the wilderness here. From Salinas, go south on US 101 to the town of Greenfield. Exit west on Greenfield–Arroyo Seco Rd. Travel roughly 13 miles and veer right, onto Carmel Valley Rd. Travel roughly 20 miles to Cachagua Rd and turn left; go 6 miles to Nason Rd. Proceed about 1 mile to the parking area and trailhead.

Horseback Riding

Packing in on horseback is a great way to take in some of the rugged beauty of this place. Sit up high and let the horse watch your step for you. Popular day trips are from Bottchers Gap toward Devil's Peak or Mount Carmel, both offering wide vistas of the wilderness and the Big Sur coast from beyond 4,000 feet elevation. Longer treks through the diverse landscapes, however, are much more rewarding, particularly during late spring when temperatures are warming and streams are running strong. Numerous

outfitters offer rentals and tour packages. Ventana Wilderness Ranch and Expeditions, 1780 Prescott, Monterey, (831) 372-4974, and Ventana Wilderness Outfitters and Guides, 38655 Tassajara Rd, Carmel Valley, (831) 659-2153, give riding tours both on a private ranch in the valley and, for the more adventurous, out in the Ventana backcountry. Molera Big Sur Trail Rides in Big Sur, (831) 625-8664, offers trail rides and pack trips into Ventana as well.

Rock Climbing

While there are some outcroppings in Ventana where rock jocks can have plenty of fun, most head inland instead to **Pinnacles National Monument,** where the fragmented remains of an ancient volcano form countless caves and spire rock formations, some up to 1,200 feet high. A few words of warning, however, before you set your sights on Pinnacles. First, extreme weather in central California severely damaged roads and other park improvements in both 1997 and 1998, and at this writing, repairs were still under way. Second, some routes are subject to closure during nesting season for the peregrine falcon, which, even though it has been recommended for removal from the federal endangered species list, will likely be on it for a few years more. Finally, rock climbing here is dangerous. Novices have no business heading out alone, unless they want to be plucked off a peak by a helicopter. Always call ahead for information on **conditions;** phone the monument at (831) 389-4485. To approach the monument from the Monterey area, take Hwy 68 east to US 101, then continue south on 101 for 18 miles to the Hwy 146 east turnoff at Soledad. Follow Hwy 146 east to the park entrance. The park is bisected by the highway and also has an entrance from the San Benito area to the east on Hwy 146. Numerous outdoors **outfitters** are willing to guide climbers here; check with the ranger station for a list of reputable guides. One is Adventure Alternatives, based out of Carmel, (831) 624-4827.

Scenic Drives

If you're looking for a pleasant way to burn a tank of gas, the 30-mile drive through Carmel Valley and then into the Santa Lucia Mountains through **Tularcitos Canyon** is a scene to behold. Be prepared for a long, careful, meandering trip requiring your full attention on switchbacks and around curves. Features along the way include vistas of Sugarloaf Peak and Pigeon Point, following the County Rd G16 route through the wilderness region. In the forest itself, take the Tassajara Rd route southwest from County Rd G16.

Wildlife

Birders venturing into the Santa Lucia Mountains and Ventana Wilderness Area are in for a treat. The rare **California condor** and **peregrine falcon** are spotted here often, as are numerous doves, songbirds, chickadees, finches, and woodpeckers that make up the forest community. As you might expect in the raw wilderness of the central coast, **deer, wild pigs, bobcats, mountain lions, rattlesnakes,** and even the occasional **mountain goat** will be sharing the forests and canyons with you. Check with the ranger station at King City, (831) 385-5434, for information. Also note that some hunting is allowed in the wilderness area; take necessary precautions during hunting season.

Fishing

The Carmel and Big Sur Rivers, as well as San Jose Creek, are a favorite for fly-fishing during the **steelhead trout** and **coho salmon** runs in winter and spring. Numerous access points to the Carmel River are along Carmel Valley Rd east of the Coast Highway. Marshall Canyon and Roach Canyon are particularly good spots along the river to consider stopping. For the Big Sur River, access is outside of Ventana along the Coast Highway south of Point Sur and Swiss Canyon. Five miles of San Jose Creek is flanked by San Jose Creek Rd, which extends from the Coast Highway just south of the Carmel River State Beach. There are also numerous other small creeks and rivers, all suitable for salmon and steelhead action during the peak season. During summer, however, many smaller creeks dry out, leaving anglers with mainly the hundreds of small lakes throughout the wilderness to choose from. With recent Endangered Species Act listings involving the central coast steelhead and coho salmon, expect fishing regulations to be more confusing and convoluted than ever on the Big Sur River. Call the state Department of Fish and Game's Monterey field office, (831) 649-2870, to check on the latest regulations.

More Information

Department of Fish and Game, Monterey field office: *(831) 649-2870.*
Forest Service reservations system: *(800) 280-2267.*
Los Padres National Forest, Monterey Ranger District: *(831) 385-5434*
Monterey Peninsula Visitors and Convention Bureau: *(408) 649-1770.*

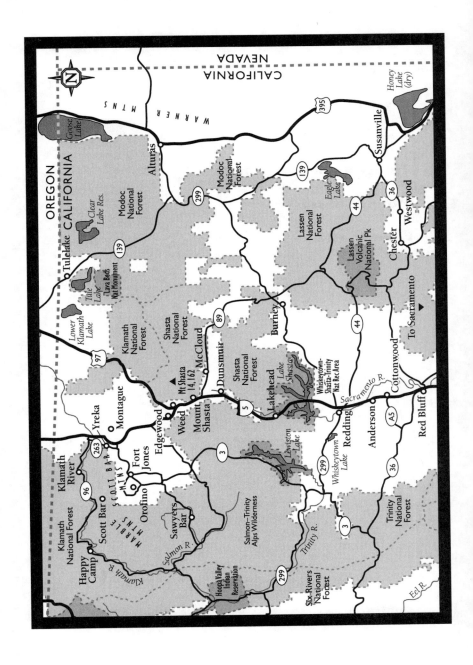

Northern
Mountains

Northern Mountains

Modoc
Region

Includes 1.6 million acres of wilderness in the Modoc National Forest, Medicine Lake and South Warner Wilderness Areas, Lava Beds National Monument, and Modoc National Wildlife Refuge.

On a state famous for its surfing and beachcombing spots, its ski resorts and glacial valleys, and its shining cities at the leading edge of modern American culture, the extreme northeast corner doesn't get much attention. That, however, is one of the nicest things about the high desert country here: despite the breathtaking mountain wilderness, seemingly boundless marsh sanctuaries for migrating birds, stunning lava-flow landscapes, and placid fishing lakes, there are no crowds. No traffic jams, no lines at the grocery store, no trouble getting a campsite, very few if any tour buses. As is the case with so much of the northern mountains and Cascade region, this is one of California's truly forgotten places.

Obscurity, however, does not presuppose unworthiness. The Modoc region, indeed, boasts a long list of "must-see" places.

Lava Beds National Monument, for example, seems more like another planet than a remote part of Northern California. Covering nearly 47,000 acres, this expanse of misshapen lava fields, dark and mysterious lava tubes and caves, and open craters on the banks of a long-dormant volcano is a geological wonder. Ironically, more Californians will fly to Hawaii for a glimpse of this kind of landscape than venture north to the Oregon border. Within Modoc National Forest, the high peaks, thick forests, wild and meandering rivers, and high mountain lakes of the 70,000-acre South Warner Wilderness are a backpacker's dream—and a challenge. The way to the highest peaks is trail-free, and at these high desert elevations (topping out at 9,000 feet), the weather is unpredictable year-round. At Medicine Lake, an old crater flooded by river water, swimming and fishing rival what you might find in the Sierra Nevada, and in an arguably more interesting setting: obsidian glass and lava fields. Finally, the Modoc region is a birder's paradise, as the marshes and wetlands of the nearly 7,000-acre Modoc National Wildlife Refuge are a haven for hundreds of species of waterfowl and other winged creatures migrating on the Pacific Flyway.

All of this spectacular wilderness is complemented by small, friendly towns like Alturas and Cedarville, built on the pioneering spirit of the Gold Rush and the transcontinental railroad. This is Mayberry, RFD, where people greet each other on the street instead of looking away. A well-planned trip to the Modoc area can be a rewarding escape not only from city life but also from the masses who flock to Yosemite and Tahoe during the peak tourist seasons.

Getting There

The preferred route is Interstate 5 north from the Sacramento Valley to Redding and the Highway 299 interchange. On Highway 299, head east to the small hamlets of Adin and Alturas. US 395 traverses the region's eastern end, and Highway 139 cuts a swath through the northwestern hinterlands between Lava Beds and Alturas. Be advised that winters can be severe in these parts—always carry chains. And if you plan to do any traveling on Forest Service roads, check first on road conditions, as many are not maintained to accommodate low-clearance vehicles. Four Forest Service ranger districts serve this area and are the main information centers for visitors: Devil's Garden Ranger District, 800 West 12th Street, Alturas, (530) 233-5811; Warner Mountain Ranger District, Highway 81 at Wallace Street, Cedarville, (530) 279-6116; Doublehead Ranger District, Modoc County Road at Wright Road, Tulelake, (530) 667-2246; and Big Valley Ranger District, Highway 139 at Cedar Street, Adin, (530) 299-3215.

Adjoining Areas

SOUTH: **Lake Shasta**

WEST: **Klamath Region**

Hiking/Backpacking

There are more than 140 miles of hiking trails on the Modoc National Forest public lands, and despite the seclusion and relatively undeveloped condition of this area (there are more mountain lakes than strip malls), we can recommend a number of day hikes that pay off in a big way—with nice vistas of the natural landscape, good up close views of odd volcanic rock formations, and even quiet lakeside strolls and fishing in mountain lakes more than 6,000 feet up. The best **maps** of the national forest are available directly from the Forest Service; write US Forest Service Information, Room 521, 630 Sansome St, San Francisco, CA 94111. There are three main maps for this national forest area: one full Modoc National Forest map, and one each for the South Warner and Medicine Lake Wilderness Areas. Access to some areas is restricted during the snowy season—until June in wet years. **Trail conditions** in any forest or wilderness area are subject to change, so check with the appropriate ranger station before setting out, particularly in spring or winter.

Glass Mountain (easy; no trail system, length varies) is one of those must-see wilderness spots, a vast area of ancient volcanic glassy obsidian, oddly shaped and immune to weather, covering about 4,000 acres. This stuff is difficult to walk on, so be careful and just meander. There is no trail system, but walkers should be sure to stay off the shiny, slick obsidian surfaces and walk on the lighter-colored rock instead. To reach the mountain and staging area, take Hwy 89 east from I-5 in Dunsmuir for 30 miles to Powder Hill Rd, then head north another 30 miles to Forest Rd 97. Six miles out, turn north on Forest Rd 43N99 and proceed to the mountain. For information, call the Doublehead Ranger District, (530) 667-2246.

Ice Caves Trail (easy; 0.25 mile round trip) is another quick, easy walk for those curious about the geologic formations caused by volcanic activity that has shaped the Modoc region. It's actually not much of a hike—more of a natural sciences field trip to look at some interesting caves. To reach the spot, take Hwy 89 east at Dunsmuir and continue 30 miles to Powder Hill Rd. Turn north and drive 20 miles to the caves on the left side of the road. For information, call the Doublehead Ranger District, (530) 667-2246.

Pine Creek Trail (moderate; 4 miles round trip) is a classic, short day hike into some stunning scenery bounded by Pine Creek canyon, Pine Creek Lake, and the Warner Mountains—about as far away as you can get from the state's urban population centers. This hike truly has that "you're out in the middle of nowhere" feel to it. To reach the trailhead from Alturas, head east for 5 miles on Parker Creek Rd, and proceed 10 miles to the turnoff to the east. Continue another 2 miles or so to the trailhead. For more information, call the Warner Mountain Ranger District, (530) 279-6116.

Mill Creek Falls Trail (easy; 0.5 miles round trip) is a short stroll to the water's edge at Modoc County's Tule Lake, a scenic mountain fishing spot in the northwestern corner of the forest. Those traveling with children who want to see the sights without having to pack in too far will appreciate this walk. To reach the trailhead from Alturas, head south on US Hwy 395 (US 395) for 19 miles to the town of Likely. Next, go 20 miles east on Jess Valley Rd to the lake, 3 miles past the fork in the road to the left. For more information, call the Warner Mountain Ranger District, (530) 279-6116.

Blue Lake Loop National Trail (easy; 2.5 miles round trip) is another easy waterside stroll by a pretty, mountainous lake that is easy to reach, even with children. The trail loops the lake, which has good fishing spots and is stocked with brown and rainbow trout. To reach the trailhead from Alturas, head south on US 395 for 19 miles to the town of Likely. From there, head 10 miles east on Blue Lake Rd, then veer south for 8 miles to the trailhead. For more information, call the Warner Mountain Ranger District, (530) 279-6116.

Backpackers wishing to take **longer treks** into the northeastern California wilderness should explore the Warner Mountain area south of Cedarville, one of the least discovered and most stunningly beautiful high-country outdoor playgrounds on the West Coast. Consult the **Warner Mountain Ranger District,** (530) 279-6116, for trail conditions and specific recommendations, and also be sure to obtain the official brochure/map. Naturally, winters are harsh here, so these hikes are best scheduled for the late spring to early autumn. With that in mind, here are a few suggestions:

Summit Trail (moderate; 12 miles round trip) is a 2,000-foot climb into the upper reaches of the South Warner Wilderness, where the secluded Patterson Lake basin sits just below 9,700-foot Warren Peak. You'll find wide vistas, nice lakeside camping, and plenty of time to listen to wilderness noises in the upper righthand corner of the state. This area is lightly traveled. To reach the trailhead from Alturas, head east for 12 miles on Parker Creek Rd. The entrance to Pepperdine trailhead is marked; turn south and proceed to this staging area, from which the Summit Trail also begins.

East Creek Trail (moderate; 15 miles round trip) is another popular route, but because there are few visitors to this lightly traveled spot, it's perfect for a well-paced trek through river canyons and over rocky peaks of the Warner Mountains, with elevations ranging between 7,000 and 8,000 feet. Backpackers taking this route may choose to make an extended loop of their journey using the prized **Summit Trail** (difficult; total possible loop 50 miles round trip), described above but approached from another vantage point, through pine forests, secluded canyons, and barren granite peaks, with elevations topping out at 9,000 feet around Patterson Lake.

East Creek Trail gets you to Poison Flat Trail, which connects easily to Summit Trail; Owl Creek Trail completes the link to two of the high peaks, connecting up again with Summit Trail on the western slopes. Rapid elevation gains and alternating terrain make this a trek to remember. To reach the East Creek trailhead from Alturas, head south on US 395 for 19 miles to Likely. From there, head east on Jess Valley Rd to S Warner Rd, then south to the Patterson staging area, where the East Creek Trail begins.

Visitors wishing to explore the unusual misshapen rock formations left behind by years of heavy volcanic activity that shaped this region 30,000 years ago should consider a walking tour of **Lava Beds National Monument,** a vast wilderness littered with such geologic oddities as lava tubes, caves, craters, and flows. There are 28,000 acres of federally protected wilderness here with 25 miles of interpretive trails, among them the **Whitney Butte Trail** (moderate; 7 miles round trip), which skirts the bizarre moonscape preserved at the Callahan Lava Flow; the less challenging **Thomas Wright Trail** (easy; 2.5 miles round trip), which covers the site of the infamous Thomas Wright battle with the Modoc Indians; and **Schonchin Butte Trail** (moderate; 1.5 miles round trip), which affords great views of the smaller Schonchin lava flow from the 5,200-foot lookout overhead. Call the monument headquarters, (530) 667-2282, for more information. The monument is about 140 miles northeast of Redding; take Hwy 299 east to Canby, then proceed northwest on Hwy 139 toward the Oregon border for about 50 miles. Follow signs to the monument entrance on the west side of the highway.

Camping

As with most of the national forests in California, camping in Modoc National Forest is allowed just about anywhere you can find a piece of ground flat enough to pitch a tent on—with just a few exceptions. The best camping areas in Modoc are near lakes, near the Lava Beds National Monument, or around the South Warner Wilderness. **Dispersed camping** is your best bet if you're backpacking in the wilderness, but be sure to get **permits** for any use of fire. The best maps are available directly from the Forest Service; write US Forest Service Information, Room 521, 630 Sansome St, San Francisco, CA 94111 (see primer at the beginning of this book). Periodic road closures are unavoidable. Check with the relevant ranger station for updated **road conditions** before deciding on a site located deep within the forest. Roads are not maintained for vehicles with low ground clearance. The Forest Service is currently reviewing its **reservations and fees** policies for this area, but generally no reservations are taken for any of the campgrounds listed below. Stays are limited to 14 days. Call the Forest Service reservations system at (800) 280-2267 or individual ranger stations for campsite availability information and reservations where applicable.

Warner Mountain Ranger District, (530) 279-6116

Cave Lake Camp contains 7 sites (no hookups; RV limit 16 feet) near the shore of Cave Lake in the remote northern reaches of the forest about 1 mile from Oregon. The lake is well stocked with rainbow trout during the summer months. The campground has piped water and vault toilets. Each site has a table and fire ring. A general store is to the north in New Pine Creek. *From Alturas, take US 395 north. Half a mile shy of the Oregon border, turn right onto County Rd 2 and proceed to the campground on the left.*

Plum Valley Camp contains 15 sites (no hookups; RV limit 16 feet) near the South Fork Davis Creek. Most visitors to this campground are planning to visit Upper Alkali Lake, several miles to the east. There is no running water in the camp area, so be sure to bring plenty of your own. Vault toilets are provided, along with fire grills and tables at each site. There's a general store nearby in Davis Creek. *From Alturas, take US 395 north to Davis Creek. Turn right on County Rd 11. Go about 2.5 miles and veer right at the fork in the road in about 2.5 miles. Proceed to the campground, on the left about 1 mile ahead.*

Stowe Reservoir Campground has 8 sites (no hookups; RV limit 21 feet) near Stowe Reservoir. The campground has piped water and vault toilets, along with fire grills and tables at each site. There's a general store to the west in Cedarville. *From Alturas, take US 395 north to Hwy 299, 2 miles south of Chimney Rock Historical Monument. Turn right (east) and proceed to the campground on the right.*

Cedar Pass Campground has 17 sites (no hookups; RV limit 21 feet) near Thomas Creek. The campground is popular with hikers because it's centrally located among several mountain peaks. There is no running water, so be sure to bring plenty of your own. Vault toilets are available, and each site has a fire ring and table. There's a general store to the west in Cedarville. *From Alturas, take US 395 north to Hwy 299, 2 miles south of Chimney Rock Historical Monument. Turn right (east) and proceed to the campground.*

Emerson Campground contains 5 sites (no hookups; RV limit 16 feet). This campground is quiet and little known even though it is the closest campground to Middle and Lower Alkali Lakes. Piped water and vault toilets are available. Each site has a fire ring and table. *From Alturas, take US 395 south to Madeline. Turn left (east) onto County Rd 510/Patterson Sawmill Rd and proceed to Hwy 81 north. Turn left onto Emerson Rd and proceed to the campground.*

Patterson Campground contains 5 sites (no hookups; RV limit 21 feet). When visitors to Middle and Lower Alkali Lakes find Emerson Campground filled, this campground is the next best alternative. The campground is also popular with hikers and those in search of solitude. Piped water and vault toilets are available; each site has a fire ring and table. *From Alturas, take US 395 south to Madeline. Turn left (east) onto County Rd 510/Patterson Sawmill Rd and proceed to the campground.*

Other districts

Indian Well Campground has 40 sites (no hookups; RV limit 15 feet) in the desirable setting of **Lava Beds National Monument.** Piped water and flush toilets are available except during the winter months. Each site is equipped with a fire ring and table. *From Tulelake, take Hwy 139 south to Perez and turn right onto County Rd 197. In 2 miles, veer right onto Lava Beds National Monument Rd/Hill Rd. Proceed into the national monument to the campground beyond. For more information, call the monument headquarters at (530) 667-2282.*

Medicine Lake and **Hogue Campgrounds** have 24 and 27 sites, respectively (no hookups; RV limit 21 feet) along the banks of Medicine Lake. The lake is well stocked with rainbow trout during the summer and freezes over most winters. The campgrounds have piped water and vault toilets. Each site has a table and fire ring. A boat ramp and general store are nearby in Bartle. *From Tulelake, take Hwy 139 south to Perez and turn right onto County Rd 197. (Do not make the turn onto Lava Beds National Monument Rd.) Proceed to Medicine Lake Rd and turn right. Continue to the campgrounds ahead. For more information, call Doublehead Ranger District, (530) 667-2246.*

Lava Campground contains 15 sites (no hookups; RV limit 34 feet) in a secluded, seldom traveled area of California. There is no running water in the camp area, so be sure to bring plenty of your own. Vault toilets are provided, along with fire grills and tables at each site. Whitehouse Reservoir to the southwest is the largest body of water in the vicinity. *From Adin, take Hwy 139 north past Harris Springs, and turn left onto Forest Rd 41N10. Turn left onto Forest Rd 42N03 in about 12 miles. Proceed to Forest Rd 42N23 and turn right. Proceed to the campground ahead. For more information, call Big Valley Ranger District, (530) 299-3215.*

McArthur Falls Campground has 130 sites (no hookups; RV limit 37 feet) along the banks of Lake Britton and near the 130-foot McArthur Falls. With its stunning location and amenities, the campground can fill up during the balmy summer season. Piped water, flush toilets, and showers are available. A sanitary dump station is provided for RVs, and each site is equipped with a fire grill and table. *From Burney, take Hwy 299 east and turn left onto Hwy 89 north. Proceed past Four Corners to the campground on* *the left. Call the campground, a state facility, at (530) 335-2777.*

Dusty Campground has 7 sites (no hookups; RV limit 21 feet) along the banks of Lake Britton. The campground, owned by Pacific Gas and Electric Company (PG&E), is sought out by those who are looking for a primitive camping experience and who want to avoid the more crowded McArthur Falls Campground. There is no running water in the camp area, so be sure to bring plenty of your own. Vault toilets are provided, along with fire grills and tables at each site. *From Burney, take Hwy 299 east and turn left onto Hwy 89 north. Proceed to Clark Creek Rd just before Four Corners and turn left. Continue to the campground ahead. For more information, call PG&E, (916) 923-7142.*

Northshore Campground contains 30 sites (no hookups; RV limit 31 feet) along the banks of Lake Britton. The campground, owned by PG&E, serves as an overflow area for McArthur Falls Campground. Piped water and vault toilets are available. Each site is equipped with a fire grill and table. *From Burney, take Hwy 299 east and turn left onto Hwy 89 north. Proceed to Clark Creek Rd just before Four Corners and turn left. Continue to the campground ahead. For more information, call PG&E, (916) 923-7142.*

Big Sage Reservoir contains 25 sites (no hookups; various RV lengths accommodated) along the banks of Big Sage Reservoir. The campground is quiet and unknown. There is no running water in the camp area, so be sure to bring plenty of your own. Vault toilets are provided along with fire grills and tables at each site. A boat ramp is adjacent to the campground. *From Alturas, take Hwy 299 west and turn right onto Airport Rd/County Rd 73. Proceed several miles and turn right onto County Rd 180. Continue to the campground ahead. For more information, call Devil's Garden Ranger District, (530) 233-5811.*

Skiing/Snowmobiling

Cedar Pass Ski Hill, a funky, 100-acre ski area in the northeast corner of the state, is a nice change of pace from the fancy resort scene—with tow ropes and T-bars in lieu of fancy high-speed lifts, no snowmaking machines, no $200 rooms for rent, and nowhere to buy a morning latte. There are 7 groomed ski runs with a 400-foot vertical drop from the summit (the longest run is 1,500 feet); 50 percent are intermediate runs, 30 percent are advanced, and 20 percent are for beginners. The area is open weekends and holidays only and is staffed by volunteers. Call the Warner Mountain Ranger District, (530) 279-6116, for conditions and contact information. The season is November to March. Cedar Pass is 20 miles west of Alturas and 160 miles west of Redding on US 299.

Cross-country skiers will find ungroomed Nordic trails around the

Cedar Pass ski area, but also look for any flat Forest Service roads during the snowy season—they make fine ski turf during weather-related road closures.

Doorknob Snowmobile Park, 1.5 miles south of Lava Beds National Monument on Forest Rd 49, provides access over groomed trails to the Medicine Lake area and other snowmobile trail systems in neighboring forests. Call the Forest Service headquarters in Alturas, (530) 233-5811, and ask for the snow activities ranger.

Wildlife

With nearly **250 species** logged, massive inundation by **migrating birds,** and a high-mountain desert position along the Pacific Flyway, the carefully managed ponds and marshes of the 6,280-acre **Modoc National Wildlife Refuge** are a great place for birding in all seasons. In summer, Canada geese, mallards, cranes, ducks, and numerous **shorebirds,** including the kildeer and avocet, are found nesting here. White pelicans, cormorants, snowy egrets, short-eared owls, and hawks are also spotted in summer. The harsh winter weather pretty much clears out the area, but some Canada geese, and mallards have been known to brave the conditions and winter here. **Bald eagles** have also been spotted in the winter months. Spring and fall bring more geese, teal, wigeon, and pintail, along with scaup, golden-eye, and tundra swans. **Guided tours** are available, weather permitting. Call the refuge office, (530) 233-3572, for more information. The refuge is south of Alturas, half a mile east of US 395 on County Rd 56.

Be on the alert, throughout the Modoc region, for **black bears** and **rattlesnakes,** the two wild creatures most feared by your typical weekend outdoor-recreationist. **Mule deer, weasels, beavers, porcupines, cougars,** and **wild horses** are also found here.

Fishing

There are literally hundreds of creeks, rivers, and lakes suitable for summertime angling in the Modoc region, many of them packed thanks to an aggressive stocking program. **Brown and rainbow trout** are the main fare. Some notable spots for shore casting or boat fishing are **Medicine Lake** and **Bullseye Lake** south of Lava Beds National Monument, along with **Mill Creek** at Tule Lake in the forest's northwestern corner. To reach Medicine Lake from Lava Beds National Monument, take Lava Beds–Medicine Lake Rd south for 30 miles; Bullseye Lake is 5 miles south on the same road. **Blue Lake** is another sleepy fishing-hole kind of place, stocked with brown and rainbow trout. Keep in mind that things chill off big-time in this part of the state during winter, so fishing is typically a summer to late-summer proposition. To reach Mill Creek from Alturas, head south on US 395 for 19 miles to the town of Likely. Next, go 20 miles east on Jess Valley Rd to the lake, 3 miles past the fork in the road to the left. To reach Blue Lake from Alturas, head south on US 395 for 19 miles to Likely. From there, head 10 miles east, then 8 miles south on Blue Lake Rd at the fork. For more information, call the Warner Mountain Ranger District, (530) 279-6116. Another option with decent trout action is **Dorris Reservoir,** 6 miles east of US 395 via County Rd 56 from Alturas.

Mountain Biking

Mountain bikes are welcome on most Forest Service roads, but we suggest using those in and around the South Warner Wilderness to avoid potential run-ins with logging trucks. One nice ride with sweeping views of Goose Lake and the Warner Mountains is along **Highgrade National Recreation Trail** (moderate; 11 miles round trip), which skirts the foothills beneath Mount Vida through fir- and pine-forested terrain that's also peppered with small buildings and other relics left from the Gold Rush era. The trail has moderate grades with the exception of one spot with a 1,000-foot elevation gain in the course of a mile—not really anything that downshifting won't handle. To reach the trailhead from Alturas, take County Rd 1 for 20 miles east to Fandango Pass, then go west on the forest road for 10 miles to Del Pratt Spring Rd. From there, go east another miles to the beginning of the trail. This is an all-terrain-vehicle route, but isn't used much except during hunting season. Check with Warner Mountain Ranger District, (530) 279-6116, for the word on road conditions and any other special circumstances before setting out.

Adventure Calendar

Modoc Ski Festival, February: *Cedar Pass Ski Hill, (530) 233-2113.*
Warner Mountain Roundup Pro Rodeo, June: *Cedarville, (530) 233-2022.*
Great Historic Hotel Bicycle Race, August: *Alturas, (530) 233-4434.*
Hot Air Balloon Festival, September: *Alturas, (530) 233-444.*

Attractions

To find out what's currently happening in the area, visit the friendly folks at **Great Basin Books,** 540 Main St, Cedarville, (530) 279-2337. In addition to selling books, this shop houses Floating Island Publications, a publisher of limited-edition poetry and prose.

Restaurants

Country Hearth Restaurant & Bakery   The Country Hearth should be called the "Country Heart" for all the love owner Janet Irene puts into the meals served in her homey, pine-paneled dining room with its wood-burning stove. *551 Main St (S of Hwy 299), Cedarville; (530) 279-2280; $.*

Nipa's California Cuisine ☆   Nipa's version of California cuisine is actually spicy Thai food—and it's the finest fare of any kind in Modoc County. Located in an old drive-in burger joint that's been transformed into a contemporary cafe decorated with Thai artifacts. *1001 N Main St (1 block S of US 299 and US 395), Alturas; (530) 233-2520; $.*

Lodgings

Dorris House ☆☆   Set on a sage-covered plain at the edge of Dorris Lake, this two-story, turn-of-the-century ranch is a pleasant home-away-from-home. The 4 immaculate guest rooms are decorated with family antiques and comfortable furnishings. *On County Rd 57 (3 miles E of US 395; on County Rd 56, turn right at County Rd 57 and drive 1 mile), Alturas; (530) 233-3786; $.*

J. K. Metzker House Bed and Breakfast ☆☆   Built in 1860, this pretty clapboard house with its white picket fence and rose-lined walkway has 4 guest rooms, 3 upstairs and 1 downstairs. Each room has a private bath and a queen-size bed (the downstairs bedroom also has twin beds). *520 Main St (turn right onto Main St from Hwy 299), Cedarville; (530) 279-2650 or (530) 279-2337; $.*

More Information

Alturas Chamber of Commerce: *(530) 233-4434.*
Big Valley Ranger District: *(530) 299-3215.*
Devil's Garden Ranger District: *(530) 233-5811.*
Doublehead Ranger District: *(530) 667-2246.*
Forest Service reservations system: *(800) 280-2267.*
Lava Beds National Monument: *(530) 667-2282.*
Modoc County Chamber of Commerce: *(530) 233-2819.*
Warner Mountain Ranger District: *(530) 279-6116.*

Lassen Region

More than 1 million acres of wilderness in the southern reaches of the Cascade range, along with Lassen Volcanic National Park, Caribou Wilderness, and Eagle Lake to the east.

Climb to what seems like the top of the world. Ski down the side of a volcano. Launch your boat from the banks of the second-largest natural lake in the state and fish its mist-shrouded waters. If it sounds like a travel brochure to some far-flung tropical paradise, you're wrong. This is Lassen County, where the northern tip of the Sierra Nevada meets the southern reaches of the Cascades. It's where mountainous peaks meet glacial valleys, and where moonscapes of hardened lava and cinder cones give way to thick forests of red fir and lodgepole pine. Turn one way and face the high desert and the great plateau; turn the other and enter Muir's "range of light."

At 10,457 feet, volcanic Lassen Peak is the dominant geologic feature, remaining snowcapped most of the year. Actually a volcanic vent on the north side of Mount Tehama, it's part of the Pacific "ring of fire" and last blew its top in 1915. It's a great area to explore for those curious about unusual landscapes, and three wilderness areas outside the volcanic park offer stunning contrast. For example, you'll find expansive plateaus, dozens of lakes surrounded by forest, and high mountain rivers teeming with rainbow trout in the 20,000-acre Caribou Wilderness—a backpacker's favorite due to its uncrowded, secluded setting. Eagle Lake, as much a water-sports area as a great big fishing hole, lies to the east; it, too, offers relative solitude compared to other summer recreation spots along the northern mountains and Sierra range. To fully explore this whole area, bring the fishing gear, the mountain bike, the snow skis, and the backpack. With more than 1,000 campsites and more than 100 miles of the Pacific Crest Trail here, there is plenty to keep the active traveler busy.

Getting There

US Highway 395 (US 395) and Highway 139 are the two primary north-south access routes through the Lassen area, and Highways 36, 32, and 70 are the main access points east from the Interstate 5 corridor. For information about forest roads, campgrounds, and other matters, call the Hat Creek Ranger District in Fall River Mills, (530) 336-5521; Eagle Lake Ranger District in the Susanville area, (530) 257-4188; and Almanor Ranger District in Chester, (530) 258-2141. Lassen Volcanic National Park can be reached at (530) 595-4444. Also call the Lassen County Chamber of Commerce, (530) 257-4323, for assistance with travel plans.

Adjoining Areas

NORTH: **Modoc Region**

WEST: **Lake Shasta**

SOUTH: **Plumas Region**

inside out

Hiking/Backpacking

With more than a million acres of forest and wilderness, and Lassen Volcanic National Park at its center, the Lassen National Forest region is another fantastic hiker's paradise. Naturally, the snow season limits the time of year when exploration is possible—high elevations are mostly a June-to-early-October proposition—but the thaw is worth waiting for. From almost-surreal lava-flow terrain to rolling forested canyons, alpine lakes, and high mountain meadows and marshlands, the stratification of the landscape here is fascinating to behold. About 120 miles of the **Pacific Crest Trail** pass through the Lassen region, bisecting the volcanic park and entering Plumas's Bucks Lake Wilderness for the next leg south toward Mexico. In addition, there are numerous wilderness area hikes within Lassen, including the **Bizz Johnson National Recreation Trail** (see below), spanning more than 400 miles.

As with most national forests and wilderness areas, camping is allowed just about anywhere it's flat enough to pitch a tent, but **permits** are required for any use of fire and for use of wilderness areas. The Pacific

Crest Trail Association, 1350 Castle Rock Rd, Walnut Creek, CA 94598, (925) 939-6111, has **maps and information** on hiking the Pacific Crest Trail. The best trail maps of the national forest areas are available directly from the Forest Service; write US Forest Service Information, Room 521, 630 Sansome St, San Francisco, CA 94111. There are four main maps for this forest: one full Lassen National Forest map, and one each for the Thousand Lakes, Caribou, and Ishi Wilderness Areas. **Trail conditions** in any forest or wilderness area are subject to change, so before setting out, check with the appropriate ranger district for up-to-date information. Many backcountry trails may be impassable during winter, and sections can be washed out or too dangerous to cross when rivers are running high.

Burney Mountain Summit Overlook Trail (easy; 0.5 mile round trip) is one of those easy-to-reach spots that's perfect for families with children who can't spend two or three days heading for higher peaks on the backcountry trails. Here, just park the station wagon and take a short stroll to the summit overlook, which at more than 7,800 feet offers panoramic views of the Modoc/Shasta/Lassen skyline. The summit can be accessed directly by car in the summer. Take Hwy 299 east from I-5 at Redding for 10 miles, then head west on Forest Rd 34N23 and continue 4 miles or so up the mountain. Contact the Hat Creek Ranger District, (530) 336-5521, for more information.

Another good short walk is the easy 1.5-mile stroll along **Spatter Cone Trail** and through **Subway Cave,** created by an underground lava flow. Both are easily found east of Hwy 89 at Hwy 44, with parking areas off the road. Other **short wilderness walks** abound for those not planning on a days-long expedition into the backcountry. From the Hwy 299 junction with Hwy 89, head south through the forest to Red Rock Hill, Sugarloaf Peak (6,552 feet), Big Pine and Twin Bridges (at Vista Point and Forest Rd 32N12), and Red Mountain, just outside the Lassen Volcanic National Park boundary. Also consider a pass through Pine Creek Valley and Crater Mountain. All of these areas offer easy roadside access to wild places in exchange for little more than a short stroll and are indicated on the trail maps recommended above.

Drakes Lake Trail (difficult; 6 miles round trip) is a steep trudge uphill that leads to one of those unbelievably pristine and pretty alpine lake basins that pocket the landscape here, this one situated at 6,400 feet, nestled in the shadows of the 7,400-foot Sifford Mountain near the southern boundary of Lassen Volcanic National Park. The hike covers an 800-foot elevation gain in less than 3 miles, so be prepared to huff and puff a little before descending into this little oasis. From Chester, located on Hwy 36, go north on the highway through Warner Valley 16 miles to the staging area. For more information, call the Almanor Ranger District,

(530) 258-2141. Another kicker of a trek is **Spencer Meadow Trail** (moderate; 10.5 miles round trip), which provides a glimpse of terrain different from the volcanic landscape that dominates this part of the state—mountainous meadows and prairies. With Morgan and Do Mountains as a backdrop, this gently sloping trail leads out of the Mill Creek Valley toward the Mill Creek Plateau area, expansive high-country grasslands dotted with small lakes and natural springs—perfectly lovely. To reach the trailhead, take Hwy 36 for 50 miles east from Red Bluff to the trailhead on the north side of the road, 6 miles past the town of Mineral. For more information, call the Almanor Ranger District, (530) 258-2141.

Magee Trail (moderate; 10.5 miles round trip) in the Thousand Lakes Wilderness section of the forest is another hearty days-long trek into some of the quietest, most pristine glacial valley settings found outside Yosemite. Most follow the trail to Magee Lake and double back, but there is always the option of continuing on as far as **Lake Eiler** in the shadow of the 7,485-foot Freaner Peak in the northern end of the wilderness (about 7 additional miles). Magee, however, is a good two- to three-day trip, with a pass over the 8,550-foot Magee Peak and Gray Cliff before you reach the lake. To find the trailhead, take Hwy 299 east from Redding for 55 miles to just past the town of Burney, then head south on Hwy 89 another 30 miles to Forest Rd 16. Follow Forest Rd 16 for 10 miles east to Forest Rd 32N48, and head northeast about 3 miles to the staging and parking area at the end. For more information, contact the Hat Creek Ranger District, (530) 336-5521.

Bizz Johnson National Recreation Trail (easy; 26 miles one way) is an abandoned railroad right-of-way that has been transformed into one of the most stunning recreation trails found anywhere, a three- to four-day journey stretching from Westwood on the northern shore of Mountain Meadows Reservoir to Susanville near Antelope Mountain, cutting a wide path through the Susan River canyon and meandering between Goodrich and Pegleg Mountains, along with numerous other peaks. There are suitable camping spots along the way. Park a car at both ends and do it in one direction. To reach the trailhead, take Hwy 36 east for 160 miles to Westwood, then head 4 miles north on County Rd A21 to the trailhead 4 miles out. To reach the Susanville end, take North Lassen Rd south from the Hwy 36 junction and go 2 miles to the staging area. For more information, call the Almanor Ranger District, (530) 258-2141.

Lassen Volcanic National Park, which covers some 108,000 acres, contains more than 100 miles of hiking trails within its boundaries. The park office can be reached at (530) 595-4444. To reach the trailhead, take either Hwy 36 east from Red Bluff or Hwy 44 east from Redding approximately 50 miles to Hwy 89, then head south from Hwy 44 or north from

Hwy 36 another 8 miles to the park entrance.

In our view, the premier hike within Lassen Volcanic National Park is the **Lassen Peak Trail** (difficult; 5 miles round trip), a gruelingly steep 2,000-foot catapult to the tip of Lassen Peak, with view of craters and expansive lava flows that would be stunningly beautiful enough without the accompanying vistas of the northern mountain region from 10,400 feet above it all. Don't be fooled by this trip's relatively short length. You will need a half day to make the climb, rest up, take in the scenery, and then follow the jagged switchbacks back down to the staging area.

While the hike to the peak is unquestionably the best the park has to offer, there are numerous other options as well. Those who want to get a close-up look at the volcanic scenery may opt for the **Cinder Cone Trail** (moderate; 4 miles round trip), which offers a nice view of both lava beds and Painted Dunes. There also are two short lakeside walks within the park, one at **Summit Lake** and the other around **Shadow Lake.** The **Nobles Emigrant Trail** (easy; 10 miles round trip) has an interesting pygmy forest section along with more curious volcanic rock-scapes. Another nice, easy walk is along the **Manzanita Lake Trail** (easy; 1.5 miles round trip), a lovely alpine lake setting that is a popular family camp-out spot during the summer (see Camping, below). Finally, check out the **Bumpass Hell Trail** (easy; 3 miles round trip), named after a mid-19th-century tour guide. Poor ol' Kendall Bumpass lost a leg on this one, but that was long before park rangers built wooden catwalks to safely guide visitors past the pyrite pools, steam vents, seething mud pots, and noisy fumaroles that line the trail.

Camping

As with most of the national forests in California, in Lassen National Forest camping is allowed just about anywhere you can find a piece of ground flat enough to pitch a tent on—with just a few exceptions. **Dispersed camping** is your best bet if you're backpacking in the wilderness, but be sure to get **permits** for any use of fire. The best **maps** are available directly from the Forest Service; write US Forest Service Information, Room 521, 630 Sansome St, San Francisco, CA 94111. Periodic road closures are unavoidable. Check with the relevant ranger station for updated road conditions before deciding on a site located deep within the forest. Roads are not maintained for vehicles with low ground clearance. The Forest Service is currently reviewing its **reservations and fees** policies for this area, but generally no reservations are taken for any of the campgrounds listed below. Stays are limited to 14 days. Call the Forest Service reservations system, (800) 280-2267, or individual ranger stations for campsite availability information and reservations where applicable.

Cave Campground contains 50 sites (no hookups; RV limit 22 feet) along Hat Creek. This campground is near Old Station and has a centralized location within Lassen National Forest. Piped water and flush toilets are available, and each site is equipped with a fire ring and table. A general store is nearby in Old Station. *From Redding, take I-5 north to Hwy 299 east. Exit onto Hwy 89 south. Proceed to the campground on the right, just before Old Station. Call Hat Creek Ranger District, (530) 336-5521, for information.*

Hat Creek Campground contains 76 sites (no hookups; RV limit 22 feet) along Hat Creek. This campground is also near Old Station. The campground has piped water and flush toilets, and each site is equipped with a fire ring and table. *From Redding, take I-5 north to Hwy 299 east. Exit onto Hwy 89 south. Proceed to the campground on the right, just before Old Station. Call Hat Creek Ranger District, (530) 336-5521, for information.*

Big Pine Campground contains 22 sites (no hookups; RV limit 23 feet) along Hat Creek. This campground is just outside the border of Lassen Volcanic National Park. The campground has well water and flush toilets, and each site is equipped with a fire ring and table. A general store is nearby in Old Station. *From Redding, take I-5 north to Hwy 299 east. Exit onto Hwy 89 south. Proceed to the campground on the left before Old Station. Call Eagle Lake Ranger District, (530) 336-5521, for information.*

Butte Creek Campground contains 12 sites (no hookups; RV limit 23 feet) nestled along Butte Creek and just 3 miles from Lassen Volcanic National Park. This campground is sought out by those looking for a primitive camping experience. Given the lack of amenities, it is generally quiet. There is no running water available. Each site is equipped with a fire ring and table, and vault toilets are available. *From Redding, take I-5 north to Hwy 299 east. Exit onto Hwy 89 south. Turn left on Hwy 44 east and proceed to Forest Rd 33N29 and turn right. Proceed to the campground. Call Eagle Lake Ranger District, (530) 257-4188, for information.*

Crater Lake Campground has 21 sites for tents (no RV access) near the banks of Crater Lake along the slopes of Crater Mountain. Location has its advantages, and this campground near the mountain summit and the lake is no exception. Well water is available, along with vault toilets. Each site is equipped with a fire ring and table. *From Redding, take I-5 north to Hwy 299 east. Exit onto Hwy 89 south. Turn left onto Hwy 44 east and turn left onto Forest Rd 33N02. Cross the railroad track and turn right. Proceed to Crater Lake and the campground. Call Eagle Lake Ranger District, (530) 257-4188, for information.*

Silver Bowl Camp has 18 sites (no hookups; various RV lengths accommodated) nestled along Silver Lake, a popular fishing spot during the summer. The campground has piped water and vault toilets; each site is equipped with a fire ring and table. *From Redding, take I-5 north to Hwy 299 east. Exit onto Hwy 89 south. Turn left onto Hwy 44 east and turn right onto County Rd A21/Mooney Rd. Turn right onto Silver Lake Rd and proceed to the campground. Call Almanor Ranger District, (530) 258-2141, for information.*

Bogard Campground contains 20 sites (no hookups; RV limit 31 feet) along Pine Creek. The campground is nicest during the spring and early summer when the creek flow is at its strongest. Piped water and vault toilets are available, and each site has a fire ring and table. *From Redding, take I-5 north to Hwy 299 east. Exit onto Hwy 89 south. Turn left onto Hwy 44 east and turn right onto Forest Rd 32N09, just past the Bogard Ranger Station. Take the first left you see and then take your second right a few hundred feet ahead. Proceed to the campground access road on the right. Call Eagle Lake Ranger District, (530) 257-4188, for information.*

Summit Lake Campground has roughly 100 sites (no hookups; RV limit 31 feet) adjacent to Summit Lake, in Lassen Volcanic National Park. The campground is not only popular for its lakeside activities, but for its exclusive setting deep inside the national park. The campground has well water and flush toilets, and each site has a fire ring and table. *From Redding, take I-5 north to Hwy 299 east. Exit onto Hwy 89 south. Turn right onto Hwy 44/89 and proceed past Old Station. Turn left onto Hwy 89 past Manzanita Lake and proceed to Summit Lake. Call Lassen Volcanic National Park, (530) 595-3262.*

Manzanita Lake Camp has 184 sites (no hookups; RV limit 37 feet) along the banks of Manzanita Lake, in Lassen Volcanic National Park. This campground is perhaps the most popular in Lassen National Forest due to the lake, considered the area's most picturesque. The campground has piped water, flush toilets, fire rings, and tables; there's a general store nearby. *From Redding, take I-5 north to Hwy 299 east. Exit onto Hwy 89 south. Turn right onto Hwy 44/89 and proceed past Old Station. Turn left onto Hwy 89 to Manzanita Lake. Follow the signs to the campground. Call Lassen Volcanic National Park, (530) 595-3262, for information.*

Crags Campground contains 45 sites (no hookups; RV limit 37 feet) in Lassen Volcanic National Park. This campground not only serves as an overflow area for Manzanita Lake Campground, but it is also sought after in its own right by those looking to avoid Manzanita's crowds and enjoy one of Lassen's prettier camping spots. The campground has piped water and pit toilets. Each site is equipped with a fire ring and table, and there's a general store nearby. *From Redding, take I-5 north to Hwy 299 east. Exit onto Hwy 89 south. Turn right onto Hwy 44/89 and proceed past Old Station. Turn left onto Hwy 89 past Manzanita Lake to the campground. Call Lassen Volcanic National Park, (530) 595-3262, for information.*

Juniper Lake Campground contains 20 tent sites (no RV access) in the southeast part of Lassen Volcanic National Park. In addition to the lakeside activity, it boasts several good trails traversing the area, in particular one that leads up to Inspiration Point. The campground has no piped water, so be sure to bring plenty of your own. Pit toilets are available, and each site is equipped with a fire ring and table. *From Susanville, take Hwy 36 east to Chester. Turn right onto Feather River Rd. Veer right onto Chester/Juniper Lake Rd. Proceed to the campground. Call Lassen Volcanic National Park, (530) 595-3262, for information.*

Gurnsey Creek Campground contains tent 34 sites (no hookups; various RV lengths accommodated) along Gurnsey Creek. The campground is most popular during the spring and early summer before the creek flow diminishes rapidly. Piped water and vault toilets are available, and each site is equipped with a fire ring and table. *From Susanville, take Hwy 36 east. About 1.5 miles past the junction with Hwy 32, look for the campground access road on your right. Call Lassen Volcanic National Park, (530) 595-3262, for information.*

Domingo Springs Campground contains 9 sites (no hookups; various RV lengths accommodated) adjacent to the Domingo Springs and near the North Fork Feather River. The campground has piped water and vault toilets, and each site is equipped with a fire ring and table. *From Susanville, take Hwy 36 east to Chester. Turn right onto Feather River Rd. Veer left onto Warner Valley Rd. Proceed to High Bridge and follow the signs to the campground. Call Lassen Volcanic National Park, (530) 595-3262, for information.*

High Bridge Campground contains 9 sites (no hookups; various RV lengths accommodated) along the north fork of the Feather River. The campground is very quiet and not well known. There is no running water, so be sure to bring plenty of your own. Vault toilets are available, and each site has a fire ring and table. *From Susanville, take Hwy 36 east to Chester. Turn right onto Feather River Rd. Veer left onto Warner Valley Rd. Proceed to Warner Valley High Bridge and turn left. Continue to the campground on the right. Call Lassen Volcanic National Park, (530) 595-3262, for information .*

Elam Campground has 17 sites (no hookups; various RV lengths accommodated) along Deer Creek. The campground is most popular during the spring and early summer months when the creek flow is strongest. Piped water and vault toilets are available, and each site is equipped with a fire ring and table. *From Susanville, take Hwy 36 east to the junction with Hwy 32. Proceed south on Hwy 32 about 3 miles to the campground on the right. Call Almanor Ranger District, (530) 258-2141, for information.*

Alder Campground has 5 tent sites (no RV access) along Deer Creek. The campground is most popular during the spring and early summer when the creek flow is strongest and it attracts campers who want to avoid RV traffic. Piped water and vault toilets are available, and each site is equipped with a fire ring and table. *From Susanville, take Hwy 36 east to the junction with Hwy 32. Proceed south on Hwy 32 about 9 miles to the campground on the right. Call Almanor Ranger District, (530) 258-2141, for information.*

Potato Patch Campground has 20 sites (no hookups; various RV lengths accommodated) along Deer Creek. The campground is most popular during the spring and early summer when the creek flow is strongest. Piped water and vault toilets are available, and each site is equipped with a fire ring and table. *From Susanville, take Hwy 36 east to the junction with Hwy 32. Proceed south on Hwy 32 about 12 miles to the campground on the right. Call Almanor Ranger District, (530) 258-2141, for information.*

Ponderosa Flat Campground has 63 sites (no hookups; various RV lengths accommodated) adjacent to Butte Valley Reservoir. This campground, which is owned by Pacific Gas and Electric Company (PG&E), has an accessible boat ramp and therefore attracts its share of boaters. Piped water and vault toilets are available, and each site is equipped with a fire ring and table. There's a general store to the north in Prattville. *From Susanville, take Hwy 36 east past Chester. Turn left onto Hwy 89. Turn right onto Prattville/Butte Reservoir Rd. Proceed to the campground. Call PG&E, (916) 923-7142, for information.*

Cool Springs Campground has 32 sites (no hookups; RV limit 37 feet) adjacent to Butte Valley Reservoir. The campground, which is owned by PG&E, serves as an overflow area for the more popular Ponderosa Flat Campground. It is also sought out by those looking for a small, quiet campground. There is piped water and vault toilets, and each site is equipped with a fire ring and table. A general store lies to the north in Prattville. *From Susanville, take Hwy 36 east past Chester. Turn left onto Hwy 89. Turn right onto Prattville/Butte Reservoir Rd. Proceed past Ponderosa Flat to the campground. Call PG&E, (916) 923-7142, for information.*

Hallsted Campground has 20 sites (no hookups; RV limit 25 feet) along the east branch of the North Fork River. Stocked with trout, the river attracts many visitors, and the campground is very popular and often crowded on summer weekends. Piped water and vault toilets are available, and each site is equipped with a fire ring and table. There's a general store nearby in Twain. *From Quincy, take Hwy 70 west, about 2 miles past Twain to the campground access road on the right. Call Mount Hough Ranger District, Plumas National Forest, (530) 283-0555, for information.*

Downhill Skiing

Ever ski down the side of a volcano? Now's your chance. **Lassen Volcanic National Park** (see Hiking/Backpacking, above, for directions to the park) has an 80-acre ski area just inside its Hwy 89 entrance, open November to March. This is a unique ski setting, on the gently sloping banks of a volcanic peak. Winter is an interesting time here, with snow transforming the lava flow terrain from black rock to a soft winter blanket. The contrast is striking enough that you'll be tempted to return after the spring melt just to see what a volcanic park is supposed to look like. There are 10 ski runs—40 percent beginner level, 40 percent intermediate, and 20 percent advanced, the longest being a half mile from top to bottom. The park has 1 triple chair lift and 2 tows. Equipment rentals and lessons are available on site. **Snowboarding** also is allowed on some ski runs. For snow conditions and information, call Lassen Volcanic National Park, (530) 595-4444.

East of the park, along Hwy 89 east of Chester, are two other ski areas. **Stover Mountain,** 70 miles east of Chico off Hwy 89 at Chester Ski Rd, has no beginner runs, but 80 percent of the runs are suitable for intermediate skiers, although the intermediate runs consist of just a 250-foot vertical drop with a tow-rope lift. The advanced run has a steep 850-foot drop from the 6,000-foot summit, with a poma lift. Call Lassen National Forest Almanor Ranger District, Chester, (530) 258-2141. **Coppervale,** a small facility of 65 acres with 8 ski runs, is 40 percent beginner, and 30 percent each advanced and intermediate. There is a poma lift and a T-bar lift, to 600-foot and 100-foot drops, respectively. Call the ski area at (530) 257-9965 for information.

Snowboarding and **tubing** are popular on Willard Hill, 5 miles east from the Coppervale ski area (see above), and at Jamesville Grade, another 28 miles south. Call the Lassen National Forest, Eagle Lake Ranger District, (530) 257-4188, for more information on both spots. Also check for snow-play areas within the Lassen Volcanic National Park ski area, above.

Cross-Country Skiing/Snowmobiling

In addition to more than 30 kilometers of ungroomed Nordic ski trails adjacent to the ski area, hundreds of miles of groomed and ungroomed ski trails are found within Lassen National Forest—without the resort crowds you will come across in the Tahoe or Shasta ski parks. This makes the forest, which receives on average 550 inches of snow each winter, a prime destination for the Nordic skier looking for a little solitude. The best is one lengthy section of the **Bizz Johnson National Recreation Trail** between Westwood and Susanville (see Hiking/Backpacking, above). For more information on the area, call the Almanor Ranger District, (530) 258-2141. Groomed and ungroomed trails, primarily set aside for Nordic skiers, are also found on forest roads at the base of Colby Mountain on Lassen Volcanic National Park's southwestern boundary, beneath **Grays Peak** at McGowan Lake. But stay on the alert for snowmobilers (see below), who tend to be plentiful in these parts.

On Saturday afternoons from January through March, a loquacious naturalist will take anyone who shows up by 1:30pm at the Lassen Chalet in Lassen Volcanic National Park on a free, two-hour **snowshoeing** adventure across the park's snowy dales. You must be at least eight years old, warmly dressed, and decked out in boots. Free snowshoes are provided (although a $1 donation for shoe upkeep is requested) on a first-come basis. Pack a picnic lunch. The chalet is at the park's south entrance, 5 miles north of the Hwy 36/89 junction. For more details, call park headquarters at (530) 595-4444.

If you're more inclined to open a throttle than to push off under your own power, Lassen National Forest just may be the definitive winter playground for you. No fewer than six areas of the forest contain a mixture of groomed and ungroomed trails open to **snowmobiles.** The most conveniently reached staging areas are at Cherry Hill near Jonesville and Colby Creek or from the western shore of **Lake Almanor** (see Plumas Region chapter) on Hwy 89, 2 miles south of Chester. From Susanville, take Hwy 36 east past Chester. Turn left onto Hwy 89 and proceed to the rest area on the west side of the road. The Lake Almanor Snowmobile Club, (530) 596-3822, and the Almanor Basin Snowmobile Coalition, (530) 258-3856, have information on outfitters and the many other trails in some of the northern reaches of the forest.

Fishing

The 24,000-acre Eagle Lake, second-largest natural lake in the state, with 100 miles of shoreline, is Lassen's most popular fishing spot, not only because it is the geologic centerpiece of the canyon but also because it is home to a rare species of **trout,** the Arschellian, that responds well to trolling, which is just plain fun. The lake is unique for its two distinct terrain zones—half is in a pretty pine and mixed conifer forest while the other is in craggy desert terrain devoid of vegetation beyond sparse shrubs. Fishing season here is late May to December 31, but keep in mind that while the lake's waters are a comfortable 62 degrees during the summer, winters are a chilly proposition—water drops to near-freezing, and winds are cold. The best time is mid- to late summer when you can combine your fishing adventure with other water sports. Four public boat ramps make access to the lake easy, and there are lodging and camping areas at the water's edge. Boat and personal watercraft rentals are available at the Eagle Lake Marina. The lake is located 15 miles northwest of Susanville on Hwy 129. For information, call the Eagle Lake Resource Area, (530) 257-0456. Southwest of Eagle is the equally popular Lake Almanor (see Fishing, Plumas Region chapter). Trout fishing is also prime in the nearby Susan River, Goodrich Creek, and Horse Lake.

Mountain Biking

Lassen forestlands and US Bureau of Land Management (BLM) desert terrain in the southeastern end of the county are prime mountain-biking turf, particularly on dry, cool mornings in early autumn. **Shaffer Mountain** is a difficult 8-mile climb or 16-mile round-trip ride, ascending 2,300 feet to a sweeping vista of the northern Sierra. The mountain is 20 miles east of Susanville on US 395. Bizz Johnson National Recreation Trail (see Hiking/Backpacking, above), is an easy and scenic bike tour on a paved national recreation trail cutting a 26-mile path through the eastern end of the county along an abandoned railroad right-of-way. Alpine Mountain Sports, 120 S Gay St, Susanville, (530) 257-3767, has bicycle rentals and other outdoor equipment. Forest Rd 30N07 east from Swain Mountain at Eagle Lake Rd is an excellent ride (moderate; 11 miles round trip) during the dry summer months after the snowmelt is complete. Forest Rd 37N02 north of Lake Britton is also a good riding area. Keep in mind that roads, and not trails, are most amenable for mountain-bike riding. Bikes are not allowed in the wilderness areas.

Adventure Calendar

Sierra Nevada Mountain Metric Bike Ride, early June: *Chester,* *(530) 258-2338.*
Mile High Century Bike Ride, September: *Chester, (530) 258-2338.*

Attractions

Surprisingly, many Californians have never even heard of **Lassen Volcanic National Park,** much less been there. In fact, it's one of the least crowded national parks in the country, forever destined to play second fiddle to its towering neighbor, Mount Shasta. This is reason enough to go, since the park's 108,000 acres (including 50 beautiful wilderness lakes) are practically deserted, even on weekends.

The heart of the park is 10,457-foot Lassen Peak, the largest plug-dome volcano in the world (its last fiery eruption was in 1915, when it shot debris 7 miles into the stratosphere). For decades Lassen held the title of the most recently active volcano in the continental United States; it lost that distinction in 1980, when Washington's Mount St. Helens blew its top. The volcano also marks the southernmost end of the Cascade Range, which extends to Canada. A visitors map calls the park "a compact laboratory of volcanic phenomena"—an apt description of this pretty but peculiar place. In addition to wildflower-laced hiking trails and lush forests typical of many national parks, parts of Lassen are covered with steaming thermal vents, boiling mud pots, stinky sulfur springs, and towering lava pinnacles—constant reminders that Lassen Peak is still active.

Free **naturalist programs** are offered daily in the summer, highlighting everything from flora and fauna to geologic history and volcanic processes. Pick up a copy of the "Lassen Park Guide," a handy little newsletter listing activities, hikes, and points of interest that you get upon entering the park, and review the Inside Out sections, above.

Restaurants

Grand Cafe   This time warp of a restaurant is furnished with green-and-black tiles, dark wooden booths, and a long Formica counter. For breakfast, try the sweet buckwheat hotcakes. At lunchtime, soup, house-baked bread, and a chocolate malt are your best bets. *730 Main St (near Gay St), Susanville; (530) 257-4713; $.*

St. Bernard Lodge ☆☆   Most Mill Creek residents come to the St. Bernard for its juicy hamburgers. You can also sink your teeth into prime rib, steak, fried chicken, and fried or sautéed fish. *On the S side of Hwy 36 (10 miles W of Chester), Mill Creek; (530) 258-3382; $$.*

St. Francis Cafe ☆   You won't hear anybody asking "Where's the beef?" in this cafe. Their specialty is prime rib, indisputably the best (and the largest servings) in the area. (Strict vegetarians should try their luck elsewhere.) *830 Main St (at Union St), Susanville; (530) 257-4820; $$.*

Lodgings

Clearwater House ☆☆☆☆   Created by a former wilderness and fishing guide, this inn features 7 rooms decorated in the style of an English angling lodge. Pick up pointers on the art of fly-fishing at a three-day fishing class, or attend the "Mastering the Art of Fly-Fishing" five-day program. *At the intersection of Hat Creek and Cassel/Fall River Rds, Cassel;* (415)381-1173; $$.

Drakesbad Guest Ranch ☆☆☆☆   Hidden in a high mountain valley inside Lassen Volcanic National Park, this mountain retreat has a waiting list for its 19 rustic rooms and cabins that's several months long. May and June are good times to call to take advantage of cancellations. *On Hwy 36 (about 17 miles N of Chester; call for directions), Drakesbad;* (530) 529-9820; $$ *(includes meals).*

Lava Creek Lodge ☆☆   Set well back from the main road at the end of a country lane, the lodge has 8 modest guest rooms with private baths, and most offer lake views. But the best accommodations are actually in the woods: 7 small, comfortable cabins were recently renovated and all have private baths. *On Eastman Lake (at the end of Island Rd), Fall River Mills;* (530) 336-6288; $$–$$$ *(includes meals).*

Mill Creek Resort ☆☆   A picture-postcard general store and coffee shop serve as this resort's center, and 9 housekeeping cabins are rented on a daily or weekly basis. The units are clean and homey, with vintage '30s and '40s furniture. *On Hwy 172 (3 miles S of Hwy 36), Mill Creek;* (530) 595-4449; $.

Spanish Springs Ranch ☆☆☆   Buckaroo wannabes should pack up their cowboy boots and head on out to this 70,000-acre working cattle ranch. Whether you want to slumber in ultimate comfort or rough it on the range, the choice is yours: accommodations vary from log cabins, Western-style suites, and a historic homestead to turn-of-the-century ranch houses. *On US 395 (40 miles N of Susanville and 6 miles S of Ravendale);* (800) 272-8282; $$–$$$.

More Information

Almanor Ranger District: *(530) 258-2141.*
Chester Chamber of Commerce: *(530) 258-2426.*
Eagle Lake Ranger District: *(530) 257-4188.*
Hat Creek Ranger District: *(530) 336-5521.*
Lassen County Chamber of Commerce: *(530) 257-4323.*
Lassen Volcanic National Park: *(530) 595-4444.*
Pacific Crest Trail Association: *(925) 939-6111.*

Klamath Region

Some 1.7 million acres of wilderness and timberlands in Klamath National Forest and surrounding areas, primarily located in Siskiyou County, extending down from the Oregon border on the north to the Marble Mountains on the south, including the Russian, Red Buttes, and Siskiyou Wilderness Areas, and the Salmon, Scott, and Klamath Rivers.

Sitting around the campfire high up in the vast Marble Mountain Wilderness one recent summer, members of a California Conservation Corps trail-building crew took turns talking about how five months in the wilderness had affected them. It was a warm August night, cloudless, with shooting stars overhead, and the end of a long work day. "The city takes your soul away," one young man from Los Angeles said. "When you come here, you get it back."

Indeed, the extreme northern reaches of the state can be a place to regain your sanity—and the wilderness areas of Siskiyou County are no exception. With its narrow, steep canyons, its thick pine and Douglas fir forests, its hundreds of high mountain lakes and meadows sprinkled across the mountains like jewels, and its three wild rivers, this is indeed a great place to drop out for a spell. Klamath National Forest, which covers some 1.7 acres of forested mountains bounded by the Oregon border, the North Coast and Interstate 5, is your place for rafting, hiking, swimming, camping, backpacking, fishing, snow adventures, and just getting away from it all. The Klamath, Scott, and Salmon Rivers, with hundreds of meandering creeks spilling into them, are three of the state's most prized recreational waterways. The Marble Mountain Wilderness—with its stunning white marble peaks for which it is named—is a sight that will make you forget you just spent two grueling days on steep trails full of switchbacks to get a look at them. You will have that same urge to return here that plagues so many who visit Tahoe and Yosemite; but unlike those beautiful places, the Klamath wilderness is one place you can still call undiscovered.

Elevations in this part of the wilds range from 600 to over 8,000 feet, so be prepared for severe weather in the high country during winter. Summers, however, are a joy to behold, with mild temperatures just high enough to warm lake waters to tolerable swimming temperature most of the season. In the Gold Rush hamlets, logging communities, and farming towns of the Klamath region, Bigfoot stories are as easy to get as rides from a stranger. "You need to come here to find out what friendly people are like," one local said. Yreka—100 miles north of Redding on Interstate 5 and a stone's throw from the Oregon border—calls itself a "Garden of Eden" for outdoors enthusiasts looking to escape the city for a time. Such a big claim deserves to be investigated.

Getting There

Because of its sheer size, travelers can use numerous different routes to reach the Klamath region. Our preferred approach is from Yreka on Interstate 5, 20 miles south of the Oregon border. Both Highway 96 and Highway 3 are accessible through Yreka. Highway 96 extends through the northern portions of the forest, while Highway 3 extends southwest through the forestlands toward the Trinity Alps. These two highways ultimately lead to the Redwood Coast region. For those interested in exploring the Siskiyou Wilderness, however, it is probably best to approach the Klamath region from the North Coast through Crescent City via US Highway 199 (US 199). The forest contains an elaborate network of county highways and logging roads, in various states of repair and disrepair. Many forest roads are unpaved and best traveled in a vehicle with high ground clearance, preferably equipped with four-wheel drive. Always check with the forest office or individual ranger stations on road conditions before setting out. The main forest office in Yreka can be reached at (530) 842-6131. The office is located at 1312 Fairlane Road. Contact ranger districts for particulars about areas you're interested in visiting to make sure roads and trails are in decent repair and the weather won't interfere too much. The Happy Camp Ranger District, (530) 493-2243, and Scott River/Salmon River Ranger District, (530) 468-5351, cover a lot of ground. The Yreka Chamber of Commerce, (530) 842-1649, and Fort Jones Chamber of Commerce, (530) 468-5442, can also provide assistance with travel planning.

Adjoining Areas
> SOUTH: **Trinity Region**
> EAST: **Mount Shasta, Modoc Region**
> WEST: **Smith River National Recreation Area**

inside out

Hiking/Backpacking

With more than 1,300 miles of trails covering every imaginable type of wilderness terrain, backcountry long hauls are obviously the big ticket outdoor recreation item here. Terrain ranges from old-growth pine and fir forests of numerous varieties to oak woods, cedar forest, and lush redwood stands scattered with ferns. In contrast, there are also barren cliffs and dry ridgelands of sage and brush, along with serpentine and marble rock formations where little or no vegetation grows. Cool and lush river canyons give way to exposed meadows above the tree line. Isolated mountain lakes found beyond each peak are irresistible during hot summer treks, as is cold spring water that flows year-round in some areas, at a constant 39 degrees.

About 120 miles of the 2,600-mile **Pacific Crest Trail** passes through Klamath National Forest regions, including Marble Mountain Wilderness, Shelley Meadows, Cliff Lake, and other areas. Access points are available at Hwy 96 in Siead Valley or Hwy 3 at Scott Mountain. Several food and mail drops for PCT hikers are found in Siead Valley and Etna. The Pacific Crest Trail Association, (925) 939-6111, has maps and information on access points and hiking routes for this and all sections of the trail.

The best **maps** of the national forest are available directly from the Forest Service. Write US Forest Service Information, Room 521, 630 Sansome St, San Francisco, CA 94111. There are four main maps for this forest: one full Klamath National Forest map and one each for the Marble Mountain, Russian, and Trinity Alps Wilderness Areas. **Trail conditions** in any forest or wilderness area are subject to change, so before setting out on any days-long adventures, check with the appropriate ranger district for up-to-date information. Many backcountry trails may be impassable during winter, and some sections could be washed out or too dangerous to cross when rivers are running high. Contact Goosenest Ranger District, (530) 398-4391; Oak Knoll Ranger District, (530) 465-2241; Happy Camp Ranger District, (530) 493-2243; Scott River/Salmon River Ranger District (includes Marble Mountain Wilderness), (530) 468-5351; and Ukonom Ranger District, (530) 627-3291.

Taylor Lake Trail (easy; 1 mile round trip) is one of those rare short treks in the national wilderness areas that pay off nicely: a quiet, beautiful mountain lake setting is yours in exchange for a 15-minute walk on a graded trail you wouldn't be surprised to see in a city park. It's wilderness, just easy to get to. This is also a good jump-in point for the Pacific Crest Trail, which links up near the lake as well. To reach the trailhead, take Hwy 3 south from Fort Jones 30 miles to Etna, then head west on Etna–Somes Bar Rd 10 miles to the trailhead.

Paradise Lake Trail (moderate; 4 miles round trip) also offers big payoffs for little work. An isolated setting at 6,000 feet and less than 90 minutes from the trailhead, the lake is still, scenic, and shallow, with camping on the banks. The fishing isn't that great, and watch out for newts when swimming. To reach the trailhead, take River Rd 18 miles west from Fort Jones to the Indian Scotty Campground, then go 5 miles south on Forest Rd 43N45 and 6 miles west on the Paradise Lake access road.

Kings Castle Trail (moderate; 5.5 miles round trip) is a good choice for a well-paced day hike with both a lovely mountain lake to take a dip in during summer and a 7,405-foot summit. Paradise Lake is the first stop, 2 miles in from the trailhead; then continue on the trail through sometimes steep terrain and numerous switchbacks to Kings Castle. For directions to the trailhead, see Paradise Lake Trail, above.

Shackleford Creek Trail (moderate to difficult; 12 miles round trip) gives backpackers a bit of everything this stunning wilderness has to offer: rocky crags, virgin forestlands, deep-cut canyons with wild creeks pouring through them, and access to high peaks overlooking seemingly endless mountainous terrain. The hike begins at Shackleford Trailhead; traverses the Shackleford Creek canyon, crossing the creek often; and tops out above 7,000 feet at Summit Lake. From there, dozens of trail options lead to smaller lakes, and privacy is plentiful. Or make it a day hike and double back. To reach the trailhead, take Scott River Rd 4 miles west from Fort Jones, and turn left at Meamber Bridge Rd. The staging area is 7 miles out from the turn.

Marble Mountain Rim Trail (moderate; 16 miles round trip) is, in our view, the premier hike in all of Klamath National Forest, a long, steady trek from Lovers Camp to the 6,000-plus-foot-elevation summit rim through the Marble Mountains, with sweeping views of mountain peaks in all directions, including Shasta and the Trinity Alps. From Lovers Camp, follow Marble Mountain Rim Trail along Canyon Creek to Marble Valley, then take the Pacific Crest Trail to the mountain, which is carved out of stunningly white marble . . . unlike anything you've ever seen. Lovers Camp is 14 miles west from Fort Jones on Scott River Rd, then south on Forest Rd 44N45. Go forward on 44N45 another 8 miles from where the road splits. The campground, where you stage from, is on the left.

Kelsey Creek Trail (moderate; 18 miles round trip) is another great choice for a moderately paced romp through the wilderness over a couple of days, complete with a nice waterfall on Kelsey Creek, a couple of mountain lakes to dip in, and a connection to the Pacific Crest Trail that could be a staging point for longer journeys. To reach the trailhead, take Scott River Rd 20 miles west from Fort Jones, cross the bridge over the creek, turn south, and drive 1 mile on the access road to the trailhead.

Haypress Meadows Trail (moderate; 20 miles round trip) is a world-class California wilderness tour, well paced but with a few difficult and steep sections, passing through old-growth Douglas fir forests and topping out at Sandy Ridge, with several nice lakes nearby for setting up camp. To reach the trailhead, take Hwy 3 for 30 miles south to Etna, then go west 35 miles on Sawyers Bar Rd, then go another 20 miles west on Salmon River Rd. Just past Somes Bar, turn left at the sign for Haypress and continue about 7 miles to the trailhead.

Spirit Lake Trail (moderate; 34 miles round trip) takes you on another grand tour hike of the Marble Mountains region; on a long steady jaunt to Sandy Ridge; and then down toward a pristine, postcard-perfect mountain lake setting with thick virgin woodlands surrounding a wide, glassy bowl of snow melt. The hike begins at Haypress Meadow.

Mule Bridge Trail (moderate to difficult; 30 miles round trip, variable) is a seemingly endless climb from the camp at Idlewild up through the Salmon River canyon into some of the most stunning and deep wilderness found anywhere in the northern mountains. Lakes, springs, old-growth fir forests, meadows brimming with wildflowers, and camping choices all abound. Just take a map with you and choose. Osprey Lake is our favorite. The trail crosses the Pacific Crest Trail, making connections to other sections of the wilderness. From Fort Jones, take Hwy 3 south to Etna, then proceed 20 miles west on Sawyers Bar Rd, then go left at Mule Bridge Rd, which leads another 3 miles to the trailhead. Siskiyou Wilderness, Happy Camp Ranger District, (530) 493-2243.

Buck Lake Trail (easy; 4.5 miles round trip) passes through forests of Douglas and white fir, wide meadows brimming with wildflowers in the spring, and ends at a small fishing lake full of steelhead at 4,300 feet elevation. To reach the trailhead, head 30 miles out of Crescent City on US 199, then south on Little Jones Creek Rd for 10 miles, and 3.5 miles west on Forest Rd 16N02 to Doe Flat.

Young's Valley Trail (easy; 4 miles round trip) is an easy walk to a pleasant meadow nestled on the west side of 4,500-foot Preston Peak, popular for camping and day outings and also a suitable staging area for longer hikes into the deep wilderness. To reach the trailhead, take US 199 east from Crescent City for 30 miles, then head 15 miles north on Forest Rd 18N07. Do not attempt this Forest Service road without proper ground clearance on your vehicle.

Rattlesnake Meadow Trail (very difficult, potentially dangerous; 12 miles round trip) is a grueling, sometimes steep, slippery, and rocky climb to the 7,309-foot summit of Preston Peak, which provides sweeping views of all the northern mountain region, particularly on clear, cool days when visibility is prime. The last leg to the summit is actually part hike and part rock climb, leaving adventurers to scramble over slick, steep, bare rock to get to the top beyond where the trail tops out. Those without mountaineering experience should get some before attempting this trek. For directions, see Young's Valley Trail, above. Follow Young's Valley Trail to Young's Meadow, and then proceed 1 mile on Clear Creek Trail to meet Rattlesnake.

Kelsey Trail (moderate; 10.5 miles round trip) is a steady but manageable all-day climb to the 5,775-foot summit of Baldy Peak, where fantastic vistas of the surrounding Siskiyou and Marble Mountains regions are your reward. Kelsey continues through to the Marbles with numerous connections to other peaks and neighboring watersheds, depending on how far you are willing to go and how much time you have to explore. To find the trailhead, drive 25 miles east from Crescent City on US 199, then go 10 miles south on Little Jones Creek Rd. Turn north on Forest Rd 16N02 and continue for 5 miles, then go 3 miles east on Forest Rd 15N34 to the trailhead on the north side of the road. The hike actually begins across the Smith River National Recreation Area border.

Wilderness Falls Trail (difficult; 13 miles round trip) is a great two-day waterfall trek through the Doe Creek and Clear Creek canyons, topping out at a magnificently wide cascade on Clear Creek that runs furiously in the spring. There is one creek crossing that will most likely get you soggy, so proper footgear is a must (as it is for any wilderness hike). There are many good camping spots along the way. The hike begins from the Doe Flat trailhead. To reach the trailhead, head 30 miles out of Crescent City on US 199, then south on Little Jones Creek Rd 10 miles, and 3.5 miles west on Forest Rd 16N02 to the Doe Flat trailhead. Take Doe Flat Trail, which connects with Clear Creek and Wilderness Falls Trail 5 miles out.

Devil's Punchbowl Trail (difficult; 13 miles round trip) is a sometimes grueling two-day climb, involving countless switchbacks, a river crossing, and plenty of slick and rocky terrain, ending at Devil's Punchbowl Lake. For directions to the trailhead, see Wilderness Falls Trail, above. Begin the hike on Doe Flat Trail, which connects with Devil's Punchbowl 3 miles out.

Camping

Some of Klamath National Forest's 30-plus developed campgrounds are open only in summer (year-round, unless otherwise noted below). Beyond the developed sites, camping is allowed—as in all national forests—just about anywhere that you can find a plot of ground flat enough to set up for the night, provided it is at least a quarter mile from developed camps. Backcountry campers prefer the forest wilderness areas but may also find suitable riverside spots. **Permits** are required for use of fire anywhere outside developed campgrounds. Visitors also are asked to pack out garbage and burn all food waste.

Oak Knoll Ranger District, (530) 465-2241

Sarah Totten Campground contains 17 sites (no hookups; RV limit 21 feet) along the banks of the Klamath River and, like Beaver Creek, is also most enjoyable during the spring and early summer when the river is high. Piped water and vault toilets are available, and each site is equipped with a fire ring and table. *From Scott Bar, take Scott River Rd north to Hwy 96. Turn left (west) and proceed to the campground on the right about 1 mile ahead.*

O'Neil Creek Campground contains 18 sites (no hookups; RV limit 21 feet) along the banks of O'Neil Creek, a feeder stream for the Klamath River. The creek's flow diminishes substantially during the dry summer and fall season. Piped water and vault toilets are available, and each site is equipped with a fire ring and table. *From Scott Bar, take Scott River Rd north to Hwy 96. Turn left (west) and proceed past Hicks Gulch, to the campground on the left.*

Grider Creek Campground contains 10 sites (no hookups; RV limit 16 feet) along the banks of Grider Creek, a feeder stream for the Klamath River, which barely flows during dry summers and falls. Piped water and vault toilets are available, and each site is equipped with a fire ring and table. *From Scott Bar, take Scott River Rd north to Hwy 96. Turn left (west) and proceed to Walker Creek Rd, just before Siead Valley. Turn left and follow the signs to the campground.*

Scott River Ranger District, (530) 468-5351

Kangaroo Lake Campground has 18 sites (no hookups; RV limit 16 feet) on the shores of a 25-acre fishing lake stocked with steelhead trout, at a 6,500-foot elevation. Open June to October only. Each site has a picnic table and fire ring, with vault toilets nearby. There is a fishing pier at the lake. *From I-5, take the Edgewood exit north of Weed and head west to Callahan Rd, then turn south onto Forest Rd 41N08 for 7 miles to the campground entrance.*

Indian Scotty Campground has 28 sites (no hookups; RVs not advised) near the Marble Mountains trail connections and good fishing spots, and is open May to October. Each site has a picnic table and fire ring, with vault toilets nearby. This camp is particularly popular during holiday weekends because of its proximity to the Marble Mountain summit, the main attraction in this section of forest for hikers. *The camp is 14 miles west of Fort Jones, via Scott River Rd.*

Lovers Camp has just 8 sites (no hookups; RVs not advised) nearest the main trail connection leading to Marble Mountain's summit. This camp is also equipped with corrals for stock and is open May to October. Each site has a picnic table and fire ring, with vault toilets nearby. *To reach the camp, take Scott River Rd 14 miles west from Fort Jones, then turn south on Forest Rd 44N45 and continue for another 8 miles to the entrance.*

Bridge Flat Campground has 4 sites (no hookups; RVs not advised) on the Scott River, right at a popular rafting put-in and good fishing spot. Open May to October. Each site has a picnic table and fire ring, with vault toilets nearby. *The campground is 17 miles west of Fort Jones via Scott River Rd. Call the Scott River Ranger Station, (530) 468-5351, for more information.*

Hidden Horse Campground has 6 sites (no hookups; RVs not advised) situated in a pleasant meadow area in the foothills below Scott Mountain, nicely equipped for staging pack trips into the wilderness, with stock corrals and access for trailers. No water troughs or feed are available, however. Open May to October. Each site has a picnic table and fire pit, with vault toilets nearby. *The camp is 25 miles south of Fort Jones. Take Hwy 3 to the Callahan–Cecilville Rd cutoff, then go 13 miles west to the entrance.*

Trail Creek Camp has 12 sites (no hookups; RVs not advised) with easy access to numerous day hikes in the Trinity Alps Wilderness, and connections to the Pacific Coast Trail. Open May to October. Each site has a picnic table and fire ring, with vault toilets nearby. *To reach the camp, take I-5 to just north of Weed, exiting at Edgewood. Turn north on the surface road, and continue to Old Stage Rd. Turn right and continue 3 miles to Gazelle/Callahan Rd. Turn right and continue 15 miles to the campground on the right.*

Tree of Heaven Campground contains 20 sites (no hookups; RV limit 16 feet) along the banks of the Klamath River. The campground is most enjoyable during the spring and early summer months when the river flow is at its strongest. Piped water and vault toilets are available, and each site is equipped with a fire ring and table. *From Redding, take I-5 north and exit west onto Hwy 96. Proceed about 7 miles, past Klamath River Rd, to the campground access road on the left.*

Mount Ashland Campground has 9 sites (no hookups; RVs not advised) near the top of Mount Ashland at 6,600 feet, near a popular resort skiing area. Each site has a picnic table and fire ring, with vault toilets nearby. Open May to October. *To reach the camp, head west from Yreka on Hwy 96 for 12 miles, then go north on Forest Rd 48N01 for 13 miles. The campground entrance is on the west side of the road.*

Salmon River Ranger District, (530) 468-5351

Idlewild Campground contains 21 sites (no hookups; RV limit 22 feet) along the Salmon River. A number of popular hiking trails traverse the area. Piped water and vault toilets are available. Each site has a table and fire ring, and a general store is to the west in Sawyers Bar. *From Sawyers Bar, take Sawyers Bar Rd east and turn left onto Mule Bridge Rd. Proceed to the campground.*

Matthews Creek Campground contains 12 sites (no hookups; RV limit 17 feet) along the South Fork of the Salmon River, a popular rafting spot during the spring and early summer season. The campground is an attractive fishing spot as it fronts a number of deep, clear pools along the river. Piped water and vault toilets are available. Each site has a table and fire grill. *From Cecilville, take Cecilville Rd west, past Cody Bar, to the campground on the left side of the road.*

East Fork Campground contains 9 sites (no hookups; RV limit 17 feet) next to the East and South Forks of the Salmon River. Several deep bedrock holes, for fishing and swimming, lie along the South Fork. There is no running water, so be sure to bring plenty of your own. Vault toilets are provided, and each site has a table and fire grill. *From Cecilville, take Cecilville Rd east, past Caribou Rd, to the campground on the right side of the road.*

Big Flat Campground contains 9 sites (no hookups; RV limit 17 feet) at an elevation of 5,760 feet. Due to the high elevation, access to this campground is usually delayed until mid-spring and generally runs until early winter. Piped water and vault toilets are available. Each site has a table and fire ring. *From Trinity Center, take Hwy 3 north past Carrville, and turn left onto Coffee Creek Rd. Proceed past Rocky Gulch to the campground.*

Wildlife

The expansive marshlands of the **Klamath National Wildlife Refuge,** although substantially altered from their pristine condition by a century of water development around Tule Lake, are perhaps the chief birding site in this portion of the northern mountains, particularly during the spring migration. Because of the refuge's adjacency to the Pacific Flyway, millions of **migrating birds** visit, including Canada geese and any variety of ducks and pintails. Nearly 300 species of bird have been recorded in this area, 10 miles west of the Hwy 97 intersection with Hwy 161. For information, call the refuge offices, (530) 667-2231.

Birders visiting the Klamath wilderness areas can expect a few sure things, and perhaps a few surprises. Year-round communities of **great blue herons, common mergansers, belted kingfishers,** and **American dippers** can commonly be spotted in the forest's riparian areas, around ponds and lakes, rivers and wetlands. Less common **waterbirds** include the **green-backed heron,** which appears during the summer, ospreys, ring-billed gulls, Pacific flycatchers, and yellow-breasted chats. With so many different species of bird documented here, however, there is no telling where or when some rare spotting will happen. In the forests, look for bitterns, great horned owls, swifts, and hummingbirds, to name a few. Open grasslands and meadows with peaks overhead are the best areas to view **raptors,** such as turkey vultures, cooper's hawks, peregrine falcons, bald eagles, and prairie falcons.

Rattlesnakes and **black bears** get a lot of attention in these parts (aside from the legendary Sasquatch, whom we have yet to spot), but other abundant wildlife includes **elk, deer, coyotes, shrews, mountain lions,** and **river otters.**

Rafting

The Class II and III rapids on the **Klamath River** between Ash Creek Bridge and the Scott River are a good run for beginning to intermediate rafters setting out with a qualified outfitter. The primary season is April to October. River access is easy all along Hwy 96. The stretch of the Klamath between the Scott River and Happy Camp is more of an adrenaline rush, with a bit of Class IV action mixed in with the Class III. Ash Creek is a good put-in spot. The **Scott** and **Salmon Rivers** can flow furiously depending on the water year, with Class IV and V stretches used only by expert rafters, or rafters accompanied by expert guides and experienced river sportsters. The runs are normally most active April to June. Noah's World of Water, (800) 858-2811, offers **raft trips** departing as often as twice weekly on the Upper Klamath and Class V stretches of the Salmon. Living Waters Recreation, (800) 994-RAFT, runs the Klamath and upper Klamath, as well as the Salmon and Scott Rivers. Access to Adventure, (800) KLAMATH, also runs all three rivers. The Happy Camp Ranger District, (530) 493-2894, has the best river information.

Fishing

With hundreds of mountain lakes, many stocked, dotting the landscape—and with three excellent steelhead/salmon rivers and numerous streams to choose from—it's pretty much a given that backpackers setting into the Klamath high country should do so with their fishing gear. On the Salmon, Klamath, and Scott Rivers, **trout** and **steelhead** fishing can be excellent. The best spots are near tributaries of the main rivers, such as Canyon, Elk, Girder, and Shackleford Creeks. During the spring, look for **king salmon** on the Klamath and on Wooley Creek, a main tributary. One particularly nice river-fishing spot is on the South Fork of the Salmon at the Cody Bar area near Cecilville, where numerous pools form on the river. Bridge Flat on the Scott River near Fort Jones (see Camping, above) is another prized river fishing location.

    Fishing lakes, naturally, are too numerous to mention. Those with developed campsites and dependable trail connections, however, include Buck Lake, outside Happy Camp, and Kangaroo Lake (see Camping, above) near Weed. Lake fishing for **brown trout** and **rainbow trout** is best in September and October. Most lakes are at elevations between 5,500 and 6,500 feet. Flyfishing Headquarters, Dunsmuir, (530) 465-3448, and Ted Fay Fly Shop, Dunsmuir, (530) 235-2969, are two reputable **guides** in the Klamath area, as is Bob Claypole's Fishing Guide Service, on the Klamath River, (530) 465-2370. Retail **bait and tackle** dealers include Chain Reaction Sports, 614 S Main St, Yreka, (530) 842-6665.

Winter Sports

While hundreds of miles of trails are open to snow play, the extensive groomed and marked Nordic trails at **Juanita Lake Cross-Country Ski Trail,** adjacent to the Butte Valley Wildlife Area 5 miles south of the Oregon border on the west side of US 97, are a favorite in this remote, snow-bound area of the state.

    Snowmobilers have the run of Deer Mountain, Lake Lava Flow, Little Horse Peak, and all the winding, looping forest roads in between. Deer Mountain Snowmobile Park and Pilgrim Creek Snowmobile Park are the easiest areas to stage from. Call Mt. Shasta Sno-Mobilers, (530) 926-2824, for a snow report. The Goosenest Ranger District, (530) 398-4391, has current information on trail conditions and road access.

    Dogsled Express is owned an operated by guide Pat Campbell out of Etna, with unique overnight **snow camping** trips in the Marble Mountains backcountry. Campers get their own dogsled while Campbell mans the pack sled: a unique experience at a reasonable price. Campbell can be reached at (530) 467-5627. Campbell also leads trips into the Mount Shasta area and the Trinity Alps.

Adventure Calendar

Siskiyou Century Bike Ride, September: *(530) 842-1649.*

outside in

Attractions

Once a boomtown, **Yreka** now mines gold from tourists who visit the town's Historic District; city maps are available at the Yreka Chamber of Commerce at 117 W Miner St, (530) 842-1649. In the summer, take a scenic round-trip train ride on the **Yreka Western Railroad,** (530) 842-4146, to the historic town of **Montague,** where you can poke around the museum in the 1887 railroad depot and get a snack at the 1904 Opera Restaurant at 170 S 11th St, (530) 459-5794.

Restaurants

Indian Creek Cafe ☆   It may be a small cafe in one of the most sparsely populated corners of California, but Indian Creek has one of the state's largest menus. Youngsters in tow will definitely be happy campers, because there's something for everyone here. *106 Indian Creek Rd (near 2nd Ave), Happy Camp; (530) 493-5180; $.*

The Old Boston Shaft ☆   You won't get the shaft at this Yreka restaurant, where a generous three- to four-course meal costs about $35 for two. What a deal! Specialties include hearty beef and veal dishes. *1801 Fort Jones Rd (W of I-5 at the Fort Jones/Hwy 3 exit), Yreka; (530) 842-5768; $.*

Sengthong's ☆☆☆   Folks from Redding to Yreka sing the praises of this unpretentious restaurant hidden in one of the most remote areas of California. This small restaurant blends the cuisines of Vietnam, Laos, and Thailand. *434 Main St (off Hwy 3, in the center of town), Etna; (530) 467-5668; $.*

Lodgings

Beaver Creek Lodge ☆☆   One of the better lodges on the Klamath River, Beaver Creek has 5 knotty pine cabins, well-groomed grounds, and a coveted riverfront location. Four cabins sleep up to three people each; a larger unit accommodates as many as five. All units have kitchens, and you can pick up groceries in town, only 2 miles away. *16606 Hwy 96 (2 miles E of town), Klamath River; (530) 465-2331; $.*

Hollyhock Farm Bed & Breakfast ☆☆☆ Though this 1902 Normandy-style stone farmhouse is easily overlooked, its charm and setting make it a required stop for visitors to the North Mountains. All the rooms are tastefully furnished with antiques and lace curtains. *18705 Old Hwy 99 (just west of I-5; from Yreka take the Grenada/Gazelle exit; from Weed take the Edgewood/Gazelle exit), Gazelle; (530) 435-2627; $–$$.*

Otter Bar Lodge ☆☆☆ Surrounded by a pond and acres of grass, this 7-bedroom ranch-style lodge features oak floors, French doors, and lots of glass—all in an effort to bring the outdoors indoors. Six-night stays are required (and the seventh night is free), although shorter visits are available in April. All meals are included in the weekly rate. *On Salmon River Rd (15 miles E of Somes Bar), Forks of Salmon; (530) 462-4772; $$$.*

Ripple Creek Cabins ☆☆ Set amid tall pines and cedars where Ripple Creek enters the Trinity River, all 7 of these well-furnished cabins have amply stocked kitchens (Wow! Corkscrews and garlic presses!) and private baths. Most of the cabins accommodate two to six people. *On Eagle Creek Loop (off Hwy 3), Coffee Creek; (530) 266-3505 or (510)531-5315; $.*

More Information

Goosenest Ranger District: *(530) 398-4391.*
Fort Jones Chamber of Commerce: *(530) 468-5442.*
Happy Camp Ranger District: *(530) 493-2243.*
Oak Knoll Ranger District: *(530) 465-2241.*
Scott River/Salmon River Ranger District: *(530) 468-5351.*
Ukonom Ranger District: *(530) 627-3291.*
Weed Chamber of Commerce: *(530) 938-4624.*
Yreka Chamber of Commerce: *(530) 842-1649.*

Trinity Region

The northern mountain ranges including the Trinity Alps Wilderness, Trinity Lake, the Highway 299 corridor along the Trinity River, the Salmon Mountains, and points south to the Mendocino National Forest border.

Coming upon Trinity Lake can be a surreal experience. One minute you're on a long, upward-sloping mountain road twisting through the Trinity Alps—seemingly in the middle of nowhere—and the next thing you know, there it is, glistening like some impossible mirage. You blink, and it's still there, this wonderfully tucked-away boating and swimming spot seemingly sprung out of nowhere.

The glittering Trinity Lake and neighboring Lewiston Lake, at the geographic core of the recreation area, look so comfortable sprawled out in the canyons northeast of Weaverville that you almost don't notice the dams. Another river corralled by impressive engineering, the Trinity River is a popular water-play spot in the Northern Mountains, and a nice alternative to Shasta. This is more than just a boater's paradise, however. The 225,000-acre Trinity Alps Wilderness, with its 9,000-foot peaks snowbound nine months out of the year, is one of the state's largest and most pristine wilderness areas. Its deep-cut glacial canyons and rugged timberlands contain hundreds of miles of hiking routes, including nearly 150 miles of the Pacific Crest Trail. Hundreds of lakes and wild streams make Trinity a favorite backpacker's destination during the short period when access to the high country is unimpeded by weather. With nearly 150 inches of snow a year, and moderate to cool temperatures year-round with the exception of late summer, the rivers of Trinity almost always run heavy. Rafters and kayakers know this and head to the long, winding Trinity River canyon, which follows Highway 299 across the state from the North Coast to the highlands. They are generously rewarded with some of the most exciting whitewater in the state. Riverside camping and healthy runs (by today's standards, anyway) of rainbow, brook trout, and coho salmon make the river as much the center of attention as the lake and the high country—a little something for everybody. There is also, however, a side to the Trinity region that you won't have to put a roof rack on your car to take advantage of—and that is the area's remarkable ability to hang on to its past. As with so many small hamlets found hidden away on the state's side roads, Trinity's heritage is an open book. Mining equipment used to wash entire mountainsides away in the mad treasure search of the Gold Rush is still on display at the river's edge, as are the visible scars—piles of rock and scoured hillsides where vegetation stops. Weaverville, the region's center, has some of the oldest buildings in the state still in use, including a drugstore on Main Street that has been there since the 1850s.

Getting There

The Trinity region is best reached by traveling west from the Interstate 5 corridor via Highway 299 out of Douglas City and Weaverville or south on Highway 3 from Fort Jones and Yreka to the north. US 299 east through the Trinity River canyon from the North Coast is an alternative approach. Highways here are passable during the winter months, but Forest Service roads and access to areas at high altitudes may be either closed or restricted. Do watch, however, for boulders and patches of ice on the highways when conditions are ripe.

This area is also an important gateway to the North Coast for those traveling out of the Shasta region headed for the redwoods. In a day, the Trinity River canyon will take you there. Those planning travel to the area, particularly the lake, should contact the Trinity County Chamber of Commerce, (530) 623-6101; Big Bar Ranger District, (530) 623-6106; and Weaverville Ranger District, Highway 299 at South Miner Street, Weaverville, (530) 623-2121, for information on current weather and road conditions, as well as pointers on what to do and when to do it.

Adjoining Areas

NORTH: **Klamath Region**

SOUTH: **Mendocino National Forest**

EAST: **Lake Shasta**

WEST: **Smith River National Recreation Area**

inside out

Hiking/Backpacking

The world-famous Trinity Alps, covering some 225,000 acres of glacial valleys, pristine forestlands, and deep-cut river canyons west of Lake Shasta, are the primary draw in these parts for hikers and backpackers looking for a big piece of solace and solitude among the crags, canyons, and mountain lakes. **Wilderness permits** are required for all overnight trips in this area, and for use of fire. The best **trail maps** of the national forest are available directly from the Forest Service. Write US Forest Service Information, Room 521, 630 Sansome St, San Francisco, CA 94111. There are three main maps for this area—one full Trinity National Forest map, and one each for Trinity Alps Wilderness and Chanchelulla Wilderness. (See the primer at the beginning of this book for precise details.) **Trail conditions** in any forest or wilderness area are subject to change, so before setting out on any days-long adventures check with the appropriate ranger district for up-to-date information. Many backcountry trails may be impassable during winter, and sections can be washed out or too dangerous to cross when rivers are running high. Most of the hikes in this region begin in river or creek canyons, then ascend easily to alpine lake basins, with lower elevations at 2,500 feet and top peaks near 8,000; access to the high country is normally impossible until midsummer. Most hikes we recommend here are overnighters or weeklong treks, but there are a few day hikes available as well.

Burnt Ranch Falls Trail (easy; 1 mile round trip) is a good short stroll along the Trinity River with a pretty but small waterfall at its conclusion. This hike is ideal for parents traveling with children, and is a good opportunity to see the river and take in some waterfall action without having to stray too far from the minivan. The trailhead is at the Burnt Ranch Campground (see Camping, below). From Weaverville, take Hwy 299 west to Burnt Ranch. Continue on Hwy 299 about a mile to the campground entrance on the right. For more information, call the Big Bar Ranger District, (530) 623-6106.

Long Gulch Trail (difficult; 5 miles round trip) is one of those hearty river canyon climbs, ending at Long Gulch Lake, a nice fishing spot in the north end of the Salmon Mountains. Deadman Peak is the dominant feature on the skyline. The trail follows Long Gulch Creek from the Carter Meadows area, and points straight up—so catch your breath and hang on. There are trail connections nearby for longer legs, or just fish awhile and hike back that day. The lake is stocked with rainbow trout. Take Hwy 3 to

Callahan, north of Trinity Center, then head 10 miles west on Cecilville Rd to the staging area. For information, contact the Klamath National Forest, Scott River Ranger District, (530) 468-5351.

Caribou Lakes Trail (moderate; 18 miles round trip) is a nice two-day jaunt out of the Salmon River canyon and over Smith Ridge to a string of lakes situated in a basin beneath the higher Sawtooth Ridge, beyond. The first leg of the hike is the most difficult, since the climb up from the Salmon is continuous, but there are big payoffs the minute the trail comes over the ridge top and begins its descent to the lakes. To reach the trailhead, take Hwy 3 to the Trinity Lake area, then drive 15 miles west on Coffee Creek Rd, which is just north of Trinity Center. Call the Scott River Ranger District, (530) 468-5351.

Hobo Gulch Trailhead (moderately difficult; 40 miles round trip) is a long backcountry journey, topping off at 8,663-foot Thompson Peak in the Trinity Alps, through the Grizzly Creek canyon to Pfeiffer Flat and Grizzly Lake. Lush canyons, lovely meadows, alpine lake settings, and white granite peaks offering wide vistas abound. It is best to pace this trip over six days or so. To reach the trailhead, take Hwy 299 for 12 miles west from Weaverville, then head 20 miles north of the highway on Hobo Gulch Rd. For information, contact the Shasta-Trinity National Forest, Weaverville Ranger District, (530) 623-2121.

Canyon Creek Trail (moderate; 15 miles round trip) is perhaps the most rewarding—and certainly one of the most popular—in the Trinity Alps Wilderness Area. The trail meanders through the Canyon Creek canyon in the shadows of Sawtooth Mountain and portions of the Salmon and Scott Ranges. Thompson Peak is also a dominant feature on the skyline. After a few creek crossings, the trail rises 3,000 feet toward the Canyon Creek Lakes area beneath Sawtooth. This hike has it all: fishing creeks, high granite peaks, meadows, waterfalls, swimming lakes (during summer), and spectacular vistas of the Northern Mountains region. To reach the trailhead, travel 8 miles west on Hwy 299 from Weaverville, then 15 miles north on Canyon Creek Rd. For information, contact the Shasta-Trinity National Forest, Weaverville Ranger District, (530) 623-2121.

Swift Creek Trail (moderate; 22 miles round trip) catapults some 3,400 feet up to Sunrise Pass at 7,400-foot elevation, overlooking Big Flat meadows along the Swift Creek canyon route. The pass is really a Gold Rush–era trading route that over the past 150 years has evolved into a popular backpacking destination through the Shasta-Trinity Wilderness. The climb from the canyon is steep in places but the trail is easy to follow. To reach the trailhead, follow Hwy 3 for 30 miles west from Weaverville, then head north on Swift Creek Rd another 7 miles. For information, contact the Shasta-Trinity National Forest, Weaverville Ranger District, (530) 623-2121.

Union Lake Trail (moderate; 11.5 miles round trip) is yet another catapult out of the canyons, over a ridge, and into a secluded and pristine alpine lake basin where you don't have to worry about Jet-skis and RVs spoiling the ambience. The hike begins at Coffee Creek in the Trinity Lake region, and follows Coffee and Union Creeks to the lake basin below the Red Rock Mountain ridgeline. To reach the trailhead, take Hwy 3 to the Trinity Lake shore frontage, then take Coffee Creek Rd 10 miles west to the staging area. For information, contact the Shasta-Trinity National Forest, Weaverville Ranger District, (530) 623-2121.

Camping

As with most of the national forests in California, camping in the Trinity National Forest is allowed just about anywhere you can find a piece of ground flat enough to pitch a tent on—with just a few exceptions. The best camping areas in Trinity are along the Trinity River and at Lewiston and Trinity Reservoirs, although **dispersed camping** in the Trinity Alps Wilderness is prime. Be sure to get **permits** for any use of fire in wilderness. The best maps are available directly from the Forest Service. Write US Forest Service Information, Room 521, 630 Sansome St, San Francisco, CA 94111. (See the primer at the beginning of this book for precise instructions.) Periodic **road closures** are unavoidable. Check with the relevant ranger station for updated road conditions before deciding on a site located deep within the forest. Roads are not maintained for vehicles with low ground clearance. The Forest Service is currently reviewing its **reservations and fees** policies for this area, but generally no reservations are taken for any of the campgrounds listed below. Stays are limited to 14 days. Call the Forest Service reservations system at (800) 280-2267 or individual ranger stations for campsite availability information and reservations where applicable.

Trinity River, Big Bar Ranger District, (530) 623-6106

Hayden Flat Campground contains 22 sites (no hookups; RV limit 27 feet) adjacent to the Trinity River. The campground has piped water and vault toilets. Each site is equipped with a table and fire ring, and a general store is nearby in Big Bar. *From Weaverville, take Hwy 299 west to Delloma. Continue about a mile to the campground entrance on the right.*

Burnt Ranch Campground contains 19 sites (no hookups; RV limit 27 feet) on a bluff above the Trinity River. The campground's location makes it popular among visitors to the Trinity River. It has piped water and vault toilets. Each site is equipped with a table and fire ring, and a general store is nearby in the village of Burnt Ranch. *From Weaverville, take Hwy 299 west to Burnt Ranch. Continue about a mile to the campground entrance on the right.*

Gray's Falls Campground has 36 sites (no hookups; RV limit 37 feet) along the Trinity River. Nestled near Gray's falls, a small waterfall, the campground is nicest during the spring and early summer months when the river is flowing at its strongest. It has piped water and vault toilets. Each site is equipped with a table and fire ring, and a general store is nearby in the village of Burnt Ranch. *From Weaverville, take Hwy 299 west to Burnt Ranch. Continue about 5 miles to the campground entrance on the right. Trinity Lake and Lewiston Reservoirs, Weaverville Ranger District, (530) 623-2121.*

Jackass Springs Camp has 20 sites (no hookups; RV limit 28 feet) northwest of Lake Shasta along Trinity Lake. This campground is popular among visitors looking for good fishing in a picturesque lake. The campground has piped water except during the winter months. Vault toilets are available, and each site is equipped with a fire ring and table. *From Carrville, take Hwy 3 south and turn left on East Side Rd/County Rd 106. Continue to County Rd 119, turn right, and proceed to the campground entrance.*

Trinity River Campground has 11 sites (no hookups; RV limit 31 feet) just north of Trinity Lake, near the Trinity River. This campground serves as an overflow area for Jackass Springs Camp. There is piped water except during the winter months. Vault toilets are available, and each site is equipped with a fire ring and table. A general store is just to the south in Carrville. *From Carrville, take Hwy 3 north about 9 miles to the campground entrance on the left side of the highway.*

Eagle Creek Campground has 19 sites (no hookups; RV limit 31 feet) north of Trinity Lake, along Eagle Creek and Trinity River. This campground is most enjoyable in the spring and early summer season when the river is flowing strong. There is piped water except during the winter months. Vault toilets are available, and each site is equipped with a fire ring and table. A general store lies just to the south in Carrville. *From Carrville, take Hwy 3 north about 15 miles to the campground entrance on the right side of the highway.*

Horse Flat Campground contains 18 sites (no hookups; RV limit 16 feet) north of Trinity Lake. The campground is used mostly by visitors who are looking for solitude and a primitive camping experience. There is no running water, so be sure to bring plenty of your own. Vault toilets are available, and each site is equipped with a fire ring and table. A general store is to the south in Carrville. *From Carrville, take Hwy 3 north past Trouble Ranch, to Forest Rd 38N27. Proceed to the camp about 2 miles ahead.*

Preacher Meadow contains 47 sites (no hookups; RV limit 35 feet) a few miles from Trinity Lake. The campground serves as an overflow area when the lakeside campgrounds fill up during the busy summer holiday weekends. The campground has piped water and vault toilets. Each site is equipped with a table and fire ring, and a general store is to the north in the town of Trinity Center. *From Trinity Center, take Hwy 3 south for 2 miles and look for the campground entrance on the right.*

Alpine View Campground has 65 sites (no hookups; RV limit 35 feet) a few miles from Trinity Lake. This campground also serves as an overflow area when the lakeside campgrounds fill up. The campground has piped water and vault toilets. Each site is equipped with a table and fire ring, and a general store is nearby in the town of Covington Mill. *From Trinity Center, take Hwy 3 south to Covington Mill. Turn left on Guy Covington Dr and proceed to the campground entrance.*

Clark Springs Campground contains 26 tent sites (no RV access) adjacent to Trinity Lake. The campground is popular with boaters because it's near a boat ramp. Clark Springs has piped water except during the winter season. There are flush toilets, and each site is equipped with a table and fire ring. A general store is to the north in the town of Covington Mill. *From Trinity Center, take Hwy 3 south to Covington Mill. Continue south 2 miles on Hwy 3 to the campground entrance on the left.*

Stoney Point Campground has 24 tent sites (no RV access) along Trinity Lake. The campground is very popular due to its lakefront setting. There is piped water and vault toilets. Each site is equipped with a table and fire ring. A general store is to the north in the town of Trinity Center. *From Trinity Center, take Hwy 3 south past Ridgeville, to the campground entrance about 1,500 feet from the Stewart Fork Bridge.*

Hayward Campground contains 100 sites (no hookups; RV limit 42 feet) along the shore of Trinity Lake. It is one of the area's most popular campgrounds because of its waterside location, and it often fills up during the busy summer holiday weekends. The campground has piped water and vault toilets. Each site is equipped with a table and fire ring. A boat ramp lies nearby and a general store is to the north in the town of Trinity Center. *From Trinity Center, take Hwy 3 south. About 1.5 miles before Ridgeville, turn left at the campground access road, just before Digger Creek Rd. Proceed to the campground entrance.*

Minersville Campground contains 21 sites (no hookups; RV limit 21 feet) near the shore of Trinity Lake. The campground has piped water, except during the winter season, and flush toilets. Each site is equipped with a table and fire ring. A boat ramp lies nearby and a general store is to the north in the town of Trinity Center. *From Trinity Center, take Hwy 3 south past Ridgeville, to the campground entrance on the left side, just past Mule Creek.*

Tannery Gulch Campground has 91 sites (no hookups; RV limit 41 feet) along the shore of Trinity Lake. The campground has a boat ramp, piped water, and flush toilets. Each site is equipped with a table and fire ring. A general store is to the north in the town of Trinity Center. *From Trinity Center, take Hwy 3 south past Ridgeville and past the Stuart Fork Bridge, and turn left on Tannery Gulch Rd. Proceed to the campground entrance.*

East Weaver Campground has 19 sites (no hookups; RV limit 18 feet) along East Weaver Creek, several miles from the shore of Lewiston Reservoir. The campground serves as an overflow area for the more popular lakeside campgrounds. There is piped water, except during the winter season, and vault toilets. Each site is equipped with a table and fire ring. A general store is nearby in Weaverville. *From Weaverville, take Hwy 3 north about 2 miles and turn left on E Weaver Creek Rd. Proceed to the campground about 4 miles ahead.*

Ackerman Campground contains 72 sites (no hookups; RV limit 44 feet) adjacent to the northern shore of Lewiston Reservoir. The campground is quite popular, particularly among RV users, as there is a dump station on the premises. A boat ramp lies south of the campground, and the fishing is great along the nearby dam. There is piped water, except during the winter season, and vault toilets. Each site is equipped with a table and fire ring. A general store is to the south in Lewiston. *From Weaverville, take Hwy 3 north and turn right on Trinity Dam Rd, just past Rush Creek Rd. Proceed past Trinity Dam to the campground entrance.*

Mary Smith Campground contains 17 tent sites (no RV access) on the southern shore of Lewiston Reservoir. The campground is quite popular with tent campers due to its very quiet and somewhat intimate setting. There is piped water available, along with vault toilets. Each site is equipped with a table and fire ring. A general store is to the south in Lewiston. *From Weaverville, take Hwy 3 north and turn right on Trinity Dam Rd, just past Rush Creek Rd. Proceed past Trinity Dam and the Ackerman Campground to the entrance.*

Ruth Lake area

Fir Cove Camp has 24 sites (no hookups; RV limit 21 feet) along the shore of Ruth Lake, a popular fishing and boating spot. There is piped water and vault toilets. Each site is equipped with a table and fire ring. A general store is to the south in Ruth. *From Mad River, take Hwy 36 east a few miles to Lower Mad River Rd. Turn right and proceed to the campground on the right side of the road. Contact the Six Rivers National Forest, Mad River Ranger District, (707) 574-6233.*

Baily Cove Campground has 27 sites (no hookups; RV limit 21 feet) along the shore of Ruth Lake, and adjacent to Fir Cove Campground. There is piped water and vault toilets. Each site is equipped with a table and fire ring. *From Mad River, take Hwy 36 east a few miles to Lower Mad*

River Rd. *Turn right and proceed to the campground on the right side of the road. Contact the Six Rivers National Forest, Mad River Ranger District, (707) 574-6233.*

Scott Mountain Campground has 10 tent sites (no RV access) nestled in a very isolated area of Klamath National Forest. This campground is sought out by hikers looking for a very quiet primitive camping experience. There is no running water, so be sure to bring plenty of your own. There are vault toilets, however, and each site is equipped with a table and fire ring. *From Callahan, take Hwy 3 south to Scott Mountain and look for the campground on the right side of the road. Contact the Weaverville Ranger District, (530) 623-2121.*

Rafting

If you're looking for whitewater action, take a drive down the **Trinity River** canyon west from Weaverville on Hwy 299—you'll find it. The Trinity's Class II and III rapids below Lewiston Reservoir through Sailor's Bar, Hell's Hole, and the Slot are ideal for beginner to intermediate rafters, but be advised that there are also some killer runs on the Trinity, namely the Class V Burnt Ranch Gorge run west of Cedar Flat. There's easy access to the river on the south side of Hwy 299, with put-in spots clearly signed by the Forest Service. Big Bar Flat, or the Pigeon Point run, is a 5-mile stretch of Class III often sought after by those who crave whitewater without having a death wish—just plain fun, not scary (depending on water releases, that is). Those who don't know the river or are inexperienced would do best to contact a **guided rafting** trip company. Turtle River Rafting Company, (800) 726-3223; Living Waters Recreation, (800) 994-RAFT, www.livingwaters.com; and River Dancers, (800) 926-5002, are all authorized outfitters on the Trinity and other rivers in the northern mountains. Whitewater fun is also available on the Klamath, Cal Salmon, Scott, and Smith Rivers (see Klamath Region and Smith River National Recreation Area chapters).

Fishing

Nestled at the base of the dramatic and sweeping Trinity Alps, **Trinity Lake** is a 17,000-acre reservoir that floods 17 miles of the Trinity River canyon, creating 145 miles of some of the prettiest shoreline in the area. Trinity is considered one of the state's best **smallmouth bass** fisheries during the spring and summer seasons, and to a lesser degree during the winter season. The southwest region of the lake hosts the best fishing according to the locals. There is also a healthy **largemouth, catfish,** and **kokanee salmon** fishery here. In particular, Mule Creek, Cedar Stock, and Buckeye Arm are sections of the lake worth checking out. However, don't fall under the mistaken impression that those areas are to be fished to the exclusion of the remainder of the lake. Myriad good fishing spots are in the creeks and coves along the lake's long eastern edge. Numerous marinas, tackle shops, and boat ramps dot the shore of the lake, particularly on the western side. From Trinity Center, take Hwy 3 south to the lake.

Swift Creek, Coffee Creek, the Trinity River below the dam, and hundreds of small mountain lakes scattered throughout the Trinity region also make for decent **trout** fishing. Trinity Fly Shop, Weaverville, (530) 623-6757, is one of numerous bait-and-tackle dealers in the vicinity and can provide general information.

Boating/Swimming

Trinity Lake is the boating center in these parts, with fishing, waterskiing, Jet-skiing, and swimming a popular draw during the summer months. Bowerman Gulch and Pole Gulch on the lake's northeast end are popular **swimming spots,** with easy access along Guy Covington Rd. There also are numerous pullouts directly off Hwy 3. The main information point for the lake complex is the Weaverville Ranger District, Hwy 299 at S Miner St, Weaverville, (530) 623-2121. There are also resorts and marinas around the lake. Wyntoon Resort, in Trinity Center, (800) 715-3337, has **rental boats,** as does the Recreation Plus Marina, (530) 266-3432. Estrellita Marina, Weaverville, (530) 286-2215, has fishing boats, ski boats, Jet-skis, and houseboats for rent. Public **boat ramps** are located around the lake, including at Clark Springs Campground on Hwy 3 at Stuarts Fork Arm, at the Minersville Campground on Hwy 105 near Trinity Dam, and at Trinity Center Boat Ramp. The lake is 18 miles north of Weaverville on Hwy 3.

Scenic Drives/Photography

Shutterbugs will enjoy the 111-mile drive north along Hwy 3, beginning in Weaverville and ending in the northern reaches at Fort Jones. This is the official **Trinity Heritage National Scenic Byway,** a self-guided auto tour of the Trinity Region that includes stops at historic buildings, mining sites, interesting geologic features, vista points, and key river crossings. The drive takes you through some of the most dramatic mountain and forest landscape in the north state, with high mountain lakes and wild river views all along the way. The trip is indeed stunning, particularly when Trinity Lake comes into view, like a jewel set deep in the mountains. Call the Weaverville Ranger District, (530) 623-2121, for an official scenic byway brochure, with an explanation of 20 significant landmarks along the way.

If you have even more time on your hands and an extra tank of gas, also check out the **Highway 299** route west from Weaverville to the North Coast. The 90-mile stretch of Hwy 3 between Fort Jones and Weaverville—running through the scenic Etna River canyon and into the expansive forestlands east of Russian Wilderness and the Trinity Alps—provide a stellar view of portions of the Northern Mountains region normally overshadowed by the Lake Shasta corridor along I-5. When the mountain peaks part, Clair Engle Lake comes into view, a particularly inviting sight during a summer heat wave. Camping and boating opportunities abound here. At Weaverville, follow Hwy 299 another 80 miles through the Trinity River canyon—with numerous easy river access points. This stretch of Hwy 299 is a popular rafting area, with numerous roadside outfitters in the Big Bar area. This drive is a good link between the Shasta region and the North Coast area for those travelers wishing to see both the northern mountain highlands and the ancient redwoods (see Humboldt Coast chapter). When scheduling such a trip, however, be sure to keep in mind that the drive between Fort Jones and Arcata will take an entire day, particularly since there are numerous interesting places to stop along the way.

Wildlife

Birders will have a time of it trying to spot the wide variety of bird life found throughout Trinity County. Jays, nuthatches, poor-wills, kingfishers, robins, chickadees, black-headed grosbeaks, woodpeckers, owls, numerous hawks and falcons, and a host of **songbirds** and **shorebirds** are commonly seen in the Trinity River canyon and surrounding forestlands. The lake basins of the unspoiled Trinity Alps Wilderness Area are among the best birding spots, but there are also good roadside spots through the Hwy 299 corridor, in particular around Ruth Lake and Trinity Lake in forested shoreline areas and creek mouths.

Naturally, **black bears** and **rattlesnakes** are on the loose in the Trinity area, where **black-tailed deer, raccoons, bobcats, coyotes, otters, gray foxes,** and numerous other wild creatures roam. Observe all snake- and bear-related precautions described in the primer at the beginning of this book.

Mountain Biking

National forests blanket 70 percent of Trinity County, so opportunities for bikers abound, though it requires some research and scouting. Mountain bikers, hikers, and horseback riders alike flock to the scenic 50-mile **Weaver Basin Trail,** which circles Weaverville. For information about the trail and other options in the area, visit the helpful staff at Brady's Sport

Shop, located on the ground floor of the Weaverville Hotel at 201 Main St, Weaverville, (530) 623-3121.

Adventure Calendar

La Grange Classic Mountain Bike Race: *a grueling Weaverville event, typically held the first weekend in June,* *(530) 623-6101 or (800) 487-4648.*

Attractions

Founded nearly 150 years ago by gold miners, the little rural town of **Weaverville** (population 4,000) is the largest town in Trinity County (an area the size of Rhode Island and Delaware combined). While cruising through the historic downtown district, keep your peepers open for the peculiar outdoor spiral staircases that grace many of the homes—they're remnants of the days when each floor was owned by a different person. For a bit of Gold Rush and Weaverville history, stroll down Main St and visit the small **Jake Jackson Museum,** 508 Main St, (530) 623-5211. Adjacent to the museum is **Joss House State Historic Park,** site of the oldest Chinese temple in the United States. The well-preserved temple was built by immigrant Chinese miners in 1874 and is worth a peek (and the nominal entrance fee); call (530) 623-5284 for information on temple tours.

Restaurants

Cinnabar Sam's ☆   Be sure to stop for a bite at Cinnabar Sam's. A popular hangout for rafters and kayakers, this restaurant is decked out in Western memorabilia; even the salad bar is in a claw-footed tub. *19 Willow Way (at Hwy 299, at the E end of town), Willow Creek; (530) 629-3437; $.*

La Grange Cafe ☆☆☆   Named after a nearby mine, La Grange Cafe serves the best food in town. An excellent and moderately priced wine list boasts more than 100 selections. And then there's the sweet stuff: divine desserts are made on the premises. *315 N Main St (on Hwy 299), Weaverville; (530) 623-5325; $$.*

Lewiston Hotel ☆   Built in 1863 as a stage stop, the Lewiston Hotel is home to one of California's oldest continuously operating restaurants. The seasonal menu includes prime rib (some of the region's best), steaks, game, fresh fish, and housemade pasta. *On Deadwood Rd (1 block from the bridge), Lewiston; (530) 778-3823; $.*

Noelle's Garden Cafe ☆☆   This snug, cheerful cafe, now located in an old two-story house, has a phalanx of windows and a sunny outside deck. Specialties include Austrian strudel and a hefty veggie melt. *252 Main St (1 block W of Oregon St), Weaverville; (530) 623-2058; $.*

Lodgings

Old Lewiston Inn ☆☆☆   This B&B has 7 guest rooms: 3 small rooms in the 1875 Baker House and 4 rooms in the adjoining inn (most have private baths). The inn accommodations have less history but more elbow room, with private entrances and decks overlooking the Trinity River. *On Deadwood Rd (½ block from the bridge), Lewiston; (530) 778-3385 or (800) 286-4441; $$.*

Red Hill Motel ☆   The Red Hill's 14 well-maintained auto-court units would have made a great set for a '40s film noir. So put on your best fedora and step back in time by booking a night or two at these cabins, decorated with authentic pre–World War II furnishings. *On Red Hill Rd (across from the US Forest Service station on Main St, at the N end of town), Weaverville; (530) 623-4331; $.*

Weaverville Hotel   This hotel has been in operation since 1861—a few fiery interruptions notwithstanding (it burned to the ground several times in the town's early days). The 8 guest rooms, located on the second floor, are a bit spare, but they're a good choice for the budget-conscious traveler who likes historic surroundings with that morning cup of coffee. *201 Main St (in the center of town), Weaverville; (530) 623-3121; $.*

More Information

Big Bar Ranger District: *(530) 623-6106.*
Forest Service reservations system: *(800) 280-2267.*
Trinity County Chamber of Commerce: *(530) 623-6101.*
Weaverville Ranger District: *(530) 623-2121.*

Mount Shasta

Mount Shasta, and the surrounding wilderness areas east of the Interstate 5 corridor and north of Lake Shasta, bounded on the east by Lassen and Modoc Counties, and including Castle Crags State Park.

Climb. At first the impulse is possible to ignore. While taking in that view of Mount Shasta, crowned in snow year-round at more than 14,000 feet above it all, a little part of you wants to do more than just look. What actually possesses people to make the grueling two-day journey to the top—without being turned back by weather, exhaustion, or altitude sickness—is something else. This crowning peak of the southern Cascades region is irresistible to us all, to varying degrees. And much is also to be found here for those satisfied to just admire the mountain from afar. Some choose to backpack in its foothills or climb lesser peaks for a look from a different angle. Others take to the forest service roads for the 50-mile bike ride around the mountain—which takes as long as the hike to the summit. Others come in winter, when Mount Shasta Ski Park with its 1,400-foot vertical drop and adjacent winter play areas, turns the whole region into a winter wonderland. In many ways, the recreation scene in the entire Shasta region depends solely on the mountain. It is even the gradually melting winter snows from the mountain that fill Lake Shasta, the largest man-made lake in the state.

Mount Shasta is the result of 250,000 years of volcanic activity in the Siskiyou region and is considered "dormant" but not "inactive" as far as volcanoes go. It towers over the neighboring peaks of the Cascade Range (though anyone who has taken an air tour of the 1,000 miles stretching from Northern California to British

Columbia knows Shasta's distant cousins loom to the north). Lava flow and ash are the building blocks of the Cascades, and while volcanic activity has leveled off in the Shasta region over the past 200 years, experts say it will, indeed, blow its top again, as it has a dozen times or so in the past 3,500 years. Evidence of past volcanic activity is seen just about everywhere, such as in the 1,000-foot towering crags at Castle Crags State Park, which the more daring among us like to climb.

Nobody is quite sure where Shasta got its name. European explorers used the French and Russian words meaning "pure" to describe the mountain—and both sound enough like "Shasta" that this could be the origin. But another story holds that an Indian tribe north of the mountain called itself by that name. Although historians haven't figured it out yet, they do know that the first recorded sighting of the mountain was in 1817, when Spanish explorer Fray Narcisco Duran spotted the white-capped summit. He gave it the name "Jesus Maria," but that didn't stick.

Had Duran or any of the other alleged Shasta-namers stopped admiring it from a distance, strapped on a set of crampons, and trudged to the summit instead, the mountain might have been named in a universal language. They would have named it "Wow."

Getting There

Mount Shasta and its surrounding wilderness areas are easily reached via Interstate 5 north from Redding, or by way of Highway 89 from the east. Everitt Memorial Highway, east from Interstate 5 at Mount Shasta City, provides the most direct access to the mountain and its main outdoor recreation destinations. During winter, however, the road is closed at the lower elevations and turned over to snowmobile action. Travelers planning to visit the Shasta region should contact the Mount Shasta Chamber of Commerce, (530) 926-6212, McCloud Chamber of Commerce, (530) 964-3113, or Dunsmuir Chamber of Commerce, (800) 386-7684, for recommendations and trip-planning help. Mount Shasta Ranger District, 204 West Alma Street, Shasta, (530) 964-2184, will have the latest on mountain access and road conditions within the wilderness.

Adjoining Areas

NORTH: **Klamath Region**

SOUTH: **Lake Shasta**

EAST: **Modoc Region, Lassen Region**

WEST: **Trinity Region**

inside out

Downhill Skiing/Snowboarding

Mount Shasta Ski Park is a privately owned and operated ski resort area on the south-facing slopes of the mountain, and arguably one of the more serene and beautiful alpine ski destinations in the state, with the towering peak as a postcard-perfect backdrop and good skiing from Thanksgiving to Easter during normal weather years (although it's tough to even imagine a Shasta without snow!). The park contains more than 400 acres, with 25 downhill runs covering 1,400 feet combined. The resort recently underwent an expansion. It has a base elevation of 5,500 feet, with the summit 1,100 feet above that. There are 2 triple chair lifts and a surface tow, with the longest run covering a distance of a little more than a mile. The ski area is geared toward the typical intermediate skier on 60 percent of its runs and trails. Beginner and advanced-ranked runs cover 20 percent each of the ski area. The more difficult runs are at Douglas Butte, while beginner runs are found at Marmot, with just under 700 feet of vertical rise. The resort has a **ski school** with a 50-foot lift, and private instruction is available at a reasonable cost. There is also a children's ski program. Rentals are available on site with restaurants and lodgings nearby. For **snow conditions** at the park, call (530) 926-8686. To reach the resort, head 10 miles east of I-5 from the Mount Shasta exit on Hwy 89. At Siskiyou Ave, turn left (north) and continue a short distance to the resort entrance. Mount Shasta Ski Park also has **snowboarding** areas, with rentals and lessons available at the ski park.

Numerous ski outfitters are found in and around the Shasta area. The Fifth Season, (530) 926-3606, 300 Chestnut St, Mount Shasta, has **rentals** for boarders and downhill and cross-country skiers, and also maintains the aforementioned weather and ski conditions hot line. House of Ski and Board, right next door, (530) 926-2359, also has the works.

Snowboarding areas are designated by gentleman's agreement in the sloping areas adjacent to Nordic ski trails at Bunny Flat (see Cross-Country Skiing/Snowmobiling, below) and Snowman's Hill, at Ski Park Hwy and Hwy 89. Castle Lake (see below) and Mount Shasta Ski Park (see above) also have snowboarding areas, with rentals and lessons available at the ski park. See above for Shasta-area ski outfitters.

Cross-Country Skiing/Snowmobiling

The best and most easily accessed Nordic ski areas around Shasta are along the Everitt Memorial Hwy east of the Shasta town site and beyond the ski resort area. There are three interlinking marked trails with graduating degrees of difficulty. **Bunny Flat Trail,** 12 miles east of I-5 on the Everitt Memorial Hwy, consists of 1.5 kilometers of marked, level trail suitable for beginners. The gently downward-sloping trail extends eastward to **Sand Flat,** where skiers can enjoy another 2.5 kilometers of flat, ungroomed trail through old-growth fir forestlands. One particularly nice route is **Overlook Loop Trail,** which begins at Sand Flat and covers just under a kilometer of ungroomed, marked trail leading to an area with sweeping vistas of Shasta Valley and the Sacramento River canyon.

More experienced skiers are encouraged to leave the trails and cover miles of countryside around Bunny Flat as well as the Old Ski Bowl area east on Everitt Memorial Hwy—but watch out for and heed any avalanche warnings. The best way to reach these areas is to head east on Everitt from Mount Shasta City, 10 miles east of I-5. Parking is at Bunny Flat and at smaller pull-offs nearby. Along Everitt, there are no commercial equipment rental outlets, so be sure to get outfitted in town (see above).

Mount Shasta Ski Park (see above) also has 25 kilometers of Nordic ski trails, from easy, machine-groomed trails to more rustic advanced routes through the woods and across open meadows adjoining the slopes. Day packages and group lessons are available at the resort's Nordic ski school, and there are equipment rentals on site. At **Castle Lake,** 1 mile east of the ski park on Hwy 89, you'll find another 48 kilometers of Nordic trails, most groomed and packed, 40 percent for advanced snow trekkers, including one route covering 11 kilometers. Call the state parks reservation system, (800) 444-7275, for reservations information. Call the Mount Shasta Ranger District, (530) 964-2184, or the Shasta road and weather and ski report hot line, (530) 926-5555, for information, particularly before heading into the wilderness on unmarked trails.

Snowmobilers who really want to put some distance between themselves and potential trail use conflicts head to the east side of the mountain and stage from the **Pilgrim Creek Snowmobile Park,** where there are more than 150 miles of marked snowmobile trails with connectors to more expansive trail systems in neighboring Klamath National Forest. It's 3 miles east of McCloud on state Hwy 89, at Pilgrim Creek Rd. Call the McCloud Ranger District, (530) 964-2184, for information. Another popular snowmobiling area is at **Deer Mountain,** 17 miles east of Weed on US Hwy 97 (US 97) and 4 miles toward the mountain on Deer Mountain Rd. Call the Shasta Ranger District, (530) 964-2184, for particulars. The snowbound Everitt Memorial Hwy, from Bunny Flat to Old Ski Bowl, also is open to snowmobilers, but they are required to stay out of the Shasta wilderness areas near the bowl—so perhaps the freedom of a wide, flat, open highway is the real draw here.

Hiking/Backpacking

Mount Shasta is within the Shasta-Trinity National Forest boundaries (also see Trinity Region chapter), which contains more than 3,000 miles of hiking trails, including nearly 200 miles of the Pacific Crest Trail and the dramatic Mount Shasta summit climb (see below). Wilderness areas covered in this chapter are Mount Shasta and Castle Crags, which contain an amazing diversity of landscapes to explore: volcanic formations, deep river canyons and waterfalls, high mountain meadows, and thick forests of ponderosa pine and Douglas fir. The best **trail maps** of the national forest areas are available directly from the Forest Service: write US Forest Service Information, Room 521, 630 Sansome St, San Francisco, CA 94111. (See the primer at the beginning of this book for details.) Trail conditions in any forest or wilderness area are subject to change, so before setting out on any days-long adventures, check with the appropriate ranger district for up-to-date information. Many backcountry trails may be impassable during winter.

Numerous day hikes on the northern and southern slopes of Mount Shasta can satisfy the urge to conquer the mountain. **Sand Flat Trail** (moderate; 3.5 miles round trip) bites off 1,000 feet of elevation, ending at Horse Camp, at 7,800 feet. Horse Camp is near the mountain's tree line, and it is from here that many adventurers choose to stage for a second-leg hike to the summit. Horse Camp can also be reached from the **Bunny Flat** trailhead. The Sand Flat and Bunny Flat Trails are east of I-5 on the Everitt Memorial Hwy, 10 and 14 miles out, respectively.

Panther Meadow Trail (easy; 3 miles round trip) has a more mild elevation gain, from 7,800 to the 8,119-foot Gray Butte overlook, which offers wide vistas of the entire Northern Mountains region. To find this trailhead, take Everitt Memorial Hwy past Sand and Bunny Flats, and continue all the way to the end to the staging area. A similar hike on the northern side of the mountain follows the **Bolam Creek Trail** (easy; 3.5 miles round trip), which tops out at 6,400 feet but provides similarly appointed vistas nonetheless. The trailhead is at the end of Forest Rd 43N21, 10 miles east of Weed off US 97. Contact the Mount Shasta Ranger District, (530) 926-4511, for more information about any of these Mount Shasta links.

Among the more fascinating geologic displays often overshadowed by

Shasta are **Castle Crags State Park**'s crags, which projected 6,000 feet through the serpentine over some 170 thousand years of volcanic activity. To jump right in for a grand tour, consider **Crags Trail** (difficult; 6 miles round trip), a grueling and sometimes steep trudge, gaining 2,500 feet in 3 miles, to the base of Castle Dome, the centerpiece at Crags. This is a great place for a geology lesson, or a picnic. Take a side trip to Indian Springs (another mile). Head straight for the spots above the forest line to get the best wide vista. Try to do any hike at Crags in the summer, as some areas can get icy in winter and spring months. Also, be careful at the trail's edge, as there are some nasty drops from the high rock edges. **Root Creek Trail** (moderate; 4 miles round trip) and a 10-mile stretch of the **Pacific Crest Trail,** running along the base of the crags, are other day hike options here. Castle Crags State Park is just west of I-5 at the state park exit, 5 miles south of Mount Shasta. Call the park, (530) 235-2684, for more information.

For a nice waterfall workout or a nature stroll in a secluded river canyon, the McCloud River area offers a welcome change of pace from the mountaintop scrambles that are the biggest draw in this area. **McCloud Nature Trail** (easy; 4.5 miles round trip) follows the river for 2 miles through a pretty forested canyon from the AtAh-Di-Na Campground (see Camping, below). To reach the trail, take I-5 north to Hwy 89 east and then to the town of McCloud. Turn right on Squaw Valley Rd (Forest Rd 11). Proceed to Lake McCloud and continue to the campground. For a waterfall hike, take the short walk to **Lower McCloud Falls,** a low but pretty waterfall that also makes a good swimming spot on hot summer days. To reach it, proceed east on Hwy 89 from McCloud, about 5 miles to the Fowler Campground entrance on the right (see below); park there and walk up the river about an eighth of a mile to the spot. Contact the McCloud Ranger District, (530) 964-2184, for more information.

The trip to the summit (see below) is certainly not the only overnighter in the Shasta region; with these expansive forestlands, there is no limit to how deep into the wilderness you can go. One favorite is the **Sisson Callahan Trail** (difficult; 16.5 miles round trip), a steep, grueling, switchback-strewn climb through Morgan Meadows to the 8,243-foot summit of Mount Eddy—a 5,000-foot elevation gain. Continue on to Deadfall Lakes, near where this trail intersects with the Pacific Crest Trail. The Sisson Callahan Trail staging area is half a mile up on Forest Rd 26, north from W. A. Barr Rd just past Lake Siskiyou. Take the Central Mount Shasta exit and head west on W. A. Barr Rd to the lake.

Castle Crags State Park is the best jump-on point in this area for the **Pacific Crest Trail.** Head east from here to the **McCloud River canyon** (moderate; 29 miles one way), topping Girard Ridge and then descending toward Squaw Valley Creek and the AtAh-Di-Na Camp on the riverbank (see Camping, below). Vistas of the entire Shasta-Cascade region are excellent from Girard, and the crags are an excellent added bonus. Hikers also may want to head west from Castle Crags through Castle Crags Wilderness, over the 6,785-foot Devil's Pocket peak, then into the Seven Lakes Basin. The section ends at Gumboot on Forest Rd 26. The Pacific Crest Trail Association, 1350 Castle Rock Rd, Walnut Creek, CA 94598, (925) 939-6111, has maps and information on access points and hiking routes for this and all sections of the trail.

Mount Shasta summit climb

Some outdoor adventurers can come to the southern end of the Cascade mountain range, take in the grand spectacle of the snowcapped, 14,162-foot Mount Shasta looming large on the skyline, say, "Isn't it pretty?" and leave it at that. Others can't let it go; they need to know what it would be like to be looking down from the top of the world.

But climbing the **Mount Shasta summit** (difficult; 12 miles round trip) should certainly not be done on a whim, by the inexperienced, or by the unprepared. What's it like at the top? First let's talk about what it's like getting there. This is not a hike; it's a climb—not a climb involving just rock and dirt and dust, mind you, but snow and ice and wind. For every thousand feet you ascend, the temperature drops 3 degrees, and once you pass what you think is the point of no return, the climate shifts. A sunny, warm day can turn to a cold, nasty blizzard in a matter of an hour, and this may send you scampering back down, defeated. In addition to your normal hiking gear, you will need (and must know how to use) an ice axe, special footgear for snow climbing (crampons), and a gutsy determination.

The hike begins in the mid-7,000 foot elevations and tops out beyond 14,000 feet. The easiest route is via **Avalanche Gulch** from the Bunny Flat, Old Ski Bowl, or Sand Flat trailheads. The climb takes about 10 hours (one way) if taken at a reasonable pace, and is best done in two days, especially since less experienced climbers will need to adjust to the altitude before they trudge all the way to infinity. **Horse Camp** or **Lake Helen** are two favorite base camp areas, at 8,000 and 10,500 feet, respectively, to hunker down for the night before completing the climb early the next day. The climb is breathtaking, both figuratively and literally. At these altitudes, there is a chance you will feel light-headed; with this strenuous a climb (gaining more than 7,000 feet), the wind will be taken out of you regardless; and once you reach the summit and look down upon a vista so high and wide that you think you can see the curvature of the Earth, whatever breath you have left is going to be history.

Three **guide services** are permitted to operate by the Forest Service:

Shasta Mountain Guides, led by Michael Zanger, in Mount Sh
926-3117; Alpine Skills International, run by Bela and Mimi Va
Norden, (530) 426-9108; and Sierra Wilderness Seminars of San Ra
led by Timothy Keating, (888)797-6867, www.swsmtns.com. Equipme
rentals, including the critical crampons, are found at The Fifth Season,
300 N Mount Shasta Blvd, Mount Shasta, (530) 926-3606, or at The
House of Ski on Ski Village Dr in Mount Shasta, (530) 926-2359.

Sand Flat and Bunny Flat each provide trail access to Avalanche
Gulch. To reach Sand Flat, take the Everitt Memorial Hwy 9.5 miles east
from Mount Shasta City, then head north on Lower Sand Flat Rd
(unpaved) a little less than a mile to the Upper Sand Flat Rd junction.
Continue on Upper Sand Flat Rd a half mile to the trailhead. Bunny Flat is
11 miles east of Mount Shasta City, on the Everitt Memorial Hwy. Continue to the end of the Everitt Memorial Hwy to reach the Ski Bowl trailhead, which at 7,900 feet is the highest access point to Avalanche Gulch
reachable by car.

For those visiting the Cascades region who perhaps need to warm up
to the idea of a mountaineering ordeal, one excellent lesser peak to consider instead of Shasta is the **Lassen Peak Trail** in Lassen Volcanic
National Park (see Hiking/Backpacking, Lassen Region chapter). It is not
quite the expedition that Shasta is, so the inexperienced may consider
tackling this climb first and doing Shasta on the next trip.

Camping

Dispersed camping in the Mount Shasta area can be more difficult than in
other wilderness areas because of snow much of the year at the high elevations and inclement weather year-round. If you aren't properly outfitted
and trained for snow camping, heading into the wilderness areas under
threat of storms is not wise. At higher elevations, particularly during hikes
to the summit, camping at designated trail camps is advised. For an
overview of the area, the best maps are available directly from the Forest
Service: Write US Forest Service Information, Room 521, 630 Sansome St,
San Francisco, CA 94111. (See the primer at the beginning of this book
for more precise details.) Periodic road closures are unavoidable. Check
with the relevant ranger station for updated **road conditions** before
deciding on a site located deep within the forest. Roads are not maintained for vehicles with low ground clearance. The Forest Service is currently reviewing its **reservations and fees** policies for this area, but
generally no reservations are taken for any of the campgrounds listed
below. Stays are limited to 14 days. Call the Forest Service reservations
system at (800) 280-2267, or individual ranger stations for campsite

ɔn and reservations where applicable.

s has 10 tent sites (no RV access) on the foothills of ɪmpground is quiet due to its size, but its proximity to es it a popular spot. Naturally, hikers love this camp. ; piped water and vault toilets. Each site is equipped ring, and there's a general store to the south in the village of Mount Shasta. *From Dunsmuir, take I-5 north to Mount Shasta. Exit east onto East Lake Rd. Proceed to Everitt Memorial Hwy and turn left. Continue to the campground's entrance on the left, about 5 miles out of town. For more information, call Mount Shasta Ranger District, (530) 926-4511.*

Panther Meadow Campground has 10 tent sites (no RV access) on the south side of Mount Shasta. Like McBride Springs, this campground is quiet due to its small size, but is also popular among hikers because of its proximity to Mount Shasta and staging areas for the summit climb. The campground has piped water and vault toilets. Each site is equipped with a table and fire ring, and there's a general store to the west in the village of Mount Shasta. *From Dunsmuir, take I-5 north to Mount Shasta. Exit east onto East Lake Rd. Proceed to Everitt Memorial Hwy and turn left. The road turns into County Rd A10. Continue past Band Flat Rd to the Bunny Flat parking area. Walk a short distance to the campground ahead. Call Mount Shasta Ranger District, (530) 926-4511.*

Toad Lake Campground has 10 tent sites (no RV access) right along Toad Lake, a beautiful alpine region. This campground is sought by those who want solitude and a beautiful setting. Tucked far away from the road, the campground is accessible only on foot (an easy 10-minute walk). There is no running water, so be sure to bring plenty of your own. Vault toilets are available, and each site is equipped with a fire ring and table. *From Mount Shasta, take I-5 south and exit at West Lake Rd. Travel west and turn left on S Old Stage Rd. Proceed to W. A. Barr Rd and veer right. The road becomes Forest Rd 26 and then Forest Rd 40N26. Proceed to where the road crosses the South Fork Sacramento River; shortly thereafter, turn right onto an unnamed dirt forest road, then left. Proceed along the very winding road about 12 miles to the camp. Call Mount Shasta Ranger District, (530) 926-4511.*

Lake Siskiyou Campground has about 400 sites (some hookups; various RV lengths accommodated) adjacent to Lake Siskiyou. This enormous campground is popular for its location and amenities, and it can get quite crowded during the summer. Piped water, flush toilets, and showers are available; each site has a table and fire grill. A general store and marina are within walking distance. *From Mount Shasta, take I-5 south and exit at West Lake Rd. Travel west and turn left on S Old Stage Rd. Proceed to W. A. Barr Rd and veer right. Continue 2.5 miles past the dam to the campground entrance on the right. Contact the campground directly, (530) 926-2618.*

Fowler Campground contains 42 sites (no hookups; RV limit 29 feet) adjacent to one of the nicer stretches of McCloud River. Popular for its central location, the campground has piped water and vault toilets. Each site is equipped with a table and fire ring, and a general store is nearby in McCloud. *From McCloud, proceed east on Hwy 89, and go about 5 miles to the campground entrance on the right. For more information, call McCloud Ranger District, (530) 964-2184.*

Castle Crags Campground consists of 67 sites (no hookups; RV limit 29 feet). Located near the Sacramento River, this is one of the area's more popular campgrounds due to its central location and amenities. Piped water, flush toilets, and showers are available. Each site is equipped with a table and fire ring, and a general store is nearby in Castella. Call the state parks reservation system, (800) 444-7275, for reservations information. *From Castella, take I-5 north to the Castle Crags State Park exit. Travel west to the park entrance and campground. For more information, call the park directly, (530) 235-2684.*

Hawkins Landing contains 11 sites (no hookups; RV limit 31 feet) at Iron Canyon Reservoir, a Pacific Gas and Electric Company facility northeast of Lake Shasta. Popular among visitors looking for some good trout fishing, the campground has piped water and vault toilets. Each site is equipped with a fire ring and table. A general store is several miles to the east in Big Bend. *From Redding, proceed east on Hwy 299 to Hillcrest. Turn north on Big Bend Rd. Proceed past Big Bend Rancheria and continue to the campground at the reservoir. Call PG&E, (916) 923-7142.*

Deadlun Campground has 30 sites (no hookups; RV limit 21 feet) near Iron Canyon Reservoir. A PG&E facility northeast of Lake Shasta, the campground serves as an overflow area for the more popular Hawkins Landing Campground at the reservoir's edge. There is no running water at the campground, so be sure to bring plenty of your own. Vault toilets are available, and each site is equipped with a fire ring and table. A general store is several miles to the east in Big Bend. *From Redding, proceed east on Hwy 299 to Hillcrest. Turn north on Big Bend Rd. Proceed past Big Bend Rancheria and continue to the campground at the reservoir. Call PG&E, (916) 923-7142.*

Sims Flat Campground contains 18 sites (no hookups; RV limit 18 feet) north of Lake Shasta, adjacent to the Sacramento River. This campground is popular among visitors looking for good fishing. The campground has piped water and flush toilets. Each site is equipped with a fire ring and table. *Take the Sims Rd exit from I-5, and follow the road southeast for a mile to the campground entrance. Call Shasta Ranger District, (530) 926-4511.*

AtAh-Di-Na Campground contains 18 sites (no hookups; RV limit

31 feet) northeast of Lake Shasta, adjacent to the McCloud River and at the base of Grizzly Peak. This campground is a naturally well-situated base from which visitors can fish or hike. The campground has piped water and flush toilets. Each site is equipped with a fire ring and table. *From Lakehead take I-5 north to Hwy 89 east. Proceed to McCloud and turn right on Squaw Valley Rd/Forest Rd 11. Proceed to Lake McCloud and continue to the campground. Call McCloud Ranger District, (530) 964-2184.*

Cattle Campground has 22 sites (no hookups; RV limit 29 feet). This campground is on the quiet side and is sought by those who want solitude in the forest. It also serves as an overflow area for Fowler Campground to the west (see above). The campground has piped water and vault toilets. Each site is equipped with a table and fire ring, and a general store is to the west in McCloud. *From McCloud, proceed east on Hwy 89 and go about 11 miles to the campground entrance on the right. Call McCloud Ranger District, (530) 964-2184.*

Harris Springs Campground contains 17 sites (no hookups; RV limit 35 feet). This campground is also on the quiet side and a good bet for solitude in a nice forest setting. The campground has piped water and vault toilets. Each site is equipped with a table and fire ring, and a general store is to the west in McCloud. *From McCloud, take Hwy 89 east to Bartle. Turn left on Old Camp Two Rd. Turn left onto Forest Rd 15/Harris Springs Rd. Proceed about 12 miles and turn right toward the Harris Springs Ranger Station. Proceed to the campground on the right. For more information, call (530) 964-2184.*

Rock Climbing

Castle Crags State Park has numerous climbing routes, some short enough for those just learning and others catapulting more than 1,000 feet up the odd granite formations, which rose skyward from being pushed through bedrock by thousands of years of volcanic activity. Shasta Mountain Guides, (530) 926-3117, leads **guided climbs** along six of the most popular routes at Crags, including the 1,000-foot Cosmic Wall. Novices should not attempt any such climb alone, lest they become stranded on the rocks or worse. See Hiking/Backpacking, above, for directions to the park.

Photography

While Mount Shasta is a stunning, often-photographed northern landmark—its snowcapped peak and surrounding storm clouds are always a winner—it is best photographed from afar. Once you're on the mountain, you lose the view. One of the best vantage points is from Castle Crags State Park, which provides not only stunning vistas of Shasta but also some interesting shots of the bizarre granite spires of the crags themselves, some of which tower more than 1,000 feet. These make for some interesting moonscape scenery, perfect for that collection of "how I spent my summer" photographs we love to fill our family albums with.

Mountain Biking

Mountain bikes are not allowed on trails within the Mount Shasta Wilderness Area, but that doesn't mean you can't enjoy the mountain by bicycle. As we say, the mountain is best viewed from afar—once you're actually on it you can't see it in all its splendor anymore—and you'd never make it to the summit on a bike anyway. Consider instead the moderately difficult 50-mile ride along **Circle of Mount Shasta**—a two-day bicycle camping trek around the southern, eastern, and northern exposures of the mountain on Forest Service roads that includes stunning vistas from all vantage points and interesting diverse landscapes, including lava flows and forested canyons. The staging area is at the intersection of Hwy 88 and Forest Rd 31, east of I-5 at Mount Shasta City. From Forest Rd 31, ride Forest Rd 19 to an immediate junction with Forest Rd N2N02. From here it's 6.5 miles to Forest Rd 42N34, which extends north to the Forest Rd 42N33 turnoff back west toward Weed. Call the McCloud Ranger District, (530) 964-2184, to check on road conditions and obtain proper maps before attempting this ride. When roads are unimpeded, this is a moderate trek suitable for novice riders in good shape, although there is a gradual 1,000-foot-elevation climb over 14 miles during the first half of the ride (the entire second half of the ride is downhill). Other good riding areas are on forest roads south and southwest of Castle Crags State Park. Shasta Cycling Adventures, (530) 938-3002, leads **guided bike tours** of the mountain area out of Weed, complete with support vans, and also **rents bicycles.**

Fishing

Lake Shasta, with its sprawling arms and nearly 400 miles of shoreline, is the biggest draw for anglers (see Lake Shasta chapter), but there are good fishing spots on rivers and creeks north of the lake as well. Fly-fishing for **rainbow** and **brown trout** on the McCloud River south of McCloud and the Upper Sacramento River directly north of the lake is good despite the obvious effect the dam has had on native fisheries. The McCloud River is best accessed along Hwy 89, at AtAh-Di-Na (see Camping, above), and the Upper Sacramento at Sims Flat off I-5 at Sims Rd. **Outfitters** include Jack Trout Flyfishing and Guide Service, (530) 926-4540, which leads regular outings on both rivers and along the Feather River (see Plumas Region chapter). Hart's Guide Service, (530) 926-2431, leads outings on the McCloud, Upper Sacramento, and Pitt Rivers. McCloud Fly-Fishing School, (530) 964-2878, is a good place to learn the best techniques for the Shasta region waterways. The state Department of Fish and Game office in Redding, (530) 225-2300, has an update or you can try to decipher a free **regulations** handbook available at most licensing locations, including bait shops.

Hot Air Ballooning

Want to get a look at Mount Shasta from a new perspective? From spring to late summer, ballooning tours of the mountain region are available out of Mount Shasta City. Shasta City Balloons, (530) 926-3612, offers half-day package deals and short flights over the valley. Jane English, a local photographer and author, also leads aerial tours, (530) 926-2751.

Adventure Calendar

Fourth of July 5-mile run, July 4: *Mount Shasta City, (530) 926-6212.*

outside in

Attractions

Magnificent, snowcapped **Mount Shasta** soars 14,162 feet into the sky and it is the largest volcano (by mass) in the contiguous 48 states and the fifth-highest peak in the state. Shasta is a dormant volcano; it's not dead, just sleeping until it decides to blow its snowy stack—something it hasn't done since the late 1700s. Although an eruption may seem long overdue, fear not; geologists constantly monitor movement within the volcano and claim they will be able to predict an eruption early enough for you to pack your bags and skedaddle.

"Lonely as God and white as a winter moon" is how author Joaquin Miller described this solitary peak in the 1870s. The mountain dominates the horizon from every angle, and on clear days it's visible from as far away as 150 miles. Some Native Americans who lived in its shadow believed Mount Shasta was the home of the Great Spirit and vowed never to climb its sacred slopes, which they viewed as an act of disrespect. Today, men and women from around the world pay tribute to the volcano by making the spectacular trek to the top. See various Inside Out sections, above, for climbing and other fun on the mountain.

While **Mount Shasta City** (population 3,700) caters to the thousands of thrill-seekers and naturalists who make the long journey here every year, it also has its share of New Agers and metaphysical folks (the Creative Harmonics Institute, Ascended Master Teaching Foundation, Shasta Buddhist Abbey, and Temple of Cosmic Religion are all here). In fact, for years, Mount Shasta has been hailed by spiritualists as one of the seven "power centers" of the world. Although city council members are loath to admit it (and you certainly won't see the words "channeling" or "crystal" in any chamber of commerce brochure), a large percentage of visitors are spiritual pilgrims who have come from around the world to bask in the majestic mountain's mysterious energy. If you're interested in learning about the mountain's alleged mystical powers, visit the delight-fully funky **Golden Bough Bookstore,** where the staff can give you the spiritual lowdown and direct you to tapes, books, and all matter of info on the topic; 219 N Mount Shasta Blvd at Lake St, (530) 926-3228.

If you've had enough spiritual enlightenment and are no longer excited about hanging by your nails from cliffs for fun, the town of Mount Shasta offers two good (and safe) attractions that won't even make a dent in your billfold: the free **Sisson Museum** showcases changing exhibits on local history, nature, geology, and Native American life, and its adjacent **Mount Shasta Fish Hatchery,** the oldest hatchery in the West, keeps thousands of rainbow and brown trout, including a few biggies, in the holding ponds. For only a quarter you can get some fish food and incite a fish-feeding frenzy; take Lake St across the freeway, turn left on Hatchery Rd, and head to 3 N Old Stage Rd, (530) 926-2215 (hatchery), (530) 926-5508 (museum). For more information on Shasta's attractions, contact the Mount Shasta Visitors Bureau, 300 Pine St at Lake St, (530) 926-4865.

A company-built milltown, **McCloud** bills itself as "the quiet side of Mount Shasta." And true to its motto, this is a relatively sleepy place, but its many sumptuous B&Bs attract a lot of anglers, hikers, and other nature lovers, as well as bleary-eyed city folk who long for little more than a warm bed and some solitude. Whatever your attraction to this neck of the woods, you can introduce yourself to the area in style by hopping aboard the **Shasta Sunset Dinner Train,** which follows a historic turn-of-the-century logging route. The steep grades, sharp curves, and a unique switchback at Signal Butte are still part of the route, though passengers now ride in cars handsomely restored in wood and brass. As you nosh on a very good dinner in your railcar, you'll be treated to views of Mount Shasta, Castle Crags, and the Trinity Alps. The 40-mile, three-hour jour-ney is run by the McCloud Railway Company from April to December, and costs about $70 for adults and $45 for children under 12, which includes dinner. Special-event train trips are scheduled throughout the year; call (530) 964-2142 or (800) 733-2141 for more details.

In the summer, you can watch—or, better yet, join—the McCloud locals as they kick up their heels every weekend from May to September in the town's two air-conditioned **dance halls.** Dancing—especially square dancing—is a favorite pastime here, so if you want to promenade your partner or swing to the beat (not to the heat), call (530) 964-2578 for the latest schedule.

When a Southern Pacific train ran off the tracks in 1991 and spilled an herbicide in the Sacramento River, it killed all aquatic life for 45 miles along the river. And it darn near killed **Dunsmuir.** But this pretty, historic railroad town has a population of 2,300 resilient residents who are bringing the place back with a vengeance. Using a financial settlement from Southern Pacific, the townsfolk have gussied up their community and hope to make Dunsmuir a major California tourist destination. They may just succeed. In addition to the beautiful natural surroundings, stylish gift shops and restaurants have sprung up on the city's streets (particularly on Dunsmuir and Sacramento Aves). Furthermore, trophy-size wild trout now abound in the Sacramento River, and the community slogan is "The Upper Sac is back." Fortunately, not all of the tourists are coming to Dunsmuir by car, thanks to the Amtrak train that stops here daily. Call the Dunsmuir Chamber of Commerce and Visitors Center, (800) DUNSMUIR, for the nitty-gritty.

Restaurants

Acacia Restaurant, Bar and Grill ☆   When the dinner bell rings, Acacia's faithful clientele comes running for entrees like juicy barbecue pork ribs and vegetarian curry pie. All-American standards are served for breakfast and lunch. *1136 S Mount Shasta Blvd (from I-5, take the Central Mount Shasta exit), Mount Shasta; (530) 926-0250; $.*

Cafe Maddalena   ☆☆☆☆   Dining at this small, intimate restaurant is similar to eating at a four-star restaurant in some little European village. Expect superb Italian cuisine with subtle differences in flavors and ingredients than what you'd find on the Italian mainland. *5801 Sacramento Ave (1 block W of Dunsmuir Ave), Dunsmuir; (530) 235-2725; $$.*

Lily's ☆☆   This popular place offers very good California cuisine with an ethnic flair. Lunch and dinner offerings are equally varied and imaginative, and if you're looking for something a little different from the usual breakfast fare, try Lily's cheesy polenta fritters. *1013 S Mount Shasta Blvd (from I-5, take the Central Mount Shasta exit), Mount Shasta; (530) 926-3372; $.*

Michael's Restaurant ☆   This estimable little restaurant has been around since 1980, which makes it an old-timer on the Mount Shasta restaurant scene. The Italian dinners will satisfy those with lumberjack-size appetites. *313 Mount Shasta Blvd (from I-5, take the Central Mount Shasta exit), Mount Shasta; (530) 926-5288; $.*

The Old Rostel Pub and Cafe ☆☆   This lively pub and cafe across the street from the Dunsmuir train station is popular with locals, anglers, and history buffs. Expect a mix of very good traditional German and not-so-traditional vegetarian dishes. *5743 Sacramento Ave (1 block W of Dunsmuir Ave), Dunsmuir; (530) 235-2028; $.*

Serge's Restaurant ☆☆☆   This classical French restaurant framed with lace curtains is Mount Shasta's best—and it's even more memorable because of the view of the grand volcano from the deck. The menu changes seasonally. *531 Chestnut St (1 block E of Mount Shasta Blvd), Mount Shasta; (530) 926-1276; $$.*

Lodgings

McCloud Bed and Breakfast Hotel ☆☆☆☆   Built in 1916, the McCloud Bed and Breakfast Hotel has earned a highly coveted spot on the National Register of Historic Landmarks. Its meticulous restoration was completed in 1995, and now the hotel offers 14 beautiful guest rooms. *408 Main St (from exit off Hwy 89, follow signs to the historical district), McCloud; (530) 964-2822 or (800) 964-2823; $$–$$$.*

McCloud Guest House ☆☆   Built in 1907, this stately two-story mansion features a game room furnished with the house's original light fixtures and a magnificent antique carved billiards table. The inn's spacious 5 guest rooms have four-poster beds and antique furnishings. *606 W Colombero Dr (at the W end of town), McCloud; (530) 964-3160; $$.*

Mount Shasta Ranch Bed and Breakfast ☆☆☆   This 70-year-old bed-and-breakfast inn with gabled windows and hip roofs offers large rooms, large baths, large views, and even large breakfasts. In addition to 5 guest rooms in the main building, there are 5 rooms in a converted carriage house and a two-bedroom cottage. *1008 W. A. Barr Rd (S of the fish hatchery), Mount Shasta; (530) 926-3870; $$.*

Mount Shasta Resort ☆☆☆   The 50 Craftsman-style chalets at this incredibly scenic resort have all the creature comforts, and they're located on the forested shore of Lake Siskiyou, where you can swim, fish, sailboard, kayak, canoe, or rent paddleboats. *1000 Siskiyou Lake Blvd (from I-5, take the Central Mount Shasta exit, go W on Old Stage Rd, veer onto W. A. Barr Rd, and turn left on Siskiyou Lake Blvd), Mount Shasta; (530) 926-3030 or (800) 958-3363 (reservations only); $$–$$$.*

Railroad Park Resort/The Caboose Motel   A must for railroad buffs but a maybe for everyone else, the Railroad Park Resort's funky Caboose Motel offers quiet, comfortable lodgings in a boxcar and 23 refurbished cabooses from the Southern Pacific, Santa Fe, and Great Northern Railroads. *100 Railroad Park Rd (1 mile S of town), Dunsmuir; (530) 235-4440; $.*

Stewart Mineral Springs ☆   Hidden in a forested canyon at the end of a twisting country road, Stewart Mineral Springs is a great place to commune with nature. You can choose between 2 tepees, 5 cabins with kitchens, a five-bedroom A-frame (perfect for large groups of up to 10 people), and 10 modest motel rooms. Camping and RV sites are available, too. *4617 Stewart Springs Rd (call for directions), Weed; (530) 938-2222; $.*

Strawberry Valley Inn ☆☆   This terrific 14-room inn, surrounded by a lush garden and towering oaks, incorporates the privacy of a motel and the personal touches of a B&B. Guest rooms are individually decorated. *1142 S Mount Shasta Blvd (from I-5, take the Central Mount Shasta exit), Mount Shasta; (530) 926-2052; $.*

More Information

Castle Crags State Park: *(530) 235-2684.*
Department of Fish and Game office, Redding: *(530) 225-2300.*
Forest Service reservations system: *(800) 280-2267.*
McCloud Ranger District: *(530) 964-2184.*
Mount Shasta Ranger District: *(530) 964-2184.*
State parks camping reservations: *(800) 444-7275.*

Lake Shasta

The waters of the 30,000-acre Lake Shasta, its 400 miles of shoreline, and the immediate surrounding area.

Before the waters of Lake Shasta help turn the deserts of the Central Valley into rice fields and the bone-dry scrub of Los Angeles into suburbs carpeted by green lawns, people get to swim in it, boat on it, and fish from it here. One of the crowning achievements of the US Army Corps of Engineers' building frenzy of the 1930s and '40s, Shasta is the largest man-made lake in the state, with nearly 400 miles of jagged shoreline following its odd-shaped arms. It is curious to consider how man-made features that alter the natural landscape complement Mother Nature's handiwork, but Shasta Dam, with the highest-placed spillway in the country, can be almost as much of a spectacle as Mount Shasta's snowcapped peaks. When record storms dumped an abnormally high snowpack in the high country in 1988, Lake Shasta filled with debris washed in from the surrounding river canyons. Dam operators opened the floodgates full bore, and people came from miles around to watch the ensuing torrent drop 600 feet into the Sacramento River below, roaring louder than any waterfall they'd ever seen.

Lake Shasta's shorelines are packed with more than 20 campgrounds and resorts, public boat launches, and marinas. Whether you prefer to spend lazy weeks on the deck of a houseboat, quiet days fishing in one of the lake's shady, coved arms, or wild, hot summer afternoons waterskiing, Lake Shasta draws all types and leaves no water-recreation enthusiast disappointed. On nice summer weekends, roads around the lake naturally become crowded, as do the public boat ramps—but there is so much room to spread out that you hardly notice it once you find your special place. The areas around the lake can be as inviting as the lake itself. The shore is made up of a varied terrain with flooded limestone canyons, rocky beaches, and caverns of odd-shaped stone and crystal awaiting the visitor who arrives without a boat.

But whether you're boatless or ready to push off, the views from the dam—the snowy peaks of Mount Shasta, reflected in a lake that shouldn't be there—will make you forget that the lake is only here because of human tinkering.

Getting There

Quite simply, Lake Shasta is easily accessible on both the east and west sides of Interstate 5, north of Redding. Travelers heading north from the Sacramento Valley can't miss it—it's the first nice scenery along the long, boring stretch of Interstate 5 extending north from the state capital, so it's bound to get your attention. Once the landscape turns from dismal and repetitive to interesting, you will know you have arrived. Those planning a visit to the Shasta area should contact Lake Shasta Information Center, (530) 257-1589, or the Redding Convention and Visitors Bureau, (800) 874-2782, for trip-planning assistance. Also stop in at the Lake Shasta Ranger District, 14250 Holiday Drive, Redding, (530) 275-1587.

Adjoining Areas

NORTH: **Mount Shasta**

SOUTH: **Sacramento Valley**

WEST: **Trinity Region**

inside out

Boating/Water Sports

Why bob around in a junky aluminum fishing boat when you can fish from a luxurious floating condominium? Bring all the conveniences and comforts of a resort suite right out onto the lake with you during a week-long **houseboat** vacation on Lake Shasta. Big, comfy houseboats are in vogue at Shasta, which has evolved into a favorite relaxation getaway for all those people who used to just check into Club Med for a week when they were feeling stressed. What could be better therapy than a lazy week on the lake, complete with a rod, reel, bathing suit, and satellite feed? And there is no need, necessarily, to go all out. Some choose to rent simple floating platforms on which to unfurl a sleeping bag and camp under the stars while adrift—not at all fancy. The lake is even equipped with floating outhouses, so there's no need to go ashore even to take care of business! Because the lake has five separate arms folding out over more than 400 miles of diverse shoreline (on both sides of I-5), it is really like several lakes in one.

The northeastern arm on the McCloud River is the most popular with skiers, while houseboaters tend to congregate at Bailey and Allie Coves near the center of the lake complex. Ski Island offshore from Marsher's Point on the lake's southeastern shore is a heavy draw for water-sports enthusiasts. The lake also has its quiet, lazy hidden spots, however—and its size proves to be its greatest asset when it comes time to get away from the crowds. Shoemaker Gulch in the lake's northwestern end (west of the interstate and north of the dam), along with many gulches in the Squaw Creek arm of the lake on the east end, tend to be quieter than other areas. Numerous resorts have the big **boats for rent,** including Antler Marina Resort at Lakehead, (800) 238-3924; Lakeshore Resort & Marina, 20479 Lakeshore Dr, Lakehead, (530) 238-2301; and Shasta Marina Resort, O'Brien Inlet Rd, (530) 238-2284. Call the Lake Shasta Information Center, (530) 257-1589, for houseboat rental advice and other information.

With so much room to move around, Shasta is one of the state's premier **waterskiing** lakes. John Steiner's Ski Center in Redding, (530) 275-6744, located at the Holiday Harbor Resort, has equipment **rentals** for skiing and wake boarding, as well as water-ski lessons. Numerous resorts also have the ski boats and **Jet-skis** for rent, including Antler Marina Resort at Lakehead, (800) 238-3924; Lakeshore Resort & Marina at Lakehead, (530) 238-2301; and Shasta Marina Resort, O'Brien Inlet Rd, (530) 238-2284. Call the Lake Shasta Information Center, (530) 257-1589, for a rundown on water-sports equipment options.

Most private resorts have **launching facilities** and rentals, but a large contingent of lake users who just want to get their own boats on the water without dealing with a resort scene would do best finding a public boat ramp. Generally, all public ramps become congested on hot summer weekends—the key is to use those away from Shasta Dam, the easiest to reach and most visible. To reach the boat ramp at the dam, exit I-5 at Shasta Dam Blvd in the town of Central Valley and head west on Shasta Dam Blvd to the ramp on the east side of the dam near Vista House. On the Pit Arm, there are two ramps—one at Squaw Creek and the other near the Packer Bay Marina. Exit I-5 at Packers Bay Rd and drive to Lakehead, 2 miles west.

Two other ramps are on the McCloud Arm, one at the end of Shasta Caverns Rd, Bailey Cove, 1 mile to the east off I-5, and the other at Hirz Bay, 10 miles east of the interstate at Gilman Rd. On the Sacramento Arm, exit the interstate at Antlers Rd and head west half a mile to Antlers Campground (see Camping, below).

Fishing

Lake Shasta, like many of Northern California's lakes, is shaped irregularly, with long arms and bays reaching outward and creating nearly 400 miles of shore. It's also California's largest man-made lake, with a surface area of more than 30,000 acres. This makes for some diverse fishing, as water depths and temperatures vary as widely as the shoreline terrain. Largemouth and smallmouth bass, bronzebacks, trout, salmon, catfish, sturgeon, crappie, and bluegill are among the main fare here, but don't try to find them all in the same lazy cove. McCloud Arm, for example, is known as the **brown trout** arm. The Pit River Arm, in the southeast part of the lake, is a year-round favorite haunt for **bass.** For **rainbows,** try the Sacramento Arm. And so on. Keep on moving and it will seem as if you've been to 20 different lakes in one fishing trip. The balmy spring and summer seasons naturally attract a large fishing crowd, while the winter attracts mostly local regulars and serious anglers. The lake is easily accessible from any one of its many boat ramps (see Boating/Water Sports, above).

Anglers also head for creeks and rivers downstream of the lakes, along Hat Creek, the McCloud River, Fall River, and the Sacramento, for **rainbows** and **king salmon.** On the Sacramento, the trout and salmon action is naturally best downstream of Shasta Dam; and with the recent high-water years, runs have been impressive of late. Several creeks along this stretch of the Sacramento are undergoing environmental restoration work, which in the long run should help reestablish fish runs on a more permanent basis. The McCloud River's confluence with Lizard Creek, accessible easily on Forest Rd 11 (Squaw Valley Rd) south from Hwy 89 in McCloud, is a prime spot. Shasta Tackle and Sportfishing, a supplier and **guide service,** (530) 275-2278, offers regularly scheduled outings. As always, check with the appropriate regulatory agencies if you are not up-to-date on current fishing laws, as they are constantly changing in this age of rampant endangered and threatened species listings. The state Department of Fish and Game office in Redding, (530) 225-2300, has an update or you can try to decipher a free regulations handbook, available at most licensing locations, including bait shops.

Caving

One of the most bizarre and fascinating geologic oddities of the Northern Mountains is found at the **Lake Shasta Caverns** site, a series of deep-set caves on the McCloud Arm containing numerous odd-shaped stone and crystal-studded stalagmites and stalactites that will remind you of melting wax. The marble and limestone caverns, which conceal underground waterfalls, were discovered in 1878 by explorer-miner James A. Richardson but were thought to be visited often by the ancient peoples of the Shasta region long before there was any European settlement (or lake, for that matter) in the north state. Getting there is an adventure in itself; after you pull off the highway and check in at cavern headquarters, you'll have to hop aboard a ferry for a 15-minute trip across Lake Shasta, then climb onto a bus for a white-knuckle ride up to the caverns (open daily year-round); from I-5, take the Shasta Caverns Rd exit (about 30 miles north of Redding) and follow the signs. Guided tours are given daily from 9am to 4pm during the summer; call (530) 238-2341 or (800) 795-CAVE.

Camping

As one would expect, there are dozens of resorts and public campgrounds dotting the nearly 400 miles of shoreline at Lake Shasta, virtually all geared to water sports and fishing. Few people realize, however, that **dispersed camping** is also allowed around the lake, with restrictions—generally, you can set up camp anywhere that is not posted as private property or with a "no camping" sign. In addition to the recommendations listed here, call Lake Shasta Information Center, (530) 257-1589, for a rundown on private resorts. All campsites run by the Forest Service are open on a first-come, first-served basis. Private resorts and privately run campgrounds on Forest Service lands must be contacted directly. The Lake Shasta Ranger District, 14250 Holiday Dr, Redding, CA 96003, (530) 275-1587, is the primary resource point for camping information.

Holiday Harbor has 26 RV sites (some hookups; RV limit 40 feet) along the northern shore of Lake Shasta. Though the campground allows tents, it is primarily for RVs, and those with tents may find it a bit noisy. Piped water, flush toilets, and showers are available, and each site has a table and fire grill. A general store and marina are within walking distance. *From Lakehead, take I-5 south and exit at Shasta Caverns Rd. Travel east 1 mile to the campground entrance. Contact the campground directly at (530) 238-2383.*

Hirz Bay Campground has 50 sites (no hookups; RV limit 31 feet) along the northern rim of Lake Shasta near the McCloud River, a popular fishing area. Piped water and flush toilets are available, and each site has a table and fire grill. A general store and marina are nearby. *From Lakehead, take I-5 south and exit east on Gilman Rd. After 10 miles, turn right on Hirz Bay Rd and proceed another mile to the campground. Call Lake Shasta Ranger District, (530) 275-1587.*

Nelson Point Campground contains 10 sites (no hookups; RV limit 18 feet) along the northern rim of Lake Shasta near the Sacramento River. This quaint spot is sought out by those looking for a primitive camping experience. There is no piped water so be sure to bring plenty of your own. Vault toilets are provided, and each site has a fire ring and table. A general store and marina are close by. *To reach the campground, head east on Salt Creek Rd from I-5. Make an immediate left turn and continue 1 mile north to the exit. Call Lake Shasta Ranger District, (530) 275-1587.*

Salt Creek Campground has 60 sites (some hookups; RV limit 40 feet) near the northern shore of Lake Shasta. This is one of the largest campgrounds near the lake and given its amenities, it is often filled to capacity. Piped water, flush toilets, and showers are available, and each site has a fire ring and table. A general store, heated pool, and volleyball court are also on the premises. *Take Salt Creek Rd east from I-5, make an immediate left, and continue half a mile to the entrance. Call the camp directly at (530) 238-8500.*

Gregory Creek Campground contains 19 sites (no hookups; RV limit 23 feet) along the Sacramento River, near Lake Shasta. As with most riverfront campgrounds in Northern California, the area is nicest in the spring and early summer when the river is flowing strong. Piped water and vault toilets are available, and each site has a table and fire grill. There is a general store nearby in Lakehead. *From Lakehead, take I-5 south and exit at the Gregory Creek Rd/Salt Creek Rd exit. Proceed 4.5 miles north on Gregory Creek Rd, turn off under the I-5 overpass and proceed to the campground entrance. Call the park directly, (530) 238-2824.*

Moore Creek Campground has 13 sites (no hookups; RV limit 21 feet) adjacent to the McCloud River, near Lake Shasta. The river is flowing at its strongest during the spring and early summer months. The campground tends to be on the quiet side. Piped water and vault toilets are available, and each site has a table and fire grill. There's a general store to the southwest in O'Brien. *From Lakehead, take I-5 south and exit east on Gilman Rd. Continue 10 miles to the campground, just past Hirz Bay Rd. Call Lake Shasta Ranger District, (530) 275-1587.*

Antlers Campground has 60 sites (no hookups; RV limit 31 feet) along the Sacramento River, near Lake Shasta. This is one of the area's larger campgrounds, and with the amenities offered, it is frequently filled to capacity. Piped water and flush toilets are available, and each site is equipped with a table and fire ring. A general store and marina are nearby to the south. *From Lakehead, take I-5 south to the Lakeshore Rd/Antlers Rd exit. Exit east onto Antlers Rd. Proceed south and turn left at the railroad crossing. Continue to the campground's entrance 1 mile up the road. Contact the campground directly, (530) 275-1512.*

Ellery Creek Campground contains 20 sites (no hookups; RV limit 31 feet) along Ellery Creek and the McCloud River, near Lake Shasta. The campground is most popular during the spring and early summer when the river flow is at its strongest. The campground tends to be on the quiet side. Piped water and vault toilets are available, and each site has a table and fire grill. There's a general store to the southwest in O'Brien. *From Lakehead, take I-5 south, exit east on Gilman Rd, and go 15 miles to the campground, beyond the intersection with Hirz Bay Rd. Call Lake Shasta Ranger District, (530) 275-1587.*

McCloud Bridge Campground contains 20 sites (no hookups; RV limit 31 feet) along the McCloud River, near Lake Shasta, and is popular for its river access and fishing. Piped water and vault toilets are available, and each site has a table and fire grill. A general store is to the southwest in O'Brien. *Exit I-5 east on Gilman Rd and continue 20 miles to the campground exit, beyond the intersection with Hirz Bay Rd. Call Lake Shasta Ranger District, (530) 275-1587.*

Pine Point Campground has 16 sites (no hookups; RV limit 23 feet) above the McCloud River, near Lake Shasta. Set amid a grove of pines, the campground offers beautiful vistas. Piped water and vault toilets are available, and each site has a table and fire grill. There's a general store to the southwest in O'Brien. *Take Gilman Rd east from I-5, and continue 16.5 miles to the campground entrance, beyond the intersection with Hirz Bay Rd. Call Lake Shasta Ranger District, (530) 275-1587.*

Lakeshore Campground has 30 RV sites (no hookups; various RV lengths accommodated) and 8 cabins. Located along the Sacramento River near Lake Shasta, this is one of the area's more popular campgrounds, particularly with boaters. Piped water, flush toilets, and showers are available. Each site is equipped with a table and fire ring, and a general store and marina are nearby. *Take the Lakeshore Rd/Antlers Rd exit west from I-5. Turn left and cross under the interstate. Follow Lakeshore Rd (south) a mile to the campground entrance. Contact the campground directly, (530) 238-2004.*

Lakeshore East Campground contains 38 RV sites (no hookups; RV limit 37 feet). Located along the Sacramento River near Lake Shasta, this campground serves as an overflow area for the more popular Lakeshore Campground (see above). Piped water and flush toilets are available. Each site is equipped with a table and fire ring, and a general store and marina are nearby. *Exit I-5 at Antlers Rd, and head west through the underpass to Lakeshore Dr. Head south (left) 3 miles to the campground entrance. Call Lake Shasta Ranger District, (530) 275-1587.*

Madrone Campground has 13 sites (no hookups; RV limit 18 feet) east of Lake Shasta along Squaw Creek. The campground is very quiet and attracts visitors looking for a primitive camping experience. There is no running water at the campground, so be sure to bring plenty of your own. Vault toilets are available, and each site is equipped with a fire ring and table. A general store is several miles to the east in Wengler. *From Redding, proceed east on Hwy 299 past Round Mountain. Turn left onto Fenders Ferry Rd. Continue about 20 miles to the campground. Call Lake Shasta Ranger District, (530) 275-1587.*

Clear Creek Campground contains 9 sites (no hookups; RV limit 21 feet) adjacent to Clear Creek, northwest of Lake Shasta. This campground is popular with those looking for solitude and a primitive camping experience. There is no running water, so be sure to bring plenty of your own. Vault toilets are available and each site is equipped with a fire ring and table. A general store is several miles to the east in LaMoine. *From Redding, exit west onto Hwy 299. Proceed to Tower House and turn north onto Trinity Mountain Rd. Proceed past Log Cabin Rd and turn right onto County Rd 106. Proceed 12 miles to the campground entrance on the right. Contact the campground directly, (530) 623-2121.*

Hiking

Several nice hiking trails on the northern arm of Lake Shasta are short and easy enough to provide some good exploration of the shore without taking more than a few hours out of the water-play day. Naturally, hardcore packers are going to head to Mount Shasta and the surrounding wildlands (see Mount Shasta chapter). **Bailey Cove Trail** (easy; 3 miles round trip) skirts the McCloud River Arm of the lake along John's Creek and Bailey Cove, providing a good overview of the flooded limestone canyon that created the lake. Take the Shasta Caverns turnoff from I-5, and follow signs to the Bailey Cove boat launch area to find this trail. **Hirz Bay Trail** (easy; 3.5 miles round trip) also skirts the shore of the lake, running between the Hirz Bay and Dekkas Rock areas, with quiet coves and nice views of the rocky shore along the way. There's good wading access on a hot summer day. This trail is at Hirz Bay, off Gilman Rd from I-5.

Wildlife

While visiting Lake Shasta, keep your eye on the sky for a glimpse of the mighty **bald eagle,** the largest bird of prey in North America. The lake is currently the home of at least 18 pairs of the endangered birds—the largest nesting population of bald eagles in California.

outside in

Attractions

As you drive north to Redding up the flat, uninspiring I-5 corridor, snow-topped Mount Shasta first appears as a white smudge at the end of the highway. Venture a little closer and the imposing volcano soon dominates the horizon. This unforgettable sight heralds your approach to the gateway to California's Northern Mountains: **Redding.** Step out of your car, and you'll feel as though you've stepped back in time to a simpler way of life. Redding isn't known so much for what's here as for what's near: prime fishing, hiking, boating, waterskiing, mountain biking, rock climbing, camping, and river rafting. For information about Lake Shasta attractions and houseboat rentals, call the Redding Convention and Visitors Bureau, (800) 874-7562 (see Inside Out sections, above).

In the town of Redding, the 6-mile-long Sacramento River Trail meanders along the riverbanks and over a stress-ribbon concrete bridge—the only bridge of its kind in the country. **The Redding Museum of Art and History** has local-history exhibits and a fine collection of Native American baskets; 56 Quartz Hill Rd, (530) 243-8801. Next door is the **Carter House Natural Science Museum,** a funky, spirited place that houses live animals as well as those that have spent some time with a taxidermist (rest assured that only animals that died accidentally or of natural causes got the glass-eye treatment). Kids will also find plenty of hands-on activities to keep them amused; 56 Quartz Hill Rd, (530) 243-5457. For an extensive selection of newspapers, magazines, and other good reading material, **The Redding Bookstore** is second to none in this part of the state; 1712 California St, (530) 246-2171. The bookstore also houses the Downtown Espresso and Coffee Roasting Company, so you can get a good cup of joe to go along with that terrific travel tome you're now reading.

If you're heading up to Lake Shasta on I-5, the monolithic 3,640-foot-long **Shasta Dam** is a great place to pull over for a lengthy pit stop. Shasta is the second-largest and second-tallest concrete dam in the United States (it contains enough concrete to build a 3-foot-wide sidewalk around the world) and one of the most impressive civil engineering feats in the nation. The visitors center and viewing area are rather ho-hum, but the free 45-minute tour of the dam is outstanding. It kicks off with a speedy elevator ride into the chilly bowels of the 15-million-ton, 602-foot-high structure—definitely not recommended for claustrophobes. Dam tours are held from 9am to 4pm daily; call (530) 275-4463 for information and winter and holiday hours (from I-5, take the Shasta Dam Blvd exit and follow the signs).

Restaurants

Buz's Crab ☆☆   Every day the bounty of the North Coast is hauled over the hills into Buz's seafood market. With Naugahyde booths and Formica tables, this ain't no pretty place for a romantic dinner for two, but Buz's earns its stars for doing what it does perfectly. *2159 East St (N of W Cypress Ave and Pine St), Redding; (530) 243-2120; $.*

Cheesecakes Unlimited & Cafe ☆☆   This place started as a wholesale cheesecake business, then added a small cafe that offers light meals—so now you can have your cake and eat croissant sandwiches and freshly made salads, too. *1334 Market St (just N of the downtown mall), Redding; (530) 244-6670; $.*

Jack's Grill ☆☆   A 1930s tavern, Jack's Grill is a beloved institution in Redding—so beloved, in fact, that few even grumble over the typical two-hour wait for a table on the weekend. But be forewarned: this is a carnivores-only club. *1743 California St (S of the downtown mall, between Sacramento and Placer Sts), Redding; (530) 241-9705; $$.*

Nello's Place ☆☆☆   The exuberant Italian murals and the bright Campari umbrellas hanging from the ceiling add a playful touch to this traditional, romantically lit Italian dinner house. Nello's menu and Italian and California wine list are vast and wide-ranging. *3055 Bechelli Lane (near Hartnell Ave), Redding; (530) 223-1636; $$.*

Lodgings

Tiffany House Bed and Breakfast Inn ☆☆   Perched on a hill above town, Brady and Susan Stewart's beautifully refurbished Cape Cod–style home offers 3 guest rooms and a cottage, a swimming pool, and a fine view. *1510 Barbara Rd (off Benton Dr), Redding; (530) 244-3225; $$.*

More Information

Lake Shasta Information Center: *(530) 257-1589.*
Lake Shasta Ranger District: *(530) 275-1587.*
Redding Convention and Visitors Bureau: *(530) 255-4100 or (800) 874-2782.*

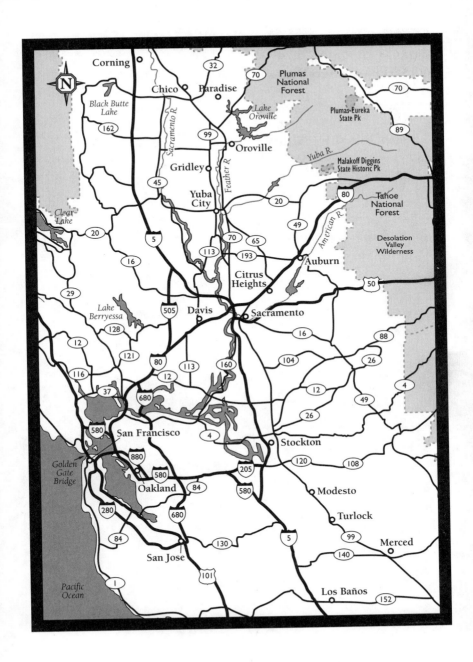

Central
State

Central
State

Sacramento Valley

The entire Sacramento Valley, from the Sacramento–San Joaquin Delta and state capital north to Redding, including the Sacramento River National Wildlife Refuge complexes, the American River Parkway trail system, and numerous riverside recreation areas.

Let's be honest. It's the flat middle of the state, sandwiched between the fabulous California coast and John Muir's "range of light." Most outdoor recreationists are going to drive right through without stopping, unless it's for gas.

But the Sacramento Valley is not a complete lost cause. The Sacramento and American Rivers provide ample opportunities for boaters, swimmers, anglers, campers, and birders. The American River Parkway trail system, extending 25 miles from Old Sacramento east to Folsom Lake, is the recreation centerpiece of the valley, meticulously cared for and passing through multiple river-access areas. Just like the Sacramento–San Joaquin Delta area to the south, the state's northern valley has been the site of extensive land reclamation and water development, leaving the two major rivers and their tributaries channelized and confined. In the past, however, they meandered and often overflowed their banks, creating huge marsh areas, and during exceptionally wet years, an inland sea. While most of the marsh habitat that resulted from these pristine conditions is gone, here and there are toeholds that can give visitors an appreciation for what once was. Chief among these are more than 23,000 acres of the Sacramento River National Wildlife Refuge, which, along with expansive wildlands owned by private duck-hunting clubs, riverfront state parks, and private lands used as floodways, still provide habitat for wintering waterfowl. And with ecosystem restoration projects currently under way, these areas promise to expand in coming decades.

Campers in the Sacramento Valley will find choice riverside and lakeside areas centered mostly around fishing, boating, and water sports during the summer. Fishing along the Sacramento River is good all year, with healthy runs of king salmon and steelhead. Chico, a university town, is one of the most bike-friendly communities in the valley, and its proximity to riverfront and country back roads make it a popular cycling destination.

While most serious outdoor adventurers will elect to drive the extra few miles to the Sierra Nevada, the Shasta region, the coast, or the High Sierra, the Sacramento Valley is a quiet and less-crowded option for a quick recreation fix.

Getting There

Interstate 5 and Highway 99 run north and south through the Sacramento Valley, both of them long, flat, and definitely less than scenic. Nonetheless, they're the main thoroughfares for exploring the middle of the state. Highways 20 and 32, among the dozens of east-west connections between these two arteries, provide most of the access to the Sacramento River recreation areas, the nucleus of outdoor activity in the region. There is no rail system, and regional transportation into the river areas is abysmal, so we suggest exploring this part of the state by car.

Adjoining Areas

NORTH: **Lake Shasta**

SOUTH: **The Delta**

EAST: **Northern Gold Rush Country**

WEST: **East Bay**

inside out

Parks

The **Sacramento National Wildlife Refuge** is the largest of four such areas in the northern Sacramento Valley popular among birders, wildlife buffs, and anglers who enjoy the river scene. The refuge covers nearly 11,000 acres of marshland, ponds, and mudflats frequented en masse by waterfowl during the winter migration. Visitors have miles of walking trails and a 5-mile driving tour to keep them occupied, along with access to riverbank fishing. This refuge is located directly east of I-5, 23 miles north of Woodland. Follow the refuge signs off the freeway and onto

County Rd 68 in Norman. The refuge office is 17 miles east of the freeway, on the left side of the road. To the south are three smaller national refuges.

The **Colusa National Wildlife Refuge** encompasses 4,000 acres of similar terrain, including ponds, marshes, and tule fields, also quite productive for birding and well appointed with walking trails. The Colusa refuge is less than a mile west of the town of Colusa on Hwy 20. Take I-5 north from Sacramento 35 miles to Williams, then head east on Hwy 20. The refuge entrance is south of the highway as you approach Colusa. At 2,500 acres, **Sutter National Wildlife Refuge** is the smallest of the four refuges, just south of Hwy 20 and west of Yuba City near the town of Meridian on the Sacramento River. Sutter is a bit more user-friendly than **Delevan National Wildlife Refuge**, 5 miles east of Maxwell on Hwy 99, which encompasses nearly 6,000 acres of similar terrain. Both Sutter and Delevan are more a destination for hunters than for bird-watchers, but the birding is decent at both if you arrive in the hunting off-season. For information about these refuge areas, call the US Fish and Wildlife Service office in Willows, (530) 934-2801.

Another good place to enjoy the riparian habitat and riverside oak woodlands of the valley is at **Woodson Bridge State Recreation Area,** which follows the Sacramento River to where Kopta Slough branches off from the western banks. The slough provides easy boating and fishing access guarded from the strong flows of the main tributary. This is a secluded and quiet spot for picnics and camping at the river's edge, though the park is used mostly by bird-watchers and anglers. The campground has 40 sites for boat-in access only. To reach the park from Corning, drive 5 miles north on I-5 to South Hwy, then head east 5 miles to Kopta Rd just before the Woodson Bridge. Turn north on Kopta Rd and continue a short distance to the park entrance. For information, call the recreation area at (530) 839-2112.

At **Colusa/Sacramento River State Recreation Area,** nearly 70 acres of marshland and riparian woodlands make for a great birding, fishing, and boating area with good river access. There is a boat launch for public use and nature trails are popular during the winter for birders. The park is also a culturally significant Patwin Indian settlement. The park is 10 miles east of I-5 at Colusa on Hwy 20. Call the recreation area at (530) 458-4927 for more information.

Bidwell/Sacramento River State Park extends along 4 miles of the Sacramento River and is a popular put-in spot for canoeing and rafting, as well as a good fishing and birding area. There are four day-use areas here, with public boat launch facilities, picnic tables, beach access, and other amenities for daylong outings on the river. The park is noted for its pristine condition; much of the terrain here is kept as it would have appeared before western settlers arrived and began using the river to irrigate farmland. To reach the park, take the Hwy 32 exit from I-5 to River Rd, and then head south on River Rd a short distance to the entrance. For more information, call the park at (530) 342-5185.

Fishing/Boating/Swimming

The **Sacramento and American Rivers,** along with their tributaries, provide the bulk of the fishing recreation in the Sacramento area, the American being the more preferred because of its accessibility and relative pristine condition. River access is available at any of numerous park, refuge, and recreation areas along the water. Colusa/Sacramento River State Recreation Area (see Parks, above) is one spot with good river access and decent fishing. River Valley Guide Service in Anderson, (530) 365-2628, runs **guided fly-fishing tours** of the Sacramento River year-round. Dan Mar Guide Service in Chico, (530) 343-3487, also has guided fishing and boat trips on the Sacramento. For fishing access along the American, look for access points along the American River Parkway (see Biking, below), or consider fishing the upper river or Folsom Lake instead (see Northern Gold Rush Country chapter), which have more amenable boating and recreation facilities.

At Bidwell/Sacramento River State Park (see Parks, above), there are four day-use areas with river access, the best being the **Big Chico Creek Recreation Area,** which is a fully equipped water recreation spot popular for canoeing, inner tubing, swimming, and Jet-skiing. **Collins Lake** near Marysville (see Camping, below) is one of numerous small lakes in the area for swimming and other water sports, with **boat rentals** and well-appointed day-use facilities for toasty summer days in the valley. The lake may be reached at (530) 692-1600.

Biking

Looking for a grand tour? Perhaps the best way to see this area is via the **American River Parkway** trail, which extends 25 miles from Old Sacramento to Folsom along the American River, and is one of the nicest recreation features in the Sacramento Valley. **Cyclists** use the paved sections of trail to bike the entire valley in a day—a great trip on cool, dry fall or spring days. Joggers and horseback riders use the unpaved section of the trail, which is well maintained and well marked to avoid conflicts between different classes of trail user. The private nonprofit American River Parkway Foundation, PO Box 188437, Sacramento, CA 95818, (916) 456-7423, can provide information and recommendations. Trail entrances are all along the river corridor, but begins at Discovery Park in Old Sacramento, just off I-5 at Richards Ave in the central Sacramento area.

From Discovery Park, the ride follows the northern riverbanks over a mostly level course, continuing to Folsom at the eastern end of the Sacramento Valley. While it makes a suitable day ride, most trail users bite it off in small chunks, as there are access points throughout the Sacramento Valley, each trail section offering something a bit different. Or do it as an endurance ride. During the summer it is a good course for cyclists training for heat conditions, but the casual rider will want to schedule the ride for more moderate spring or fall weather, since the Sacramento Valley can heat up unbearably in the warmer months. The trail enters numerous small community parks that make good picnic spots. One good **outfitter** with locations at several points along the trail route is American River Bicycle Center, 9203 Folsom Blvd, Sacramento, (916) 363-6271; 3291 Truxel Rd, Sacramento, (916) 641-8640; and 391 Riverside Blvd, Sacramento, (916) 427-6199.

While the American River Parkway trail system is the longest and best developed and maintained, there also are numerous suitable rides along the Sacramento River, which runs north through the valley from the city center. **River Road,** west of Chico, is a relatively flat 20-mile riverside trail course that runs through walnut and almond orchards. Begin the ride going west out of downtown Chico, which is where you will find equipment and **rentals.** Campus Bicycles, on Main St at Fifth St in downtown Chico, is one of several good outfitters, (530) 345-2081, as is Bike Lane, 364 Broadway, (530) 342-2453. The Chico Velo Cycling Club, (800) 482-2453, schedules regular **outings and events** in the area.

While the American River Parkway trail system has dirt sections parallel to the paved, it is not an ideal **mountain-biking** place for two reasons: there are too many other types of trail users to conflict with, and there are no mountains. Mountain bikers who really want to rough-and-tumble it are best advised to head east to the Sierra foothills or north to the Lassen National Forest region (see Lassen Region and Northern Gold Rush Country chapters).

Wildlife

There was a time, way back before water development and land reclamation began changing the look and landscape of the Sacramento Valley, when it was one of the most productive wintering destinations for waterfowl migrating along the Pacific Flyway. To repeat the old cliche, there were so many of them that when they took flight the sky darkened. As alteration of the landscape took hold, however, bird populations dwindled. Now, with the state in the midst of a gigantic environmental restoration program, things may be looking up. Some populations of birds, both local and seasonal, have begun increasing in recent years—and biodiversity experts say that may be in part because of restoration and enhancement of river basin marshes and wetlands, many of them owned by hunting clubs. Birders in the Sacramento Valley, in fact, should make certain they are not walking into hunting season when they take to the levee roads and sanctuary walking paths. Look for **ducks,** ducks and more ducks—but also for **Canada geese, great blue herons, jays, quail, hawks, falcons,** and **owls** in either the river marshes or riparian woodlands found along the river. Woodson Bridge State Recreation Area, Colusa/Sacramento River State Recreation Area, and Bidwell/Sacramento River State Park (see Parks, above) are among the best locations for the casual birder. Also consider one of the valley's national wildlife **refuges** (see Parks, above) for a more pristine and natural birding experience, but either go prepared to share space with hunters or wait until the off-season. Call the US Fish and Wildlife Service, (530) 934-2801, for more information.

Walking/Hiking

This being a flat, hot valley with no mountain peaks, riverside recreation is also the best bet for those wanting to take a stroll. The American River Parkway trail system (see Biking, above) is the most often used walking area in the valley—but be prepared to share the trail with bikes, horses, strollers, and every other kind of trail user imaginable. A quieter and more scenic walk may be had at the Sacramento River National Wildlife Refuge, with more than 5 miles of nature trails for exploring riverside marshlands and tule fields. Any of the Sacramento-area wildlife refuges are a good place for a walk, but check first to make sure trail access is not limited because of duck hunting. Call the US Fish and Wildlife Service office in Willows, (530) 934-2801, for information and recommendations. Looking for a more strenuous hike? Check out Lassen Region, Mount Shasta, and Northern Gold Rush Country chapters, all describing areas adjacent to the valley.

Camping

In the immediate state capital area, virtually all camping is at small private resorts catering mostly to RVers. But there's plenty of suitable camping north, south, and east of the city (see also Northern Gold Rush Country and The Delta chapters). In the northern Sacramento Valley, most camping is lakeside or riverside, near boating, fishing, and bird-watching.

The **Colusa/Sacramento River State Recreation Area** has 15 sites (no hookups; RV limit 30 feet) in an excellent bird-watching, boating, and fishing area on the Sacramento River north of the city near Colusa. Each site has a picnic table and fire grill, with running water, showers, and flush toilets nearby. This is a particularly well-equipped campground for its size. Take note that hunters also frequent the general vicinity and use the campground. *Take I-5 north from Sacramento 32 miles to Williams, then head east on Hwy 20 another 10 miles to 10th St in Colusa. Turn right on 10th and continue to the campground. Call the campground, (530) 458-4927, for information, and state parks reservations, (800) 444-7275, for reservations.*

Boaters who don't want to contend with the overly popular **Englebright Lake Boat-In Camp** should try **Collins Lake Campground,** which has 160 sites (partial hookups; RV limit 30 feet) on a pretty fishing lake near Marysville. Each site has a picnic table and fire grill, with piped water, flush toilets, and showers nearby. Lakeside sites are premium here, but all of the camping area is well appointed for boating, fishing, and other summertime sports. There is a full-service marina at the lake with rental boats, along with adjacent day-use swimming areas. *To reach the lake, depart east from Marysville for 20 miles on Hwy 20, then go another 10 miles north on Marysville Rd. To reserve a spot, call the lake at (530) 692-1600.*

Lake Red Bluff Campground has 30 sites (no hookups; RV limit 30 feet) on a small lake at the Sacramento River near Red Bluff. Picnic facilities, running water, showers, and flush toilets are provided at this waterside retreat, which is popular with water-skiers and anglers. The campground is managed by the National Forest Service. *The campground is east of I-5 at Lassen Park in Red Bluff; go 2 miles south on Sale Lane from the highway exit. Contact Forest Service reservations, (800) 280-2267, or Corning Ranger District, Mendocino National Forest, (530) 824-5196.*

Woodson Bridge State Recreation Area Campground has 40 sites (no hookups; RV limit 30 feet) at a good boating and fishing spot on the Sacramento River east of I-5 in Corning. Each site has a picnic table and fire grill with running water, showers, and flush toilets nearby. *The campground is 10 miles east of the interstate along South Ave. To reserve a site, call the state parks reservations at (800) 444-7275. For more information, call Woodson Bridge State Recreation Area, (530) 839-2200.*

There are two large campgrounds at **Whiskeytown Lake** west of Redding, a popular fishing, boating, and water-sports area near both the Trinity and Shasta National Forests. **Brandy Creek Campground,** the smallest of the two, has 45 sites (no hookups; RV limit 30 feet), each with tables and fire pits, with a boat launch and running water nearby. **Oak Bottom Campground** is more than twice as large, with 150 sites (no hookups; RV access at only 50 sites; RV limit 30 feet), each with picnic tables and fire pits, with running water, flush toilets, and showers nearby. Beach access is adjacent to the campground, as are access to forested areas around the lake and boat rental facilities. In addition to these two camp-grounds, there is a group campground at the lake for large events. *To reach the lake, take Hwy 299 west from Redding for 10 miles to the lake area entrance. Contact Forest Service reservations, (800) 280-2267. For information, call Shasta-Trinity National Forest, Whiskeytown Unit, (530) 241-6584.*

McCumber Reservoir Campground is a small, out-of-the-way spot with fewer than 20 sites (no hookups; RV access limited; RV limit 22 feet) on a small fishing lake owned by Pacific Gas and Electric Company (PG&E) east of Redding. Each site has a picnic table and fire grill, with vault toilets and running water nearby. With the electric deregulation situation in California, PG&E is preparing to offer a number of its electric generation facilities for sale, so be sure to check on this one before heading up there expecting a campsite, as it may have a new owner. *To reach the lake, go east of Redding on Hwy 44, then north on Lake McCumber Rd. For information, call (916) 923-7142.*

Adventure Calendar

Chico Wildflower Century, April: *a 100-mile bicycling marathon,* (530) 891-5556.

outside in

Attractions

Sacramento has long been regarded as the second-class stepsister of San Francisco, but with its increasing number of skyscrapers, upscale restaurants, and swanky hotels (not to mention the NBA's Sacramento Kings and the Sacramento Monarchs, a women's NBA team), California's capital city is no longer the sleepy little valley town folks whiz through on their way to Lake Tahoe. Located 90 miles northeast of the Bay Area, the city is best known for its dual status as the seat of state government and the epicenter of California's biggest industry: agriculture (locals affectionately call Sacramento the Big Tomato, Sacratomato, and the River City). But disregard any disparaging words you may have heard about this agricultural hot spot: there are no cows (or even cowboy hats) within city limits, and most of the city slickers do not pick tomatoes for a living.

A former Gold Rush boomtown, Sacramento sprang up where the American and Sacramento Rivers meet—a tourist area now known as Old Sacramento. In 1839 Swiss immigrant John Sutter traversed both rivers, built his famous fort, and established his colony called New Helvetia

("New Switzerland"). But his hopes that the thriving colony would evolve into his own vast empire were dashed when gold was discovered up near his sawmill in 1848. Sutter's colonists deserted New Helvetia to search for the precious nuggets, and as word of the gold discovery spread, thousands more wound their way to the hills above Sacramento to seek their fortune. Ironically, Sutter himself never prospered from the Gold Rush and he died a bitter, penniless man.

Today, Sacramento is home to more than a million people, many of whom play politics with the capital crowd or practice law. They dote on their spectacular Victorian homes and fine Craftsman-style bungalows, and are justly proud of the tree-lined streets and thick carpets of grass that surround their houses and parks.

To best appreciate the Big Tomato, start your tour of the town in **Old Sacramento** (aka Old Sac), the historic district. Perched along the Sacramento River, the four-block-long stretch is filled with dozens of restaurants, gift shops, and saloons. An Old Sac highlight is the **California State Railroad Museum,** a grand monument to the glory days of locomotion and the Big Four, and the largest museum of its kind in the nation; 125 I St at Second St, (916) 323-9280. The granddaddy of Old Sac attractions is the **Sacramento Dixieland Jubilee,** the world's largest Dixieland jazz festival, which attracts thousands of toe-tappers and bands from around the world each Memorial Day weekend, (916) 372-5277. One mile south of this historic district is the **Towe Ford Museum of Automotive History,** which boasts the largest antique Ford collection in the world; 2200 Front St, (916) 442-6802. Nearby is the **Crocker Art Museum,** home of the region's largest art collection, including a fine selection of contemporary California art by local talents who made the big time such as Wayne Thiebaud and Robert Arneson. The museum also holds a stunning collection of European master drawings; 216 O St at Third St, (916) 264-5423. Also of special interest to art lovers is **La Raza Galleria Posada,** a Chicano, Latino, and Native American arts center located in a beautifully restored Victorian house. Within this complex are a cultural center, a contemporary-art gallery, a bookstore, and a gift shop stocked with wonderful Mexican folk arts; 704 O St at Seventh St, (916) 446-5133.

A few blocks northeast of the gallery is the awe-inspiring **State Capitol,** restored in the 1970s to its original turn-of-the-century magnificence. You may wander around the building on your own, but you really shouldn't miss the free tours given daily every hour between 9am and 4pm. Tours include an overview of the legislative process and, if you're lucky, a chance to see the political hotshots in action. Tickets are handed out a half hour before the tour on a first-come, first-served basis in the basement of room B-27 in the Capitol; it's located on 10th St, between L and N

Sts, (916) 324-0333. While you're getting your tickets, pick up a copy of the "State Capitol Tree Tour" brochure and after your indoors tour you can saunter through marvelous Capitol Park and admire more than 340 varieties of trees from around the world.

If you're a big history buff, step back in time by strolling through **Sutter's Fort,** where you can view the restored self-contained community that Sutter built in the wilderness in 1839. On the same grounds is the **California State Indian Museum,** with artifacts from more than 100 California Indian tribes, including one of the finest basket collections in the nation; it's located between K and L Sts and 27th and 28th Sts, (916) 445-4422 (fort) or (916) 324-0539 (museum).

Performing Arts. The Sacramento Community Convention Center is the regular venue for the local symphony, as well as big-name jazz and classical groups and dance troupes; 1421 K St, (916) 264-7777 or (916) 264-5181 (box office). Just up the road is the Crest Theater, a refurbished art deco palace that hosts rock, folk, reggae, and World Beat concerts and runs classic movies; 1013 K St, (916) 442-7378. Sacramento has a thriving live theater scene, and two top venues are the Sacramento Theater Company, 1419 H St, (916) 446-7501, and B Street Theater, co-founded by TV and film star Timothy Busfield (of *thirtysomething* fame) and his brother Buck; 2711 B St, (916) 443-5300. One of the city's most popular summer pastimes is the Music Circus—an annual festival of Broadway musicals presented under a big-top tent. Every July and August the Sacramento Light Opera Association continues this 50-year-old summer musical tradition by reviving the music of Cole Porter, the Gershwins, and Stephen Sondheim using professional casts from Broadway and Hollywood; 1419 H St, (916) 557-1999.

If you're cruising through town during the last two weeks of August, set aside a hot day or night to visit the **California State Fair,** Sacratomato's grandest party. The carnival rides and games are predictably head-spinning and not for the faint of stomach, but everyone agrees the livestock exhibits and wine tastings (featuring winners of the prestigious State Fair wine competition) are worth the admission price. Other fair highlights include daily horse races, nightly rodeos, free nightly concerts by big-name groups of all persuasions, and a wild variety of events ranging from Western art and Web page competitions to the State Fair film festival; located at Cal Expo, off the I-80/Capital City Freeway (north of the American River) at Expo Blvd. Call (916) 263-3000 for more details or visit the State Fair's Web site at www.bigfun.org.

The University of California at Davis (UCD) is this little city's claim to fame, particularly the college's respected veterinary science and enology schools. A former farming town, **Davis** is also famous for its city officials who pride themselves on finding more ecological ways of living on the planet. For example, to encourage people to move their feet up and down on bicycle pedals instead of gas pedals, the city has built 67 miles of bike lanes and trails. The great minds of Davis get their world-shaking ideas while sipping espresso at Mishka's Cafe, 514 Second St, (530) 759-0811, and they spend their spare hours pawing through the works of other great minds at Bogey's Books, 223 E St, (530) 757-6127. The urban-village atmosphere of downtown Davis draws shoppers, diners, and browsers to its charming streets, and on the southeastern outskirts of town is The Palms Playhouse, an intimate, down-home spot that features nationally known blues, country, jazz, and folk acts that will save you a trip to Austin; 726 Drummand Ave, (530) 756-9901.

Chico is a pretty little college town that gained a national reputation when *Playboy* magazine named the California State University at Chico (aka Chico State) the number-one party school in the nation. Horrified by this label, most of the local gentry tried to put an end to it by doing away with Chico's biggest college celebration, Pioneer Days—a weeklong beer bust rivaling spring break in Palm Beach. Of course, the college crowds still party hearty here, but they don't take over the town once a year as they used to. When the warm weather rolls in, plan a picnic or a stroll among the trees in the 2,400 acres of pretty Bidwell Park. To find out what's currently going on around town, settle in at Caffe Paulo with a pastry and espresso and thumb through the *Chico News and Review*, the city's fine alternative-press newspaper; 642 W Fifth St, (530) 343-0704.

Restaurants

Alexander's Meritage ☆☆☆☆   French inspired, if not strictly French, Meritage has some appetizers that alone are worth the visit. But don't lick the plate—this is a classy joint. The wines are engaging, especially Meritage's rare cabernets. *6608 Folsom-Auburn Rd, Suite 9 (in the Ashland Station Center), Folsom; (916) 988-7000; $$$.*

Biba ☆☆☆☆   Biba is a study in understated neo-deco design—the sort of place where you'd expect precious, trendy foods to dominate the menu. Fortunately, they don't. What comes out of the kitchen is classical Italian cooking. *2801 Capitol Ave (at 28th St), Sacramento; (916) 455-2422; $$$.*

The Buckhorn ☆☆   You know you're in serious meat-eating country when you see the glassy eyes of the Buckhorn's small herd of mounted deer, a moose, and a goat gazing down at you. *210 Railroad Ave (at Main St), Winters; (530) 795-4503; $$.*

Christophe's French Restaurant ☆☆☆☆ This traditional French restaurant is open, light, and airy, with a courtyard, a pond, gardens, and a dramatic fountain. Best of all, the tables are so far apart you can actually have a private conversation. *2304 E Bidwell St (between Creekside Dr and Oak Ave), Folsom; (916) 983-4883; $$$.*

City Cafe ☆☆☆ By golly, Yuba City's gone trendy with this chic little cafe smack-dab in the middle of the town's historic section. The lunch menu focuses on an assortment of panini; dinner is a more ambitious affair. *667 Plumas St (at Colusa Hwy), Yuba City; (530) 671-1501; $$.*

Cory's Sweet Treats & Gallery ☆☆ This cheerful little daytime cafe adorned with the work of local artists serves lumberjack-size sandwiches with generous layers of meats such as roast beef, baked ham, and pastrami. *230 W 3rd St (between Broadway and Salem St, downtown), Chico; (530) 345-2955; $.*

Crêpe Bistro ☆ Tucked into a row of small shops, this tiny, brightly lit cafe is a favorite hangout of the university crowd—and there is always a crowd here. True to its name, the specialty is crêpes. *234 E St (between 2nd and 3rd Sts), Davis; (530) 753-2575; $.*

David Berkley ☆☆☆ This is essentially a delicatessen—but, wow, what a deli! Just about everything served here is perfect: perfect salads, perfect sandwiches, perfect produce, perfect desserts. *515 Pavilions Lane (in the Pavilions shopping center, on the N side of Fair Oaks Blvd, between Howe and Fulton Aves), Sacramento; (916) 929-4422; $$.*

Dos Coyotes Border Cafe ☆☆ This distant outpost of Southwestern cuisine is one of the hottest places in Davis (with a branch in Sacramento, too). The crowds come for the fresh, consistently good food, such as the house-made salsas, shrimp tacos, and ranchero burritos. *1411 W Covell Blvd #108 (in the Marketplace shopping center, just E of Hwy 113), Davis; (530) 753-0922; $. 1735 Arden Way (at Market Square in the Arden Fair shopping mall), Sacramento; (916) 927-0377; $.*

El Rio Club ☆ Once you're safely ensconced in this small dining room (beyond the bar haunted by mounted moose, deer, and antelope heads), all entrees come with fresh veggies, pasta, and a salad. *1198 3rd St (just E of the Sacramento River and S of Hwy 20), Meridian; (530) 696-0900; $$.*

The Fox and Goose ☆☆☆ You'll see chaps chugging down pints of bitter and having a jolly good time over a game of darts at this bustling British pub, almost as genuine as any neighborhood spot you're likely to find in the United Kingdom. *1001 R St (at 12th St, just S of the Capitol), Sacramento; (916) 443-8825; $.*

Granzella's, Inc. ☆   This culinary emporium houses everything from a restaurant and an ice-cream parlor to a sports bar and a bakery. Its fine Italian deli is packed with a large selection of wine and beer, olive oils, and Granzella's own exquisite olives. *451 6th St (just W of I-5), Williams; (530) 473-5496; $.*

Jammin' Salmon ☆☆   Built on a barge, this small but delightful restaurant gently rocks when boats pass by, creating a rather soothing environment for nibbling such fare as blackened ahi tuna seared with wasabe and Chinese mustard. *1801 Garden Hwy (on the river), Sacramento; (916) 929-6232; $$.*

Kramore Inn ☆☆   This inn's food has kept people coming back for more than 20 years. The Kramore specialty is crêpes. You'll find 30 different kinds—everything from a shrimp-and-broccoli combo to the old favorite ham-and-cheese crêpe. *1903 Park Ave (at W 19th St), Chico; (530) 343-3701; $.*

Lemon Grass ☆☆☆☆   This elegant restaurant, offering a unique blend of Vietnamese and Thai cooking, keeps getting better and better and is approaching nirvana. Many of the culinary masterpieces use little or no oil. *601 Monroe St (just N of Fair Oaks Blvd, near Loehmann's Plaza shopping center), Sacramento; (916) 486-4891; $$.*

Louis Cairo's ☆   Louis Cairo's offers the warm atmosphere of a traditional Italian cafe, a large variety of entrees, and a good wine list. Burgundy-checkered tablecloths and matching napkins top the tables of the simple dining room. *558 7th St (downtown), Williams; (530) 473-5927; $.*

Ludy's Main Street BBQ and Catering ☆   From the outside it looks a lot like any small-town restaurant, but step inside and you'll feel as though you've been transported to the heart of Texas, complete with barnwood walls, wagon wheels and antlers. *667 Main St (downtown), Woodland; (530) 666-4400; $.*

Merchant and Main Grill and Bar ☆☆   Belly up to this grill and bar and order the steak sandwich, the rich, buttery, grilled crab-salad sandwich, or the Asian chicken salad. This restaurant is very popular, so reservations are advised. *349 Merchant St (take the Alamo/Merchant St exit off I-80), Vacaville; (707)446-0368; $$.*

Morrison's Upstairs ☆☆   Tucked into the attic of one of Woodland's most striking buildings, an 1891 Queen Anne Victorian, Morrison's Upstairs combines old-fashioned elegance with a pre-dinner aerobic workout; guests must climb three flights of stairs. *428½ 1st St (at Bush St), Woodland; (530) 666-6176; $$.*

Paragary's Bar and Oven ☆☆☆   Paragary's Bar and Oven restaurants (there are three in Sacramento and one in Folsom) are well known for zesty pizzas cooked in wood-burning ovens and mesquite-grilled entrees that typically have a strong Italian accent. *1401 28th St (at N St), Sacramento; (916) 457-5737; $$$. 2384 Fair Oaks Blvd (between Howe and Fulton Aves), Sacramento; (916) 485-7100; $$$. 2220 Gold Springs Court (at the corner of Sunrise Blvd and Gold Expwy), Sacramento; (916) 852-0214; $$$.*

Pasquini's ☆☆   Pasquini's is a warm, welcoming, and sometimes raucous dinner house, where the tables are draped with red-checkered cloths and the favored seats are the two well-padded booths. The menu is as thick as a magazine. *6241 Live Oak Blvd (on Hwy 99, about 5 miles N of Yuba City), Live Oak; (530) 695-3384; $$.*

Redwood Forest Restaurant ☆☆   Come to this kick-back college-town cafe for a good lunch of vegetarian lasagna; the dinner menu features grilled or poached salmon, filet mignon, and several veggie selections. *121 W 3rd St (between Broadway and Main St, downtown), Chico; (530) 343-4315; $.*

Rio City Cafe ☆☆   Located on the Sacramento River, the Rio City Cafe has a pleasantly light, airy, and attractive dining room. The fare here is primarily Southwestern with a dash of California and a soupçon of New Orleans. *1110 Front St (between J and K Sts), Sacramento; (916) 442-8226; $$.*

Ruthy's Bar and Oven ☆☆   If you're a big breakfast eater, make a beeline to Ruthy's. For lunch, head straight for the salad bar or order a sandwich served on house-made bread. Dinner is a more elaborate affair. *229 Clark Ave (in the Hillcrest Plaza mini-mall, S of Franklin Ave), Yuba City; (530) 674-2611 or (800) 455-LAKE; $$.*

Siam Restaurant ☆   This admirable tiny Thai restaurant located in a redeveloping part of town turns out delicious soups, unusual salads, fiery-hot curry dishes, and seafood entrees such as steamed clams cooked with fresh ginger. *5100 Franklin Blvd (at 26th Ave, in the south-central part of town), Sacramento; (916) 452-8382; $.*

Sicilian Cafe ☆☆   Settle in beneath the vineyard mural, order some good Italian wine, and prepare yourself for a simple but tasty Italian meal. The Sicilian's specialties are its fresh pasta dishes and calamari. *1020 Main St (between W 9th and W 11th Sts), Chico; (530) 345-2233; $$.*

Silver Dollar Saloon ☆   This restaurant and saloon is a lively relic of Marysville's frontier past, with Western memorabilia scattered throughout the building. You can watch 'em cook your order on the open-pit grill here or, heck, even cook it yourself. *330 1st St (in Old Town, between C and D Sts), Marysville; (530) 743-0507; $.*

The Snack Box ☆   Residents of Red Bluff gladly stand in line to eat the jumbo servings of freshly made food offered for breakfast (served all day) and lunch in this pretty little Victorian house. *257 Main St (at Ash St), Red Bluff; (530) 529-0227; $.*

Soga's Restaurant ☆☆☆   If you didn't know about this exquisite slip of a restaurant you might pass right by it (look for the British telephone booth out front). Word of mouth has transformed the classy, 16-table, wood-paneled restaurant into a bustling establishment. *222 D St (between 2nd and 3rd Sts), Davis; (530) 757-1733; $$.*

The Symposium ☆☆   Ancient Greeks cavort across the mural-covered walls of this lively Greek restaurant—and after one taste of the Symposium's deliciously different Greek pizza, you may want to do a bit of cavorting yourself. *1620 E 8th St (at M St, near Albertson's), Davis; (530) 756-3850; $$.*

33rd Street Bistro ☆☆☆   This bistro combines a casual, trendy ambience—a handsome red-brick wall, high ceilings, polished wood floors, and vibrant oversize paintings of vegetables—with terrific food at reasonable prices. *3301 Folsom Blvd (at 33rd St), Sacramento; (916) 455-2282; $$.*

Lodgings

Abigail's Bed and Breakfast ☆☆☆   A 1912 Colonial revival mansion, Abigail's is a prime example of home-building and hospitality from an era when both were art forms. It is located in the heart of midtown's Boulevard Park district, a neighborhood with some of the city's most opulent Victorian homes. The 5 handsome bedrooms are furnished with antiques. *2120 G St (between 21st and 22nd Sts), Sacramento; (916) 441-5007 or (800) 858-1568; $$.*

Amber House ☆☆☆☆   Amber House is actually three restored historic homes—two set side by side (a 1905 Craftsman and a 1913 Mediterranean) and one across the street (an 1895 Colonial revival). The houses have been exquisitely restored, and the 14 guest rooms are artfully decorated with a mix of antiques and contemporary furnishings. *1315 22nd St (between Capitol Ave and N St), Sacramento; (916) 444-8085 or (800) 755-6526; $$.*

Emma's Bed and Breakfast ☆☆☆   Perched on a hill overlooking rolling farmlands dotted with grazing horses and llamas doing whatever it is that llamas do, this stately manor situated on 45 acres is impressively furnished and decorated. Three of the suites are in the immaculately renovated 1912 farmhouse and two are in a new, matching building next door. *3137 Taylor Rd (between King and Penryn Rds), Loomis; (916) 652-1392; $$.*

The Esplanade Bed and Breakfast ☆ This B&B is located on one of Chico's most beautiful boulevards, The Esplanade, which is lined on both sides with lush lawns, tall trees, and stately Victorian mansions. The charming turn-of-the-century house has 5 guest rooms, each with a cable TV and a private bath. *620 The Esplanade (near Memorial Way), Chico; (530) 345-8084; $.*

The Faulkner House ☆☆ No use looking for the *Absalom, Absalom* room or the *As I Lay Dying* suite in this 1890 Queen Anne Victorian, for it was named after a local doctor who practiced here in the '30s, not the writer. The Faulkner House features a red-velvet parlor, a casual living room, and a spacious dining room. Each of the 4 guest rooms has a private bath. *1029 Jefferson St (off Union St), Red Bluff; (530) 529-0520 or (800) 549-6171; $$.*

Harkey House ☆☆ This beige 1874 Victorian Gothic B&B trimmed in blue and red offers 4 guest rooms with private baths, as well as such diversions as a spa, a chess table, and an antique Chickering piano. In the solarium-style dining area, guests are treated to a full breakfast. *212 C St (in old downtown, across from the courthouse), Yuba City; (530) 674-1942; $$.*

Hyatt Regency Sacramento ☆☆☆ This is the only lodging in Sacramento that truly feels like a big-city hotel. It boasts a vaulted marble entryway; the nightclub Busby Berkeley's on the 15th floor; a sumptuous, light-filled atrium lounge; 500 beautifully appointed rooms with pretty views of palm-tree-lined Capitol Park; and excellent service. *1209 L St (at 12th St, across from the Capitol), Sacramento; (916) 443-1234 or (800) 233-1234; $$$.*

The Inn at Shallow Creek Farm ☆☆ Who would have thought there'd be an elegant and absolutely peaceful refuge so close to I-5? This ivy-covered farmhouse, surrounded by citrus trees and set at the end of a long drive, offers 4 guest rooms. *4712 County Rd DD (take the Chico-Orland exit off I-5, drive 2½ miles W, then turn right on County Rd DD and drive ½ mile), Orland; (530) 865-4093 or (800) 865-4093; $.*

The Old Flower Farm Bed and Breakfast Inn ☆☆☆ Set in a bucolic countryside and oozing charm from every cranny, the 3-room Old Flower Farm looks out over (what else?) a flower farm. With its century-old architecture lovingly painted and restored, it looks like a cover shot for

Sunset magazine. And inside it's even more impressive. *4150 Auburn-Folsom Rd (halfway between the towns of Auburn and Folsom, at Horseshoe Bar), Loomis; (916) 652-4200; $$–$$$.*

Palm Court Hotel ☆☆☆   This chic, unobtrusive jewel is reminiscent of a fine little boutique hotel. The lobby is small and intimate with a kind of Raffles Hotel look (English with a dash of East Indian) and some very classy antiques artfully scattered about. The 28 suites have an East Indian/English flair, too, with dark wooden blinds and Regency furnishings in hues of rust, maroon, and gold. *234 D St (at 3rd St), Davis; (530) 753-7100 or (800) 528-1234; $$.*

Sterling Hotel ☆☆☆☆   This striking, turn-of-the-century Victorian inn with its beautiful garden immediately draws attention. Inside, it's a sleek luxury hotel aimed at corporate travelers. The Sterling's interior is awash in Asian-influenced, neo-deco flourishes, and the artwork has a decidedly Zen twist. The 16 guest rooms are large, airy, and spotless. *1300 H St (at 13th St), Sacramento; (916) 448-1300 or (800) 365-7660; $$$.*

More Information

The American River Parkway Foundation: *(916) 456-7423.*
Chico Chamber of Commerce: *(530) 891-5556.*
Colusa–Sacramento River State Recreation Area: *(530) 692-1600.*
Corning District Chamber of Commerce: *(530) 824-5550.*
Red Bluff Chamber of Commerce: *(530) 527-6220.*
Sacramento Chamber of Commerce: *(916) 444-6670.*
Shasta-Trinity National Forest, Whiskeytown Unit: *(530) 241-6584.*
US Fish and Wildlife Service office, Willows: *(530) 934-2801.*
Woodson Bridge State Recreation Area: *(530) 839-2112.*

The Delta

The sloughs, rivers, and waterways of the Sacramento–San Joaquin Delta, at the confluence of the Sacramento and San Joaquin Rivers, including Brannan Island State Recreation Area, Rio Vista, Grizzly Island, and Suisun Marsh.

At one time, it was a perfect system. Heavy winter snows in the Sierra Nevada would drop high enough and deep enough on the mountain peaks that the rivers coursing their way through the foothills and toward the Central Valley floor would run wild and uncontrolled year-round. The result? At times when the snow melted too fast under the weight of a warm rain, the valley floor would fill like a bathtub as rivers overspilled their banks and melded into a giant inland sea. The marshes and meadows attracted millions upon millions of waterfowl migrating along the Pacific Flyway. Two of the state's largest rivers, the Sacramento and the San Joaquin, formed the estuary that today carries a constant flow of Sierra runoff to the San Francisco Bay, where it meets and mixes with salt water from the Pacific moving through the Golden Gate. For much of the winter and spring, this area was like a standing pool.

All of this began changing during the Gold Rush years, when farmers began diking the Delta islands. Small towns, some of them below sea level, cropped up behind high levee roads. The rivers were contained. Upstream, huge reservoirs were built to store water for the dry months, making the flows through the Delta more predictable. The inland sea was gone—replaced by what today has emerged as a patchwork quilt of farmland, burgeoning suburbs, duck-hunting blinds, and beaches, connected by levee roads and drawbridges. And while it is by no means a natural

environment—nor pristine, thanks to runoff from Central Valley farms—
it has become the state's premier water-sports playground. Call it Water
World, or call it the Delta; all we know is that anglers, water-skiers, windsurfers, beachcombers, and bird-watchers can't stay away—whether it's
the official outdoor season or not (in the winter, they just water-ski with
wet suits on). This is bass fishing central, with a thousand miles of
labyrinthine waterways to get lost in—sloughs connecting riverways and
slicing between islands, some of them in Contra Costa County, others in
Sacramento, and still more in Solano and San Joaquin. Park your car on
the side of a levee road and sit under a bridge fishing all day. Ride a paddle
wheeler from Old Sacramento and you'll swear you're somewhere along
the Mississippi. Roll into the sleepy town of Isleton, where the police chief
has been criticized for doling out concealed weapons permits too liberally
and an annual festival honors the crawdad, and you will know you've
arrived. Most of the property in the Delta region is privately owned, but
there is enough public access to the water, like the lovely Brannan Island
State Recreation Area, that it is not 100 percent necessary to visit a private
resort while here. The best way to do the Delta is to simply pack up and
hit Highway 160, the Delta Highway. Everything you need will unfold
before you if you give it time.

Getting There

*Highway 160 runs the entire length of the Delta region from Sacramento on
the north to the Antioch Bridge, which crosses the San Joaquin River to Contra
Costa County and the Bay Area. The Delta region is also bisected by Highway
12, which crosses from the Interstate 80 corridor at Fairfield and Suisun City,
through Rio Vista, and on east to the Interstate 5 corridor at Lodi. Highway
160 in particular has numerous drawbridge crossings between Antioch and
Sacramento, so allow extra time. Use extra caution around bridges; some drivers have been known to get confused and find out the hard way that their cars
don't float when they hit the river. Finally, the river roads are packed to the
rafters on hot summer days when the boating and water-sports season is in
full swing. Watch for intoxicated or reckless drivers and for pedestrians on the
highway.*

Adjoining Areas

NORTH: **Sacramento Valley**

SOUTH: **San Joaquin Valley**

EAST: **Southern Gold Rush Country**

WEST: **East Bay**

inside out

Parks/Beaches

Most of the recreation areas in the Delta region are privately owned, many by hunting clubs. Waterfront resorts with beaches are the main fare; most have marinas and boat rentals. See Boating/Water Sports, below, for contacts. There are a few good public areas as well, however.

Brannan Island State Recreation Area is by far the best-appointed public property in the entire Delta region, with camping areas, swimming beaches, wide-pooled flooded areas for boating and waterskiing, and a public boat launch. The park is set in a pleasant riparian wood and meadow. Adjacent is **Franks Tract,** more of the same, accessible only by boat. The park is located 3 miles south of the Hwy 12 bridge at Rio Vista, on Hwy 160. Call the recreation area, (916) 777-6671.

Sandy Beach County Park, just south of the Rio Vista waterfront on the Sacramento River, provides a full swimming and water-sports recreation experience, complete with a well-appointed campground and picnic facilities, as well as places to fish offshore (the best way to fish in these parts is from a boat). This is a favorite put-in for windsurfers as well. To reach the park, go 15 miles east of Fairfield on Hwy 12 to Rio Vista. Exit the highway east on Main St into the downtown. Turn south on Second St, and follow it a few blocks to Beach St. Turn east on Beach St and proceed to the park on the waterfront. Call the park, (707) 374-2097, for more information.

Across the water in Contra Costa County, **Antioch Regional Shoreline** is a quaint 7-acre waterfront park on the Delta with a 500-foot pier. Striped bass fishing is best from November through January, and flounder move in during the warm summer months. Or just have a waterside picnic here, if you can't make it to the quieter Browns Island Regional Shoreline, which we recommend because of its location away from the city of Pittsburg. From Oakland take Hwy 4 east to Antioch. Exit north at Bridgehead Rd. For additional information contact the East Bay Regional Park District at (510) 562-PARK. **Browns Island Regional Shoreline,** covering 595 acres, is located at the confluence of the state's two largest rivers, the Sacramento and the San Joaquin, which meet to form the Delta leading to the San Francisco Bay. Wildlife viewing is a favorite activity here, as is picnicking—but be certain to bring something to sit on, as this is a primitive site with no facilities of any kind. We're talking remote, quiet, and rustic. Six species of rare and endangered plants are found on the island, which is also a suitable spot. The island is located off the Pittsburg shoreline. From

Oakland, take Hwy 24 east to I-680, continue to Hwy 242, then go east on Hwy 4 toward Stockton. Exit east on Railroad Ave, and follow it to the waterfront and marina area. For additional information, contact the East Bay Regional Park District at (510) 562-PARK.

Boating/Water Sports

The labyrinth of sloughs winding and twisting between the Delta islands are a boater's dream, with literally hundreds of miles to explore and ideal conditions for everything from dropping anchor in that favorite fishing spot to water-skiing at nearly the speed of sound (well, maybe not quite that fast, since there is a speed limit).

For a true Delta experience, rent a **houseboat** and cruise the water for a few days alongside snowy egrets, sandhill cranes, and Swainson's hawks. Houseboat rentals are available several miles north of Stockton off I-5: at Little Connection Slough, at Herman and Helen's Marina at the west end of 8 Mile Rd, (209) 951-4634, (800) 676-4841, www.house-boats.com; and Paradise Point Marina, located at Bishop Cut near Stockton, off Eight Mile Rd, 8095 Rio Blanco, (209) 952-1000 or (800) 752-9669 (reservations). Also call the Delta Houseboat Rental Association for rental/outfitter recommendations, (209) 477-1840.

Here is also where the high-speed adventure begins. While hardcore **water-skiers** take to the Delta year-round, the peak season is naturally summer. The Delta is considered one of the premier ski areas of the West Coast because of pocketed wind protection and stillwater conditions in some spots where river flows are broken by the levees. Most of the action is in the southern sloughs and riverways around the Contra Costa/San Joaquin County border and Discovery Bay. Middle River and Old River are particularly active. One drawback, however, is the crowds. Summers on the water are packed, making the Delta a place for alert boaters only. Discovery Bay Water Ski School, 5901 Marina Rd #3, Byron, is a suitable place for beginners to check for instruction and equipment, (925) 634-0412. Numerous marinas and boat rental outfits (see below) rent ski equipment, as does Larson Marine, 1325 W Fremont St, Stockton, (209) 465-5801.

The high winds that kick up off the Pacific and fan through the San Francisco Bay and estuary create perfect **windsurfing** conditions on the Delta. Sacramento County Park on Sherman Island has some good shallow areas for beginners to practice in; watch out, however, for submerged rocks. Martin's Marina, adjacent to the park, is also a good launch area, as is Windy Cove, across the highway from the entrance to Brannan Island State Recreation Area (see Parks/Beaches, above), which requires intermediate boarding skills because of its exposure. Near the Rio Vista Bridge on the Sacramento is another spot with easy access to the water, Sandy Beach County Park (see Parks/Beaches, above). Most of the action is between Sandy Beach and Sherman Island—just drive that stretch of Hwy 160 and look for the parked cars and sails. Be careful if you choose to park on the side of the levee road; traffic moves quickly through the area. The Rio Vista Windsurfing Association, (925) 778-2345, can recommend outfitters and provide further information.

There are several places to rent **fishing boats** and **ski boats** out here. Both Paradise Point Marina and Herman and Helen's Marina (both noted above) rent them. Korth's Pirates Lair Marina on Andrus Island also rents aluminum fishing boats, (916) 777-6464. Another way to get out on the water is on a **chartered paddle wheeler,** just like the one on Huck Finn's Island at Disneyland. Contact Riverboat Cruises in Old Sacramento, (800) 433-0263, for a seat. **Boat launches** and **guest moorings** are available throughout the river and slough system, including at Brannan Island State Recreation Area (see Parks/Beaches, above); Boathouse Marina, on the Sacramento River at the town of Locke, (916) 776-1204; Herman and Helen's Marina (see above), on Little Connection Slough; King Island Resort, on Disappointment Slough, (209) 951-2188; Suisun City Marina, on Suisun Slough, (707) 429-2628; and Vieira's Resort, on the Sacramento River near Rio Vista, (916) 777-6661.

Before you take to the waters and begin soaking up the fun, however, there are a few things to keep in mind. First of all, boating can be dangerous. During the regular boating season from April to September, the Delta can expect to see numerous injuries and deaths caused by recklessness on the water. According to the state Department of Boating and Waterways, more than 50 percent of fatal boating accidents out here involve alcohol, of particular concern because summer days in the area routinely heat up beyond 100 degrees. Short lecture: don't drink and boat, don't drink and swim, don't drink and drive. Winding levee roads and two-lane highways without passing lanes, potentially strong river currents, and inexperienced boaters are all the ingredients you need to brew trouble.

That aside, the object here is to get out on the water.

Fishing

Once you're out on the water, the natural next step is to go fishing. And aside from providing drinking water for about two-thirds of the state's residents, that's what the Delta is used for most. Take your pick. **Catfish, largemouth bass, sturgeon,** and to a certain extent **shad** can be found here year-round, and the catfish action is so dependable that it's the ideal draw for families who want to give children the thrill of a first catch, no matter how easy. Most common is bait fishing. For catfish, bottom fishing in coves works best, with crayfish as bait. In the spring and summer, look for the **salmon** and **striped bass** fishing to pick up. Good spots are near the Sacramento River mouth or the mouth of the Mokelumne. Another neat trick is to park near one of the fish screens at the federal and state pumping plants in the southern Delta. Fish straying toward the pumps are captured, sorted, and released—and sometimes they head back to the open river, confused and hungry. Naturally, you can get **bait-and-tackle supplies** just about anywhere on the Delta where the highway passes through a town. A few places to stop include Bob's Bait Shop, 302 Second St, Isleton, (916) 777-6806, and the Bridgetender Bait Shop, 14164 Hwy 160, Walnut Grove, (916) 776-3969. It is more fun, however, to trap your own bait—if you can wait overnight for a load of crayfish. Naturally, all state fishing laws and limits apply here, so be sure to pick up a copy of the latest regulations at any bait-and-tackle dealer or check with the state Department of Fish and Game office in Sacramento, (916) 653-6281.

Scenic Drives

The best quick tour of the Delta region is to simply drive the whole stretch of **Highway 160** from the foot of the Antioch Bridge at Sherman Island to the Freeport area of the Sacramento River, a distance of about 45 miles with numerous drawbridge crossings and pleasant river towns and beaches along the way. Isleton is a favorite stop, but also be sure to check out the sights at Steamboat Landing, which has a private beach and quaint roadhouse restaurant at the Sutter Island Rd intersection with the highway near Courtland. Hood-Franklin Rd east will take you back to I-5 to continue the drive to Sacramento.

Camping

While there are several suitable public campgrounds, all with good river frontage, in the Delta region **private resorts** also occupy key spots along the shore. These are lazy places where it's okay to lounge around doing little more than drop a line into the river and then forget it's there. The California Delta Chambers, (916) 777-5007, can provide information about riverside resorts.

Brannan Island State Recreation Area on the Sacramento River near Isleton, the crawdad capital of the Delta region, has 100 sites (no hookups; RV limit 36 feet), each with picnic tables and fire grills, with showers, running water, and conveniences nearby. This is a favorite beach, boating, and family outing spot, with easy access to good water recreation and beaches.

Public slips are also available. *To reach the campground from Fairfield, head 15 miles east to Rio Vista, cross the river to the Hwy 160 intersection, then head west (toward Antioch) 3.5 miles to the entrance on the left side of the road. For reservations, call the state parks reservations system, (800) 444-7275. To contact the park, call (916) 777-6671.*

Sandy Beach County Park on the Sacramento River near Rio Vista has 40 sites (partial hookups; no RV limit) near a popular beach play area and fishing spot. Each site has a picnic table and fire grill, with running water, flush toilets, and showers nearby. *The campground can be reached via Hwy 12. From Fairfield, head east 15 miles to Rio Vista, and exit the highway east on Main St into the downtown. Turn south on Second St, and follow it a few blocks to Beach St. Turn east on Beach St and head to the park on the waterfront. For reservations, call (707) 374-2097.*

Westgate Landing County Park, at Terminous on Sycamore Slough, has 14 sites (no hookups; no RV limit) and is a popular but nice, quiet, out-of-the way fishing spot where you don't stand too much of a chance of being overrun by the masses. Boat slips are available for day rentals. *From Fairfield, take Hwy 12 east 15 miles to Rio Vista, cross the Rio Vista Bridge, then continue another 9 miles east to Terminous. At Terminous, turn left from Hwy 12 on Glasscock Rd and continue north a short distance to the clearly marked park entrance on the left side of the road. Call the San Joaquin County Parks Department, (209) 953-8800.*

On the San Joaquin River near Stockton, **Dos Reis Park** has 25 sites (no hookups; no RV limit) in a popular river access spot for waterskiing and fishing during the summer. Each site has a picnic table and fire grill, with flush toilets, showers, and piped water nearby. There also is a boat ramp at the river. *The campground is west of I-5 outside the town of Lathrop. Take I-5 south from Stockton 3 miles to the Lathrop Rd exit, head north for a few blocks to Dos Reis Rd, and follow it west to the river and the park entrance. For reservations, call the San Joaquin County Parks Department, (209) 953-8800.*

Wildlife

Birders have a field day out here. Sure, the vast majority of the marshlands that existed in the Delta region before 1850 have been diked off as farmland—and there most certainly are fewer Pacific Flyway stopovers here than before the Delta was reclaimed. But that doesn't mean there's nothing to look at. **Egrets, pelicans, geese, swans, coots, grebes,** and **ducks**—millions and millions of ducks, it seems—can be seen in the tules and marshlands that remain.

Hogback Island, south of Howard Landing on Country Rd 220,

Snodgrass Slough near Walnut Grove, and Grizzly Island in the flats west of Rio Vista and Suisun are three of the best viewing areas. Before setting out, be sure to check with the state Department of Fish and Game, (916) 653-6281, to find out if it's hunting season. Many flats are privately owned by duck-hunting clubs.

Adventure Calendar

Bethel Island Frozen Bun Run, New Year's Day: *winter water-ski event, (925) 684-3220.*

Western Buddy Bass Open Tournament, early March: *Brannan Island, two-day event, (209) 333-7000.*

Isleton Crawdad Festival, third weekend of June: *proves crawdads are good for more than just fish bait, (916) 777-5880.*

25th Annual Crawdad Races, early August: *at Mossdale Marina, near Manteca, (209) 982-0512.*

Rio Vista Bass Derby, early October: *the river town goes all out for the fish with parade and the works, (707) 374-2700.*

outside in

Attractions

The birthplace of Caterpillar tractor inventor Benjamin Holt and, more recently, heartthrob rock star Chris Isaak, **Stockton** used to be a simple blue-collar town—home to a multicultural mix of European, Mexican, and Asian immigrants who worked the fields, stockyards, and docks. As the Deep Water Channel was being dredged to accommodate grain carriers during the 1930s, however, this inland city was gradually transformed into an international seaport, growing by leaps and bounds, particularly over the last decade (as did the crime rate and gang activity). Despite suburbanization and its inherent problems, agriculture is still king here—fruit stands continue to dot the roadsides from April to October, and fresh local produce still draws crowds to Stockton's farmers markets. The **open-air markets** offer superb produce and are held on Thursday and Sunday from 8:30am to 1pm in the Weberstown Mall parking lot at March Lane and Pacific Ave, in front of Sears; Friday from 10am to 2pm in Hunter's Square downtown, by the courthouse; and Saturday from 7am to 11am underneath the freeway, across from St. Mary's church. For more information on the farmers markets call (209) 943-1830. If you're in town on Friday, Saturday, or Sunday, don't miss the huge outdoor flea market (open from 8am to 5pm), where everything that can be sold is sold. Great ethnic food stands and a summertime carnival for kids are additional flea-market attractions; 3550 N Wilson Way, off Hwy 99, (209) 465-1544.

The Sacramento River Delta is dotted with quaint, old-fashioned little island towns connected by drawbridges and ferries. You'll find a good, if pricey, Sunday brunch in the Delta at **Grand Island Mansion,** a Gatsby-esque inn with 58 rooms and a private bowling alley and cinema, located on the west end of Grand Island, 3 miles west of Hwy 160, at 13415 Grand Island Rd, (916) 775-1705.

Locke was the first town in the United States built solely by Chinese laborers for Chinese residents (even though the Chinese businesspeople and workers who built it were forbidden to own any of the land). During its heyday at the beginning of the century, Locke was a town of gambling houses, opium dens, and speakeasies. Now the tiny town is owned by a Hong Kong corporation, and the businesses are much tamer (and certainly more legal) than in years past. Note the old wooden sidewalks lining the streets, a remnant of Locke's early days.

Restaurants

Al the Wops ☆   The food is simple but adequate here, and the assorted tourists, boaters, and local characters who hang out at the long tables and benches like it that way. Al's dinners are limited to chicken and New York steaks (12 or 18 ounces). *13943 Main St (the first street off the levee), Locke; (916) 776-1800; $.*

Giusti's ☆☆   Opened in 1910, this family-run restaurant continues the tradition of serving good food in an old-fashioned, laid-back atmosphere. Except for the 1,500 baseball caps hanging from the ceiling, Giusti's looks as if it has been frozen in time for the last 50 years. *14743 Walnut Grove–Thorton Rd (4 miles W of I-5), Walnut Grove; (916) 776-1808; $.*

Nena's Restaurant ☆   Nena's started out as a tiny cafe on the south side of Stockton and was an instant hit, especially with Stockton's large Latino population. The restaurant moved to bigger digs in a central part of town, and the crowds still come. *1064 E Waterloo Rd (at Solari St), Stockton; (209) 547-0217; $.*

Primavera Ristorante ☆   This traditional Italian restaurant features tables topped with crisp linens and candles, handmade pasta, and a host of waiters spouting Italian accents. *856 W Benjamin Holt Dr (in the SE corner of Lincoln Center, at Pacific Ave), Stockton; (209) 477-6128; $$.*

Yen Ching ☆   Ornate wall carvings and bright red partitions set the mood for the authentic Peking, Hunan, Sichuan, and Mandarin Chinese cuisine served here. Standout entrees include the Shandong steamed bread. *6511 Pacific Ave (in the SE corner of Lincoln Center, at Benjamin Holt Dr), Stockton; (209) 957-0913; $.*

Yoneda's Japanese Restaurant ☆   This pleasantly decorated restaurant retains a hint of old Japan, and offers a wide selection of sushi and sashimi, as well as the traditional sukiyaki, tempura, and teriyaki dishes. *1101 E March Lane (in the Calaveras Square shopping center on the NW corner of March and West Lanes), Stockton; (209) 477-1667; $.*

Lodgings

The Ryde Hotel ☆☆   Originally built as a boardinghouse, this four-story, pink stucco inn on the banks of the Sacramento River became famous as a speakeasy during Prohibition. The inn now has 32 guest rooms decorated in a 1920s art deco style with a pink, gray, and mauve color scheme. In late 1997, the hotel changed hands, and renovations were in progress. *14340 Hwy 160 (3 miles S of Walnut Grove), Ryde; (916) 776-1318; $$.*

Stockton Hilton ☆   Tucked away in a quiet corner of Stockton, this five-story hotel with 198 one- and two-bedroom suites is certainly nothing to swoon over, but it offers the most pleasant (and safest) accommodations you'll find in town. Room service, a spa, and free access to the athletic club across the street round out the Hilton's amenities. *2323 Grand Canal Blvd (from I-5 take the March Lane exit and head E), Stockton; (209) 957-9090 or (800) 444-9094; $$$.*

Wine and Roses Country Inn ☆☆☆   This ivy-covered 1902 farmhouse is surrounded by 5 acres of cherry trees, rose gardens, and towering 100-year-old deodar cedars, and the interior is covered with flowers and lace. The inn's 10 guest rooms (named after songs) have queen-size beds, turn-of-the-century decor, and handmade comforters. *2505 W Turner Rd (5 miles E of I-5, 2½ miles W of Hwy 99), Lodi; (209) 334-6988; $$.*

More Information

California Delta Chambers of Commerce: *(916) 777-5007.*
Discovery Bay Chamber of Commerce: *(925) 634-9902.*
San Joaquin County Parks Department: *(209) 953-8800.*
State Department of Fish and Game, Sacramento: *(916) 653-6281.*
Stockton Chamber of Commerce: *(209) 547-2770.*

San Joaquin Valley

The San Joaquin River basin south of the Delta, including select adjacent reservoirs, camping areas, and wildlife refuges as far south as Merced.

If you could have seen the San Joaquin River during the first half of the 19th century, it would have looked more like a huge lake than a confined river draining from farmlands to the Delta. That's because the river was untamed, and rain would send it over its banks, while currents would send it meandering about the Central Valley floor to find its own path. Today, as water development has defined the California way of life, not to mention its economic power, the river is confined behind flood-control levees that keep it from drowning crops and flooding burgeoning central California suburbs. The taller and more magnificent the levees get, the less often the river manages to escape and behave as it did naturally. The last time the river flooded big-time was during the New Year's floods of 1997, when the San Joaquin actually sat above flood stage for nearly two months as record amounts of rainfall inundated reservoirs, mountain tributaries, and the river itself.

Because of the river's predicament, it is not looked upon as a prime destination for water recreation. Just as we have confined the river and dumped our wastewater, pesticides, and silt into it by the billions of gallons, we have also thumbed our noses at it, preferring man-made reservoirs for recreation instead.

There is, however, an emerging interest in environmental restoration and rehabilitation along the river's diked wetlands and marshlands. Before the land was reclaimed, this was the single most productive wintering ground for migrating waterfowl in the northern hemisphere. Wildlife experts say it will never be that again, but they have been successful at restoring or protecting numerous areas of marsh, wetlands, ponds, and riparian forested areas suitable for wintering habitat. Bird-watching and nature walks are the premier outdoor activities in these areas, with more than 200 species of raptor and waterfowl on record.

Getting There

Interstate 5 and Highway 99 extend south through the Central Valley, with numerous river access points and cross-highway cutoff points along their length. Highway 152 between Los Baños and Merced, Highway 132 between the Altamont Pass and Modesto, and Highway 33 between Vernalis and Gustine also provide direct access to key points along the river.

Adjoining Areas

NORTH: **The Delta**

EAST: **Southern Gold Rush Country**

WEST: **San Francisco, Peninsula and South Bay, Monterey Bay**

inside out

Wildlife/Walking

The **Central San Joaquin Valley National Wildlife Refuge** complex comprises three vast river marsh restoration areas and floodways that are being maintained for the benefit of millions of **migratory waterfowl** that winter in the Central Valley each year. This whole area was at one time a vast inland sea. Years of water reclamation and levee building have decimated a large portion of the wildlife habitat in the valley, making refuges such as these vital to sustaining at least a semblance of the natural ecosystem and wildlife web. The **Merced National Wildlife Refuge** covers 4,500 acres of wetlands and hillsides adjacent to the river for a variety of wildlife management purposes. As with most of these sanctuary areas, wildlife officials artificially flood and drain the fields to mimic as closely as possible the natural conditions that existed prior to damming and irrigation. This marsh area is 9 miles downstream from Merced on Hwy 59. Some 40 miles east of Merced on Hwy 140 is the infamous 10,700-acre **Kesterson National Wildlife Refuge,** where Fish and Game officials discovered horrifyingly deformed birds in the early 1980s, victims of apparent selenium poisoning caused by rampantly uncontrolled agricultural drainage. The area is still recovering and is returning to normal, but new land management practices have yet to run their full course, meaning the health of the ecosystem here still hangs in the balance as permanent solutions are pursued. Nonetheless, Kesterson on the surface is a popular wintering area for migrating waterfowl stopping over on the Pacific Flyway. To reach Kesterson, take Hwy 140 west from Merced for 40 miles. At the intersection with Hwy 165, head south (left) into the refuge. At the **San Luis National Wildlife Refuge,** covering some 15,000 acres of marsh and riverfront at the San Joaquin, walking paths extend through the expansive marshlands and wetlands being restored here. An interpretive driving tour is also offered in this area. The San Luis refuge is just south of Kesterson on Hwy 165, on the east side of the road.

The **bird species** seen throughout the valley and at these main refuge outposts number over 200 and include tundra swans, shorebirds, cranes, snowy plovers, sandpipers, egrets, and on occasion nesting **Swainson's hawks,** a protected species. The San Luis portion of the refuge is 10 miles north of Los Baños on Wolfsen Rd. Take Mercy Springs Rd northeast from Hwy 152 for 7.5 miles, then head up Wolfsen Rd another 2.5 miles to the refuge entrance. For more information, call the US Fish and Wildlife Service, (209) 826-3508.

Great Valley Grasslands State Park, 5 miles east of Gustine on Hwy 140, is another prize wildlife viewing area, with nearly 3,000 acres of grasslands and riparian forestlands, where more **shorebirds** and other varieties of **migrating waterfowl** can be spotted during the winter migration. Call the state parks office, (209) 632-1852, for more information. Finally, the **Los Baños State Wildlife Area** and the **Mendota State Wildlife Area,** near Los Baños and Mendota, respectively, cover a combined area of nearly 20,000 acres, with marshes, mudflats, wetlands, and ponds well suited to birding. Look for grebes, herons, teals, mallards, sandpipers, flickers, snipes, and rails, depending on the time of year. Los Baños is the best appointed of the two, offering extensive walking paths and allowing dispersed camping with limitations. Call the state Fish and Game office, (209) 826-0463, for more information on both.

Boating/Fishing/Water Sports

What will it be, lake action or river action? Actually, most anglers stick to the numerous reservoirs upstream of the San Joaquin (also see Southern Gold Rush Country chapter), since the river itself is stressing under the weight of pesticide runoff from farms and years of uncontrolled silting and wastewater disposal. Health advisories suggest the fish from the San Joaquin may be perilous to your health if consumed beyond certain amounts. Reservoirs tend to be cleaner because they are closer to the natural source of the water in most cases. **San Luis Reservoir State Recreation Area** (see Camping, below), primarily a **bass** fishing lake adjacent to the vast Los Baños wildlife area (see Wildlife/Walking, above), is among the most popular. The reservoir is on Hwy 152, 12 miles east of Los Baños and 10 miles west of I-5, and is equipped with boat launch facilities. **Waterskiing** and **windsurfing** are popular activities here, with rentals and lessons available on-site. Call the reservoir, (209) 826-1196, for more information. While the San Joaquin River is a suitable fishing and boating river for some, with public access points throughout the area, its tributaries—such as the Merced, Tuolumne, and Mokelumne Rivers—are more popular because of the issues mentioned above. But there are numerous public river access points for those who opt to use the river anyway.

Swimming and **waterskiing** on valley reservoirs are popular summer activities, most notably at the San Luis Reservoir State Recreation Area (see above). Swimming in the San Joaquin River, however, is not advisable because of pesticide runoff and wastewater disposal.

Camping

The best camping in the San Joaquin Valley is lakeside or riverside. Dispersed camping is allowed during the summer at the Los Baños State Wildlife Area (see Wildlife/Walking, above), probably a more pleasant choice than many of the others. Frankly, much of the camping in these parts is best suited to the RV set—retirees on a mission to fish every lake in the state or see all 49 to complete their bumper-sticker collections. In addition to the campgrounds listed below, there are numerous private campgrounds along the I-5 and Hwy 99 corridor, some little more than highway hookups where people rest up while on their way elsewhere.

Caswell Memorial State Park has 65 sites (no hookups; RV limit 24 feet) in a nice secluded fishing spot at the confluence of the Stanislaus and San Joaquin Rivers south of Stockton. This is a nice river floodplain wildlife area, best visited before the dead of summer when temperatures in the valley begin jumping past the century mark. Each campsite comes equipped with a picnic table and fire pit, and showers, toilets, and running water are nearby. *To reach the campground, take I-5 south for 15 miles, then go east 5 miles on Austin Rd. Call the state parks reservations office, (800) 444-7275, or the campground directly, (209) 599-3810.*

Frank Raines Park has 35 sites (full hookups; no RV limit) near the San Joaquin River at Modesto—mostly used by highway travelers who need a place near the interstate to hook up, but also by those interested in exploring the river floodplain nature areas and the foothills west of the valley. *The campground and park are west of I-5 on Puerto Canyon Rd. Take* *the Patterson Pass Rd exit from I-5 just south of Tracy and then head south on Puerto Canyon Rd another 15 miles. To reserve a site, call the park, (408) 897-3127.*

George Hatfield State Park (no hookups; RV limit 32 feet) has 20 sites near where the Merced and the San Joaquin Rivers meet, a popular fishing and camping spot for RVers. Each site has a picnic table and fire grill, with running water, flush toilets, and other amenities and conveniences nearby. *To reach the campground, take I-5 south to Stur Rd near Merced, head east on Stur Rd for 4 miles to Hills Ferry Rd, then head east another 6.5 miles to the campground and park. Call state parks reservations, (800) 444-7275, or the park, (209) 826-1196, for information and to reserve a site.*

There are three nice campgrounds at **San Luis Reservoir State Reservation Area** west of the San Joaquin River, with nearly 500 sites in all. The reservoir is a popular fishing and water-sports spot during the summer and fall. The smallest campground of the three is **San Luis Campground,** which is actually located on Los Baños Creek, with 50 sites (partial hookups; no RV limit). **Madeiros Campground** is enormous, with 350 sites (no hookups; RV limit 28 feet) above the lake; **Basalt Campground,** with 80 sites (no hookups; RV limit 32 feet), is on the lakeshore. The sites are equipped with tables and fire grills, with running water nearby. The lake campgrounds have boat ramps. *To reach the reservoir, take Hwy 152 west 12 miles from Los Baños, or west 10 miles from I-5. To reserve a site, call the reservoir, (209) 826-1196, or the state parks reservation system, (800) 444-7275.*

Cycling

The river wildlife refuges and public levee roads in the valley are a suitable cycling destination, but not during the valley's frequent summer heat waves. The San Luis National Wildlife Refuge and Los Baños State Wildlife Area (see Wildlife/Walking, above) are the best choices, both with more than 10 miles of roads and trails. Bike Haus, 1343 W 18th St, Merced, (209) 383-4251, is a local source for rentals and equipment.

outside in

Attractions

Merced has claimed the title "Gateway to Yosemite" for more than a century, and the majority of its visitors are San Francisco Bay Area residents just passing through. Those who stop long enough to look around usually end up at Applegate Park, a 23-acre greenbelt with more than 60 varieties of trees, an immaculate rose garden, a small free zoo, and, in the summer, amusement rides to whirl and twirl you and the kids; it's located between M and R Sts. On Thursday evening local farmers sell their fresh produce from 6pm to 9pm on Main St (between N and K Sts), a good place to buy picnic basket ingredients. One of the more interesting sights in the area is the Old Courthouse Museum, the pride and joy of Merced and a monument to the early settlers of the Great Central Valley; 2222 N St, (209) 723-2401.

Oakdale would be just another sleepy Central Valley cow town were it not for the monolithic Hershey Chocolate Factory located on the south side of the city. Believe it or not, some 150,000 annual visitors line up for the free 30-minute tours of the chocolate-making plant, offered Monday through Friday from 8:30am to 3pm (excluding major holidays). Tours depart from the Hershey Visitors Center, which has a few low-tech displays on the history of Milton Hershey's chocolate empire, but it's mostly crammed with Hershey teddy bears, Hershey coffee mugs, Hershey toy trucks, Hershey beer mugs, Hershey sweatshirts, Hershey . . . well, you get the point; 120 S Sierra Ave, at the intersection of Yosemite Ave and E F St, (209) 848-8126. Another town highlight is the Saturday Oakdale Livestock Auction, which is best enjoyed with a big piece of pie from Cheryl's Cafe; for more details see Restaurants, below.

Surrounded by four major highways—I-5 and Hwys 152, 33, and 165—the sleepy town of **Los Baños** calls itself the "Crossroads of California." A more accurate nickname would be "California Pit Stop," since it's nearly impossible to drive through this sparsely populated part of the state without stopping for something—food, gas, or simply to use *los baños*. If you decide to hang around town for a while, you can see remnants of America's halcyon days at the soda fountain at Los Baños Drugs, which looks like a set for *Happy Days*, right down to the cherry phosphate; 601 J St at Sixth St, (209) 826-5834.

Restaurants

Branding Iron Restaurant ☆   This paean to the American Beef Council has delighted Mercedites for nearly half a century. The ambience is Old West, with rough-hewn redwood walls decorated with registered livestock brands from all over California. *640 W 16th St (next to the Santa Fe Railway Depot), Merced; (209) 722-1822; $$.*

Cheryl's Cafe ☆   Every Saturday, ranchers from all around come to the Oakdale Livestock Auction to bid on a heifer or two and talk business over a Cattleman's Sandwich (beef, of course) and a slice of pie, but the real treat is the auction itself. *6001 Albers Rd (S of town, just past the Hershey Chocolate Factory), Oakdale; (209) 847-1033; $.*

Christopaolo's ☆☆ If there were ever a reason to roll your wheels into Ripon, this is it. Many of the original fixtures have been kept in this handsome, high-ceilinged 1886 edifice, and the menu offers a large array of Italian dishes. *125 E Main St (at Stockton Ave), Ripon; (209) 599-2030; $$.*

Deva Café & Bistro ☆☆ If you're looking for a good, reasonably priced breakfast, lunch, dinner, or simply a decent cup of coffee, head directly for Deva, a swank, very popular little cafe in Modesto's downtown district. *1202 J St (at 12th St), Modesto; (209) 572-3382; $.*

El Jardín ☆☆ If you ignore the Wells Fargo Bank sign across the street, you could easily imagine you were basking in the sun at a cozy cantina on the plaza in Guadalajara. The authentic south-of-the-border fare is offered at south-of-the-border prices. *409 E Olive St (1 block W of Golden State Blvd, 1 block N of Main St), Turlock; (209) 632-0932; $.*

El Ranchito ☆☆ A good way to tell whether a Mexican restaurant's food is truly authentic is to sample the refried beans—nothing has the taste or the texture of hand-mashed frijoles, which is what you'll find at this family-run landmark. *3048 Atchison St (at 1st St), Riverbank; (209) 869-0196; $.*

España's Mexican Restaurant ☆ España's offers a full range of traditional Mexican dishes such as house-made tamales, enchiladas, tacos, and flautas, plus a small selection of steak, chicken, and seafood entrees. *1460 E Pacheco Blvd (E of Hwy 165), Los Baños; (209) 826-4041; $.*

Hazel's ☆☆ This old pink house, converted about 30 years ago into a restaurant, is a favorite romantic weekend retreat for many Modesto residents. In this part of the valley Hazel's is the place to be for a candlelit dinner. *513 12th St (between E and F Sts), Modesto; (209) 578-3463; $$.*

H-B Saloon and Bachi's Restaurant ☆ For a real Central Valley experience, don your shitkickers and cowboy hat and head for the H-B Saloon, a decidedly funky old bar. Dinner is served family style in the adjacent Bachi's Restaurant. *401 E F St (next to the Hershey Chocolate Factory), Oakdale; (209) 847-2985; $.*

La Morenita ☆ This restaurant brought fajitas to the Modesto area and it still serves the best in this part of the valley. Expect to wait for a table at this typically crowded restaurant, especially on weekends. *1410 E Hatch Rd (from Hwy 99 take the Hatch Rd exit and head E), Ceres; (209) 537-7900; $.*

The Mansion House ☆☆   This aging grande dame may have seen more glamorous days in years past, but now the house has an unabashedly casual interior and serves as the site of one of Merced's better restaurants. The menu features a wide variety of Italian dishes. *455 W 20th St (at Canal St), Merced; (209) 383-2744; $$.*

Marty's Inn ☆   A favorite on the west side of Stanislaus County, this rustic, wood-paneled steak house has a mellow, lodgelike atmosphere and a simple menu that has kept its unpretentious clientele satisfied since 1955. *29030 Hwy 33 (just S of town), Newman; (209) 862-1323; $$.*

Out to Lunch ☆☆   Word got out a long time ago about the delicious thick sandwiches that emerge from this little veranda-wrapped cottage. Almost anything piled between the warm, sweetly spiced slices of house-made zucchini bread is a good bet. *1301 Winton Way (at Drakely St; from Hwy 99, take the Applegate exit), Atwater; (209) 357-1170; $.*

Tresetti's World Caffe ☆☆   This popular hangout is chic with its burgundy drapes, matching cement floor, pale yellow walls, and only a dozen tables. The chef strives for a global culinary theme, focusing on classic dishes from around the world. *927 11th St (at J St, adjacent to Tresetti's Wine Shop), Modesto; (209) 572-2990; $$.*

Wool Growers Restaurant ☆   This old-time Basque restaurant is a Los Baños institution. If you've never experienced a real Basque feast, it's a great place to start. The question is, will you be able to wolf it all down? *609 H St (between 6th and 7th Sts), Los Baños; (209) 826-4593; $.*

Lodgings

Doubletree Hotel Modesto ☆   Towering 14 stories above the Modesto landscape, the Doubletree is the Central Valley's premier business/luxury accommodation. Guests are pampered with such amenities as a spa, sauna, sun deck, heated outdoor pool, weight room, two restaurants, two bars, and extensive conference facilities. The 258 guest rooms are dull but comfortable. *1150 9th St (at K St), Modesto; (209) 526-6000 or (800) 222-TREE; $$$.*

Ramada Inn ☆   Your best bet for lodging in Merced is the impeccably clean Ramada Inn. Although the inn's exterior is painted a garish pink and green, within its 61 capacious mini-suites you'll find attractive cherry-wood furnishings, brass lamps, love-seat sofa beds (in addition to regular beds), large showers, and coffee-makers. *2000 E Childs Ave (off Hwy 99), Merced; (209) 723-3121; $.*

More Information

Great Valley Grasslands State Park: *(209) 632-1852.*
Gustine Chamber of Commerce: *(209) 854-6975.*
Los Baños Chamber of Commerce: *(209) 826-2495.*
Merced Chamber of Commerce: *(209) 384-3333.*
Modesto Chamber of Commerce: *(209) 577-5757.*
State parks camping reservations: *(800) 444-7275.*
State Fish and Game office: *(209) 826-0463.*
US Fish and Wildlife Service: *(209) 826-3508.*

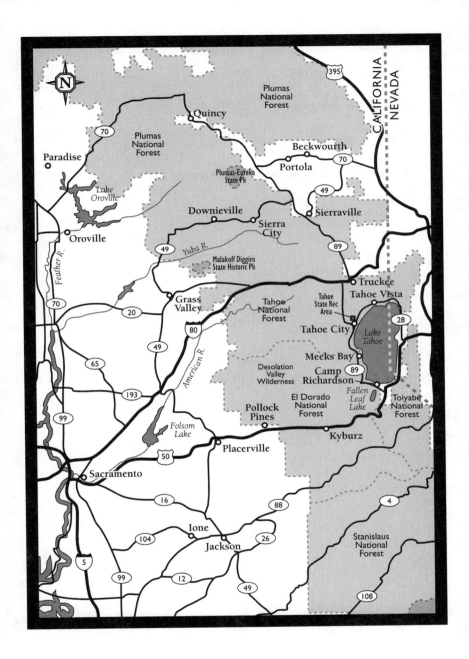

**Northern
Sierra**

Northern Sierra

Plumas Region

Plumas National Forest lands, including Bucks Lake Wilderness, Feather River canyon, Lake Oroville, Lake Almanor, and Plumas-Eureka State Park.

Plumas National Forest is like a forgotten stepchild. It's not really part of the Sierra Nevada because the landscape quite frankly is not as scenic, and it doesn't fit well with the Cascades because there is, alas, no volcano here. What this area does have, however, is the least-used trail system in all of the national forests, the least-known (and possibly the first existing) ski park in the state, hundreds of small fishing lakes and a few large reservoirs to keep anglers happy, and the scenic Feather River canyon—offering secluded waterfall hikes and whitewater rafting runs ideal for beginners.

And if you can't be in the thick of the Sierra Nevada with all the other tourists, it is at least possible to get a good look at the mountain range from here—by scrambling to the 7,447-foot summit of Eureka Peak in Plumas-Eureka State Park, which also contains 73 miles of the Pacific Crest Trail. Plumas not only serves as the intersection between the West Coast's two most prominent mountain ranges, it's also the gateway to the state's core Gold Rush country. According to historians, that's the reason a small ski resort—the Plumas Ski Bowl—exists at the park: miners, they say, started skiing here 150 years ago, using cut pieces of timber as skis.

Pine, fir, and cypress make up most of the forested areas, which are interspersed with lakes—both man-made and natural—that have become the region's most stable draw for tourists. Lake Almanor, Lake Oroville, and the more remote Bucks Lake each have waterside campgrounds and full boating and fishing facilities—and Bucks is surrounded by 20,000 acres of designated wilderness. Of the half dozen or so small cities and towns here, the largest, Quincy, has fewer than 7,000 residents; countywide, just 22,000 people call Plumas home. So while the Plumas region may seem forgotten, it's actually very much here and worth your while to remember.

Getting There

Plumas is bisected by Highway 89, from Chester to the northwest to the Sierra-ville area to the southeast, and many of the area's key features are found along the route. There is also easy access from the northern Sacramento Valley. From Chico, take Highway 32 east. From Oroville, take Highway 162 east to Lake Oroville, and from Red Bluff, head east on Highway 36 to meet Highway 89 near Chester. Forest Service roads here, as in any other area, are generally not maintained for vehicles with low ground clearance. It is a good idea to call ranger stations before trying to drive deep into the forest. For general highway information, call (800) 427-7623. Travelers to the Plumas region should con-tact the Quincy Main Street Chamber of Commerce, (530) 283-0188, for assistance with travel plans; Plumas-Eureka State Park may be reached at (530) 836-2380; and the Lake Oroville State Recreation Area is at (530) 538-2200. The Forest Service headquarters is in Quincy, (530) 283-2050. The national forest has four ranger districts: Beckwourth Ranger District, on Mohawk Road, PO Box 7, Blairsden, (530) 836-2575; Feather River Ranger District, 875 Mitchell Avenue, Oroville, (530) 534-6500; Mount Hough Ranger District, 39696 Highway 70, Quincy, (530) 283-0555; and Milford Ranger District, in Milford, (530) 253-2223; and the Lake Almanor Ranger District, in Chester, (530) 258-2141.

Adjoining Areas

NORTH: **Lassen Region**

SOUTH: **Tahoe Basin**

WEST: **Sacramento Valley**

inside out

Hiking/Backpacking

Despite being overshadowed by the more popular Shasta and Tahoe regions on either side, the Plumas County wildlands have plenty to offer outdoor lovers—particularly those who want to avoid the masses. The trails here are less traveled than in most of the state's outdoor recreation areas, and that means fewer minivans, kids, Winnebagos, and novices than in Yosemite or Tahoe (no white sneakers and soda pop on the trails here!). Most of the activity here centers around Feather Falls, Bucks Lake Wilderness, Lake Oroville, and the Feather River canyon, which bisects the national forest. Some 73 miles of the **Pacific Crest Trail** are also found here. (The Pacific Crest Trail Association, 1350 Castle Rock Rd, Walnut Creek, CA 94598, (925) 939-6111, has maps and information on access points and hiking routes for this and all sections of the trail.) In Plumas-Eureka State Park, in the forest's south end, conquer the 7,447-foot Eureka Peak for a spectacular panorama of the northern Sierra range. Waterfall walks and lakeside strolls top off the menu. The best **trail maps** of the national forest areas are available directly from the Forest Service; write US Forest Service Information, Room 521, 630 Sansome St, San Francisco, CA 94111. See the primer at the front of this book for more detailed ordering instructions. **Trail conditions** in any forest or wilderness area are subject to change, so before setting out on any days-long adventures, check with the appropriate ranger district for up-to-date information. Many backcountry trails may be impassable during winter.

The premier hike for this area, naturally, is the trek to Feather Falls along **Feather Falls National Trail** (difficult; 8 miles round trip), a killer climb of almost 2,500 feet in 4 miles, up the Feather River canyon beginning at Bryant Ravine. Two river crossings and four wicked switchbacks later, the 640-foot falls make the huffing and puffing well worth it, especially if you need the spray to cool yourself off. This is your cardio workout for the day. To reach the trailhead, take Hwy 162 for 11 miles east, past Lake Oroville, to Forbestown Rd, then go 5 miles more to Lumpkin Rd, which signs designate as the route to Feather Falls. Turn right on Lumpkin Rd and continue 9 miles to the clearly marked staging area. For more information, call the La Porte Ranger District, (530) 675-2462.

The 20,000-acre **Bucks Lake Wilderness** is another must-see within Plumas. Look for the section of Pacific Crest Trail passing through the wilderness beginning at Bucks Summit near Meadow Valley. Here, make connections with numerous other routes down to Bucks Lake or hop from peak to peak, looking down upon the lake basin from the 7,000-foot perch at Mount Pleasant. The area is managed by Plumas National Forest, Mount Hough Ranger District, (530) 283-0555. To reach this area, take Spanish Ranch/Butte County Rd northeast from Four Trees and Coyote Gap, off Hwy 70 from Pulga.

The **Eureka Peak Trail** (moderate; 3 miles round trip), within Plumas-Eureka State Park, is one of those short but somewhat difficult hikes that pays off big in exchange for just a little sweat, rising 1,100 feet in just 1.5 miles. The payoff is a lovely view of the northern Sierra foothills and plateau—vistas that don't quite rival those in more heavily traveled areas such as Tahoe and Yosemite, but are memorable nonetheless. From Quincy, head southeast on Hwy 70 to the park entrance on your right. The park covers some 6,500 acres of pine forest and foothills and is adjacent to the Plumas National Forest wilderness areas, meaning the backpacking possibilities from here are boundless. Call Plumas-Eureka State Park, (530) 836-2380, for more information.

Camping

As with most of the national forests in California, camping in Plumas National Forest is allowed just about anywhere you can find a piece of ground flat enough to pitch a tent on. The best camping areas in Plumas are near lakes and within Plumas-Eureka State Park. **Dispersed camping** is your best bet if you're backpacking in the wilderness, but be sure to get **permits** for any use of fire. The best trail maps are available directly from the Forest Service; write US Forest Service Information, Room 521, 630 Sansome St, San Francisco, CA 94111. See the primer at the beginning of this book for more detailed ordering instructions. Periodic **road closures** are unavoidable. Check with the relevant ranger station for updated road conditions before deciding on a site located deep within the forest. Roads are not maintained for vehicles with low ground clearance. The Forest Service is currently reviewing its reservations and fees policies for this area, but generally no reservations are taken for any of the campgrounds listed below. Stays are limited to 14 days. Call the Forest Service **reservations** system, (800) 280-2267, or individual ranger stations for campsite availability information and reservations where applicable. For state facilities at Lake Oroville and Plumas-Eureka, call state camping reservations at (800) 444-7275.

Plumas-Eureka State Park Campground has 64 sites (no hookups; RV limit 31 feet) and is popular due to its amenities. It frequently fills to capacity on weekends. Piped water, flush toilets, and showers are available. Each site is equipped with a fire ring and table, and a sanitary dump station is on the premises for RVs, along with a general store. *From Quincy, take Hwy 70 east. Turn right onto Hwy 89 south, and in half a mile, turn right again onto County Rd A14. Proceed to the Plumas-Eureka State Park entrance and the campground beyond. For more information, call the park, (530) 836-2380, or state parks reservations, (800) 444-7275.*

Beckwourth Ranger District, (530) 836-2575

Crocker Campground has 10 sites (no hookups; RV limit 34 feet) along Lake Davis. This campground is sought by visitors to Lake Davis who are looking for solitude and a primitive camping experience. There is no running water, so be sure to bring plenty of your own. Vault toilets are provided, and each site is equipped with a fire ring and table. *From Beckwourth, take Hwy 70 west and turn right (north) onto Grizzly Rd. Turn right on Crocker Mount Rd, just before reaching the lake. Proceed to the campground. For more information, call (530) 836-2575.*

Frenchman Campground has 41 sites (no hookups; various RV lengths accommodated) along the banks of pretty Frenchman Lake. The campground has piped water, vault toilets, and a sanitary dump station for RVs. Each site is equipped with a fire ring and table. A boat ramp is nearby. *From Beckwourth, take Hwy 70 east and turn left (north) on Hwy 284 in Chilcoot. As you approach the lake, turn right onto the campground access road.*

Grizzly Campground has 53 sites (no hookups; RV limit 34 feet) along Lake Davis, a popular trout-fishing spot in the early fall. The campground has piped water, flush toilets, and a sanitary dump station for RVs. Each site is equipped with a fire ring and table. A general store and a boat ramp are nearby. *From Beckwourth, take Hwy 70 about 1 mile west and turn right (north) onto Grizzly Rd. Just past Lake Davis Rd, on the left, is the campground access road.*

Bucks Lake area

Haskins Valley Campground has 70 sites (no hookups; various RV lengths accommodated) along Bucks Lake. The alpine lake is stocked with trout, and the area often fills to capacity on summer weekends. Piped water and vault toilets are available, and each site is equipped with a fire ring and table. There is a boat ramp close by, as well as a general store, in the village of Bucks Lake. *From Quincy, take Bucks Lake Rd west 17 miles to Bucks Lake. Look for the campground access road on the right. Call the Pacific Gas and Electric Company (PG&E), (916) 923-7142, for information.*

Whitehorse Campground has 21 sites (no hookups; various RV lengths accommodated) near Bucks Lake. This campground serves as an overflow area when the more popular Haskins Valley Campground is full. Piped water and vault toilets are available, and each site is equipped with a fire ring and table. A general store is nearby in the village of Bucks Lake. *From Quincy, take Bucks Lake Rd west 15 miles. Look for the campground access road on the right about 2 miles before Bucks Lake. For more information, call the Mount Hough Ranger District, (530) 283-0555.*

Sundew Campground has 18 sites (no hookups; RV limit 37 feet) along the banks of Bucks Lake. Like Whitehorse, this campground also attracts those looking to avoid the crowds at Haskins Valley Campground. Piped water and vault toilets are available, and each site is equipped with a fire ring and table. A general store is nearby in the village of Bucks Lake.

From Quincy, take Bucks Lake Rd 10 miles west to Bucks Lake. Turn right on Bucks Lake Dam Rd and proceed to the campground on the right. Call the Mount Hough Ranger District, (530) 283-0555, for more information.

Lake Almanor Ranger District, (530) 258-2141

Lake Almanor Campground has 140 sites (no hookups; RV limit 32 feet) adjacent to Lake Almanor, one of the region's larger lakes. This campground is massive by local standards. A sanitary dump station is available for RVs. Piped water and vault toilets are available, and each site is equipped with a fire ring and table. *From Susanville, take Hwy 36 east past Chester. Turn left onto Hwy 89 and proceed about 2 miles to the campground access road on the left.*

Almanor Campground has 100 sites (no hookups; various RV lengths accommodated) next to to Lake Almanor. This campground has an adjacent boat ramp and therefore attracts a lot of boating activity. Those looking for solitude are advised to check out Last Chance Creek Campground instead. Piped water and vault toilets are available, and each site is equipped with a fire ring and table. *From Susanville, take Hwy 36 east past Chester. Turn left onto Hwy 89 and proceed about 2 miles to the campground access road on the left.*

Last Chance Creek Campground has 14 sites (no hookups; RV limit 37 feet) adjacent to the area where Last Chance Creek meets Lake Almanor, one of the region's larger lakes. This campground provides solitude for those who want to avoid the lake's busier campgrounds. Piped water and vault toilets are available, and each site is equipped with a fire ring and table. *From Susanville, take Hwy 36 east. Just before crossing the bridge to Chester, turn right on an unmarked road. After 5 miles, turn left and continue half a mile, then go right again. Proceed about 4 more miles along the lake to the campground ahead on the creek.*

Lake Oroville State Recreation Area, (530) 538-2200

Loafer Creek Campground contains 140 sites (no hookups; RV limit 42 feet) along the banks of Lake Oroville. The campground can get quite busy during the spring and early summer bass and trout season. Piped water, showers, and flush toilets are available. A sanitary disposal station is available for RVs and a boat ramp lies adjacent to the campground. Each site is equipped with a table and fire ring. *From Oroville, take Hwy 162 north 1.5 miles and turn left onto Loafer Creek Rd, just past Forestown Rd. Proceed to the campground ahead. For reservations, call state parks reservations at (800) 444-7275.*

Loafer Creek Group Camp contains 6 group tent sites (no RV access). Each site accommodates up to 25 people. Piped water is provided, along with showers and flush toilets. A boat ramp lies adjacent to the campground and each site is equipped with a table and fire ring. *See directions for Loafer Creek Campground, above. For reservations, call state parks reservations at (800) 444-7275.*

Bidwell Canyon Campground contains 70 sites (full hookups; RV limit 42 feet) along the banks of Lake Oroville. This campground is one of the few public campgrounds in Northern California with full hookups for RVs. That alone is enough to make it a major draw for RVers passing through; tent campers are advised to look for shelter at Loafer Creek. Piped water is provided, along with showers and flush toilets. A sanitary disposal station is available for RVs, and a boat ramp and marina lie adjacent to the campground. Each site is equipped with a table and fire ring. *From Oroville, take Hwy 162 north 8.5 miles and turn right onto the signed campground access road, just past Loafer Creek Rd. For reservations, call state parks reservations at (800) 444-7275.*

Mount Hough Ranger District, (530) 283-0555

Black Rock Campground has 22 sites (no hookups; various RV lengths accommodated) along the banks of Little Grass Valley Reservoir, plus another 10 walk-in sites for people with tents who are looking for a more remote area. The walk is a short distance from the campground parking area. Piped water and vault toilets are available, and each site is equipped with a fire ring and table. A boat ramp and a general store are nearby, and the campground has a sanitary dump station for RVs. *From Quincy, take Hwy 162 east for 8.5 miles and turn right onto Quincy/La Porte Rd. Proceed to the town of La Porte and turn right onto Little Grass Valley Rd. Continue on to the campground.*

Boulder Creek and **Lone Rock Campgrounds** have 73 and 84 sites, respectively (no hookups; various RV lengths accommodated), on the banks of Antelope Lake. This area of Plumas is remote and sought by those looking for a lakeside setting without many people. The campgrounds have piped water and vault toilets. Each site is equipped with a fire ring and table, and a general store is nearby. *From Susanville, head south on S Wheatherlow Rd. Turn right onto Richmond Rd, and after 4 miles, turn left onto Gold Run Rd. Continue for half a mile and then turn left onto Skyline Mountainway. Turn right onto Diamond Mountain Rd. Proceed past Bear Valley, and turn left onto Fruit Growers Rd. Proceed to the campgrounds at Antelope Lake.*

Little Beaver Campground has 122 sites (no hookups; various RV lengths accommodated) on Little Grass Valley Reservoir, due east of other campgrounds. This is the area's largest campground and can get quite busy. Piped water and flush toilets are available. Each site is equipped with a fire ring and table, and a boat ramp and a general store are nearby.

From Quincy, take Hwy 162 east for 8.5 miles and turn right onto Quincy/La Porte Rd. Past Black Rock Campground, proceed to the Little Beaver entrance. **Milsap Bar Campground** has 223 sites (no hookups; RV limit 37 feet) along the Middle Fork Feather River, a prime spot for whitewater rafting. The campground has no running water, so be sure to bring plenty of your own. Vault toilets are available, and each site is equipped with a fire ring and table. A general store is nearby in Merrimac. *From Quincy, take Bald Rock Rd a half mile south from Hwy 162 to Milsap Bar Rd. Turn east (left) and continue 7.5 miles to the campground entrance on the right side of the road.*

Running Deer Campground has 44 sites (no hookups; RV limit 21 feet) along the banks of Little Grass Valley Reservoir. Piped water and vault toilets are available, and each site is equipped with a fire ring and table. A boat ramp and a general store are nearby. *From Quincy, take Hwy 70 east and turn right onto Quincy/La Porte Rd. Proceed to La Porte and turn right onto Little Grass Valley Rd. Proceed to the campground.*

Skiing

Plumas-Eureka Ski Bowl, within Plumas-Eureka State Park southeast of Quincy, is a 300-acre volunteer-run ski park in the heart of Gold Rush country, with 75 percent well-groomed intermediate runs and 10 percent ungroomed advanced runs, the longest being 1 mile with a 650-foot vertical drop. Early folklore in these parts says gold miners began using this area as a snow-play destination way back in the mid-1800s, with boards of lumber strapped on in place of skis. There is no ski school here, nor are rentals available, so bring your own. In areas of the ski park where it will not interfere with downhill, **snowboards** are welcome, as are tubes and toboggans. There are poma lifts to the 2,650-foot advanced run and bunny tows to the 700-foot beginner's area. The season is December to April. Call the ski area, (530) 836-2380, for information and conditions. The park is 120 miles east of Truckee. Take Hwy 89 120 miles east to Hwy 70.

Madora Lake Trail and **Jamison Mine Trail,** north of Graeagle on Hwy 89, are ungroomed **cross-country ski** routes suitable for beginners, together offering 6 kilometers of ground between the two of them through a pretty forested area with a "white Christmas" sort of feeling. Groomed trails are found adjacent to the Plumas-Eureka Ski Bowl (see above), along with 15 kilometers of intermediate to advanced deep-wilderness trails. Plumas National Forest maintains a supreme network of ungroomed Nordic trails on Forest Service roads and trails near Bucks Summit, Snake Lake, and Antelope Lake. Call ahead to the Forest Service headquarters in Quincy for conditions; (530) 283-2050. Mountain Adventures of Nevada

City, (530) 274-0644, and Chico Sports Ltd, 240 Main St, Chico, (530) 894-1110, are two reputable **outfitters** in the region.

You'll also find some 100 miles of groomed **snowmobile trails** around Bucks Lake, with two staging areas. Ungroomed turf is plentiful as well. Stage from Four Trees, 10 miles south of the lake, or Bucks Summit, 3 miles south, on Bucks Lake Rd. Call the Forest Service headquarters in Quincy, (530) 283-2050, for trail conditions.

Rafting/Kayaking

Radical Class II and III rapids on the **Feather River's north fork**, with put-in sites all along Hwy 70, are moderate enough in normal water years for beginning rafters and kayakers between the Hwy 89 junction and Virgilia. Downstream of Virgilia through to Belden is an expert Class III run. Call the Feather River Ranger District, (530) 534-6500, for information and leads on any good **outfitters** leading trips down the Feather. As of this writing, it is a do-it-yourself proposition—meaning if you don't know what you're doing, don't.

Fishing/Boating

If you want to fit in around Plumas County, you have to park an aluminum fishing boat in your driveway and make sure you use it. There are hundreds of lakes and more than 1,000 miles of streams and rivers to keep anglers busy. Rainbow, brown, and brook trout are the main fare, but smallmouth and largemouth bass, king salmon, and catfish also are well established.

Lake Almanor, formed by a dam built in 1914, measures 13 miles in length and up to 6 miles in width. But it's relatively shallow, with its deepest points only about 60 feet, so the fish don't get as big as one might expect. Popular catches here are **bass, king salmon, rainbow** and **brown trout,** and **chinook.** The fishing season on this lake slows up in the winter with the drop in temperatures. During late spring and summer, however, the fish are biting in the lake's deeper areas during the day and in the shallower, warmer areas at night. The most popular fishing spots are along the dam and where the lake meets Baily Creek. Several marinas and tackle shops line the shore of the lake, and boaters have no trouble finding access. From Red Bluff, take Hwy 36 east 60 miles; the highway runs along the shore, so the lake is impossible to miss. There are two public boat launches: one on the south end of the lake near the dam, and another on the west side near Prattville. Knotty Pine Resort in Lake Almanor, (530) 596-3348, has fishing boats, ski boats, and pontoons for **rent.** Call the Almanor Ranger District, (530) 258-2141, for information.

Lake Oroville is shaped irregularly, with long arms and bays reaching outward and creating nearly 170 miles of shoreline. While at its widest the lake is only about 3 miles across, it is quite deep and encompasses over 15,000 acres of surface area. Largemouth and smallmouth, spotted, and red-eye **bass** were reintroduced to the area in the early 1980s; the spring and summer seasons hence attract a large contingency of serious bass anglers. During the spring, **bronzebacks** and **northern pike** are also a popular catch. Three boat ramps in the southern part of the lake make for easy access. Large camping areas are available (see Camping, above) in addition to a small number of boat campsites. There is also a boat ramp on the north shore of the lake, near Glory Hole. The lake has two full-service **marinas:** Bidwell Canyon at the south end and Lime Saddle at the north. From Oroville, take Hwy 162 north to the south shore of the lake. For more information, call the Lake Oroville State Recreation Area at (530) 538-2200. Huntington's Sportsman's Store, 601 Oro Dam Blvd, Oroville, (916) 534-8000, and McGrath's Fishing and Divers Supplies, 751 Oro Dam Blvd, West Oroville, (916) 533-8564, are two reputable **bait-and-tackle** dealers in the lake area, although there are many others.

Bucks Lake is quieter and more secluded than the larger Oroville and Almanor but still gets packed on nice summer weekends, with healthy **rainbow** and **salmon** fisheries, two full-service marinas with boat launch, and campgrounds along the 17-miles of shore. Despite the lake's small size, Jet-skiers and water-skiers enjoy it for its out-of-the-way feel. Take Bucks Lake Rd from Quincy direction to the lake access. Public ramps are right off the road when you reach the area. Call the marina at Bucks Lake, (916) 923-7142.

The middle fork of the **Feather River** offers the best **trout** fishing downstream of the lakes because much of it is unimpeded by major dams. Along the north fork of the Feather at Berry Creek and at Canyon Creek, fisheries are also quite productive. Yellow Creek in Humbug Valley is another good fishing destination in spring and summer. As always, check with the appropriate regulatory agencies if you are not up-to-date on current fishing laws, as they are constantly changing in this age of rampant endangered and threatened species listings. The state Department of Fish and Game office in Redding, (530) 225-2300, has an update, or you can try to decipher a free regulations handbook available at most licensing locations, including bait shops.

There are numerous **guides** working the Plumas County region, including Roger's Guide Service, (530) 258-2283; Out West Guide Service, (530) 283-2733; and Golden Eagle, (530) 836-4868.

Scenic Drives

Highway 70 through the Feather River canyon is a popular scenic route, with nice views of riparian terrain in the Sierra foothills region, along with a number of impressive man-made structures like the Pulga and Tobin railroad bridges, hydroelectric power houses on the river, and tunnels blasted through granite mountainsides. Begin the drive in Quincy and follow the highway southeast through the canyon. You will have the option of turning back and following the canyon out the way you came in, or joining US Hwy 395 (US 395) for a drive along the Sierra mountains to points north or south.

The scenic **Gold Lake Road** (Hwy 89), which starts several miles south of Graeagle and ends at Hwy 49 just east of Sierra City, is a spectacular 14-mile-long stretch of tarmac that zigzags through verdant valleys dotted with farms, historic buildings, deer, cows, and horses, and passes nearly a dozen sky-blue lakes (there are 30 lakes within the basin), most of them either visible from the highway or within easy walking distance. The Lakes Basin Campground, located right off the road, offers 24 sites available on a first-come, first-served basis; call the Mohawk ranger station for details at (530) 836-2575. In the winter, the basin closes and the unplowed road becomes a haven for snowmobilers.

Biking

A 10-mile paved trail for touring surrounds **Lake Almanor** (see Fishing/Boating, above), but country roads and byways traversing all of Plumas County are ripe for tar heads to rip it up. Call Bodfish Bicycles in Chester, (530) 258-2338, for equipment and tour suggestions. The ride to the top of Crystal Peak, with a 2,000-foot elevation gain over 10 miles on **Crystal Peak Route** (moderate; 20 miles round trip), is another popular mountain-bike trek. To reach Crystal Peak, take Hwy 70 east from Quincy through Feather River canyon to US 395, and then head north 5 miles to Constantina Rd; stage anywhere along the road, which is west of the highway.

Horseback Riding

Pack trips into the forest and wilderness areas, particularly on long multi-day hauls, are a pleasant way to enjoy the Plumas countryside. Numerous stables provide this service, chief among them Bucks Lake Stables, (530) 283-2532, and Gold Lake Stables, (530) 836-0940. Both stables do shorter, one-day and half-day rides as well.

Gold Panning

This being Gold Rush country, numerous mining clubs and companies offer recreational panning, which is a hoot for children learning about California history. The Rich Bar Mining Company west of Quincy on Hwy 70 leads **guided panning trips** along the Feather River. Call (530) 283-1730.

Adventure Calendar

Indian Valley Bike Tour, mid-May: *Greenville, (530) 284-6633.*
Round Valley Bluegill Derby, June: *(530) 284-6633.*
Sierra Summerfest Century Bike Ride, June: *Quincy, (530) 283-3490.*
Feather River Bull Riding Classic, August: *Quincy, (530) 283-6272.*

Attractions

The charming, tiny town of **Johnsville** was established by the Sierra Buttes Mining Company in the 1870s and is a California treasure. It was built for the gold miners and their families who didn't want to live next to the brothels and gambling centers in the nearby mining camps. Surrounded by the densely forested Plumas-Eureka State Park, Johnsville is a mix of old, abandoned miner's shacks and restored ones that serve as private residences. In between the historical buildings are some new homes, most built to meet the Johnsville Historical Society's strict design guidelines. As you drive down Main St, note the striking old barn-red Johnsville Hotel, now a private home, and the toylike firehouse across the street with a bell in its steeple and a horse-drawn fire wagon inside. Among the many wonderful artifacts at the **Plumas-Eureka State Park Museum** are a working blacksmith shop and a five-story 60-stamp mill where gold was processed. Across the street from the museum is the diminutive Moriarity House, a completely restored miner's home with furnishings and equipment used by the 10-member Moriarity family in 1901. For museum information, call (530) 836-2380.

About a quarter mile south of Blairsden is the picturesque little city of **Graeagle,** a former company town of the California Fruit Growers Exchange. Fruit Growers once had a lumber mill here that made wooden boxes for storing its produce, but the old mill is gone and the millpond has been converted into a family swimming area with grassy banks, gravel beaches, brown trout, and paddleboat rentals; in the winter, the pond is often a resting ground for flocks of Canada geese. Graeagle modestly bills itself the "Home of the World's Finest Golf Clubs" (there's a custom golf-club store here) and there are five golf courses in the area; for golfing information, call or stop by Williamson Realty in the Graeagle Village Center on Hwy 89, (530) 836-0112. The rest of the town consists of a little grocery store, a tearoom, an antique shop, and a handful of other small businesses—and most are located in former company houses painted barn-red with white trim. For more information and a brochure on the area, call the Plumas County Visitors Bureau at (800) 326-2247. If you're looking for a place to stay, numerous condos that double as vacation homes are available for rent; call (530) 836-0313 or (530) 836-2525 for rental information.

Oroville has been largely, and undeservedly, overlooked by tourists. This historic Gold Rush town (site of the second major gold discovery after Coloma) and center of a rich agricultural industry (cattle, citrus, nuts, olives) has lots for the traveler to investigate. The Oroville Chinese Temple and Garden was built in 1863 to serve the 10,000 Chinese who worked the mines here. It has an extensive collection of tapestries, costumes, and puppets used in Chinese opera, and its lovely gardens, planted exclusively with plants from China, offer a great place for meditation; 1500 Broderick St, (530) 538-2496. The 770-foot-tall Oroville Dam is the tallest earthen dam in the country, and Lake Oroville (see Inside Out sections, above) is a houseboaters' paradise, with 24 square miles of surface area and 167 miles of shoreline; to reach the dam and lake from Hwy 70, head east on Oroville Dam Blvd, (530) 534-2306.

Restaurants

BJ's Bar-B-Que & Deli ☆   Barbecue basics—beef, pork, and chicken—reign at this unassuming roadside spot. The ribs are thick, tender, meaty, and slathered with a tangy sweet sauce, and the baked beans and barbecued pork sandwiches are good, too. *3881 Hwy A-13 (Hamilton Branch), Lake Almanor; (530) 596-4210; $.*

Creekside Grill ☆☆☆   This fine restaurant has upped the ante in the Chester cuisine game with its fresh, bistrolike menu. This comfortable place with lots of natural wood and a great stone fireplace attracts tourists and locals alike. *278 Main St, Chester; (530) 258-1966; $–$$.*

Ernest and Jessie's Coffee Lounge and Tea Room ☆   Don't let the rather stark facade of this establishment deter you. If you're looking for a spot to have a cup of tea or an informal meal, this friendly place with its pretty furniture and colorful plants is perfect. *346 Main St, Chester; (530) 258-2238; $.*

Grizzly Grill Restaurant and Bar ☆☆☆   This place is a true pioneer in this neck of the woods: they've introduced baby greens, sun-dried tomatoes, and Asiago cheese into the meat-and-potato belt. Their light, woodsy, and relaxed restaurant is a fine spot to have dinner. *250 Bonta St (near the junction of Hwys 70 and 89), Blairsden; (530) 836-1300; $–$$.*

The Iron Door ☆☆   The Iron Door restaurant has occupied the century-old general store and post office building since 1961, and it hasn't changed much since then. The bar and dining room are decorated with antique farm equipment, and the main bill of fare is heavy with beef, lobster, and fowl. *5417 Main St (in Plumas-Eureka State Park, 5 miles W of Graeagle), Johnsville; (530) 836-2376; $$.*

Moon's   A popular local hangout since the mid-'70s, Moon's is a roomy, ramshackle, rustic wooden building. The strong scent of garlic and yeast is a dead giveaway to the house specialties: pizza and pasta. *497 Lawrence St (at Plymouth St), Quincy; (530) 283-0765; $.*

Morning Thunder Cafe ☆   With its stained-glass window, vine-laced trellis, and macramé plant holder, the Morning Thunder Cafe looks a bit like a hippie haven. Breakfast has always been the draw here. The restaurant also serves lunches of enormous hamburgers and freshly made soups. *557 Lawrence St (downtown), Quincy; (530) 283-1310; $.*

Mount Tomba Inn ☆☆   This place is a hoot. It's not only a restaurant, it's a shrine to John Wayne. Every dish is named after one of the Duke's movies (well, except for the nameless vegetarian plate). *Off Hwy 70 (½ mile E of town, 17 miles from both Quincy and Portola), Cromberg; (530) 836-2359; $–$$.*

Sardine Lake Resort ☆☆☆   The food here is good—perhaps the best in the Plumas-Eureka area—with a small but nicely rendered selection of meat, seafood, and poultry dishes. Restaurant reservations are a must. *At the end of Sardine Lake Rd at Lower Sardine Lake (off Gold Lake Rd, 2 miles N of Hwy 49), Lakes Basin Area; (530) 862-1196 (summer), (916) 645-8882 (winter); $$.*

Ten-Two ☆   Ten-Two is built right over a rushing flume, and although it's off the beaten track, many Quincy residents make the trek here for dinner. The menu offers sturdy standbys as well as fancier fare. *8270 Bucks Lake Rd (10.2 miles E of Quincy), Meadow Valley; (530) 283-1366; $$.*

Wilson's Camp Prattville & Carol's Cafe ☆   Certainly the oldest and funkiest place at Lake Almanor, Camp Prattville offers breakfast, lunch, and dinner in a small dining room crowded with knickknacks. The menu is prodigious, and breakfasts are served until 1pm. *2932 Almanor Dr W (on the lake's W shore), Lake Almanor; (530) 259-2464; $.*

Lodgings

The Bidwell House Bed and Breakfast Inn ☆☆☆   The beautifully restored Bidwell House has 14 guest rooms (most have private baths) furnished with antiques. A few have wood-burning stoves; 7 units are equipped with Jacuzzi tubs. A cottage that sleeps up to six people makes an ideal family retreat. *1 Main St (E end of town), Chester; (530) 258-3338; $$.*

The Cinnamon Teal ☆☆☆   From the carved pineapple finials on the four-poster beds to the vintage floral wallpapers and colorful quilts, no touch has been spared to make this bed and breakfast feel as homey as a visit to Grandma's—that is, if Grandma has excellent taste in fabrics. *227 Feather River Dr (near Main St), Chester; (530) 258-3993; $$.*

Dorado Inn ☆☆   All of the Dorado's 6 cottages (4 two-bedroom cottages and 2 one-room units) are near the water's edge, and they have fully equipped kitchens, private bathrooms, electric heat, and wood-burning stoves. Spectacular Mount Lassen and lake views can be seen from the cottage decks. *4379 Hwy 147 (on the lake's E shore), Lake Almanor; (530) 284-7790; $$.*

Gold Lake Lodge ☆   Gold Lake Lodge is in the heart of the Lakes Basin Area and within hiking distance of stunning High Sierra scenery, wildflower-filled meadows, and numerous lakes. Eleven tidy little cabins line the edge of a pretty meadow and a stand of old-growth red fir trees. *On Gold Lake Rd (7 miles S of Hwy 89), Lakes Basin Area; (530) 836-2350 (July 1 to Sept 30), (530) 836-2751 (Oct 1 to June 30); $$–$$$.*

Gray Eagle Lodge ☆☆☆   This resort's 18 refurbished cabins are set in the heart of spectacular scenery at the northern edge of the Lakes Basin Area. Ironically, there isn't a lake nearby, but you will see a lovely stream, a waterfall, and Sierra trails trimmed with wildflowers. *On Gold Lake Rd (5 miles S of Hwy 89), Lakes Basin Area; (530) 836-2511 or (800) 635-8778; $$.*

Lake Oroville Bed and Breakfast ☆☆☆   This B&B sits in lonely splendor on 40 acres high above the lake, with views in every direction. Built in 1992, the inn has 6 guest bedrooms. *240 Sunday Dr (from Hwy 70 take Oroville Dam Blvd/Hwy 162 E for 1.7 miles, turn right at Olive Hwy and continue for 13.5 miles, then turn left at Bell Ranch Rd, bear right, and drive a half mile to Sunday Dr), Berry Creek; (530) 589-0700 or (800) 455-LAKE; $$.*

Packer Lake Lodge ☆☆   What separates the 1926 Packer Lake Lodge from its neighbors is its combination of good food and—at a 6,218-foot elevation—great scenery. Accommodations are in 14 simply furnished cabins, ranging from rustic log cabins to three-room buildings. Each cabin has its own rowboat, too. *On Packer Lake Rd (off Sardine Lake Rd, 4½ miles*

N of Hwy 49), Lakes Basin Area; (530) 862-1221 (mid-May to Oct), (415) 921-5943 (Oct to mid-May); $$.

River Pines Resort ☆☆   Set alongside the Feather River, this resort is a popular family retreat that folks return to year after year. It's fun and affordable, and it offers enough activities to keep any vacationer entertained. The resort has 62 units, including 18 cabins. *8296 Hwy 89 (at the NE end of Graeagle, on the Feather River's S side), Graeagle; (530) 836-0313 or (800) 696-2551; $$.*

Salmon Lake Lodge ☆   The 10 tent cabins at this 1920s resort offer canvas roofs, rough-wood walls, built-in double beds and single bunks, mini-refrigerators, and electric stoves; you need to bring a sleeping bag, towels, dishes, cooking gear, an ice chest, and groceries (showers and a washing machine are available in a separate building). *At the end of Salmon Lake Rd (off Gold Lake Rd, 3 miles S of Gold Lake, 6 miles N of Hwy 49), Lakes Basin Area; (530) 842-3108 (summer), (530) 757-1825 (winter); $$.*

Twenty Mile House ☆☆☆   This two-story brick building is set amid 250 acres of wildflowers, evergreens, and wildlife, and 2 miles of the Feather River run through the inn's private property. The 1854 house has been carefully restored, and offers 3 guest bedrooms with private bathrooms. *On Old Cromberg Rd (1 mile S of Hwy 70, 7 miles N of Graeagle, 18 miles SE of Quincy), Cromberg; (530) 836-0375; $$.*

White Sulphur Springs Ranch Bed and Breakfast ☆   The ranch's large restored wood-frame house with a two-story porch offers 6 guest rooms decorated with period antiques. During the day, you can dive into the inn's huge 78-degree mineral-water pool. *On Hwy 89 (2 miles S of town), Clio; (530) 836-2387 or (800) 854-1797; $$.*

More Information

Beckwourth Ranger District: *(530) 836-2575.*
Feather River Ranger District: *(530) 534-6500.*
Forest service reservations system: *(800) 280-2267.*
Indian Valley Chamber of Commerce: *(530) 284-6633.*
Lake Oroville State Recreation Area: *(530) 538-2200.*
Mount Hough Ranger District: *(530) 283-0555.*
Plumas-Eureka State Park: *(530) 836-2380.*

Truckee
Region

Wilderness areas north and east of Lake Tahoe, including ski resorts along the Interstate 80 corridor and Donner Lake, the Truckee River, Donner Summit, and Donner Memorial State Park.

To fully take advantage of all there is to do in the Donner Summit/Truckee region of the Sierra Nevada, you need more footwear than Imelda Marcos. Ski boots for the slopes. Cross-country skis for the sno-parks. Snowshoes for the trails in winter, and hiking shoes for the trails in summer. Climbing shoes for the granite walls, and Tevas for fun in the water.

And finally, water-skis to take a power glide across the "gem of the Sierra," Donner Lake.

As much as the Truckee area has been looked upon for years as a backdoor entrance to the more popular Lake Tahoe, it is not without its own fine appointments—high mountain peaks and deep-cut glacial valleys, small dispersed lakes, and deep river canyons. These natural features have been spared the heavy use seen in the Lake Tahoe basin and Yosemite, partly because there haven't been enough facilities to entice outdoor enthusiasts to pull off Interstate 80. That, however, has begun to change.

The funky railroad and lumber communities that grew out of the Comstock silver mines and the Gold Rush have been trying to transform themselves into upscale winter resort destinations—and it's starting to work. The booming popularity of snow sports and the Truckee area's relative accessibility during inclement weather have drawn increasing numbers of ski visitors the past few years, and resorts are beginning to respond by investing big money in expanded facilities and modernized ski lifts.

In a way, it is almost a return to the area's lost beginnings. Sugar Bowl Ski Resort erected the state's very first ski lift way back in 1939 and for years served as a winter playground for Hollywood and big-money jet-setters. Then, after World War II, Tahoe began to establish itself as the premier ski destination on the West Coast. When the 1960 Winter Olympics came to Tahoe at Squaw Valley, however, a new momentum caught on for the Truckee region to reap some of the benefits. With improved resorts and more winter skiers beginning to explore, it's only a matter of time before the secret places tucked within the northern reaches of Tahoe National Forest are discovered too. For now, however, the outdoors scene in the Donner Summit and Truckee area still languishes in the shadows of the big blue lake to the south—and that means it's still possible to wear out all those shoes while enjoying a little bit of privacy.

Getting There

The most direct access to the Truckee/Donner area is along Interstate 80 west from Reno or east from the Sacramento Valley—often a more sure bet when US Highway 50 (US 50) into the Tahoe Basin is affected by heavy snowfall. Interstate 80 is less prone to closures and also is an easier drive, with a reasonably direct connection to the Tahoe Basin through the Truckee River canyon along Highway 28. During winter, always observe road restrictions related to snow; chains are advised in moderate to heavy snowfall. For current road conditions, call the state Department of Transportation, (800) 427-ROAD (7623). Check on the Internet in advance at www.dot.ca.gov/hq/road-info/. For help planning a winter visit, call Ski Lake Tahoe at (800) 588-SNOW or go to www.SkiLakeTahoe.com on the Web. The Tahoe National Forest Truckee Ranger District, 10342 Highway 89 North, Truckee, (530) 587-3558, is the main information center for area wilderness and forestlands, including public sno-parks. Also contact the Foresthill Ranger District, 22830 Foresthill Road, Foresthill, (530) 367-2224, and the Nevada City Ranger District, 631 Coyote Street, Nevada City, (530) 265-4531.

Adjoining Areas

NORTH: **Plumas Region**

SOUTH: **Tahoe Basin**

WEST: **Northern Gold Rush Country**

inside out

Downhill Skiing/Snowboarding

Even before you learn to get on skis and start tearing up the downhill runs, it is first necessary to learn how to get behind the wheel of a car and drive on mountain highways in winter conditions without causing an accident. So with any trip to the ski areas around Donner Summit and Truckee, the first challenge is getting there. Because I-80 is an easier drive than US 50, winter travelers headed to the Donner Summit and Truckee areas generally have a better time of it than those headed for Tahoe. Winter sports enthusiasts will find plenty of downhill, Nordic, and snowboarding action here, despite the lower billing the area receives, compared to Tahoe. During winter travel, always observe road restrictions related to snow; chains are advised in moderate to heavy snowfall. For current **road conditions,** call the state Department of Transportation, (800) 427-ROAD (7623). Check on the Internet in advance at www.dot.ca.gov/hq/roadinfo/. For help planning a winter visit, call Ski Lake Tahoe at (800) 588-SNOW or go to www.SkiLakeTahoe.com on the Web.

A favorite **snowboarding** and snow-play area is just west of the Truckee Bridge; others are Granlibakken Ski Area, Mount Rose, and Northstar-at-Tahoe (see Tahoe Basin chapter).

A plethora of ski outfitters in the greater Truckee area, outside the main resorts, offer all varieties of **equipment for rent.** Three reputable places are Dave's Ski Shop, 10200 Donner Pass Rd, Truckee, (530) 582-0900; Truckee Board Works, 11921 Pine Forest Rd, Truckee, (530) 587-0603; and Paco's Truckee Bike & Ski, 11200 Donner Pass Rd, Truckee, (530) 587-5561.

Sugar Bowl Ski Resort

Marketing people will have you believe that a major renovation and expansion alone has helped bring nostalgic Sugar Bowl—where the first ski lift in the state was constructed in 1939—to the attention of California's burgeoning supply of downhill weekend warriors. And they may be partly right. We think, however, it must also have something to do with the resort's location away from the bumper-to-bumper US 50 corridor, which on ski weekends and holidays can make a trip to the Tahoe region more of a road-rage festival than a serene winter getaway. Sugar Bowl, you see, is closer to the Bay Area than any of the other major resorts and away from the Tahoe madness. The facility really has spruced up in the past few years, however. In 1996, the resort opened 400 new acres of intermediate trails, 2 high-speed lifts, and an entire new mountain—8,238-foot **Mount Judah.** But it also brought in cars with construction of a spiffy new parking lot. (Before, you could enter the ski area only by gondola.)

It may not excite those looking to re-create the "agony of defeat" ski-crash scene from the *Wide World of Sports* trailer, but our favorite Sugar Bowl run is the **Crow-Traverse,** via the Crow's Nest Lift, down the western slopes of Mount Disney, which in a little over 2 miles of groomed, moderate-sloped trail runs the summit ridge of the mountain, enters a pretty wooded area, spills into a wide-open meadow, and takes a final leg through the forest to the base. The longest run is **Lakeview,** on the Silver Belt line. In total, there are 80 miles of trail, 40 percent groomed, with snowmaking on 13 percent. Seventeen percent of runs are rated for beginners, 43 percent are intermediate, and 40 percent are advanced. There are 4 quad lifts, 5 doubles, 2 surface lifts, and 1 gondola. Lodgings, restaurants, rentals, and a ski school are on-site, but the main attraction away from the slopes is the historic Sugar Bowl Lodge, designed by noted architect William Wurster and the winter playground for the Hollywood elite of the 1940s and '50s. It was later overshadowed by the more modern developments that cropped up around the Tahoe Basin, though there may have also been some reluctance by the original investors, who included Walt Disney, to make it more inviting to the masses. To reach the resort from Truckee, take I-80 west 14 miles to the Soda Springs/Norden exit, then head south across the freeway and drive 3 miles to the gondola exit on the right side of the road. The new drive-in entrance is up another quarter mile. For a **snow report** at Sugar Bowl, call (530) 426-1111. To reach the resort, call is (530) 426-9000, or go to www.skisugarbowl.com on the Web. The season is typically November to April.

Donner Ski Ranch

Inexperienced skiers who don't want to look foolish in front of the fully equipped are drawn to this 350-acre ski complex just a mile east of Sugar Bowl (see above). It has 40 runs over a 720-foot vertical drop to a base elevation of 7,031 feet, with snowmaking and some groomed and some packed powder. Fifty percent of trails are rated intermediate, with 25 percent each beginner and advanced. The longest run is 1 mile long. For many, the drawback to Donner, aside from its size and lower elevation, is that it has just 4 chair lifts. Nordic downhill skiing lessons are offered on site, as are rentals. While there is no lodge here, there is RV parking. For information and a snow report, call (530) 426-3635.

Soda Springs

This 200-acre ski area, under the same management as at Boreal (see below), is open weekends (Friday to Monday) and holidays only, and rented out to private parties during the remainder of the week. There are 16 runs with a 652-foot vertical drop to a base elevation of 6,700 feet. The trails are ranked 30 percent beginner, 50 percent intermediate, and 20 percent advanced, and are mostly groomed, with no snowmaking on-site. A ski school, ski rentals, and private lessons are available, as is overnight RV camping. There is no lodge. The ski area is 2 miles west of Sugar Bowl on Soda Springs Rd; from Truckee, take I-80 west 14 miles to the Norden/Soda Springs exit. The typical season is from late November to mid-April. Call (530) 426-3666 for information, (530) 426-3663 for a snow report.

Boreal

Also in the process of an expansion, Boreal has long been a favorite stopover for skiers from the San Francisco Bay Area who don't want to contend with frustrating road closures and long traffic jams getting into the Lake Tahoe basin. There are 380 acres containing 41 runs, 30 percent ranked beginner, 55 percent intermediate, and 15 percent advanced. The base elevation is 7,200 feet with a vertical drop of 600 feet, and a 1-mile run is the longest. There are 10 chair lifts and 1 quad, with a ski school, ski rentals, day lodging, and RV parking area on-site. The resort is off I-80 at Castle Peak 10 miles west of Truckee, near both Soda Springs and Royal Gorge. The season is November to April. For information and a snow report, call (530) 426-3666.

Tahoe Donner

This 120-acre ski area with no tree runs and no unpacked, ungroomed trails is a perfect place to learn how to ski without feeling like an idiot. Half the trails are ranked beginner and half ranked intermediate. More advanced skiers may want to go elsewhere. There are 11 runs with a vertical drop of 600 feet from the 7,350-foot summit. There's also a ski school on-site, rentals, a day lodge, and RV parking. The ski area is 5 miles west of Truckee. Take I-80 to Hwy 89 north, then head west on Donner Pass Rd to the entrance. Open December to April. Call (530) 587-9400 for information and a snow report.

Cross-Country Skiing

Royal Gorge at Soda Springs resort (see Downhill Skiing/Snowboarding, above), has 90 trails covering 120 kilometers, groomed and ready, with warming shacks, a lodge accessible only by skis, and all the amenities you would expect in an Aspen resort setting. Royal Gorge covers 7,000 acres of gently sloping wilderness descending toward the American River canyon. The resort is between the Soda downhill area and Boreal (see Downhill Skiing/Snowboarding, above). Call (530) 426-3871 for a **snow report** and other information.

The **Tahoe Donner Cross-Country Ski Area** is located next to the Tahoe Donner alpine ski resort (see Downhill Skiing/Snowboarding, above). There are 24 kilometers of groomed trails evenly divided among the three skill levels.

Donner Memorial State Park has a little less than 2 kilometers of beginner and intermediate trails. From Truckee, travel south on Hwy 89 about 2 miles to the park on your right. North of I-80 at **Castle Peak**, an expansive public outdoor recreation area, a little under 2 kilometers of ungroomed trail and a big cross-country ski area are available. Trails and courses are evenly divided among skill levels.

Northstar-at-Tahoe (see Tahoe Basin chapter) has 15 kilometers miles of groomed trails at its cross-country center at mid-mountain, primarily beginner and intermediate runs. There is also a Nordic ski clinic at the center. Call (530) 562-1010 for information.

Snowmobiling

Snowmobilers will find more than 100 miles of marked snowmobile trails between Hwy 89 and **Bald Ridge Loop**, Yuba Pass, and Webber Lake within the Tahoe National Forest. There is also an expansive sno-park area with snowmobile runs 5 miles east of Donner Ski Ranch (see Downhill Skiing/Snowboarding, above), off I-80 at **Castle Peak**, a large public snow-play area maintained by the Forest Service. Eagle Ridge Snowmobile Outfitters, (530) 546-8667, on Little Truckee Summit, has forest **tours** throughout the Donner region.

Hiking/Backpacking

The vast uplands surrounded the Truckee area, most within Tahoe National Forest, are a winter wonderland during the snow season but also a summertime play area, with good lake access and a well-developed trail system through glacial valleys and expansive (but not untouched) forests. As with most national forests and wilderness areas, camping is allowed just about anywhere the ground is flat enough to pitch a tent, but **backcountry permits** are required for any use of fire and for use of wilderness areas. Nearly 100 miles of the **Pacific Crest Trail** are found in the Tahoe wilderness areas, stretching from Donner Summit near Truckee to the Mokelumne Wilderness boundary near Caples Lake on Hwy 88. The Pacific Crest Trail Association, 1350 Castle Rock Rd, Walnut Creek, CA 94598, (925) 939-6111, has maps and information on access points and hiking routes for this and all sections of the trail. The best **trail maps** of the national forest areas are available directly from the Forest Service; write US Forest Service Information, Room 521, 630 Sansome St, San

Francisco, CA 94111. (See the primer at the beginning of this book for more explicit ordering instructions.) Always check on **trail conditions** before leaving on extending backcountry treks; the Truckee Ranger District, (530) 587-3558, has the most up-to-date information. In normal years, the high country is generally inaccessible until early summer because of snow cover.

The short, easy walk to Lola Montez Lake on **Lola Montez Lake Trail** (easy; 3 miles round trip) used to be a best-kept secret among the Donner/Truckee area faithful. What could be more wonderful than a secluded, quiet, placid lake nobody knew about that you can reach with just a short walk? Alas, you'll probably find others there these days, but this is still the kind of setting people will scramble over 7,000-foot mountains in the most far-flung national forests to find, so don't complain too much. The trail is actually a walking path that follows two dirt road sections and a stream bed up to the lake. To find the trailhead, take I-80 west from Truckee for 7 miles, and exit at Soda Springs. Staying on the north side of the highway, drive east on the frontage road a little less than half a mile to the trailhead. Call the Truckee Ranger District, (530) 587-3558, for more information.

Another nice hike-in lake—often less crowded because it involves a longer walk, but still reasonably easy to get to—is at **Loch Leven Lakes Trail** (moderate; 7 miles round trip to the third lake), a sometimes steep trek through a Douglas fir forest that descends into a pretty, glaciated valley occupied by a string of lakes with decent fishing and (when the weather is particularly warm) good swimming holes as well. This hike is of variable length and difficulty depending how far into the valley you want to venture. Our advice is to skip the first lake, inviting as it looks, and continue to the third—more work, but a quieter outdoor experience since many don't resist the temptation to jump in at the first body of water they see. To find the trailhead, take I-80 west from Truckee for about 20 miles, and exit at Big Bend. Just past the highway exit, watch for the Big Bend Visitor Center. The trailhead is a little less than a mile east of the center. For information, call the Truckee Ranger District, (530) 587-3558.

For an even more rewarding payoff, **Summit Lake Trail** (easy; 4 miles round trip), a tributary of the Pacific Crest Trail just west of I-80, takes you over a ridge and down into the Summit Lake basin to a lovely fishing and swimming spot in the shadows of the 9,103-foot Castle Peak to the northwest. Continue on **Warren Lake Trail** (easy; 12 miles round trip, Summit Lake included) over another forested ridge in the Castle Peak foothills, and descend into the Warren Lake basin—bigger, better, and more secluded. This hike is long enough that you should plan it as an overnighter or a weekend stay rather than trying to complete it as a day trip. Both hikes begin at the Pacific Crest Trail staging area just past the Castle Peak/Boreal exit from I-80 about 7 miles west of Truckee. The Summit Lake Trail intersection with Pacific Crest is 1 mile out from the staging area. For information, call the Truckee Ranger District, (530) 587-3558.

The leg of **Pacific Crest Trail** extending from Donner Pass south to the Lake Tahoe basin at Barker Pass (difficult; 32 miles one way) is perhaps the best opportunity in the Truckee region to get a good overview of the glaciated valleys, deep river canyons, sparkling alpine lakes, and wildflower meadows that dominate the landscape here. The trail leg passes over two Truckee region peaks—the 8,243-foot Mount Judah, over looking Donner Lake, and 8,683-foot Anderson Peak, overlooking Goose Meadows and the Truckee River canyon. The trail then enters the Granite Peak Wilderness as it moves toward the Tahoe Basin (see Tahoe Basin chapter). Even if you have no desire to hike all the way from Canada to Mexico, biting off a portion of this trek is a crowning achievement for any visit to the Truckee region. The hike to **Mount Judah** alone, for example, is a 6.4-mile round trip with moderately difficult grades—doable in half a day. To reach the staging area, take I-80 west 5 miles from Truckee and exit the highway at Donner Pass. Look for a parking area south of the highway. You can also take a short nature walk from this trailhead along the **Glacier Meadow Loop Trail** (easy; 0.5 mile round trip), an interpretive trail with signs explaining how the granite-walled valleys were formed by glaciers moving through the Western Hemisphere. Contact the Truckee Ranger District, (530) 587-3558.

Camping

The campgrounds in national forestlands north and east of Lake Tahoe are abundant, and many provide a truer wilderness experience than the crowded, busy Tahoe Basin can offer during the height of winter and summer sports activity. Camping on public grounds within the national forests is allowed anywhere you choose to set up, although **dispersed camping** must be a suitable distance from developed campgrounds and permits are required for any use of fire. The best maps are available directly from the Forest Service. Write US Forest Service Information, Room 521, 630 Sansome St, San Francisco, CA 94111. (See the primer at the beginning of this book for more explicit ordering instructions.) Periodic road closures are unavoidable. Check with the relevant ranger station for updated **road conditions** before deciding on a site located deep within the forest. Roads are not maintained for vehicles with low ground clearance. The Forest Service is currently reviewing its **reservations** and fees policies for this area, but generally no reservations are taken for any of the campgrounds listed below. Stays are limited to 14 days. Call the Forest Service reservations system at (800) 280-2267, or individual ranger stations for campsite availability information and reservations where applicable. In the listings below, campgrounds are run by the Forest Service unless otherwise noted.

Truckee Ranger District, (530) 587-3558

Lower Little Truckee Camp has 15 sites (no hookups; RV limit 21 feet) along the Little Truckee River at an elevation of roughly 6,000 feet. The campground is quiet compared to its neighbor, Upper Little Truckee Camp (see below). Piped water and vault toilets are available, and each site has a table and fire grill. There is a general store north in Sierraville. *From Truckee, take Hwy 89 north, cross Little Truckee River, and look for the campground on the left.*

Upper Little Truckee Camp contains 25 sites (no hookups; RV limit 21 feet) along the Little Truckee River at an elevation of roughly 6,000 feet. The campground is a bit busier than Lower Little Truckee Camp (see above) and has piped water and vault toilets. Each site has a table and fire grill. There is a general store north in Sierraville. *From Truckee, take Hwy 89 north, cross Little Truckee River, and look for the campground on the left past Lower Little Truckee Camp.*

Cold Creek Campground contains 13 sites (no hookups; RV limit 21 feet) just north of the Little Truckee River, also at an elevation of roughly 6,000 feet. The campground is quiet and has piped water and vault toilets. Each site has a table and fire grill. There is a general store a few miles north in Sierraville. *From Truckee, take Hwy 89 north, cross Little Truckee River, pass Rioe Canyon, and look for the campground on the left.*

Lakeside Campground has 30 sites (no hookups; RV limit 31 feet) along the Prosser Creek Reservoir at an elevation of roughly 6,000 feet. The quiet campground and attracts visitors who enjoy canoeing and fishing. Piped water and vault toilets are available, and each site has a table and fire grill. There is a general store a few miles west in Hobart Mills. *From Truckee, take Hwy 89 north 3 miles. Turn right toward Hobart Mills at the campground entrance and proceed to the campground.*

Logger Campground contains 252 sites (no hookups; RV limit 38 feet) along the banks of Stampede Reservoir. This beautiful alpine lake is a popular spot for fishing, swimming, and boating. The campground can get quite busy, and those who prefer quieter settings are advised to stay at Lakeside Campground (see above), a few miles west. Piped water, flush toilets, showers, and a dump station for RVs are available. There's a general store to the west in Hobart Mills. *From Truckee, travel east on I-80 to the Boca/Hirschdale exit. Head north on Stampede Dam Rd. Turn left onto Dog Valley Rd at Stampede Reservoir. Proceed to the campground. Call the US*

Bureau of Land Management (BLM), (530) 582-0120.

Emigrant Group Camp contains 4 group sites (no hookups; RV limit 31 feet). Two of the sites accommodate up to 25 people; the other two up to 55. Set along the banks of Stampede Reservoir, a beautiful alpine lake popular for fishing, swimming, and boating, the campground has piped water and flush toilets. A general store lies to the west in Hobart Mills. *From Truckee, travel east on I-80 to the Boca/Hirschdale exit. Head north on Stampede Dam Rd. Turn left onto Dog Valley Rd at Stampede Reservoir. Proceed to the campground. Call the BLM, (530) 582-0120.*

Davies Creek Campground has 10 sites (no hookups; various RV lengths accommodated) about half a mile from Stampede Reservoir, a popular spot for fishing, swimming, and boating. The primitive campground is quiet due to its lack of amenities. There is no running water, so be sure to bring plenty of your own. Pit toilets are nearby. *From Truckee, travel east on I-80 to the Boca/Hirschdale exit. Head north on Stampede Dam Rd. Turn left onto County Rd S460 at Stampede Reservoir's northeast corner. Proceed to the campground. Call the BLM, (530) 582-0120.*

Boca Rest Camp contains 29 sites (no hookups; RV limit 21 feet) adjacent to Boca Reservoir. This alpine lake is a popular spot for fishing, swimming, and boating during the spring when water levels are at their highest. Piped water, vault toilets, tables, and fire grills are provided. A general store is nearby in Truckee. *From Truckee, travel east on I-80 to the Boca/Hirschdale exit. Head north on Stampede Dam Rd. Proceed to the campground on the right. Call the BLM, (530) 582-0120.*

Boca Springs Campground has 16 sites (no hookups; RV limit 15 feet) in a rustic setting near Boca Reservoir. Piped water, vault toilets, tables, and fire grills are provided. A general store is nearby in Truckee. *From Truckee, travel east on I-80 to the Boca/Hirschdale exit. Head north on Stampede Dam Rd and, after a quarter mile, turn right on County Rd 73 and continue another mile to the campground. Call the BLM, (530) 582-0120.*

Donner Memorial State Park Campground has 150 sites (no hookups; RV limit 31 feet) adjacent to Donner Lake, near the ominous site where the Donner party, traveling west in the 1800s, tragically fell victim to an unexpected early winter. The lake is a popular boating site, particularly for sailboats. Piped water, flush toilets, showers, tables, and fire grills are provided. A general store is nearby in Truckee. *From Truckee, travel west on I-80 to the Donner Memorial State Park exit. Proceed to the park and the campground beyond. Call the park directly at (530) 582-7892; for reservations, call the state reservations system, (800) 444-7275.*

Granite Flat Campground has 75 sites (no hookups; RV limit 31 feet) near Donner Memorial State Park. The campground serves as an overflow area when the Donner Memorial State Park Campground (see above) reaches capacity. The campsites near the highway can be a bit noisy, so it is advised to stay at the sites deeper in. Piped water, vault toilets, tables, and fire grills are provided. A general store is nearby in Truckee. *From Truckee, travel south on Hwy 89 about 2 miles to the campground on your right.*

Goose Meadows Camp has 26 sites (no hookups; RV limit 31 feet) along the banks of the Truckee River. The campground serves as an overflow area when the area's more popular campgrounds reach capacity. It also attracts visitors who like fishing in the Truckee River. The campground is on the noisy side as the highway is close by. Well water, vault toilets, tables, and fire rings are provided. A general store is nearby in Truckee. *From Truckee, travel south on Hwy 89 about 4 miles to the campground on your left.*

Silver Creek Campground contains 30 sites (no hookups; RV limit 38 feet) near the banks of the Truckee River. The campground serves as an overflow area when the more popular campgrounds, closer to Lake Tahoe, reach capacity. The campground is on the noisy side, as the highway is close by; however, the fishing in the Truckee River is excellent. Well water and vault toilets are available. Tables and fire rings are provided. A general store is to the north in Truckee. *From Truckee, travel south on Hwy 89 about 7 miles to the campground on your left.*

Foresthill Ranger District, (530) 367-2224

French Meadows Campground contains 73 sites (no hookups; RV limit 36 feet) along French Meadows Reservoir, a popular spot for boating and fishing. A boat ramp lies nearby. This campground is enormous by area standards. Piped water, vault toilets, tables, and fire rings are provided. *From Westville, take Forest Hill Rd east, past Sailor Flat. About 1.5 miles past Sunflower Hill, turn right onto the access road for French Meadows Reservoir. Proceed to the campground on the northeast side of the reservoir.*

Lewis Campground contains 40 sites (no hookups; RV limit 36 feet) across the highway from French Meadows Reservoir. This campground serves as an overflow area for the more popular French Meadows Campground (see above). Piped water, vault toilets, tables, and fire rings are provided. *From Westville, take Forest Hill Rd east, past Sailor Flat. About 1.5 miles past Sunflower Hill, turn right onto the access road for French Meadows Reservoir. Proceed to the campground on the northeast side of the reservoir.*

Ahart Campground contains 14 sites (no hookups; RV limit 21 feet) near French Meadows Reservoir. This campground is popular with visitors to the French Meadows area who are looking to avoid crowds. There is no running water in the campground, so bring plenty of your own. Vault toilets are provided, along with tables and fire rings. *From Westville,* *take Forest Hill Rd east, past Sailor Flat. About 1.5 miles past Sunflower Hill, turn right onto the access road for French Meadows Reservoir. Proceed to the campground on the northeast side of the reservoir.*

Nevada City Ranger District, (530) 265-4531

Lodgepole Camp contains 20 sites (no hookups; RV limit 21 feet) along Lake Valley Reservoir. The lake is a popular canoeing spot, and several good hiking trails traverse the area. Piped water, vault toilets, tables, and fire rings are provided, and a boat ramp is nearby. *From Emigrant Camp, take I-80 east about 2.5 miles and exit south onto Lake Valley Rd. Proceed about 1 mile and veer right onto Sky Mountain Rd. Proceed a few hundred feet to the campground. Call Pacific Gas and Electric Company (PG&E), (916) 923-7142.*

Lake Spaulding Campground contains 27 sites (no hookups; RV limit 21 feet) along Lake Spaulding, a tiny granite-enclosed alpine lake. The cobalt-blue water makes this lake picturesque and attractive to visitors. Piped water, vault toilets, tables, and fire rings are provided, and a boat ramp is nearby. *From Emigrant Camp, take I-80 east and exit onto Hwy 20 at Yuba. Proceed 2 miles and turn right onto Lake Spaulding Rd. Proceed a few hundred feet to the campground. Call PG&E, (916) 923-7142.*

Indian Springs Campground contains 35 sites (no hookups; RV limit 29 feet) along the banks of the South Yuba River. The campground is most popular during the spring and early summer when the river flow is at its strongest. The campground has piped water and vault toilets. Tables and fire rings are provided. *From Emigrant Camp, take I-80 east, past Yuba. Exit onto Eagle Lakes Rd and proceed to the campground about a mile and a half ahead.*

Woodchuck Campground contains 10 sites (no hookups; RV limit 16 feet) along the banks of Rattlesnake Creek. Most enjoyable during the spring and early summer when the creek flows at its strongest, the campground attracts visitors who are looking for a primitive camping experience and solitude. There is no running water, but vault toilets are provided, along with tables and fire rings. *From Emigrant Camp, take I-80 east, past Yuba. Exit north onto Fordyce Rd and proceed to the campground about 2 miles ahead.*

Big Bend Campground contains 16 sites (no hookups; RV limit 16 feet) along the banks of the South Yuba River. The campground is most popular during the spring and early summer when the river flow is at its strongest. The campground has piped water and vault toilets. Tables and fire rings are provided. *From Emigrant Camp, take I-80 east, to Cisco Grove. Exit south onto Hampshire Rocks Rd. Proceed to the campground ahead.*

North Fork Campground contains 18 sites (no hookups; RV limit 16 feet) along the banks of the North Fork American River. The campground is little known and a good place to escape to if solitude is what you are looking for. The river's flow diminishes rapidly as the summer season progresses. The campground has piped water and vault toilets. Tables and fire rings are provided. *From Emigrant Camp, exit I-80 south onto Emigrant Gap Rd. Proceed about 6 miles (the road name changes to Texas Hill Rd) to the campground.*

Bowman Lake area

Canyon Creek Camp contains 21 tent sites (no RV access) along the banks of Canyon Creek and near Lake Faucherie. The area attracts an eclectic array of travelers since it's centrally located among several trailheads, a lake, and river. There is no running water at the campground, so be sure to bring plenty of your own. Vault toilets, fire grills, and tables are provided. *From Marsh Mill, take Meadow Lake Rd, east. Veer left at the fork in the road and continue to Bowman Lake. Just past Bowman Lake, turn right toward Sawmill and Faucherie Lakes. Proceed about 2 miles to the campground on the right. Call Nevada City Ranger District, (530) 265-4531.*

Jackson Creek Camp contains 15 tent sites (no RV access) along the banks of Jackson Creek and near Bowman Lake. The campground is sought by those looking for a primitive camping experience and solitude. There is no running water at the campground, so be sure to bring plenty of your own. Vault toilets, fire grills, and tables are provided. *From Marsh Mill, take Meadow Lake Rd, east. Veer left at the fork in the road and continue to Bowman Lake. Proceed to the campground on the left, about 1 mile past Bowman Lake. Call Nevada City Ranger District, (530) 265-4531.*

Bowman Lake Campground contains 9 tent sites (no RV access) along Bowman Lake at an altitude of roughly 5,500 feet. The granite-enclosed alpine lake is popular for canoeing and fishing. There is no running water at the campground, so be sure to bring plenty of your own. Vault toilets, fire grills, and tables are provided. *From Marsh Mill, take Meadow Lake Rd, east. Veer left at the fork in the road and continue Bowman Lake. Upon reaching the lake, just past Bowman Rd, look for the campground on the right. Call Nevada City Ranger District, (530) 265-4531.*

Woodcamp Campground contains 10 sites (no hookups; RV limit 24 feet) near Jackson Meadow Reservoir. The campground is adjacent to a boat ramp and attracts a crowd looking for boating and fishing activity. Piped water, vault toilets, tables, and fire rings are provided, and there's a general store to the east in Truckee. *From Marsh Mill, take Meadow Lake Rd, east. Veer left at the fork in the road and continue past Bowman Lake toward Jackson Meadow Reservoir. Just before the reservoir, turn right onto the campground access road. Contact the BLM, (530) 582-0120.*

Fir Top Campground contains 13 sites (no hookups; RV limit 24 feet) adjacent to Jackson Meadow Reservoir, a popular spot for boating and fishing. A boat ramp lies about 1 mile away in Woodcamp. Piped water, vault toilets, tables, and fire rings are provided, and a general store is to the east in Truckee. *From Marsh Mill, take Meadow Lake Rd, east. Veer left at the fork in the road and continue past Bowman Lake toward Jackson Meadow Reservoir. Just before the reservoir, turn right onto the campground access road. Contact the BLM, (530) 582-0120.*

Pass Creek Campground contains 15 sites (no hookups; RV limit 24 feet) near Jackson Meadow Reservoir. The campground is adjacent to a boat ramp and attracts a crowd looking for boating and fishing. Piped water, vault toilets, tables, and fire rings are provided, along with a sanitary dump station for RVs. A general store is to the east in Truckee. *From Marsh Mill, take Meadow Lake Rd, east. Veer left at the fork in the road and continue past Bowman Lake toward Jackson Meadow Reservoir. Cross the reservoir dam and County Rd 8301. Turn right onto the campground access road near the eastern shore of the lake. Contact the BLM, (530) 582-0120.*

East Meadow Campground contains 48 sites (no hookups; RV limit 45 feet) near Jackson Meadow Reservoir. This campground is particularly popular with RV users, as most of the area's campgrounds cannot comfortably accommodate larger RVs. Piped water, flush toilets, tables, and fire rings are provided, and a general store is to the east in Truckee. *From Marsh Mill, take Meadow Lake Rd, east. Veer left at the fork in the road and continue past Bowman Lake toward Jackson Meadow Reservoir. Cross the reservoir dam and County Rd 8301. Turn right onto the campground access road near the eastern shore of the lake. Contact the BLM, (530) 582-0120.*

Rafting/Kayaking

The **Truckee River** has 10 miles of Class III rapids, north of Truckee, that are perfect for those with intermediate skills who want to see the excitement of a wild river canyon without being tossed about too badly. The section of the Truckee north of Tahoe City has a long stretch that is calm enough for **tubing** and other soft-core water play, including novice rafting, so long as releases, snowmelt, and weather aren't out of the ordinary. The run stretches from the Hwy 28/89 interchange to the River Ranch Resort. The best put-in spots are along Hwy 89, at Rampant and at numerous turnouts from the highway in the 5 miles out of Tahoe City. Check with Fanny Bridge Raft Rentals in Tahoe City, (530) 581-0123.

Another relatively calm river when there isn't abnormal weather is along the **east fork of the Carson River** along the Hwy 89 corridor east of Markleeville, with mostly Class II and a few Class III rapids. Take Hwy 89 for 2 miles west of Markleeville to Hangman's Bridge and beyond Mogul

Canyon for river access. The **middle and south forks of the American River** (see Northern and Southern Gold Rush Country chapters) are also favorites, with good whitewater runs upstream of Folsom Lake, including some radical Class IV and V runs.

Fishing/Boating

Year-round fishing for **rainbow** and **Mackinaw trout** and **kokanee salmon** is the main draw at **Donner Lake,** known as the "gem of the Sierra" because of the way its mirrored glassy surface (on still summer mornings, that is) reflects the sky and surrounding ridgeline. The lake can, however, become quite crowded, with anglers lined up elbow to elbow on nice spring and summer days, partly because of the ease with which they can get to the lake, 26 miles west of Truckee directly off I-80. There are a number of less-crowded alternatives in the Truckee region, ranging from small, secluded alpine lakes that take a little more work to reach by car to high, backcountry lakes and streams that only anglers willing to hike a ways are going to get to enjoy. **Prosser Creek Reservoir,** 8 miles north of Truckee off Hwy 89, is a good rainbow and brown trout lake year-round, as are **Stampede Reservoir** and **Boca Reservoir.** All three have boat access and well-appointed marinas and lack the crowded feeling of Donner. To reach Stampede from Truckee, travel east on I-80 to the Boca/Hirschdale exit. Head north on Stampede Dam Rd a short distance to Dog Valley Rd and head left to the lake. To reach Boca Reservoir from Truckee, travel east on I-80 to the Boca/Hirschdale exit. Head north on Stampede Dam Rd to the lake area. Hikers may choose to settle into a high-mountain backcountry setting, such as those found along the **Loch Leven Lakes** and **Warren Lake** trails (see Hiking/Backpacking, above).

The **Truckee River** north of the city also boasts a decent brown and rainbow fishery in spring and summer, easily accessible from Hwy 89 (see Tahoe Basin chapter). The California School of Flyfishing, Truckee, (530) 587-7005, has schooling and reasonably priced **guided trips.** Bud's Sporting Goods, 10043 Donner Pass Rd, Truckee, (530) 587-3177, is a **bait-and-tackle** dealer. As always, check with the appropriate regulatory agencies if you are not up-to-date on current fishing laws, as they are constantly changing in this age of rampant endangered and threatened species listings. The state Department of Fish and Game office in Rancho Cordova, (916)358-2900, has an update, or you can try to decipher a free regulations handbook available at most licensing locations, including bait shops.

Donner Lake is the most popular and best-appointed boating and **waterskiing** lake in the area. The Donner Lake Marina, (530) 587-6031, has fishing boats and ski equipment for **rent.** Dispersed boating on any local reservoirs or lakes mentioned previously is more oriented toward fishing, as many of these places do not allow gasoline motors.

Mountain Biking

Many of the major ski resorts in the Truckee and Tahoe Basin areas have mountain-bike courses open during the off-season. **Donner Ski Ranch** (see Downhill Skiing/Snowboarding, above) has more than 20 miles of trails. The ski terrain essentially provides a downhill thrill ride rather than the serene nature experience of cross-country. Ski resort riding is simple: take your bike instead of your skis to the summit, and ride down instead of skiing down. This can be fun, but it's not unlike a waterslide: two or three times, and you're ready to get distracted by something else. Call the ski ranch at (530) 426-3635 for information about the summer program there.

Rather than spend so much time on the resort properties, we suggest that you also explore the logging roads, which reach for hundreds of miles through the Donner Summit and Truckee region forest areas. The Tahoe National Forest, Truckee Ranger District, (530) 587-3558, should have the most up-to-date information on what roads are in the best condition for riding and are safely away from logging activity.

The **Truckee River Recreation Trail,** as the name would suggest, follows the Truckee River from the Alpine Meadows area just east of Squaw Valley for 4.5 miles to Tahoe City. Paco's Truckee Bike & Ski, 11200 Donner Pass Rd, Truckee, (530) 587-5561, has **rentals** available.

Wildlife

Birders exploring the expansive forests of Jeffrey pine, juniper, live oak, and hemlock and the granite-walled river canyons of the forestlands around Truckee should watch for **quail** and **coots** near waterways and marshes, and a long list of usual suspects in the forested areas, including swallows, great horned owls, Cooper's hawks, western meadowlarks, blackbirds, warblers, sage grouse, and sparrows. The best viewing places for birds tend to be along riverbanks in the riparian forest areas; try the Donner Creek area at Donner Memorial State Park. The Truckee Ranger District, (530) 587-3558, has an official bird list.

The ever-present **black bears** and **rattlesnakes** join **raccoons, bobcats, mountain lions, skunks,** a numerous variety of **squirrel,** and even **porcupines** to round out the list of reptiles and mammals often spotted in these parts. Campers and backpackers are asked to use extreme caution and care in black bear areas, so as not to attract them with food and other goodies. Food should be properly packed and stored and all garbage packed out of the wilderness.

Rock Climbing

There are a variety of climbing routes at the granite-walled **Donner Summit** and **Lover's Leap** near Strawberry on US 50—but these are not places novices should go to try to prove a point. Another advanced climbing spot nearer Donner Lake is at Cave Rock, east of Zephyr Cove. Be sure to contact a licensed **guide service** for proper instruction and equipment before jumping on the rocks. Contact the Truckee Ranger District, (530) 587-3558, for information on the climbing routes and any guide services working the area.

Adventure Calendar

Truckee Ski Race, early March: *covers 30 kilometers of Nordic trails, (530) 583-9353.*

Donner Swim Race, mid-August: *covers nearly 3 miles across Donner Lake, (415)892-0771.*

Donner Hike, mid-September: *retraces the course taken by the ill-fated Donner party, at Donner Memorial State Park, (530) 582-7892.*

outside in

Attractions

Truckee is a popular little city—packed with quaint shops, restaurants, and some terrific bed-and-breakfast inns—that started out in the mid-1800s as a railroad-lumber town with the construction of the first transcontinental railroad over Donner Summit. Its transformation from a dirty, run-down, one-horse town to a bustling city began in the 1970s. Today visitors arrive by car, bus, or the eastbound or westbound Amtrak passenger trains that stop at the yellow depot. If you need hiking, rock-climbing, and cross-country skiing guidebooks or topographical maps and hiking supplies, stop by **Sierra Mountaineer,** housed in the stone building that was once a livery and garage; located on Bridge St at Jibboom St, (530) 587-2025. Another notable shop is the **Bookshelf at Hooligan Rocks,** one of the Sierra Nevada's best bookstores (it's named after a nearby outcropping of rocks where miscreants were once tarred and feathered); 11310 Donner Pass Rd, at the west end of the Safeway shopping center, (530) 582-0515 or (800) 959-5083. The Bookshelf also has a separate children's bookstore called Kidsshelf, (530) 582-5437, at the opposite (east) end of the shopping center. In the summer, popular Truckee attractions include the Cannibal Car Cruise in June, the Fourth of July Parade, and the Truckee Championship Rodeo in August. The Truckee River Regional Park, half a mile south of town on Hwy 267, has softball diamonds, picnic tables, tennis courts, and an outdoor amphitheater offering music programs (many are free) throughout the summer.

In December, when snow blankets the wooden boardwalks and bright little white lights twinkle in the windows of the century-old facades along Commercial Row, Truckee truly looks like a picture from a fairy tale. All winter long the town swarms with skiers who take advantage of its proximity to many first-rate alpine and cross-country ski areas (see Inside Out sections, above). Others brave the freezing temperatures to engage in such winter activities as the Sled Dog Races in February and the 10-day winter carnival called Snowfest in March. For more information on the town, call the Truckee Chamber of Commerce, (530) 587-2757.

A whirl of white in the wintertime, the **Donner** region was named after the 89 members of the ill-fated Donner party, who journeyed by wagon train to the area in October 1846. They had come from the Midwest and were bound for the West Coast, but were trapped here by an early winter storm. The **Emigrant Trail Museum** in Donner Memorial State Park tells their grim story of starvation, cannibalism, and (for some members) survival. The 350-acre state park, located at 12593 Donner Pass Rd (south of I-80), also offers campsites, picnic tables, and hiking trails (see Inside Out sections, above); for general park information call (530) 582-7894 or (530) 582-7892.

Restaurants

Andy's Truckee Diner   Andy's classic diner feels like it's been here forever. Perhaps that's because the 1940s diner lived on the rails until it was relocated and restored here in 1995. The copious menu will surely offer something to please everyone. *10144 W River St (junction of Hwy 267), Truckee; (530) 582-6925; $.*

Cottonwood ☆   Cottonwood stands high on a hill, affording a great view of the bright lights of Truckee from its spacious dining room. The eclectic seasonal menu ranges from Southwestern to Creole and Mediterranean fare. *10142 Rue Hilltop (above town, right off Hwy 267 at Hilltop Lodge, just beyond the railroad tracks), Truckee; (530) 587-5711; $$.*

Engadine Café ☆☆☆   Some of the best food in the region is served at this charming and cozy cafe. Breakfasts feature a wide range of choices, lunches are simple and satisfying, and in the evening the kitchen turns out an eclectic mix. *On Rainbow Rd at the Yuba River (½ mile W of I-80), Soda Springs; (530) 426-3661; $$.*

Jordan's ☆☆☆ Housed within an austerely attractive Queen Anne Victorian house on the town's main drag, Jordan's dishes out terrific fare. The Italian pastas are particularly noteworthy. *10292 Donner Pass Rd (1 block west of Commercial Row), Truckee; (530) 587-7815; $$.*

Monte Vista Inn ☆ For about 60 years, the Monte Vista has been a roadhouse catering to locals—and to travelers lucky enough to find it. The comfortable inn is built of logs and indigenous stone, and serves generous portions of California cuisine. *Off I-80 at the Dutch Flat exit (9 miles E of Colfax), Dutch Flat; (530) 389-2333; $$.*

The Passage ☆☆☆ Tucked inside the landmark Truckee Hotel (see Lodgings, below), the Passage offers consistently well-prepared food. The wine list has won at least a dozen awards of excellence from *Wine Spectator* magazine. *10007 Bridge St (in the Truckee Hotel, at Donner Pass Rd), Truckee; (530) 587-7619; $$.*

Truckee Trattoria ☆ Conveniently located right off I-80, this good, casual Italian cafe focuses primarily on pastas—and garlic! Truckee Trattoria is both intimate (read small) and popular (despite its steep prices), so you should make a reservation. *11310-1 Donner Pass Rd (at the W end of the Safeway shopping center), Truckee; (530) 582-1266; $$.*

Lodgings

Donner Country Inn ☆☆ Decorated with country pine furnishings and Laura Ashley prints, this inn, built in 1986, sits in a grove of pine trees just across the road from Donner Lake. The 5 guest rooms have private entrances and baths, queen-size beds with down comforters, and wood-burning stoves. *10070 Gregory Pl, Donner Lake; (530) 587-5574 or (925)938-0685; $$.*

Loch Leven Lodge ☆ If you want to get away from the crowds in Tahoe but would like easy access to the area, this quiet, simple lodge might be for you. Each of its 8 units faces beautiful Donner Lake and all but 1 have a kitchen. The lodge also has picnic tables, a barbecue, a spa, and a rowboat. *13855 Donner Pass Rd (from I-80, take the Donner Lake exit and turn left on Donner Pass Rd; it's 1½ miles from I-80), Donner Lake; (530) 587-3773; $$.*

Richardson House ☆☆☆☆ The lavishly restored Richardson House (built in 1886) sets the standard that other B&Bs in the area will have to strive for. Its 8 beautiful guest rooms are elegantly appointed with plush carpeting, color-coordinated drapes and wallpaper, vintage fixtures, feather beds and comforters, and claw-footed tubs. *10154 High St (at Spring St), Truckee; (530) 587-5388 or (888) 229-0365; $$–$$$.*

Royal Gorge's Rainbow Lodge / Wilderness Lodge ☆☆   The 1922 Rainbow Lodge, built of hand-hewn timbers and local granite at a bend in the Yuba River, has 32 simple, pine-paneled rooms. Royal Gorge also offers cross-country skiers accommodations at its Wilderness Lodge, a handsome wood lodge that's tucked away in a remote part of the cross-country course. *On Rainbow Rd (from I-80, take the Rainbow Rd exit and drive ½ mile W), Soda Springs; (530) 426-3871, (530) 426-3661, or (800) 500-3871 (outside Northern California only); $$.*

The Swedish House Bed and Breakfast ☆☆☆   This charming European inn has 11 lovely rooms, with custom furniture and fabrics and sparkling, private bathrooms. And what else would you expect at the Swedish House B&B but a delicious breakfast of Swedish pancakes garnished with lingonberries? *10009 E River St (at Bridge St), Truckee; (530) 587-0400 or (888) 302-0400; $$.*

The Truckee Hotel ☆☆   Built in 1873, this handsome hotel is one of the oldest operating hotels in the Sierra Nevada. Upstairs there are 37 guest rooms with antique dressers, glass chandeliers, and full-, queen-, or king-size beds; 8 rooms have private baths and the other 29 have basins and share bathrooms. *10007 Bridge St (at Donner Pass Rd), Truckee; (530) 587-4444 or (800) 659-6921; $–$$.*

More Information

Boreal: *(530) 426-3666.*
Donner Ski Ranch: *(530) 426-3635.*
Foresthill Ranger District: *(530) 367-2224.*
Nevada City Ranger District: *(530) 265-4531.*
Road conditions: *(800) 427-ROAD or www.dot.ca.gov/hq/roadinfo/.*
Ski Lake Tahoe: *(800) 588-SNOW or www.SkiLakeTahoe.com.*
Soda Springs: *(530) 426-3666.*
Sugar Bowl Ski Resort: *(530) 426-1111.*
Tahoe Donner: *(530) 587-9400.*
Truckee Ranger District: *(530) 587-3558.*

Tahoe
Basin

Lake Tahoe and its immediate surroundings, including Emerald Bay, D. L. Bliss State Park, Tahoe City, the South Lake Tahoe shore, Sugar Point State Park, Truckee Marsh, and select spots on the Nevada shore of the lake. Also includes nearby ski resorts, Tahoe and El Dorado National Forests, Desolation Wilderness, and Granite Chief Wilderness.

Lake Tahoe may be the quintessential summer sports playground in California, but the mountains surrounding it are the place to be when winter snows move in. Ever since the 1960 Winter Olympics at Squaw Valley anointed Tahoe as a ski resort destination, it has been compared to Aspen, Colorado, and other alpine settings where bumpy, powdery chutes pointing 3 miles through the tree runs get the adrenaline pumping through your veins. Tahoe has become too popular for its own good, however. Northern Californians love to ski Tahoe and do it in record numbers each year. Resorts have responded by investing millions of dollars in new equipment, including high-speed lifts designed to move larger numbers of people to the summits more quickly. But bumper-to-bumper traffic on Echo Summit and long lines at the lifts have pushed some downhill action away from the Tahoe Basin. The Donner/Truckee region, for example, also has been reaping the benefits of the winter sports craze (see Truckee Region chapter), as has Kirkwood in Carson Pass. Still, as much as people complain about the crowds, it is a cycle that feeds on itself and shows no sign of slowing.

Each resort has a distinct personality. Heavenly, considered by many to be the premier resort in the area, is the downhill race spot for those looking for a rush. Smaller, more low-key and out-of-the-way spots, such as Granlibakken near Tahoe City, are where beginners can fall down without feeling humiliated in front of the "pros." The ski resorts also try to draw summer visitors with such amenities as mountain-bike runs.

The vast open reaches of El Dorado and Tahoe National Forests, with the serene Desolation and Grant Chief Wilderness Areas overlooking the Tahoe Basin, also make the forested and high-country areas a summer haven for those who want to enjoy the lake from afar rather than contend with its crowded shores. Dispersed camping and hundreds of miles of backcountry trails among high mountain lakes, glacial valleys, rivers, streams, and meadows supply outdoors folks with the solitude they crave. Rock climbers and bird-watchers, cyclists and river rafters can enjoy the Tahoe hinterlands during the summer with just as much gusto as the winter weekend road warrior—it's all a matter of timing.

When explorer John C. Frémont caught his first glimpse of Lake Tahoe in 1844, he fell in love, mesmerized by its beauty. At 1,600 feet deep, the glacier-carved lake holds many mysteries. Its 72 miles of shoreline, however, is no mystery at all to millions who descend into the basin each year to enjoy holidays and weekend frolicking. Some turn to the casinos, with their high-rise hotels crowding the south shore like a city block of Los Angeles. Others hit the beaches—choosing between fully developed sandy shores with volleyball courts, marinas, picnic tables, and campgrounds or more pristine settings adjacent to marshes and streams, the shores lined with boulders instead of sand. Waterskiing, lakeside camping, swimming, fishing, boating, and biking are all prized activities along the shore. Motor into Emerald Bay, and dive from the rocks on Fannette Island. Ride an inflatable tube down the swollen Truckee River. Take a walk through a field of granite boulders at D. L. Bliss State Park . . . but good luck doing any of it without a lot of company.

Alas, Tahoe is being loved to death. Indeed, the big blue lake that is the crown jewel of the Sierra Nevada is slowly losing its legendary water clarity to polluted runoff and nutrients from developed property within its watershed. Its trees, environmentalists say, are diseased from exposure to automobile exhaust and other contaminants. All these problems came to a head in 1997, when Bill Clinton became the first sitting president to visit the lake for the sole purpose of focusing on its environmental health. Dr. Charles Goldman, a researcher for the University of California, has been measuring water quality on the lake for 30 years and has documented its slow decline; Goldman took the president for a ride on the lake to demonstrate his findings, and the effort to reverse the trend received some important nods of encouragement. Some want to put a tollgate on US Highway 50 and limit the number of cars allowed to enter the Tahoe Basin. Others look toward marsh restoration around the lake, elimination of forest roads that wash downstream, or a ban on motorized watercraft. For now, however, the lake is still blue as far as the eye can see—and Jetskis have yet to be outlawed.

And some point out that Lake Tahoe is resilient. After the pine forests surrounding it were cut down to be used as support beams for the Comstock silver mines, so much silt rolled into the lake that its waters were transformed from that trademark blue to a murky brown. But within 50 years after reforestation began to take hold, the water clarity returned, and the lake changed back to its brilliant, shockingly beautiful cobalt blue.

Getting There

There are three major highway approaches to the Tahoe area, none of them foolproof. If you have a bit of extra time and the weather is good, drive to the Tahoe Basin via Highway 88 through Carson Pass. This lesser-known backdoor entrance is more relaxing and equally as scenic as US Highway 50 (US 50), without as many crazy drivers. US 50, which follows the American River canyon from the Sacramento Valley through the Sierra foothills and into the Tahoe Basin through Echo Summit, is by far the most popular route because it is the most direct. The road, however, is the least navigable and the most crowded, much of it two lanes. The highway is also heavily used by trucks. The third approach is via Highway 89 from Truckee. Take Interstate 80 east from Sacramento instead of US 50, then head south from the Truckee area to Tahoe City. For current road conditions, call the state Department of Transportation, (800) 427-ROAD (7623). Check via the Internet in advance at www.dot.ca.gov/hq/roadinfo/. For help planning a winter visit, call Ski Lake Tahoe at (800) 588-SNOW or go to www.SkiLakeTahoe.com on the Web. El Dorado National Forest, headquartered at 100 Forni Road, Placerville, (530) 622-5061, is the main information center for the Tahoe forest and wilderness areas.

Adjoining Areas

NORTH: **Plumas Region**

SOUTH: **Southern Gold Rush Country**

WEST: **Northern Gold Rush Country**

inside out

Downhill Skiing/Snowboarding

Speed. Downhill thrills. The bite of icy wind on your cheeks, brushing against the rush of adrenaline that comes with pointing the skis toward

Earth and letting go. This is the Tahoe experience. As Northern California's premier winter play area, it is of the reasons so many living in the Bay Area 'burbs have four-wheel-drive SUVs and even trucks. (Look for the ski rack and the dirt bath on their vehicles each Monday.) Every winter warrior can find a little bit of snow play in Tahoe: crazy, radical downhill death-drop runs used 30 years ago by Olympic athletes; mild beginner runs where it's okay to fall down; snowboard hills and cross-country trails, skating lanes, open bowls, and places to teach children how to slide around in those big shoes. The typical **snow season** is November to April at most locations, but heavy snowfall in recent winters has extended skiing well into June. Never assume California weather is going to be normal every year; it is possible to ski and get a tan at the same time. For current **road conditions,** contact the state Department of Transportation at (800) 427-ROAD (7623) or www.dot.ca.gov/hq/roadinfo/. For help with planning a winter visit, call Ski Lake Tahoe at (800) 588-SNOW or go to www.SkiLakeTahoe.com on the Web.

Tahoe area resorts are beginning to warm up considerably to **snowboarding,** and all have areas designated for boarder action. Squaw Valley USA (see below), with its Central Park area between Emigrant and Squaw Peaks, is perhaps the best place to have free run with all the goodies included. There are boarding areas in virtually all public parks as well. In Tahoe, most private property is not fenced off or signed, so if you go solo, be considerate of private property owners.

Heavenly

Aside from some of the most dramatic, steep, expert runs available in the Tahoe Basin, Heavenly (formerly Heavenly Valley) boasts that it draws the most non-skiers of any other resort in the area. Why? With a comfy, modern **summit tramway** rising to more than 10,000 feet, it's the easiest way for couch potatoes to get a grand view of the Tahoe Basin from way on high without having to break much of a sweat. Restaurants, viewing decks, and other amenities are what attract the non-skiing masses. If they'd put on skis, however, they would find more than just pretty scenery. The runs, scattered among two faces of the mountain at **Monument Peak** straddling the California/Nevada state line, are dispersed over 4,800 acres with a 3,500 foot vertical drop from the 10,040-foot summit—the longest in the Tahoe region. There are 82 miles of trails, with two bowls, served by 27 lifts including a tramway, 5 high-speed quads, 8 triple chairs, 8 surface lifts, 5 doubles, a high-speed quad that seats six, and 2 "magic carpet" lifts at the **children's school.** Snowmaking is done on two-thirds of the skiable area. The runs are ranked 20 percent beginner, 47 percent intermediate, and 33 percent advanced. Expert runs (drops is probably more accurate) are found out of the Mott Canyon lift, beneath the Milky Way bowl. The longest run is 5.5 miles.

Heavenly is a full-service resort with lodging, ski school, rentals, restaurant, RV parking—the works. It is in the process of being spruced up, with $10 million in improvements this season, including the replacement of two lifts with high-speed quad chairs on the Gunbarrel and Stagecoach runs and new or expanded day care and children's play areas. There are plans to construct a new resort hotel at the summit, along with a gondola lift to the resort from the South Lake Tahoe strip. The resort has two bases, one on the California side and one in Nevada. The California base is at the end of Ski Run Blvd, half a mile from South Lake Tahoe on US 50. To approach from the Nevada side, take US 50 past the state line, then go 3 miles on Kingsbury Grade Dr. For information, call (800) 2HEAVEN, or go to the Web site at www.skiheavenly.com. For a snow report, call (530) 541-SKII (7544).

Squaw Valley USA

Advanced skiers who don't want to fool around with kid's stuff should head directly to Squaw Valley USA, where they can retrace the tracks of Olympic athletes who competed here during the 1960 Winter Olympics. The world-famous KT-22 and Palisades are found here, as are 4 lifts originally used when this was Olympic Village—Papoose, the KT-22 Olympic Lady Express, Headwall, and Siberia Express—all spread across three of the resort's five peaks. One of the largest ski resorts in the country, Squaw Valley USA operates 30 lifts including a cable car, a gondola, 5 quads, 9 triplets, 10 doubles, 3 surface lifts, and 1 pulse lift. It covers 4,000 skiable acres downhill from the 7,550-foot **Snow King,** the 8,200-foot **KT-22,** the 8,020-foot **Broken Arrow,** the 8,700-foot **Granite Chief,** and the 8,900-foot **Squaw Peak.** Despite its reputation as a hard-core chute-run destination, however, 25 percent of the trails here are ranked beginner and 45 percent are intermediate, with extensive open-bowl skiing and a large snowboarding area. There are also more than 15 kilometers of Nordic trails in the resort's cross-country ski center, many of which are suitable for families with children. Other conveniences include a snow school and ski rentals. The resort also rents snowboards and offers an instruction package. There is on-site lodging and a convention center, all quite pricey but very nice. For a snow report or other information, call (530) 583-6955, or go to www.squaw.com on the Web. To reach the resort, take Hwy 89 south 10 miles from Truckee, or north 7.5 miles from Tahoe City, and look for the clearly marked entrance on the west side of the road.

Alpine Meadows

With more than 100 runs covering widely diverse terrain, including six bowls, and a vertical drop of 1,800 feet to its 6,835-foot base elevation, Alpine Meadows is a good choice for intermediate skiers looking for downhill action that isn't too steep or loaded down with difficult-to-navigate ski runs. The resort, nestled against **Scott's Peak,** has a few good chutes and tree runs to keep advanced skiers occupied, but the mostly roomy, gently sloping open runs are perfect for teens and adolescents who have advanced beyond the family ski-park stage. Alpine has a dozen lifts, including 1 six-passenger high-speed lift, 1 high-speed quad, 2 triples, 7 doubles, and 1 surface tow. There is snowmaking on 185 of the ski area's 2,000 acres of skiable terrain, spread out over all but two of the 12 lift areas. The runs are ranked 25 percent beginner, 40 percent intermediate, and 35 percent advanced. For information and a snow report, call (800) 441-4423 or (530) 581-8374. The resort is easy to reach from Truckee (12 miles south on Hwy 89) or Tahoe City (5 miles north on Hwy 89).

Northstar-at-Tahoe

With a vertical drop of nearly 2,300 feet from the summit of **Mount Pluto,** Northstar-at-Tahoe is one of those downhill excitement spots. The mountain is a full-service resort with lodging, restaurants, ski clinic, rentals, **snowboarding areas,** and instruction (as well as tennis courts, a golf course, and a mountain-bike park for summer). There are 63 downhill runs rated 50 percent intermediate, 25 percent beginner, and 25 percent advanced. The base elevation is 6,400 feet, and the longest run is nearly 3 miles. The runs are interestingly situated so that most are on the top half of the mountain, converging at the bottom three runs to the base. There are a dozen lifts, including 1 gondola, 4 quads, 2 doubles, 2 triples, 2 surface, and 1 magic carpet. The resort is equidistant from Truckee and Tahoe City, 6 miles in on Hwy 267. Call (530) 562-1010 for information, or (530) 562-1330 for a snow report. The resort Web site is www.skinorthstar.com.

Sierra-at-Tahoe

Beginning skiers who hate to drive in the snow make out like bandits at the Sierra-at-Tahoe resort. It's closer to the Bay Area and Sacramento Valley than any other ski area on the US 50 corridor, and it has the longest beginner-rated ski run in the area: the 2.5-mile Sugar and Spice run off the West Bowl Express and Puma lifts. Sierra's 46 runs cover 2,000 acres and are ranked mostly for intermediate skiers, with 25 percent beginner and 25 percent advanced from a base elevation of 6,640 feet with a 2,212-foot vertical drop. There are 10 lifts, including 3 quads, 1 triple, 5 doubles, and 1 magic carpet. There are, however, no steep death-drop runs like those found at more rowdy resorts closer to Tahoe—which is fine with those who are still a little wobbly on the alpine track. This is a full-service resort with ski instruction and rentals, lodging, restaurants, and a large **snowboarding area.** It's directly off US 50 just east of Echo Summit and easy to spot. Call (530) 659-7453 for information, or (530) 659-7475 for a snow report.

Kirkwood

Alpine skiers have two great reasons to try Kirkwood. First, it is outside of Tahoe proper along Hwy 88 at Carson Pass—so they can avoid the bumper-to-bumper US 50 shuffle out of the Sacramento Valley. Second, it has the highest base elevation (7,800 feet) of any resort in the Tahoe region, meaning more consistent quality snowfall on its 2,300 acres of skiable terrain. The resort's 12 runs, ranging from gently sloped bowl to steep expert level chutes, are ranked 15 percent beginner, 50 percent intermediate, and 35 percent advanced, with a 2,000-foot vertical drop from the 9,800-foot summit. There are 65 trails, seven bowls, and runs of every imaginable type, including several expert tree runs from the Wagonwheel Lift. The 12 lifts include 7 triples, 3 doubles, and 2 surface lifts. Kirkwood is a full-service resort with lodging, restaurants, a ski school and rentals, **snowboard center,** and extensive Nordic trail system (see Cross-Country Skiing, below). Check on road conditions before heading up Hwy 88, as it is more subject to closures during heavy snowfall. From Tahoe, take Hwy 89 southwest for 11 miles, then go 16 miles west to Carson Pass. From the Sacramento Valley, take Hwy 88 east from Stockton for 100 miles, instead of cutting over from US 50 in the foothills, which is cumbersome and time-consuming. For information, call (209) 258-6000. For a snow report, call (209) 258-3000.

Diamond Peak (Incline Village, Nevada)

Diamond Peak, on the northeast shore of Lake Tahoe in Incline Village, Nevada, is another ski resort that has invested heavily in new lift equipment in recent years. Here, you will find more than two dozen runs and an impressive 1,840-foot vertical drop to the 6,700-foot base elevation. One downhill run is 2.5 miles long! The runs are rated 46 percent intermediate, 36 percent advanced, and 18 percent beginner. Snowmaking is found on 80 percent of the developed area. Because Diamond Peak is in a more exclusive area of the Tahoe lakeshore and away from large casinos found on the south end, the scene here tends to be a bit more serene and family oriented. There are 8 lifts on the mountain face, including 6 doubles, 1 quad, and a new conveyor belt lift unique to the Tahoe area and said to be exquisitely efficient at moving people. The downhill runs include the infamous **Great Flume** (advanced). There are also 35 kilometers of cross-country trails divided evenly among skill levels. Skating lanes also have been added, as has an expansive snowshoeing area. Diamond Peak has no overnight lodging but has a ski school, rentals, and a suitable base lodge. The resort, located at 1210 Sky Way Dr in Incline Village, is 17 miles southeast of Tahoe City, with a clearly marked turnoff from Hwy 28. Call (702) 832-1177 for general information or (702) 831-3211 for a snow report. The regular season is November to April.

Granlibakken

One of the least costly ski areas, Granlibakken Ski Resort near Tahoe City is popular among beginners because of its simplicity. Two chair lifts and one ski run are divided evenly between beginner and intermediate terrain that covers some 10 acres. With a base elevation of 6,330 feet and a summit of 6,610, you will find no death-drops or places to do a helicopter twirl in midair. And because the resort is part condominium development and part lodge, the crowd tends to be more resident than at the larger resorts. There are also 2 kilometers of Nordic trails and a snow hill for **boarding.** In addition to the lodging, conveniences include a ski school and rentals. To reach the resort, take Hwy 89 half a mile south of Tahoe City, then turn left on Granlibakken Rd and proceed to the resort entrance. For information or a snow report, call (530) 583-4242. The regular season is December to April.

Ski Homewood

Also closer to Tahoe City and less crowded than the higher-profile resorts, Ski Homewood has a summit elevation of 7,880 feet—enough to give skiers panoramic views of the lake as they descend the more than 50 runs covering nearly 1,300 acres of developed mountain terrain. The vertical drop here is 1,650 feet to the base elevation of 6,230. There are 8 lifts, including 4 surface lifts, a double chair, a quad chair, and 2 triples. The runs are 35 percent advanced, 50 percent intermediate, and 15 percent for beginners. The steep and tree-lined Nose—the most radical downhill run—is for advanced to expert skiers only. There are also 40 kilometers of cross-country ski trails, divided fairly evenly among difficulty levels, as well as a terrain park with varied grades for **snowboarding.** Other conveniences include a ski school, rentals (including snowboards), children's programs, and child care. There are two day lodges but no overnight lodging on-site. Parking at the resort is very limited. To reach the resort, take Hwy 89 south from Tahoe City for 6 miles, or go 20 miles north on Hwy 89 from South Lake Tahoe, and turn west at the Ski Homewood entrance. For a snow report, call (530) 525-2900. For general information, call (530) 525-2992.

Cross-Country Skiing

Most of the major resorts described in Downhill Skiing/Snowboarding, above, have extensive cross-country skiing areas, but we prefer the 16 kilometers of intermediate and beginner groomed trails at **Sugar Pine Point State Park** (see Parks/Beaches, below). Numerous sections of **Tahoe Rim Trail** (see Hiking/Backpacking, below) also double as wide, flat Nordic areas during the winter—which is just as well since much of the trail itself is inaccessible until after the spring melt. Check with the Tahoe Rim Trail Organization, (702) 588-0686, for up-to-date information on the best location, since winter conditions can vary widely along the trail's 240 kilometers and some areas may be avalanche-prone.

Of the resorts, Kirkwood's 80-kilometer cross-country center is the most extensive, with nicely groomed beginner and intermediate marked trails, warming huts, and ski patrol in the wide-open meadow at the resort base. Near Truckee, the Royal Gorge at Soda Springs (see Truckee Region chapter) covers 7,000 acres of gently sloping wilderness descending toward American River Canyon and has 90 trails, groomed and ready, covering 320 kilometers, with warming shacks, ski-in lodging, and all the pampering you would expect in Aspen. There is also a Forest Service sno-park at **Echo Summit** on the north side of US 50—a good place to stretch and get your feet in the snow before dropping into the Tahoe Basin. Watch out, however, for cross traffic when stopping there.

Skiers exploring on their own will find no shortage of shops with equipment **rentals,** such as the reputable Alpenglow Sports, 415 N Lake Blvd, Tahoe City, (530) 583-6917; Breeze Ski Rentals, 1019 Ski Run Blvd, South Lake Tahoe, (530) 583-4123; Carson Tahoe Rents, 2724 Lake Tahoe Blvd, South Lake Tahoe, (530) 541-2130; and Tahoe Paradise Sports, 3021 US 50, South Lake Tahoe, (530) 577-2121.

Parks/Beaches

By the time you get to **Kings Beach State Recreation Area,** near the northern tip of Lake Tahoe—especially if you're making the trip on a busy weekend—you will already be acclimated to the Los Angeles–style traffic. Because of this, you will be less disappointed when you see this place and realize that it is the *Baywatch* Sierra Nevada franchise: bikini babes and muscle jocks playing volleyball and frolicking on the sand and in the water; paddle boats, kayaks, Jet-skis, picnic facilities, and 3,000 feet of sand. You get the picture. The beach is about 12 miles northeast of Tahoe City on Hwy 28. For information, call the North Tahoe Recreation and Parks Department, (530) 546-7248. A quieter shore access point (without all the amenities) is at **Lake Forest Beach,** a popular camping spot (see

Camping, below) with a public boat ramp and a small beach and picnic area that gets surprisingly little use, since boaters tend to camp, launch, and head out. To find the beach, take Hwy 89 to Tahoe City, then head east on Hwy 28 about 2 miles to Lake Forest Rd. Turn right and proceed to the entrance. Call the beach at (530) 583-3074 for information.

Tahoe State Recreation Area is another beachfront setting, more heavily used than Lake Forest Beach but better appointed, with a campground twice the size (see Camping, below) and nicer picnic facilities. This is a good place for a waterside lunch outdoors (we took a pizza there once). The facility is off Hwy 28, 1 mile north of the Hwy 89 intersection at Tahoe City.

The rocky lakeshores, while certainly not much of a beach "scene," can also be an enjoyable way to take in the Tahoe waterfront. Diving from the rocks is, of course, dangerous—the water is too darn cold anyway—but it's interesting to see how well humans can adapt from a sand to a rock habitat when it comes to finding a good sunbathing spot. **William Kent Beach** and **Kaspian Beach** are two places where you get to observe this. The campgrounds (see Camping, below) and adjacent picnic areas, run by the US Forest Service, are 3 miles south of Tahoe City on Hwy 89. Call (530) 583-3642.

The shoreline at **Sugar Pine Point State Park** is more of a museum setting than a beach experience—with several historic buildings as the main attraction—but Sugar Pine Point and the grounds of the Erhman Mansion, where a nature center is located, make this 2,000-acre mixed conifer forest/stream drainage a fantastic ecology study spot, as well as a place to camp (see Camping, below) and enjoy the lake. During the winter, there are several cross-country skiing trails (see Cross-Country Skiing, above), groomed regularly. You can't miss the park, on Hwy 89, 10 miles south of Tahoe City. Although most of the grounds are upstream from the highway, the shoreline area to the east is the highlight, in our view. Call the park, (530) 525-7232, for information.

Simply put, **D. L. Bliss State Park** is our favorite spot on the Lake Tahoe shore, with a bit of sandy beach and a wonderful stretch of giant boulders sitting on the water's edge. Skip the beach, the picnic areas, the campgrounds, and the hiking trails and instead head for the rocks. You will have a blast climbing from boulder to boulder, and maybe find a good pooled cove for swimming. There are 4 miles of fantastic shoreline, and this is a popular anchor spot for boaters looking for a lazy, outrageously gorgeous place to bob in the water a while. The waterfront is not the only draw, here, however. Some 900 acres of odd granite rock lands, with stunted trees growing haphazardly and sparsely among the boulders, make for some fascinating cross-country hiking. The terrain is odd, interesting, almost tragically beautiful. This land is named for a railroad owner and financier who settled the Tahoe Basin during the Comstock silver boom. The park was dedicated to the state by the Bliss family for use as an outdoor recreation area and natural preserve. It's 1.5 miles south of Meeks on Hwy 89, on the shore side of the road. Call the park, (530) 525-7277, for more information.

Just south of Bliss is perhaps the most heavily traveled portion of the Tahoe shoreline, **Emerald Bay State Park,** which, if it weren't for the hordes of people who flock to it relentlessly on busy summer weekends, would be quite wonderful. Our advice is this: if you can't make it on a weekday when things are a bit slow, skip it. Either that or approach the bay by boat instead. Otherwise, prepare to wait ages for a parking space just for the pleasure of walking like a herd of cattle down the trail to the waterfront to look at the sights. (Yawn.) This is not to suggest that if you're lucky enough to stumble upon Emerald Bay State Park, somehow, at a time when it's not overflowing with tourists, there won't be anything to look at. Waiting for you are fantastic views not only of the bay itself but of **Fannette Island** offshore (go by boat and you can dock at the island and swim off the rocks while avoiding the crowds). There's a little bit of everything here. Vikingsholm is a miniature Scandinavian castle, constructed at the bay's edge, home in the late 1920s to Lora Josephine Knight, who built both the castle on the mainland and a teahouse on the island before the property was passed on to the state for its beauty and historical significance. Geologists say the bay was formed when glaciers moved through the Tahoe bowl, leaving a gouge almost completely encircled by granite shores. Fannette Island is a geological oddity of sorts. It is the only island in all of Lake Tahoe, although similar peaks on the lake bottom—fully submerged—were recently mapped by the US Geological Survey. In our view, the island is a superb choice. Not only is it more secluded than most other public areas, with nicer coves off the rocks, but the view of the lakeshore and blunt peaks beyond is best from out on the water. From here you can also see Eagle Falls.

The southern tip of the lakeshore is a 2-mile stretch of three heavily used public beaches (with some private property intermixed) managed by the US Forest Service. This is pretty much a swim/sunbathe/picnic/enjoy-the-view destination during the summer. If it weren't for the high mountain peaks on the horizon, summer days here would seem a lot like a small tropical island. Just close your eyes and pretend. **Kiva Beach,** the westernmost of the three, is located at the base of the Mount Tallac stream drainage, and adjacent to the Forest Service visitors center. Take Hwy 89 to half a mile north of Camp Richardson, and turn toward the lake at Baldwin Beach Rd. Both Kiva Beach and **Pope Beach** are adjacent to

Camp Richardson. **Baldwin Beach** is just north of Kiva, and at times is a bit more secluded because its not to near the most easily accessed parking areas. To reach Kiva, take Kiva Beach Rd north from the highway. For Pope, the busiest and most popular of the three, take Pope Beach Rd. Call the Forest Service, (530) 573-2675, for more information about these beaches.

Feel like a nature stroll? Perhaps the finest spot at Tahoe to get a feel for what the lakeshore must have looked like way back when, before waterfront development swallowed up most marshlands and meandering streams, is at the mouth of the **Truckee River,** ironically near what many consider to be the Tahoe Basin's biggest urban development blunder, the Tahoe Keys subdivision. Drive through the seemingly endless tract-home-lined suburban mecca on Tahoe Keys Blvd, following it all the way to the end. There you will find not only all that is left of the marsh (increasing in size, thanks to an impressive restoration project in the works), but walking paths and footbridges meandering through, from which you can observe waterfowl and other marsh-dwelling critters. West of the marsh on the lakeshore is a small public beach. The first time we stumbled upon this place, we were startled to find something so lovely tucked away in such an ugly corner.

Two miles east of the marshes, **Nevada Beach** is a spacious, sandy spot with a campground at the mouth of Folsom Spring. It's a good place for a picnic, beachcombing, and more lake views, with a boat dock area to boot. Take US 50 east from Tahoe Village 1 mile, and turn left on Elks Point Rd. Proceed to the end to find the beach area. Call the beach, (530) 573-2674, for information. **Zephyr Cove** is a privately operated lakeshore resort with nearly 2 miles of sandy beach, volleyball courts, a campground, restaurants, and a marina with boat rentals. Rent Jet-skis on the beach, paraglide, swim, and frolic. It's certainly not pristine or "natural," but if you're looking for full amenities on the waterfront, this is the spot—so nice you won't mind the crowds (as much). Both are on the Nevada side of the lake. Call the resort at the Zephyr Cove Marina, (702) 588-3833.

Hiking/Backpacking

The vast terrain surrounding Lake Tahoe—glacial valleys, high mountain meadows, secluded alpine lakes, stream canyons, expansive marshlands, and forests consisting of pine, Douglas fir, incense cedar, and other conifers—is a hiker's dream. Cars pour into the Tahoe Basin in the summer just as during the ski season, for both trail action and water sports, making this a year-round outdoor play area. Most of this mountainous region is within Tahoe and El Dorado National Forests, and Desolation and Granite

Chief Wilderness Areas are the prime backcountry destinations not only because of their seclusion but also their proximity to the lakeshore population centers. One minute you can be in bumper-to-bumper traffic breathing exhaust fumes while heading to the famous lake vista, and the next you may be trucking up an unnamed forest road, ditching your car and scrambling over a ridge top to a tiny alpine lake, and not a soul in sight.

As is the case with most national forests and wilderness areas, camping is allowed just about anywhere the ground is flat enough to pitch a tent, but **permits** are required for any use of fire and for use of wilderness areas. Nearly 100 miles of the **Pacific Crest Trail** pass through the Tahoe wilderness areas stretching from Donner Summit near Truckee to the Mokelumne Wilderness boundary near Caples Lake on Hwy 88. The Pacific Crest Trail Association, 1350 Castle Rock Rd, Walnut Creek, CA 94598, (925)939-6111, has information and maps about access points and hiking routes for sections of the trail. The best **trail maps** of the national forest areas are available by writing to US Forest Service Information, Room 521, 630 Sansome St, San Francisco, CA 94111. There are five main maps for this region: one each for Tahoe and El Dorado National Forests, one for the Tahoe Management unit, and one each for Desolation and Granite Chief Wilderness Areas. (See the primer at the beginning of this book for explicit ordering instructions.) **Trail conditions** in any forest or wilderness area are subject to change, so check with the appropriate ranger district for up-to-date information before setting out on any dayslong adventures. Many backcountry trails may be impassable in winter, and sections wash out or are too dangerous to cross when rivers are running high. In Tahoe, some trails are not usable until the spring melt is finished in early June. Call the Tahoe Rim Trail Organization, (702) 588-0686, or the Forest Service's Lake Tahoe Basin Management Unit in South Lake Tahoe, (530) 573-2674, for current information.

The nearly complete **Tahoe Rim Trail** (150 miles when finished) encircles the lake, on both the Nevada and California sides, with legs over some of the most awesome peaks in the region. Development of the trail began in 1984 and has been funded and constructed mostly by volunteers. Much of the trail is open in winter for cross-country skiing, but the best time to hike it is from early June, after the spring melt, through October. As of this writing, volunteer trail builders are putting the finishing touches on a 4-mile section from **Tahoe City to Twin Peaks,** where it meets the Pacific Crest Trail within Desolation Wilderness (see below). Next year, the final leg from **Brockway Summit to Mount Rose** in Nevada (north of Incline Village) may also be finished, depending on how the Forest Service–led planning process goes. Our favorite section is from **Tahoe City to Brockway Summit** (easy to moderate; 19 miles one way, best done over two days), which skirts the 7,754-foot Painted Rock, the 8,424-foot Mount Watson summit overlooking the Burton Creek canyon and the lake, and then 8,617-foot Mount Pluto before descending to the trailhead at Brockway Summit—no slouch of a view itself at 7,199 feet. Elevation gains are gradual, as the trail straddles the northern peak ridgeline for its entire length. To reach the trailhead, take either Hwy 89 north from Tahoe City 3.5 miles to the staging area on the east side of the road, or Hwy 267 northeast from Brockway Vista on the lakeshore 7 miles to the Brockway guard station on the west side of the road. For trail maps and information about specific trail segments, contact the Tahoe Rim Trail Organization, (702) 588-0686. Day-use permits are not required for sections of the trail outside of wilderness areas, but if you plan to camp, you must check in with the Forest Service at Lake Tahoe Basin Management Unit in South Lake Tahoe, (530) 573-3674.

Desolation Wilderness, more than 63,000 acres of high-country wilderness, includes peaks nearly 10,000 feet high, glaciated granite walls, valleys, domes, more than 100 alpine lakes (naturally too cold to swim in, but good for cooling off), forested river canyons, and pristine high mountain meadows. Desolate indeed yet easy to get to, this is a place to get lost. The best way to explore this area is to take a two- to three-day backpacking trip, but any of the trail segments are suitable for shorter day hikes, and many of the lakes are accessible by car. One option is the **General Creek Trail** (moderate; 7 miles round trip), which ascends toward Desolation Wilderness from Sugar Pine Point State Park (see Parks/Beaches, above). **Tahoe-Yosemite Trail** (easy; 10 miles round trip) is a steady climb through the Meeks Creek canyon to a chain of pretty, secluded mountain lakes nestled in the forested Desolation Wilderness. There you may encounter Lake Genevieve, Crag Lake, Shadow Lake, Hidden Lake, Stony Ridge Lake, and Rubicon Lake. Numerous lakeside camping spots are along this route in the canyons below the 9,234 Phipps Peak, near the Tahoe section of the Pacific Crest Trail. (You'd have to scale the peak to reach the PCT from here, however . . . probably not a good idea.) The Tahoe–Yosemite trailhead is near Meeks Bay on Hwy 89, 18 miles north of South Lake Tahoe, at the end of an unnamed forest road just west of the highway. Look for the trailhead sign along the roadside. If you reach Log Cabin Rd, you've gone too far.

Mount Tallac Trail (moderate; 11 miles to the top) offers panoramic views of Fallen Leaf Lake and the adjacent forested canyons. Catapult straight up to Tallac Summit, 9,735 feet, for a sweeping vista of the Lake Tahoe Basin. Just southwest is the Gilmore Lake basin, nestled in at 8,300 feet, near the trail's junction with the Pacific Crest Trail. The Mount Tallac staging area is 3 miles north of South Lake Tahoe on Hwy 89 on the west of the road. Watch for signs for Desolation Wilderness.

Barker Pass, at the 8,166-foot Barker Peak west of Tahoe Pines, is the access point for the **Pacific Crest Trail** segment (difficult; 32 miles one way) that extends south through Desolation Wilderness to the Echo Summit area on US 50. This section passes through mostly 7,000- to 8,000-foot elevations, with suitable camping spots in the Velma Lakes basin, at Dicks Pass, and at the Lake Aloha basin outside Desolation Valley. Camp Harvey on the northern banks of Echo Lake is also a favorite spot to roll out a sleeping pad in late summer. In winter and spring, this trail is too snowed in to make the three- to four-day trek across, so check on trail conditions before setting out. Remember, wilderness permits are required on this segment of the PCT, and use of fire is prohibited within the Desolation Wilderness boundaries. To reach the staging area at Barker Pass, take Hwy 89 west to the Blackwood Canyon Rd turnoff, just north of Eagle Rock at Tahoe Pines, and continue through the Blackwood Creek Canyon on Forest Rd 15N03 for 8 miles to the trailhead. Contact the Lake Tahoe Basin Management Unit in South Lake Tahoe, (530) 573-2674.

Like Desolation Wilderness, the isolated backcountry of **Granite Chief Wilderness** features stunning glaciated valleys, peaks topping out at over 9,000 feet, forested canyons, and high mountain lakes. While less than half the size of Desolation Wilderness, it is more secluded since no vehicles are allowed within the wilderness boundaries. The **Shanks Cove Trail/Five Lakes Canyon Trail** corridor (moderate; 11 miles round trip) is a butt-kicking, switchback-strewn trek through the dead center of Granite Chief, with a great view of the Tahoe Basin and an easy connection to Pacific Crest Trail. Watch out for steep sections and damaged trail runs. The staging area is at the end of Squaw Valley Rd, 6 miles west from Hwy 89. The segment of **Pacific Crest Trail** passing through Granite Chief from Barker Pass (difficult; 32 miles one way) to the infamous Donner Summit (at Boreal Ridge) is a tremendous spring wildflower walk through Barker Meadow (14 miles in) and offers spectacular vistas from several peaks, including the 9,000-foot Granite Peak. This section has some wicked, rugged climbs before and after descending the American River canyon. Watch for tricky switchbacks between Mount Judah and Donner Ski Ranch. Allow three to four days to complete this section, and don't even think about trying it until after the spring thaw. To reach the staging area at Barker Pass, take the Blackwood Canyon Rd turnoff west from Hwy 89 just north of Eagle Rock at Tahoe Pines, and continue through the Blackwood Creek canyon 8 miles on Forest Rd 15N03 to the trailhead. Contact the Lake Tahoe Basin Management Unit in South Lake Tahoe, (530) 573-2674.

Walking

Once you've seen it from afar, it's time to get a close-up look at Lake Tahoe from its shore. This is where the scores of lakeside walking paths and nature trails come into use. Naturally, these are found at all of the shore access points described in Parks/Beaches, above. Tahoe Trips and Trails, Tahoe City, (530) 583-4506, offers **guided hiking and walking tours** of the lake region. The best lakeside walking areas are as follows:

Lighthouse Trail (easy; 1 mile round trip) is an interesting stroll through the stunted-growth forests and rocky terrain of D. L. Bliss State Park to Rubicon Point on the lake's northern shore. Because of its open exposure on three sides, Rubicon is one of the best spots along 72 miles of waterfront to view the clear blue waters of the lake and the mountainous skyline on the Nevada side. While at D. L. Bliss, also check out **Balancing Rock Nature Trail** (easy; 1 mile round trip), an interpretive walk through more of the unusual rocky forest terrain—a great opportunity to learn about the unique ecosystem here. The trail is named for the infamous rock formation in which the lower half has eroded faster than the upper, which precariously dangles in place. Finally, while at Bliss, explore the rocky shoreline south of the beach. It's an experience you won't want to miss.

Vikingsholm Trail (moderate; 1 mile round trip) is unquestionably the most heavily traveled in all of the Tahoe Basin, a short walk down a steep grade to the site of the most unusual example of Scandinavian architecture on the West Coast of the United States. The house is interesting, but take the walk for the views of Emerald Bay (see Parks/Beaches, above). Do this walk only on weekdays or in so-so weather unless you really enjoy waiting a while to park your car and then sharing the scenery with many others. In Sugar Pine Point State Park (see Parks/Beaches, above) **Dolder Trail** (easy; 1 mile round trip) is a looping trail that reaches the lakeshore at Sugar Pine Point, another great vista because of its open exposure and protrusion. One of the most interesting nature walks in all of the Tahoe Basin is at **Truckee Marsh Trail** (easy; 2 miles round trip, variable), a telling glimpse into Tahoe's past with its vistas of the expansive marsh areas at the mouth of the Truckee River east of Tahoe Keys. To reach the trailhead, take Tahoe Keys Blvd north from US 50 just before the state line and follow it all the way to the end. Parking areas are along the road, just east of the marina. The trail begins at the end of the road, east of the pavement, and is clearly marked.

Swimming/Diving

Even during the dead of summer, lowering yourself into the cobalt blue waters of Lake Tahoe can be a cold slap in the face. That's one of the reasons our favorite swimming area on the entire 72-mile shore is at **D. L. Bliss State Park** (see Parks/Beaches, above)—because there you can just jump in off the rocks and get it over with (but be sure to be extra-careful if you do). Our second choice, because of its nice amenities, is at **Zephyr Cove Resort** (see Parks/Beaches, above), just across the state line from South Lake Tahoe and past casino row. While we would rarely suggest a commercial operation jammed with *Baywatch* clones as a place to have fun, this one is different . . . take our word for it. It's also a great place for water sports, with Jet-ski and boat rentals available from the marina. Call the resort at the Zephyr Cove Marina, (702) 588-3833. **Kings Beach State Recreation Area** (see Parks/Beaches, above) is another well-appointed place to make body contact with the water and also has water-sports rentals on site. Call the North Tahoe Recreation and Parks Department, (530) 546-7248.

There is an **underwater park** in **Emerald Bay,** but the most interesting features divers will come across when they plop into the chilly waters of the lake weren't put there by Mother Nature: sunken boats, old rusted boat trailers, and barges used during the Comstock mining era mark much of the course, along with an unbelievable amount of junk tossed into the cobalt blue waters in more modern times—like last week. Access is from the southern shore of Emerald Bay. Take Hwy 89 north from South Lake Tahoe 7 miles to the Emerald Bay area. Parking is very limited. Either find parking in the main lot at the park and hike down to the south shore of the bay, or continue along Hwy 89 to any area where parking is allowed on the side of the road, and then hike back. There's simply no easy way to get there.

Boating/Sailing

The best way to see Lake Tahoe and reach some of its most beautiful inlets is by boat—as politically incorrect as it may be to go buzzing around on a beautiful and environmentally sensitive body of water. As a matter of fact, environmentalists have led a valiant effort to ban motorboats and Jet-skis from Tahoe's waters completely. That hasn't happened yet (we just got back from a wild boating tour of the lake a few weeks ago), so public boat launches are easy to find around the lake perimeter, either at private resorts or public campgrounds. On the north end of the lake, **Kings Beach State Recreation Area** (see Parks/Beaches, above) has everything you need to get out onto the big blue—boat, kayak, and Jet-ski rentals plus a public ramp. Call (530) 583-3074 for information. **Zephyr Cove Marina** (see Parks/Beaches, above) on the south shore, just across the state line in Nevada, also has a good selection of boats and a public ramp. Call (702)

588-3833. Once you're on the water, head to the stunningly beautiful **Emerald Bay** on the lake's west shore, dock at **Fannette Island,** and go for a swim. Be sure to adhere to speed restrictions and traffic control at the bay entrance. **D. L. Bliss State Park's** 4 miles of mostly rocky shore is another favorite haunt. The **Tahoe Keys marina** is also a reliable access point to the water, with two public ramps. Other public boat ramps are also at Sand Harbor at Nevada Beach (see Parks/Beaches, above) and at Cave Rock.

If you really want to draw sneers and jeers from environmentalists, rent a Jet-ski and have as much fun as humanly possible on the seemingly boundless waters. **Kings Beach** and **Zephyr Cove** (see Parks/Beaches, above) rent both Jet-skis and ski boats, as does the High Sierra Water Ski School at Sunnyside Marina in Tahoe City, (530) 525-1214.

The winds can really pick up out on the lake's center, and that is good news for boaters who want to get sideways. Action Watersports of Tahoe, in South Lake Tahoe, has **sailboat rentals** from the Timber Cove Marina on the US 50 waterfront, at 3411 Lake Tahoe Blvd, (530) 544-3411.

Canoeing/Kayaking

Sure, you can shove off from the beaches of Lake Tahoe under paddle power. It's more environmentally responsible and better exercise than all the other alternatives—and it's a great way to view the shore without the sound of a jet engine screaming in your ears. For an even more serene experience on the water, however, take your gear to one of the numerous smaller lakes in the Tahoe wilderness areas, such as Echo Lake, Fallen Leaf, or even Donner Lake (see Truckee Region chapter). **Rent** kayaks at Kings Beach (see Parks/Beaches, above), or call Tahoe Paddle & Oar in Tahoe City, (530) 581-3029, for rentals and/or lessons.

Camping

Camping on public grounds within the national forests is allowed anywhere, although **dispersed camping** must be a suitable distance from developed campgrounds and permits are required for any use of fire. Periodic road closures are possible, and roads are not maintained for vehicles with low ground clearance, so check with the relevant ranger station for updated **road conditions** before deciding on a site deep within the forest. The Forest Service is currently reviewing its **reservations and fees** policies for this area, but generally no reservations are taken for any of the campgrounds listed below. Stays are limited to 14 days.

Campers have numerous options around the lakeshore and in forested areas, with easy access to the lake, but direct shore access is prime real estate and hard to come by. The key to a good camping experience here, however, is to avoid two things: highway noise and overcrowded campgrounds. A few years back on the Fourth of July weekend, we decided at the last minute we would like to see the Lake Tahoe fireworks (by some standards, the best fireworks display on the West Coast) and we were hell bent on camping—even though every public campground was jammed. We ended up at a private campground much too close to US 50—nothing like the sound of big rigs thundering through the trees to make your camping experiences memorable. On poorly planned trips, campgrounds full of shrieking children and barking dogs can also be common. D. L. Bliss State Park is the prime camping location on the shore; if you can't get a site there or at Sugar Pine Point, it is probably best to head for the hills and try dispersed camping in the national forest or dropping into a national forest developed site. Call the Forest Service reservations system at (800) 280-2267 or individual ranger stations for campsite availability information and reservations where applicable. For state facilities, call well in advance for reservations, (800) 444-7275.

El Dorado National Forest, (530) 644-6048

Northshore, Loon Lake Camp has 15 sites (no hookups; various RV lengths accommodated) serves as an overflow area for the area's more popular camp areas, as it is near Lake Tahoe. There is no running water, so be sure to bring plenty of your own. Tables and fire rings are provided. *From Pollock Pines, take US 50 east, just past Riverton, and turn left onto Ice House Rd. Travel the long curvy road past Wentworth Springs Rd and Schlein Ranger Station to the campground on the right.*

Loon Lake Campground contains about 50 sites (no hookups; RV limit 21 feet) along the banks of Loon Lake's northwest shore. The campground's proximity to the lake's boat ramp makes it a popular destination. Piped water, vault toilets, tables, and fire rings are provided. *From Pollock Pines, take US 50 east, just past Riverton, and turn left onto Ice House Rd. Travel the long curvy road past Wentworth Springs Rd and Schlein Ranger Station to the campground on the right.*

Wrights Lake Campground has 75 sites (no hookups; RV limit 21 feet) along the banks of a beautiful and very quiet alpine lake. About half the sites are exclusively for RVs. The campground has piped water and vault toilets. Tables and fire rings are provided. *From Pollock Pines, take US 50 east. Continue about 16 miles east of Ice House Rd, then turn left onto Wrights Lake Rd. Proceed to the campground along the lake at the end of the road.*

Sunset Campground contains 165 sites (no hookups; RV limit 21 feet) along Union Valley Reservoir. This campground is enormous by local standards. If you want to escape the crowds, 30 walk-in sites (100 yards in) are at the back end of the campground. The campground has piped water and vault toilets, and each site is equipped with a table and fire ring. A boat ramp and sanitary disposal station for RVs are nearby. *From Pollock Pines, take US 50 east to Riverton and exit north onto Ice House Rd. Go past Ice House Reservoir to the south shore of Union Valley Reservoir. Continue past Jones Fork Powerhouse Rd over Jones Fork Silver Creek to the campground access road on the left.*

Yellowjacket Campground contains 42 sites (no hookups; RV limit 21 feet) along Union Valley Reservoir. The campground serves as an overflow area for Sunset Campground (see above). It has piped water, vault toilets, tables, and fire rings. A boat ramp is adjacent to the campground, making it popular with people wanting to fish. *From Pollock Pines, take US 50 east to Riverton and exit north onto Ice House Rd. Go past Ice House Reservoir to the north shore of Union Valley Reservoir. Turn right and proceed along the northern shore to the campground.*

Ice House Campground contains 17 sites (no hookups; RV limit 23 feet) along Ice House Reservoir. This campground is sought by visitors to the area who wish to avoid the larger crowds typically found at Union Valley reservoir. Piped water, vault toilets, tables, and fire rings are provided. A boat ramp is nearby. *From Pollock Pines, take US 50 east to Riverton and exit north onto Ice House Rd. Go 6 miles to Big Hill Lookout Rd and turn right. Proceed to the campground ahead*

Northwind Campground has 11 sites (no hookups; RV limit 26 feet) on a high ridge along Ice House Reservoir, a popular fishing spot. The campground has piped water and vault toilets. Each site is also equipped with a table and fire ring. A boat ramp is nearby. *From Pollock Pines, take US 50 east to Riverton and exit north onto Ice House Rd. Go to Big Hill Lookout Rd and turn right. Proceed to the campground ahead.*

China Flat Campground contains 21 sites (no hookups; RV limit 22 feet) across the highway from the south fork of the American River. The campground has piped water and vault toilets, and each site has a table and fire ring. A general store is to the west in Riverton. *From Pollock Pines, take US 50 east to Kyburz and turn right (south) onto Silver Fork Rd. Turn left onto Redwing Rd, then go right for 4 miles to the unmarked forest road. Continue to the campground another 3 miles ahead.*

Sand Flat Campground contains 21 sites (no hookups; RV limit 22 feet) adjacent to the south fork of the American River. The campground has piped water and vault toilets, and each site has a table and fire ring. A general store is to the west in Riverton. *From Pollock Pines, take US 50 east, about 4 miles past the junction with Ice House Rd. Look for the campground on the right just before Dutch Camp.*

Highway 88/Carson Pass area, (530) 644-6048

Kirkwood Lake Camp has 12 tent sites (no RV access) along the banks of small, placid Kirkwood Lake. The campground is popular with visitors looking for solitude. Piped water, vault toilets, tables, and fire rings are provided. *From Markleeville, take Hwy 89 north to Hwy 88 west. Proceed to Kirkwood Lake on the right, just past Caples Lake.*

Caples Lake contains 45 sites, 15 of which are for RVs (no hookups; RV limit 21 feet) along the banks of Caples Lake. Unfortunately, the highway is nearby, so the sites close to the road can be a bit noisy. The campground has piped water and vault toilets. Tables and fire rings are provided, and a laundromat and general store are a short distance away. *From Markleeville, take Hwy 89 north to Hwy 88 west. Go past Red Lake to the campground access road on the left.*

Silver Lake East has 30 sites (no hookups; RV limit 28 feet) along the western shore of Silver Lake, a beautiful alpine lake with numerous coves and a small island in its center. A popular spot among visitors to the Sierra, this region has a number of small lakes, and, as one might imagine, great fishing, canoeing, and hiking. The campground has piped water and vault toilets. Tables and fire rings are provided. *From Markleeville, take Hwy 89 north to Hwy 88 west. Go past Caples Lake to the campground access road on the left.*

Silver Lake West has 65 sites (no hookups; RV limit 28 feet), 25 of which are exclusively for tents. Nestled along the western shore of Silver Lake, this area is popular for fishing, canoeing, and hiking. The campground has piped water and vault toilets. Tables and fire rings are provided. *From Markleeville, take Hwy 89 north to Hwy 88 west. Go past Caples Lake to the campground access road on the left.*

Woods Lake Campground contains 25 tent sites (no RV access) adjacent to Woods Lake. This campground is set far off the highway, which allows visitors to enjoy a feeling of being out in the middle of nowhere. The lake is great for canoeing, swimming, and fishing. Piped water, vault toilets, tables, and fire rings are provided. *From Markleeville, take Hwy 89 north to Hwy 88 west. Go past Red Lake and turn left onto Woods Lake Rd. Proceed to the campground.*

Toiyabe National Forest, (702) 882-2766

Kit Carson Campground has 15 sites (no hookups; RV limit 21 feet) tucked away in the High Sierra south of Lake Tahoe along Carson River. The campground is serene and quiet. Piped water, vault toilets, tables, and fire rings are provided. *From Markleeville, take Hwy 89 north and turn left onto Hwy 88. Go past Shingle Mill Flat about 1.5 miles to the campground access road on the right.*

Hope Valley Campground contains 20 sites (no hookups; RV limit 21 feet) tucked away in the High Sierra south of Lake Tahoe along Carson River. The campground is popular with visitors who enjoy fishing in a very quiet and undisturbed area. Piped water, vault toilets, tables, and fire rings are provided. *From Markleeville, take Hwy 89 north and turn left onto Hwy 88. Go past Maxwell Creek and turn left onto Blue Lakes Rd. Continue to the campground ahead.*

Crystal Springs Campground has 23 sites (no hookups; RV limit 21 feet) on the Carson River. The campground is serene, quiet, and popular among visitors who enjoy fishing. Piped water, vault toilets, tables, and fire rings are provided. A general store is just east in Woodfords. *From Markleeville, take Hwy 89 north and turn left onto Hwy 88. Go about 1 mile and turn left onto Crystal Springs Rd. Proceed to the campground.*

Turtle Rock Campground has 30 sites (no hookups; RV limit 28 feet) and serves as an overflow area for the more popular campgrounds to the west, along the Carson River. Piped water, vault toilets, tables, and fire rings are provided. A general store is just east in Woodfords. *From Markleeville, take Hwy 89 north about 5 miles and turn left into Turtle Rock County Park. Proceed to the campground.*

Grover Hot Springs State Park has about 80 sites (no hookups; RV limit 28 feet) of which 30 are for tents only and 13 are for RVs only. The campground is popular not only because of its proximity to the Grover Hot Springs (see Attractions, below) but also for its amenities. It has piped water, flush toilets, showers, and a swimming pool. Tables and fire rings are provided, and a laundromat and general store are a short distance away. *From Markleeville, turn west onto Montgomery Rd. Veer right onto Hot Springs Rd and proceed to the campground.*

Markleeville Campground has 12 sites (no hookups; RV limit 21 feet) and serves as an overflow area for the Grover Hot Springs Campground to the west (see above). Piped water, vault toilets, tables, and fire rings are provided, and a general store is northwest in Markleeville. *From Markleeville, take Hwy 89 south a few hundred feet to the campground on the left side of the highway.*

Northwest Lake Tahoe area

Sugar Pine Point State Park has 180 sites (no hookups; RV limit 31 feet) near the shore of Lake Tahoe. The campground is quite popular due to its amenities and proximity to Tahoe City. Piped water, flush toilets, and showers are available. Tables and fire rings are provided. A general store is within walking distance at Tahoe City. *From Truckee, go south on Hwy 89 to Tahoe City. Turn right on Hwy 89 and proceed past Tahoma to the campground* *on the right. Call the park, (530) 583-3642, or the state reservations system, (800) 444-7275.*

Tahoe State Recreation Area Campground has 32 sites (no hookups; RV limit 21 feet) a short walk from Lake Tahoe. The campground serves as an overflow area when the more popular campgrounds closer to the banks of the lake are at capacity. Located close to the highway, the campground can be a bit noisy. Piped water, flush toilets, showers, tables, and fire rings are provided. A general store is within walking distance. *From Truckee, go south on Hwy 89 to Tahoe City. Turn left and proceed north on Hwy 28 about 1 mile to the campground on the left. Call the campground, (530) 583-3074, for information. For reservations, call the state reservations system, (800) 444-7275.*

William Kent Campground contains roughly 100 sites (no hookups; RV limit 21 feet) across the highway from Lake Tahoe. Regularly used as an overflow area, the campground is busy. Piped water, flush toilets, tables, and fire rings are provided. A general store is within walking distance at Tahoe City. *From Truckee, go south on Hwy 89 to Tahoe City. Continue on Hwy 89 to the campground on the right about 3 miles ahead. Call the campground, (530) 583-3642, for information and reservations.*

Lake Forest Campground contains 20 sites (partial hookups; RV limit 31 feet) near the banks of Lake Tahoe. It seems this popular campground is always busy, perhaps because it is adjacent to the only boat ramp in the northwest Tahoe area. Piped water, flush toilets, tables, and fire rings are provided. A general store is a short distance south in Tahoe City. *From Truckee, go south on Hwy 89 to Tahoe City. Turn left and go north on Hwy 28 about 2 miles to Lake Forest Rd. Turn right and proceed to the campground. Call the campground, (530) 583-3074, for information and reservations.*

Sandy Beach Campground has 44 sites (partial hookups; RV limit 21 feet) a short walk from Lake Tahoe's northern rim. As with all campgrounds near the lake, it is a popular spot and can get crowded, particularly since it is the only campground near the lake along its northern rim. Piped water, flush toilets, and showers are available. Tables and fire rings are provided. A general store is to the east in Tahoe City. *From Truckee, go south on Hwy 89 to Tahoe City. Turn left, go north on Hwy 28, and proceed to Carnelian, about 7 miles ahead. Look for the campground on the left. For information and reservations, call the campground, (530) 546-7682.*

Southwest Lake Tahoe area

Meeks Bay Camp contains 40 sites (no hookups; RV limit 21 feet) on Lake Tahoe's western shore. Though the campground is close to the highway and therefore gets traffic noise, it is a popular spot and can be crowded. Piped water, flush toilets, showers, tables, and fire rings are provided. A general store is nearby in Meeks Bay. *From Truckee, go south on Hwy 89 to Tahoe City. Turn right on Hwy 89 and proceed to the campground just outside of Meeks Bay. For information and reservations, call the campground, (530) 583-3642.*

D. L. Bliss State Park Campground has 170 sites (no hookups; RV limit 21 feet) on Lake Tahoe's western shore. The campground is nestled in a grove of pines in one of Tahoe's most beautiful landscapes. The lake is a short walk from the camp. Piped water, flush toilets, showers, tables, and fire rings are provided. *From Truckee, go south on Hwy 89 to Tahoe City. Turn right on Hwy 89 and proceed past Meeks Bay to the park on the right. Enter the park and proceed to the campground. For information, call the park at (530) 525-7277. For reservations, call the state reservations system, (800) 444-7275.*

Emerald Bay State Park has roughly 100 sites (no hookups; RV limit 21 feet) near Lake Tahoe's western shore. The campground is very popular, as it lies adjacent to Emerald Bay. Piped water, flush toilets, and showers are available. Tables and fire rings are provided. *From Truckee, go south on Hwy 89 to Tahoe City. Turn right on Hwy 89 and proceed past D. L. Bliss State Park, around to Emerald Bay's southern shore, to the campground's access road on the right. Call the park, (530) 541-3030, for information. For reservations, call the state reservations system, (800) 444-7275.*

Camp Richardson Resort contains 340 sites (some hookups; various RV lengths accommodated) a short walk from Lake Tahoe's southern shore. This is the largest campground in the Tahoe area, and certainly the busiest due to its proximity to the lake and the casinos. Piped water, flush toilets, and showers are available. Tables and fire rings are provided. A general store is nearby. Pets are not allowed at this camp. *From South Lake Tahoe, take US 50 south to Hwy 89. Proceed on Hwy 89 north to the campground on the right. Call the resort for information and reservations, (530) 541-1801.*

El Dorado Recreation Area Campground has 190 sites (some hookups; RV limit 21 feet) near Tahoe's southern shoreline. Proximity to the casinos on the Nevada border, along with the hustle of Stateline, make this campground busy. If you are in search of solitude, look elsewhere. Piped water, flush toilets, and showers are available. Tables and fire rings are provided. A general store is nearby. *From the junction of Hwy 89 and US 50, take US 50 north to South Lake Tahoe and turn right onto Lyons Rd. Proceed to the campground. For information and reservations, call the campground, (530) 542-6096.*

Fallen Leaf Campground consists of about 225 sites (no hookups;

RV limit 38 feet) along the banks of Fallen Leaf Lake. About 75 of the sites are exclusively for tents. Make no mistake about it, this lake is one of the most beautiful in the Tahoe area, and its proximity to Lake Tahoe makes the campground a prime spot. The campground has piped water and flush toilets. Tables and fire rings are provided, and a laundromat and general store are a short distance away. *From South Lake Tahoe, take US 50 south to Hwy 89. Proceed on Hwy 89 north to the sign for Fallen Leaf Lake on the left, near Camp Richardson. Follow the sign to the campground. Call the Tahoe Ranger District, (530) 544-0426, for information. For reservations, call the Forest Service reservations system, (800) 280-2267.*

Tahoe Valley Campground has 80 sites (some hookups; various RV lengths accommodated) just south of Lake Tahoe. The campground is quite popular due to its conveniences and amenities. Piped water, flush toilets, and showers are available. Tables and fire rings are provided, and the facility has a general store, laundromat, and swimming pool. *From South Lake Tahoe, take US 50 west past Meyers to the campground on the right. Call the campground, (530) 544-0426, for more information. It is privately run on Forest Service land.*

Scenic Drives/Photography

Carson Pass National Scenic Byway is a beautiful ride through the Sierra Nevada foothills that gives you a little taste of Gold Rush country, wide and sweeping views of the El Dorado National Forest's southern boundaries, nice lakeside resting places to stretch your legs, and beautiful High Sierra wetlands and meadows. The Byway includes much of our favorite highway into the Lake Tahoe Basin, Hwy 88 (and, best of all, spares you the white-knuckled craziness of US 50). Numerous stopping points along the highway are choice places to photograph. First, pull into Jackson at the junction of Hwy 88 and Gold Rush Highway (Hwy 49), and head slightly north for a quick peek at **Sutter Creek,** a small Gold Rush town brimming with its original old-time charm. As the highway ascends out of the foothills toward Kirkwood Ski Resort (see Downhill Skiing/ Snowboarding, above), watch for Silver Lake and Caples Lake, before and after the resort turnoff. Stop on the east side of Caples Lake dam to take in a magnificent view of **Caples Creek Canyon.** The next lake in the chain is Red Lake, and following it on Hwy 89 to US 50 are **Grass Leaf Lake** and **Grass Leaf Creek,** which spills into open marshes and postcard picture–perfect meadows blooming with wildflowers in spring. Naturally, you will want to save plenty of film for Lake Tahoe itself.

Biking

If you haven't figured it out yet, there are two different ways to enjoy Tahoe. One is to meld into the crowds and do the obvious. The other is to put a little distance between yourself and others by hiking a ways, getting out onto the water in a boat, or finding a quiet spot within the madness. Well, if you want to ride a bicycle on the shores of the lake, forget about doing it without company. Sure, the trails are nice. Sure, they're paved. You just have to share them and get over it if you want to enjoy them. There are four main trail segments on the west side of the lake, with the leg up going to the Truckee River canyon toward Squaw Valley at Tahoe City. From Tahoe City and the Truckee River, working south, the trail connections parallel Hwy 89. There are long-range plans to someday encircle the lakeshore with easy-to-use contiguous trail segments, but the day you see the entire 72-mile shoreline trail finished will be the day that neighboring city, state, county, and regional government agencies figure out how to cooperate with each other . . . so it may take time. If it's a nature ride you're looking for, head for the mountains; you will stand a better chance of finding some peace and quiet that way. The lakeshore, however, is so darn nice that it may well be worth putting up with a few indelicacies for.

The **Truckee River Recreation Trail,** as the name would suggest, follows the Truckee River from the Alpine Meadows area just east of Squaw Valley for 4.5 miles to Tahoe City, where it drops into the Hwy 89 corridor and connects with the **West Shore Bike Path**—the longest and nicest cycling tour you're going to find anywhere along the lakefront area. The staging area for this trail segment is just west of where Hwys 28 and 89 meet in Tahoe City. The trail extends from Tahoe City 10 miles south to Sugar Pine Point State Park at Meeks Bay. This stretch of trail meanders the highway, passing through wooded areas, lake vista points, and a few commercial spots on the highway between South Lake Tahoe and Tahoe City. But remember, this portion of Hwy 89 is wall-to-wall cars on warm weekend days. As such, be aware that there are some trail crossings at the highway—and on busy days that could spell bad news for anyone on a bike. Use extra caution in places where the trail and the highway come together. This is also the most crowded section of trail, not only because it is so scenic but also because it is nearest to where most visitors camp, rent their bicycles, and park their minivans. The best medicine is to just ride, fan out as far and wide as you can, and try to find some breathing room.

The 3.5-mile stretch of paved cycling trail between the Hwy 89 interchange with US 50 at South Lake Tahoe and the Forest Service visitors center at Tallac—**Pope Baldwin Bike Path**—is another very busy stretch of pavement straddling the lakeshore, with pretty scenery all around. To find the trailhead, take Hwy 89 north from the US 50 interchange for 4 miles; the visitors center is on the right side of the highway. Parking, again, is limited in this area and throughout this section of the lakeshore, so be resourceful.

Finally, the 5-mile stretch of **South Lake Tahoe Bike Path** extending from the US 50/Hwy 89 interchange, east across the south lakeshore to the Truckee marsh, traverses the busiest and most populated areas of the Tahoe Basin—but there are beach and picnic stops along the way, and the marsh area is interesting from an ecological point of view, since it is one of the largest remaining sections of lakeshore marshlands still around. The best access is from the interchange business district, where there is plenty of parking. Also pick up the trail from Bijou Park, which is at the end of Ski Run Blvd—make a left turn from US 50, 4 miles east of the Hwy 89 interchange. Virtually all of these trail sections are easy and level, with the exception of a portion near the Truckee River connections through Tahoe City. In addition to the access points described above, it is possible to hop onto the trail system from just about any public beach or shorefront area mentioned in this section.

There are numerous **bicycle rental** outfits throughout the Hwy 89/US 50 corridor, including several very visible ones at the highway split in South Lake Tahoe's commercial section. Anderson's Bicycle Rental, 545 Emerald Bay Rd, (530) 541-0500, and Sierra Cycle Works, 3430 US 50, South Lake Tahoe, (530) 541-7505, are two reputable places near staging areas for both the South Lake Tahoe and Pope Baldwin paths. Camp Richardson, 1900 Jameson Beach Rd, South Lake Tahoe, (530) 542-6584, also has bicycle rentals. In the Tahoe City area, try Olympic Bike Shop, 620 North Lake Tahoe Blvd, (530) 581-2500.

The scores of logging roads in El Dorado and Tahoe National Forests create a backcountry playground of unimaginable proportions for avid **mountain bikers.** Just be sure to stay out of designated wilderness areas, public property where you're not welcome, and areas where logging operations are under way (having a run-in with a logging truck is no fun). Most major ski resorts (see Downhill Skiing/Snowboarding, above) also have some trails open to mountain bikes in the off-season. Kirkwood, for example, boasts a vast network of dirt roads and single-track trails meandering down the face of the mountain (you ride the lifts to the top). Rentals are available on-site. Call (530) 258-7283 for information. Squaw Valley, Northstar, Heavenly, and other resorts are similarly appointed.

Fishing

With literally hundreds of small, secluded lakes and reservoirs to choose from, anglers who know for certain they don't want to join the masses on Lake Tahoe have a number of options. The El Dorado National Forest alone has 600 miles of streams and hundreds of lakes and reservoirs dotting the high-country landscape. Depending on how well Mother Nature is cooperating, **rainbow, brown,** and **eastern brook trout** fly-fishing action can be a crowning highlight to a backpacking trip across the Tahoe Basin wildlands. Lake Genevieve, Crag Lake, Shadow Lake, Hidden Lake, Stony Ridge Lake, and Rubicon Lake all are situated in the Desolation Wilderness Area of El Dorado National Forest along the Tahoe-Yosemite Trail—nice scenery if you're willing to hike in with your gear (see Hiking/Backpacking, above). Also fish the adjoining creeks. Woods Lake, in the Carson Pass region near Markleeville, off Woods Lake Rd from Hwy 88 east of Hwy 89, is another quiet spot in the high country you can actually drive to. Union Valley Reservoir, off US 50 near Pollock Pines at Ice House Rd, is another out-of-the-way drive-in lake in the foothills. Closer to Tahoe and moderately crowded because of its location, Fallen Leaf Lake (see Camping, above) can be a good spot to fly-fish for **rainbows, browns,** and **Mackinaw.** Call the El Dorado National Forest headquarters in Placerville, (530) 622-5061, for the latest word on road and trail access before setting out for far-flung areas. As always, check with the appropriate regulatory agencies for up-to-date fishing laws. The state Department of Fish and Game office in Rancho Cordova, (530) 358-2900, has an update, or you can try to decipher a free regulations handbook available at most licensing locations, including bait shops.

Mackinaw and **rainbow trout** are the main game for anglers casting into Lake Tahoe itself, but shore fishing can be a waste of time if you really expect to catch anything. The lake is big, deep, and cold, and most good fishing spots are accessible only by boat. Still, fishing from one of the lake's numerous coves, with piers or suitable spots to anchor, can be enjoyable. Consider boating from Zephyr Cove (see Boating/Sailing, above) just west to Marla Cove, much quieter and often suitable for fishing. Also remember that the points around the lake where creeks and river mouths meet the blue waters are particularly productive during the winter migration. Still, you'd do best to opt instead for one of the hundreds of small fishing lakes in the Tahoe wilderness areas, where **rainbows, browns,** and **golden trout** are the main fare. The **Truckee River,** north of Truckee along Hwy 89, is a dependable spot for **rainbow** during spring through November, and the stretch between Truckee and Tahoe City is a good run for **rainbows** and **browns.** Access is all along Hwy 89, which follows the river out from Tahoe City. Rampart, 10 miles north of Tahoe City, is a good place to stage in search of a spot.

The Outdoor & Flyfishing Store, 3433 Lake Tahoe Blvd, South Lake Tahoe, (530) 541-8208, and True Value Hardware, 200 North Lake Blvd, Tahoe City, (530) 583-3738, are good **bait-and-tackle** stops around the lake. Dennis's Eagle Point Sport Fishing, (530) 577-6834, and O'Malley's Fishing Charters, (702) 588-4102, are two of a few dozen **guide services** working the lake area.

Wildlife

Birders exploring the expansive forests of Jeffrey pine, juniper, live oak, and hemlock and the granite-walled river canyons around Tahoe and its wilderness areas should watch for **quail** and **coots** near waterways and marshes. A long list of frequently spotted birds in the forested areas includes swallows, great horned owls, Cooper's hawks, western meadowlarks, blackbirds, warblers, sage grouse, and sparrows.

The ever-present **black bears** and **rattlesnakes** join **raccoons, bobcats, mountain lions, skunks,** numerous **squirrels,** and even **porcupines** to round out the list of reptiles and mammals often spotted in these parts. Campers and backpackers are asked to use extreme caution in black bear areas so as to not attract them with food and other goodies. Food should be properly packed and stored, and take all your garbage out of the wilderness.

Rafting/Kayaking

The **Truckee River,** the **east fork of the Carson River** along the Hwy 89 corridor east of Markleeville, and the **middle and south forks of the American River** all offer good whitewater runs. See Rafting/Kayaking, Truckee Region chapter.

Adventure Calendar

Death Ride Tour of the California Alps, mid-July: *a grueling 128-mile bike trek over five mountain passes (15,000 feet of climbing) that's renowned among bicyclists as one of the top 10 cycling challenges in America; limited to the first 2,500 prepaid applicants, (530) 694-2475 or alpcnty@telis.org.*

Attractions

Frontiersman Kit Carson was guiding General John Frémont's expedition across the Sierra Nevada in 1844 when he stumbled on an immense, deep-blue body of water, a lake so vast the native Washoe Indians were calling it *tahoe* ("big lake"). Carson was the first white man to see **Lake Tahoe,** North America's largest alpine lake and the eighth-deepest in the world (1,645 feet at its deepest point). If completely drained, Tahoe would cover the entire state of California with 14 inches of water.

The California/Nevada border runs straight through the heart of the lake, leaving its west side in California and its east side in Nevada. Despite this east/west state division, the lake is more commonly referred to in terms of its north and south shores. The South Shore area is the most populous and urban, where you'll hear all those slot machines ringing and coins tinkling. If you'd rather steer clear of the one-armed bandits, head for the North Shore. There you'll find fewer casinos (and tourists) and more of everything else, including Tahoe's best alpine and cross-country ski resorts, first-rate restaurants, and luxurious lodgings.

When you first arrive at **North Lake Tahoe,** make a quick stop in Tahoe City at the **Tahoe North Visitors and Convention Bureau** and sort through the mountain of brochures on local attractions ranging from indoor wall climbing to ice skating and horseback riding. If you plan to hike or ride bikes here, load up on the free trail maps, too. This is also the place to visit or call if you're having trouble finding a hotel room or campsite (a common problem during peak seasons) or need information on ski packages; 950 North Lake Blvd, above McDonald's, Tahoe City, (530) 581-6900 or (800) 824-6348. If you weren't able to pack all your recreational toys, Porter's Ski & Sport in Tahoe City has the best prices in town for **outdoor equipment rental**—everything from bikes to skates to rackets, as well as a full line of snow skis, water-skis, and snowboards; 501 North Lake Blvd, Tahoe City, (530) 583-2314.

To try your luck at blackjack or spinning the big wheel, make the short drive to Nevada, where the folks in the **casinos** will be delighted to see you. Although the North Shore's casinos are more subdued and less glitzy than the South Shore's high-rolling high-rises, the dealers are still adept at taking your money. If you're a greenhorn, this is a good place to learn the ABCs of the games, especially during off-hours. North Shore casinos include the Tahoe Biltmore Hotel, (702) 831-0660; Cal-Neva Lodge and Casino, (702) 832-4000; Hyatt Regency Lake Tahoe, (702)

831-1111; and Crystal Bay Club Casino, (702) 831-0512.

North Lake Tahoe also offers a few nocturnal alternatives to the dice and the slots. You can dance any night of the week at Pierce Street Annex, which caters primarily to a thirtysomething crowd but attracts swingers of all ages; 850 North Lake Blvd, behind Safeway, Tahoe City, (530) 583-5800. Humpty's, on the other hand, resembles (and smells like) a college-town hangout, though this is where you'll find some of the area's top dance bands and the cheapest drinks; 877 North Lake Blvd, across from Safeway, Tahoe City, (530) 583-4867. During the ski season, the lounge of the River Ranch Lodge (see Lodgings, below) has a raging après-ski scene, with ski bums from all over kicking back and chowing down on cheap hors d'oeuvres.

Three premier attractions separate sassy **South Lake Tahoe** from its sportier northern counterpart: glitzy casinos with celebrity entertainers, several sandy beaches, and the massive Heavenly ski resort (see Downhill Skiing/Snowboarding, above), the only American ski area that straddles two states. If 24-hour gambling parties or schussing down the slopes of Heavenly is your idea of paradise, then you're in for a treat.

Most of the weekend warriors who flock here on Friday afternoons book their favorite lodgings weeks—if not months—in advance. Follow their lead and plan early. For long-term stays, consider renting a condo with a group of friends. As soon as you roll into town, stop at the **South Lake Tahoe Chamber of Commerce,** where you'll find an entire room filled with free maps, brochures, and guidebooks to the South Lake region. And if you risked traveling to Tahoe without a hotel reservation, ask the staff to help you find a room; 3066 Lake Tahoe Blvd, (530) 541-5255.

Tahoe's brilliant blue lake is so deep it never freezes, so it's navigable even in the dead of winter. Capitalizing on that fact, the *Tahoe Queen,* an authentic Mississippi stern-wheeler regularly used for scenic lunch and dinner cruises, doubles as a ferry for South Shore skiers who want to explore the North Shore's resorts. Skiers hop aboard at the base of Ski Run Blvd in South Lake. The 25-mile ride takes about two hours, ending at the West Shore's tiny town of Homewood, where a waiting shuttle transports riders to Squaw Valley USA ski resort (see Downhill Skiing/Snowboarding, above). Passengers return to South Lake the same way they came; however, on the trip back the bar is open, the band is playing, and the boat is rockin'. The round-trip fare is reasonable, and for an extra fee skiers can fill up on a big breakfast on the morning ferry. Reservations are required; call (530) 541-3364 for more details.

In the summer, droves of tourists and locals arrive by bike, car, or boat at The Beacon restaurant and bar (see Restaurants, below) to scope out the beach, babe, and bar scene—easily the best on the lake. The South

Lake's number-one nighttime entertainment is—you guessed it—the **casino**. The three top guns on this side of the lake are Harrah's, Caesars Tahoe, and Harveys, which are squeezed next to each other on US 50 in Nevada and burn enough bulbs to light a small city. Even if you can't afford to gamble away your money, stroll through the ruckus to watch the high rollers or gawk at those "just-one-more-try" players mesmerized by the flashy money machines. If you want to try your luck, a mere $10 can keep you entertained for quite a while on the nickel slots. Or spend the night kicking up your heels on the dance floor at Nero's 2000 Nightclub in Caesars; 55 US 50, Stateline, Nevada, (702) 588-3515. Or visit Turtle's Sports Bar and Dance Emporium in the Embassy Suites; 4130 Lake Tahoe Blvd, South Lake Tahoe, (530) 544-5400.

For more than a century, **Walley's Hot Springs Resort** in Nevada has been the place for South Lake residents to unwind after a hard day of skiing or mountain biking, even though it's about an hour-long drive from town. For less than the price of a pair of movie tickets, you can jump into the six open-air pools (each is set at a different temperature) and watch ducks and geese at the nearby wildlife area. If a good soak doesn't get all the kinks out, indulge in a rubdown at the resort's massage center. No children under 12 are allowed in the resort; 2001 Foothill Blvd, 2 miles north of the east end of Kingsbury Grade, near Genoa, Nevada, (702) 782-8155.

The only place worth visiting in the tiny mountain town of **Markleeville** is the Cutthroat Bar, located in the Alpine Hotel and Cafe downtown. Belly up to the bar, order a whiskey or two (skip the food), and contemplate why the owners decided to hang a collection of brassieres from the bar's ceiling. (By the way, women are encouraged to add their bras to the display; payment is a free Cutthroat Bar T-shirt. Whoopee!) Just outside of town is the popular Grover Hot Springs State Park (see Camping, above), where you may soak in the ugly but soothing cement **mineral pools** year-round (bathing suits are required); open 9am to 9pm daily in the summer, and 2pm to 9pm weekdays and 9am to 9pm weekends in the winter; located 4 miles west of Markleeville at the end of Hot Springs Rd, (530) 694-2248. The town's main claim to fame is the annual Death Ride Tour of the California Alps; see Adventure Calendar, above, for details on this bike trek.

Restaurants

The Beacon　☆☆　On a warm summer afternoon there is no better place on the lake to sit outside. The lunch fare is mostly salads, hamburgers, sandwiches, and the like; dinner specialties include fresh seafood. *1900 Jamison Beach Rd (off Hwy 89, 2½ miles N of the US 50 junction, at Camp Richardson), South Lake Tahoe; (530) 541-0630; $$.*

The Boulevard Cafe & Trattoria ☆☆   The breads, pastas, and just about everything else on the Boulevard's menu are made here, in the North Shore's only Italian trattoria. It's a small, casual, roadside restaurant. *6731 N Lake Blvd (on Hwy 28, 1½ miles W of Hwy 267), Tahoe Vista; (530) 546-7213; $$.*

Bridgetender Tavern and Grill ☆   Tahoe's foremost tavern, a rough-hewn log-and-stone structure built around a trio of healthy ponderosa pines, is frequented by folks who know each other on a first-name basis. The menu is basic but the food is filling and cheap. *30 W Lake Blvd (on Hwy 89 at Fanny Bridge, downtown), Tahoe City; (530) 583-3342; $.*

Christy Hill ☆☆☆   Perched high above the lake in one of the most romantic fireside settings in Tahoe, the venerable Christy Hill restaurant is one of the finest—and most expensive—restaurants in Tahoe City. The menu changes seasonally. *115 Grove St (off Hwy 28/N Lake Blvd, behind the Village Store), Tahoe City; (530) 583-8551; $$$.*

Evan's American Gourmet Café ☆☆☆   This is not the most attractive restaurant in Lake Tahoe, but the food is its raison d'être. The ever-changing menu features an eclectic and impressive mix of Italian, Caribbean, Asian, and Southwestern cuisine. *536 Emerald Bay Rd (on Hwy 89, 1 mile N of the US 50 junction, at 15th St), South Lake Tahoe; (530) 542-1990; $$$.*

Fire Sign Cafe ☆☆   This converted old Tahoe home has been a favorite breakfast stop for locals since the late 1970s. Just about everything here is made from scratch. Expect a long wait on weekends. *1785 W Lake Blvd (on Hwy 89, 2 miles S of town), Tahoe City; (530) 583-0871; $.*

Jake's on the Lake ☆☆   If you're in the mood for steak and seafood, Jake's serves some of the best in Tahoe. One link in a wildly popular California and Hawaii chain, this handsome lakefront restaurant offers consistently good food and service. *780 N Lake Blvd (on Hwy 28, downtown), Tahoe City; (530) 583-0188; $$.*

Le Petit Pier ☆☆☆   One of Tahoe's more exclusive French restaurants is elevated just above the shore with a dazzling view of the lake. Order from the prix-fixe menu gastronomique or the à la carte menu. *7238 N Lake Blvd (on Hwy 28 at the W end of town), Tahoe Vista; (530) 546-4464; $$$.*

The Red Hut ☆   This all-American coffee shop, complete with an L-shaped Formica counter, booths, and a bubble-gum machine, has become so popular the owners have added a waiting room. *2723 US 50 (¼ mile S of Al Tahoe Blvd, 3.5 miles from Stateline, Nevada), South Lake Tahoe; (530) 541-9024; $.*

Rosie's Cafe ☆☆   Most folks who spend a few days or more in North Lake Tahoe eventually wind up at Rosie's for breakfast, lunch, dinner, drinks, or all of the above. This humble Tahoe institution serves large portions of traditional American fare. *571 N Lake Blvd (on Hwy 28, downtown), Tahoe City; (530) 583-8504; $$.*

Samurai ☆☆   Despite Tahoe's far-from-the-sea location, there is decent seafood in the area, and you'll certainly find some of the freshest sea creatures at Samurai, one of the best Japanese restaurants in South Lake Tahoe. *2588 US 50 (1½ miles E of the Hwy 89 junction), South Lake Tahoe; (530) 542-0300; $$.*

Scusa! on Ski Run ☆☆   Don't let the restaurant's tacky casino lights and "Pasta Power" sign scare you away. Though the decor leaves much to be desired, this is the place where South Lake Tahoe foodies come for Italian fare. *1142 Ski Run Blvd (off US 50), South Lake Tahoe; (530) 542-0100; $$.*

Sprouts Natural Foods Cafe ☆☆   You don't have to be a granola-loving long-haired type to figure out that Sprouts is among the best places to eat in town. Almost everything is made on the premises. *3123 Harrison St (on the corner of US 50 and Alameda St), South Lake Tahoe; (530) 541-6969; $.*

Sunsets on the Lake ☆☆☆   Rare in Tahoe is a lakeside restaurant serving food that's equal to the spectacular view. Yet even the Kodak Moment beyond the window panes is humbled by the superb Northern Italian/California menu. Built with gleaming beams of pine, the restaurant has a rustic and romantic ambience. *7320 N Lake Blvd (on Hwy 28 at the E end of town), Tahoe Vista; (530) 546-3640; $$.*

Swiss Lakewood Restaurant ☆☆   This handsome Swiss-style edifice, first opened in 1920, is the home of the oldest operating restaurant in Lake Tahoe, offering fine French-Continental cuisine in a traditional Swiss setting. *5055 W Lake Blvd (on Hwy 89, 6 miles S of Tahoe City, next to Ski Homewood), Homewood; (530) 525-5211; $$$.*

Villa Gigli ☆☆☆   Every Friday, Saturday, and Sunday morning, Ruggero Gigli rolls pasta dough, bakes breads, and stuffs cannelloni in preparation for his two dozen or so nightly guests, most of whom have traveled hours to get here—it's that special. *145 Hot Springs Rd (about ¼ mile W of downtown), Markleeville; (530) 694-2253; $$.*

Wolfdale's ☆☆☆   This casually elegant restaurant is well known for its innovative California cuisine that's often accented with Japanese touches. The short, frequently changing menu offers an intriguing mix of dishes that vary from very good to sublime. *640 N Lake Blvd (on Hwy 28, downtown), Tahoe City; (530) 583-5700; $$$.*

Za's ☆☆   Za's is one of the most popular restaurants in Tahoe, serving very good Italian food at bargain prices. There are only a dozen tables, so during peak hours you'll have to join the line of salivating patrons snaking out the door. *395 N Lake Blvd (on Hwy 28, across from the fire station), Tahoe City; (530) 583-1812; $.*

Lodgings

Christiania Inn ☆☆   Located only 50 yards from Heavenly's main chairlift, this European-style bed-and-breakfast inn, built in 1965 as a Scandinavian ski dormitory, has 4 suites that are frequently occupied by honeymooners. Each suite has a wood-burning fireplace, a dry sauna or a whirlpool, and a king-size bed. *3819 Saddle Rd (off Ski Run Blvd, at the base of Heavenly ski resort), South Lake Tahoe; (530) 544-7337; $$.*

The Cottage Inn ☆☆   This is one of the more appealing places to stay in Tahoe City. Each of the inn's 15 cabins has Swedish-pine furniture, a stone fireplace, a private bath with a ceramic-tile shower, a thick, colorful quilt on the bed, and a TV with a VCR. After breakfast, kick back in the Scandinavian sauna or at the nearby beach and dock. *1690 W Lake Blvd (on Hwy 89, 2 miles S of town), Tahoe City; (530) 581-4073 or (800) 581-4073; $$.*

Franciscan Lakeside Lodge ☆   The best of the area's motel scene, the Franciscan offers access to many recreational opportunities. Its 51 plain but adequate units feature one or two bedrooms, full kitchens, private bathrooms, TVs, phones, and daily housekeeping service. *6944 N Lake Blvd (on Hwy 28, 1 mile W of Hwy 267), Tahoe Vista; (530) 546-7234, (530) 546-6300, or (800) 564-6754; $$.*

Lakeland Village Beach & Ski Resort ☆☆   This 19-acre resort has more than 1,000 feet of beachfront property, two tennis courts, and two swimming pools. The Village's 208 units, ranging from studios to five-bedroom town houses, are individually owned. All units have fireplaces, fully equipped kitchens, and daily housekeeping service. *3535 Lake Tahoe Blvd (between Ski Run Blvd and Fairway Ave), South Lake Tahoe; (530) 544-1685 or (800) 822-5969; $$$.*

PlumpJack Squaw Valley Inn ☆☆☆   This is Tahoe's most stylish and sophisticated hotel. Draped in muted tones of taupe and soft greens, the 60 guest rooms are loaded with comforts and all boast mountain views. The hotel also has a swimming pool, two spas, a retail sports shop, ski rentals and storage, and complimentary parking. *1920 Squaw Valley Rd (off Hwy 89), Squaw Valley; (530) 583-1576 or (800) 323-7666; $$$.*

Resort at Squaw Creek ☆☆☆   This $130-million super-luxury resort is a paradise for skiers, golfers, and tennis players. Tucked away in an inconspicuous corner of Squaw Valley, the nine-story resort opened in 1990, offering a plethora of amenities and 405 rooms, suites, and bi-level penthouses. *400 Squaw Creek Rd (off Hwy 89), Squaw Valley; (530) 583-6300 or (800) 327-3353; $$$.*

Richardson's Resort ☆   This log lodge offers 29 sparsely furnished rooms with private baths and is only a five-minute walk from the lake. Even closer to the water are 39 homey cabins and the small 7-room Beach Inn. Staying at Richardson's Resort is sort of like being at camp again, and it's a great place to take the kids. *At Jamison Beach Rd and Hwy 89 (2½ miles N of the US 50 junction), South Lake Tahoe; (530) 541-1801 or (800) 544-1801; $$.*

River Ranch Lodge ☆☆   This rustic, wood-shingled lodge stands on the banks of the picturesque Truckee River. All 19 rooms have private baths and antique furnishings. A continental breakfast is included in the surprisingly reasonable rates. The ski/lodging combo packages offered by River Ranch in Alpine Meadows are often outstanding. *On Hwy 89 (at Alpine Meadows Rd, 3½ miles from Lake Tahoe and Tahoe City), Alpine Meadows; (530) 583-4264 or (800) 535-9900; $$.*

Rockwood Lodge ☆☆☆   This native stone and timber lodge, located just across the street from the lake, has 5 rooms, each furnished with antiques, feather beds, and down comforters covered in Laura Ashley fabrics. The extravagant private bathrooms feature brass fixtures, hand-painted tiles, and double showers. *5295 W Lake Blvd (on Hwy 89, next to Ski Homewood), Homewood; (530) 525-5273 or (800) LE-TAHOE; $$$.*

Sorensen's Resort ☆☆   This resort's cluster of 30 cabins, nestled among the meadows and aspen groves of alpine Hope Valley, offers first-rate cross-country skiing in the winter, prime hiking in late spring and summer, and a terrific display of colors in the fall. There's good trout fishing here, too. Accommodations range from inexpensive, rustic-but-comfy cabins to grand, modern chalets. *14255 Hwy 88 (5 miles NW of Woodfords), Hope Valley; (530) 694-2203 or (800) 423-9949; $$.*

Sunnyside Restaurant & Lodge ☆☆☆   Restored about a dozen years ago, this beautiful mountain lodge has 23 rooms, each with a deck. All but four have an unobstructed view of Lake Tahoe. The Chris Craft Dining Room serves well-prepared California cuisine and specializes in fresh seafood. *1850 W Lake Blvd (on Hwy 89, 2 miles S of town), Tahoe City; (530) 583-7200 or (800) 822-2SKI; $$$.*

Tahoma Meadows Bed & Breakfast ☆☆   This B&B consists of 11 private cabins perched on a gentle forest slope among sugar pines and flowers. Each cozy cabin is individually decorated, and all rooms have a private bath, a discreetly placed TV, and comfy king-size, queen-size, or twin beds; four have gas-log fireplaces. *6821 W Lake Blvd (on Hwy 89, 8.5 miles from Tahoe City), Tahoma; (530) 525-1553 or (800) 355-1596; $$.*

More Information

Alpine Meadows: *(800) 441-4423 or (530) 581-8374.*
Basin Management Unit, South Lake Tahoe: *(530) 573-2674.*
Diamond Peak: *(702) 832-1177.*
El Dorado National Forest, supervisor's office: *(530) 622-5061.*
Forest Service reservations system: *(800) 280-2267.*
Granlibakken: *(702) 583-4242.*
Heavenly: *(800) 2HEAVEN or www.skiheavenly.com.*
Kirkwood: *(209) 258-6000.*
North Lake Tahoe Chamber of Commerce: *(530) 581-6900.*
Northstar-at-Tahoe: *(530) 562-1010 or www.skinorthstar.com.*
North Tahoe Recreation and Parks Department: *(530) 546-7248.*
Sierra-at-Tahoe: *(530) 659-7453.*
Ski Homewood: *(530) 525-2992.*
Ski Lake Tahoe: *(800) 588-SNOW or www.SkiLakeTahoe.com.*
South Lake Tahoe Chamber of Commerce: *(530) 541-5255.*
Squaw Valley: *(530) 583-6955 or www.squaw.com.*
State parks camping reservations: *(800) 444-7275.*
Tahoe Rim Trail Organization: *(702) 588-0686.*
Toiyabe National Forest: *(702) 882-2766.*
Truckee Ranger District: *(530) 587-3558.*

Northern Gold Rush Country

The northern Sierra foothills region between Yuba Pass and Jackson, including the American River canyon, the Yuba River, Malakoff Diggins State Historic Park, the Marshall Gold Discovery State Park at Coloma, Auburn State Recreation Area, and portions of Tahoe and El Dorado National Forests.

As much as outdoorspeople prefer to spend their time admiring Mother Nature's handiwork, the High Sierra, there is something to be said for human handiwork too—and the Sierra foothills, home of the infamous Gold Rush mining centers that transformed California 150 years ago, is a perfect example of that. Here, in place of Tahoe's wonderfully blue, glacier-carved lake, you find enormous reservoirs where dams have been used to flood river canyons for the sake of water storage and flood control—places where people today also fish, swim, and boat. Partly because flows on virtually every major river in this area are controlled by scheduled water releases, river runs for rafters and kayakers are predictable, meaning people of all skill levels can find rapids to enjoy. In fact, the American River is the most popular rafting river in the state, and the very spot where gold was first discovered in January 1848, now part of a state park, is the most-used put-in. Stretches of landscape scarred from years of over-mining—including the largest hydraulic mining site in the world, at Malakoff—are interesting not only historically but also as recreational attractions; this is one place where you can camp overlooking an environmental calamity and still come away with a "wilderness experience" feeling.

Not that you can't also find wild areas that look just as they might have before the Gold Rush fervor took hold. The American River canyon between Auburn and the Tahoe Basin, for example, offers a taste of deep wilderness where forces other than political boundaries and pavement hold sway.

Gold Rush country also makes for an interesting driving tour, with Highway 49—the Gold Rush Highway—cutting a meandering path across nearly the entire length of the Sierra foothills. Historic townships like Nevada City, Placerville, Amador City, and Sutter Creek retain much of the flavor of pioneering days, with many of the original Gold Rush–era buildings still intact and handsomely restored.

So, as tempting as it may be to bypass the foothills and head straight for the High Sierra, the canyons and ridges of the Gold Rush area are a worthy detour or even full-fledged destination. They're also a convenient day trip, given their proximity to the Sacramento Valley and the San Francisco Bay Area—up to two hours closer than the Tahoe or Truckee basins. El Dorado and Tahoe National Forests occupy much of the northern Gold Rush country, but you'll find numerous state parks and historic sites as well.

Getting There

Highway 49 runs the entire length of Gold Rush country beginning in the northern tip at Sierra City and Yuba Pass and continuing south through the foothills for 100 miles to Oakhurst, just west of Yosemite National Park's Mariposa entrance. The northern Gold Rush portion of Highway 49 is most easily accessed via Interstate 80 between Reno and San Francisco, US Highway 50 (US 50) between Sacramento and Lake Tahoe, or Highway 88 between Stockton and Carson Pass. Check with chambers of commerce in major foothill towns like Auburn, 601 Lincoln Way, Auburn, (530) 885-5616, and Placerville, 542 Main Street, Placerville, (530) 621-5885, for help planning a specific outing or visit. The El Dorado National Forest ranger station east of Placerville on US 50, (530) 644-6048, has the best information on dispersed camping and trails, as well as such historically oriented activities as gold panning. Also check with the Foresthill Ranger District, 22830 Foresthill Road, Foresthill, (530) 367-2224, or the Nevada City Ranger District, 631 Coyote Street, Nevada City, (530) 265-4531, for information on the outdoors.

Adjoining Areas

NORTH: **Plumas Region**

SOUTH: **Southern Gold Rush Country**

EAST: **Tahoe Basin**

WEST: **Sacramento Valley**

inside out

Parks

As crazy as it sounds, the environmental damage caused by hydraulic mining during the Gold Rush has resulted in some of the most unusual and strangely beautiful landscapes in all of Northern California. All you have to do is forget for a moment that rivers of mud and mercury once flowed in torrents through the streams and rivers of the Sierra foothills, leaving a toxic legacy with lingering aftereffects even 150 years later. Sometimes a scar—even one as huge as this—can belie what it truly is; the grotesque can be breathtaking. **Malakoff Diggins State Historic Park** consists of what at first appear to be rolling forested hills cut by streams and rivers like those of the Sierra Nevada. It is here, however, where the most devastating scars from the mad search for gold have been preserved—naked cliffs standing over 600 feet tall where mountainsides once stood, a wide man-made canyon with meandering streams still carrying sediment to the rivers. On a quiet day, you can hear the pebbles falling off the barren canyon walls. Some 41 million cubic yards of earth were washed away during the hydraulic mining period, which left an open pit more than a mile long. The 3,000-acre preserve is more than a history tour, however. It also comes equipped with a well-appointed campground and hiking trails through both the devastated and preserved natural areas. This is the antithesis of undisturbed wilderness, but it is still a wonder to see. To reach Malakoff, take Hwy 49 north from Nevada City 10 miles to Tyler Foote Crossing, and head east on Tyler Foote Crossing to the park entrance via Cruzon Grade or N Bloomfield Rd. For more information, call (530) 265-2740.

Just west and contiguous with Malakoff is the **South Yuba River Recreation Area,** a mostly forested river canyon traversed by an 11-mile stretch of national recreation trail. The canyon is a popular hiking, biking, horseback riding, and fishing spot. To get there, take Hwy 49 north from Nevada City 8 miles, then go west on Yuba Recreation Rd 3 miles to the staging lot. At **Empire Mine State Historic Park** near Grass Valley, shaft mines from the Gold Rush era, tunneling thousands of feet below ground, are preserved at the site of one of the state's most productive mines, where more than 2 billion ounces of gold were extracted from deep pits. The park is mostly a walking tour and picnic destination, featuring old mining-operation buildings and educational materials on the Gold Rush era. The visitors center is on Empire St between Colfax and Grass Valley, a mile southeast of Hwy 20. For information, call the park at (530) 273-8522.

Farther south, **Auburn State Recreation Area** encompasses some

42,000 acres of the American River canyon area, including more than 50 miles of some of the most popular whitewater rafting runs in the state (see Rafting/Kayaking, below), dozens of miles of hiking trails, and numerous spots for dispersed riverside camping. There is also a lake with a marina and boat launch facilities. The recreation area is located along Hwy 49, south of the city of Auburn, with key river access points marked throughout. Call the recreation area office at (530) 885-4527.

At the **Marshall Gold Discovery State Park** in Coloma, the history tour along Hwy 49 continues at the town site on the American River where the gold discovery that shaped California's statehood took place on January 24, 1848. The exact spot where John Marshall made the discovery is not difficult to find, just a short walk from the main parking area on the east side of the highway. The entire town of Coloma is now owned by the state, with historic buildings and artifacts the main attraction. There's also the small Gold Discovery Museum displaying artifacts and memorabilia. Just as the Malakoff site gives the curious explorer an appreciation for the effects of hydraulic mining, the surrounding countryside at Coloma still bears the scars of riverbed mining gone awry, including deep trenches cutting through what used to be open meadows. In fact, miners so rampantly picked through the Coloma area that when they had exhausted their search for gold in all open spaces around the town, they tore down town buildings to search for gold underneath. A recent excavation turned up foundations and artifacts indicating where the demolished buildings had stood. Most of the park is an easy walking tour centered around historical events and ecology. But there's another draw as well. Coloma is a favorite put-in spot on the American River for whitewater rafters and kayakers taking the river west toward Auburn. To reach Coloma, head north on Hwy 49 from Placerville for 8 miles; the highway bisects the park, so you can't miss it. In the hills just west of the park is John Marshall's grave site and monument. Call the park office at (530) 622-3470 for information.

Boating/Fishing

While environmentalists decry the manner in which California's rivers have been harnessed by dams for the benefit of cities and farms, the dozens of reservoirs built since the turn of the century are a water recreationist's dream, a playground for anglers, boaters, swimmers, waterskiers, and more. Actually, this engineering legacy started on a smaller scale in the mid- to late 1800s, as gold miners who needed water to keep their operations going reined in rivers and streams with primitively constructed dams. Some of these abandoned dams can still be found throughout the foothills region, most in poor repair.

Folsom Lake on the American River is one of the most heavily traveled lakes in the state, not only because it's so accessible to Northern California's major population centers along US 50, but also because it is a well-appointed recreation spot. The lake is huge, with nearly 50 miles of shoreline, hundreds of camping spots (see Camping, below), easy-to-reach public boat ramps, and full amenities for anglers at the **Folsom Lake State Recreation Area.** There are six public boat ramps around the lake; some, however, are not in service all year because of the lake's fluctuating water level. Boaters should call the recreation area office for information about ramps and the water level before deciding what part of the lake to launch from. While the area certainly contains trails and other amenities, fishing is the main activity. (Hikers would be better off continuing on to nearby forests and state parks, particularly within the American River canyon.) Fishing here is good year-round, but best in the winter. Take your pick of fare: **trout, bass, salmon, perch, catfish.** . . . The recreation area office can be reached at (530) 988-0205.

Near Nevada City, **Bullards Bar Reservoir** covers some 16 miles of the scenic Yuba River canyon on the north fork. You'll forget you're at a man-made lake here; the shores are surrounded by forests and canyon walls of granite. Campsites, a fully outfitted marina with boat rentals, and two public boat ramps make this another favorite destination for anglers and water sportsters. **Salmon, trout,** largemouth and smallmouth **bass, crappie, catfish,** and **bluegill** fishing is best here in winter. Coves and stream mouths seem to yield the best results, particularly during trout and salmon season. Contact the Emerald Cove Marina resort, (530) 692-3200, for information and rentals. To reach the lake, take Marysville Rd from Hwy 49 to the midpoint between Marysville and Nevada City.

Trout fishing is also popular along the **Yuba** and **American Rivers** and their tributaries, although given the way state fishing regulations continually change to comply with federal endangered species listings, anglers should always check with state fish and game officials or bait-and-tackle retailers for the latest rules before setting out. Easy-to-reach, productive fishing spots on the Yuba are along the Hwy 49/Indian Valley Rd junction 10 miles west of Downieville, for those who want to just pull over and lounge on the banks for a spell. On the American River, you can find places to pull off Hwy 49 between Auburn and Cool.

Rafting/Kayaking

The Sierra foothills and Gold Rush country are the prime whitewater rafting and kayaking destination of the state, and, once you've put in, it doesn't take long to figure out why. The **American River**'s three forks—along with the **Mokelumne, Stanislaus, Tuolumne,** and **Merced Rivers**—contain some of the best whitewater runs, through steep and rugged hidden canyons so far from the nearest patch of pavement that they seem like passageways to another time. Couple this with the fact that the range of difficulty makes these rivers inviting to all skill levels, and you have yourself a true whitewater playground. While the American is by far the most sought-after rafting river in the state, the others do not skimp on adrenaline-pumping excitement; there is plenty of room for everybody.

American River

Of those who nowadays come upon the spot where John Marshall discovered gold at Sutter's Mill, an impressive number make the visit by raft and kayak instead of by car—they jet past the historic spot on the first leg of a 20-mile mostly Class III **south fork** run that is indeed one of the most invigorating and stunningly beautiful outdoor experiences in the Golden State. The first leg begins at **Chili Bar,** just north of Placerville on Hwy 193 (an east turnoff from Hwy 49, 2 miles north of US 50). The Chili Bar run is the tame half of the ride; there are a few dips and spills, but for the most part the heart-stopping sections are few and far between, enough so that a novice who is in decent physical condition can make the run with no problem. The second half of the south fork run, however, is a bit more exciting. Known as The Gorge, this stretch of the American is famous for its abrupt Class IV death drops—one of which is known affectionately as Satan's Cesspool. While the south fork runs are not technically difficult, beginners should not attempt them unless supervised by a qualified guide and outfitter, particularly since these runs are so darn popular it can begin to look like bumper boats on busy peak-season weekends, especially in summer when the river (in normal weather years) doesn't seem scary at all. Don't be surprised to see families with children running Chili Bar during the warmer months.

The American's **middle fork** is another matter altogether. In fact, while the south and middle forks are both part of the same river system, they are nothing alike. If these were roadways, the south fork would be a quiet country road whereas the middle fork would be more akin to the German autobahn, with radical Class III and IV rapids—including a 20-foot drop through a tunnel known as Tunnel Chute. The middle fork passes through some of the most remote and secluded river canyons in all of the Sierra foothills. The easiest way to reach the middle fork put-ins is to take Hwy 49 south from I-80 at Auburn for 3 miles to Old Foresthill Rd, which follows the river through much of its wild American River canyon wilderness runs.

Like the middle fork, the American River's **north fork** is reserved for the more daring paddlers, preferably those in good physical condition who have at least some prior experience. The north fork is an even wilder ride, with steep wooded canyon runs that twist, turn, and drop relentlessly down waterfall drops and rocky staircase rapids. These, again, are mostly Class IV; novices need not apply.

There are numerous **outfitters** running the American—dozens, in fact, since it is the easiest-to-reach river run adjacent to Northern California's large population centers and suitable for family outings. Earthtrek Expeditions, (530) 642-1900, has good river run packages, including family specials. Gold Rush Whitewater Rafting, (800) 900-7238, is another good choice for American River runs.

Yuba River and others

Hwy 49 follows much of the **north fork of the Yuba River** through the Yuba canyon from Union Flat to Bullards Bar Reservoir, nearly 30 miles west. This stretch of river is most often taken in two legs or as a two-day trip. The upper portion, however, is strictly an expert Class V run, not suitable for beginners or even necessarily those with intermediate skills, as there are numerous chutes, falls, boulder-strewn obstacle courses, and almost 10 miles of continuous whitewater to contend with. The character of the river begins to change at Goodyear's Bar, just southwest of Downieville off Hwy 49. It is a two-day run from here to Bullards containing mostly Class III and IV rapids, with the exception of one Class V leg at Maytag that novices can easily skip by just taking out and putting in below. Many see the Yuba as the next logical step up for whitewater enthusiasts who have cut their teeth on the less cantankerous American and are ready for something a bit more challenging. Whitewater Voyages, (800) 488-RAFT offers fully **guided three-day trips** following the entire river (beginning with the rough stuff and calming down gradually), as well as one-day trips that can be custom-designed for those not ready for the Class V action.

For those don't want to fight the masses putting in on the American, the **Mokelumne River** is another river system with a little something for every type of rafter, with Class II runs perfect for novices and families with children, along with more radical Class IV and V whitewater upstream for the more adventuresome. The **Merced** and **Tuolumne Rivers** offer Class III and IV whitewater runs leading from the Yosemite area through the southern Sierra foothills. See Southern Gold Rush Country chapter in the Southern Sierra section for detailed information on the Mokelumne, Merced, and Tuolumne.

Hiking/Backpacking

The Sierra foothills contain some of the loveliest wild landscape in the state, although it's often overshadowed by more popular hiking areas in the High Sierra. Here is plenty of opportunity for a wilderness experience, whether among the forested river canyons, mid-range peaks, or wide meadows and plateaus. Tahoe, El Dorado, and Stanislaus National Forests encompass most of the Gold Rush country, which extends from Sierra County 150 miles south to Mariposa County along Hwy 49. Historical and interpretive walking tours and long riverside treks abound. The best **trail maps** of the national forest areas are available directly from the Forest Service; write US Forest Service Information, Room 521, 630 Sansome St, San Francisco, CA 94111. (See the primer at the beginning of this book for more explicit ordering instructions.) Two local businesses well suited to help with **outdoor supplies** and guidance are located in Placerville. They are Kyburz Ski Hut & Sports, 87 Fair Lane, (530) 622-0237, and Lrp's Sports Kingdom, 442 Main St, (530) 622-8401.

John Marshall's 1848 gold discovery at Sutter's Mill on the American River transformed California overnight from a sleepy, sparsely populated rural settlement in the far reaches to a promised land that lured big dreamers west. Most of the early western settlers landed in hastily constructed mining towns that flourished overnight and languished quickly when miners moved on to new claims. Today, numerous **historical walking tours and hikes** visit landmarks that go a long way to bring the Gold Rush era to life: an abandoned mill, a stone hut that once served as the town jail, meadows cut with wide trenches, mountainsides washed away. There are a number of easy hikes, centered around historical points of interest; we have chosen a few favorites.

First, **Pioneer Trail** (easy; 24 miles round trip) is a two-day history tour—a trip back in time following an original wagon train route through the northern Sierra. It ambles through plateaus past overlooks, and toward the forested Yuba River canyon. The route passes numerous historic buildings (in various states of disrepair) still standing and ready to explore, with good camping spots and great overlooks of the northern Gold Rush country along the way. The Yuba is perhaps one of the most abused rivers in the western region, having served as a garbage disposal for rampant hydraulic mining operations of the late 1800s, which sent piles of sediment and toxic tailings downstream. Evidence of this is still visible today, should you carefully examine the riverbed for rocks fused together by silt and piled higher than the natural river bottom. This is a crowded trail, but once you cover a couple of miles, the stragglers will be gone. The best sights await you beyond the first few miles, so if you don't feel like walking, you miss out. The trailhead is 7 miles east of Nevada City on Hwy 20, on the southeast side of the road.

Naturally, the most often traveled history hikes in the northern Gold Rush country are in and around the **Marshall Gold Discovery State Historic Park,** in the town of **Coloma,** 8 miles north of Placerville on Hwy 49. The state owns the entire town, which is made up of numerous Gold Rush–era buildings, including a classic one-room schoolhouse, a riverside trading post, and ruins of a crude jail cell. Walking trails on both sides of the highway cover a lot of historical ground. On the riverside, you will stumble on the precise spot where John Marshall is believed to have first spied something shiny in the water on January 24, 1848. The mill site and numerous remnants of the township are scattered about. Archaeologists have been excavating some portions of the town in search of artifacts trampled by the search for gold: miners, it seems, tore down most of the town's buildings at the height of the gold craze to make sure they didn't leave a stone unturned. The walking trails also highlight numerous examples of the Gold Rush's aftereffects on the Sierra foothills ecology. This is a good stop for explorers with children because the park is easy to get to and not difficult to walk in. In the hills west of the main park complex, John Marshall's grave and monument are on display; the **monument walk** is the one spot where you'll contend with hilly terrain, although it covers just a few miles. It should be a breeze for anyone in reasonably good physical shape, though. For more information, call the park at (530) 622-3470.

The hydraulic mining sites at **Malakoff Diggins State Historic Park** (see Parks, above) are the most dramatic Gold Rush–era relics in the state. The best view is from the canyon overlook on the south edge of the park campground, a sweeping and impressive vista. There are also numerous access points to the canyon itself, with extensive interpretive trails throughout. Items of historical interest include a couple of hydraulic water cannons left from the height of the mining rush in these parts. Overlooking the park is the semirestored mining town of **North Bloomfield,** where you can hike along a 3-mile loop trail that shows hydraulic-mining memorabilia. Park rangers lead tours on weekends year-round (every day in the summer) and rent out campsites and replicas of miners' cabins; for more details call the park at (530) 265-2740.

American River Canyon

The more than 100 miles of trails following the north and middle forks of the American River provide access to some of the most stunning and secluded scenery in the foothills. Numerous staging areas are off I-80 near Auburn in the **Auburn State Recreation Area** (See Parks, above), which covers some 35,000 acres of steep river canyons with forested slopes and dramatic rocky cliffs and contains a third of the trail system. Because the canyon covers quite a large area, stretching from the Tahoe Basin to just east of the Sacramento Valley, trail connections here can be difficult without proper **maps**; in fact, it's best not to embark on long treks without them, since many trails are nameless and elaborately interconnected. Maps may be obtained at the recreation area office or at the Forest Service offices covering the canyon area: the Foresthill Ranger District, 22830 Foresthill Rd in Foresthill, (530) 367-2224, and the Nevada City Ranger District, 631 Coyote St in Nevada City, (530) 265-4538.

Camping

Dispersed camping is allowed throughout the El Dorado and Tahoe National Forests—and with numerous stretches of secluded river canyon terrain and fishing lakes to choose from, settling on a spot can be a dilemma. Call the El Dorado National Forest ranger station just east of Placerville, (530) 644-6048, for recommendations along the US 50 corridor. The Downieville Ranger District, (530) 288-3231, and the Nevada City Ranger District, (530) 265-4538, are the resources for dispersed camping information in Tahoe National Forest areas along the I-80 corridor. For camping **reservations** at developed sites, call the state parks reservations system, (800) 444-7275, or the Forest Service reservations system, (800) 280-2267, for reservations where applicable. You'll also find developed sites at many lakes and reservoirs in the foothills.

Malakoff Diggins State Historic Park Campground contains 32 sites (no hookups; RV limit 25 feet) near a lake but, more important, near a fantastic lookout spot for the man-made canyon that is a relic of the Gold Rush and the hydraulic mining era. The campground is most popular during the summer when many vacationing families stop in to learn about California history (see Parks, above). The campground has piped water and flush toilets, except during the winter months. Each site has a table and fire grill. There is a general store nearby in North Bloomfield. *From Nevada City, take Coyote Rd north about half a mile and turn right onto North Bloomfield/Graniteville Rd. Proceed to the state park about 12 miles ahead. Enter the park and follow signs to the campground. For more information, call the park at (530) 265-2740 or the state parks reservations system at (800) 444-7275.*

Farther north, **Moonshine Campground** contains 25 sites (no hookups; various RV lengths accommodated) near the middle fork of the Yuba River, a popular place to cool off during the hot summer months. The private campground has piped water and vault toilets; each site has a table and fire grill. There is a general store nearby in North San Juan. *From*

North San Juan, take Hwy 49 north to Moonshine Rd, which is about a quarter of a mile past Byron Rd and just past the middle fork of the Yuba River. Turn left and proceed to the campground ahead. Call the campground directly at (530) 288-3585.

A less conspicuous riverside location is **South Yuba Campground,** with 17 sites (no hookups; RV limit 30 feet) along Kenebee Creek and near the Yuba River's south fork. This campground is very quiet and not well known. Piped water and pit toilets are available; each site has a table and fire grill. There is a general store to the west in Nevada City. *From Nevada City, take Coyote Rd north about half a mile and turn right onto North Bloomfield/Graniteville Rd. Proceed to North Bloomfield and turn right onto Relief Hill Rd. Proceed to the campground. Call the Bureau of Land Management at (530) 985-4474.*

For the RV set there are 134 sites (full hookups; various RV lengths accommodated) adjacent to the **Nevada County Fairgrounds.** Though tents are allowed, this campground is better suited to RVs; those with tents should look elsewhere. Showers, flush toilets, and a sanitary dump station are provided. *From Nevada City, head south on Golden Center Fwy, to Grass Valley. Exit at Empire St and follow the signs to Hwy 20, Mill St, and the fairgrounds beyond. Call Nevada County Fairgrounds, (530) 273-6217.*

Auburn State Recreation Area Campground contains 75 tent sites (no RV access) nestled in the American River canyon. One of the sites is a group site, and 21 are boat-in sites. This campground is quite beautiful, surrounded by some 45,000 acres of wilderness, including numerous hiking and riding trails (see Parks, above). There is no running water, so be sure to bring plenty of your own. Pit toilets are provided, and each site has a table and fire grill. There is a general store nearby. *From Auburn, take Hwy 49 south about 1 mile to the state recreation area and follow the signs to the campground beyond. For more information, call the recreation area at (530) 885-4527.*

Folsom Lake (see Boating/Fishing, above) is a popular camping spot for anglers and water sportsters. There are two large lakeside campsites. **Beal's Point Campground** contains 74 sites (no hookups; RV limit 33 feet) and is equipped with a boat ramp. Piped water is provided, along with showers, flush toilets, and a sanitary dump station for RVs. Each site has a table and fire ring. A marina and general store are nearby at the Folsom Lake Marina. *Folsom Lake is 25 miles east of Sacramento on US 50. From Auburn, take I-80 west to Roseville. Exit at Douglas Rd and turn left. Travel on Douglas about 5 miles and turn right onto Auburn-Folsom Rd. Proceed about 1 mile and turn left onto the campground access road.* Also at the lake, **Peninsula Campground** contains 100 sites (no hookups; RV limit 43 feet) in what tends to be a quieter spot than Beal's, despite the larger size. A boat ramp lies adjacent to the campground. Piped water is provided, along with showers, flush toilets, and a sanitary dump station for RVs. Each site has a table and fire ring. A marina and general store are nearby at the Folsom Lake Marina. *From Auburn, take Hwy 49 south and turn right onto Rattlesnake Bar Rd, just before reaching Pilot Hill. Proceed to the campground at the lake. For more information on both campgrounds, call Folsom Lake State Recreation Area at (530) 988-0205 or the state parks reservations system at (800) 444-7275.*

Other camping spots in the foothills include **Sly Park Campground,** with 154 sites (no hookups; RV limit 33 feet) along Jenkinson Lake, in the Sly Park Recreation Area. A boat ramp is nearby. The campground has piped water and pit toilets; each site has a table and fire ring. A marina and general store are nearby. *From Placerville, take US 50 east. Exit at Pollock Pines and turn right onto Gold Ridge Trail. Proceed a few hundred feet, turn right onto County Rd E16, and proceed to the campground access road at the lake. For information and reservations, call Sly Park Recreation Area, (530) 644-2545.*

Gold Panning

When record rainfall in January 1997 turned Sierra rivers and creeks into raging torrents, the ensuing floods did more than just wash out highways and trample riverside cabins: they caused a mini gold rush. So much earth was displaced by the floods that previously undisturbed gold deposits were dispersed throughout the foothills. This, naturally, brought treasure hunters out of the woodwork and into some of the region's most popular recreational panning areas. Panning is the most primitive of gold mining techniques, used in earnest only by the original forty-niners before more lucrative, high-volume techniques such as hydraulic, dredge, pit, and shaft mining were developed. Now, however, it has emerged as both a tradition and an outdoor pastime. **Marshall Gold Discovery State Historic Park** at Coloma (see Parks, above) has designated areas along the American River for panning, and each October it's the site of the national gold panning championships. Instruction is available at the park visitors center, and panning equipment is sold at riverside shops. Contact the park at (530) 622-3470.

Panning is also allowed along Humbug Creek at **Malakoff Diggins State Historic Park** (see Parks, above), where the most impressive scars on the landscape caused by Gold Rush–era hydraulic mining are found. Call the park, (530) 265-2740, for information. The **South Yuba River** area, being developed as a state park west of Nevada City, also has a popular mining spot, at the Pleasant Valley Rd river overcrossing, 9 miles north of where the road meets Hwy 20; call the ranger station at (530) 432-2546. No permit is required for gold panning in national forestlands, but recreational panners who want to explore the river canyons on their own are advised to take extra care to stay off private property and avoid interfering with commercial mining claims still in effect along the foothill rivers. State law allows panning—no claim or permit required—anyplace that a state highway crosses a waterway. Look for small-operation commercial dredge miners at some of these spots. The El Dorado National Forest headquarters just east of Placerville on US 50 has information on numerous recreational mining sites throughout the forest canyons; call (530) 644-6048. For additional panning sites, see Southern Gold Rush Country chapter.

Biking

Hwy 49 between Auburn and Coloma, a distance of 25 miles through the **American River canyon,** is a terrific scenic and historical tour, covering varied terrain that is relatively flat with the exception of the canyon entrance at I-80. This is best taken as a weekday ride, however—particularly in the summer, when rafters and other sightseers flock to Coloma via Hwy 49. On weekends, the 15-mile drive on **Highway 193** from Placerville north to Georgetown is a better choice; this ride is also fairly flat except for the hills entering the canyon.

The extensive logging roads of Tahoe and El Dorado National Forests are a **mountain biker**'s dream, but be sure to check with appropriate ranger stations before setting out to avoid run-ins with logging trucks and motorcycles, which also use the forest roads in earnest.

Bicycle **supplies and rentals** are available at Jason's Bike Shop, 424 Placerville Dr, Placerville, (530) 621-1273, and Placerville Bicycle Shop, 1307 Broadway, Placerville, (530) 622-3015. From the Auburn side, try Auburn Bike & Hike Shop, 1440 Canal St, Auburn, (530) 885-3861, or the Emporium, 483 Grass Valley Hwy, Auburn, (530) 823-2900.

Scenic Drives/Photography

Hwy 49, aka the **Gold Rush Highway,** the main artery linking the Gold Rush country communities, is the best route for touring this section of the Sierra foothills (see also Attractions, below). Naturally, there is a lot to look at and photograph architecturally, historically, and within the natural landscape. The **American River canyon** area around Auburn, with its dramatically high, steep walls and impressive bridge crossings, are a wonder to see. Points of interest at the Coloma gold discovery site and the John Marshall Monument west of it also provide ample photo ops for sightseers interested in California history. But Hwy 49 also has another side. Many rural stretches between communities are rustic and sparsely developed; old broken barns, rickety fences, abandoned Studebakers with the windows and headlights busted out, wood-frame farmhouses with weathered shingles and broken screen doors . . . all of this is extremely photogenic. The drive from **the Buttes to Oakhurst,** while optimally a three-day trip, is a fascinating journey full of discovery and well worth the time and gasoline!

Wildlife

The Sierra foothills are an interesting place for **birders,** whose dilemma is to choose between man-made waterways and nature-built forested river canyons for spotting grounds. At reservoirs such as Folsom Lake (see Boating/Fishing, above), look for woodpeckers, kestrels, Swainson's thrush, goldfinches, and sparrows, along with the occasional Canada geese during the winter migration. In some of the forested river canyons such as the American and the Yuba, look for mergansers, Cooper's hawks, scrub and Stellar's jays, woodpeckers, sparrows, warblers, kinglets, and finches, depending on the type of forest. Contact the appropriate local ranger station for a bird list. Birders looking for seclusion and a unique natural experience should check out the Auburn State Recreation Area (see Parks, above) along the I-80 corridor for the best viewing. Another nice spot is where the American River meets Salt and Knickerbocker Creeks, just south of Auburn along Hwy 49.

A woman jogging in the Auburn State Recreation Area at the American River was attacked and killed by a **mountain lion** in 1994, raising concern that the protected species might be repopulating to a potentially dangerous level. As a result, a state initiative was proposed to revoke the creature's protected status and open the forests up to lion hunting. The initiative lost in 1996, and there have been no lion attacks since, so wildlife experts are treating the incident as one of those freak incidences that might only rarely if ever reoccur. While the lions get the most notoriety, they most certainly are not the only wildlife tramping around the foothills—and they are so reclusive that it's easier to find a forest ranger who has never seen one than it is to find a lion! Also look for the ever-present **black bear, red fox, skunks, squirrels, deer,** and **raccoons.** Bear-related precautions are advised.

Horseback Riding

Equestrians flock to the South Yuba River Recreation Area and the Auburn State Recreation Area (see Parks, above) for their well-appointed riding trails and horse-friendly trailheads. Call the South Yuba Recreation Area office, (530) 885-4527, for information about riding options. There are no stock outfitters permitted in the area, however, so this tip is for those who just happen to have their own.

Adventure Calendar

National Gold Panning Championships, early October: *Marshall Gold Discovery State Park, (530) 622-3470.*

outside in

Attractions

By 1849, word had spread throughout the United States, Europe, and other corners of the globe that gold miners were becoming millionaires overnight in California. In just one year, more than 80,000 eager souls stampeded across water and land to reach the hilly terrain now known as the Gold Country and the Mother Lode. By 1852, more than 200,000 men were working the mines. Many of the "forty-niners" had to fight for their claims to the land, claims that left the average miner with little more than dirt and grime in his pocket. Crime and starvation were rampant, and when the exhausted miners put away their picks and pans for the night, most sought comfort in drinking, gambling, and prostitutes. It was a wild and heady time that brought riches to relatively few, but changed the Golden State forever.

You can follow in the miners' footsteps (geographically, at least) by cruising along the aptly numbered Hwy 49, the zigzagging, 321-mile Gold Rush Highway that links many of the mining towns (see also Scenic Drives/Photography, above). You'll find some of the most authentically preserved towns in the northern Gold Rush country, including Grass Valley, where more than a billion dollars in gold was extracted, and Nevada City, former home of one of the region's more famous miners, President Herbert Hoover. The rolling hills of the southern Gold Country are honeycombed with mysterious caverns and abandoned mines, including the deepest gold mines on the continent (see Southern Gold Rush Country chapter).

The mining boom went bust by 1860, and most of the Gold Rush towns were abandoned by the 1870s. Some have survived by mining for tourist dollars instead, and as a result it's not always easy to steer clear of tourist trappings. A scenic little mountain town at the junction of the Yuba and Downie Rivers, **Downieville** hasn't changed much since the

1850s: venerable buildings still line the boardwalks along crooked Main St and trim homes are cut into the canyon walls above. Downieville's population hovers around 350 now, though during its heyday 5,000 prospectors panned the streams and worked the mines here. The lusty gold camp even had the dubious distinction of being the only place in California where a woman was lynched.

A former Gold Rush–era Chinese store houses the Downieville Museum (open daily in the summer, and on weekends in the spring and fall); 330 Main St, no phone. The Sierra County Courthouse displays gold dug out of the rich Ruby Mine, 100 Courthouse Square, (530) 289-3698, and next door stands the only original gallows in the Gold Country. For more Gold Rush history and lore, check out the Sierra County Historical Park, just north of Sierra City, where the restored Kentucky Mine and a stamp mill still stand (open Wednesday through Sunday in the summer, and on fall weekends); on Hwy 99, 1 mile north of Sierra City, (530) 862-1310. For local news and current Downieville events, pick up a copy of the *Mountain Messenger,* a weekly newspaper published since 1853.

If you're driving anywhere near the remote town of **Brownsville,** consider making a reservation for a tour of the **Renaissance Vineyard & Winery,** a spectacular 365-acre winery with rose gardens fit for a queen's palace. Located in the village of Oregon House, Renaissance is at an elevation of 2,300 feet and is one of the largest mountain vineyards in North America. It is owned and operated by a wealthy religious group known as the Fellowship of Friends. The visitors' schedule is subject to change, but tours and tastings are usually available on Friday and Saturday and appointments are essential, even if you just want to smell the roses; 12585 Rice's Crossing Rd, 7 miles south of Brownsville (call for directions), Oregon House, (530) 692-3104 or (800) 225-7582. If you're in town on the weekend, the best place for a bite in Brownsville is at **Lottie Brennan's Bakery & Eating Establishment,** which serves an eclectic mix of great food, although (much to the chagrin of the locals) the restaurant is now open only for lunch on Saturday and brunch on Sunday. Don't miss Brennan's aebleskivers (Scandinavian pancakes with cardamom, Grand Marnier syrup, and French custard) or her sumptuous Swedish princess cake with marzipan; 9049 La Porte Rd, (530) 675-1003.

Established in 1849 when miners found gold in Deer Creek, **Nevada City** occupies one of the most picturesque sites in the Sierra foothills. When the sugar maples blaze in autumn, the town resembles a small New England village, making it hard to believe this was once the third-largest city in California. This is also B&B heaven, and with so many beautifully restored houses to choose from, you'll have a tough time selecting a favorite. To understand the lay of the land, put on your walking shoes and pick up a free walking-tour map at the chamber of commerce; 132 Main St at Coyote St, (530) 265-2692. Town highlights include the National Hotel, where the cozy Gold Rush–era bar is ideal for a cocktail or two, and the white, cupola-topped Firehouse Number 1 Museum, featuring Gold Rush memorabilia, a fine Chinese altar from a local 1860s joss house, and relics from the infamous and ill-fated Donner party; 214 Main St at Commercial St, (530) 265-5468.

And consider an afternoon of beer-tasting: you can sample some of the Gold Country's finest microbrews at the **Nevada City Brewing Company**. Free tours and tastings are offered Friday from 1pm to 5pm, Saturday from 10am to 4pm, and by appointment (or whenever you can talk the staff into taking a break to show off their suds); 75 Bost Ave at Searls Ave, (530) 265-2446.

Once known for rich quartz mines, Cornish pasties, and Gold Rush entertainers like dancers Lola Montez and Lotta Crabtree, **Grass Valley** has a historic and slightly scruffy downtown that's a pleasure to explore, as well as elegant bed-and-breakfast inns and good restaurants. Stop at the chamber of commerce for a free walking-tour map of the town and two terrific brochures listing more than two dozen scenic walking, hiking, and mountain biking trails; 248 Mill St, (530) 273-4667 or (800) 655-4667. As you tour the town, be sure to stop at the 10-ton Pelton Waterwheel (at 30 feet in diameter, it's the world's largest) on display at the exemplary **North Star Mining Museum.** The museum building was once the powerhouse for the North Star Mine (open daily from May through October); located at the south end of Mill St at McCourtney Rd, (530) 273-4255. Just outside of town is the 785-acre **Empire Mine State Historic Park,** the oldest, largest, and richest gold mine in California (see also Parks, above); its underground passages once extended 367 miles and descended 11,007 feet into the ground. A museum occupies a former stable, and the impressive granite and red brick Empire Cottage, designed by San Francisco architect Willis Polk in 1897 for the mine's owner, is a prime example of what all that gold dust could buy; 10791 E Empire St, (530) 273-8522.

If you've ever visited downtown Nevada City or Grass Valley on a weekend, you know how hard it is to find a parking spot (and to think you came here to get away from it all!). This time, why not leave the car at the inn and let the **Gold Country Stage** shuttle drivers do all the navigating? A couple bucks buys you an all-day shuttle pass good for both towns as well as rides to major attractions in outlying areas. Call (530) 477-0103 for a free map and riders' guide.

After touring Grass Valley, head about 5 miles west on Hwy 20 for a pleasant side trip to the tiny town of **Rough and Ready,** which once chose to secede from the Union rather than pay a mining tax. Then continue on Hwy 20 for another couple of miles and turn north on Pleasant Valley Rd; 15 miles up the road is **Bridgeport,** home of California's longest covered bridge. Built in 1862, the bridge provides a good spot for dangling your fishing line—or pretending you're Clint and Meryl in a scene from *The Bridges of Madison County.*

The Gold Country's largest town, **Auburn** is sprawled on a bluff overlooking the American River and has been the seat of Placer County since 1850. Nowadays, Auburn serves mainly as a pit stop for vacationers headed for Lake Tahoe. Its few noteworthy sights, including **Old Town** and the impressively domed Placer County Courthouse, 101 Maple St, (530) 889-6550, are best seen out the car window as you head toward the far more congenial towns of Grass Valley and Nevada City to the north. But if you're here to stretch your legs or get a bite to eat (there are some very good restaurants), stroll by the numerous bustling shops and restaurants that grace Old Town's streets. Many of these enterprises are housed in historic Gold Rush buildings, including the Shanghai Restaurant, a Chinese establishment that has been open continuously since 1906 and displays a wonderful collection of memorabilia in its bar (where part of the movie *Phenomenon* was filmed with John Travolta); 289 Washington St, (530) 823-2613. A gigantic stone statue of Claude Chana, who discovered gold in the Auburn Ravine in 1848, marks the historic section. Other Old Town highlights include the whimsical firehouse (on Lincoln Way at Commercial St), the former 1852 Wells Fargo Bank (on Lincoln Way, 1 block south of the firehouse), and the post office that first opened its doors in 1849 (on Lincoln Way at Sacramento St).

One of the first camps settled by miners who branched out from Coloma, **Placerville** was dubbed Dry Diggins because of a lack of water. Its name was changed to Hangtown in 1849 after a series of grisly lynchings; it became Placerville in 1854 to satisfy local pride. Home to an unassuming array of gas stations, budget chain hotels, and 24-hour coffee shops, Placerville doesn't have much to offer visitors except some Gold Rush–era relics, Old Town gift shops, and its famous "Hangtown fry"—a concoction of bacon, eggs, and oysters popular with early miners—which nowadays is dished out at the Bell Tower Cafe at 423 Main St, in Old Town, (530) 626-3483.

Among the town's historical highlights is the brick-and-stone City Hall, which was built in 1860 and originally served as the town's firehouse; 487 Main St, (530) 642-5200. Another noteworthy edifice is Milton's Cary House Hotel, where Mark Twain once lodged; 300 Main St. Across the street, note the dangling dummy that marks the location of the town's infamous hanging tree. A mile north of downtown Placerville is

Gold Bug Park, home of the city-owned Gold Bug Mine; guided tours of the mine lead you deep into the lighted shafts; located on Bedford St, call (530) 642-5238 for tour details. **El Dorado County Historical Museum,** adjacent to the county fairgrounds, showcases Pony Express paraphernalia, an original Studebaker wheelbarrow, a replica of a 19th-century general store, a restored Concord stagecoach, plus other mining-era relics (open Wednesday through Sunday); 104 Placerville Dr, (530) 621-5865.

Every autumn, droves of people—about a half a million each year—come to a small ridge just east of Placerville called **Apple Hill Orchards.** What's the attraction? Why, apples, of course. Baked, fried, buttered, canned, candied, and caramelized apples, to name just a few variations. Dozens of apple vendors sell their special apple concoctions, and on weekends the atmosphere is positively festive, with everyone basking in the alpine sunshine while feasting on such treats as hot apple pie à la mode. In September and October (peak apple-harvest season), it's definitely worth a stop. From US 50, take the Carson Rd exit and follow the signs.

Three miles south of Placerville on Hwy 49 sits the small town of **El Dorado,** whose denizens tolerate but in no way cultivate tourism. In fact, most travelers pass right on through—except for those who know about Poor Red's, a bar and restaurant that may not look like much from the outside (or the inside, for that matter), but is known throughout the land for its famous cocktail, the Golden Cadillac.

Amador City is the smallest incorporated city in California. Lined with false-fronted antique and specialty shops, this block-long town is a good place to stop, stretch your legs, window-shop, and eat dinner.

Sutter Creek is the self-proclaimed "nicest little town in the Mother Lode" and was named after sawmill owner John Sutter. "Big Four" railroad baron Leland Stanford made his millions at Sutter Creek's Lincoln Mine, then used his wad to invest in the transcontinental railroad and fund his successful campaign to become governor of California. The town boasts some beautiful 19th-century buildings that you can admire from the street, including the landmark Knight's Foundry, the last water-powered foundry and machine shop in the nation (81 Eureka St off Main St, no phone), and the Downs Mansion, the former home of the foreman at Leland Stanford's mine (this private residence is on Spanish St, across from the Immaculate Conception Church). Also worth exploring: the Asian furnishings and Native American and Mexican folk art at the Cobweb Collection, 83 Main St, (209) 267-0690; the contemporary and traditional American handicrafts at Fine Eye Gallery, 71 Main St, (209) 267-0571; and the prints, watercolors, and stone carvings at Sutter Creek Gallery, 35 Main St, (209) 267-0228.

Restaurants

Bootlegger's Old Town Tavern & Grill ☆☆☆ Located in a handsome old brick building, Bootlegger's offers a large, eclectic seasonal menu that's so chock-full of interesting choices you'll want to come back several times to sample them all. *210 Washington St (in Old Town), Auburn; (530) 889-2229; $$.*

Cirino's ☆ Nevada City folk come to ever-popular Cirino's for its large, family-style Italian dishes. Expect a loud, bustling environment that's kid-friendly and full of the wonderful aroma of roasted garlic. *309 Broad St (just past Pine St), Nevada City; (530) 265-2246; $$.*

Country Rose Cafe ☆☆ Within this tall, stately brick building you'll find some mighty fine French country fare. Fortunately, sunny days are in abundance here, enabling diners to sit on the cafe's pretty walled-in garden patio. *300 Commercial St (at Pine St), Nevada City; (530) 265-6248; $$.*

Cowboy Pizza ☆ This pizza joint is gussied up with cowpoke kitsch. But before you even walk through the door of this wacky place, you'll smell the garlic loaded onto the Gilroy Pizza, cooked in an old stone-floor oven. *315 Spring St (near the Miners Foundry Cultural Center), Nevada City; (530) 265-2334; $.*

The Haven ☆ This modest restaurant of polished wood and stained glass just may be the best-kept secret in the mountains. While most out-of-towners don't know it exists, the Haven is famous among locals for its scallops, thick-cut steaks, and mountainous salads. *6396 Pony Express Trail (½ mile W of Safeway), Pollock Pines; (530) 644-3448; $$.*

Herrington's Sierra Pines Resort ☆☆ In a log and wood-paneled dining room on the gorgeous north fork of the Yuba River, the Herrington family serves house-baked bread and their specialty: fresh trout reeled right out of their trout pond. *On the S side of Hwy 49 (at the W end of town), Sierra City; (530) 862-1151 or (800) 682-9848; $$.*

Kirby's Creekside Restaurant & Bar ☆☆☆ This attractive restaurant is perched precariously over Deer Creek. The fare here is excellent. Kirby's takes its wine list as seriously as its food and maintains a very good selection. *101 Broad St (at Sacramento St), Nevada City; (530) 265-3445; $$.*

Latitudes ☆☆☆ Latitudes, which the owner/chefs call their "world kitchen," is located in a lovely Victorian building just above Auburn's Old Town. Most of their cuisine is truly adventurous and wide-ranging. *130 Maple St, #200 (across from the courthouse), Auburn; (530) 885-9535; $$.*

Le Bilig ☆☆☆☆ This small jewel-box restaurant with 10 rough-hewn pine tables specializes in hearty, rustic French comfort food. The menu changes every few months to accommodate available ingredients. *11750 Atwood Rd (off Hwy 49, 1 block W of the Bel Air Shopping Center, at the N end of town), Auburn; (530) 888-1491; $$.*

Lil' Mama D. Carlo's ☆☆   This pleasant, unpretentious Italian restaurant across from the city courthouse features old-fashioned food based on the recipes of four generations of a Neapolitan-American family. *482 Main St, Placerville; (530) 626-1612; $$.*

Main Street Cafe & Bar ☆☆   Contemporary, casual, and colorful, the Main Street Cafe is appreciated for its standard but accomplished American lunch menu, featuring a variety of burgers, sandwiches, and salads. *213 W Main St (across from the Holbrooke Hotel), Grass Valley; (530) 477-6000; $$.*

The Stewart House ☆☆☆   An elegant, classic Victorian manse on the edge of downtown, the Stewart House was built in 1891 by the owner of the local sawmill and now it's one of the town's best restaurants. *124 Bank St (off S Auburn St), Grass Valley; (530) 477-1559; $$.*

Sweetie Pies ☆☆   Stop for lunch at this cute little house on Main Street and order one of the freshly made soups, or a slice of the vegetable quiche and a freshly tossed garden salad. Whatever you choose, save room for the pie. *577 Main St, Placerville; (530) 642-0128; $.*

Tofanelli's ☆☆   This is one of Grass Valley's cultural and culinary meeting places. Tofanelli's whips up several vegetarian dishes, and each week the chefs prepare a new dinner menu. *302 W Main St (next to the Holbrooke Hotel), Grass Valley; (530) 272-1468; $.*

Weird Harold's ☆   Tucked under a grove of towering ponderosa pines, this pale blue chalet-style restaurant serves thick cuts of prime rib and hefty platters of steak, pasta, and fresh seafood. *5631 Pony Express Trail (at the W end of town), Pollock Pines; (530) 644-5272; $$.*

Zachary Jacques ☆☆☆☆   The decor at Zachary Jacques may be Western, but the cuisine is definitely French country and it's superb. The wine list has received an award of excellence from the highly respected *Wine Spectator* magazine. *1821 Pleasant Valley Rd (3 miles E of Diamond Springs), Placerville; (530) 626-8045; $$$.*

Zinfandels ☆☆☆   Zinfandels brings light (but not meatless) California cuisine to the Gold Country. The menu changes weekly, incorporating the best local farm produce and seasonal ingredients. The only sour note here is the rather blasé decor. *51 Hanford St (downtown), Sutter Creek; (209) 267-5008; $$.*

Lodgings

American River Inn ☆☆   The innkeepers have done an exemplary job of maintaining this inn's 25 guest rooms, which are spread out between three well-appointed buildings dating back to the 1850s. The hotel has a pool and spa, as well as bicycles, a putting green, horseshoes, table tennis, badminton, a driving range, and a croquet ground. *At the corner of Main and Orleans Sts, Georgetown; (530) 333-4499 or (800) 245-6566; $$.*

Chichester–McKee House ☆☆   This gracious Victorian was the finest house in Placerville when it was built in 1892. Today the refurbished home still has the look and feel of the late 1800s—except, of course, for its updated plumbing. All 4 guest rooms have Victorian-era bedsteads, stained glass, and fireplaces trimmed with carved wood and marble. *800 Spring St (on Hwy 49, ½ block N of US 50), Placerville; (530) 626-1882 or (800) 831-4008; $$.*

Coloma Country Inn ☆☆☆   This intimate 1852 hotel is set in the heart of the lovely Marshall Gold Discovery State Historic Park. The inn has 7 guest rooms (including a two-bedroom suite), and every weekend the adventure-seeking innkeepers offer their guests and other visitors one of the thrills of their lives: whitewater rafting trips and hot-air balloon rides. *345 High St (in Marshall Gold Discovery State Historic Park), Coloma; (530) 622-6919; $$.*

Downey House ☆☆☆   The exterior of this impeccably restored house is traditional; inside, however, its personality is more contemporary. Each of the 6 pastel guest rooms features built-in beds, comfortable reading chairs, and an aquarium. Guests may make themselves at home in the upstairs sun room or in the downstairs garden room. *517 W Broad St (just beyond the historic district at Bennett St), Nevada City; (530) 265-2815 or (800) 258-2815; $$.*

Emma Nevada House ☆☆☆☆   Although it was built in 1856, the immaculately restored Emma Nevada House is one of the newer stars in Nevada City's fine array of bed-and-breakfast inns. Many of the home's antique fixtures have been refurbished and modernized, and the 6 guest rooms have private baths and new queen-size beds. *528 E Broad St (on the right side of the Y), Nevada City; (530) 265-4415 or (800) 916-EMMA; $$–$$$.*

Fitzpatrick Winery and Lodge ☆☆   If you've never experienced true Irish hospitality, reserve a night at this country-style winery and lodge to see (and taste) for yourself why Irish eyes are always smiling. Sitting atop a hill with a commanding 360-degree view of the countryside, the lodge has 5 guest rooms. *7740 Fairplay Rd (off Mount Aukum Rd, 6 miles SE of town), Somerset; (530) 620-3248 or (800) 245-9166; $$.*

The Foxes in Sutter Creek Bed and Breakfast Inn ☆☆☆   This is the finest B&B in Sutter Creek. An immaculate garden fronts the Gold Rush–era foundation, and from there it only gets better. Each of the 7 guest rooms is furnished with antiques, including massive, elaborate Victorian headboards and armoires that seem too priceless to actually use. *77 Main St (downtown), Sutter Creek; (209) 267-5882 or (800) 987-3344; $$.*

The Gold Quartz Inn ☆   If you enjoy the ambience of a B&B but are reluctant to give up the comfort and privacy of a hotel, the Gold Quartz Inn is a good compromise. Both the strengths and the weaknesses of this 24-room Queen Anne replica stem from its relative newness: it delivers the amenities, but with aesthetic sacrifices. *15 Bryson Dr (at Hwy 49, just S of town), Sutter Creek; (209) 267-9155 or (800) 752-8738; $$.*

Grandmère's Inn ☆☆☆☆   Generally considered the grande dame of Nevada City's hostelries, Grandmère's Inn is indeed a showplace, with quite a history to boot. This three-story Colonial revival mansion is set amid old terraced gardens and offers 7 guest rooms. The wonderful breakfast spread consists of hot dishes, baked goods, and fresh fruits. *449 Broad St (at Bennett St), Nevada City; (530) 265-4660; $$$.*

Grey Gables Inn ☆☆   This adorable Victorian retreat is run by two ever-friendly British expatriates dripping with genuine hospitality. Surrounded by terraces of colorful, meticulously manicured gardens, the two-story inn has 8 plushly carpeted guest rooms named after British poets and writers. *161 Hanford St (on Hwy 49, at the N end of town), Sutter Creek; (209) 267-1039 or (800) 473-9422; $$.*

Historic Cary House Hotel ☆   Originally built in 1857, refurbished in the late 1980s, and redecorated in 1997, this four-story brick building is centrally located on Main St. All 31 of the simple, comfortable guest rooms are decorated with antiques and have received a fresh coat of paint and new beds and drapes; each has a private bath, a remote-control TV, and a phone. *300 Main St (between Bedford and Spring Sts), Placerville; (530) 622-4271; $$.*

The Holbrooke Hotel ☆☆☆   Mark Twain slept here. But don't be intimidated; despite its rugged Gold Rush grandeur, the 140-year-old brick Holbrooke Hotel is a relaxed and accommodating establishment. All 27 rooms offer antiques and contemporary bathrooms with those delightful (though not so contemporary) claw-footed bathtubs. *212 W Main St (between S Church and Mill Sts), Grass Valley; (530) 273-1353 or (800) 933-7077; $$.*

Imperial Hotel ☆☆☆   This century-old brick hotel, restored in 1988, strikes a marvelous balance between elegance and whimsy. The 6 guest rooms house numerous antiques as well as hand-painted furnishings by a local artist. The elegant Imperial Hotel Restaurant offers first-rate California cuisine. *14202 Hwy 49 (downtown), Amador City; (209) 267-9172 or (800) 242-5594; $$.*

Murphy's Inn ☆☆☆   This 19th-century inn has become one of Grass Valley's premier B&Bs. A topiary garden with bubbling fountains, a fish pond, and a giant 140-year-old sequoia surrounds the elegant Victorian mansion. And in true Victorian style, all 8 guest rooms are tastefully gussied up in an understated floral motif. *318 Neal St (at School St, 1 block from Main St), Grass Valley; (530) 273-6873 or (800) 895-2488; $$–$$$.*

National Hotel   The National Hotel is a California institution. It opened in the mid-1850s, and is the oldest continuously operating hotel west of the Rockies. Sure, the place shows its age, and the decor is a mishmash from every era. But that ain't all bad. Plus, there's lots to see, and the 42 guest rooms are furnished with exquisite antiques. *211 Broad St (center of town), Nevada City; (530) 265-4551; $–$$.*

Piety Hill Inn ☆☆☆   Originally built in 1933 as an auto court, Piety Hill Inn has been imaginatively and charmingly restored and redecorated. The inn consists of 9 cottages clustered around a grassy, tree-shaded courtyard and garden. Each of the cottages has a kitchenette, a private bath, cable TV, and air conditioning. *523 Sacramento St (2 blocks SE of Hwy 49), Nevada City; (530) 265-2245 or (800) 443-2245; $$–$$$.*

Power's Mansion Inn ☆☆   Built at the turn of the century, the charming, pink Power's Mansion Inn, located on a hill in the heart of downtown Auburn, has 11 antique-filled guest rooms with big brass beds and private baths. The innkeepers serve a full breakfast in the attractive dining room. *164 Cleveland Ave (between Lincoln Way and High St; call for directions), Auburn; (530) 885-1166; $$–$$$.*

The Red Castle Historic Lodgings ☆☆☆☆   A towering, four-story red brick manse detailed with lacy white icicle trim, the Red Castle is a gothic revival gem. The 7 guest rooms (3 of them are suites) have either a private porch or a garden terrace. The Red Castle's ever-changing breakfast (prepared by an in-house chef) is a feast. *109 Prospect St (call for directions), Nevada City; (530) 265-5135; $$$.*

Sierra Shangri-La ☆☆   Sierra Shangri-La sits beside the Yuba River at the base of Jim Crow Canyon. The comfortable lodge has 3 guest rooms with brass bedsteads, but it's the 7 riverside cottages—with decks, patios, kitchens, barbecues, and wood-burning stoves—that keep people coming back year after year (making it difficult to get a reservation in the summer). *On Hwy 49 (2½ miles E of town), Downieville; (530) 289-3455; $$–$$$.*

Strawberry Lodge ☆☆   Wedged between the giant conifers and granite headwalls of Lake Tahoe's southwestern rim, Strawberry Lodge has been the headquarters for a cornucopia of year-round outdoor activities for more than a century. The 45 rooms aren't lavish (and have no TVs or phones), but then neither is the price. *17510 US 50 (43 miles E of Placerville, 9 miles E of Kyburz), Kyburz; (530) 659-7200; $.*

More Information

Amador County Chamber of Commerce: *(209) 223-0350.*
Auburn Chamber of Commerce: *(530) 885-5616.*
Bass Lake Chamber of Commerce, Mariposa: *(559) 642-3676.*
Colfax Area Chamber of Commerce, Colfax: *(530) 346-8888.*
Eastern Madera County Chamber of Commerce, Oakhurst: *(559) 683-7766.*
El Dorado Hills Chamber of Commerce: *(530) 933-1335.*
El Dorado National Forest ranger station: *(530) 644-6048.*
Foresthill Ranger District: *(530) 367-2224.*
Grass Valley–Nevada County Chamber of Commerce: *(530) 273-4667.*
Nevada City Chamber of Commerce: *(530) 265-2692.*
Nevada City Ranger District: *(530) 265-4531.*
Placerville Chamber of Commerce: *(530) 621-5885.*

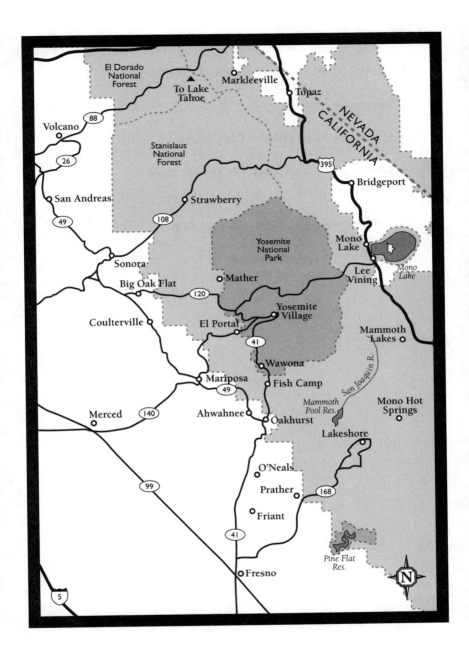

Southern Sierra

Southern
Sierra

Yosemite National Park: Overview

More than 1,200 square miles of wilderness and developed parklands in the southern Sierra high country, including Yosemite Valley, the Yosemite uplands to the north, east, and west, Mono Lake, and portions of Stanislaus and Sierra National Forests.

It is almost ridiculous to try to describe Yosemite National Park. It is simply one of those places you can read about, look at photographs of, see in films, and listen to firsthand accounts of and still just not get it. It is too beautiful for words, and impossible to envision sight-unseen without being ridiculously inaccurate. Imagine, if you will, walls of granite so high and magnificent that they stop your heart, and mighty waterfalls carrying an endless supply of icy, pristine melt into the Merced River. Take the worst cliched image of the Garden of Eden—something off the front cover of a romance novel—make it even more impossible, and that might be Yosemite.

Places like this really do exist. And as much as people whine and complain about the crowds it attracts and fighting your way into this place, all it takes is a short walk down a path or trail off the main drag and you're here alone, admiring the grandeur.

While most of the 4-million-plus visitors Yosemite receives each year head to Yosemite Valley for the legendary views of its granite peaks and its pristine falls, there are also more than 1,200 square miles of wilderness to explore. Hiking and backpacking routes into the Yosemite high country are sparsely populated because the National Park Service does a terrific job of regulating the number of people on the trails. Those adventuresome enough to climb get to see this place from two perspectives. From the valley floor, the waterfalls and granite walls seem miles off and silent. Climb out of the valley along one of the hiking routes ascending the falls, however, and the forces that carved this place out of glaciers and rock millions of years ago can almost be known to you. The roar of the falls deafens you to almost all other sound, and the spray soaks you to the bone.

Sure, there are rows of RVs in the campgrounds and a couple of four-star hotels in the valley, along with cable TV and cellular phones. But this is not civilization. Take away the highways and other creature comforts and look at the meadows, the wild rivers and streams, the ample wildlife. Rock slides and wildfires, uncontrolled floods and sudden storms. Ice sheets dropping from the valley walls in the morning thaw. We call this place a park, but it is really nature in the raw.

Getting There

See Vehicles and roads, below.

Adjoining Areas

Portions of Yosemite National Park are described in each chapter of the Southern Sierra section.

inside out

Yosemite National Park Rules and Regulations

Considering there are more than 1,200 square miles of dazzlingly beautiful wilderness within its boundaries alone, it's difficult to fathom why Yosemite National Park and the surrounding areas have such insurmountable **crowd control problems.** Yet Yosemite is way up there in the ranks of outdoor national treasures getting a few too many visits from those clamoring to admire it. John Muir predicted all of this. When he first learned it would be possible to bring automobile traffic all the way into **Yosemite Valley,** he scoffed and said it was a lousy idea that would ultimately spoil the place. Many are sorry they didn't heed his warning way back in the early 20th century; if they had, road rage and wilderness would have nothing to do with each other. That's the reality now, however, and with any trip through Yosemite's gates, you're going to be competing with scores of the park's 4-million-plus annual visitors. Be prepared for the sound of bus motors drowning out the sound of running rivers, and for gridlock in place of serenity during peak season. While it's still possible to catch Yosemite on a sunny weekend in the off-season, there are a few things the weary traveler should know that could make the experience more pleasant. First, while Yosemite National Park is equated with high granite canyon walls, famous rock faces, and stunning waterfalls dropping into Yosemite Valley, there are **lesser-known areas** that don't draw nearly the crowds. **Wawona, Tuolumne Meadows, Mariposa Grove,** and even **Mono Lake** (outside the park boundaries) all have a lot to offer. Explore waterfalls, unusual rock formations rising out of a lake, or the fabulous Grand Canyon of the Tuolumne hidden deep in the park's northeastern reaches, with granite walls higher than Yosemite Valley's cutting a narrow path toward **Hetch Hetchy Valley,** where San Francisco's water supply is stored. Tuolumne Meadows allows you to enter Yosemite National Park through the upland routes and hike down into the valley rather than the other way around—often preferable, as fewer visitors opt for this route (overnight wilderness permits are issued in daily rations to keep the trails from getting too crowded). If you plan to visit Yosemite, be smart. Explore the alternatives rather than making a beeline for the valley, and be sure to either make reservations for camping and wilderness hikes well in advance or show up early enough in the day to get a walk-in spot.

When John Muir and some of the early western travelers and outdoor adventurers first stumbled on Yosemite and Yosemite Valley, they made up their own rules and regulations—because there weren't any. Today, with the federal government in charge, there are rules aplenty to keep track of, most of them centered around either protecting wildlife and wildlife habitat from humans or protecting humans from potentially dangerous animals and the elements in the wild. The rest concern traffic control, crowd control, and collecting fees.

Vehicles and roads

Naturally, automobiles are to remain on paved designated roads only. Occasionally during the peak spring and summer seasons, the park is closed to additional vehicle traffic until congestion and parking availability return to acceptable levels. High-country roads such as Tioga and Badger Pass are closed during the winter because of severe weather. **Highways 120, 141, and 41** are the main access to the park via the four main entrances. Once you're in Yosemite Valley, however, all three highways merge onto **Southside Drive and Northside Drive.** These roads carry one-way traffic only: Southside Dr is the entrance road and Northside Dr is the exit road. The connecting roads between them are at Yosemite Village. Because of this orientation, visitors who want to see areas of the valley on the north side must drive through the valley and access Northside Dr first.

Fees

The park entry fee is $20 for each vehicle and is good for seven days. Individuals who ride public transportation into the park or hike in through the fee stations are charged $10 each. An annual pass costs $40. Campsites are $18 a night, and wilderness permits cost $4.

Visitors centers

Yosemite National Park has four main visitors centers offering wilderness permits and park program information: one at each of the park's three main entrances and a fourth in Yosemite Valley. While park visitors are given a complete guide and park map upon entry at the toll gates, the visitors centers are the places to stop for updates on trail conditions, additional maps, and wilderness permits. The **Valley Visitors Center** is the main information resource for the entire park. To find it, drive into Yosemite Valley (there is only one route in and one route out, so you can't get lost) and follow the signs along Southside Dr to the Yosemite Village area. At the point where Southside Dr turns left toward the buildings, you will see a parking area for the Village Store. It is best to park here and walk to the visitors center just beyond the store, since spaces in the store lot are easier to find and parking in the village area is limited. The visitors center phone number is (209) 372-0299 (for all locations). If you are entering the park from the US 395 corridor on Hwy 120 to Tuolumne Meadows, stop at the **Tuolumne Meadows Visitors Center** on the south side of Tioga Rd, 5 miles west of the entrance. This visitors center usually opens by late May and stays open until wintertime. The other two visitors centers, open May 1, are located just beyond the Hwy 120 and Hwy 41 entrances at **Big Oak Flat** and **Wawona,** respectively. Business hours at all of the centers are 9am to 4:30pm. In addition to the maps available at the entry gates and the visitors centers, hiking guides published by the Wilderness Press are available through the Yosemite Fund. These are pocket-size and include recommended hikes. Map sales benefit the park. Check at the park bookstore in Yosemite Village.

Pets

Pets are not allowed on paths other than the paved trails in Yosemite Valley and must be leashed at all times. This does not, however, apply to guide dogs for the disabled, per federal law. Pets are not allowed in the North Pines, Lower Pines, or Tamarack Flat Campgrounds.

Camping/Backpacking

Reservations

Those heading to Yosemite hoping to have a serene wildlife experience had better think again if they plan to stay in Yosemite Valley. At just 7 square miles and with upward of 4 million visitors each year, most of them during peak summer months, campsites and even wilderness permits can come at a premium. There are ways to get around this, however. First, it is advisable to plan any trip to Yosemite—even if it doesn't involve camping in one of the park's popular developed valley campsites—as far in advance as possible. Campground reservations for most of the prized Yosemite Valley sites are taken up to **five months in advance,** and during peak season they sell about as fast as tickets to a Backstreet Boys concert . . . only so many spaces, and an overabundance of fans. There are several tricks to getting in. First, it is important to know that bookings for any Yosemite reservable campsite are taken both by telephone and by mail. So those who don't want to play the speed-dial game can instead mail a check or money order to the National Park Service well in advance of the date wanted; five months before the arrival date, reservations will be processed. Of course, there are bound to be more people turned away than those who luck out, but *somebody* has to get in, and it may as well be you. To reserve a site by phone, be sure to begin dialing at 7am Pacific Standard Time, and be diligent about trying to get through. Speed-dial, busy signal, hang up, speed-dial, busy signal, hang up, and so on . . . the **reservations phone** is (800) 436-7275. **Mail reservations** should be addressed to NPRS, PO Box 1600, Cumberland, MD 21502, but be sure to call the number above first to find out the exact price of the campsite of your choice.

Actually, there's no need to go through any of this if you're willing to get up extra early to claim a prized **walk-in campsite,** either in the valley or in the Yosemite uplands along Tioga Rd, which accesses Tuolumne Meadows (a non-winter option only, since weather closes the pass annually). To do this requires timing and perseverance; only those who show up at the right moment at the specific campground—particularly during peak season—will get a chance to pitch a tent. At the Sunnyside camp in Yosemite Valley, which is exclusively held for walk-in campers, six people are crammed into each site whether they show up together or not. So don't opt for Sunnyside during the peak April to September camping season if privacy is what you're looking for. There are also first-come, first-served campsites throughout the Yosemite uplands, including at Wawona south of Yosemite Valley, Bridalveil Creek off Glacier Point Rd, Hodgdon Meadow near Big Oak Flat, White Wolf and Yosemite Creek on Tioga Rd, and at Tuolumne Meadows. Note that many upland campsites may be closed in winter and walk-in sites are limited. (See Camping in Yosemite Valley, Yosemite Northern Uplands, and Yosemite Southern Uplands and Mono Lake chapters).

Wilderness permits

To manage the hordes of people descending upon Yosemite's wilderness areas during the peak backpacking season, all overnight backpackers are required to obtain a wilderness permit before venturing off into the hinterlands. The park accomplishes this by regulating the number of backpackers it allows to stage from each trailhead daily, meaning the most popular hikes fill up first, while less desirable staging areas are more readily available. Permits may be reserved **up to 24 weeks in advance.** Half of the permits for each trailhead are reserved for drop-in backpackers and doled out on a first-come, first-served basis at the visitors centers; early risers who get there ahead of the masses are virtually guaranteed access. Dispersed camping is allowed only at least 4 miles away from developed areas of the park, and at least 1 mile away from roads. Groups are limited to 15 people on trails, and 8 people for cross-country bushwhacking. It's best to reserve a wilderness permit up to 24 weeks in advance. Call the permit office at (209) 372-0740, or write Wilderness Permits, PO Box 545, Yosemite, CA 95389. For wilderness information, call (209) 372-0200.

If you've always wanted to backpack in Yosemite but don't have the equipment or experience, here's your chance. Call Southern Yosemite Mountain Guides at (559) 658-TREK and ask for a free brochure of their **guided and catered backpacking adventures,** which range from leisurely weekend family outings to challenging two-week treks. Guided mountain bike tours, fly-fishing excursions, and rock-climbing clinics are also available.

Campfires

During peak season, from May to October, campfires are allowed in Yosemite Valley only between 5pm and 10pm and only in designated fire rings and pits. Wood gathering is strictly prohibited both within the valley and in wilderness areas above 9,600 feet. Even burning of wood debris such as pine cones or needles is prohibited, as is building a fire in any sequoia grove. Fires are not allowed in the backcountry, so backpackers who insist on cooking should be sure to carry stoves. Stoves are to be refueled only when cool.

Wildlife

Don't feed the bears. If you were to forget every park rule except one, park officials would probably prefer that you adhere to the set of regulations regarding **black bears** and food. Campers and backpackers are required to store and pack food properly to avoid attracting bears into developed campsites and areas frequented by long-haul trekkers. Developed campsites are equipped with bear-proof food storage lockers; backpackers are required to store all food in **bear-proof canisters.** In fact, in camp situations where fires are permitted, it is best to burn all food waste rather than throw it in the trash or try to pack it out. A special note to car campers: do not store food in your car thinking it will be safe. Bears at Yosemite know that if a Honda or Toyota smells like a doughnut or a bag of potato chips, all they have to do is peel the car open like a sardine can to get at the goodies. While bears are normally not likely to attack humans (the only park visitor ever to be killed by an animal in Yosemite was by a deer's antlers), park officials are becoming increasingly concerned with the aggressive behavior of bears that have figured out that humans camping in the parks are an easy source of snacks. Numerous bears each year must be destroyed as a result.

Naturally, the "do not feed" rule does not apply to bears alone. In Yosemite, **it is unlawful to feed any animals.** Even bait fishing in the Merced River is not allowed. It also is against the rules to approach or otherwise harass park wildlife.

Bicycles

Cycling is allowed only on paved, designated biking paths and roads. No off-road biking is allowed in the park. Mountain bikers should consider opting for Stanislaus or Sierra National Forests.

Rock Climbing

Some climbing routes are closed during bird nesting seasons for a number of protected species, including the peregrine falcon. It is best, however, to check with the park for the latest information since federal protection status and nesting seasons are likely to change. Call the Yosemite rock-climbing school at (209) 372-8435 for information.

outside in

Attractions

What was once the beloved home of the Ahwahneechee, Mi-Wuk, and Paiute Indians is now a spectacular international playground. Designated a national park in 1890, thanks in part to Sierra Club founder John Muir,

1,170-square-mile Yosemite is only slightly smaller than the state of Rhode Island. During the peak season, however, Yosemite seems more like a 1,200-square-foot park. Crowds more typical of Disney World clog the 7-square-mile valley for a glimpse of some of nature's most incredible creations, including 4,500-foot-high El Capitan, the largest piece of exposed granite on earth, and 2,425-foot-high Yosemite Falls, the highest waterfall in North America and fifth highest in the world.

To avoid most of the crowds, visit in the spring or early fall, when the wildflowers are plentiful and the weather is usually mild. This grande dame of national parks is most dazzling, and least crowded, in the winter, the time of year Ansel Adams shot those world-renowned photographs of the snow-laced valley.

No matter what the time of year, be sure to tour the **Yosemite Valley Visitors Center,** which houses some mildly interesting galleries and museums. The center's **Indian Cultural Museum** hosts live demonstrations of the native Mi-Wuk and Paiute methods of basket weaving, jewelry making, and other crafts. Nearby are a reconstructed Mi-Wuk–Paiute village, a self-guided nature trail, and an art gallery showcasing the master photographer whose name is almost synonymous with this place: Ansel Adams.

If you're partial to viewing Yosemite by car, pick up a copy of the Yosemite Road Guide or the **Yosemite Valley Tour** cassette tape at the Yosemite Valley Visitors Center. It's almost as good as having Ranger Rick in the back seat of your car.

Restaurants and Lodgings

While the sightseeing in Yosemite is unparalleled, the dining is not. Bring as much of your own food as possible, because most of the park's restaurants offer mediocre (or worse) cafeteria-style food; the only exception is the lofty Ahwahnee Hotel restaurant (see Lodgings, Yosemite Valley chapter), but you'll have to fork over a bundle to eat there.

Park accommodations range from less than $15 per night for a campsite to more than $200 nightly for a room at the Ahwahnee Hotel. Reservations are required for most Yosemite campsites—only a few are available on a first-come, first-served basis; see Reservations under Camping/Backpacking, above, and Camping in the other Yosemite chapters for details. Moderately priced motel rooms are available at the valley's bare-bones but adequate Yosemite Lodge (a quick walk from Lower Yosemite Falls). Spartan cabins (some are nothing more than wood frames with canvas covers, others are heated in the winter) offer inexpensive alternatives to camping, and they're popular with families. There are also 69 tent cabins at

Tuolumne Meadows Lodge. For reservations at Yosemite National Park's non-camping accommodations, call (559) 252-4848.

Vacation-home rentals (with full kitchens) can also be reserved, but they cost a pretty penny; for more information call Yosemite West Condominiums at (209) 372-4240, and for rental reservations call (800) 640-9099. Also check out the Web site www.yosemitepark.com for additional lodgings information.

More Information

Road and weather conditions: *(209) 372-0200.*

Visitors centers (at entrances to park): *(209) 372-0299.*

Yosemite campground reservations: *(800) 436-7275 or www.reservations.nps.gov.*

Yosemite concessionaires: *(559) 252-4848.*

Yosemite on the Web: *www.nps.gov/yose/ and www.yosemitepark.com.*

Yosemite Wilderness Center: *(209) 372-0740.*

Yosemite Valley

The Yosemite National Park core, including Yosemite Valley, El Capitan, Eagle Peak, Yosemite Point, Half Dome, Glacier Point, and Cathedral Rock.

When floodwaters washed away campsites and damaged roads leading into Yosemite Valley in the winter of 1997, National Park Service officials had no choice but close the park while they patched one of America's most beloved places back together again. It took three months, Yosemite's longest closure ever. Yet even as new road sections were constructed in place of those washed away and storm-lashed trees lodged in bridge railings were removed, something magnificent happened in Yosemite Valley that had never been witnessed perhaps since the time of John Muir: it got quiet. So quiet, in fact, that it was possible to hear sheets of ice crash off the granite valley walls in the morning thaw. Afternoons passed without the rush-hour traffic jams that turned this wild, ancient place into road rage central. No longer was there the constant buzz of auto-winders, the rumble of tour bus motors, the hum of electric generators mounted to the tops of Winnebagos. Visiting the park shortly before it reopened to see how it had weathered the closures, we were stunned. Never had recent visitors seen this Yosemite. It was the one Muir wrote of, long ago lost in the crush of so many others who wanted to share his experience.

Since then, Yosemite Valley has returned to "normal." Campgrounds again fill to the brim during peak season, and traffic still piles up on valley roads in the afternoons. Despite a long-range plan to alleviate all of that by busing more visitors in from feeder cities, progress comes slow. But the other reality is this: it is still possible to escape the masses in Yosemite Valley. All you have to do is hike away from the 7-mile-long valley and into some of the 1,200 square miles of surrounding wilderness, and you stand a chance of hearing the rush of waterfalls, rivers, and the wind over the sounds that are imported. It doesn't hurt to try.

True, a trip to Yosemite Valley seems at times more about crowd control and careful planning than about reconnecting with nature. Reservations for campgrounds are made at lease three months in advance, and the few walk-in sites that are available get snapped up fast. But to be there is well worth the trouble, as the waterfalls dazzle and the views of Half Dome, El Capitan, Glacier Point, and other peaks never fail to amaze and inspire. Short walks or long treks out of the valley pay off big-time. Bicycle tours of the valley's nature areas, while the trails are often crowded, are relaxing and good for the soul, and the Merced River, when it is not engorged with floodwaters, makes a nice swimming hole. Plan carefully and forget about the hassles of dealing with crowds. Relax and enjoy a beautiful place.

Getting There

As vast as Yosemite's wilderness and developed areas are, combined, national parks officials do a good job of making sure visitors entering by vehicle get counted and pay their entrance fees. There are four main driving routes into the park, including Highways 140, 120, and 41 from the California side out of the Gold Rush country; and Highway 120 from US Highway 395 (US 395) in Nevada, via Lee Vining. A fifth entrance is at Hetch Hetchy Valley. Because of concerns about overuse of the park by humans, an effort to reduce the number of cars entering the park (particularly Yosemite Valley) has been picking up steam in recent years. Yosemite, however, is very difficult to get to and around in without a car unless you're planning to backpack into the hinterlands. Those who want to brave public transportation can catch the VIA/Yosemite Gray Line from either Merced or Fresno to Yosemite Valley, and then backpack into the high country from there. Call (888) PARK-BUS for schedules and rates. It is always a good idea to check on road conditions; call (209) 372-4726 or (209) 372-0467 for up-to-date information.

Adjoining Areas

NORTH: **Yosemite Northern Uplands**
SOUTH: **Yosemite Southern Uplands and Mono Lake**
WEST: **Southern Gold Rush Country**

inside out

Hiking/Backpacking

When it comes to the outdoors, intensity and extremes are what really make a lasting impression—and there is perhaps no better way to have an intense experience than by taking a waterfall hike, particularly in Yosemite Valley. A waterfall begins to attack the senses even before you set out to get a close-up look. From a distance, the ferocious velocity with which falls pour over Yosemite's granite walls is not apparent. You can fool yourself into dismissing them as far-away silent trickles, barely visible and certainly not powerful. Stand right beneath one, however, and you are drenched and freezing, in the midst of a crashing thunder. Seeing a waterfall up close is both beautiful and frightening—it is the point at which a river seems most alive, while at the same time potentially destructive. You are afraid of getting too close, but then again you can't resist. We have done the hike to Vernal Falls on particularly warm summer days and found ourselves overheating one moment from the strenuous climb in the sun and then huddling, drenched, with chattering teeth—soaked to the bone by the ice-cold blizzard of spray along Mist Trail. Dry off in the sun and soon you are warmed again. It is like a cold slap in the face, a blunt reminder that this is wilderness, not Disneyland. Waterfall hikes beginning in Yosemite Valley range from short and easy to long and difficult. You choose.

Bridalveil Fall Trail (easy; 0.5 mile round trip) is a quick and easy walk up a roadside footpath at the side of Wawona Rd—just stop the car, get out, and walk no more distance than you would from a pretty good parking spot at the mall. You won't even get your white tennies dirty if you're careful. You'll have trouble believing this waterfall is real at first. It is so perfect and orderly that it reminds you of an elaborate fountain sitting in front of a Las Vegas casino. Don't be fooled, though; no human tinkering went into this. The trailhead is just south of El Portal Rd, the park's gateway entrance, right past the intersection with Tunnel View. Look for the parking area and sign to the right of the one-way road.

Lower Yosemite Falls Trail (easy, 0.5 mile round trip) is another short walking path to the base of the valley's other easy-to-reach waterfall. Expect major neck-craning as you take in a view of both the lower and upper falls from the point where the lower fall spills into Yosemite Creek, a tributary to the Merced River. The trailhead is just west of the Valley Visitors Center on Hwy 120 and well marked. Now, those who are willing to break a little sweat should consider the steep 1,000-foot climb up **Columbia**

Rock Trail (difficult; 2 miles round trip) for a close-up look at **Upper Yosemite Falls.** If after you've huffed and puffed your way to this point you feel as if you've got it in you to continue to the top (another 4.5 miles round trip), have at it. Your climb will take you another 2,700 feet to where the fall begins its awesome 2,425-foot drop into the valley. You will wonder where all of this water could possibly be coming from, especially if you make the trip during the spring runoff when the fall is fully engorged.

John Muir Trail to Vernal Falls and Nevada Falls (difficult; 7 miles round trip) is in our view the premier waterfall hike not only in Yosemite Valley but anywhere. The long, strenuous climb from the Happy Isles trailhead should be attempted only by those in decent shape—it really is hard work from the trailhead, ascending 1,000 feet to the **Vernal Falls overlook.** Our preferred route is to pick up **Mist Trail** (named that for a reason, and clearly marked with trail signs) for the climb along Vernal Falls, and then continue to Nevada Falls via the Mist Trail's upper leg, which rejoins John Muir Trail at 5,900 feet. Mist Trail is essentially a long, wet granite stairway—and easier to climb than it is to descend. Get wet and cold going up, then dry off at the edge of Emerald Pool, where Vernal Falls begins its violent drop. The top leg of John Muir Trail loops from Nevada Falls back toward the trailhead without your having to get drenched twice. Don't wanna get drenched the first time? Bring a rain poncho (or avoid Mist Trail altogether). Incidentally, the hike to Nevada Falls is also the first leg to the infamous climb to Half Dome (see below). The Happy Isles/John Muir trailhead is in the eastern end of Yosemite Valley. Use the parking area near Curry Village. There is also the option of continuing on the John Muir Trail the entire 22 miles to Tuolumne Meadows (see Yosemite Northern Uplands chapter).

Despite the ease with which you can reach and complete the **Happy Isles Interpretive Trail** (easy; 0.5 mile round trip), we consider it one of the most fascinating nature walks in the Yosemite region. That's because in 1996 a huge section of granite came crashing down from the valley walls east of Glacier Point, striking the valley floor with such force that a wind blast more powerful than a hurricane ripped through Happy Isles. The force of the wind blast ripped the forest apart, sending trees sailing through the air like javelins, the result a bizarre moonscape of broken twigs. Because the slide and wind blast were a natural event, park officials decided to leave Mother Nature's handiwork as is. Walk this trail and what you see is a fascinating process of reforestation—it will take hundreds of years for the forest to reestablish itself. The trailhead is at the eastern end of Yosemite Valley; use the parking area near Curry Village.

Mirror Lake Trail (easy; 3 miles round trip) is a pleasant walk up a slight grade to what used to be a stunningly brilliant small lake on Tenaya

Creek at the foot of Half Dome. Because of silting, the lake now dries up during the summer—and an adjacent meadow makes for a nice ecology tour during the spring bloom. Head up here before late summer and the lake may even look like a lake, as an added bonus. The trail is paved most of the way, so watch out for bicyclists (or join them by riding up yourself). To reach the Mirror Lake trailhead, stage from Yosemite Village and walk 1 mile east on any of the three access trails—all of them lead to the Mirror Lake trail system. There is no vehicle access to this part of the park—so ditch the car and hoof it.

Valley Floor Loop (moderate; 6.5 miles or 13 miles round trip) is a grand tour of the Yosemite Valley floor, not only a great way to become acquainted with the meadows, springs, riverbanks, and forests here but also a good opportunity to get the best views of Yosemite's dominant features—Cathedral Rock, El Capitan, Half Dome, Three Brothers, and the falls. Take the wide view and the narrow view all at once, and you come away from this walk with a better feel for what Yosemite is—a life web with each feature contributing to its complexity and beauty. To use this trail system, it is best to look for parking near the valley headquarters complex off Southside Dr, and stage from there. The trail covers most of the valley floor, and parking outside the village is limited. If parking is available, also try staging a hike through the meadows from the Lower Yosemite Falls parking area, a half mile west of Yosemite Village on the north side of Northside Dr. Because this section of Northside Dr is a one-way road heading west, you'll need to enter and turn back to reach this area.

No matter how many times you visit and see it, that first glimpse of Yosemite Valley when you come around the bend on Oak Flat Rd or through Tunnel View Overlook is going to leave you awestricken. Then a couple of things happen. At first, taking in the wide overview is enough— El Capitan, Half Dome, Glacier Point, Yosemite Falls, the high walls of granite bathed in the morning sunlight. Then, you begin to feel small and temporary in the presence of these strange and stunning surroundings. This is about the time a primal urge arises . . . and you know you've got to climb. You've got to be "up there." This is why so many of us choose to put ourselves through the agony of huffing and puffing 3,000 feet up the relentlessly steep trails leading out of Yosemite Valley. Some of us can't help ourselves. We not only need to see this place from as many vantage points as possible, we need to conquer this place by at least being able to say we climbed it. Any one of the following three hikes should quench this urge. Remember, however, to get a wilderness permit if you plan to camp out.

Four Mile Trail (difficult; 9.5 miles round trip) will take you 3,200 feet above the valley floor to the **Glacier Point summit** (this is a summer hike only), but there is a price to pay. This is a difficult, steep, strenuous, butt-kicker of a hike with 20 jagged switchbacks, topping out at 7,214 feet. In exchange for your hard work, you'll get the pleasure of being able to look Half Dome right in the eye instead of having to crane your neck to look up at it—and we must say, viewing it this way is a whole new experience. Those who are making an overnighter of this may consider continuing another 3.5 miles to the 8,122-foot Sentinel Dome . . . but you probably won't feel like it after such a rigorous climb. You can, by the way, drive to Glacier Point through Badger Pass, but what would be the fun in that? The trailhead is 2.5 miles west of Curry Village, on Southside Dr. Park a car at the top ahead of time and you can get back down the easy way. To reach the 7,569-foot summit of El Capitan, drive to the trailhead off Tioga Rd (closed during winter): **North Rim Trail** (difficult; 14.5 miles round trip) will lead you through zigs and zags, catapulting skyward through forested highland terrain to the El Capitan summit, at 7,569 feet. Pitch a tent, scarf some instant food, and sleep now. You won't be in the mood to walk back down till morning. From the valley, take Hwy 120 west to Tioga Rd, then take the Tamarack Flat entry road to the end.

The **John Muir Trail** to Half Dome (difficult; 17 miles round trip) is the Yosemite Valley hike you are most likely to brag to your friends about once you're completed it. The first leg of the hike is identical to the Vernal Falls/Nevada Falls trek described above—you decide whether to bring Mist Trail into the equation. It is best to do the first leg of the hike on day one, then camp out at Little Yosemite Valley and continue on to the **Half Dome overlook** in the morning, when weather conditions are favorable. The rock itself is equipped with handrails and climbing cables. Hang on tight and be careful. The view from up here (you have climbed 4,800 feet by this point, to 8,842) is going to make you dizzy.

Camping

The key to camping in Yosemite National Park is not choosing the best site, or getting outfitted with the perfect sleeping bag and hiking shoes, or even coming up with the best-ever recipe for campfire stew—it's all about using speed-dial. That's because if you don't dial in soon enough to make a reservation, you don't have a prayer. The phone number is (800) 436-7275. Campsites become available exactly five months in advance. The reservations office opens every morning at 7am, Pacific Standard Time. That means if you want to go camping on September 15, you'd better start on April 15. Call the park at (209) 372-0200 for information on current conditions. For detailed information on reservations and other matters, see Yosemite National Park: Overview chapter.

Upper Pines Campground has 238 sites (no hookups; RV limit 38 feet), **North Pines Campground** has 85 sites (no hookups; RV limit 38 feet), and **Lower Pines Campground** has 60 sites (no hookups; RV limit 38 feet). Upper Pines and North Pines are adjacent, and Lower Pines is slightly to the west. These campgrounds are probably the most sought-after campgrounds in the United States. Crowded they are, and why expect otherwise given their location? Located in the heart of Yosemite Valley, the camp areas have piped water, flush toilets, and shower rooms. A general store is nearby in Yosemite Village. *The campgrounds are in the eastern end of Yosemite Valley. To reach them, take Southside Dr 3 miles through the valley and follow the signs to the camp areas, which are all north of the road. For Upper River, turn left at Curry Village and cross the river. The camp area is on the right just past the bridge. Open year-round.*

Hodgdon Meadow Campground has about 100 sites (no hookups; RV limit 33 feet) and is the primary campsite for backpackers visiting the Hetch Hetchy Valley and preparing to embark on one of the many trails traversing the area. The campground has piped water, flush toilets, tables, and fire grills. *At the Big Oak Flat Rd entrance to the park, directly off Hwy 120. Open year-round.*

Sunnyside Campground has 35 tent sites (no RV access) in Yosemite Valley. No reservations are taken; instead, sites are doled out daily on a first-come, first-served basis. During the peak season, it is guaranteed to fill up every day—and park service officials are so determined to make sure as many people as possible get to enjoy it that they will pack six people into every site, whether those people came to the park together or not. Got three in your party? You may have three new friends camping with you, then! The campground is approachable only on foot (a short walk) and while one may think this would discourage potential visitors, it doesn't. The camp area has piped water and flush toilets, with a shower room and general store nearby. *Drive to Yosemite Valley and proceed to the campground's parking area near the base of Yosemite Falls, near the Valley Visitors Center. Open year-round.*

Wawona Campground has roughly 100 sites (no hookups; RV limit 34 feet) at the southern end of the park. The campground serves as an overflow camp for the Yosemite Valley campgrounds, and is also popular among visitors to the Mariposa Grove just south of the campground. Set along the South Fork Merced River, the campground has piped water, flush toilets, tables, and fire grills. *From the Hwy 41 entrance to the park, east out of Oakhurst, take Wawona Rd north 6 miles to the campground on the left side of the road, 2 miles past the river crossing. To reach the campground from the valley, take Wawona Rd 10 miles south from the Tunnel View area and look for the entrance on the left side of the road. Open year-round.*

Rafting

The Merced River has Class III whitewater runs below El Capitan bridge, and outside of the park. See Southern Gold Rush Country chapter for complete information.

Skiing

Roads leading into the Yosemite uplands and high country are closed to automobile traffic during the snow season—and open to cross-country skiers. See Yosemite Northern Uplands chapter for information about this and about the Badger Pass Ski Area, where downhill skiing is also available within the park.

Fishing

The Merced River through Yosemite Valley is a successful fly-fishing spot for **brown** and **rainbow trout,** but serious anglers be advised—rainbows are catch-and-release only in the valley, and there is a five-fish daily limit on browns. Bait fishing is not allowed. Season is April to November. Also be advised that Yosemite National Park no longer stocks lakes, as has been the practice in the past, for fear of introducing exotic species to the park's streams and rivers, thereby slowing the recovery of the declined trout fishery. No permits or fishing licenses are required within the park boundaries.

Rock Climbing

Of the 4 million-plus people who pour into Yosemite Valley to get a look at El Capitan and Half Dome, for some looking just isn't enough. Therefore, they climb. The **Salathe Wall** up the face of **El Capitan** is one of the most sought-after climbs in the world—that's why invariably you can scan the face of "the Cap" and see legs dangling out of the small openings in the side of the wall face where climbers sleep at night as they make their way to the top (the climb can take several days). Naturally, novices should not try to scale El Capitan—while the park has a good network of volunteers who regularly rescue stranded climbers, it's not worth the embarrassment. Shorter climbs are available in the high country areas, such as Lembert Dome. Yosemite Mountaineering School and Guide Services, (209) 372-8435, offers **instruction** and **guided climbs.** Call them before scaling any walls freestyle.

Scenic Drives/Photography

All of Yosemite National Park is a "scenic" drive—but naturally we have our favorite spots. The turnout at Tunnel Overlook out of Wawona to the valley is one of the best easy-to-reach spots in the park to get a wide-angle overview of the peaks. Good luck, however, getting a shot without a tour bus in it! For more nice vantage points, assuming it's summer, take the Tioga Rd and/or Badger Pass Rd corridors to the Yosemite uplands. Glacier Point and North Point also have terrific wide vistas of the valley and its environs. Wannabe Ansel Adams types also may get a chance to practice wildlife photography techniques, as mule deer and black bear are not an uncommon sight. (For inspiration, stop by the Ansel Adams gallery/gift shop in Yosemite Valley.)

Cycling

Pedal power is closely monitored and regulated in Yosemite National Park—and it's allowed only on paved roadways and trails. There are 12 miles of paved cycling paths in the valley, a pleasant way to see the sights without having to walk or drive. The Yosemite Valley bikeway trails extend from the east end of the valley near Mirror Lake to the western end, crossing the meadows between Northside and Southside Dr. This is a great way to take in all the Yosemite peak views without having to drive and repark several times or walk for hours. With the exception of the path leading up to Mirror Lake, these trails are level and easy. Mountain bikes, naturally, are banned in the Yosemite high country. **Rentals** for low-impact tours of the valley are available at Curry Village.

Horseback Riding

Yosemite Trails Pack Station, Inc., has **guided horseback tours** of the meadows and canyons in the south end of the park, ending with a tour of the Mariposa Grove. Expeditions through Sierra National Forest areas adjacent and contiguous with Yosemite are also available. There is no horseback riding in Yosemite Valley itself. For information, call the stables at (559) 683-7611 or (559) 683-7426.

Swimming

Pools that form in the **Merced River** around the Happy Isles Nature Center are popular spots to cool off on hot summer days—but don't be fooled by the river's seemingly placid surface. In spring and sometimes well into the summer, snowmelt can create river currents that are much more powerful than they appear. That means small children should never be allowed to wade in unattended, and also that common sense should prevail at all times. Because the river is divided into several channels around the islands in the eastern end of the valley and because there are numerous trees across the water and coved areas on the banks, the Happy Isles portion of the Merced is the most swimmable. We suggest keeping any body contact with the water limited to this area; if unsure about the velocity of the river, definitely check with park rangers.

outside in

Lodgings

Ahwahnee Hotel ☆☆☆   The majestic Ahwahnee Hotel stands regally against the soaring cliffs of Yosemite. Built in 1927 with native granite boulders and redwood-hued concrete, the multitiered six-story building blends comfortably into its surroundings. The 123 rooms are spacious. If money's no object, request one of the hotel's luxury suites or private cottages. The Ahwahnee Restaurant's food is decent, but the view is the main draw. *In Yosemite Valley, Yosemite National Park; (559)252-4848 (hotel), (209) 372-1489 (restaurant); $$$.*

Wawona Hotel ☆   Four miles from the park's entrance, the rustic Wawona is the oldest resort hotel in the state. A pair of century-old white buildings, adorned by pillars and a veranda, face an expansive manicured lawn, giving the Wawona the look of an antebellum mansion. The majority of its 104 rooms are small, and about half of them have private bathrooms. *On Hwy 41 (SW corner of the park, 27 miles from Yosemite Valley), Yosemite National Park; (209) 375-6556; $$.*

More Information

Road conditions: *(209) 372-4726 or (209) 372-0467.*
Transportation information: *(888) PARK-BUS.*
Valley Visitors Center: *(209) 372-0299.*
Yosemite camping reservations: *(800) 436-7275.*
Yosemite general information: *(209) 372-0200 or
    www.yosemitepark.net/.*
Yosemite Mountaineering School and Guide Services: *(209) 372-8435.*

Yosemite Northern Uplands

The backcountry and wilderness areas north of Yosemite Valley, including Hetch Hetchy Reservoir, Tuolumne Meadows, Tioga Pass, Merced Lake, and Little Yosemite.

Simply put, outdoor enthusiasts who insist on visiting Yosemite National Park during peak season have two choices: they can fight the crowds down in Yosemite Valley and spend their time wandering 7 confined and crowded square miles, or they can trek out into the deep reaches of the park—which covers 1,200 square miles of the High Sierra wilderness and offers room to spread out and fewer people to share the space with. The dispersed Yosemite visit is the most rewarding. Those who don't head for higher ground, for example, will never set eyes on the Grand Canyon of the Tuolumne River, a steep, V-shaped granite trench with walls higher than those of Yosemite Valley itself, carrying the high-country snowmelt down to Hetch Hetchy Valley. Hetch Hetchy is another sight to behold. Though it was once touted as equivalent to Yosemite Valley in its grandeur, environmentalists long ago lost the fight to prevent the city of San Francisco from damming the Tuolumne at Hetch Hetchy—turning what had been a pristine meadow enclosed by granite walls into a man-made lake. In the late 1980s, some activists scaled the dam and painted a huge crack down the front—a sight so frightening to water department workers that they reported in a panic that the dam was about to burst. "Free the river," the graffiti artists also scrawled (the white splotches where the cover-up paint was applied are still visible). Tuolumne Meadows, home of the meandering creeks and rivers feeding Yosemite Valley's grand waterfalls, is another upland treasure, as are the scenic 45 miles of wilderness accessible by Tioga Road.

On the south end of the park, the vistas from Glacier Point, accessed through Badger Pass by car during summer, are something else you can't see without either climbing or driving away from the park's populated center. In winter, when Badger is snowed in, overnight cross-country ski outings to Glacier Point are a favorite activity, paying off with winter views that provide a whole new perspective on Yosemite.

Getting There

With much of the Yosemite National Park uplands, getting there is the big challenge. Tioga Road, which provides the easiest access to Tuolumne Meadows and alternative access to Tuolumne River canyon and the Pacific Crest Trail, is typically closed from November to May because of snow, as is Glacier Point Road out of Badger Pass. These seasonal road closures aside, all high-country roads are subject to periodic closure due to rock slides, freak unseasonable snowstorms, and any number of unforeseeable events. There are four main entrances to the park, but to reach the areas covered in this chapter the best points of entry are from Tioga Road, Hetch Hetchy, or the US Highway 395 (US 395) corridor east of Yosemite. To reach the Tioga Road corridor to Tuolumne Meadows, enter Yosemite National Park via Highway 120 from Sonora and China Camp. The Tioga Road turnoff is 5 miles past the Big Oak Flat entrance. To reach Hetch Hetchy Reservoir, take Evergreen Road north from just before the Big Oak Flat entrance and drive approximately 6 miles to the less frequently used Hetch Hetchy entrance. The Tioga Pass entrance from the US 395 corridor in Nevada provides the most direct access to Tuolumne Meadows, but is subject to the same seasonal road closures as the Big Oak Flat entrance from Highway 120. Use the Highway 140 entrance from El Portal if you wish to visit Yosemite Valley before continuing to an upland area. If your destination is the Badger Pass Ski Area, Glacier Point, Mariposa, or Wawona, the Highway 41 entrance from Oakhurst and Fresno is most direct. There is also the option of using your hiking shoes to reach the outlying areas of Yosemite. See Hiking, Yosemite Valley chapter, and Hiking/Backpacking, below, for a description of options. It is always a good idea to check on road conditions. Call (209) 372-4726 or (209) 372-0467 for up-to-date information. For additional information on entrances, fees, and public transportation, see Yosemite National Park: Overview chapter.

Adjoining Areas

NORTH: **Tahoe Basin**

WEST: **Southern Gold Rush Country**

inside out

Hiking/Backpacking

The largest misconception people have about Yosemite National Park is that it is, indeed, a park. Perhaps the name should be changed. Despite the paved highways, developed campgrounds, and park service buildings, the wilds here are far from tamed. We stress this point because Yosemite's popularity draws hordes of people who have spent little or no time in the wild. They are people who don't understand that a river can look peaceful and placid from its banks but become a violent torrent once you jump in, or that you can't hike 30 miles wearing a pair of tennis shoes and carrying a straw picnic basket. Yosemite covers more than 1,200 square miles of deep, uncharted wilderness and 900 miles of trails—including some areas that are still unnamed and have never been visited by humans. In 1993, as a matter of fact, hikers found the wreckage of a small plane—skeletons still strapped into their seats—that had crashed in an area so remote that it was nearly 30 years before anybody came upon it. Weather in the remote northern uplands can be severe not only during winter but at any time of year; a sunny, warm day can become engorged in a cold blizzard in a matter of hours. During winter, the high country is buried beneath heavy snows, remaining inaccessible for five or more months each year until the spring melt releases the submerged trails and camping areas. Visiting the uplands will give you a true appreciation for the fact that Yosemite is actually two places—a valley full of tourists, and a far-flung wilderness where if you're lucky (and properly outfitted, not only with equipment but with survival skills) you can walk for days without seeing another soul.

Black bears are a big problem through all of the Yosemite wilderness, and the valley as well, because they have become accustomed to human visitors and understand that backpackers carry tasty snacks. Food must be properly stored according to park regulations. Also watch out for rattlesnakes. **Wilderness permits** are required for visiting the backcountry and using trail camp areas. If you're planning a trip during the peak outdoor season, you're advised to reserve a wilderness permit up to 24 weeks in advance. Call (209) 372-0740, or write Wilderness Permits, PO Box 545, Yosemite, CA 95389. For information on trails, call (209) 372-0200. Novices who really want to explore may want to consider checking in with Yosemite Mountaineering School and Guide Services, (209) 372-8344, for a **guided backpacking trip.** For more explicit information on planning a hike or backcountry trip, see Yosemite National Park: Overview chapter.

Tuolumne Meadows

It is here that the meandering, wild high-country rivers and streams spill into the largest high-country meadow you will find in all of the Sierra range. The water passing through the Tuolumne region collects into two river basins—the Tuolumne River canyon, which drains into Hetch Hetchy Reservoir. This is also the headwaters for the Merced River and Tenaya Creek, the spigots feeding the mighty waterfalls that bring the life force to Yosemite Valley. Following are some of our favorite hikes in the Yosemite uplands.

May Lake Trail (moderate; 3 miles round trip) is a pleasant day hike through forested terrain and over granite slabs to a pretty and pristine fishing, swimming, and camping spot in the shadows of Tuolumne's most impressive peaks—Mount Hoffman and Tuolumne Peak, both towering to just above 10,800 feet. This, naturally, is a staging area for longer backpacking trips to the peaks. Dispersed camping south of the lake is possible if you can't get a reservation at the developed campground. **Mount Hoffman Peak Trail** (difficult; 6 miles round trip) leaves from the southern end of May Lake, passes through meadows at the base of the climb, and then begins a strenuous and sometimes steep ascent, more than 1,500 feet to one of the best views in all of Yosemite National Park. Because the elevation nears the 11,000-foot mark, standard warnings apply: turn back if it looks as if a storm is approaching, be sure to acclimate to the high altitude gradually—no need to sprint to the top—and wear sunglasses to protect yourself from the ultraviolet rays found this high up. For both these trails, stage from the May Lake Trailhead, a little less than 4 miles west of Tenaya Lake. Look for the sign from Tioga Rd.

Waterwheel Falls (difficult; 11 miles round trip) is one of those "must-do" hikes out of Tuolumne Meadows. If you don't have time for anything else, this would be an excellent choice (note, however, our bias toward waterfall over peak experiences). The long trek through the enchanting Grand Canyon of the Tuolumne River begins from the northwest corner of the Tuolumne Meadows Visitors Center on Tioga Rd. Follow the Pacific Crest Trail to Glen Aulin Camp, and then from the camp jump off to the falls trail following the Tuolumne River through its deep, V-shaped, granite-walled canyon past California Falls, Le Conte Falls, and, ultimately, the main attraction—Waterwheel Falls, a spot where the river spills in a wide band down a sloping, rock-strewn granite flat. When the river is fully engorged with spring runoff, water passing over the falls soars high, creating noisy whitewater sprays. Try to get here before June for the best sights. To find the Tuolumne Meadows Visitors Center, enter the park from the US 395 corridor in Nevada and continue easily to the visitors center complex 7 miles east of the gate, or enter at Big Oak Flat and take the long, meandering Tioga Rd to the east side of the park.

The 6-mile hike to the **Glen Aulin Camp** from the visitors center offers a spectacular spot for pitching a tent, or stay in one of 8 canvas cabins (for four to six occupants) available to backpackers; prices average $150 for two per night and include breakfast, dinner, and a shower. These cabins, and others in the park, are booked through an annual lottery each fall; call (559) 454-2002 for details.

Lembert Dome (moderate; 9 miles round trip) is a great climb for those who want to be able to say they conquered "the dome" in Yosemite but who perhaps don't have it in them to scale Half Dome (see Hiking/Backpacking, Yosemite Valley chapter). Begin by heading up **Dog Lake Trail** from the northeast corner of the Tuolumne Meadows Visitors Center. Take the 3-mile trek through the forested crest, down toward Dog Lake Basin. You can stop here and take a dip, or continue immediately east on Young Lakes Trail to the Lembert Dome access path. Then, it is as simple as walking on to the rock for a vista of the meadows and surrounding peaks. This is not as exciting as Half Dome, but most certainly an interesting walk for those who enjoy looking at the handiwork of slow-moving glaciers so many millions of years after they passed over this section of North America. See Waterwheel Falls, above, for directions to Tuolumne Meadows.

Pohono Trail (difficult; 20 miles round trip) is a long, meandering ramble through fir and pine forestlands, rock gardens, and sometimes steep mountain terrain between Glacier Point and Inspiration Point overlooking the south rim of Yosemite Valley. This hike is best taken over two days and is not advisable during the winter because of inaccessibility, depending on the weather. While the jaunt is quite a lot of hard work, this hike encapsulates all that is Yosemite and provides a great overview of both the uplands and the valley, with spectacular views of the valley's northern peaks. The hike begins near Glacier Point, and ascends sharply toward Sentinel Falls and Taft Point, which provides an interesting perspective on Cathedral Rocks and Cathedral Spires to the northwest (these features are actually 2,000 feet below the 7,000-foot elevation of the trail). The trail is equipped with a footbridge over Bridalveil Creek and then skirts to the northwest over Dewey, Stanford, and Inspiration Points. The vicinity of the creek is generally the best place to camp, since there is level ground and a consistent water supply throughout the summer. At Inspiration Point, there is the option of continuing another 4 miles to Wawona Tunnel and making this a one-way (14 miles total) hike. The trailhead is easy to find—simply drive to the very end of Glacier Point Rd and look for the trail staging area on the left side of the parking lot. Special note: Because of its accessibility, this hike can be a bit more crowded than other jaunts through the Yosemite uplands and backcountry.

John Muir Trail to Little Yosemite Valley, Nevada Falls, Vernal Falls, and ultimately Yosemite Valley (difficult; 32 miles round trip, best done one way) is essentially the two-day grand tour of the best that Yosemite has to offer. It begins among the meandering creeks and rivers draining toward the mighty waterfalls that engorge Yosemite Valley with thunder and spray, passes through meadows and forests of hemlock, over stream beds, past Cathedral Peak, Cathedral and Sunrise Lakes, and then descends into Little Yosemite Valley via the Sunrise Creek Canyon. Camp at Little Yosemite and continue to Half Dome in the morning, then descend toward Yosemite Valley itself, perhaps along the breathtaking Mist Trail for part of the way. (See Hiking, Yosemite Valley chapter, for valley hiking information.)

Two sections of the **Pacific Crest Trail** meet in Tuolumne Meadows at a three-way intersection with John Muir Trail. Whatever name the trail goes by, the hike to **Agnew Meadows** (difficult; 28 miles one way) is a strenuous and long three- to four-day trip across the southeastern reaches of the Yosemite wilderness. It exits the park through Lyell Canyon, then hopscotches from secluded lake to secluded lake, scrambling to more than 11,000 feet through Donohue Pass, skipping through creek and river crossings, past waterfalls—so deep into the wilds you'll suffer a major attitude adjustment. The journey ends just outside Mammoth Lakes. Don't attempt this one without proper gear and information. Many hike it the other direction because it's less of a climb.

The northern section of the Pacific Crest Trail leads from Tuolumne Meadows to **Sonora Pass** (difficult; 77 miles one way) and is only for expert mountaineers who have at least a week on their hands to spend trouncing around the Sierra wilderness. Most Yosemite visitors will bite off a smaller chunk and make a weekend of it. This leg of the trail enters some of the most secluded and rugged high country found within Yosemite, crossing Virginia, Matterhorn, Rodgers, Kerrick, and Stubblefield Canyons and cutting a crazy roller-coaster zigzag up and down peaks, across rivers, into secluded lake basins, and (if you really want to go the whole way) through the Stanislaus Wilderness toward Gold Rush country. The Pacific Crest Trail Association, 1350 Castle Rock Rd, Walnut Creek, CA 94598, (925) 939-6111, has maps and information available on access points and hiking routes for this and all sections of the trail.

Hetch Hetchy Reservoir/Tioga Road area

Tuolumne Canyon Trail (difficult; 36 miles round trip) to Muir Gorge begins at the White Wolf trailhead and delivers you via Lukens Lake Trail to the **Grand Canyon of the Tuolumne River,** perhaps the most unsung feature of Yosemite National Park were you to weigh its magnificence (it is more than 5,000 feet deep in some places) against the number of visitors it gets as compared to Yosemite Valley. Naturally, the reason for the discrepancy is that you can't drive your RV here—you can only get here using foot power and that means walking long, hard, and far to see one of the deepest granite river canyons in the world. Watch out for difficult river crossings and tiring switchbacks as you pass through pine, fir, and manzanita forests toward the river canyon, entering just beyond Morrison Creek. While this is a beautiful experience, being cast into the northern reaches of the deep Yosemite wilderness can also be dangerous. The trail ascends and declines sharply, and the river, although inviting, is potentially dangerous. Use bridge crossings and common sense. The White Wolf trailhead is 15 miles out from the Big Oak Flat entrance to Yosemite National Park on Hwy 120.

Smith Peak Trail (difficult; 18 miles round trip) catapults you to the 7,751-foot summit of Smith Peak for a grand vista of Hetch Hetchy Reservoir and the vast uncharted northern wilds of Yosemite National Park. The first leg of the strenuous two-day hike begins at the White Wolf trailhead and is a pleasant jaunt through meadows and forests of fir and pine on Harden Lake Trail. After checking out the lake and perhaps camping there, continue to Smith Peak Trail via White Wolf Mather Trail, and jet on up through the steep, switchback-infested western slopes of the peak. This may also be done as a one-way day hike (all day, that is) to Hetch Hetchy Reservoir if you choose to descend the peak on the same trail down the northeast slopes instead of turning back. The long, meandering descent to the edge of **North Dome** from Porcupine Flat on Tioga Rd (easy; 10 miles round trip) may not be the most invigorating in the park, but it makes up for that in what you get at the end—a wide, sweeping, impressive view of Yosemite Valley and all of its accessory parts. Take Tioga Rd east from the Big Oak Flat entrance to the park and head for a parking area just past the Porcupine Flat area. The hike is along an old campground access road, then straight out beyond the Tenaya Trail junction.

Scenic Drives

Due north of Yosemite Valley is the famous **Tioga Pass** (Hwy 120), the highest automobile pass in California, which crests at 9,945 feet (and is closed in the winter). The ideal time to tour the 60-mile-long east-west stretch is in early summer, when the meadows are dotted with wildflowers and you can occasionally spot some wildlife lingering near the lakes and exposed granite slopes. Numerous turnouts offer prime photo opportunities, and roadside picnic areas are located at Lembert Dome and Tenaya

Lake. This is also the route to Tuolumne Meadows, the gorgeous sub-alpine meadows along the Tuolumne River.

Camping

One of the best-kept "secrets" in Yosemite National Park is that while it's nearly impossible to get a campsite in Yosemite Valley, many sites in the Yosemite uplands are held exclusively for walk-ins. Additionally, dispersed camping is allowed throughout the vast wilderness area outside the valley for backpackers (see Hiking/Backpacking, above). For information on any of these campgrounds, call the park at (209) 372-0200. To reserve a site, call 90 days before the date of arrival, (800) 436-7275; see Yosemite National Park: Overview chapter for more detailed information.

White Wolf Campground has about 90 drop-in sites (no hookups; RV limit 33 feet) and is the primary campsite for backpackers visiting the Hetch Hetchy Valley and preparing to hike on one of the many trails traversing the area. The campground has piped water, flush toilets, tables, and fire grills. *From Groveland, take Hwy 120 west about 19 miles east of the junction with Hwy 41. Turn left onto White Wolf Rd and proceed to the campground. Open July to September.*

Tuolumne Meadows Campground contains 314 sites (no hookups; RV limit 33 feet) in the park's eastern reaches. Though the campground is a fair distance from Yosemite Valley, it is very popular as it is the park's only camp area in Tuolumne Meadows. The camp area has piped water, flush toilets, tables, and fire pits. There is a dump station for RVs. *From Groveland, take Hwy 120 west about 45 miles east of the junction with Hwy 41. Turn right into the campground. Open July to September; 25 drop-in sites available.*

Crane Flat Campground has 166 sites (no hookups; RV limit 33 feet) along the park's western border. The campground has piped water, flush toilets, tables, and fire grills, and a general store is nearby in the village of Crane Flat. *From Groveland, take Hwy 120 west, pass the junction with Hwy 41, and continue to the Crane Flat Ranger Station on the left. Proceed to the campground. Open June to September.*

Tamarack Flat Campground contains 52 tent sites (no RV access) about 10 miles from Yosemite Valley. As one might imagine, this is the very first of the overflow campgrounds from the valley to fill up, despite the fact that it has no running water and only pit toilets. In the minds of most visitors, the proximity to the valley more than compensates for the lack of conveniences. Each site is equipped with a fire pit and table. *From Groveland, take Hwy 120 west to about 3 miles east of the junction with Hwy 41. Turn right onto Old Big Oak Flat Rd and proceed to the campground. Open July to September.*

Yosemite Creek Campground has 75 tent sites (no RV access) along Yosemite Creek, due north of Yosemite Village, available on a drop-in basis only. The campground's lack of amenities make it less popular among tourists and more sought-after by visitors who are looking for solitude. The camp area has no running water so be sure to bring plenty of your own. Pit toilets, tables, and fire pits are available. *From Groveland, take Hwy 120 west about 19 miles east of the junction with Hwy 41. Pass White Wolf Rd on the left and proceed to the campground access road on the right. Open July to September.* (209) 372-0200.

Bridalveil Creek Campground has 115 drop-in sites (no hookups; various RV lengths accommodated) near Glacier Point. Originally used as an overflow camp for the Yosemite Valley campgrounds, the camp today is generally always booked during the spring and summer months. It has piped water, flush toilets, tables, and fire grills. *From Groveland, take Hwy 120 west and turn right at Hwy 41. Proceed to Glacier Point Rd and turn left. Drive to the campground access road on the right past Peregoy Meadow.*

Cross-Country Skiing/Snowshoeing

If you're going to do the winter experience in Yosemite, you're best off spending as much of your time as possible on Nordic skis. With so many of the park's roadways, trails, and wildlands prime for winter exploration and the Yosemite scenery so stunning when covered in its winter blanket, Nordic is indeed the way to explore. The wide, flat, gradual sloping surface of **Tioga Road** is the perfect Nordic experience (the road is closed every winter rather than plowed out), and you'll have a blast if you just have at it there, but be prepared for a primitive experience if you choose to. Because the area is inaccessible by car during the winter months, most of the activity is limited to those areas adjacent to staging areas on main highways both at Tioga Pass and Big Oak Flat. Trails are not maintained or groomed but, rather, used informally by winter visitors who don't mind hiking in. In addition to the 45-mile Tioga Rd, there are 350 miles of paved roadways within the park closed to cars during the snow season.

The premier cross-country action, however, is in the uplands on the other side of the valley out of Badger Pass. From Badger, it is a 17-kilometer jaunt out to **Glacier Point** and **Sentinel Dome.** Many choose to make the trip with a guide, spend the night at the point, and return the next day, but it is also a reasonable day trip for those with experience and who allow enough time to do it. There also are more than 50 kilometers of marked trails, including 12 kilometers groomed, around Badger. The **Yosemite Cross-Country Ski School,** (209) 372-1244, schedules guided weeklong Nordic skiing excursions through Tioga Pass, as well as the Glacier Point overnight outing. Call the school for general information. Unless you are participating in a guided ski excursion, it is necessary to pick up rental equipment outside the park or bring your own.

Downhill Skiing

Downhill skiers looking for advanced runs head for **Badger Pass Ski Area**'s 9 ski runs. With a total vertical drop of 800 feet, almost exclusively tailored for beginner to intermediate use, this is one of those rare spots where you may feel out of place if you don't show up with a minivan full of children. The ski area, developed in 1935 after road access toward Glacier Point was created, has 11 lifts and is best for family ski outings, particularly those with kids ready to learn. A ski school and rentals are on-site. Call the ski area at (209) 372-1000 for information and a snow report.

Those looking for more advanced downhill in the southern Sierras who are willing to trade the grandeur of Yosemite for an equally scenic (but arguably not quite as stunning) spot looking over the Mokelumne River valley east of Stockton should head instead to **Bear Valley Ski Area.** Advanced runs are found on nearly half the trails at Bear, which has 60 runs and 11 lifts: 7 double, 2 triple, and 2 surface tows. Most of the expert runs are in Grizzly Bowl, the centerpiece of the resort, with 1,000 feet of vertical drop. Snowmaking is used on a third of the ski runs. Trails are ranked 30 percent beginner, 25 percent intermediate, and 45 percent advanced or expert. The resort is equipped with a ski school, rentals, restaurants, and lodging. From Stockton, take Hwy 4 east for 107 miles to Bear Valley; the way is clearly marked with road signs. Call (209) 753-2301 for information or (209) 753-2308 for a snow report.

outside in

Lodgings

Bear Valley Lodge and Restaurant ☆☆   Bear Valley Lodge is a full-service, year-round resort catering to families and sports enthusiasts. There are cross-country and downhill ski facilities nearby, and plenty of mountains, trails, lakes, and streams to explore. There are 53 guest rooms (including 3 suites). The restaurant offers standard American fare. *On Bear Valley Rd, Bear Valley; (209) 753-BEAR; $$.*

Lake Alpine Lodge ☆   This quaint Sierra resort situated on Lake Alpine was built in the '20s and remodeled in the '30s. Seven of the eight rustic, fully equipped cabins have kitchens and outdoor barbecues, and all come with a shower, a deck, and a view of the lake. The lodge also offers "upscale camping" via 3 tent cabins (available mid-June through Labor Day only). *On Hwy 4 (at Ebbets Pass/Lake Alpine), Bear Valley; (209) 753-6358; $$.*

More Information

Badger Pass Ski Area: *(209) 372-1000 for information and a snow report.*

Bear Valley Ski Area: *(209) 753-2301 for information, or (209) 753-2308 for a snow report.*

Road conditions: *(209) 372-4726 or (209) 372-0467.*

Wilderness permits: *(209) 372-0740.*

Yosemite general information: *(209) 372-0200 or www.yosemitepark.net/.*

Yosemite Mountaineering School and Guide Services: *(209) 372-8344.*

Yosemite
Southern
Uplands
and Mono Lake

The areas south and east of Yosemite Valley, including Mono Lake, Mammoth Lakes, and Bodie State Historic Park.

Until they start selling tickets to the moon, the crags, spires, and boulders of Mono Lake will have to do ... and they do a pretty good job. The lake and surrounding shore basin cover 100 square miles in the highlands southeast of Yosemite and represent one of a wide range of fantastic nature areas that rival better-known park destinations. Nature photographers adore the unusual Mono moonscapes; bird-watchers are mesmerized by the colonies of migrating waterfowl attracted by the lake's briny and alkaline ecosystem, which makes for a great place to feed. The eastern Sierra and the foothills south of Yosemite offer a change of pace from the hustle and bustle of paradise. And yet exploring these parts, while it doesn't require the extensive planning of a visit to Yosemite, takes a little preparation. Most of the best-appointed wilderness areas, such as Chilnualna Creek canyon with its waterfalls and swimming holes, take days of backpacking treks to reach and fully enjoy. You can only get to destinations such as Mono Lake and the Bodie Hills after hours of driving beyond Yosemite proper. In fact, it may be better to view Mono Lake as an add-on to a trip to Lake Tahoe than to Yosemite. Nonetheless, it shares with Yosemite the Sierra and Inyo National Forests, which surround the southern and eastern national park boundaries; these are a wilderness camper's paradise, with hundreds of campsites, thousands of miles of high mountain creeks and streams, dozens of lakes, and impressive peaks for hiking and taking in the views.

Mammoth Lakes, just south of the Mono Lake basin, is another strangely beautiful destination within the eastern Sierra, not only because of its interesting volcanic landscapes and natural hot springs but also because of its isolation from some of the better-known mountain destinations. A swarm of recent earthquake activity in Mammoth has geologists on edge, speculating that Mammoth Mountain may blow its top sometime soon, but they are unable to say for sure.

Some other areas, however, can still draw crowds. For example, Yosemite's southern gate at Mariposa offers the most direct access point to the world-famous Mariposa Grove of sequoia redwoods, among the biggest living things on earth. It's more of a tram tour of a tree museum than a wilderness experience, but the trees are impressive and worth it.

While some of these sights are a good distance from Yosemite Valley, those who don't mind road-tripping it and who plan their time wisely can get the best of both worlds by combining a trip here with a trip to Yosemite. Find a quiet out-of-the way camp in the national forest wilderness and spend one day touring Yosemite Valley just to see it. When you return to your camp, the peace and quiet of wilderness will be there waiting for you.

Getting There

US Highway 395 (US 395) south from Carson City, Nevada, or from the interchange of Highways 4 and 89 in the Topaz Lake area, is the most direct route to the mountains east of Yosemite National Park. The Wawona and Mariposa Grove areas of Yosemite are most directly accessed via Highway 41 east from Fresno through Oakhurst. There is a $20 fee to cross the park boundary, even if you're just passing through. All highways in this portion of the Sierra range are subject to weather closures during winter, although Highway 41 is not at a high enough elevation to generally get much serious snow most winters. The best approach to the Mono Lake area is also from US 395: Take Highway 108 east through the foothills to the US 395 junction, then head south to the lake area south of Lee Vining and Bridgeport. Those exiting Yosemite National Park from Tuolumne Meadows on Highway 120 can also easily reach Mono Lake by heading south on US 395. Winter conditions in this area can restrict travel. For road conditions, call (800) 427-ROAD (7623) or visit www.dot.ca.gov/hq/roadinfo/ on the Web. For more information on travel and access to the Yosemite region, see Yosemite National Park: Overview chapter. Because Mono Lake is within the Inyo National Forest, the best information source for the area is the Mono Basin Visitors Center, in Lee Vining, (760) 647-3044, off US 395 half a mile northeast of town. For the Mammoth Lakes area, contact the Mono County Chamber of Commerce in Mammoth Lakes, (760) 924-3699. Also check with *the Inyo National Forest, Mammoth Lakes Ranger District, on Highway 203, 3 miles west of US 395, (760) 924-5500. The Mono County Tourism Commission can be reached at (800) 845-7922.*

Adjoining Areas

NORTH/WEST: **Southern Gold Rush Country, Yosemite Valley, Yosemite Northern Uplands**

inside out

Parks

In the far eastern reaches of the south Sierra is some of the most unusual and tragically beautiful countryside an outdoor explorer can hope to find, not only because it lives in the shadow of the world-famous Yosemite National Park, but because of the unique features of the landscapes themselves, with bowl-shaped volcanic upwellings and spires protruding from lake bottoms. The northern boundary of this area features **Bodie State Historic Park,** which includes the abandoned Gold Rush town of Bodie and covers some 85,000 acres of rolling hills, forested slopes, steep cliffs, and high mountain peaks. To reach Bodie, take Hwy 270 15 miles east from the intersection with US 395, just south of Bridgeport. Call the park, (760) 647-6445, for more information.

Mono Lake is distinctive for its water's high saline and alkaline content—unusual in an alpine setting. The lake, which covers about 100 square miles of the mountains southeast of Yosemite National Park, has no drainage outlet. Its intriguing moonscapelike scenery is great fodder for landscape photographers, and its waters are a popular boating and swimming destination during the summer.

The Bodie area is operated mostly by the US Bureau of Land Management (BLM), Mono Lake by the US Forest Service. To reach both, take US 395 south from Hwy 4 in the Topaz Lake area or from the Carson City, Nevada, corridor. Hwys 120, 167, and 270 are the east-to-west access points through the region. Call the BLM, (760) 872-4881, or Inyo National Forest, (760) 647-3044, for information.

The southern portion of **Yosemite National Park,** less traveled than Yosemite Valley and the Tuolumne Meadows/Tioga Pass areas, has a significantly different character from the scenery Yosemite is most often associated with. In place of the high granite peaks and dramatically powerful waterfalls are stunning old-growth stands of sequoia redwoods at Mariposa Grove and rolling forested hills and river canyons of Wawona, a good visitor-overflow area for Yosemite Valley, with camping on the south fork of the Merced River. **Wawona,** once an encampment for Native Americans, also serves as a staging area for many of Yosemite's lesser-known high-country destinations, including Chilnualna Falls, Buena Vista Peak (9,709 feet), Horse Ridge, and the Buena Vista Creek canyon and is surrounded on three sides by Sierra National Forest. **Mariposa Grove** south of Wawona is the largest grove of sequoia redwoods in Yosemite, including the 2,700-year-old Grizzly Giant. These trees are the largest living things on the planet by all accounts. Round-trip guided tram tours of the forest are available, but it is best to ditch the tram halfway through and explore on foot. Both Wawona and the Mariposa Grove are found near the Hwy 41 entrance to Yosemite National Park east from Fresno and Oakhurst. Call the Wawona Information Station, (209) 375-9501, for more information.

Devil's Postpile National Monument is an area of fascinating lava flow terrain, including columns of rock pointing to the sky, covering some 800 acres west of Mammoth Lakes along the San Joaquin River's middle fork. The 60-foot-tall, slender basalt columns rise 7,560 feet above sea level and were formed nearly 100,000 years ago when molten lava from the erupting Mammoth Mountain cooled and fractured into multisided forms; they've become such a popular attraction that, between June 15 and September 15, rangers close the access road to daytime traffic and require visitors without a special permit to travel by shuttle. Shuttles pick up riders every 15 minutes at the Mammoth Mountain Ski Area parking lot on Minaret Rd, west off Hwy 203, and drop them off at a riverside trail for the less-than-half-mile walk to the monument; (760) 934-2289. After you've seen the Postpile, follow the trail for another 2 miles to the beautiful Rainbow Falls, where the San Joaquin River plunges 101 feet over an ancient lava flow into a deep pool, often creating rainbows in the mist. If you follow the trail to Red's Meadow, you'll be at one of the entrance points to the 228,500-acre Ansel Adams Wilderness, a popular backpacking destination highlighted by the jagged Minarets, a series of steep, narrow volcanic ridges just south of massive Mount Ritter. Take Hwy 203 for 11 miles west from US 395 to the monument entrance. The monument is another 8 miles down a narrow road leading from the entrance off the highway. The area is managed by Sequoia and Kings Canyon National Parks, (559) 565-3341.

Hiking/Backpacking

This section of the Sierra Nevada offers a potpourri of different landscapes, climates, vegetation, and character for those who want to hit the trails. On a whole, it contains some of the most interesting wilderness in the state—the surreal Mono Lake rock islands, the round-topped volcanic upwellings at Bodie Hills, the enormous sequoia giants at Mariposa Grove, and far-flung river canyons and waterfalls of Horse and Horizon Ridges in Yosemite's little-traveled southwestern reaches. Because some of these areas are within the national forests surrounding Yosemite and others are in the national park itself, it is important to keep in mind that one area's ground rules for backpackers differ quite a bit from the other's. It's also crucial to understand that there is a 5,000-foot elevation difference between the Wawona/Mariposa area and the Mono Lake/Bodie Hills area. **Weather** and **trail conditions,** therefore, may vary greatly as you travel. Very important: Backpackers within Yosemite National Park boundaries who intend to take overnight treks must obtain wilderness permits in advance; call (209) 372-0740 for information, and see Yosemite National Park: Overview chapter for details. Rules for dispersed camping and hiking within the Mono Lake and Bodie Hills areas, as well as in the Sierra National Forest areas south of Yosemite, are similar to those allowed in other national forests: backpackers must set up camp away from developed campgrounds and be careful to minimize their impact on the land, particularly in wilderness areas. For Mono Lake information, call the Inyo National Forest, Mono Lake Ranger District, (760) 647-3044. The BLM, (760) 872-4881, has jurisdiction over much of the Bodie area.

Want to get a good close-up look at some really big trees? The **Mariposa Grove Loop Trail** (moderate; up to 7 miles round trip) is a fascinating nature stroll through the largest stand of old-growth sequoias in Yosemite. These awesome creatures are well worth a half day of exploration. The walking tour is complete with good interpretive signage that explains the complex forest ecosystem and history of the grove, which contains some trees in excess of 3,000 years old, including the **Grizzly Giant** and **Bachelor,** as well as the **Fallen Monarch,** three of the most famous trees in the world. Many opt to take a guided tram tour of the park, then walk out on the nature trails, cutting the distance spent on foot by half. While the grove is stunning, this is by no means a secluded wilderness experience, particularly during the peak outdoor season—it's more of a family stop and a tourist attraction, attractive only because of the magnificence of the trees. You can get an overview of the grove from the summit of 1,200-foot **Wawona Point Trail** (moderate; 3 miles round trip). The trailhead is at the visitors center just east of the Yosemite south entrance.

Chilnualna Falls Trail (difficult; 8 miles round trip) follows Chilnualna Creek canyon from the Wawona area of Yosemite high into some of the most secluded yet easily accessed wilderness in the park. While most park visitors flock to Yosemite Valley to gawk at the waterfalls there, the falls along this creek get attention only from those park visitors who have it in them to take on steep, sometimes slippery trails and contend with a maze of switchbacks to have a similar experience without standing shoulder-to-shoulder with gaggles of tourists. The trailhead is at the end of Chilnualna Rd, which leads east from the Wawona Rd corridor at the South Merced River crossing. But even if you do it as a day hike, it is imperative to be properly outfitted and skilled, as some sections of the trail are steep and potentially hazardous. Resist the urge to climb up through the riverbed itself. Those wishing to make this a two-day trek to Glacier Point can continue from Chilnualna Falls to Bridalveil Creek, via the same trail system (also difficult; add 19 miles round trip). **Buena Vista Pass Trail** to the Chilnualna Lakes area (difficult; 30 miles round trip) follows the Chilnualna waterfall hike described above, then continues on to the Buena Vista Pass ridges overlooking the Wawona area wilderness from 9,000-plus feet. Grouse Lake, the most inviting of the three lakes, is a suitable camping spot for the second night. This and adjoining areas show the adventurous backpacker another side of Yosemite. Plan this as a summer hike, as the area is snowed in during winter. Call (209) 372-0740 for additional information on this hike and permits.

Mono Lake area

Lee Vining Creek Trail (easy; 3 miles round trip) leaves the Mono Lake visitors center on US 395 and follows the creek through a lush canyon teeming with interesting plants, wildflowers in spring, and all varieties of wildlife. This is a favorite birding spot, and an easy walk for seniors and families with children. It is best to take the trail at least a mile in to get away from highway noise and trailhead congestion. To reach the trailhead, take US 395 to the intersection with Hwy 120 at Lee Vining on the northwestern shore of the lake near Old Marina.

A great overview of Mono—one of the most photogenic of all Sierra lakes—is available from Parker Lake, which you can reach via the **Parker Lake Trail** (moderate; 10 miles round trip), a hearty day hike through forested canyons and meadows into the Ansel Adams Wilderness in Sierra National Forest. To reach the trailhead, take US 395 2.5 miles south from Lee Vining to Hwy 158. Turn right (west) on Hwy 158 and follow it another 6 miles to Forest Rd 1S25A. Turn right on the Forest Service road and follow it to the end.

Another outstanding overview of Mono is from Crystal Lake, northwest of Lee Vining. Take **Lakes Canyon Trail** (moderate; 6.5 miles round trip) through Lundy Canyon and onward past several lakes, including Oneida, toward Mount Scowden. The trailhead is at the end of Lundy Canyon Rd, west from US 395 just north of Lee Vining.

While short, the hike along **South Tufa Trail** (easy; 1 mile round trip) is a must for first-time visitors to Mono Lake who want to get an eye-ful of the bizarre rock formations, including spires rising out of the lake's waters like something out of *The X Files*. You'll think you've reached the rendezvous point. The trailhead is on the south end of the lake. Take Hwy 120 for 5 miles southeast from China Ranch and look for the tufa area on the left side of the road as you draw toward the water's edge. Call (760) 647-3044 for more information.

Mammoth Lakes area

Minaret Lake Trail (moderate; 15 miles round trip) is an awesomely beautiful two-day trip into the high reaches of the Ansel Adams Wilder-ness that ascends nearly 2,000 feet in less than 8 miles along the Minaret Creek Canyon. It is a long, steady climb but well worth it. At 9,800 feet, this small lake, left by glaciers that carved out the surrounding peaks, is a great place to rest up and take in some quiet solitude. The trailhead begins from the Minaret Falls Campground (see Camping, below). From Lee Vining, travel south on US 395 and exit west onto Hwy 203. Proceed past the Devil's Postpile National Monument entrance and continue to the campground entrance.

Camping

Read Yosemite National Park: Overview chapter for information on camp-ing and campground reservations within the park boundaries. Camping on public grounds within the national forests is allowed anywhere you choose to set up, although dispersed camping must be a suitable distance from developed campgrounds and permits are required for any use of fire. Get maps directly from the Forest Service. Write US Forest Service Infor-mation, Room 521, 630 Sansome St, San Francisco, CA 94111. (See the primer at the beginning of this book for explicit ordering instructions.) Periodic road closures are unavoidable. Check with the relevant ranger station for updated road conditions before deciding on a site located deep within the forest. Roads are not maintained for vehicles with low ground clearance. The Forest Service is currently reviewing its reservations and fees policies for this area, but generally no reservations are taken for any of the campgrounds listed below. Stays are limited to 14 days. Call the Forest Service reservations system at (800) 280-2267, or individual ranger stations for information on campsite availability and reservations where applicable.

    Wawona Campground has roughly 100 sites (no hookups; RV limit 34 feet) at the southern end of the park. The campground serves as an overflow camp for the Yosemite Valley camp areas, and is also popular among visitors to the Mariposa Grove just south. Set along the south fork of the Merced River, the campground has piped water, flush toilets, tables, and fire grills. *From Groveland, take Hwy 120 west and turn right at Hwy 41, pass Glacier Point Rd, cross Adler Creek, and continue to Wawona on the right side of the highway.* Open year-round. Contact the park at (209) 372-0200 for information, or call (800) 436-7275 for reservations.

Inyo National Forest, Mono Lake Ranger District, (760) 647-3044

Big Bend Campground contains 17 sites (no hookups; RV limit 28 feet) along Lee Vining Creek. The campground serves as an overflow area for the more popular campgrounds to the west in Yosemite. Piped water is available during the summer season, along with vault toilets. Tables and fire grills are provided as well. *From Lee Vining, travel south on US 395 a few miles to Horse Meadows Rd. Turn right and proceed to the campground.*

Saddlebag Lake Campground contains 21 sites (no hookups; RV limit 21 feet). There is also 1 group site available, which can accommodate up to 20 people. Though the campground is a short walk from Saddlebag Lake, for many the lure of this campground is its altitude. At 10,000 feet, above the tree line, the barren environment is one you don't encounter very often. Piped water is available during the summer season, along with vault toilets. Tables and fire grills are also provided, and a general store is nearby. *From Lee Vining, travel south on US 395 and exit west onto Hwy 120. Proceed to Saddlebag Lake Rd, just after Ellery Lake, and turn right. Proceed to the campground.*

Tioga Lake Campground has 13 tent sites (no RV access) adjacent to Tioga Lake and near Ellery Lake. Encircled by granite, these two lakes at nearly 10,000 feet provide a pristine playground where visitors enjoy canoeing and fishing. The campground has piped water available during the summer season, along with vault toilets. Tables and fire grills are provided as well. *From Lee Vining, travel south on US 395 and exit west onto Hwy 120. Proceed west of Ellery Lake, to the campground on the left side of the road.*

Junction Campground contains 13 sites (no hookups; RV limit 21 feet) near Saddlebag Lake, also at an elevation of nearly 10,000 feet. The campground serves as an overflow area for the more popular Saddlebag Lake campground (see above). Piped water is available during the summer season, along with vault toilets. Tables and fire grills are provided as well. *From Lee Vining, travel south on US 395 and exit west onto Hwy 120. Proceed to Saddlebag Lake Rd, just after Ellery Lake, and turn right. Make an immediate left onto the campground access road.*

Ellery Lake Campground has 13 sites (no hookups; RV limit 21 feet) near Ellery Lake, at an elevation of roughly 9,500 feet. Stocked with trout, the lake is a popular fishing spot. Piped water is available during the summer season, along with vault toilets. Tables and fire grills are provided, and a local grocery store is nearby. *From Lee Vining, travel south on US 395 and exit west onto Hwy 120. Proceed to Saddlebag Lake Rd, just after Ellery Lake, and turn right.*

Minaret Falls Campground has 30 sites (no hookups; various RV lengths accommodated) along the San Joaquin River. Several excellent trails exist throughout the beautiful landscape in this stretch of the forest. Piped water, vault toilets, tables, and fire grills are provided, and a general store is nearby. *From Lee Vining, travel south on US 395 and exit west onto Hwy 203. Proceed past the Devil's Postpile National Monument entrance and continue to the campground entrance.* Call Inyo National Forest, Mammoth Lakes Ranger District, (760) 924-5500.

Toiyabe National Forest, Bridgeport Ranger District, (760) 932-7070

Sonora Bridge Campground has 25 sites (no hookups; RV limit 36 feet) near West Walker River, at an elevation of roughly 7,000 feet. Stocked with trout, the stream serves as a popular fishing spot. Piped water is available during the summer season, along with vault toilets. Tables and fire grills are provided as well. *From Bridgeport, travel north on US 395 and turn left onto Hwy 108 at Sonora Junction. Proceed a few miles to the campground entrance.*

Obsidian Campground has 15 sites (no hookups; RV limit 29 feet) tucked in the forest at an elevation of roughly 8,000 feet. The campground is sought by those looking for solitude and a primitive camping experience. There is no running water, so be sure to bring plenty of your own. Tables and fire grills are provided, and vault toilets are available. *From Bridgeport, travel north on US 395 a few miles to the campground access road on the left.*

Robinson Creek Campground has 55 sites (no hookups; RV limit 43 feet) along Robinson Creek and near Twin Lakes. The creek is well stocked with trout during the summer. The campground has piped water, along with vault toilets, tables, and fire grills. *From Lee Vining, travel north on US 395 and turn left onto Twin Lakes Rd in the town of Bridgeport. Proceed to the campground entrance about 10 miles ahead.*

Bootleg Campground has 63 sites (no hookups; RV limit 43 feet) adjacent to West Walker River, a popular trout fishing spot during the summer. The campground has piped water, along with vault toilets, tables, and fire grills. *From Bridgeport, travel north on US 395, past the junction with Hwy 108, to the campground on the right side of the highway.*

Buckeye Campground has 65 sites (no hookups; RV limit 28 feet) and is quite popular. Near Buckeye Hot Spring and a few rivers and lakes that provide good fishing, the campground can fill up rather quickly during the summer season. The campground has piped water, along with vault toilets, tables, and fire grills. *From Lee Vining, travel north on US 395 to Bridgeport. Turn left onto Twin Lakes Rd. Continue 7 miles to Buckeye Rd and turn right. Proceed to the campground.*

Crags Campground has 27 sites (no hookups; RV limit 43 feet), also adjacent to West Walker River. The campground has piped water, along with vault toilets, tables, and fire grills. *From Lee Vining, travel north on US 395 to Bridgeport. Turn left onto Twin Lakes Rd. Proceed to Lower Twin Lakes and turn left, over the bridge crossing Robinson Creek. Turn left again and proceed to the campground.*

Honeymoon Flat Campground has 35 sites (no hookups; RV limit 43 feet) adjacent to Robinson Creek and near Twin Lakes. The creek is well stocked with trout during the summer. The campground has piped water, vault toilets, tables, and fire grills. *From Lee Vining, travel north on US 395 to Bridgeport. Turn left onto Twin Lakes Rd. Proceed to the campground.*

Paha Campground contains 22 sites (no hookups; RV limit 38 feet) near Robinson Creek and Twin Lakes, at an elevation of roughly 7,000 feet. The campground tends to be a bit more crowded than others in the area due to the amenities available. Along with piped water, there are also flush toilets, tables, and fire grills; a boat launch, general store, laundromat, and shower room are close by. *From Lee Vining, travel north on US 395 to Bridgeport. Turn left onto Twin Lakes Rd. Proceed to the campground about 11 miles ahead.*

Lower Twin Lakes Campground contains 15 sites (no hookups; RV limit 38 feet) adjacent to Twin Lakes, at an elevation of roughly 7,000 feet. The campground tends to be a bit more crowded than others in the area due to the amenities. Piped water, flush toilets, tables, and fire grills are available; in addition, a boat launch, general store, laundromat, and shower room are close by. *From Lee Vining, travel north on US 395 to Bridgeport. Turn left onto Twin Lakes Rd. Proceed to the campground about 12 miles ahead.*

Leavitt Meadows Campground has 16 sites (no hookups; RV limit 38 feet) near West Walker River, at an elevation of roughly 7,000 feet. There are also two feeder streams in the area and a pack station for horseback riding. The campground has piped water, along with vault toilets, tables, and fire grills. *From Bridgeport, take US 395 north to Hwy 108 west. Proceed to Leavitt Station and turn left onto the campground access road just before the S curve in the road.*

Green Creek Campground has 11 sites and 2 group campsites (no hookups; RV limit 21 feet) along Green Creek, a trout-filled creek that flows into the larger Green Lake. The group campsites can accommodate up to 20 people. The campground has piped water, vault toilets, tables, and fire grills. *From Bridgeport, proceed south on US 395 for 4 miles and turn* left onto Green Lake Rd. Proceed to the campground half a mile before the road's end.

Chris Flat Campground has 16 sites (no hookups; RV limit 38 feet) along West Walker River. The picturesque river is well stocked with trout during the summer season. The campground has piped water, vault toilets, tables, and fire grills. *From Bridgeport, take US 395 for 3 miles north of the junction with Hwy 108. The campground is on the right.*

Trumbull Lake Campground contains 45 sites (no hookups; RV limit 42 feet) adjacent to Trumbull Lake, at an elevation of roughly 9,500 feet. The campground has piped water during the summer season. Tables, vault toilets, and fire grills are provided. A general store is close by. *From Bridgeport, take US 395 south to Virginia Lake Rd (about 5 miles north of the junction with Hwy 167). Turn right and proceed to the campground.*

Sierra National Forest, Mariposa Ranger District, (559) 683-4665

Summit Campground has 6 tent sites (no RV access). This little-known campground just outside Yosemite is more like a private club for the few people who are aware of its existence. Most are those who prefer the solitude of a quieter campground and don't mind the road trip to Yosemite Valley. Mariposa Grove is only a short drive away. Piped water, vault toilets, tables, and fire grills are available. *From Fish Camp, take Hwy 41 east for 17 miles to Forest Rd N1402, turn right and continue for 7 miles to Chowchilla Mountain Rd. Turn left and continue another 3.5 miles to Battalion Pass and the campground on your right.*

Summerdale Campground has 30 sites (no hookups; RV limit 21 feet) and is used as an overflow area for the larger and more popular Wawona Campground (see above). Mariposa Grove and the entrance to Yosemite are both a short drive away. Piped water, vault toilets, tables, and fire grills are provided. *From Mariposa, take Hwy 49 east. Turn left at Hwy 41 and continue to Fish Camp. Proceed to the campground on the left, not far outside of town.*

Jerseydale Campground has 10 sites (no hookups; RV limit 21 feet). Several good trails exist in the camp area, which is popular among visitors to Mariposa Grove, when the Wawona Campground fills up (see above). Piped water, vault toilets, tables, and fire grills are provided. *From Mariposa, take Hwy 140 north to Triangle Rd (2 miles south of Briceburg). Turn left onto Triangle Rd. Drive to Darrah and turn left onto Jerseydale Rd. Proceed to the campground.*

Mountain Biking

Mountain biking is another hugely popular sport here in the summer, when the entire **Mammoth Mountain Ski Area** is transformed into one of the top bike parks in the country. The national Norba mountain-bike championship race takes place here, too, on Minaret Rd, off Hwy 203 W; call (760) 934-0606 or (800) 367-6572 for details. You can buy an all-day pass to 60 miles of single-track trails and a gondola that will zip you and your bike up to the top of the mountain. From there it's downhill all the way (be sure to wear a helmet), with trails ranging in difficulty from the mellow "Paper Route" ride to the infamous "Kamikaze" wheel-spinner. If you don't want to pay to ride a bike, call the Eastern Sierra Visitors Center, (760) 932-5281, for trails in the area where mountain bikes are permitted.

Downhill Skiing/Snowboarding

While the north Sierra is known as the state's premier ski region, the high mountains of the south Sierra contain some of the best skiing west of Aspen. Just as Northern Californians in the San Francisco Bay Area and Sacramento Valley flock to the Lake Tahoe basin for weekend ski adventures, Los Angeles weekend warriors jet up to the 11,053-foot Mammoth Mountain for their downhill thrills. With runs high above the tree line, and altitude high enough that the chill factor keeps things frosty well into the summer, the ski season in this area some years extends from September to June or beyond. **Mammoth Mountain Ski Area** is the main draw here, with its 150 runs covering 3,500 acres of outstanding ski turf. There are 30 lifts, including 3 high-speed quads, 2 gondolas, a surface lift, 11 double chairs, and 7 triple chairs. The terrain is 30 percent beginner, 40 percent intermediate, and 30 percent advanced, with a base elevation of nearly 8,000 feet and a 3,100-foot vertical drop from the summit. The ski area features machine-groomed and packed powder terrain, with expert runs, numerous hidden chutes, tree runs easy enough for intermediate skiers, and large bowl areas for beginners. There is simply so much room here that, if you tried, you could ski all day without covering the same run more than once. The resort features a day lodge, ski school, equipment rentals, and child-care center. Night skiing and a **snowboarding** area (with rentals) are also found here. The ski resort anchors the entire Mammoth Lakes region, which is a straight shot up US 395 from the Yosemite and Tahoe regions. To reach Mammoth Mountain Ski Area, take US 395 south from Lee Vining for 32 miles to the Hwy 203 interchange. Turn west on Hwy 203 and continue 12 miles to the mountain and resort area, all well signed along the way. For a snow report, call (888) SNOW-RPT. To contact the ski area, call (888) 4MAMMOTH.

Cross-Country Skiing/Snowshoeing

Winter road closures throughout the Yosemite, Mono Lake, and Sierra National Forest regions are good news for cross-country skiers, who have free run of lakeside trails and take advantage of the absence of cars to explore such areas as Yosemite's Glacier Point (see Yosemite Northern Uplands chapter). Inyo National Forest has vast trail systems set aside for Nordic skiers in winter, and there are numerous equipment rental businesses in surrounding communities. Particularly popular Nordic skiing areas are found directly off US 395, 7 miles south of Mono Lake at **Obsidian Dome** and just east of June Lake at **South June Lake Junction.** Some 30 kilometers of ungroomed trails are open for exploration here. Call forest headquarters in Bishop, (760) 873-2400, or the Mono Lake Ranger District, (760) 647-3044, for information on trail conditions, road closures, and access.

Mammoth Lakes also has mile upon mile of perfectly groomed cross-country ski trails, winding through gorgeous stretches of national forest and immense meadows. Nordic skiers of all levels favor the Tamarack Cross-Country Ski Center at Tamarack Lodge in Twin Lakes, which offers 40 kilometers of groomed trails, extensive backcountry trails, lessons, rentals, and tours; it's on Lake Mary Rd, 2.5 miles southwest of town, (760) 934-2442.

Wildlife

Because of Mono Lake's unique alkaline and saline water conditions, brine shrimp and invertebrates flourish, making the lake a great spot for wintering gulls, grebes, snowy plovers, and numerous other varieties of **migrating birds,** including Canada geese and tundra swans. In forested areas around the lake, look for red-tailed hawks, great horned owls, thrashers, warblers, hummingbirds, chickadees, and mountain quail. The best viewing areas, naturally, are the lakeside marshes and the river and creek canyons traversing the southern end of Yosemite and all of Sierra and Inyo National Forests. One good viewing area near Mono Lake is directly off US 395 at Cemetery Rd, which dead-ends 8 miles east of the highway in an open marsh and wetland area. Also look for birds along Lee Vining Creek Trail (see Hiking/Backpacking, above).

Black bears, coyotes, raccoons, bobcats, and **gray foxes** inhabit the forested areas around Mono Lake and upland from the Wawona and South Merced River canyons. But for those who thought the Rocky and Bullwinkle cartoons were based on fiction and not fact, **flying squirrels** are the big attraction here. Keep an eye out for them darting out of the trees!

Photography

Mono Lake is by far the most interesting of landscapes in the southern and eastern Yosemite wilderness areas—its briny and placid waters are reflecting pools for the bizarre spires and boulders that create the Mono moonscape. In summer, lakeside marshes come alive with brilliant blooms; in winter, blankets of snow envelop the shoreline and the surrounding ridges, creating an Ansel Adams wannabe's dream subject. Also irresistible and often photographed are the giants of the **Mariposa Grove** (see Parks and Hiking/Backpacking, above)—everyone and his or her cousin has got to come back from a vacation at Yosemite with a "big tree" shot.

Fishing

Fishing within Yosemite National Park is closely regulated and monitored. In Yosemite Valley, for example, bait fishing is not allowed. The Merced River's south fork through Wawona is a good **trout-fishing** spot. The river is most easily accessed along Hwy 41 near Wawona along Chilnualna Rd. The countless streams and lakes throughout the Yosemite, Inyo, and Sierra forest regions yield **kokanee salmon,** large- and smallmouth **bass, bluegill, crappie,** and **catfish.** Lake Crowley and Mammoth Lake Reservoir near the San Joaquin River headwaters are particularly popular as **high-country fishing** holes during the spring and summer. Silver Lake, June Lake, and Agnew Lake are all easily accessed from the Hwy 158 loop just south of Mono Lake (off US 395). Rush Creek, which spills into Agnew, is a particularly nice spot.

Swimming

There are numerous swimming holes in the southern and eastern Yosemite region wilderness areas, including at the base of the 50-foot **Chilnualna Falls** (see Hiking/Backpacking above), a welcome dip for summer backpackers contending with the heat. **Mono Lake's Navy Beach and County Park** are popular swimming spots, but be sure to keep in mind that because Mono is not a freshwater lake, swimming here can be more like taking a dunk in a small sea . . . be prepared for salt! From US 395 at Lee Vining, take Picnic Grounds Rd to the lakeshore and continue along the western shore to Forest Rd 1N51. The beaches are next to each other, about 5 miles east of where these two roads intersect. The south fork of the **Merced River** near the Wawona Campground is another fine place to take a dip, although parents should use extreme caution—particularly during the spring runoff—when it comes to allowing young children into the water. From the Hwy 41 entrance to the park, east out of Oakhurst, take Wawona Rd north 6 miles to the campground on the left side of the road, 2 miles past the river crossing. To reach the campground from the valley, take Wawona Rd 10 miles south from the Tunnel View area and look for the entrance on the left side of the road.

outside in

Attractions

Set at the eastern foot of the craggy Sierra Nevada and ringed with fragile limestone tufa spires, **Mono Lake** is a hauntingly beautiful 87-square-mile desert salt lake and a stopover for millions of migratory birds that arrive each year to feed on the lake's trillions of brine shrimp and alkali flies (*mono* means "flies" in the language of the Yokuts, the Native Americans who live just south of this region). While numerous streams empty into Mono (pronounced "MOE-no") Lake, there is no outlet. Instead, the lake water evaporates, leaving behind minerals washed down from the surrounding mountains. The result is an alkaline and saline content that is too high for fish but ideal for shrimp, flies, and swimmers (the brackish water is three times saltier than the sea). Right off US 395 is the **Mono Basin Scenic Area Visitors Center,** a modern, high-tech edifice that would make any taxpayer proud. The center offers scheduled walks and talks, and it has an outstanding environmental and historical display with hands-on exhibits that will entertain even the kids; open daily in the summer and Thursday through Monday in the winter, (760) 647-3044. After touring the visitors center, head for the South Tufa Area at the southern end of the lake and get a closer look at the tufa formations and briny water.

At the base of 11,053-foot Mammoth Mountain are nearly a dozen alpine lakes and the sprawling town of **Mammoth Lakes**—a mishmash of inns, motels, and restaurants primarily built to serve patrons of the popular Mammoth Mountain Ski Area (see Downhill Skiing/Snowboarding, above). Ever since founder Dave McCoy mortgaged his motorcycle for $85 in 1938 to buy his first ski lift, folks have been coming here in droves (particularly from Southern California) to carve turns and navigate the moguls at one of the best downhill ski areas in the United States.

Whether you've migrated to the Mammoth area to ski, fish, golf, play, or simply rest your weary bones, stop by the **Mammoth Lakes Visitors Center/Ranger Station** on Hwy 203, just before the town of Mammoth Lakes; (760) 924-5500. You'll find wall-to-wall maps, brochures, and day planners, as well as copies of the Forest Service's excellent (and free) "Winter Recreation Map" and "Summer Recreation Map," which show the area's best routes for hiking, biking, sledding, snowmobiling, and cross-country skiing. If you need to rent ski gear or practically any other athletic and outdoor equipment, visit the bustling Kittredge Sports shop on Main St, next to the Chevron gas station, in Mammoth Lakes; (760) 934-7566.

Dozens of natural hot springs dot the Mammoth area, although most of the remote ones are kept secret by tourist-weary locals who probably wouldn't make you feel very welcome even if you discovered one. The more accessible springs, however, definitely welcome visitors, including the free **Hot Creek Geologic Site,** where the narrow creek feeds into a series of artificial pools—some only big enough for two, others family-size. These pools are equipped with cold-water pipes that usually keep the water temperature toasty yet not unbearably hot. The Forest Service discourages soaking in the pools because of sporadic spurts of scalding water—yes, there is a small risk of getting your buns poached—but most people are more concerned about whether or not to show off their birthday suit (swimsuits are optional). Open daily from sunrise to sunset; take the Hot Creek Hatchery Rd exit off US 395 (at the north end of Mammoth Lakes Airport) and follow the signs. Call the Mammoth Lakes Visitors Bureau (see below) for more details.

Granted, life is often one big outdoor party in Mammoth Lakes, but when the annual **Mammoth Lakes Jazz Jubilee** swings into gear in July, hold on to your Tevas—nearly everyone in this toe-tapping town starts kicking up their heels when a dozen world-class bands start tootin' their horns. Opening day is free (after that it's about $25 or more per day). A much more sedate but definitely worthwhile musical event is the annual **Sierra Summer Festival,** a tribute to everything from chamber to classical music that begins in late July and winds down in early August. For more details on all of Mammoth's year-round activities, call the Mammoth Lakes Visitors Bureau at (760) 934-8006 or (800) 367-6572, or visit its Web site at www.visitmammoth.com.

The town clock in the two-story **Mariposa** County Courthouse has been marking time since 1866. Another town landmark is St. Joseph's Catholic Church, built in 1863, and behind it lies the entrance to the Mariposa Mine, discovered by Kit Carson in 1849 and later purchased by John C. Frémont, who owned most of the land around these parts.

Two miles south of Mariposa is the **California Mining and Mineral Museum,** a state geology center. One wing showcases 20,000 glittering gems and minerals; another holds artifacts and photos that tell California's mining story; 5007 Fairgrounds Rd, (209) 742-7625.

Restaurants

Carson Peak Inn ☆☆   This barn-red building, located a few miles past the town of June Lake, is one of the better restaurants in the area, serving hearty dinners such as a melt-in-your-mouth filet mignon smothered with sautéed mushrooms. *On June Lake Loop (off US 395), June Lake; (760) 648-7575; $$$.*

Charles Street Dinner House ☆☆   This 18-year-old landmark isn't as formal as its name might suggest. Rather, it's a hoot—a fun, funky place where the Old West reigns over decor, food, and service. *5043 Charles St (at Hwy 140 and 7th St), Mariposa; (209) 966-2366; $$.*

Erna's Elderberry House ☆☆☆☆   Ever since *The New York Times* praised Erna's as "one of the most elegant and stylish restaurants in the nation," epicureans from around the world have made the pilgrimage. The prix-fixe dinner is a six-course affair that changes daily. *48688 Victoria Lane (off Hwy 41, just W of town), Oakhurst; (559) 683-6860; $$$.*

The Mogul ☆   Your server skillfully charbroils fresh fish, shrimp, and steak under your watchful eye here at the Mogul, the steak house voted Mammoth's best by *Mammoth Times* readers several years in a row. *1528 Tavern Rd (1 block S of Main St off Old Mammoth Rd), Mammoth Lakes; (760) 934-3039; $$.*

The Mono Inn ☆☆   This historic inn—split into a lower-level restaurant, and an upper-level arts and crafts gallery and lounge—has rustic charm, stellar views of Mono Lake, and hearty California-style cuisine. There's also a good wine list. *On US 395 (4 miles N of Lee Vining), Mono Lake; (760) 647-6581; $$.*

Narrow Gauge Inn ☆☆   An attractive old inn and restaurant nestled in the thick of the Sierra National Forest at a 4,800-foot elevation, the Narrow Gauge is one of the Mariposa Grove area's best restaurants. *48571 Hwy 41 (4 miles S of Yosemite National Park's south gate), Fish Camp; (559) 683-7720; $$.*

Nevados ☆☆☆   Mammoth's finest restaurant is packed almost every night with an equal split of locals and Los Angelenos on their annual ski or summer holiday. The cheerful dining room melds well with the often crowded and boisterous dinner scene. *On Main St (at Minaret Rd), Mammoth Lakes; (760) 934-4466; $$.*

The Restaurant at Convict Lake ☆☆☆   The anglers who toss their lines into Convict Lake have kept this restaurant a secret for many years. Their secret, however, is slowly slipping out, as others have begun to journey here for a meal at this glorious lakeside locale. *At Convict Lake* *(from US 395 take the Convict Lake exit, 3½ miles S of Mammoth Lakes), Convict Lake; (760) 934-3803; $$$.*

Lodgings

The Cain House: A Country Inn ☆☆ Set in one of the most picturesque valleys in the eastern Sierra, this modest turn-of-the-century inn combines European elegance with a Western atmosphere. Each of the 7 individually decorated guest rooms has a private bath, a king- or queen-size bed with a quilt and down comforter, and a TV tucked inside an armoire. *340 Main St (at the N end of town), Bridgeport; (760) 932-7040 or (800) 433-CAIN; $$.*

Château du Sureau ☆☆☆☆ The opulent Château du Sureau (*sureau* is French for "elderberry") enables Erna Kubin-Clanin to offer her guests a magnificent place to stay after indulging in the exquisite cuisine at her Elderberry House (see Restaurants, above). The 9 guest rooms come replete with goose-down comforters, canopy beds, antiques, tapestries, and fresh flowers. *48688 Victoria Lane (off Hwy 41, just W of town), Oakhurst; (559) 683-6860; $$$.*

Mammoth Mountain Inn ☆ This inn is a popular haven for downhill skiers—it's just steps away from the chair lifts at the ski area—and in the summer the guests are primarily mountain bikers, fly-fishers, hikers, and horseback riders. The 214 rooms have a predictably humdrum decor, but they come with all the usual amenities. *On Minaret Rd (at Mammoth Mountain Ski Area, 4 miles from downtown), Mammoth Lakes; (760) 934-2581 or (800) 228-4947; $$$.*

Mariposa Hotel Inn ☆ This two-story building is featured on the National Register of Historic Places and was once the LeGrand stage stop, serving stagecoach passengers in the early 1900s. Attractively restored in an Early American style complete with lace curtains, it has 5 individually decorated rooms with private baths, cable TV, and air conditioning. *5029 Hwy 140 (at 6th St), Mariposa; (209) 966-4676 or (800) 317-3244; $$.*

Sierra Lodge ☆☆ Unlike most lodges in the area, Sierra Lodge, built in 1991, has no rustic elements in any of its 35 spacious rooms. The decor here is quite contemporary: soothing earth tones, framed modern prints, track lighting, blond wood furnishings, and big comfy beds. *3540 Main St (at Sierra St), Mammoth Lakes; (760) 934-8881 or (800) 356-5711; $$.*

Tamarack Lodge Resort ☆☆ Built in 1924, the 6-acre Tamarack Lodge sits on the edge of Twin Lakes, two and a half miles above Mammoth Lakes. Come summer or winter, it's an extremely romantic retreat, nestled deep within the pines and overlooking a serene alpine lake. The resort's 11 rooms and 25 cabins have pine furnishings and soft-hued fabrics. *On Twin Lakes Rd (off Lake Mary Rd, 2½ miles above town), Mammoth Lakes; (760) 934-2442 or (800) 237-6879; $$.*

Tenaya Lodge ☆   What Tenaya Lodge lacks in charm and originality, it makes up for in location—it's just two miles from the entrance to Yosemite National Park. Built in 1990, the lodge has 244 rooms, all with mountain and forest views, private baths, and tasteful Southwestern decor. *1122 Hwy 41 (2 miles S of Yosemite National Park's southwest gate), Fish Camp; (559) 683-6555 or (800) 635-5807; $$$.*

Yosemite Gateway Inn ☆   Across town from the Château du Sureau, this Best Western motel's lures (besides the inexpensive prices) are the indoor and outdoor pools that keep the kids entertained while Mom and Pop soak in the spa. Some of the 119 rooms have kitchens, and all have cable TV, phones, and air conditioning. *40530 Hwy 41 (1 mile E of the intersection of Hwys 49 and 41), Oakhurst; (559) 683-2378; $.*

More Information

Forest Service reservations system: *(800) 280-2267.*
Inyo National Forest, Mammoth Lakes Ranger District: *(760) 924-5500.*
Inyo National Forest, Mono Lake Ranger District: *(760) 647-3044.*
Mammoth Lakes Visitors Bureau: *(760) 934-8006 or (800) 367-6572, or www.visitmammoth.com.*
Mono County Chamber of Commerce: *(760) 924-3699.*
Road conditions: *(800) 427-ROAD or www.dot.ca.gov/hq/roadinfo/.*
Sierra National Forest, Mariposa Ranger District: *(559) 683-4665*
Toiyabe National Forest, Bridgeport Ranger District: *(760) 932-7070.*
US Bureau of Land Management: *(760) 872-4881.*
Yosemite camping reservations: *(800) 436-7275.*
Yosemite wilderness permits: *(209) 372-0740.*

Southern
Gold
Rush
Country

The southern Sierra foothills region, from Jackson at the intersection of Hwys 49 and 88 south through Calaveras, Stanislaus, Mariposa, and Madera Counties; including Calaveras Big Trees State Park; Columbia State Historic Park; the southern foothills lakes; the Stanislaus, Merced and Tuolumne River Canyons; Stanislaus National Forest; and portions of Sierra National Forest.

As much as outdoor enthusiasts often look at the southern end of Gold Rush country as little more than a gateway to Yosemite National Park, this area has more to offer than its Yosemite overflow campgrounds, though indeed there is an exceptional amount of camping here. Do not overlook the wild and scenic rivers of Stanislaus National Forest, encompassing the Tuolumne and Clavey River canyons, the Clavey being one of the last truly pristine and undammed rivers in the state. There are also numerous other natural sites and attractions to keep you occupied before you actually get within a stone's throw of Yosemite itself. Wander through the enormous sequoias at Calaveras Big Trees State Park. Raft and kayak the Merced, Mokelumne, and Tuolumne Rivers, passing through otherwise unreachable wilderness and past steep, stunning walls of granite.

The area is also a gateway to the San Joaquin Valley for those headed west, with numerous water storage reservoirs tucked away in the foothills featuring well-appointed campgrounds and boating facilities (which seem popular with the RV/aluminum fishing boat/retiree set). Pardee and Camanche Reservoirs, which supply water to the eastern San Francisco Bay Area, are premier bass-fishing lakes, as are the stretches of the Tuolumne River downstream of the dams.

Just as it is farther north, Hwy 49 here is a living history tour of California's gold mining legacy, with interesting towns and old mining sites.

From Mark Twain's story of the legendary Calaveras jumping frog to the scenic Mariposa Highway to the classic cowboy/miner culture of Jamestown and Sonora, the foothills are truly an outdoor playground languishing in the shadows of their more popular surroundings, with much more to offer than meets the eye.

Getting There

Highway 49 runs the entire length of Gold Rush country, beginning in the northern tip at Sierra City and Yuba Pass and continuing south through the foothills for 100 miles to Oakhurst, just west of Yosemite National Park's Mariposa entrance. The southern Gold Rush country portion of Highway 49 is most easily accessed via Highways 88, 26, or 4 east from Stockton, Highway 120 east from Manteca, Highway 140 east from Merced, or Highway 40 east from Fresno. Much of this area is within the boundaries of Stanislaus National Forest. The forest headquarters at 19777 Greenley Road, Sonora, (209) 532-3671; the Summit Ranger District, at #1 Pinecrest Lake Road, Pinecrest, (209) 965-3434; and the Groveland Ranger District, at 24525 Old Highway 120, Groveland, (209) 962-7825, are your main check-in points for information and permits for forest and wilderness areas. In the northern end of the forest, the Calaveras Ranger District, on Highway 4 at Hathaway Pines, (209) 795-1381; and the Mi-Wok Ranger District, on Highway 108 in Mi-Wuk Village, (209) 586-3234, are the resources for information. For the portions covered here that are part of Sierra National Forest, the main information point is the Sierra National Forest supervisor's office at 1600 Tollhouse Road, Clovis, (559) 297-0706; the Mariposa Ranger District, 43060 Highway 41, in Oakhurst, (559) 683-4665; and the Pineridge Ranger District, 29688 Auberry Road, North Fork, (559) 877-2218.

Adjoining Areas:

NORTH: **Northern Gold Rush Country**

EAST: **Yosemite Northern Uplands**

WEST: **San Joaquin Valley**

inside out

Parks

Nature lovers who want to get a good idea of what the mid-elevation foothills around Gold Rush country looked like before heavy logging should consider stopping in at **Calaveras Big Trees State Park,** which contains two large groves of old-growth sequoia redwoods, among the largest living things on earth by volume, not to mention among the oldest, rivaled only by the Mariposa Grove in Yosemite National Park (see Yosemite Southern Uplands and Mono Lake chapter). There are easy self-guided nature strolls, campgrounds, picnic facilities, and good wildlife viewing areas along Beaver Creek. The park is 5 miles east of Arnold on Hwy 4, within Stanislaus National Forest; take Hwy 4 east from Hwy 49 at Angels Camp. For information, call the park at (209) 795-2334. While Coloma in the northern end of the Gold Rush corridor (see Northern Gold Rush Country chapter) gets most of the attention, there are also numerous history-oriented destinations in the southern corridor along Hwy 49. The best appointed is **Columbia State Historic Park,** which has numerous Gold Rush–era buildings and offers history tours, gold panning, working gold mine tours, and stagecoach rides along with nice picnic facilities and regularly scheduled costumed reenactments of Gold Rush–era scenes. The historic park is 3.5 miles north of Sonora on Hwy 49. Call (209) 532-0150.

Another historic point of interest that predates westerners' mad search for gold is **Indian Grinding Rock State Historic Park,** in Pine Grove north of Jackson on Hwy 88. This is a Mi-Wuk Indian village, named for the grinding mortars carved into the rocks by early Americans. The park features campsites, interpretive walks, and a Native American education center—another good trip for parents who want their children to get an appreciation for California history beyond the abstractions of textbooks. To reach the park, from Hwy 49 at Jackson take Hwy 88 east for 10 miles, then take Volcano Rd another 1.5 miles north from the highway to the park entrance. For more information, contact the park at (209) 296-7488.

Boating/Fishing

The Hwy 88 corridor east of Stockton, particularly through the Mokelumne River watershed, is a great place to be if your idea of a good time happens to be spending a lazy afternoon by the lake. Amador, Camanche, and Pardee Reservoirs are like a chain of Wobegons, heaven for freshwater fans. **Lake Amador,** the smallest of the three, is like a little fishing village with campground, marina, bait shop, and grocery store—almost a self-contained paradise. **Largemouth bass, trout, crappie, bluegill,** and **catfish** are the main fare here, with the trout stocking program being the most aggressive. There really is no way to get lost. To reach the lake, go 35 miles east of Stockton on Hwy 88, then south on Jackson Valley Rd to the Amador turnoff on your left. Call the RV park and marina for information, (209) 274-4739.

Camanche Reservoir is part of the East Bay Municipal Utility District's (EBMUD's) water system, with more than 50 miles of shoreline spread over 15 square miles of Mokelumne River canyon countryside. To an extent, Camanche is like Amador on a larger scale. RV camps, two public boat ramps, and a good **trout** and **bass** stocking program make this a great place to drop anchor and forget what day of the week it is. Indeed, it is an escape in the truest sense of the word. Because gasoline motors have been banned from the lake due to concerns about contamination, it is a wonderfully quiet spot . . . the kind of place where you can fall asleep during the day. To reach the lake, head east 30 miles on Hwy 88 from Stockton, then go south on E Liberty Rd, which intersects with Camanche Pkwy, the main road encircling the reservoir. Call (209) 763-5121 or (209) 763-5178 for information.

Pardee Reservoir, about 3 miles east of Camanche, is also owned and operated by EBMUD. With nearly 40 miles of shoreline and well-maintained campgrounds, RVers are perfectly at home here. Bring along the fishing boat and have at it. There is a fully equipped marina, along with a public boat ramp. Fishing for **trout** and **salmon** is best spring to fall, but the **catfish** and **bass** action is consistent—a perfect spot to introduce children to the sport. Call the Pardee Lake Marina at (209) 772-1472 for information.

Trout fishing is also popular along the **Stanislaus, Merced, Tuolumne,** and **Mokelumne Rivers,** although because of ongoing changes to state fishing regulations to comply with federal endangered species listings, anglers should always check with state fish and game officials or bait-and-tackle retailers for the latest rules before setting out. On the Mokelumne, fly-fishing is most popular upstream of Pardee Reservoir. There are numerous river access points off Hwy 49 where it crosses the river at Big Bar. North of the bridge, take Electra Rd east alongside the river for 1 mile to Volunteer Gulch or continue on for another 7 miles to Hundred Ounce Gulch for suitable fishing spots. The Merced River is also easily accessed from Hwy 49, on the south side of the bridge at Hell Hollow near Ragby. Take the service road at Hell Hollow east along the south banks of the river to Rocky Gulch. The Tuolumne River southeast of Sonora is another good spot to lounge out on the banks. Take Hwy 108 south from Sonora for 7 miles, then turn off (right) at Old Wards Ferry Rd. Follow the road to Wards Ferry Bridge and the river. The Stanislaus River parallels Hwy 4 east through the foothills. To reach fishing spots, take Hwy 4 east from Angels Camp to Murphys, and head south to the river on Candy Rock Rd.

Rafting/Kayaking

The Sierra foothills and Gold Rush region are the prime whitewater rafting and kayaking destinations in the state, and it doesn't take long to figure out why. The Mokelumne, Stanislaus, Tuolumne, and Merced Rivers together contain some of the best whitewater runs, through steep and rugged canyons. Couple this with the fact that the range of difficulty makes these rivers inviting to all skill levels, and you have yourself a true whitewater playground. While the American is by far the most sought-after rafting river in the state, the others do not skimp on adrenaline-pumping excitement.

For those who want a novice run but don't want to fight the masses putting in on the American, the **Mokelumne River** is another river system with a little something for every type of rafter. The 5.5-mile Electra run between the end of Electra Rd southeast of Jackson to the Big Bar takeout at Hwy 49 and Butte Canyon is a tame, fun Class II run perfect for novices and families with children. It has easy access to put-ins southeast of Jackson off Hwys 49 and 88, at Electra Rd. The Mokelumne also has a whole other personality, however. Head east to the Devil's Nose and Tiger Creek Dam runs, and you will find radical Class IV and V whitewater, waterfall drop action that will have your heart leaping even more than the beautiful surroundings already do. Check with the outfitters listed below or the Stanislaus National Forest supervisor's office, (209) 532-1381, for qualified guide services.

The granite-walled **Merced River** Canyon running west from Yosemite Valley is a great way to cap off a visit to the Yosemite National Park region. There are some 30 miles of Class III and IV whitewater runs leading from the Yosemite feeder city of El Portal west to the Hwy 49 crossing at Flyaway Gulch and Hell Hollow. The first leg of the run out of El Portal follows Hwy 140, making for easy put-in access, but departs for more secluded sections of the canyon at Briceburg. It is here that the paddler gets a greater appreciation not only for this small section of river but also for the whole Yosemite region watershed—an intricate life web where the rocks, trees, water, and weather combine to carve out a paradise of high granite peaks, thundering waterfalls, and wide, marshy meadows. The Merced runs west of Yosemite are among the most popular in the state after the American, so plan carefully, especially during peak late spring–early summer rafting season.

Among the dozens of **outfitters and guide services** running the Merced are Ahwahnee Whitewater in Columbia, (800) 359-9790; Mariah Wilderness Expeditions, in Point Richmond, (800) 462-7424; and Zephyr River Expeditions, also in Columbia, (800) 431-3636.

Daredevils who want to raft Yosemite are best served by heading to the northern end of the Yosemite region for a Class V thrill ride. The **Tuolumne River** and two of its most pristine tributaries—Cherry Creek and the Clavey River—drop, twist, roll, and chute relentlessly through equally stunning and even more secluded scenery amid the Stanislaus National Forest wilderness. The highlight is the Clavey Falls death drop, about as high as even the most confident paddler is going to want start out when it comes time to get vertical. Forest Rd 1N07, northeast from Hwy 120 at Colfax Springs, has the most direct access to the river system, but it is not advisable to attempt these runs without an experienced guide who knows the river system itself, as the zigs and zags through boulder country require advanced technical skills. Sierra Mac River Trips, Sonora, (800) 457-2580, is the place to go for Tuolumne action. See Northern Gold Rush Country chapter for information on the American River.

Hiking/Backpacking

The old-growth redwood groves at **Calaveras Big Trees State Park** (see Parks, above) are among the largest by circumference in the state and are the focal point of two nature walks within the park's boundaries. **North Grove Loop Trail** (easy; 1 mile round trip) is the shortest of the two, making it a favorite for families traveling with children and elderly relatives. But because there is not much room to spread out—which is vital at a park this popular—those who can would be best advised to opt for **South Grove Loop Trail** (easy; up to 5 miles round trip), which contains the largest trees in the park. The park is 5 miles east of Arnold on Hwy 4, within Stanislaus National Forest; take Hwy 4 east from Hwy 49 at Angels Camp. For information, call the park at (209) 795-2334.

Stanislaus National Forest, which covers more than a million acres of wilderness southwest of the Yosemite region, has more than 700 miles of trails within its boundaries, many linking into the park. Stanislaus encompasses secluded canyons, challenging peaks, and more than 1,000 small lakes and ponds. Much of the wooded area is primarily ponderosa pine and Douglas fir. The 112,000-acre Emigrant Wilderness, which includes the 11,570-foot Leavitt Peak, and the Mokelumne and Carson-Iceberg Wilderness Areas, covering vast sections of Stanislaus, El Dorado and Toiyabe National Forests, are the prime hiking and backpacking destinations—look for challenging peak climbs at Leavitt and Mokelumne Peak, as well as interesting volcanic rock formations along Hwy 108. Contact the forest headquarters in Sonora, (209) 532-3671, or the Calaveras Ranger District at Hathaway Pines, (209) 795-1381, for trail condition information and recommended hikes.

One particularly nice day hike is the **Clark Meadow Trail** (difficult; 6 miles round trip), in the Carson-Iceberg Wilderness near Bridgeport. The terrain here is steep and there are difficult stream crossings, even in midsummer during big snow years, so those setting out along this trail should be extra-cautious and novices simply should not try it. There is a connection to the Pacific Crest Trail here, as well as an optional excursion to Boulder Lake (an additional 2.5 miles) on Boulder Lake Trail. Stage from the Clark Fork Trailhead. Take Hwy 108 east from Pinecrest 7 miles to Tuolumne County Rd, and continue to the end.

Sierra National Forest, also southwest of Yosemite, covers some 1.3 million acres of foothills wilderness just beyond Gold Rush country borders. The John Muir Wilderness, which accounts for more than 600,000 acres of the forest, Ansel Adams Wilderness, Kaiser Wilderness, and South Fork Wilderness are the most suitable for backpackers and day hikers alike, although access is not such a breeze since many of these areas are road-free. Contact the forest headquarters in Clovis, (559) 297-0706, for information and guidance on longer backpacking trips.

As with most national forests, dispersed camping is allowed throughout both Stanislaus and Sierra National Forests, with standard limitations and rules. The best trail maps of the national forest areas are available directly from the Forest Service. Write US Forest Service Information, Room 521, 630 Sansome St, San Francisco, CA 94111.

Camping

Dispersed camping is encouraged in this area, just as it is in all national forests. Because of the overabundance of developed sites in the southern Sierra foothills, however, it is hardly necessary to rough it. Sites are given on a first-come, first-served basis. Reservations are taken for most of this area through the Forest Service reservations system, (800) 280-2267. There are also local campgrounds and those operated by reservoir managers. These can be contacted directly at the phone numbers listed with each individual site description.

Highway 49, San Andreas to Oakhurst

Tuttletown Campground contains 160 sites (no hookups; various RV lengths accommodated) adjacent to New Melones Lake. A third of the sites are for RVs only. Those with tents are advised to camp in the rear of the campground where it tends to be quieter. The campground lies near a boat ramp and has a sanitary dump station for RVs. It also has piped water, flush toilets, and showers, along with tables and fire rings at each site. *From Sonora, take Hwy 49 north to Tuttletown. Turn left onto Reynolds Ferry Rd. Proceed to the campground at the reservoir. For more information, call the US Bureau of Reclamation, (209) 536-9094.*

Woodward Reservoir Campground contains 155 sites (some hookups; various RV lengths accommodated) along Woodward Reservoir. The campground lies near a boat ramp and marina. There is a sanitary dump station for RVs on the premises, and the campground has piped water, flush toilets, showers, tables, and fire rings. *From Oakdale, take Hwy 120 north for a mile and a half, and turn right onto County Rd J14. Proceed about 3 miles and turn right onto 26 Mile Rd. Proceed a few hundred feet to the campground. For more information, call the park at the reservoir, run by the county, at (209) 847-3304.*

Moccasin Point Campground contains 80 sites (full hookups; various RV lengths accommodated) along Don Pedro Reservoir. Fifteen of the sites are for RVs only and, due to the hookups, they fill up easily. The reservoir is a popular fishing and boating spot, and a boat ramp lies near the campground. A sanitary dump station for RVs is on the premises, along with piped water, flush toilets, and showers. Each site is equipped with a table and fire ring. *From Coulterville, take Hwy 49 north. About 3 miles past Hwy 120, turn right onto Jacksonville Rd. Proceed to the campground ahead. For more information and reservations, call the reservoir at (209) 852-2396.*

Horseshoe Bend Campground contains 110 sites (some hookups; various RV lengths accommodated) along Lake McClure, a popular fishing and boating spot. Conveniently, a boat ramp lies near the campground, along with a general store. A sanitary dump station for RVs is on the premises, along with piped water, flush toilets, and showers. Each site is equipped with a table and fire ring. *From Coulterville, take Hwy 132 west about 3.5 miles to the campground access road on the left. For more information and reservations, call the lake at (209) 878-3452.*

McClure Point Campground contains 100 sites (some hookups; RV limit 33 feet) along Lake McClure and lies adjacent to a boat ramp and general store. A sanitary dump station for RVs is on the premises, along with piped water, flush toilets, and showers. Each site is equipped with a table and fire ring. *From Coulterville, take Hwy 132 west about 7 miles and turn left onto Merced Falls Rd. Proceed to Merced Falls and turn left onto Lake McClure Rd. Proceed to the campground ahead. For more information and reservations, call the lake at (209) 878-3452.*

Sierra National Forest, Mariposa Ranger District, (559) 683-4665

Big Sandy Campground contains 14 sites (no hookups; RV limit 17 feet) in the Sierra National Forest. The campground, though remote, acts as an overflow area when the Yosemite campgrounds fill up, which is often. There is no piped water, so be sure to bring plenty of your own. Vault toilets are provided, and each site is equipped with a table and fire ring. *From Oakhurst, take Hwy 41 north to Fish Camp. Turn right onto Jackson Rd. Proceed about 5 miles and veer right onto County Rd 632. Proceed about 19 miles to the campground.*

Fresno Dome Campground contains 16 sites (no hookups; RV limit 21 feet) in the Sierra National Forest. The campground lies at the base of Fresno Dome, and there is a nearby trail heading up the mountain. There is no piped water, so be sure to bring plenty of your own. Vault toilets are provided, and each site is equipped with a table and fire ring. *From Oakhurst, take Hwy 41 north to Fish Camp. Turn right onto Jackson Rd. Proceed about 6 miles to the campground.*

Chilkot Campground contains 15 sites (no hookups; RV limit 23 feet) in the Sierra National Forest. There is no piped water, so be sure to bring plenty of your own. Pit toilets are provided, and each site is equipped with a table and fire ring. *From Oakhurst, take Hwy 41 north 3 miles and turn right onto Bass Lake Rd. Veer left onto Malum Ridge Rd, which turns into Beasore Rd. Proceed to the campground on the left.*

Forks Campground contains 30 sites (no hookups; RV limit 23 feet) nestled in a canyon along the banks of Bass Lake. Only 6 of the sites are for RV use, making the campground popular among those with tents. The campground has piped water and vault toilets. Each site is equipped with a table and fire ring. The campground closes during the winter. *From Oakhurst, take Hwy 41 north 3 miles and turn right onto Bass Lake Rd. Veer right onto South Shore Rd. Proceed to the campground ahead.*

Lupine-Cedar Campground contains 115 sites (no hookups; RV limit 43 feet) along the banks of Bass Lake. This campground is enormous by local standards and sometimes serves as an overflow area when the campgrounds in Yosemite fill to capacity. The campground has piped water and flush toilets. Each site is equipped with a table and fire ring. A boat ramp lies nearby. *From Oakhurst, take Hwy 41 north 3 miles and turn right onto Bass Lake Rd. Veer right onto South Shore Rd. Proceed to the campground ahead.*

Stanislaus National Forest, Calaveras Ranger District, (209) 795-1381

Upper Highland Lake Campground contains 35 sites (no hookups; various RV lengths accommodated) situated between Upper and Lower Highland Lakes, both of which offer good trout fishing and swimming. There is piped water in the camp area, along with vault toilets, fire grills, and tables. To the south of the campground, Hiram Peak looms at 10,000 feet and offers hikers fantastic views over the Sierra. *From Markleeville, take Hwy 89 south a few miles and turn right onto Hwy 4. Proceed past Kinney Reservoir. Just west of Ebbetts Pass, turn left onto Highland Lake Rd. Proceed to the campground.*

Union Reservoir Campground has 15 tent sites (no RV access) and is one of the area's quieter campgrounds. Nestled in Stanislaus National Forest adjacent to Union Reservoir (a great place for swimming), this quiet walk-in campground has vault toilets, fire grills, and picnic tables. A boat ramp leading into the reservoir is nearby, as are a few trailheads leading back into the wilderness. Be sure to bring your own water. *From Markleeville, take Hwy 89 south a few miles and turn right onto Hwy 4. Proceed to Lake Alpine and turn left onto W Lake Alpine Rd/Forest Rd 7N17. Proceed to Union Reservoir and turn left onto Forest Rd 7N75. Proceed to the campsite parking area.*

If you like swimming, Pine Marten, Silver Valley, and Alpine Campgrounds are the three places to camp. Located near the banks of beautiful Lake Alpine, set in a granite canyon at an altitude of 7,300 feet, these campgrounds are a favorite with visitors to Stanislaus National Forest who are looking for boating, fishing, and swimming. **Pine Marten Campground** has 30 sites (no hookups; RV limit 22 feet). **Silver Valley** has 25 sites (no hookups; RV limit 22 feet). **Alpine Camp** consists of 22 sites (no hookups; RV limit 22 feet). All three campgrounds have piped water, fire grills, picnic tables, and flush toilets. Alpine is the most crowded, as it lies adjacent to a boat ramp leading into the lake. You can avoid the crowds by camping at the other two campgrounds, both of which are in reasonable proximity to the boat ramp. Several hiking trails are easily accessible from these campgrounds, making them popular with hikers too. General supplies are available at a local store, and a laundry is close by. *From Markleeville, take Hwy 89 south a few miles and turn right onto Hwy 4. Just east of the Village of Lake Alpine, turn left and cross Silver Creek. Proceed to the campgrounds.*

Silver Tip Campground has 25 sites (no hookups; RV limit 21 feet) about 1.7 miles from Lake Alpine. This is one of the area's higher-altitude camps, at 7,500 feet, and it is usually used as an overflow campground for the camp areas closer to Lake Alpine. Flush toilets and piped water are provided, and each site is equipped with a fire ring and table. *From Markleeville, take Hwy 89 south a few miles and turn right onto Hwy 4. Just west of the Village of Lake Alpine, turn left on Silver Tip Campground Rd. Proceed to the campground.*

Big Meadow Campground contains 60 sites (no hookups; various

RV lengths accommodated) in the forest near Lake Alpine and a few reservoirs. Each site is equipped with a fire grill and table, and vault toilets and piped water are available. Additionally, a laundry and grocery store are close by. *From Markleeville, take Hwy 89 south a few miles and turn right onto Hwy 4. Proceed to Big Meadow and look for the campground on the south side of the road.*

Stanislaus River Campground consists of 25 sites (no hookups; RV limit 16 feet) along the North Fork Stanislaus River at an altitude of 6,000 feet. Popular with visitors looking to fish, this campground has piped water and vault toilets. Each site is also equipped with a fire ring and table. *From Markleeville, take Hwy 89 south a few miles and turn right onto Hwy 4. Proceed past Tamarack. Just before Hells Kitchen Vista, turn left onto Forest Rd 7N01 and proceed to the campground.*

Spicer Reservoir Campground has 65 sites (no hookups; various RV lengths accommodated) on Spicer Reservoir, a popular fishing area. Protected by steep canyon walls, the campground has vault toilets and piped water, and each site is equipped with a fire grill and table. A boat ramp lies adjacent to the camp and several good hiking trails traverse the area. *From Markleeville, take Hwy 89 south a few miles and turn right onto Hwy 4. Proceed past Tamarack. Just before Hells Kitchen Vista, turn left onto Forest Rd 7N01. Travel to Forest Rd 7N76 and turn right. Proceed to the campground.*

Stanislaus National Forest, Summit Ranger District, (209) 965-3434

Mill Creek Campground has 18 sites (no hookups; various RV lengths accommodated). If you enjoy trout fishing, take note: This campground sits at an elevation of 6,312 feet close to the middle fork of the Stanislaus River, Beardsley Reservoir, and Pinecrest Lake. Though the campground has vault toilets, fire grills, and tables, there is no water in the camp area, so be sure to bring plenty of your own. *From Hot Springs, travel west on Hwy 108, past Donnell Vista Point, to Forest Rd 5N21 on the left, west of Niagara Creek. Travel a few hundred feet on Forest Rd 5N21 and turn left onto the campground access road.*

Niagara Creek Campground has 9 sites (no hookups; RV limit 21 feet). Campers looking for solitude may be in luck here because there are 3 additional walk-in tent sites. There is no water in the camp area, so be sure to bring plenty of your own. Vault toilets, fire grills, and tables are provided. *From Hot Springs, travel west on Hwy 108, past Donnell Vista Point, to Forest Rd 6N24 on the left, just west of Niagara Creek. Proceed to the campground on the left.*

Pigeon Flat Campground has 7 walk-in tent sites (no RV access). Campers looking for a primitive camping experience appreciate this remote outreach. Accessible only on foot (a short walk), the campground has no running water, so be sure to carry plenty of your own. Each site is equipped with fire grills and tables. One vault toilet serves the camp area. General supplies can be purchased in nearby Dardanelle. *From Hot Springs, travel west on Hwy 108. Just east of Dardanelle, the campground is on the left side of the highway, west of the Columns of the Giants.*

Fence Creek Campground has 34 sites (no hookups; RV limit 21 feet) adjacent to Fence Creek at an elevation of 6,209. Fence Creek joins the middle fork of the Stanislaus River, a nice fishing spot. There is no water in the camp area, so be sure to bring plenty of your own. Vault toilets, fire grills, and tables are provided, and general supplies can be purchased 9 miles away in Pinecrest. *From Markleeville, take Hwy 89 south a few miles and turn right onto Hwy 4. Proceed past Columns of the Giants, to Wagner. Turn right onto Clark Fork Rd. Turn left onto Forest Rd 6N06. Proceed to the campground.*

Boulder Flat Campground has 22 sites (no hookups; RV limit 21 feet) and lies adjacent to the middle fork of the Stanislaus River at an elevation of roughly 5,580 feet. Campers looking to fish enjoy this stretch of river, as it is stocked with trout. Boulder Flat has piped water in the camp area, vault toilets, fire grills, and tables. In nearby Dardanelle, general supplies can be purchased. *From Markleeville, take Hwy 89 south a few miles and turn right onto Hwy 4. Proceed past Columns of the Giants. Just east of Wagner, turn right onto Boulder Flat Rd. Proceed to the campground.*

Eureka Valley Campground has 27 sites (no hookups; RV limit 21 feet) and lies on the middle fork of the Stanislaus River. There is no water in the camp area, so be sure to bring plenty of your own. Each site has a fire grill and table, and there is a vault toilet for the camp area as well. In nearby Dardanelle, general supplies can be purchased. *From Markleeville, take Hwy 89 south a few miles and turn right onto Hwy 4. Proceed just east of Dardanelle and turn left onto the campground access road.*

Baker Campground contains 45 sites (no hookups; RV limit 21 feet) on the middle fork of the Stanislaus River, a popular fishing spot close to Dardanelle. The campground has piped water, vault toilets, fire grills, and picnic tables. General supplies can be purchased in Dardanelle. *From Markleeville, take Hwy 89 south a few miles and turn right onto Hwy 4. Proceed past Chipmunk Flat to the campground entrance on the left side of the highway, just east of Baker Station.*

Brightman Flat Campground has 30 sites (no hookups; various RV lengths accommodated). Located near the middle fork of the Stanislaus River, this campground is popular with anglers. The Dardanelle area, where the river is stocked with trout, is a mere mile and a half away. Campers will also find a general store there. Though the campground has vault toilets, fire grills, and tables, there is no water in the camp area, so be sure to bring plenty of your own. *From Markleeville, take Hwy 89 south a few miles and turn right onto Hwy 4. Proceed west of Dardanelle to the campground access road on the right.*

Dardanelle Campground has 28 sites (no hookups; various RV lengths accommodated), and is *the* place to stay if you like fishing. Located on the middle fork of the Stanislaus River, within walking distance of the quaint village of Dardanelle, the campground is on a stretch of river stocked with trout. The campground has piped water, vault toilets, fire grills, and tables. *From Markleeville, take Hwy 89 south a few miles and turn right onto Hwy 4. Proceed west to Dardanelle. The campground access road is on the right.*

Clark Fork Campground has 88 sites (no hookups; RV limit 21 feet) and is located on the Clark Fork of the Stanislaus River. This campground is larger and more popular than most others in Stanislaus National Forest, particularly among RVers because there is a sanitation disposal station. The campground has flush toilets, fire grills, and tables, as well as piped water. In nearby Dardanelle, general supplies can be purchased. *From Markleeville, take Hwy 89 south a few miles and turn right onto Hwy 4. Proceed past Columns of the Giants to Wagner. Turn right onto Clark Fork Rd. Veer right at the fork in the road. Proceed to the campground.*

Sand Flat Campground has 50 sites (no hookups; various RV lengths accommodated) and is one of the more popular camp areas in Stanislaus National Forest. Located on the Stanislaus River, the campground attracts visitors looking for swimming and fishing. For those looking to get away from the campground's main area, there are an additional 15 tent sites deeper in the forest, reachable only on foot. The camp area has vault toilets, fire grills, and tables, as well as fresh well water. In nearby Dardanelle, general supplies can be purchased. *From Markleeville, take Hwy 89 south a few miles and turn right onto Hwy 4. Proceed past Columns of the Giants, to Wagner. Turn right onto Clark Fork Rd. Veer right at the fork in the road. Proceed to the campground access road, on the left about 6 miles ahead.*

Deadman Campground has 17 sites (no hookups; RV limit 22 feet) and is one of the quieter campgrounds in Stanislaus National Forest. Situated on the middle fork of the Stanislaus River, the campground has piped water, fire grills, and picnic tables, as well as flush toilets. Several hiking trails are easily accessible from this campground, making it a favorite among hikers. Dardanelle, about 7 miles away, is a nice fishing spot and has general supplies at its local store. *From Markleeville, take Hwy 89 south a few miles and turn right onto Hwy 4. Proceed past Chipmunk Flat to the Kennedy Meadow access road on the left. Turn onto the access road and proceed to the campground entrance.*

Hull Creek Campground has 20 sites (no hookups; RV limit 21 feet) adjacent to Hull Creek. The campground is generally sought by visitors who are looking for solitude. It also serves as an overflow area for Fraser Flat Campground (see below). There are vault toilets, as well as fire grills and picnic tables for each site. *From Markleeville, take Hwy 89 south a few miles and turn right onto Hwy 4. Proceed to Long Barn Rd and turn left onto Long Barn Rd. Proceed to North Fork Rd and turn right. The road turns into Forest Rd 3N01; proceed to the campground entrance on the right side of the highway.*

Fraser Flat Campground has 30 sites (no hookups; RV limit 21 feet) adjacent to the South Fork Stanislaus River, a popular fishing spot. There are vault toilets, as well as fire grills and picnic tables for each site. *From Markleeville, take Hwy 89 south a few miles and turn right onto Hwy 4. Proceed west to Cold Springs and turn right onto Forest Rd 4N14. Proceed to the campground entrance.*

Meadowview Campground contains roughly 100 sites (no hookups; RV limit 22 feet) near the very popular Pinecrest Lake. Stocked with trout, the lake attracts visitors who like fishing and boating. There is a beautiful 1-mile trail leading from the camp to the lake. The campground has flush toilets, as well as fire grills and picnic tables for each site. *From Markleeville, take Hwy 89 south a few miles and turn right onto Hwy 4. Proceed west of Strawberry and turn left onto Pinecrest Lake Rd. Take your next right and proceed to the campground.*

Pinecrest Campground contains 200 sites (no hookups; RV limit 21 feet), also near Pinecrest Lake. The campground's amenities make it a popular spot. There are flush toilets, as well as fire grills and picnic tables for each site. *From Markleeville, take Hwy 89 south a few miles and turn right onto Hwy 4. Proceed west of Strawberry and turn left onto Pinecrest Lake Rd. Proceed to the campground.*

Stanislaus National Forest, Groveland Ranger District, (209) 962-7825

Lumsden Campground has 11 tent sites (no RV access) a short walk from the Tuolumne River. A popular spot among experienced rafters, Lumsden has no running water, so be sure to bring plenty of your own. Vault toilets are available, and each site is equipped with a fire pit and table. *This campground is difficult to find. Take Hwy 120 east from Groveland for 7.5 miles. You will see Buck Meadows to your right. A short distance after Buck Meadows, turn left on a dirt road. The road forms a loop, and the campground is just beyond the midway point in the loop.*

Diamond Campground has 38 sites (no hookups; RV limit 32 feet) along the western edge of Yosemite National Park and serves as an overflow campground for the Yosemite Valley. Piped water is available during the summer season, along with vault toilets. Tables and fire pits are provided. *From Buck Meadows (see Lumsden Campground, above), travel east on Hwy 120. Turn left onto Evergreen Rd and proceed to the campground entrance 6 miles ahead.*

Cherry Lake Campground has 46 sites (no hookups; various RV lengths accommodated) situated on the banks of Cherry Lake at an altitude of 5,000 feet. The campground attracts visitors who enjoy boating, swimming, and fishing. Piped water, fire grills, picnic tables, and vault toilets are available. Unfortunately, the piped water is turned off during the winter season. A boat ramp lies about a mile and a half from the campground, and there are several beautiful hiking trails in the area. *From Buck Meadows (see Lumsden Campground, above), travel east on Hwy 120. Just past Colfax Spring, turn left onto Forest Rd 1N07 and proceed to the lakeside campground at the end.*

Lost Claim Campground has 10 sites (no hookups; RV limit 18 feet) near a stream. The campground tends to be quiet and generally serves as an overflow area for the busier camps toward the south. Well water is available during the summer season, along with vault toilets. Tables and fire grills are also provided, and a general store is nearby. *From Buck Meadows (see Lumsden Campground, above), travel east on Hwy 120 about 1 mile to the campground on the left side of the highway.*

Sweetwater Campground contains 13 sites (no hookups; RV limit 21 feet) near the South Fork Tuolumne River, and serves as an overflow campground for the Yosemite Valley. Piped water is available during the summer season, along with vault toilets. Tables and fire pits are provided, and a general store is nearby. *From Buck Meadows (see Lumsden Campground, above), travel east on Hwy 120 about 5 miles to the campground on the left side of the highway.*

Mountain Biking

There are boundless **mountain-biking** opportunities on the forest roads in Sierra and Stanislaus National Forests. Do not, however, take bikes into designated wilderness areas, as all mechanical vehicles—even those without motors—are prohibited. Pinecrest Lake, because of its day-outing amenities, is a popular mountain-biking destination; access to trails there is limited, however, because of the large number of pedestrians sharing them. Check with individual ranger districts regarding current prohibitions and logging activities before choosing a road.

Gold Panning

At **Columbia State Historic Park** (see Parks, above), panning lessons and demonstrations are offered regularly at Hidden Treasure Mine. For more information, call the park at (209) 532-9693. In Jamestown, private **gold prospecting expeditions** are led on Wood's Creek, at Jimtown Gold-mining Camp. GPE, the outfit that runs the camp, also leads dispersed panning trips throughout the Gold Rush region; call (800) 596-0009 for information. Little Valley Gold Prospecting in Mariposa also offers mining expeditions, (800) 889-5444.

outside in

Attractions

The tiny town of **Volcano,** with fewer than 100 residents, is so wonderfully authentic that it borders on decrepit (it doesn't get more Gold Rush–genuine than this, folks). During the heady mining days, this unusually sophisticated town built the state's first library and its first astronomical observatory. Nowadays you can see some preserved buildings and artifacts, including a Civil War cannon. An outdoor amphitheater, hidden behind stone facades along Main St, is the site of popular summer theatricals performed by the Volcano Theatre Company; 1 block north of the St. George Hotel, (209) 296-2525. After touring the town, take the side trip up winding Ram's Horn Grade to cool off in the funky, friendly bar at the St. George Hotel (see Lodgings, below). Or, in early spring, picnic amid the nearly half-million daffodils (and more than 100 varieties) in bloom on Daffodil Hill, a 4-acre ranch 3 miles north of Volcano (follow the signs on Ram's Horn Grade; there is no phone).

Just beyond an enormous Georgia-Pacific lumber mill lies **Jackson,** the seat of Amador County. Jackson hides most of its rowdy past behind modern facades, but old-timers know the town (once called "little Reno") as the last place in California to outlaw prostitution. For a trip back in time, take a gander at the National Hotel, which has been in continuous operation since 1862 and has built up quite a guest list: Will Rogers, John Wayne, Leland Stanford, and almost every other California governor in the last century stayed here. Ragtime tunes and classic oldie sing-alongs are played on the grand piano, and guests register for the spartan rooms with the bartender through a wooden cage at the back of the saloon; 2 Water St at Main St, (209) 223-0500.

A sight Gold Rush buffs shouldn't miss is the **Amador County**

Museum, which has scale models of the local hard-rock mines. It's open Wednesday through Sunday; 225 Church St, (209) 223-6386. There's also **Kennedy Tailing Wheels Park,** site of the Kennedy and Argonaut Mines, the Mother Lode's deepest. Though these mines have been closed for decades, their headframes and huge tailing wheels (some are 58 feet in diameter) remain to help show how waste from the mines was conveyed over the hills to a settling pond. The park is also home to the white, picturesque St. Sava's Servian Orthodox Church, built in 1894 and surrounded by a cemetery; to reach the park, take Main St to Jackson Gate Rd, just north of Jackson (there is no phone).

In 1883, the law finally caught up with the famous gentleman-bandit Black Bart at **San Andreas,** the former grungy mining camp. The legendary stagecoach robber was famous for being extremely polite to his victims and leaving poetry at the scene of his numerous crimes. He served five years in San Quentin prison and was never heard from again after his release in 1888. There isn't much to see in San Andreas, the seat of the Calaveras County government, except for the very good **Calaveras County Historical Museum,** full of gold-mining relics, Mi-Wuk Indian artifacts, and the courtroom where Black Bart was convicted; 30 N Main St (in the old courthouse), (209) 754-6579.

Cruise right through the overcommercialized and truly uninspiring town of San Andreas, and you'll eventually pull into **Angels Camp,** made famous by Mark Twain's short story "The Celebrated Jumping Frog of Calaveras County." Every year on the third weekend in May, thousands of frog fans flock to the Calaveras County Fair to witness the Jumping Frog Jubilee, one of the premier frog-jumping contests in the world. The festival takes place at the county fairgrounds, 2 miles south of town, (209) 736-2561, and features a rodeo, carnival rides, live music, and—for those of you who forgot to bring one—frogs for rent. Ribbit.

Gingerbread Victorian homes peek from behind white picket fences and tall locust trees border the streets of **Murphys,** a former trading post set up by brothers Dan and John Murphy in cooperation with local Native Americans (John married the chief's daughter). It's worth taking the detour off Hwy 49 just to stroll down Murphys' tree-lined Main St or, better yet, to sample a pint of Murphys Brewing Company's outstanding Murphys Red, served on tap at the Murphys Historic Hotel and Lodge (see Lodgings, below).

Many of the numerous **caverns** in the area were discovered in the mid-1800s by gold prospectors and can now be toured, including Mercer Caverns, (209) 728-2101, which has crystalline stalactites and stalagmites in a series of descending chambers; Moaning Cavern, (209) 736-2708, where a 100-foot stairway spirals down into a limestone chamber so huge it could house the Statue of Liberty; and California Caverns, (209) 736-2708 (reservations required), the West's first commercially developed cave and the largest single cave system in Northern California (it has yet to be fully explored). For more information on the caverns, plug into the Web site at www.caverntours.com.

Some mighty fortunate forty-niners unearthed a staggering $87 million in gold in **Columbia,** a former boisterous mining town once the state's second-largest city (it was only two votes shy of becoming the state capital over Sacramento). But when the gold no longer panned out in the late 1850s, Columbia's population of 15,000 nearly vanished. In 1945, the entire town was turned into Columbia State Historic Park, a true Gold Rush country treasure; see Parks, above.

When the traffic starts to crawl along Hwy 49, you're probably closing in on **Sonora.** In forty-niner days, Sonora competed with Columbia for the title of wealthiest city in the southern Mother Lode. Today, it is the Gold Rush country's largest and most crowded town and the Tuolumne County seat. If you have time to spare, search for a parking space along Washington St (no easy feat on weekends), feed the meter, and take a look at the well-preserved 19th-century St. James Episcopal Church, at the top of Washington St, and the Tuolumne County Museum, located in the century-old jail at 158 W Bradford St, (209) 532-1317. If you really have time to kill, take a leisurely drive along the picturesque Detour Route 108, which heads west into the Sierra Nevada over Sonora Pass, and through several scenic alpine communities.

Jamestown has been preoccupied with gold since the first fleck was taken out of Woods Creek in 1848; a marker even commemorates the discovery of a 75-pound nugget. For a fee, you can pan for gold at troughs on Main St or go prospecting with a guide. But gold isn't Jamestown's only claim to fame. For decades, this two-block town lined with picturesque buildings has been Hollywood's favorite Western movie set: scenes from famous flicks like *Butch Cassidy and the Sundance Kid* were shot here, and vintage railway cars and steam locomotives used in such TV classics as *Little House on the Prairie, Bonanza,* and *High Noon* are on display at the **Railtown 1897 State Historic Park.** You can view the vehicles at the roundhouse daily or ride the rails on weekends from April to October and during holiday events, such as the Santa Train in December; located on Fifth Ave at Reservoir Rd, near the center of town, (209) 984-3953.

A side trip off Hwy 49 leads to **Hornitos** (Spanish for "little ovens"), a name that refers to the shape of the tombs on Boot Hill. This formerly lawless burg is nearly a ghost town, though it was once a favorite haunt of Gold Rush country *bandido* Joaquin Murrieta, whose pickled head was turned over to state authorities in a glass jar for a $1,000 reward in 1853.

Weathered old buildings (saloons, fandango halls, and gambling dens) stand around the plaza, some flaunting bullet holes from bygone battles.

Restaurants

B of A Cafe ☆☆   This 1936 Bank of America building has been converted into a bright, lively cafe that attracts crowds of tourists and locals alike. At dinner, the chef caters to local meat eaters with her juicy rotisserie lemon-rosemary chicken. *1262 S Main St (near the intersection of Hwys 4 and 49), Angels Camp; (209) 736-0765; $$.*

Banny's ☆   The innkeeper at the Ryan House B&B around the corner (see Lodgings, below), has been sending her guests here for years and has yet to hear a complaint about the food. As for the decor, well . . . decor aside, Banny's is a good bet. *83 S Stewart St, Suite 100 (in Old Town), Sonora; (209) 533-4709; $$.*

Camps ☆☆☆   Camps is ensconced within a sprawling golf resort on the western fringes of Angels Camp, but it's definitely worth seeking out. The fusion cuisine pairs local produce with European, Asian, and Caribbean cooking techniques. *676 McCauley Ranch Rd (½ mile W of the junction of Hwys 4 and 49, off Angel Oaks Dr), Angels Camp; (209) 736-8181; $$$.*

Columbia House Restaurant ☆   This American restaurant has had its ups and downs over the years, but locals still come to Columbia House for its hearty breakfasts. Lunch is just as filling, and should be washed down with the locally made sarsaparilla. *On the corner of State and Main Sts (downtown), Columbia; (209) 532-5134; $.*

Good Heavens: A Food Concern ☆☆   This historic building lined with old-fashioned paintings is the setting for a delightful boutique cafe noted for its very good daily lunch specials. *49 N Washington St (downtown), Sonora; (209) 532-3663; $.*

Grounds ☆☆   This fantastic coffeehouse and cafe is bright and airy with pine furnishings, wood floors, and an open kitchen. The dinner menu changes frequently. To spice things up a bit, only Mexican food is served on Mondays. *402 Main St (downtown), Murphys; (209) 728-8663; $$.*

Kamm's ☆   Chinese restaurants are few and far between in the Gold Rush country. Kamm's is one of the better ones. You'll see a mix of locals and tourists here ordering from the large selection of mild Cantonese dishes and the spicier Hunan and Mongolian fare. *18208 Main St (downtown), Jamestown; (209) 984-3105; $.*

Mel and Faye's Diner ☆   Mel and Faye have been churning out good eats at their highwayside diner since 1956, and the place is still a favorite, primarily because you pay small prices for big burgers. *205 Hwy 49 (at Main St, at the bottom of the hill), Jackson; (209) 223-0853; $.*

North Beach Cafe ☆☆ This former auto parts store has been turned into one of Sonora's most popular restaurants. The simple lunch menu features chicken and steak sandwiches, burgers, soups, and salads, while the dinner menu is predominantly Italian. *14317 Mono Way/Hwy 108 (from central Sonora, drive 3 miles E on Hwy 108 to John's Sierra Market and turn into the parking lot), Sonora; (209) 536-1852; $$.*

Smoke Cafe ☆☆ One of Jamestown's liveliest restaurants, the Smoke Cafe is an ex-slot-machine saloon. Creative Mexican fare dominates the menu, and favored dishes include the black bean burritos, fajitas, and spicy corn chowder. *18191 Main St (downtown), Jamestown; (209) 984-3733; $.*

Steam Donkey Restaurant ☆ This popular barbecue house is usually packed with Sonorans, who make the 32-mile trek every weekend for the highly rated ribs, steaks, and chicken. *421 Pinecrest Lake Rd (off Pinecrest Ave and Hwy 108), Pinecrest; (209) 965-3117; $.*

Upstairs Restaurant & Streetside Bistro ☆☆ The bright, cheery Streetside Bistro offers soups, salads, and gourmet sandwiches for lunch. For dinner, take the stairway to the Upstairs Restaurant, which features a small, contemporary American menu. *164 Main St (downtown), Jackson; (209) 223-3342; $$.*

Lodgings

Barretta Gardens Inn ☆☆ Expansive gardens of native flowering shrubs surround this small, 5-room country inn on a hillside southeast of downtown Sonora. The wraparound porch is perfect for curling up with a good book (or your honey) in spring or autumn. Winter conversation takes place on soft sofas around the fireplace in the comfortable living room. *700 S Barretta St (a few blocks E of Washington St), Sonora; (209) 532-6039 or (800) 206-3333; $$.*

City Hotel ☆☆☆ City folk who frequented this opulent hotel in 1856 called it the Gem of the Southern Mines. When the town was turned into a state historic park in 1945, visitors once again returned to this venerable landmark. The lobby is fitted with period settees and marble-top tables, and 6 of the 10 high-ceilinged rooms face a central parlor, the setting for an elaborate continental breakfast. *On Main St (between Jackson and State Sts), Columbia; (209) 532-1479 or (800) 532-1479; $$ (hotel), $$$ (restaurant).*

Cooper House Bed and Breakfast Inn ☆ This 1911 restored Craftsman-style bungalow is the only B&B in town, nestled in a quaint garden setting well away from the main highway. The names of the 3 suites (Zinfandel, Cabernet, and Chardonnay) are indicative of the influence the winemaking community has had on this town. *1184 Church St (from Main St, turn E on Raspberry Lane), Angels Camp; (209) 736-2145 or (800)225-3764 ext. 326; $$.*

Court Street Inn ☆☆   Dave and Nancy Butow's pretty 1872 Victorian inn, with its tin ceilings, redwood staircase, and marble fireplace, has earned a well-deserved spot on the National Register of Historic Places. A two-minute stroll from Main Street, the inn's 7 guest rooms (all with private baths) are loaded with vintage furnishings. *215 Court St (just off Church St), Jackson; (209) 223-0416 or (800)200-0416; $$.*

The Dorrington Hotel and Restaurant ☆☆   This country hotel, built in 1860, is surrounded by some of the largest pines and sequoias in California. The 5 antique-filled rooms, which share bathrooms, have brass beds with homemade quilts. The hotel's casual dining room offers Northern Italian–style dinners. *3431 Hwy 4, Dorrington; (209) 795-5800; $$.*

Dunbar House, 1880 ☆☆☆   Without question, Dunbar House is among the finest B&Bs in the Gold Rush country. Century-old gardens adorn this lovely Italianate home built in 1880. The lush grounds are complemented by a gazebo, a rose garden with benches, and a swing. All 4 guest rooms are furnished with wood-burning stoves, heirloom antiques, and vases of fresh flowers. *271 Jones St (just off Main St), Murphys; (209) 728-2897 or (800)692-6006; $$.*

Fallon Hotel ☆☆   In 1988, this 1850s hostelry was beautifully refurbished to a more elegant 1890s splendor with embossed wallpapers, antique oak furnishings, ornate porcelain basins, and pull-chain toilets. Fallon Hotel's 14 bedrooms are quite small, so request one of the 5 larger balcony rooms. *On Washington St (at Parrots Ferry Rd), Columbia; (209) 532-1470; $$.*

Groveland Hotel ☆☆   Constructed in 1849, the adobe Groveland Hotel is one of the Gold Rush country's oldest buildings; the place still manages to retain some of the charm of yesteryear. Its 17 guest rooms aren't large, but down comforters and private baths make them quite comfortable, and they're furnished with attractive European antiques. *18767 Main St, Groveland; (209) 962-4000 or (800) 273-3314; $$.*

Hotel Charlotte ☆   This roadside hotel, built in 1918, serves gold panners and folks on their way to Yosemite. Each of the 11 guest rooms is pleasantly dressed up with an iron bedstead, lace curtains, and floral wallpaper; 8 rooms have private baths. *18736 Main St, Groveland; (209) 962-6455 or (800) 961-7799; $.*

Jamestown Hotel ☆☆   Built at the turn of the last century and converted into a hospital in the 1920s, this two-story brick charmer with its Western facade and wood veranda was transformed into a country inn more than a decade ago. Upstairs, each of the 8 engaging guest rooms—named after female Gold Rush personalities—are furnished with antiques and private Victorian baths with brass showers. *18153 Main St, Jamestown; (209) 984-3902 or (800) 205-4901; $$.*

Lodge at Manuel Mill ☆☆☆   This remote bed-and-breakfast lodge cantilevers over Old Mill Pond in the Stanislaus National Forest. Originally the site of a century-old lumber mill, the 43-acre resort opened in 1989 as a Western frontier-style lodge with 5 comfortable, individually furnished guest rooms. *On Dunbar Rd (off Hwy 4), Arnold; (209) 795-2622; $$.*

Lulu Belle's Bed and Breakfast ☆☆   One of the few Gold Rush country B&Bs that welcome families, this century-old Victorian is surrounded by a spacious lawn and rose garden. Located only a few blocks from historic downtown Sonora, the inn has 5 guest rooms—2 inside the main house and 3 in a quiet carriage house—all with private baths. *85 Gold St (off Washington St, downtown), Sonora; (209) 533-3455 or (800) 538-3455; $$.*

McCaffrey House Bed & Breakfast Inn ☆☆☆   Located in the Stanislaus National Forest, this gorgeous, sprawling 7-room, three-story country home was built specifically as a B&B, and it's one of the top 10 in the Gold Rush country. Nowhere else in this region will you find such a winning combination of amenities, style, and service for such reasonable prices. *23251 Hwy 108 (11 miles E of Sonora), Twain Harte; (209) 586-0757 or (888) 586-0757; $$.*

Murphys Historic Hotel and Lodge ☆   This national- and state-registered landmark opened in 1856 and still maintains its hold as Murphys' social center. The main building has 9 historic guest rooms that reflect turn-of-the-century lifestyles (that is, no phones, televisions, or private baths), while the newer building offers 20 modern rooms with private bathrooms. *457 Main St (downtown), Murphys; (209) 728-3444 or (800) 532-7684; $$.*

National Hotel ☆☆   The restoration of the 1859 National Hotel was so impressive that both the Tuolumne Visitors Bureau and the Tuolumne County Lodging Association bestowed awards for its new look. The restorers of the 9 guest rooms did an admirable job of blending 19th-century details (handmade quilts, lace curtains, brass beds) with 20th-century comforts (private bathrooms). *77 Main St (downtown), Jamestown; (209) 984-3446 or (800) 894-3446; $$.*

Serenity ☆☆   It's not easy to find this secluded inn, tucked away at the end of a country road just outside Sonora. The antique-filled house combines the gracious atmosphere of the past with the modern conveniences of the present. All 4 guest rooms have private baths and color-coordinated floral furnishings, as well as a private sitting area. *15305 Bear Cub Dr (6 miles E of downtown, off Phoenix Lake Rd), Sonora; (209) 533-1441 or (800) 426-1441; $$.*

St. George Hotel   In its heyday in the 1860s, the burgeoning village of Volcano offered a tired miner his choice of 17 hotels. Those whose pockets held the largest nuggets chose the St. George. Although its elegance has faded considerably over the last century, this three-story, 14-room hotel is still a gold mine for anyone spending an evening in this little town. *2 Main St (can't miss it), Volcano; (209) 296-4458; $$.*

More Information

Amador County Chamber of Commerce: *(209) 223-0350.*
Bass Lake Chamber of Commerce: *(559) 642-3676.*
Calaveras Big Trees State Park: *(209) 795-2334.*
Columbia State Historic Park: *(209) 532-0150.*
Eastern Madera County Chamber of Commerce: *(559) 683-7766.*
Indian Grinding Rock State Historic Park: *(209) 296-7488.*
Sierra National Forest, Mariposa Ranger District: *(559) 683-4665.*
Sierra National Forest, Pineridge Ranger District: *(559) 877-2218.*
Sierra National Forest supervisor: *(559) 297-0706.*
Stanislaus National Forest, Calaveras Ranger District: *(209) 795-1381.*
Stanislaus National Forest, Groveland Ranger District: *(209) 962-7825.*
Stanislaus National Forest headquarters: *(209) 532-3671.*
Stanislaus National Forest, Mi-Wok Ranger District: *(209) 586-3234.*
Stanislaus National Forest, Summit Ranger District: *(209) 965-3434.*

Index